RUSSIAN ROULETTE

Also by Richard Greene

Selected Letters of Edith Sitwell

Graham Greene: A Life in Letters

Edith Sitwell: Avant Garde Poet, English Genius

RUSSIAN ROULETTE

The Life and Times of Graham Greene

RICHARD GREENE

Little, Brown

LITTLE, BROWN

First published in Great Britain in 2020 by Little, Brown

1 3 5 7 9 10 8 6 4 2

A CIP catalogue record for this book
is available from the British Library.

Hardback ISBN 978-1-4087-0397-7
Trade Paperback ISBN 978-1-4087-1344-0

Typeset in Goudy by M Rules
Printed and bound in Great Britain by Clays Ltd, Elcograf S.p.A.

Papers used by Little, Brown are from well-managed forests
and other responsible sources.

MIX
Paper from
responsible sources
FSC
www.fsc.org FSC® C104740

Little, Brown
An imprint of
Little, Brown Book Group
Carmelite House
50 Victoria Embankment
London EC4Y ODZ

An Hachette UK Company
www.hachette.co.uk

www.littlebrown.co.uk

In Memory of Bernard Diederich
1926–2020

CONTENTS

Introduction   xi

1. The Dog in the Pram   1
2. Flight   13
3. Backwards Day   23
4. The Revolver   30
5. Casual Corpses   36
6. Marriage   46
7. Rats in the Thatch   52
8. The Devil Looks After His Own   63
9. Minty Stepped on Board   73
10. In Zigi's Town   80
11. Raven   91
12. My Worst Film   97
13. Shirley Temple   101
14. Real Brighton   104
15. The Lawless Roads   111
16. Doll   124
17. Bombs and Books   132
18. The House in the Swamp   137
19. The Ministry of Fear   146
20. Canaries and Defectors   149
21. Mrs Montgomery   158
22. Hot Irons   163

23.	Mother of Six	167
24.	Banned in the Republic of Ireland	173
25.	Lime	179
26.	A Piece of Grit	187
27.	Points of Departure	190
28.	Malaya	200
29.	Shoulder Flash	204
30.	The Cards in his Wallet	209
31.	'C'	211
32.	The Bell Tower	214
33.	Visas	224
34.	The Splinter	228
35.	Mau Mau	235
36.	Dien Bien Phu	241
37.	No One Expects the Inquisition	248
38.	A Reformed Character	252
39.	Accidents Can Always Happen	256
40.	Anita	263
41.	Our Man on the Potomac	269
42.	The Filthiest Book I Have Ever Read	272
43.	6½ Raves	277
44.	A Mixture of Petrol and Vodka	284
45.	Handshakes and Contracts	288
46.	Bombs and Daiquiris	291
47.	The Whole Trouble	297
48.	Taxidermy Everywhere	301
49.	The Separating Sickness	306
50.	Alone in a Lift	319
51.	Changes	322
52.	Death and Taxes	328
53.	The End of a Long Rope	335

54.	Plastiques	341
55.	Masks	343
56.	The Real End of the World	351
57.	Statues and Pigeons	361
58.	The New Life	368
59.	Fidel at Night	373
60.	Papa Doc Honoured Me	378
61.	Morse Code on the Water Pipes	381
62.	Behind the Sand Dune	388
63.	A House Surrounded by Orange Trees	394
64.	No One's Poodle	404
65.	Light Bulbs	413
66.	About my Best	419
67.	Long Spoons	422
68.	Effervescence and Vibration	428
69.	The Diplomatic Passport	436
70.	Storming the Palace	450
71.	The Bomb Party	457
72.	Three Hostages	462
73.	J'Accuse	472
74.	I Am the Message	477
75.	Better a Bad Man	483
76.	Two Faces	488
77.	The Late Rounds	497
78.	A Sense of Movement	501
	Notes	509
	Acknowledgements	559
	Index	561

INTRODUCTION

It was mid-December 1951, and French colonial forces were fighting the nationalist Viet Minh for control of Vietnam. In the years that followed the French withdrew and American forces would come in ever greater numbers to pursue their own futile war. Phat Diem was a strategic enclave on the Gulf of Tonkin about 75 miles south of Hanoi, and it was now surrounded by Viet Minh guerrillas firing from a range of 600 yards. Wading ashore from a landing craft that also transported a French commando unit, the forty-seven-year-old Graham Greene, a tall man and perhaps an easy target, could see buildings that had been blasted by bazookas and a market in flames.

It reminded him of the Blitz, but with many more corpses, some sticking up out of a canal.[1] In a sight he would never forget, he came upon a mother and her tiny son dead in a ditch. They had wandered into the field of fire between the French and the Viet Minh and been brought down by just two shots, apparently French. Greene remembered especially the 'neatness of their bullet wounds'.[2] These were his people – Catholics. Greene wondered what panic they must have felt, and then knew it for himself when he became separated from his companions and stumbled, very briefly, between the lines of the Foreign Legion and the Viet Minh.[3]

Catholics and Buddhists from the town sheltered in and around the cathedral, bringing with them whatever they treasured – photographs, pots, pans, pieces of furniture. A friend of Greene's from an earlier visit, a Belgian priest named Willichs, had perched in the bell tower and was reading his breviary. With mortars firing and planes dropping bombs and supplies, a distressed Greene, thinking that this day he might die, asked to have his confession heard. Around 1980, he spoke of this as the last time he had received the sacrament, but soon after renewed the practice. On this memorable occasion in Phat Diem, he was given as a penance one 'Our Father' and one 'Hail Mary', and the priest handed him a Tintin book so that he would have something to read.[4]

Greene learned that the attack had begun with an advance party slipping into a procession in honour of Our Lady of Fatima. There was then a surprise attack on the officers' quarters, although it turned out that only one of the dead was an officer – twenty-five enlisted men were killed.[5]

No other journalist had got near this shambles, and the French were anxious to keep it a secret. Greene got the impression that they regarded the Belgian priest as a spy – he belonged to the Société des Auxiliaires des Missions, which existed specifically to aid the transition from colonial to national churches in Asia, an objective that hardly endeared them to the French in Vietnam.[6] In any event, Greene and the priest were both independent witnesses to what had happened, so having spent just one night there – he slept in his clothes with a revolver on his pillow[7] – he accepted an offer to get away and spend twenty-four hours with the navy. But the officer who escorted him upriver to the city of Nam Dinh left him there and hurried back to Phat Diem. Returning to Hanoi, he could see that it was all a cover story and that he had been got rid of.[8]

Getting rid of Graham Greene was never going to be an easy proposition. Vietnam is perhaps the best known of his political and literary involvements. He made four winter visits to Vietnam, and in 1955 the fight for Phat Diem provided a pivotal scene in his novel *The Quiet American*, which provoked outrage in the United States by revealing how deeply the country was involved in the bloodshed, in the belief that a distant colonial conflict was a front line in the Cold War. This brave and prescient novel foresaw the American war in Vietnam, the horrors of which continued until 1975.

Half a century later, the novel still causes awkward moments along the Potomac. In 2007, former president George W. Bush, a man sometimes thought a prisoner of his own innocence, gave a speech to the Veterans of Foreign Wars, which included an odd remark, indicating that the novel's criticism of American foreign policy retained its sting in the time of the Iraq War: 'In 1955, long before the United States had entered the war, Graham Greene wrote a novel called "The Quiet American." It was set in Saigon, and the main character was a young government agent named Alden Pyle. He was a symbol of American purpose and patriotism – and dangerous naivete. Another character describes Alden this way: "I never knew a man who had better motives for all the trouble he caused."[9] When a later president, Donald Trump, arrived in Hanoi, where crowds and cameramen were kept at a distance, he tweeted of 'Tremendous crowds, and so much love!', and checked into the Hotel Metropole where Greene had once stayed. He was immediately dubbed 'the unquiet American'.[10]

Graham Greene continues to speak to an unquiet world. This biography will unravel the public and private lives of this most admired novelist. Shirley Hazzard spoke of him as 'one of the writers of the century', and John le Carré believes that in his time Graham Greene 'carried the torch of English literature, almost alone'.[11]

This book takes a very high view of Graham Greene's accomplishments, and so endorses the common opinion of three generations of writers and critics that he is one of the most important figures in modern literature. In course of time, our sense of even a great author's work will contract to a few defining books. That is how canons are formed. And yet, the process is wasteful. It is easy enough to boil Graham Greene's accomplishment down to, say, five essential books of his middle years: *Brighton Rock* (1938), *The Power and the Glory* (1940), *The Heart of the Matter* (1948), *The End of the Affair* (1951), and *The Quiet American* (1955). Once we do this, however, other first-rate novels, especially those written after 1960, not to mention his plays, short stories, journalism, essays, letters, memoirs, film scripts, and travel books, are shunted off into lists of 'Further Reading'. In fact, Graham Greene is one of the very few modern writers in English who can be valued for a whole body of work. As a craftsman, he was a perfectionist rarely content with something he had written, and so we can sometimes be misled by his criticisms of his own books. Like any writer, he could occasionally be uneven; still he maintained an extraordinarily high technical standard in his writing, and many of his insights into human character and motivation, politics, war, human rights, sexual relationships, and religious belief and doubt remain compelling and provocative. It is hard to think of a recent writer in English who comes as close to greatness as he does.

A NEW BIOGRAPHY

There is already a three-volume authorized biography of Graham Greene by Norman Sherry (1989–2004) and a more prosecutorial work by Michael Shelden (1994), as well as several fragmentary or partial works. Both completed biographies occasioned controversy when published, not least because they focused to a remarkable degree on the minutiae of his sexual life, provoking some reviewers to regard parts of the works as prurient and trivial. Broadly speaking, the complaint against these works was that in the midst of all the lurid details they had lost sight of what mattered in the life of Graham Greene.

And yet the strengths and flaws of existing biographies may be almost moot, as the body of evidence has grown enormously since those works appeared; the landscape of his life has a different outline. In recent years, many thousands of pages of new letters and documents have become available, among them letters to his family, friends, publishers, agents, and close associates. In one instance, lost letters to his immediate family were discovered in a hollow book. His daughter, Caroline Bourget, has made available her collection of private letters from her father and participated in extended interviews, allowing a rich new perspective on his family life. The many letters Greene wrote to Father Leopoldo Durán, his confessor and companion on journeys through Spain and Portugal that gave rise to his entertaining and meditative novel *Monsignor Quixote*, have now been deposited in an archive, as have his letters, amounting to over a thousand pages, to his French agent Marie Biche, and a comparable collection of letters to the publisher Max Reinhardt – developments that allow for a much deeper knowledge of two of his most valued friendships, but also of the very complicated way he earned his living. A memoir by his wartime colleague at MI6 Tim Milne forces a careful reconsideration of the novelist's relationship with the double agent and defector Kim Philby.

A political memoir by Bernard Diederich, Greene's guide through Haiti and Central America, has, by itself, transformed our sense of the second half of his career, when his eye turned to politics and human rights in the southern hemisphere.

Oliver Walston has written a detailed and revealing memoir of his mother Catherine, Greene's lover in the 1950s and the inspiration for

Sarah in *The End of the Affair* – he has made that unpublished work and many private papers available as sources for this biography. Catherine has been written about by several authors, but often speculatively; her son's memoir corrects and widens the record on many particular points and allows for a more serious reflection on her relationship with Graham Greene. Yvonne Cloetta, Greene's last lover, published a memoir that revealed her private life with the novelist over thirty-two years, a period earlier researchers had to approach often through second-hand reports. A large collection of the papers of the novelist's friend Gillian Sutro contains, extraordinarily, many transcriptions of private conversations with Greene and Cloetta, and even surreptitious tape recordings, as Sutro secretly hoped to write a book about them – these include some of Greene's private recollections of the women in his life, including the stage designer and children's author Dorothy Glover.

Intrepid bibliographers have tracked down hundreds of Greene's fugitive publications. A group of expert researchers delving in archives has added greatly to what we know about particular aspects of his career, especially his sojourns in war-torn places.[12] New secondary works have changed our sense of what was going on in the countries Greene visited – a notable example being the new historiography of Mexico in the 1930s. Accordingly, it is not only possible but imperative to bring these sources together and to retell the story of Graham Greene's life and times.

That well-worn phrase, 'life and times', is actually the essence of this book. There is no understanding Graham Greene except in the political and cultural contexts of dozens of countries. And in an odd sense the reverse is also true: we fail to understand something about modern times if we ignore Graham Greene. Here is a single life on which much of the history of a century is written.

In his later books, Greene used the term 'involvement' to describe a kind of loyalty, passion, and commitment that can overtake a person who observes suffering and injustice – as a character remarks in *The Quiet American*, 'Sooner or later, one has to take sides. If one is to remain human.'[13] Greene travelled to many of the most afflicted places in the world and drew close to the sorrow and oppression he observed. His characters and plots emerged from his observing eye, his curiosity, and his sense of involvement. This process becomes the central narrative of Graham Greene's life – how politics, faith, betrayal, love, and exile become great fiction.

Broadly speaking, even as this biography narrates, with much new detail, the key events and patterns in his private life, it swings the balance away from obscure details of his sexual life, which have captivated earlier biographers, to an account of his engagement with the political, literary, intellectual, and religious currents of his time.

And so, what follows is a story of 'involvements' – Graham Greene risked his life in such places as Sierra Leone, Liberia, Mexico, Malaya, Vietnam, Kenya, Cuba, the Congo, Haiti, Paraguay, Panama, and Nicaragua. He needed constant stimulation to keep boredom, a debilitating feature of 'manic depression' (now known as bipolar illness), at bay. But that only explains so much. He had strong political principles, not least that American foreign policy was a threat to the whole world. He refused to accept the reasoning of the Cold War – he was not going to choose between East and West, but looked south to some of the world's poorest countries, where the urgency of each day made human nature that much more discernible. As Scobie in *The Heart of the Matter* speaks of Sierra Leone: 'Here you could love human beings nearly as God loved them, knowing the worst.'[14] He was vigorous in defence of dissidents everywhere, from behind the Iron Curtain to the United States, and of writers imperilled by their beliefs.

In a sense, this is not one narrative but several braided together. It looks at the psychological history of a man who was traumatized as an adolescent over questions of loyalty and betrayal, and then suffered a mental illness that brought him to the point of suicide on several occasions. It is the story of a traveller, whose restlessness caused him to seek out troubled places, where his concerns were politics, poverty, and human rights. It is the story of a man who struggled to believe in God and yet found himself described, against his will, as a great Catholic writer. It is the story of a private life in which loves and passions ended in one ruin after another, until his sixth decade when he found constancy and peace in an unconventional relationship. It is a story of politicians, battlefields, and spies. More than anything, it is the story of a novelist mastering his craft, and exercising it in ways that changed the lives of millions.

THE DOG IN THE PRAM

'The first thing I remember is sitting in a pram at the top of a hill with a dead dog lying at my feet.' So wrote Graham Greene in the memoir, *A Sort of Life*, that he published in his sixties. The dog was his sister's pug, killed on the road, and the nurse could think of no better way to get its corpse home than to load it in with the baby. When he was five years old, he saw a man run into one of the town's almshouses intent on slitting his throat – his elder brother Raymond recalled that Graham did witness the man slashing himself but Graham had no recollection of it.[1] For many writers, an Edwardian childhood was a lighted thing, the last lovely time before fathers and brothers marched off to the Great War.

Raymond, who became a leading physician, once remarked drily of their childhood: 'I saw nothing horrible in the woodshed, perhaps because we had no woodshed.'[2] Graham wrote more lyrically of the years before his troubled adolescence: 'The clouds of unknowing were still luminous with happiness. There was no loneliness to be experienced, however occupied the parents might be, in a family of six children, a nanny, a nursemaid, a gardener, a fat and cheerful cook, a beloved head-housemaid, a platoon of assistant maids, a whole battalion of aunts and uncles, all of them called Greene, which seemed to bring them closer . . . The six birthdays arrived, the Christmas play, the easter and summer seaside, all arrived like planets in their due season, unaffected by war.'[3]

Looking back, Graham suggested that he never knew a world without pointless death, but his early years passed in an atmosphere of affection, ease, and security. His Edwardian parents were distant, in the fashion of the times, but the siblings remembered them always as loving and beloved. Of course, he did observe the troubles of people who lived in the town of Berkhamsted in Hertfordshire, but his own world was protected.

He did suffer some of the gruesome medical practices of the time: when he was five, he had his adenoids and tonsils removed in an oper- ation carried out at home – he saw a tin basin full of his own blood and remained fearful of blood, until he took on rescue work during the Blitz.[4] As a child, he fell into the hands of a dentist who must have trained under Torquemada, and he later suffered from pleurisy, which left him with a fear of drowning.[5]

For all that, there is still a contrast between the outward facts of Greene's early life and his grim descriptions of it in *A Sort of Life*. That memoir was actually begun on the instructions of a psychiatrist trying to avoid giving Greene electro-shock therapy for depression in the 1950s (see p. 369) – writing seemed the safer therapy. One can even hear in the remark about the dead dog an address to the psychiatrist. Nonetheless, Greene does allow, here and there, for comfort: 'From memories of those first six years I have a general impression of tranquil- lity and happiness, and the world held enormous interest, even though I disappointed my mother on my first visit to the Zoo by sitting down and saying, "I'm tired. I want to go home."' This passage is followed by an account of his terrors of birds, bats, and house fires, and a series of nightmares in which a witch digs her fingernails into his shoulders until finally he drives her off for good.[6]

'If I had known it,' he wrote, 'the whole future must have lain all the time along those Berkhamsted streets.'[7] A pleasant Hertfordshire market town with a population of about seven thousand,[8] it had a large Norman church, St Peter's, where Greene recalled a duke's iron helmet, of which there is no other record,[9] hung 'on a pillar like a bowler hat in a hall'.[10] The local magnate was Earl Brownlow, a member of the Egerton family. His 5000-acre estate, Ashridge Park, included extensive gardens, as well as woodlands where in spring bluebells still grow in dreamlike profusion.[11] An important site in Greene's early life and then in his fic- tion was the ruined Berkhamsted Castle on its high mound. Originally, it was built of timber after the Norman Conquest, and Thomas Becket rebuilt it in stone. In the fourteenth century Edward, the Black Prince, often stayed there,[12] but by the twentieth century only sections of wall stood, like broken teeth.

The Grand Junction Canal ran through the town, and there was a constant traffic of barges carrying freight. But Graham feared the canal as there always seemed to be another drowning, and the many canal workers and their children struck him as grimy and menacing. Twice a day, commuters to London, clutching attaché cases, trudged up and down Kings Road like figures out of *The Waste Land*. In a remark that tells us more about Greene than about Berkhamsted, he said that anywhere in the world he would recognize people from the town, their 'pointed faces like knaves on playing cards, with a slyness about the eyes, an unsuccessful cunning'.[13]

There was nothing sly about his father, Charles Greene, who came to Berkhamsted in 1888. He had studied at Bedford Grammar School and gone up to Wadham College, Oxford, as an exhibitioner in 1884, obtaining a third in Classical Moderations in 1886 and a second in Modern History in 1888. He was athletic, charming, and good looking, and had spent time in France, where he mastered the language. On their travels, he and a schoolmaster friend were approached in Naples by an oddly familiar man who asked to join them as they drank their coffee. He ordered something stronger and entertained them for an hour with his witty talk, then left them to pay for his drink. Only after he had gone did they realize that this was Oscar Wilde, not long out of prison. Charles would retell this story with the observation: 'how lonely he must have been to have expended so much time and wit on a couple of schoolmasters on holiday'.[14]

Hoping to become a barrister in London, Charles took a temporary position at Berkhamsted School, but then stayed for thirty-nine years, serving as headmaster from 1910 until 1927. The school had been founded by Dr John Incent, a Dean of St Paul's, in 1544. Although good things happened from time to time, its history reads as a series of cash-grabs by kings and by officials of the school looting the foundation. By the early 1800s, the headmaster did nothing but enjoy his perks since there was just one scholar enrolled.[15] Things were gradually set right, and after 1864 a reforming headmaster decided that Berkhamsted should be primarily a boarding school[16] – an arrangement, very common at the time, that would later cause grief to Graham Greene. This headmaster was succeeded in 1887 by the extremely energetic Thomas Charles Fry, a future Dean of Lincoln, who promptly hired his former student and relative by marriage Charles Greene. He was very generous to Charles, appointing him housemaster of the newly established St John's House and grooming him to be the next headmaster.[17] The impact he made on the small boy was long-lasting. He would later hear from his Oxford tutor Kenneth Bell that Fry was a flogger, and from Father George Trollope, who received Graham into the Catholic church, that he was harshly anti-Catholic. Still, Graham's description of him as 'sinister' and 'sadistic' has mystified those who researched Fry's life and found him, in general, benevolent. In any event, Graham recalled him vividly as a 'Manichean figure in black gaiters'[18] (buttoned gaiters still being part of the garb of senior Anglican clergy).

At the end of 1895 Charles married his cousin, the slim, elegant, six-foot-tall, intellectual, and somewhat remote Marion Greene.[19] Charles was the grandson and Marion the great-granddaughter of Benjamin Greene, the brewer of Bury St Edmunds, whose name lives on in pints of Greene King IPA. Benjamin had thirteen children, so the bloodlines are hard to follow. One line of descent includes the novelist Christopher Isherwood.[20] Benjamin had business on St Kitts in the West Indies, and, in a discreditable episode in the family history, owned 225 slaves there, as well as another six in Monserrat, according to the records of compensation paid in 1834 to masters under the Slavery Abolition Act.[21] One of his sons, Charles, is said to have fathered about thirteen children in St Kitt's before dying at the age of nineteen[22] – the mothers were evidently former slaves still living in a form of servitude. In the 1960s, Graham's younger brother Hugh researched this branch of the family and published an article frankly disclosing the history of slaveholding and sexual exploitation.[23] Following up, Graham himself visited the island and met some of his very distant cousins in 1970.[24]

The marriage of the cousins, Charles and Marion, rolled the dice on inherited illnesses. Charles's father, William, suffered from what Graham judged, very reasonably, to be manic depression, a disease long known to run in families – it has now been established that in a family where one person has the disease the likelihood of others suffering from it increases tenfold.[25] William died on an impulsive visit to St Kitts, after long absence from the island, in 1881. Marion's father, the Reverend Carleton Greene, also had a mental illness; he suffered from extreme guilt, and as Graham wrote, 'when his bishop refused his request to be defrocked, proceeded to put the matter into effect himself in a field'. That is, he stripped naked before the watching villagers.[26] 'We were never told anything about that grandparent and I had always assumed he was dead before I was born.'[27] In fact, he survived until 1924, and Graham later supposed that this man posed 'a living menace' to his daughter's family.[28]

A more cheerfully embraced piece of family history was that Marion's mother, of the Scottish Balfour family, was a cousin of the novelist Robert Louis Stevenson. The young Graham Greene liked to think of Stevenson's great adventure novel *Kidnapped*, with its young hero, as taking place on 'the wild, open stretches' of Berkhamsted Common. Marion may have met Stevenson when he came to visit her mother;[29] she certainly knew his friend and editor Sidney Colvin, and the child Graham was once permitted to play bagatelle – a game like billiards – on a board that had belonged to Stevenson.[30] His own fiction was influenced in important ways by Stevenson, and in 1949 Heinemann commissioned Greene to write a biography of him; he soon abandoned it as another author was working on a similar book.[31] Greene gestures towards that abandoned project in *The End of the Affair*, when the novelist Bendrix decides to write a biography of Gordon of Khartoum.

Charles and Marion Greene had six children: the first, Alice Marion, known as 'Molly' (1897–1963), went on to live a quiet domestic life after falling off a mountain she was climbing into the arms of a man below, who became her husband; Herbert (1898–1968) was athletic in youth but alienated much of the family with his drinking, idleness, and fascist opinions; Raymond (1901–82) became a leading endocrinologist, and his life included a successful ascent of Mount Kamet in the Himalayas in 1931 and a nearly successful attempt on Everest two years later; Henry Graham, the future novelist, came as the fourth child on 2 October 1904; Hugh (1910–87) was a journalist of formidable intellect and eventually became Director-General of the BBC; and Elisabeth (1914–99) served in Admiralty intelligence through the war and in later years became Graham's private secretary.

The children saw a good deal of Marion's sisters Maud and Nora (known as 'Nono'), and in the summer holidays stayed at the home of Charles's unmarried elder brother Sir (William) Graham Greene at Harston Hall, Cambridgeshire. Sir Graham himself hated children so fled to London during the visits. He rather resembled Sir Arthur Conan Doyle's character Mycroft Holmes, the elder brother of Sherlock – he was an expert at everything. A close associate of Winston Churchill, he had a hand in setting up naval intelligence and advised on defence matters until the end of his life. In old age he survived falling under a train on the London Underground by remaining very still until he was rescued. At the age of ninety-one he fell, without great harm, from a tree he was pruning. It was apparently a garden chair that finally killed him: he tripped over it, injured a foot, and gangrene took hold – the sign that he was at the end was a toe that came off with his sock.[32]

Uncle Eppy – Charles's younger brother Edward – who had made a fortune in the coffee business in Brazil, also set up home in Berkhamsted with his German wife Eva, in a house with seventeen bedrooms. Arriving in 1910, they became known as the 'Hall Greenes' in contrast to the poorer and more bookish 'School Greenes'. Eppy and Eva also had a brood of six: Benjamin, the eldest, was something of a dreamer, and in adult life he dabbled in extreme politics and was detained in 1939 as a possible Nazi sympathizer; Eva, called 'Ave', on whom Graham had a crush in his teenage years; and Barbara, who would save his life when they later trekked together through the Liberian jungle; Edward, or 'Tooter', who was a month younger than Graham and his closest friend among his cousins; the brilliant but erratic Felix, who became a journalist, pseudo-mystic, and apologist for Mao's Great Leap Forward (Graham despised him); and Katharine, a late child. The Hall Greenes learned German from their mother, and had ways that seemed strange to the School Greenes.[33]

Until Graham was six, his home was the red-brick St John's House in Chesham Road, which Charles had purchased in 1896.[34] According to the practice of the time, he ran the house as a business. David Pearce, a former master of the school, observes: 'That was why the characters of the housemaster and his wife were so important. A skinflint could keep his boys on thin rations, whereas a generous couple would become renowned for keeping a good table.'[35] St John's was a busy place. A matron and six female servants looked after more than forty borders in the somewhat severe dormitories with their pitch-pine partitions.

The Greene children were looked after in the family quarters by a much-loved nurse from Wiltshire named Annie Hyde. Graham remembered her as an old woman with a white bun holding a sponge over him in the bath. She had been hired when Molly was born and remained for many years, until her cantankerousness made her impossible and she was let go with a pension. There was also a series of nursery maids who did not hold up against Annie's temper. Graham wrote: 'I never remember being afraid of her, only impressed by that white bun of age.'[36]

The children would be brought down to play with their mother for an hour after tea, Graham fearing that his mother would tell them, yet again, the story of the Babes in the Wood, in which children are abandoned and birds cover their bodies with leaves – the story would make him cry. Remembering this, he later remarked: 'My tear-ducts in childhood, and indeed for many years later, worked far too easily, and even today I sometimes slink shame-faced from a cinema at some happy ending that moves me by its incredibility.'[37] This is the same writer who fashioned the dark ending of *Brighton Rock* and tried to stamp out sentimentality in his fiction as if at war with something in himself.

Although the adult Graham Greene disliked children, portraying them often as cruel and treacherous, he was himself a pleasant little boy, especially after he had his adenoids and tonsils out. Alice Greene, another of Charles's sisters, visited at Christmas 1909 and wrote of the five-year-old:

... how shall I describe little Graham? He is an utterly different child – evidently since that operation. Can you imagine little Graham with Raymond's charm? He is bright, sunny & gay, chatters all day long, has pretty manners, & a certain pretty little serious grace of his own which is altogether charming. I expect you have heard how he once said to his mother 'I am for Votes for Women,' & now I have seen him I can quite realize him saying it.

On Sunday afternoon Dr. Fry and Julia called. 'So Graham would give Women the Vote?' said Dr. Fry. 'No, if he had them he would keep them for himself' said someone & then Dr. Fry said 'Come, Graham, you would give Women the Vote, would you not? You are for Votes for Women?' Graham laughed uneasily, writhed a little when he realized that everyone was looking at him & said with a burst of charming frankness 'I believe in them!'[38]

He was late learning to read. His parents, using such primers as *Reading without Tears*, found him resistant to all their efforts. Then, suddenly, on a visit to Harston Hall, he was able to penetrate 'a real book. It was paper-covered with the picture of a boy, bound and gagged, dangling at the end of a rope inside a well with water rising above his waist – an adventure of Dixon Brett, detective.' Not wanting to be discovered, he took it up to the attic. His mother seems to have guessed, and gave him a copy of R. M. Ballantyne's *The Coral Island* for the train home, but to keep his secret he determinedly stared at the book's single illustration the whole way. In retrospect, he wondered whether he feared being sent to the preparatory school if it was known that he could read.[39]

Greene believed that 'early reading has far more influence on conduct than any religious teaching'.[40] As the son of the headmaster, he had access to plenty of books, and even as an old man he still had on his shelves many he had read in childhood. His imagination always drew on this bank of reading. It is commonly observed, for example, that his fascination with men on the run has its roots in the works of Robert Louis Stevenson and John Buchan. When Greene revised *The Ministry of Fear*, he added a series of epigrams from *The Little Duke* by Charlotte M. Yonge. Before finishing *The Human Factor*, he went to the Transvaal see the Rain Queen, who figures in Rider Haggard's *She*.[41] Captain Gilson's *The Pirate Aeroplane* contains a scene in which the young hero, expecting to be killed in the morning, plays cards with his captor; this influenced the portrayal of a game of cards in *England Made Me*, and, apparently, a key episode in *The Power and the Glory*, where the whisky priest spends the night in charged dialogue with the Lieutenant.

In their nursery, the Greene children pored over books by G. A. Henty, who specialized in heroic warfare and rejoiced in such titles as *Under Drake's Flag*, *With Wolfe in Canada*, and *With Clive in India*. Henty's books permeated the minds of boys in Britain a century ago, and while the adult Greene repudiated the lessons of Empire and noble warfare he remained obsessed with travel, believing life to be more urgent in troubled places. His conversation with Henty never quite ended.[42]

One book stood out among all the others, a historical novel set in

Italy: 'But when – perhaps I was fourteen by that time – I took Miss Marjorie Bowen's *The Viper of Milan* from the library shelf, the future for better or worse really struck. From that moment I began to write. All the other possible futures slid away: the potential civil servant, the don, the clerk had to look for other incarnations.' He saw in the book's villain, Visconti, the Duke of Milan, the cruelty and charisma of a bullying friend named Carter: 'He exercised terror from a distance like a snow-cloud over young fields. Goodness has only once found a perfect incarnation in a human body and never will again, but evil can always find a home there. Human nature is not black and white but black and grey. I read all that in *The Viper of Milan* and I looked round and I saw that it was so.' After reading that story, he began filling exercise books with similar tales; he was now launched on the life of a writer, and even sixty years later, the sinister Visconti would still fire his imagination as he gave the name to the war-criminal lover of Aunt Augusta in *Travels with My Aunt*.

In the autumn of 1910, Thomas Fry resigned as headmaster in order to become Dean of Lincoln. Even though Charles Greene was Fry's favoured candidate to succeed him, it took three ballots for the governors to elect him out of a field of thirty. Once it was settled, Fry, a small man with a large beard, was seen dancing for joy as he led Charles Greene into the school quadrangle. Although recalled as a 'brilliant and inspiring' teacher, Charles lacked Fry's magnetism and his understanding of boys. But his colleagues admired many things about him, not least his lucid prose style. Moreover, he was an orator and could make a fine impression upon the parents; this was invaluable as sometimes other speakers made a mess of things. In an episode that brings to mind P. G. Wodehouse's character Gussie Fink-Nottle, the Earl Brownlow gave out prizes on Founder's Day in 1912 and offered this consolation to those who got nothing: 'Some of the most successful men were stupid boys at school. Wellington's mother used to say what a stupid boy he was . . .'[43] Perhaps his drink had been spiked.

From time to time, Charles brought in celebrities, such as Sir Ernest Shackleton who told the boys about polar exploration.[44] Fascinated, Graham dreamed of joining an expedition to Antarctica. At the age of about ten, he wrote to the explorer William Speirs Bruce, correcting supposed errors in his book *Polar Exploration*. 'I received a courteous and defensive reply'.[45]

With Charles's promotion, the family moved into School House in Castle Street. At first Graham shared a room with the always-crying baby Hugh, then with Raymond – they quarrelled daily and he tried 'very hard' to kill Raymond with a croquet mallet.[46] In calmer moments, Graham was entranced by the walled garden and its clouds of butter-flies. In the larger of two greenhouses were Charles's rare orchids, one worth more than £300; they all died one night when a drunk gardener allowed the temperature to drop. Charles bore the loss and allowed the gardener to keep his job. A white cat inhabited an adjoining cemetery and Charles told Graham it was the ghost of an absentee headmaster from the eighteenth century.[47]

As a young man, Graham was dismissive of his father, but once he had children of his own he realized that his father's affection for him and interest in him had been authentic.[48] However, it does seem that Charles was a little out of touch with the world. A classmate of Graham's, W. A. Saunders, remembered the headmaster making an announcement: '"I have here a request from some boys who want to see the film 'Tarzan of the *Alps*'," said Charles breathing over the note. Masters to right & left & rear lean toward him and gratingly whisper, "Apes".[49]

Graham's affection for his mother, whom he and his siblings called 'Mumma', is not difficult to see, as hundreds of his candid letters to her survive. However, he was ultimately more critical of her than of his father. She was a snob while he was not. Graham remembered her absorption in news of the royal family, and her disgust when the daughter of a tripe-seller married a member of the Inns of Court Officer Training Corps (OTC) stationed in Berkhamsted.[50]

The school had its own snobberies, which Graham learned about when he entered the new Junior School in the summer term of 1912, just before he turned eight. For years, local boys had been charged £6 per year in tuition fees and boarders £9. In 1907 the governors raised the fee to £12 for everyone, while setting up a system of scholarships, and bursaries for boys who needed them.[51] The writer Peter Quennell, Graham's contemporary at the school, recalled the pecking order: 'Below an aristocracy of boarders lay a middle-class, which included myself, of easy-going day-boys, and, yet lower, a despised proletariat, the "train-boys", so called because they arrived by train from various adjacent towns.' Also called 'train bugs', this last group attended the school with financial assistance and were mocked for their accents, bad clothes, and supposed smell.[52]

Some sixty years later, in his memoir *A Sort of Life*, Greene wrote of the caning of such a boy, whose name he could not remember.[53] After it was published, he received a letter from a county councillor and governor of the school, Hilary Rost, speaking of how her father, Arthur Mayo, had been traumatized by his years at Berkhamsted. Greene remembered then that *this* was the boy who had been so severely caned. Mayo's daughter told him of her father's experience with one master in particular who 'would make the scholarship boys stand up, while he told the rest of the class that they must watch these characters carefully as their fathers were paying their fees and they should make sure that they were not wasting their money. They were verbally abused and most of the staff evidently condoned this.' Her father had told her how Graham would make a point of coming up to him after these sessions and engaging him in discussions about some academic subject, 'making it quite clear that he respected him and would have nothing to do with the invitation to bully'. At the time Rost contacted him, her father was in hospital. Graham sent a signed copy of the book to him, which he finished reading just before he died.[54]

Charles Greene did what he could to make the train-boys feel at home by establishing a house for them, and tried to encourage a sense of social responsibility among the more privileged. Inspired by what Graham later called 'rather noble old liberalism',[55] Charles gave his backing to the Cavendish Association, formed in 1913 to promote understanding between classes, and between capital and labour. He allowed them to recruit in the school, as they did at other public schools and at universities, and the school magazine carried an editorial supporting their mission: 'A man who lives on a meagre diet in the slums of Whitechapel is neither physically nor mentally fit to perform his duties as a citizen. It is our duty to find a remedy for a state of affairs which permits this. Social service is as necessary for the welfare of our Empire as military service.'[56] By today's standards, the Cavendish Association was cautious and paternalistic, but it represented a generous social impulse.

The most active recruiting was military. The OTC enlisted two hundred boys, half of the school, in the last year of peace. There were plenty of musketry competitions, and the reason was no secret: 'Exactly the same preparation is required to ensure success in the Messum Cup as is necessary for success in war.'[57] The school magazine carried a letter from a colonel in the Royal Artillery asking school leavers to join up.[58]

When war was declared in August 1914, the Greenes were at Harston. Soldiers marched past. The boys seized on every scrap of news that suggested the fighting would go on for years and that they might have a part in it. In fact, only Herbert signed up and he did not see action. In November, the school magazine reported that almost four hundred Old Berkhamstedians were already in service and it pressed the 'imperative claims of OTC', including five parades per fortnight. It added bluntly, 'as the war drags on its slow course still more of us will go forth to take the places of those who fall'.[59] By now, all the boys in the senior school were enlisted in the OTC. There was always some group of boys marching on the Common or crawling through the trenches carved into it.

It took a long time for the boys to grasp what was going on, especially as they did not know many of the OBs who were going to the front. The first was killed on 30 October 1914,[60] and by March 1915 there were still just three dead and thirteen wounded.[61] In June, there was an example of great valour to report: twenty-one-year-old Lieutenant Inglis Miller had been found with two wounds on the battlefield at Cambrai, surrounded by dead and dying Germans; he died in August.[62] By December, forty-three had been reported dead.[63] The slaughter intensified during the Battle of the Somme, as forty-six died between 1 July and 17 November 1916.[64] On Founder's Day, 22 July 1918, Charles Greene reported that of 1145 OBs who had by then entered service, 184 had been killed and 177 wounded; 121 had been mentioned in despatches, seventy-eight had received the Military Cross, seventeen the Distinguished Service Order, and twenty-eight had been granted foreign and other honours. There was one recipient of the Victoria Cross.[65] There were terrible sorrows, too, in Berkhamsted as three brothers named Sprunt, respectively aged twenty-four, twenty-two, and twenty-one, were all killed.[66]

2

FLIGHT

'If you pushed open a green baize door in a passage by my father's study, you entered another passage deceptively similar, but none the less you were on alien ground. There would be a slight smell of iodine from the matron's room, of damp towels from the changing rooms, of ink everywhere. Shut the door behind you again, and the world smelt differently: books and fruit and eau-de-Cologne.'

That door marked the border of separate countries, home and school: 'I had to remain an inhabitant of both countries.'[1]

Unlike his popular and athletic brother Raymond, who was at home on either side of the baize door and eventually became a prefect, Graham felt an exile in the school. The other boys thought he must be a Judas – betraying them to his father, the headmaster. Bookish, he was frequently excused games because of his flat feet – this too marked him as an outsider. And once the war started, there were plenty of objective reasons to find the dormitories and classrooms grim. Many of the best masters enlisted and their temporary replacements were, often enough, the dregs of the profession, even brutes. The quality of the food fell off – different dormitories had different systems of rationing but eventually everyone had to accept porridge as a substitute for bread.[2] Depression was in the air.

At thirteen, Graham had a difficult year. He spent a term at the bottom of his form, suffered a lapse in confidence, and was experiencing depression. He entered the senior school in the autumn of 1918, when he was about to turn fourteen. His parents sent him to board at St John's House, where he had spent his earliest years. Their intentions are not clear, but perhaps they thought the experience would bring him closer to the other boys. Herbert and Raymond had been sent away to Marlborough College, and they hated it.[3] For Graham, there was evidently no question of another school.

Torn between loyalty to his father and to the boys in the dormitory, Graham was guilt-ridden and alienated, and so became a loner. *The Lawless Roads*, his account of a persecution of the Catholic church in Mexico, starts with a brief description of his own school life and the cruelties committed by boys against one another. Like Mexico, he saw the school as a place 'of lawlessness' where no one is cared for or protected.[4] And in this atmosphere of harm, Graham attempted self-harm. One morning, he listened to the other boys heading down the stairs for early prep or breakfast, and took a dull knife to his knee. He did not have the nerve to cut deeply,[5] but worse things were to follow.

He was not often attacked apart from being jabbed with a pair of dividers, but was subject to sly verbal abuse and was tagged with nicknames. He became friends with a boy named Lionel Carter, his Visconti, who secured his trust by gestures of friendship then played on his troubled loyalties to a degree that Greene later recalled as torture. Having written about Carter in *A Sort of Life*, Greene was interested in his old schoolmate W. A. Saunders's recollection: 'pale red hair, snake-like skull who curled the lip & distended the lip at the approach of buggy Saunders et al.'[6] Greene's memories of this whole episode were intense, but uncertain – the details he set down in *A Sort of Life* are consistently mistaken, as if blurred through decades of retelling and myth-making. He was reassured to learn from Saunders that Carter was indeed the boy's name, and not one he had himself invented along the way. He had referred to him as Collifex in *The Lawless Roads* – presumably an effort to avoid a libel suit.

Carter had a sidekick named Augustus Wheeler, and the two of them caused Greene enormous pain when he was between the ages of thirteen and seventeen. It is not clear what forms the bullying took, but Greene saw in Carter's cruelty a kind of 'finesse', an implied promise that the pain would end and friendship become secure. It appears that Wheeler was hurtful in a cruder way, deserting Greene on several occasions for friendship with Carter. Wheeler came from a military background; his father was dead and his mother had sent him to boarding school – this mixture could easily lead a boy into bullying. For years afterwards, Greene yearned to settle scores with Wheeler. But when, by a weird coincidence, the opportunity finally arose around Christmas 1950, he did nothing (see p. 202).

Greene spent eight terms, of thirteen weeks each, as a boarder at St John's House. He performed badly at the weekly OTC parade, where he was goaded by Carter and Wheeler. Solitary and often a truant, he gave up on the OTC, and as the headmaster's son he got away with it; Peter Quennell was also given permission to leave, but very few others. As Colonel Wilson, who oversaw the OTC, recalled: 'There were only four boys in the School who were not members of the Corps. Two of them were cripples, and one was the son of the headmaster.'[7] Although bucked up by a kindly matron and a master, Greene was experimenting with methods of suicide. He later said that he consumed 'hypo' (presumably hyposulphite of soda), a bottle of allergy drops, and deadly nightshade gathered on the Common, and that he swallowed a fistful of aspirin before getting into the school baths.

Many years later, he was diagnosed as manic depressive (bipolar) by an accomplished psychiatrist named Eric Strauss, and there is no reason to dispute the diagnosis. While he was at school, the mental illness was beginning to assert itself. Over the years, he was always restless and inclined to boredom; suicidal depressions would sometimes give way to euphoria; he was thrill-seeking, promiscuous, and hard drinking; he misused drugs – common enough features of the illness. Late in life he remarked: 'I have always been cyclothymic. In the past, I used to go through bouts of deep depression, followed by a period of great euphoria. It appears that I have now reached a plateau.'[8] Cyclothymia is a variation on bipolar illness, but the symptoms are not so intense or long-lasting.[9]

We do not possess Greene's psychiatric records, so caution needs to be exercised. And yet there is no denying that his moods were extreme and variable – he could be by quick turns irritable, wildly playful, urgently sexual, or suicidally depressed. Journalists looking for easy copy have sometimes condemned Graham Greene's character, but the disasters, especially of his marriage and sexual life, are generally more pitiable than culpable. Indeed, his survival itself is something of a triumph, for, as Dr Kay Redfield Jamison, an expert on bipolar illness, has observed, given his early behaviour it is remarkable that he did not succeed in killing himself.[10]

Eventually, Greene made a run for it. A *Sort of Life* offers an unreliable account of what happened, placing events at the end of the summer of 1920, after his eighth term as a border – which would in fact have been Easter 1921. A different timeline, compiled by David Pearce, a former master at Berkhamsted School, reconciles most of the existing evidence.[11] In *A Sort of Life*, Greene says that after breakfast on the last day of the summer holidays he left a note for his parents under the whisky tantalus, saying that he would remain hidden until they promised he would never have to live in St John's again. He says that he planned to conceal himself in the trenches that had been dug on the Common and eat blackberries, 'an invisible watcher, and a spy on all that went on'.[12] Greene describes the Common in late summer in considerable detail and the notion of eating blackberries would belong to that time of year.

His mother later described the episode: 'I cannot date when the crisis occurred but between 19 & 20 I think. Graham was not well the morning he should have gone back to St. John's – slight temperature & eyes peculiar. Doctor could not understand eyes. I kept him in bed. Went to do house-keeping & returned to find he was not there & a note to say he could not go back to St. John's – had tried to poison himself with eye-drops (accounts for eyes) in vain & had gone & we should not see him again. You can imagine how we felt. We did not want to go to the police at once. Uncle Eppy set his bailiff whom he could trust to hunt along canal. Dr. McB. took me all over golf-links in his car – we searched woods calling all the time. Then after lunch Molly said she had a feeling she could find him & taking Miss Arnell & some food they set out. *And* they found him sitting in the little wood where M. thought he might be. They brought him home & I put him to bed & told him he should never go back. Said why had he not told us.'[13]

Charles tried to understand what had happened. Graham spoke incoherently of 'filth' at St John's, meaning chiefly that boys were farting all the time. Charles thought he was referring obliquely to sex and concluded that Graham had been somehow victimized by a circle of masturbators. According to Graham, this was a bizarre misunderstanding as he had not yet discovered the practice. We have to accept his word that he was not sexually abused, as there is no other evidence to call on. Charles launched enquiries through the school, putting on the spot boys who had nothing to do with Graham's troubles: it is likely that these enquiries began after the late-summer flight to the Common. In his memoir, Graham downplays all this as a 'comedy of errors' – there may have been errors, but it was no comedy. Indeed, Greene generally writes with a suave flippancy of his inclination to suicide, and it is never really convincing. If Marion's recollection of the events was right, Graham could easily have ended up in a coffin.

Charles evidently persuaded him to go back to the boarding house, where he would remain for two more terms. In the late summer of 1920, Charles could reasonably promise that things would be better in the coming year. Graham would have less to do with Carter and Wheeler, as he had passed his School Certificate in June and was entering the sixth form while they were stranded in the fifth. It seems that some good things happened that Michaelmas Term. The improvement in his state of mind, later attributed solely to psychoanalysis, must have owed something to the liberties of the sixth form – he was engaged in more independent study and he had more literary companionship with people like Quennell. He was older and growing more worldly.

He was also open to hope, but of an odd sort. He described a particular Saturday night, perhaps 14 December 1920.[14] Loitering near School House, he could hear from across the quad the school orchestra playing Mendelssohn – he was supposed to be with the other boys listening to it. But for now he was alone on the croquet lawn. He could hear a rabbit in its hutch. For the first time, he felt that prayer was possible and that God was near: 'And so faith came to me – shapelessly, without dogma, a presence about a croquet lawn, something associated with violence, cruelty, evil across the way.' He could only imagine Hell, not yet a heaven, and it was founded on the squalor and hopelessness of the dormitories: 'The rabbit moved among the croquet hoops and a clock struck: God was there and might intervene before the music ended.' That night he was standing on a border between home and school: 'When people die on the border they call it a "happy death".' But death was not the solution. He went back to his dormitory.[15]

It is likely that Hilary Term 1921 was difficult for Greene and that he was again depressed around Easter. His parents put him on suicide watch in the spare bedroom next to their own. However, one good thing happened: Lionel Carter left the school at the end of term. But this was not quite the fall of Flashman, as he kept in touch with the school and played cricket for the Old Berkhamstedians.[16] We will likely never know whether his departure owed anything to the headmaster's enquiries into sexual practices in the school. It is possible that he was quietly told to leave and the matter hushed up. In any event, it must have been a relief to Graham Greene to be rid of his tormentor.

Finished with the dormitories, Graham was well enough to appear in a school play named *Lost Silk Hat* in Trinity Term. Charles was still afraid of an outbreak of the old family madness, so summoned Raymond back from Oxford, where he was studying medicine, to discuss Graham's condition. Raymond made a proposal, surprising for the time, that his younger brother be psychoanalyzed, and even more surprisingly his parents agreed. The field was very new, it was generally frowned upon by the reticent English of their generation, and it was no easy thing sorting out effective therapists from quacks. But Raymond made arrangements, and the sixteen-year-old Graham was sent by the end of June 1921 to London for a six-month course of treatment with a psychoanalyst 'of no known school' named Kenneth Richmond. Trained by Maurice Nicoll, a sometime Jungian and the main commentator on Ouspensky's and Gurdjieff's works, he was himself a spiritualist and became a leading light in the Society for Psychical Research.[17]

Although actually living with his mother's sister, Aunt Nono,[18] Greene spent spent much of the rest of the year in the house of Richmond and his beautiful wife Zoë at 15 Devonshire Terrace, near Lancaster Gate. He would regard this time as possibly the happiest in his life. He was suddenly free of the school regime; he was treated as an adult, had pocket money, and was able to wander about London. In late June, he went to see the Cubist works at the Tate, and was especially struck by Christopher Nevinson's images of the First World War. Richmond had a wide acquaintance among writers, and through him Greene met the novelist J. D. Beresford, as well as Naomi Royde-Smith, the literary editor of the *Westminster Gazette*, which would publish some of Greene's early poetry, and Royde-Smith's former lover Walter de la Mare, who happened to be Greene's favourite poet. In a game of charades at the Richmonds', de la Mare turned himself, very convincingly, into an asparagus. He was soon superseded in Greene's esteem by Ezra Pound, whose *Personae* he purchased from a small bookshop on the

Embankment. Greene attempted some lines in an imagist manner for a ballet dancer named 'Isula ... a future Pavlova' he had met through the Richmonds, but did not show them to her. Nothing came of this infatuation, and she disappeared from his life.[19]

Spiritualism was an important element in the Richmonds' life and Zoë's mother tried to convince him of the reality of angels, saying she knew officers who had seen them at Mons. Despite his spiritual experience the preceding winter, Greene was not convinced – he was already manifesting the mixture of belief and doubt that would characterize his adult life.[20]

While in London, he was to keep up with his studies. He spent most mornings revising medieval history in Kensington Gardens. When he heard the church bell ring eleven, he would return to Devonshire Terrace for his session with Richmond. Greene kept a dream diary, a practice he resumed in later years. If he could not remember a dream, at Richmond's suggestion he invented one – usually involving a pig. Richmond, holding a stopwatch, would then ask him what he associated with the main image and count the seconds till he answered.

An embarrassing moment came when he had only an erotic dream of Zoë to report. Not wanting to cheat, he decided he had better reveal it: he was lying in bed when she came into his room naked; one of her breasts came close to his mouth and he woke. Unfazed, Richmond asked what he associated with breasts and started his stopwatch. Greene answered, 'Tube train.' Richmond noted, 'Five seconds.'[21]

Believing in the power of dreams to illuminate wide areas of experience, Greene later adopted J. W. Dunne's theory, expounded in *An Experiment with Time* (1927), that dreams could provide glimpses of the future.[22] He also absorbed Dunne's fascination with 'serial' dreams, and precognitive dreams: he pointed to his own experience of dreaming at the age of five about a shipwreck on the night of the sinking of the *Titanic*, with the image of 'a man in oilskins bent double beside a companion-way under the blow of a great wave'. While with Richmond, he dreamt that he was in a shipwreck on the Irish Sea, only to learn a couple of days later that the SS *Rowan*, on its way from Glasgow to Dublin, had gone down at the time of his dream with the loss of twenty lives.[23]

The immediate benefit Greene derived from this course of

psychoanalysis likely did not lie in the decoding of his dreams, but in the deep affirmation involved in the therapeutic relationship. Richmond took his feelings seriously and built up his confidence. In the long run, however, attention to dreams became an aspect of Greene's method as a writer. He said that his early novel *It's a Battlefield* originated in a dream. So too a dream helped him resolve an impasse in the plot of *A Burnt-Out Case*: 'It was like coming to a river bank and finding no bridge. I knew what would happen on the other side of the bridge but I couldn't get there. I then had a dream which seemed to me to belong entirely to the character in the book rather than to myself and I was able to insert it in the novel and bridge the river.' In the 1960s he returned to keeping a dream journal: 'My experience bears out the fact that one dreams at least four or five times a night when once one has disciplined oneself to have a pencil and paper beside one in bed!'[24] After his death, selections from the dream journals were published as *A World of My Own*.

At the beginning of September 1921, he took a holiday from treatment and went with his Aunt Eva and his pretty cousin Ave on a short voyage to Spain. The Greenes were distantly related to the Napoleonic hero Sir John Moore, subject of one of G. A. Henty's biographies, *With Moore at Corunna*. They visited his grave at Corunna, a trip Greene repeated in 1976 as he was taking the journeys with Father Leopoldo Durán that gave birth to *Monsignor Quixote*.[25] After their return, Ave joined him at the Richmonds', as her parents had decided that she too needed to be analyzed. A few years later, Graham, Raymond, and Herbert all paid court to her, leaving their Aunt Eva unnerved for a time at the prospect of another marriage between cousins.[26]

Back in London, Greene witnessed one of the great commemorations of the war. On 17 October 1921, the American Chief-of-Staff General John Pershing laid the Congressional Medal of Honor on the grave of the Unknown Warrior at Westminster Abbey. Prime Minister Lloyd George attended, as did Winston Churchill, now Colonial Secretary, and Earl Haig, in whose face the young writer thought he could discern the lineaments of militarism. Greene sat beside a man who read a dreary poem to him about the League of Nations, 'But it was worth being bored because of the waiting period beforehand. The Abbey itself lighted up brilliantly, but outside the door nothing but a great bank of mist, with now and again a vague steel helmeted figure appearing, only to disappear again. The whole time the most glorious music from the organ, with the American band outside, clashing in at intervals. Then the feeling of expectancy through the whole people, the minds of everyone on tip-toe. It got back the whole atmosphere of the war, of the endless memorial services; I'd never realised before how we had got away from the death feeling.'[27]

Efforts to unravel what was troubling Graham took a strange turn that autumn. One evening, conversation at the Richmonds' dinner table turned to a road accident, which caused him to think of an incident involving two women thrown from a carriage on the Royston Road in Hertfordshire: a long hat pin was driven into the brain of one of them. Recalling this, he simply fainted. At school, he had fainted occasionally, but thought nothing of it. Richmond took him to a specialist who diagnosed epilepsy, a condition with a terrible stigma at the time, commonly connected with madness and demonic possession. Richmond wrote to Charles Greene explaining the diagnosis but did not tell Graham, who was simply given medication and told to consume malt.[28] Richmond attempted to put Charles Greene's mind at ease: 'Epilepsy, in its milder forms, is much less dangerous than measles or scarlet fever. And it is often associated with genius – a divine complaint from which I think your son also suffers.'[29]

The beginning of 1922 saw Greene back at Berkhamsted for his last term at school, with Richmond's encouragement to keep writing. He was not sent to St John's House, but lived with his family. Carter and Wheeler were gone from his life, and he spent time with Cockburn, Peter Quennell, and Eric Guest, who later became a magistrate. A little 'vain and knowing', he was able to discourse on Freud and Jung. Claud Cockburn says that Greene, with the bacon cooling on his breakfast plate, would encourage other members of the family to describe their dreams: '"It's amazing," he said to me once, "what those dreams disclose. It's startling – simply startling," and at the thought of it gave a low whistle.'[30]

This was a much briefer time than *A Sort of Life* suggests. It was his last term at school. He had been reading diligently while in London, but his studies were undirected. Back in Berkhamsted he began cramming for the scholarship examination at Balliol, a college chosen because one of the dons, Kenneth Bell, was an Old Berkhamstedian and protégé of Charles Greene. Graham offered papers in medieval history, with French and Latin as languages. His subsidiary subject was English literature. Despite two attempts, he failed to win a scholarship.

The Oxford examiners did not know what to make of Graham Greene: on one of his scholarship exams they gave him marks ranging widely – between $\acute{\alpha}$- and γ+. Three examiners, including Bell and F. F. 'Sligger' Urquhart (Evelyn Waugh's *bête noire*) inclined to the higher mark as, in Bell's words, 'it was highly imaginative stuff, sometimes thin and fantastic but written with real power over words. This boy had only done history for six weeks before coming in and his efforts to disguise his ignorance, though not very convincing, were extremely ingenious.'[31] It was not enough, of course. But at least he won a place at the college, and was then awarded a less lucrative exhibition, which gave him £50 in his second and third years, helping him reduce the generous £250 allowance from his father. So he went up to Oxford 'a muddled adolescent who wanted to write but hadn't found his subject, who wanted to express his lust but was too scared to try, and who wanted to love but hadn't found a real object'.[32]

3

BACKWARDS DAY

'I have now turned violent Conservative, & wander round canvass-ing the unfortunate poor.'[1] Graham Greene plunged into the life of Oxford University as soon as he arrived there in October 1922. He joined the Union and other organizations. With a general election looming on 15 November, he and his friends put forward a bogus can-didate named Jorrocks, who made speeches in a mask and had his own campaign literature: 'Old Wine in Old Bottles! A Plague on Promises! Personality Pays! ... Ask the Returning Officer where to put your X for Jorrocks The Independent Independent! Only Triangular Candidate for Oxford.'

He was with the playful Mantichorean Society when its members descended on Wallingford in costume. One, a Scottish versifier named Robert Scott, went to the vicarage and played the part of a distressed clergyman searching for a runaway wife – he was given tea and prayed with, and told to forgive the woman; for his part, he left a bunch of bananas in the piano. There was a second clergyman, a monk, and a prince in uniform with his fiancée. Greene himself set up an easel in the market and drew people's souls for a fee; he also composed poems on the spot on any subject proposed to him. On occasion he went to the Hysteron Proteron Club for a 'Backwards Day': 'the morning', he said of one these events, 'started with bridge in dinner jackets' and at day's end, after porridge, 'we then returned backwards to Balliol'.

Despite being a prankish undergraduate, he was now very serious about his literary ambitions. In the spring before going up to Oxford, he had had his first publication in the *Berkhamstedian*, a short story called 'Tick Tock' about a solitary old woman who at her death is assured of 'love eternal'. The story was picked up by a London newspaper, the

Star, which paid him three guineas, his first literary earnings. He could not do better than the school magazine again until Naomi Royde-Smith published one of his short stories in the *Westminster Gazette* in May 1922, then five of his poems over the next two years. At Oxford he quickly became involved with an undergraduate review, *Oxford Outlook*, which also featured David Cecil, L. P. Hartley, William Gerhardi, Edward Sackville-West, and Christopher Isherwood; he became sub-editor the next year and editor at the end of 1924, and he made a point of publishing many of his own poems.

In his first term at Oxford he went to nearby Islip to see Robert Graves, who had been stationed for a time at Berkhamsted with the Artists' Rifles during the war. Graves had heard of 'great doings there. Wedding in the school chapel', and was amused to discover that this was the recent wedding of Greene's sister Molly to Lionel Walker.[2] Soon after, his schoolfriend Claud Cockburn took Greene to meet his cousin, Evelyn Waugh. A year older than Greene, Waugh had been a fairly conventional member of Hertford College since January. At the same time as meeting Greene, he discovered the aesthetes Harold Acton and Brian Howard, and entered the phase of his life that would provide the material for *Brideshead Revisited*. Although Greene and Waugh became close friends in middle age, they were merely acquaintances at Oxford. Waugh thought Greene looked on his circle as 'childish and ostentatious', but Greene felt that the difference lay elsewhere: 'I belonged to a rather rigorously Balliol group of perhaps boisterous heterosexuals, while your path temporarily took you into the other camp.'[3]

In the early 1920s, the poet Edith Sitwell and her brothers were leading figures in the modernist movement. In March 1923 Graham Greene told his mother that he had been converted to Sitwellism, which meant experimentation with prosody, a sly humour, and a touch of obscurity. In April he invited Sitwell to read poems to the Balliol College Society of Modern Poetry and Drama. She could not make it, but decided that this young man deserved her attention.[4] Greene then read her new collection, *Bucolic Comedies*, published in April 1923, and told his mother it was absolutely 'out middle stump'.[5] He wrote an essay on her work and sent it to the *Westminster Gazette*. Royde-Smith told him they had had enough articles on Edith Sitwell lately, but sent the piece directly on to Sitwell,[6] who wrote back to him: 'I am not used to people understanding anything whatever about my poetry, excepting perhaps an occasional image, and that only partially, as they do not understand the spiritual impulse behind the image. You have understood it all. Your comprehension appears to be absolutely complete. And this has given me the greatest possible pleasure.'[7] By June, he was drinking tea in her flat in Bayswater, and in November she gave him a poem to publish in *Oxford Outlook*.

Early in June, Greene and his friends had dinner with one of his favourite novelists, John Buchan, author of *The Thirty-Nine Steps*. Despite his own long association with the Scottish publisher Thomas Nelson, Buchan advised them against such careers because there is 'no opening in a publishing office. Unless you marry the publisher's daughter!' He recommended journalism and described his own successes at Reuters,[8] where he had become a director in 1919.

Greene's first effort at serious journalism followed shortly after, and it brought him to the first of his 'trouble spots'. The Irish Civil War had been fought over the Anglo-Irish Treaty signed in December 1921, providing for a Free State in the Catholic south and allowing the more Protestant north to remain in the Union. The new Free State was to be a dominion and not a republic, and its leaders would swear loyalty to the king. Republican forces regarded the treaty as a betrayal. The ensuing conflict involved numerous atrocities. The Chairman of the Provisional Government, Michael Collins, had himself been killed in an ambush on 22 August 1922, and the war itself continued until May 1923.

Greene had got to know members of the Nationalist Society in Oxford, who arranged for him to have contact with one of the Sinn Féin leaders, and he also managed to get an introduction to a Free State senator. In fact, he volunteered to send confidential reports to the Free State government, but his offer was ignored. The *Daily Express*, however, was interested in a series of five articles on the condition of Ireland.[9] Accompanied by his cousin Tooter, he went to Ireland in mid-June, just after the war's end, and spent a week hiking from Dublin to Waterford. His enduring image of the trip was 'broken bridges all the way'. He later talked down the danger involved, but it was a mad outing, since two young men with English accents were bound to be objects of hostility in a place where any number of spies and informers had come to a bad end. In one town they had stones thrown at them.[10]

The *Daily Express* did not run his articles, and it appears he had difficulty placing them anywhere. Nine weeks after his return a single piece showed up in his old stand-by, the *Westminster Gazette*. That article is vivid but lacks focus, instead presenting a series of tableaux, among them a soldier dumping a pot of red paint on the head of a Republican slogan-painter. He concluded: 'It is like that most nightmar-ish of dreams, when one finds oneself in some ordinary and accustomed place, yet with a constant fear at the heart that something terrible, unknown and unpreventable is about to happen.'[11] All his life he would use the language of dream interpretation in his journalism and fiction. For Greene, the unknown and the unconscious were sometimes the same thing.

The walking tour in Ireland was a serious matter, but Greene also had a taste for simple shenanigans. In late 1923, he and Cockburn rented a barrel organ and disguised themselves as tramps, working their way through five Hertfordshire towns where, as often as not, they were given money to take their noise down the road. They met true tramps and tinkers, who treated them as comrades and warned them of 'skinflints'. They were well treated wherever they went, except at Abbots Langley, near Watford, where they were turned away from the inns and forced to sleep in a frosty field before discovering a half-built house, where they were alarmed in the night by a strange repeated sound: 'We woke again before dawn in the grip of cramp, and finally left the suspicious and uncharitable town for the comparative warmth of walking between high hedges, followed on our right hand by a spec-trally coughing cow – and so trundled out of the profession forever.'[12]

Journeys with the possibility of intrigue were what the nineteen-year-old Greene wanted most of all. Having read the recently published *Defeat*, a collection of short stories by Geoffrey Moss about the state of Germany after the war, he was disgusted, like many others in Britain, to learn that in 1922 the French had tried to divide and exploit the country by setting up a separatist 'Revolver Republic' in the occupied Ruhr; they had assembled a loose fighting force composed of thugs from German jails and brothels to assist the collaborators. The English and Americans prevented the French from carrying out the plan, but the Germans believed they would try again. Around the beginning of March 1924, Greene wrote 'on a blind & impudent off chance' to the

German embassy saying that many people in Oxford were pro-German and that he would like to write articles on the crisis for university publications following a visit to the Ruhr; however, he would need accommodation while there. Albrecht Graf von Bernstorff, the counsellor at the embassy, agreed to meet him during a visit he was making to Oxford.

Greene, going to his rooms at Balliol at the appointed time, found the blond, six-foot-six, twenty-stone Bernstorff already installed and polishing off the brandy. Born to a family of politicians and diplomats, he was becoming a fashionable figure in London. He was soon a regular presence at literary parties, including those of Edith Sitwell. The novelist Enid Bagnold was in love with him for many years. Prejudging Bernstorff somewhat because of his appearance and his frequenting of homosexual clubs, Greene did not then realize that this was a person of extraordinary character. An opponent of Hitler, he later found himself hated by Joachim von Ribbentrop, who served as ambassador to the United Kingdom and then Foreign Minister in Nazi Germany. During the war, Bernstorff helped to run an escape route for Jews to Switzerland and was executed in April 1945.[13]

Bernstorff gave Greene £25 for expenses – telling him to burn the envelope, which of course he instead kept as a souvenir – asking him to spend three weeks in Germany, and to focus on the Rhine and the Palatinate, observing that 'the Ruhr would be a transient problem, the Rhine a perpetual one'. The embassy gave him a series of briefings and numerous letters of introduction. Meanwhile, Greene obtained letters from Oxford newspapers identifying him as a journalist. At this time, or perhaps a little later, Greene tried to play 'double agent' by asking the *Patriot*, a right-wing and pro-French publication run by the Duke of Northumberland, to make him its correspondent in Trier; his plan was to report back to the Germans, but his offer came to nothing.[14]

Meanwhile, Charles Greene objected to the whole plan, on the grounds that too close an association with the Germans could ruin his son's reputation and prospects.[15] Nonetheless, in early April, Greene, Cockburn, and the German-speaking Tooter made their way to Cologne. Throughout their journey a German intelligence officer appeared from time to time to monitor their progress. In Cologne they picked up more letters of introduction and met industrialists and politicians. In Essen they stayed at the private Krupp hotel and spoke with one of the firm's directors. They discovered that the German population was angry with all foreigners, supposing them French occupiers. One evening they went to a cabaret and watched a nude dancer symbolizing Germany bursting out of her chains. They went on to Bonn, seeing few signs of trouble there. However, Trier, occupied by the French, was another story. Soldiers were everywhere – they had bullied the police and recently made a mounted charge against small groups of civilians. In Mainz they saw many drunken soldiers. In Heidelberg, Greene met a man whose organization for the relief of exiles from the Palatinate was actually in the business of kidnapping collaborators from the French zone. In the course of their travels, the three young men dreamt up a novel in the manner of John Buchan about occupied Germany.

Back in England, Greene wrote an angry article about the behaviour of the French forces, publishing it in *Oxford Outlook* in June. In one important respect he reproduced too closely the opinions of his sponsors: he does refer to the problem of colour prejudice, yet he accepts uncritically the complaint that the presence of black soldiers failed to respect the sensitivities of the Germans – an idea that would have been intolerable to him just a few years later.[16]

Germans passed in and out of his life for some time. Greene offered to carry money into the French zone for pro-German groups, but the offer was turned down. In October, Bernstorff showed up in Oxford 'hopeful' of disturbances in the Rhineland, and a plan was afoot for Greene to go to the French zone, contact separatist leaders, and find out about their plans. Then came a menacing man from the Berlin Foreign Office who had been going to the theatre in London: 'You must see all kinds of plays, in order to sympathise with all types of people, for only by sympathising with them, can you dominate them.' Greene felt that during lunch the man was trying to gauge his weaknesses, so resolved to do a little dominating of his own. He led the obese man around Oxford 'at the speed of an express'.[17] The plan for Greene to make this second journey fell apart after the Dawes Agreement, providing for the evacuation of occupying troops and softening reparation payments, took effect shortly after. This was just as well, since the nineteen-year-old Greene was on the verge of becoming a spy for the Germans. He also looked to the French embassy in London for introductions in such a manner that he would have become something of a double agent. Looking back on all this forty years later, he remarked: 'Today, I would have scruples about the purpose I served, but at that age I was ready to be a mercenary in any cause so long as I was repaid with excitement and a little risk. I suppose too that every novelist has something in common with a spy: he watches, he overhears, he seeks motives and analyses character, and in his attempt to serve literature he is unscrupulous.'[18]

The same sense of mischief and the desire for travel led Greene, along with Cockburn, to join the small Oxford branch of the Communist Party, which served both the university and the city. Neither of them had any belief in communism and their plan was to get control of the branch and perhaps to secure a trip to Leningrad or Moscow. At least one member spotted them as impostors, and their active membership lasted little more than a month. Nonetheless, they managed to get sent to Paris in early January 1925. They visited the Communist headquarters and were invited to a meeting near Ménilmontant, where they sat through a dreary reading of messages from branches abroad. Greene found it all intolerably boring and went back to his hotel to read the copy of Joyce's *Ulysses* he had bought at Shakespeare and Company as soon as he had reached Paris – in later years he broke with critical orthodoxy in thinking the book over-rated. He visited the Casino de Paris to see the singer and entertainer Mistinguett, whose legs were insured for half a million francs. He also went to see cabaret acts at Le Concert Mayol, and on the way back to his hotel he was called to by the middle-aged prostitutes near La Madeleine.

Greene's university years were filled with pranks; however, his joining the Communist Party would have consequences in the 1950s. Under American law, a person with such a history was forbidden to enter the country. Despite being, by then, one of the world's leading novelists, not to mention a prominent Catholic, he had to fight hard for visas, and when he did step onto American soil his comings and goings were noted by the FBI, which looked upon him as a likely subversive.

4

THE REVOLVER

'We lived in those years continuously with the sexual experience we had never known ... And in between the periods of sexual excitement came agonizing crises of boredom.'[1] Early in his time at Oxford, Greene fell for women in a 'twilight world of calf love'. Apart from fantasies about his tennis-playing cousin Ave, he had, back in Berkhamsted, taken to exchanging kisses with his younger siblings' somewhat tyrannical nurse. She sought to improve the experience by giving him his first razor. One evening, he came to the nursery, found his mother there, but went ahead anyway with a kiss on the young woman's lips 'to show that I was not ashamed of what I did on other occasions'. She was soon sacked.[2] He had also conceived a passion for Clodagh O'Grady, the golden-haired daughter of his father's secretary. In Oxford, he fell in love with a waitress at the George pub. But something more painful was in store.

Like most freshmen he overspent his budget on the purchase of books and beer. He lived for his first two terms at 52 Beechcroft Road in north Oxford, so there were late-night taxis to pay for. By the end of term he was broke, despite his father's allowance, and decided very reluctantly that he must spend the summer with his family rather than go to Paris as he had hoped. The family went on holiday to the seaside town of Sheringham in Norfolk. His younger siblings Hugh and Elisabeth were past the age of needing a nurse so there was now a governess named Gwen Howell, about ten years older than Graham. At first, he paid no attention, but then one day saw her lying on the sand, her skirt pulled up showing 'a long length of naked thigh. Suddenly at that moment I fell in love, body and mind. There was no romantic haze about this love, no make believe.'[3]

It was, for him, 'an obsessive passion', for her, a flirtation. Although they did no more than kiss, she became afraid of the strength of his feelings. Meanwhile, he took dancing lessons so that they could go to 'hops' during the winter holiday. She was tenuously engaged to a man who worked abroad for Cable & Wireless. With his return anticipated, she wept, telling Graham she would have to leave Berkhamsted before long to be married. It had lasted about six intense months, 'though even today', he would write five decades later, 'it seems to have endured as long as youth itself'. From Oxford, he continued to exchange letters with Gwen each week, and thirty years later when she wrote to him asking for tickets for his play *The Living Room* the sight of her hand-writing on the envelope caused his heart to beat faster.[4]

There is nothing remarkable about a young man falling in love with an unattainable woman. However, Greene's mental state was still troubled. Following his return from Kenneth Richmond's in early 1922, he had begun to experience the terrible boredom that would afflict him all his life and that he would do almost anything to relieve. This was likely a symptom of manic depression, although he claimed that it was the result of psychoanalysis: 'For years, after my analysis, I could take no aesthetic interest in any visual thing: staring at a sight that others assured me was beautiful I felt nothing. I was fixed, like a negative in a chemical bath.' By the autumn of 1923 he was also engrossed in his impossible passion for Gwen Howell, but 'The boredom was as deep as the love and more enduring'.[5] One relief was alcohol – he told Evelyn Waugh that much of his time at Oxford passed in a 'general haze of drink' – more than he consumed at any other time in his life.[6]

He also played a reckless game. He says that he discovered in the deal cupboard of the bedroom he shared with Raymond a revolver – 'a small ladylike object with six chambers like a tiny egg-stand' – and 'a small cardboard box of bullets'. He took them and set out across Berkhamsted Common as far as Ashridge Beeches. There, he says, he loaded a bullet into the gun and spun the chambers round. He says his intentions were to escape rather than to commit suicide, and that he was intent on the gamble: 'The discovery that it was possible to enjoy again the visual world by risking its total loss was one I was bound to make sooner or later.' He writes: 'I put the muzzle of the revolver into my right ear and pulled the trigger. There was a minute click, and looking down at the chamber I could see that the charge had moved into the firing position. I was out by one.' His survival thrilled him: 'My heart knocked in its cage, and life contained an infinite number of possibilities. It was like a young man's first successful experience of sex – as if among the Ashridge beeches I had passed the test of manhood. I went home and put the revolver back in its corner-cupboard.'[7]

But when the holiday ended, he took the revolver with him back to Oxford. There, three times, he chose a country lane beyond Headington to continue the game. The thrill diminished, and by Christmas 1923, after a total of six plays, he gave up Russian roulette.

This is one of the most famous episodes in Graham Greene's life. However, it may not be entirely true. Certainly, his mother rejected the whole story. Raymond, the owner of the gun, reportedly maintained that there was no box of bullets in the cupboard. This account is indirect – Raymond speaking to his wife, who passed it on to their son Oliver Greene.[8] Graham's own versions of the story were not consistent.

As late as 1981 he claimed to have learned 'recently' that the bullets were not blank – with the implication that he supposed they were when he pulled the trigger.[9] As we have seen, A Sort of Life is not entirely reliable on some important points. It is reasonable to believe that this story is at least embellished, that Graham Greene did play Russian roulette but with blanks, or, more likely, empty chambers. Indeed, his poems at the time provide a little evidence on the subject. One describes a bullet being loaded into the chamber, but another suggests that the game involved a good deal of fantasy:

> How we make our timorous advances to death, by
>   pulling the trigger of a revolver, which we already
>   know to be empty.
> Even as I do now.
> And how horrified I should be, I who love Death in
>   my verse, if I had forgotten
> To unload.[10]

In the course of his life, Greene did many things at least as dangerous as Russian roulette, and perhaps that is the point of the story. It is not simply a tall tale but a personal myth, a story that allows Greene to explain a recurrent pattern: 'A kind of Russian roulette remained too a factor in my later life, so that without previous experience of Africa I went on an absurd and reckless trek through Liberia; it was the fear of boredom which took me to Tabasco during the religious persecution, to a *léproserie* in the Congo, to the Kikuyu reserve during the Mau-Mau insurrection, to the emergency in Malaya and to the French war in Vietnam. There, in those last three regions of clandestine war, the fear of ambush served me just as effectively as the revolver from the corner-cupboard in the life-long war against boredom.'[11]

Greene had close friends at Oxford, among them Joseph Macleod (pseudonym Adam Drinan), a Scottish poet of considerable gifts who was soon to be published by T. S. Eliot at Faber & Faber. After leaving Oxford, Macleod qualified as a barrister and then ran an experimental theatre; however, he was best known as a news presenter on the BBC: during the Second World War he became a national figure as he managed to deliver even terrible news – such as the sinking of HMS *Hood* in May 1941 – in a voice that was deep, resonant, and reassuring.[12] At Oxford, the two would go on evening walks and talk about their plans for the future, and Macleod would often come to Greene's rooms and leave poems for him to publish in *Oxford Outlook*. One evening he appeared in a state of misery over a young woman. Greene jokingly offered him the revolver so that he could commit suicide. When Macleod appeared ready to accept, he hurriedly put it away and offered whisky instead.[13]

Greene and Macleod were two of the poets from Oxford who read their verses on BBC Radio on 22 January 1925. With them were Harold Acton, Brian Howard, Patrick Monkhouse, T. O. Beachcroft, and A. L. Rowse. They were placed in a room full of sofas and armchairs and directed, each in turn, to a box covered in blue fabric where they would recite. In a humorous account published in the *Oxford Chronicle* a week later, Greene wrote: 'As Earl Harold at William's court spoke over the casket of saints' bones, I spoke over this box that I hoped contained the great heart of the British public.' One rather exposed heart was among the audience – in one of those acts of insensitivity of which he would often be guilty, he had urged Gwen to listen, and so she sat embarrassed with his parents beside the radio, as he poured out endearments in blank verse.[14]

*

At Oxford, Greene was very quickly noticed as a writer of promise. At the end of Trinity Term 1923, he sent a manuscript of poetry and prose to the publisher Basil Blackwell, who responded to it in November, saying he would be delighted to produce a book of Greene's work. Blackwell was not seeking to immortalize the effusions of Greene's youth. What he wanted was future work, so he required 'first refusal' on his next two books. In May 1925, almost two years after Greene's initial approach, Blackwell released *Babbling April*, a thirty-two-page collection of poems. Three hundred copies were printed, and one came into the hands of Harold Acton. Reviewing for the *Cherwell*, he dismissed it as 'a diary of average adolescent moods'. As for a poem about Russian roulette that featured trembling hands, Acton said it made him want to throw the book down and cry, '"For God's sake, be a man!"'[15] The *Cherwell* allowed Greene a response, and in a phrase that makes the contemporary reader cringe, he wrote that most readers would find comic the idea of Acton 'as a professor of Manliness'.[16] Soon, however, Greene accepted Acton's view of the book, never allowing it to be reprinted. As for Acton himself, Greene became devoted to him, remarking to Evelyn Waugh in 1950: 'How nice & dear he is, & how I didn't realise it at Oxford.'[17]

By early 1925 Greene was working hard on his fiction and had drawn the interest of the agent A. D. Peters, who was building up the client list for his new firm, with a novel he had written on a rather odd subject: 'By a mistaken application of the Mendelian theory', Greene says, he created a protagonist who was genetic freak, the black child of white parents. He lived a lonely life at home, and one shaped by racial prejudice at school. Peters was anxious for a happy ending – to have Sant marry the prostitute he loves. After some resistance, Greene undertook a rewrite: 'I made the young man find a kind of content by joining a ship at Cardiff as a Negro deckhand, so escaping from the middle class and his sense of being an outsider.'[18] Peters had high hopes, but the manuscript was rejected by Blackwell, Grant Richards, John Lane, Heinemann, and others.

While 'Anthony Sant' was making the rounds, Greene pushed on with a thriller, or as he called it a 'shocker', about separatist Germans. He was soon able to provide Peters with twenty thousand words of it in the spring for the purposes of serialization, though again the work did not sell.[19] A year later, he wrote five chapters of a country-house murder mystery, 'The Empty Chair', in the manner of Agatha Christie. This story was rediscovered and published in *The Strand* in 2009.[20] Greene was a young man in a hurry, but it would take years for him to learn his craft – what he had written so far had little to recommend it.

5

CASUAL CORPSES

'Did I tell you of my other excitement about a week ago, seeing a body carried up out of the Thames, as I was crossing Albert Bridge? All very dramatic, deep dusk, the two lights burning on the little quay below the bridge, & a couple of policemen carrying the covered stretcher across to the embankment steps. Then the police boat, diving back into the shadows, as though to pick out other casual corpses.'[1] It was 2 August 1925, and these remarks in a letter to his mother reveal the fascination with danger, seediness, and disorder that would characterize Greene's writing for more than sixty years.

He had just finished at Oxford, taking a second in history. He was training in London for a position with the British American Tobacco Company, which would send him to China – a troubled country where he could expect to see plenty of corpses. But there was also the threat of boredom. He would be required to stay in that post for four years before being entitled to any leave, so he resigned.

In the months before going down from Oxford he had looked into a variety of careers, especially ones that would allow him to travel abroad. One possibility was the Levant Consular Service, but that would first send him to Cambridge for another two years of study. He had an interview with Asiatic Petroleum for a position most likely in Calcutta. In late May he went to see Geoffrey Dawson, editor of *The Times*, who could offer him nothing and suggested that if he wanted to enter journalism he should first spend some time working with a provincial newspaper. So he kept applying for jobs.[2]

A year earlier the idea of a posting abroad would have been irresistible, but things had changed. In February Greene had written an article on 'The Average Film' for *Oxford Outlook*. It contained this short rant:

'We are most of us nowadays considerably over-sexed. We either go to church and worship the Virgin Mary or to a public house and snigger over stories and limericks; and this exaggeration of the sex instinct has had a bad effect on art, on the cinematograph as well as on the stage.'[3] His statement prompted a letter from a fervent and knowledge-able Catholic, the twenty-year-old Vivienne Dayrell-Browning, Basil Blackwell's private secretary. She was annoyed that anyone would speak of the 'worship' of the Virgin Mary. She informed him that the correct expression was 'hyperdulia' – the technical term for a degree of vener-ation less than that owed to God. Bemused, he apologized for his error, claiming he had been in a hurry and was trying to be provocative. Ever the flirt, he asked that she come to tea as a sign of forgiveness.[4] He met her on the 17 March 1925 and they had their tea together three days later. On 4 April, they went to see a film.[5] Greene fell in love with her.

Born, like him, in 1904,[6] Vivien (she later simplified the spelling of her name) had long brown hair and classic features. She was clever and high-minded – a tumultuous childhood had predisposed her to be conservative and otherworldly. She and a younger brother Patrick had been born to Sydney Dayrell-Browning and his wife Marion (née Green-Armytage) on a property in Rhodesia that included an unprof-itable gold mine which had to be worked 364 days a year to break even.[7] Her own first memory was, like Graham's recollection of the dead dog, violent: 'Men were always nannies in Rhodesia then. The women carried water for miles and dug the ground; the men discussed politics round a tree and were nannies. I had a nice one called Malachi. Malachi was killing a black snake on the path in front of me. I didn't feel sorry for it or frightened. It was just a happening.'[8] Her mother, an avid horsewoman and watercolourist, was a difficult character, and her father may have been no better. They hardly knew each other before marriage, and separated when Vivien was about seven. Marion took her back to England, leaving Patrick behind – Vivien did not see him again until he was at university. Eventually, Marion required Vivien to write a letter to Sydney breaking off all contact. He lived out his years in southern Africa and was buried near Salisbury (now Harare).[9]

As a child, the uprooted Vivien was bounced from school to school, and this experience, though not as traumatic as Graham's, was unpleas-ant. She spent some time during the First World War at a progressive school in Hemel Hempstead, near Berkhamsted, though she and the young Graham did not meet. Her mother chose this institution housed in an old Dominican priory for the sake of its architecture, without enquiring deeply into the curriculum, which was based largely on the anthroposophical system of Rudolf Steiner. The diet there was vegetarian and sparse; she recalled, perhaps melodramatically, that the children went searching in farmers' fields for turnips: 'The boys had knives and peeled the turnips, which were eaten raw to stave off hunger.'[10]

She finished school in South Hampstead, then went to a secretarial college. Widely read and a gifted stylist, she turned her hand to poetry. When she was just seventeen, her mother organized the publication of a collection of her poems and essays, with an introduction by G. K. Chesterton, but in later years Vivien found the book embarrassing.[11]

As a Catholic, Vivien had a very high view of consecrated virginity, but, in any event, her early life had taught her to distrust sex and marriage. She might have been better suited to a convent than to a relationship with a man, especially one as troubled as Graham Greene. He, however, was prepared to do almost anything to please her. Within a few weeks of their first meeting she persuaded him to accompany her to church, an experience he described to his mother as 'rather fun'[12] – an odd phrase given that he would later tend to view Catholicism from the perspective of the damned.

By the end of the month he had crept into a church to light a candle and felt himself under the inquisitorial eye of a woman supposedly at prayer.[13] About four years before, Greene had had a striking perception of God on the croquet lawn but afterwards had not been much interested in matters of belief. In 1923, he had published a short story, 'The Trial of Pan', in which the pagan deity appears before the aged Judaeo-Christian God and pities him. Pan defends himself against the charges only by his music. At the end the courtroom is emptied, leaving a 'white-bearded God, sitting alone in the empty hall, on a high judgment seat, under a bright blue canopy, playing noughts and crosses with himself on his blotting pad'.[14] Under Vivien's influence, he would have to think again about religion.

Over the next two years Graham would inundate Vivien with love letters, which are now embarrassing to read – as if one were listening in on thousands of hours of adolescent phone calls. He pours out clumsy endearments, picks fights, and begs for forgiveness almost cyclically. He was not yet a mature enough writer to make a good job of love letters, and on any given day he might write three of them.

The romance did not run smoothly. Graham was in a romantic frenzy and proposed marriage, so on 20 June she broke with him at Wolvercote, a village just north of Oxford. She wanted to preserve her ideal of celibacy and 'round off' their friendship pleasantly.[15] The correspondence continued somewhat awkwardly. Graham went to London to be trained for the job in China, which, if he stayed with it, meant a certain end to the relationship. On 7 August 1925 he made a new offer – of 'a monastic marriage' involving 'companionship & companionship only'.[16] He urged her to consider that God had brought them together and that they might now embark on a new adventure. At almost the same time, he quit his position with British American Tobacco and started applying to provincial newspapers. For her part, Vivien took the offer cautiously, remarking a few weeks later, 'The World soils what it touches.'[17] On 16 September, Greene again asked for an engagement, promising to become a Catholic.[18] This was an important concession, and, very tentatively, she accepted.

Greene's willingness, even in theory, to separate sex and marriage in his dealings with Vivien had a complicated background. Not long before *A Sort of Life* was published in 1971, Greene deleted some pages on the subject of the sex trade. Those pages survive in files at the Harry Ransom Center in Austin, Texas. He says that he remained a virgin until around 1925 (no precise date is given), when he deliberately decided to find out about sex. First, he picked up a prostitute and went with her to a hotel near Leicester Square. He said he felt no desire and was so nervous that nothing happened. On a second occasion, he went with a young prostitute to another hotel in the same area and experienced 'release and happiness. As I sat on the bed and saw the girl naked in front of the looking-glass combing her hair, I took us both by surprise with my unpremeditated exclamation, "How beautiful you are"; I can see her now, as she turned from the glass, smiling and pleased by such a tribute rare enough after the act was over. Ten years later, on the way to the Empire cinema, I would sometimes spy her on her old beat from which she had never graduated. She was almost unrecognizable by then, she had stepped right into middle age, and no young man would ever again exclaim at the sight of her.'[19]

He took a private tutoring job in Ashover, a village near Chesterfield, and for several weeks he was paid by a widow to amuse her lazy ten-year-old. Boredom continued to afflict him; he claims that to escape it he pretended to suffer from toothache and tricked a dentist into etherizing him; he says he lost a good tooth but secured a brief interlude free of the terrible mood.[20] It is a good story but not to be believed, as he reported to his mother at the time that he had a cyst in his mouth and an abscessed tooth[21] – there was no need to sacrifice a healthy one. But, in the evenings, back in his hotel room, he kept himself busy. He had submitted a new manuscript of poems called 'Sad Cure' to Basil Blackwell, who liked it but could not publish it except on a 'mutual responsibility' basis – that is, sharing the financial risk – since *Babbling April* had sold poorly. Greene declined.[22]

He had also completed close to thirty thousand words of a historical novel called 'The Episode', set in 1871 among Carlist refugees who lived in the area of Leicester Square.[23] The Carlists, a conservative and legitimist movement supporting the claims to the Spanish throne of a branch of the Bourbons descended from Carlos V, were an important faction in the nineteenth-century wars over Spanish succession – Greene's story is set just before the third and last of these. At the time he was writing, there was still a Carlist claimant to the throne, the elderly Duke of Anjou and Madrid, who lived in exile in Paris.[24]

Greene had become interested in the subject through Carlyle's biography of the poet John Sterling, who was tangled up with the Carlists,[25] but he was also following in the tracks of Joseph Conrad, whose novel *The Arrow of Gold* dealt with Carlists in Marseilles in the 1870s.

His search for a job on a newspaper finally bore fruit in an unpaid position at the *Nottingham Journal*, beginning in November. The city itself reminded him of Dickens's London,[26] and he wrote to Vivien about the most extraordinary fog he had ever seen: 'If I stretch out my walking stick in front of me, the ferrule is half lost in obscurity. Coming back I twice lost my way, & ran into a cyclist, to our mutual surprise. Stepping off a pavement to cross to the other side becomes a wild & fantastic adventure, like sailing into the Atlantic to find New York, with no chart or compass. Once where the breadth of the road was greater than the normal, I found myself back on the same pavement, as I started, having slowly swerved in my course across the road.'[27]

Although he complained of it at the time, he was moved by the city's air of accustomed failure and later thought of it as a second home, making it the setting for parts of A Gun for Sale and The Potting Shed. In Nottingham he lived as a boarder at the down-at-heel Ivy House on All Saints Terrace. For a companion, he had a mongrel named Paddy, who was frequently sick on the floor. Greene described the atmosphere of the newspaper office to his mother: 'one table with the News Editor, a dear old man, at the head, & smoke & work & talk &, at about 10, eat potato chips out of paper bags'. He would start work at 5:30 p.m. and finish at half-past midnight, sorting through telegrams, correcting grammar and punctuation, and trimming copy. He enjoyed the puzzle aspect of writing headlines with a limited number of letters in various sizes of type depending on the importance of the story.[28] He was particularly pleased with his handling of a large headline about a bigamous vicar and getting the type size correct.[29]

Greene was also still trying to launch a writing career, consistently turning out five hundred words per day on his novel, following a discipline he maintained until old age, when he reduced the count. He contributed some reviews to the Westminster Gazette and the Times Literary Supplement.[30] He made the acquaintance of Cecil Roberts, a former editor of the Nottingham Journal who had become a popular novelist – 'Nottingham's Tin God', as he described him to his mother, a local literary dictator who had pull at Heinemann, where Greene wanted to have his own fiction published.[31] In A Sort of Life he described Roberts, who he had gradually come to like,[32] as a 'Micawber in reverse' for telling him how risky the future looked, and speculated on whether he was actually the son of one of the dukes in the Dukeries.[33] It had not occurred to him that Roberts might still be alive. Roberts wrote a review fuming over the conjecture about his paternity and complained at length that the young Greene had had more advantages than he had had – Roberts rather specialized in putting on the poor mouth. He also asserted, wrongly, that he had only met Greene once in Nottingham.[34] Greene cut the offending passages from subsequent printings of the memoir.

Having promised Vivien that he would become a Catholic, he sought out instruction soon after his arrival in Nottingham. In A Sort of Life, he says, 'Now it occurred to me, during the long empty mornings, that if I were to marry a Catholic I ought at least to learn the nature and limits of the beliefs she held. It was only fair, since she knew what I believed – in nothing supernatural. Besides, I thought, it would kill the time.'[35] This statement is essential to his account of his reception into the church, and it is false. Vivien certainly did not understand him to be a confirmed atheist. Introducing that element into the story allowed him to present a more dramatic tale with a sharper struggle over belief and disbelief and a much shorter timeline for his conversion, but it also makes it much more difficult to know what actually happened.

As soon as he reached Nottingham, he wrote asking her what exactly should he do to be received – just walk up to a priest's house and ask for instructions? He added: 'And, darling one, though I admit that the idea came to me because of you, I do all the same feel I want to be a Catholic now, even a little apart from you. One does want fearfully hard for something firm & hard & certain, however uncomfortable, to catch hold of in the general flux.'[36]

In his memoir, he describes walking Paddy to the 'sooty' cathedral, which possessed for him a 'gloomy power because it represented the inconceivable and the incredible'. He dropped a note into the wooden enquiries box[37] and so made contact with Father George Trollope,[38] the tall, portly administrator of the cathedral, in whom Greene at first thought he recognized the smug and well-fed priest of Protestant propaganda, but soon he saw beyond the priest's belly and jowls to an extraordinary sincerity and devotion. Indeed, this man had sacrificed a good deal for his faith.

Born in 1879 and educated at Merchant Taylors' School, Trollope became an actor with the Ben Greet players, a well-known repertory company, where he learned to play many parts interchangeably – for example in *The Sign of the Cross* he had to play sometimes a Christian, sometimes a pagan. He said he 'had to roar like a lion one day, be eaten by one the next'. Trollope went on to a solid career in the West End, appearing with such actors as Herbert Beerbohm Tree. He was received into the Catholic church in 1905 and ordained a priest five years later. He had a very gentle nature and his years on the stage prepared him to be an excellent preacher. His one notable eccentricity was that he refused to wear socks, as he thought that when they became damp they would give him a cold.

Greene detected a sorrow in Trollope, a yearning for his old life.[39] Plays competed with theological works for space on his bookshelves. Sadly, he could only read them now as priests were forbidden to attend theatres in their own dioceses – and Nottingham had good theatres. Still his background in the arts probably made him an ideal person to lead this potential convert through the alien ground of theology – and despite being an actor, he argued with precision. After their first session, Graham reported to Vivien: '[I] have quite changed my mind about Father Trollope. I like him very much. I like his careful avoidance of the slightest emotion or sentiment in his instruction.'[40] It soon turned out that the priest had a surprising connection with Greene's world – his father's closest friend was Dr Thomas Fry, the former headmaster of Berkhamsted School. Trollope resented Fry for trying to turn his family against him when he converted to Rome, and he is said to have regarded the baptism of Graham Greene as a kind of revenge against Dr Fry.

According to *A Sort of Life*, Greene's problem in approaching the church had little to do with fine points of doctrine: 'Bishop Gore in his great book on religious belief wrote that his own primary difficulty was to believe in the love of God; my primary difficulty was to believe in a God at all. The date of the gospels, the historical evidence for the existence of the man Jesus Christ: these were interesting subjects which came nowhere near the core of my disbelief. I didn't disbelieve in Christ – I disbelieved in God.' His years at Oxford had made him an agile debater – he said he lost this ability in time – and he went many rounds with Father Trollope, sometimes on trams or in the sitting rooms of convents as the priest went about other duties. He wrote in the memoir: 'It was on the grounds of a dogmatic atheism that I fought and fought hard. It was like a fight for personal survival.' Of course, it is hard to know whether this was precisely true at the time, or a touch of drama added decades later to what was, in fact, mostly an exposition of the details of Catholic belief and observance rather than extended debates about the existence of God. As the sessions – usually once or twice a week – continued, Greene became captivated by the priest himself in whom he detected 'an inexplicable goodness', which in itself became a potent argument for belief.[41]

In later years he said repeatedly that he did not feel the emotional side of his faith until he witnessed the persecution of Catholics in Mexico. But his letters at the time suggest that there was an emotional component to his struggle – at least in a negative sense. On 7 December 1925, he wrote to Vivien describing his racing thoughts: 'Darling, I've got nothing to say & yet I daren't stop. I feel there's something awful in sealing up the envelope, not being able to add to this. I feel as if I must go on talking, talking, talking to you hard, until I've got back control. Chatter, chatter, chatter, chatter. On & on & on.' In this letter he describes his rage against God, and his despair: 'Don't you ever wonder, in moods, now & again, what the use of going on is? Religion doesn't answer it. One can believe in every point of the Catholic faith, & yet at times like this hate the initiator of it all, of life I mean. Justice can be just as hateful as injustice, more so often enough, because injustice puts us on a level with the wielder of it, whilst justice is more hateful because it emphasizes our own inferiority.'[42]

Greene says that he decided in January 1926 that he would enter the church – this is not actually true as he had already told Vivien in September that he intended to do it. Presumably, in January he put aside lingering doubts and made his final decision. He teased his mother about it – 'I expect you have guessed that I am embracing the Scarlet Woman' – and about his choice of baptismal name, hinting that he might go for Joan. The new name would, in any event, allow him to get rid of his first name, 'Henry', which he hated. In the end, he chose Thomas – not for Aquinas, but for the doubting apostle.[43] For all the teasing, he knew he 'was laughing to keep his courage up'.[44]

He also decided that he should end his newspaper apprenticeship and return to London. By 21 January, Greene had had twenty-six lessons with Father Trollope and was only halfway through the full instruction.[45] Father Trollope accelerated the lessons, and made arrangements for Greene to see in London the man by whom he had himself been received into the church, Father James Christie of the Brompton Oratory.[46]

On 28 February[47] Greene made a general confession, but not to Father Trollope as it would have been too embarrassing. It covered the sins of his whole life and it was 'a humiliating ordeal. Later we may become hardened to the formulas of confession and sceptical about ourselves: we may only half intend to keep the promises we make, until continual failure or the circumstances of our private life, finally make it impossible to make any promises at all and many of us abandon Confession and Communion to join the Foreign Legion of the Church and fight for a city of which we are no longer full citizens.[48] That was the voice of a man in his sixties, who had as a matter of conscience withdrawn from the sacraments rather than make empty promises to reform his life. But on this first occasion he took the promises seriously and carried them down 'like heavy stones' into a dark corner of the cathedral for his baptism, which was observed only by a woman dusting the chairs. He came out of the cathedral not joyful but full of 'sombre apprehension', unsure what these ceremonies might entail for his hoped-for marriage to Vivien. He was not then sure whether involvement with God might lead him, as it had led Trollope, to the priesthood. That fear would later seem quaint, even absurd, but in February 1926 he had no idea where his faith might take him.[49]

6

MARRIAGE

London was in turmoil, and Graham Greene was thrilled. Hired as a sub-editor on *The Times* just two months before, he found himself at one of the flash points of the General Strike. With coal miners fighting against reduced wages and longer hours, the Trades Union Congress called the long-anticipated strike, which lasted from 3 to 12 May 1926. The government seized paper supplies in an effort to prevent the TUC from publishing its strike newspaper, *The British Worker*. Most of the country's newspapers were unable to publish, but *The Times* put out a reduced edition – the only paper that continued to be issued without interruption.

Overnight on 4–5 May, Greene worked a sixteen-hour shift. With all the print workers on strike, the editorial staff produced a single-sheet issue of the newspaper using three Roneo machines. The papers were loaded under police guard. The next night, strikers poured petrol into the basement and set fire to a large roll of paper. Then, as Greene and others were loading newspapers into private cars parked along Victoria Street for transport out of London, there was a 'scrimmage' with strikers, with one man getting concussion after being hit with his own bundle of papers. The next night, some MPs came to help, but there were only peaceful pickets and the loading of cars was better organized.[1]

Greene had taken a room at 141 Albert Palace Mansions near Battersea Park, but for much of the strike he stayed with Raymond in Pimlico, and was seldom in bed before 5 a.m. He also signed up as a special constable 'for curiosity', as he said, rather than any wish 'to support the establishment',[2] patrolling Vauxhall Bridge with a regular policeman. The feared revolution never took place as the government was well prepared and the middle classes were opposed to the General

Strike. By 12 May 1926, the leaders of the TUC had lost hope and called off the strike. When it was over, Greene was given a silver matchbox by the *Times* management, and he lamented the end of free beer at the office.[3]

The *Times* recruit found himself, as a newspaper man putting out the news, a strike-breaker. At Oxford he had had his dalliance with communism, but in the midst of the strike he wrote to Vivien, who disapproved of the left: 'Darling, you talk as if I was labour. I'm not. I'm really conservative now – especially after labour tried to burn us all.'[4] In *A Sort of Life*, he tells us that just a few years later he would have taken the side of the strikers: like many others of the middle classes, the sight of hunger marchers had opened his eyes.[5] And yet, in the 1980s, he took yet another view: since *The Times* was obliged to fight off both the strikers as well as Churchill and the extreme right, he did not regret his loyalty to the newspaper.[6]

Now that he had a job, he and Vivien could make firmer plans for a wedding, but as the summer went on, her mother objected to the proposed marriage, as did Vivien's close friend in Oxford, Stella Weaver.[7] The idea of the celibate marriage was fading away, but Greene expressed a preference not to have children. He also suggested to Vivien that the creative and sexual instinct were closely related, and on one occasion compared the erotic contact of bodies to receiving the Eucharist.[8] He may just have been trying to convince her of the artistic and spiritual benefits of sleeping with him.

But these were discouraging months for his writing career. One of his sonnets won a competition judged by Humbert Wolfe in the *Saturday Review*,[9] but his collection of poems, *Sad Cure*, went from publisher to publisher without finding a home. He took some comfort from a note sent by J. C. Squire when he rejected the manuscript, and saw a little hope when Jonathan Cape said no to the poems but asked to see his prose. *Sad Cure* never did find a publisher. Meanwhile, he completed 'The Episode' at the beginning of August and borrowed £5 from his mother to have two copies typed.[10] A. D. Peters, who had put a great effort into 'Anthony Sant', told him at the end of September that this new novel was simply not publishable. Greene submitted it to William Heinemann, where it got lost in the slush pile until late April. When the managing director, Charles Evans, wrote to apologize for the delay he said he had received contrary readers' reports, but he too rejected the novel in the end.[11]

Some books are written from the heart. Greene's third novel came from his appendix. Walking in Battersea at the end of September, he felt a lingering pain in his side grow suddenly sharper, so went into the office of a down-at-heel doctor, who gave him some medicine and sent him on his way – all at a cost of six shillings. That evening things were still bad, so he called Raymond, who had him examined and then admitted at Westminster Hospital, where he was himself studying anatomy and physiology. Graham spent 2 October 1926, his twenty-second birthday, in Chadwick Ward, with his appendectomy taking place three days later. *The Times* gave him six weeks' medical leave, three of which he spent in hospital, the rest in Berkhamsted.

While in hospital, Greene saw some terrible things, including the unexpected death of a nine-year-old boy named Royston who had undergone surgery on a broken leg. The boy's mother was distraught and cried out: '"Why did you go without saying goodbye to your mother? . . . Sister, Sister, don't tell me we're parted."' This was followed by the death of an old man whose skull had been fractured in a car accident. Greene asked Vivien: 'Are people who write entirely & absolutely selfish, darling? Even though in a way I hated it yesterday evening – one half of me was saying how lucky it was – added experience – & I kept on catching myself trying to memorise details – Sister's face, the faces of the other men in the ward. And I felt quite excited aesthetically. It made one rather disgusted with oneself.'[12]

During his time in hospital, Greene began to plot out a new novel. Like 'The Episode', it would be romantic and historical. He had been reading Lord Teignmouth's and Charles Harper's historical work, *The Smugglers*, and was struck by an ugly letter written to revenue officers by an informant who called himself 'Goring'; it revealed the activities of a Sussex gang and the means to capture them: 'Do but take up some of the Servants, they will soon rout the Masters, for the Servants are all poor.'[13] Greene saw a challenge in making such a character sympathetic.

Once he was back in Berkhamsted, he started writing. He would remember decades later, when other better sentences from better books were forgotten, the opening of *The Man Within*: 'He came over the top of the down as the last light failed and could almost have cried with relief at sight of the wood below.' He wrote these words on lined foolscap while half-listening to his mother discuss chores with a parlour maid.[14] This novel contained much that would stay with Greene through his career, especially the figure of the hunted man and the problem of the 'Judas'. Just as Greene had shopped Lionel Carter to his father, so does Francis Andrews, his main character, inform on his friend, the similarly named Carlyon. The parallels are broad, of course, and *The Man Within* should not be read as a close autobiography. Greene wrote only a few paragraphs at first, then worked fitfully on it over the next eighteen months. With two failed novels behind him, he felt that this book had to succeed or he must forget about a writing career.

On his first night back at *The Times*, around 17 November,[15] he fainted and was given another week of medical leave. He decided to go to Brighton, where one night as he was sitting alone in a shelter on the front a deluded man introduced himself as 'Old Moore' of the almanac. In retrospect, Greene thought he should have suspected an omen. He had received an odd letter from his mother telling him to visit Kenneth Richmond when he returned to London. At the end of their six months of psychoanalysis, Richmond had told Greene, very amicably, that they should go their separate ways to avoid any sense of dependency. By 1926, Richmond was no longer practising psychology and instead teaching a system of shorthand.

When Greene visited him, Richmond offered to help find a publisher for the unpublishable 'Episode', then got to the point. He reminded Greene how he had once fainted at the dinner table during their period of psychoanalysis. In fact, Greene had fainted before that; he had lost consciousness on a total of three occasions. Richmond had taken him to see the leading neurologist George Riddoch,[16] who diagnosed epilepsy (see p. 21). The matter was revealed to Charles and Marion, but not to Graham himself. In Britain and many other countries, the disease was legal grounds for a marriage to be annulled or prohibited. While Greene was angry at the concealment, it was the likelihood of losing Vivien that devastated him. Indeed, he had earlier compared his pursuit of her, quite accurately, to 'monomania'.[17]

The next day, he went to an Underground station and watched the trains passing as he got ready to jump. He could not finally bring himself to do it, and after a while 'took the moving staircase to the upper world'.[18] He sought out Father Christie at the Brompton Oratory. In *A Sort of Life* Greene calls him Talbot. Greene felt that under no circumstances should he have children, yet wanted to be married according to the church. A man of considerable education,[19] Father Christie was an enlightened priest for the time and Greene found him a person of great sympathy, but his hands were tied. He took Greene out in a taxi and they rode back and forth between the Brompton Road and Bayswater, 'just as we crossed and recrossed the same lines of argument'.[20] Marriage was not forbidden, but contraception most certainly was. This was a scorching experience for Greene, and was likely on his mind when he signed letters of protest in 1968 against Pope Paul VI's encyclical *Humanae Vitae*, which upheld the prohibition against artificial contraception.

Another visit to Riddoch saw the diagnosis confirmed, but Raymond thought it was all nonsense, as did the *Times* medical correspondent Dr McNair Wilson, who had witnessed the recent fainting episode and saw no evidence that it was an epileptic seizure. By mid-February, Riddoch conceded that he had been 'too hasty'.[21] In future, Greene would faint from time to time,[22] but it was no longer attributed to epilepsy.

Relieved about his own health, Greene saw that the time was coming to worry about his father's. At sixty-one, Charles Greene had passed the normal age of retirement for his post, but his appointment had been extended at the request of the governors of the school. However, he was suffering from diabetes and could not remain. An advertisement for the headmastership appeared in January 1927, and he left the school finally in Trinity Term.[23] This was momentous for Graham, as his father and mother left Berkhamsted altogether for a house in Crowborough, Sussex, which they named Incents, after the founder of the school. Within two years, Uncle Edward had sold the Hall as well, and Berkhamsted was no longer home to the Greene family.

Graham Greene felt that his parents had always been generous towards him, and after a visit to them in the following year wrote in a letter that despite his 'terribly undemonstrative nature' he needed to thank them: 'I hope I become a success, if only so that all you've both done for me isn't wasted. There comes a time when gratitude wells up to a height above flood level, & as it's hard, owing to some kink in my nature, to speak it, I have to write it.'[24]

*

Meanwhile, with his thoughts very much on the longed-for marriage, he set up a home for himself and Vivien. At the end of March 1927 he moved into a flat at 8 Heathcroft, Hampstead Way, which they would share after the wedding, nicknaming it 'The Basket'. Having a private bathtub was a particular treat after years in boarding houses. Meanwhile, Vivien's mother, a very difficult character, was making a last stand, advising her daughter that sex was hell and that giving birth would probably kill her. At this time, Vivien was living with the Weavers in Oxford. Greene did not particularly like Stella Weaver, and at one point spoke of her as a 'reptile',[25] but he was very grateful that she told Vivien to ignore her mother's outbursts.[26] Stella, a thirty-three-year-old Catholic, was happily married and pregnant herself, so spoke with authority. The twenty-two-year-old Vivien was very much in love and wanted the marriage to go ahead – she had wept at the thought of breaking the engagement during the epilepsy scare. A formal announcement appeared in *The Times* on 5 July 1927, conspicuously omitting the name of Vivien's estranged father.

On 15 October 1927, Graham and Vivien were married at St Mary's, a tiny Catholic church in Hampstead. According to a newspaper account, Vivien wore 'an ivory satin Florentine robe, draped with silver lace and cut with a square neck. The satin train was also trimmed with silver lace. A wreath of orange blossom and silver leaves secured her long tulle veil, and she carried a sheaf of Madonna lilies, tied with silver tissue. The train bearer, Miss Elisabeth Greene, wore a rose-pink taffeta frock, trimmed with silver.' Vivien was given away by her maternal grandfather, Alfred Green-Armytage, and Raymond was best man. Among the guests was Father Christie,[27] a sign that Graham bore no ill will about their conversation on epilepsy and contraception. In an odd gesture, Vivien's mother, attempting to dictate terms for the consummation, sent a letter for Graham to read on the wedding night – he read it and tore it up.[28] Graham and Vivien took a two-week honeymoon in the South of France, spending much of their time swimming. When they returned to 'The Basket' on 29 October, they found that Stella had filled it with flowers.[29]

7

RATS IN THE THATCH

'I can think of no better career for a young novelist than to be for some years a subeditor on a rather conservative newspaper,' Greene wrote long after.[1] Apart from providing a modest income, the hours – four in the afternoon until eleven at night – left him plenty of time to get on with his fiction. It also gave him the company of older men who worked together cheerfully – Greene says no one was ever sacked from *The Times*.[2]

The chief sub-editor, George Anderson, a quiet Scot with a sarcastic wit, was somewhat remote, and was heard to say 'I am not a social man'.[3] He pushed Greene hard, especially in the first part of a shift. When the pubs opened at half-past five, Anderson would don his bowler hat and disappear from the office for about thirty minutes, returning with his face a little redder and his manner more genial. Greene later learned that he had once been a poet and guessed that literary disappointment lay behind the sarcasm. He loved roses and would usually have one on his desk or in his buttonhole. Greene says that in his three years with the newspaper he went from hating Anderson to almost loving him. In contrast, Anderson's assistant, Colonel A. H. Maude (grandfather of the Conservative MP Francis Maude) was kind to a fault and would never challenge a young sub-editor with a difficult task.[4]

The editors at *The Times* noticed Greene's talent. They ran several articles he had written, including an account of a walking tour in Sussex, which was a spin-off from the sixth chapter of *The Man Within*, where Francis Andrews is making his way across the downs to Lewes. It was a curiously written piece, employing verse rhythms to create something close to a prose poem. More entertaining was his account of how he and Cockburn had gone barrel-organing in 1923.[5]

The Times also trusted him to speak his mind about the film industry. He had written about films while at Oxford, and would, of course, go on to become one of the finest scriptwriters of his time. The Cinematograph Films Act came into force on 1 April 1928 with the intention of building up a British industry through a system of quotas. Shortly after, he produced an article on how to save money in the making of films. He also argued that critics and producers were misunderstanding the medium as somehow competing with the stage: 'The film is more truly comparable with the novel, the progress of which it has followed from action to thought ... The object of the film should be the translation of thought back into images.'[6] In June, he argued that film-makers, apart from Chaplin and one or two others, had not grasped the formal possibilities of the medium. He insisted that it needed 'a rhythm of time and of space', by which he meant that the pacing of action and the movement from one scene to another needed to be more tightly controlled, so that films would have aesthetic coherence.[7]

Like other critics, Greene was uneasy about the coming of talkies – *The Jazz Singer*, with some scenes of dialogue and music, had been released in London in September 1928 and was soon followed by a murder mystery, *The Terror*, with continuous sound.[8] Writing the following March, he suggested that since films were now a big business, experimentation was rare and the chief improvements merely mechanical. He proposed that film was especially suited to epic, fantasy, and the representation of mental process. He observed, memorably: 'It is the part of the films, in their epic province, either to regard collective life – the life of a crowd – as an end in itself or to cause an individual of more than individual significance to emerge from the crowd.' He thought that films could render worlds that existed nowhere, offering the Felix the Cat films as an example. In the years to come, he would remain interested in film fantasies, and would, perhaps surprisingly, have good things to say about Walt Disney.[9]

In the early winter of 1928, he sent typescripts of his just-finished novel about the Sussex smugglers to Heinemann and the Bodley Head, and settled down for a long wait. Soon afterwards he was lying in bed with flu, when the telephone rang. Vivien told him it was a man named Evans. At first Greene did not feel like talking to anybody, but then realized that this was Charles Evans, the chairman of Heinemann. He hurried to the phone, and listened to the words he had been longing to hear: 'I've read your novel ... We'd like to publish it. Would it be possible for you to look in here at eleven?'

He hurried to Great Russell Street and went into Evans's office imagining himself surrounded by the famous authors the firm had published. Indeed, 'The bearded ghost of Conrad rumbled on the rooftops with the rain.' The ghosts would be of less value to Greene than some of the living, especially one of the directors, A. S. Frere – known simply as Frere. With a background in the Royal Flying Corps, then journalism, he was an engaging man (and skilled tap-dancer) who would soon become managing director of the firm and a lifelong friend. For the next fifty years, Frere was the one person from whom Greene consistently took literary advice.

Charles Evans told the young novelist that he could not guarantee success for his book, 'but all the same we have hopes'.[10] He recommended him to the literary agent David Higham, then with the firm of Curtis Brown.[11] Greene soon came to an agreement with Heinemann, and Doubleday, Doran took the American rights. He was told to get to work on another novel right away, and that he could expect to be at the top of the profession in five years – heady stuff for a twenty-four-year-old who described the book to Raymond as 'terribly second-rate'.[12] There was a search for a title and Greene came up with a telling phrase from Sir Thomas Browne's *Religio Medici*: 'There is another man within me, that's angry with me ... '

The Man Within was published in Britain on 13 June 1929,[13] and by the end of the month Graham reported to his younger brother Hugh, who was by then at Oxford, that it had gone into a second impression – indeed, it would soon sell eight thousand copies:[14] 'I've had very good reviews so far in The Times, Times Lit Supp., Sunday Times, Bystander, Piccadilly (with photo!), Spectator & Daily Telegraph. The provincial papers have been inclined to sniff. We went to a terribly grand party at the American publishers the day before publication, with people like the Duchess of Devonshire, Rudyard Kipling etc. floating about. We drank a lot of champagne & felt happy.'[15]

He and Vivien had every reason to feel happy but he would later wish that he had had a mentor when writing his early fiction, and wondered what advice his cousin Robert Louis Stevenson might have given him.[16]

He was about to make some mistakes. To produce *The Man Within*, he had worked eleven hours a day: he wrote about smugglers in the morning and then went to *The Times* in the mid-afternoon. In the summer of 1929 he wrote a letter to Evans which was an obvious bluff. He said he could not continue to write fiction and to work as a journalist. Evans was wagering on his protégé, so came up with a plan that would allow him to write full time. In early August they had lunch at the Savoy with Greene's American publisher George Doran, who was more cautious and wanted to see how the book did when it was published in the United States the following month. In the meantime, Evans handed over a large cheque that allowed Graham and Vivien to go on a three-week Hellenic Club cruise. At the beginning of October, the publishers presented a firm offer of £650 in advance of royalties on *The Man Within* and his next two books, payable in monthly instalments over two years once he left other employment. He decided to accept.

It was not an easy thing for him to leave *The Times*. He loved the men he worked with, and would ever after remember them in their green eye shades. He had felt a little patronized by an editor who told him he had 'a pretty pen' and might attempt some leading articles, but he was certainly valued by his superiors and was being groomed to take over as correspondence editor, even though for a time he feared being shunted off to the court page. But on 7 October, he wrote his letter of resignation.[17] George Anderson begged him to reconsider and arranged for him to talk to the editor, Geoffrey Dawson, but Dawson delayed their meeting again and again, presumably in the hope that Greene would just abandon the whole notion. When they did meet, Dawson pointed out that other members of staff, among them the novelist Charles Morgan, went about their writing careers in their spare time. Greene stood his ground and left on 31 December 1929.

Financially, he had blundered: the success of his first novel turned out to be a fluke. The book has some good moments, but Greene later said that if he had been the publisher's reader he would have rejected it.[18] This was not false modesty. It is somewhat overwritten and melodramatic, and at the end of his life he allowed it to remain in print merely as a kind gesture to his younger self.

But now the pressure was on – to be a writer he would have to keep writing. Charles Evans told him not to allow more than a year between

his first and second novels. When Greene met him at a party, Arnold
Bennett, having praised *The Man Within* in the *Evening Standard*,
urged him to publish a book at least once a year.[19] This was bad advice.
He had written *The Man Within* in a year and a half and he was now
being told to accelerate the pace. In his maturity, Greene sometimes
committed three years to the writing of a novel. At twenty-five, he did
not yet realize how much care was needed to write a good book.

Once *The Man Within* had been accepted he decided to mine his
experiences in Germany for a new story. He went back to the Continent
to refresh his memories, and reported to his mother on 4 April 1929
that he had seen ten thousand French troops occupying a town of fifty
thousand: 'I feel more and more pro-Teuton every day.'[20] Back home,
he set to work and had sixteen thousand words written by 24 May.[21]

'I was trying to write my first political novel, knowing nothing of
politics.'[22] It imagines a dictatorship arising in the city of Trier once
the French troops have abandoned their attempts to establish an independent state in the Palatinate. The hero, Oliver Chant, a wealthy and
idealistic Englishman, decides to go there and help finance some rebels,
who turn out to be rather peaceful. A Jewish poet named Kapper and
his artist friend grind out political satires and cartoons in the belief
that the dictator will fall once he becomes a laughing stock. Chant
wants them to use his money to buy arms, which eventually they do.
Meanwhile, Chant meets the dictator, Demassener, and admires the
man despite his cruelty. He then sleeps with the dictator's wife Anne-
Marie, who reveals that her husband is impotent. Later Greene felt that
his scenes failed to communicate suspense because they were laden
with adjectives and metaphors. The revolution comes partly as a result
of Kapper revealing to the populace that the tyrant is a cuckold and
therefore a joke, Chant leaves the Palatinate, not with Anne-Marie but
with the wounded Demassener, who is sent into exile.

By the first week of April 1930, after a further research trip to
Germany, he was ready to deliver a draft to Evans. While waiting for
his response he took a commission from the *Graphic* to write about the
passion play at Oberammergau, which Vivien longed to see, and they
took a ten-day trip together in May to Innsbruck, Baden, Cologne, and
Constance.[23] Upon his arrival at Oberammergau, he found a telegram
from Evans: 'Your book magnificent. Congratulations.'[24] Evans was

not alone in praising the young author's latest effort – the novelist and playwright Clemence Dane read the manuscript, thought it very good, and came up with a title out of *Hamlet: The Name of Action*.[25] She suggested some revisions and then tried, unsuccessfully, to get it selected by the Book Society, which had ten thousand members and would have guaranteed the book's success.[26]

Released on 6 October 1930, *The Name of Action* took a trouncing from the critics. One wrote: 'Despite a supple prose and an unconventional ending, the abuse of coincidence and theatrical props makes his narrative hollow and factitious.'[27] This was typical. Greene wrote to his mother: 'I'm getting tired of kind friends who tell me they like this, but of course they much prefer the other!! *The Man Within*, I'm convinced, is a moderately bad book, while this, I'm equally certain, is a moderately good one.'[28]

Still, the literary world was noticing him. The society hostess Lady Ottoline Morrell invited him to tea: 'It appears that Aldous Huxley recommended her to read *The Man Within*! The bugbear again! I'm beginning to hate the sound of it!'[29] She would encourage Greene through the next few years, when his books were cutting no ice with reviewers or readers. He and Vivien visited her occasionally at Garsington, her home near Oxford. He remained always grateful for her kindness and drew her portrait as Lady Caroline in *It's a Battlefield*, a decidedly sympathetic character.

Evans arranged for him to meet established authors such as Michael Arlen, Marie Belloc Lowndes, and Maurice Baring. Most importantly, Greene also met the historian Cunninghame Graham, an expert on the Jesuit reductions in eighteenth-century Paraguay, a subject that more than forty years later would provide part of the background for *The Honorary Consul*.

In the autumn of 1930, he got to work on another novel, to which he would give the title *Rumour at Nightfall*. Just as he had returned to an old interest in Germany for *The Name of Action*, now he went back to the Spanish material that had already failed him in 'The Episode'. The Spanish wars had served Conrad as a subject, as well as G. A. Henty, whose book *With the British Legion: A Story of the Carlist Wars* came out in 1902, but Greene was hurrying. He started on 5 September and finished the ninety-one-thousand-word draft manuscript on 27 April

1931.[30] In a late burst of productivity in April, he wrote twenty-four thousand words.[31] As it turned out, *Rumour at Nightfall* was by far the worst novel Greene ever published.[32]

In a remote way the story anticipates *The Quiet American*. An English journalist, Chase, is covering the army's attempt to capture a Carlist commander named Caveda. Meanwhile Chase and his friend Crane are both in love with Eulelia Monti, who also happens to be Caveda's mistress. Late in the story, Crane manages to marry Eulelia very suddenly in the middle of the night. Chase changes his loyalty from the government side to that of Caveda, and arranges for the death of Crane. It is commonly thought – and the elderly Greene did nothing to discourage this – that he did not deal with Catholic subjects before *Brighton Rock*. In fact, *The Name of Action* had portrayed Catholics in the Rhineland; *Rumour at Nightfall* went somewhat further in its reflection on Christ's relations with Judas. In a distant parallel with Greene's life, Crane's marriage leads him to Catholicism: 'I have married her, and God knows whether I don't share her faith.'[33] In this novel, Greene, for the first time, compares a priest, however fleetingly, to Don Quixote, an idea that would lie at the heart of one of his last novels, *Monsignor Quixote*.[34]

Again, the reviewers were unimpressed. He was particularly stung by Frank Swinnerton's observation in the the *Evening News* that his characters spent all their time hinting.[35] Greene believed that the sales of the book were an abysmal twelve hundred, but his bibliographers have found evidence that it sold about three thousand for Heinemann and a further thousand for Doubleday in the United States.[36] So both *The Name of Action* and *Rumour at Nightfall* were aesthetic rather than commercial failures. He never allowed them to be reprinted, and at the end of his life he left specific instructions to his literary executor that there must be no new editions.[37]

The last part of Greene's apprenticeship as a novelist was conducted in public. If he had failed to publish *The Man Within*, he might have lost hope, so there is no regretting what happened. And it is worth noting that in this period there was at least one clear success, though on a small scale. In 1929 he had written a short story called 'The End of the Party' about twin brothers, one of whom is terrified of the dark. At a birthday party they are obliged to play hide-and-seek, in the course of which the fearful brother is overwhelmed by his panic and dies. This pared-down tale shows that Greene was actually maturing as a writer.

Three bad novels had made their way into print, while, oddly enough, a competent biography would have to wait forty years for publication. On 15 November 1930, having recently begun *Rumour at Nightfall*, Graham wrote to Hugh from the British Library: 'You find me, as it were, deeply engaged working on my *magnum opus*, "Strephon: The Life of the Second Earl of Rochester" – that is to say I am waiting in patience while half a dozen books of varying shades of indecency are brought to me.'[38] Adding to an already excessive workload, Greene was researching the life of one of the major poets of the Restoration – a figure often thought of in the 1930s as a pornographer.

Throughout his life, Greene was devoted to the poets of the seventeenth century and often carried with him a much-marked copy of Sir Henry Newbolt's anthology *Devotional Poets of the XVII Century*, which furnished him with the phrase from George Herbert that became the epigraph to *Our Man in Havana*: 'And the sad man is cock of all his jests.'[39] Indeed, he made the first notes for *The Living Room* inside its back cover. The argument that he would make for Rochester reveals a sensitivity to this period of English poetry: 'Rochester had inherited from Donne a poetry of passionate colloquialism. Donne's studied roughness of metre has the hesitancy and the thoughtfulness of speech; even at its most musical his poetry is that of a man speaking. Rochester's individual characteristic was to pour the passionate colloquialism of Donne, extended to include the rough language of the stews, into the mould of the Restoration lyric without shattering the form.'[40]

The choice of Rochester as a subject also reflected Greene's private worries. A notorious rake and unbeliever, Rochester died young and surprisingly repentant at thirty-three. Although he lived for eighty-six years, Greene had always expected to die young. He knew the frailty of his own faith and felt that he was in a constant state of mortal sin owing to his sexual life. There is plenty of evidence, not least the obsession in *Brighton Rock* with a change of heart 'between the stirrup and the ground', that Greene thought his own best hope lay in a deathbed repentance. It had worked for Rochester; it might work for him.

Greene's reading of Rochester's religious views is underpinned by what became one of the touchstones of his own life. As he grew older and more troubled about his Catholic beliefs, he felt at the same time that unbelief requires a certainty that cannot be justified. Rochester, he says, saw 'the cracks in the universe of Hobbes, the disturbing doubts in his disbelief'.[41] As the years went by, he found that he himself could never share the tidy confidence of an atheist.

He wrote a draft of the book between June and November 1931 and sent it for comment to his old friend the historian Kenneth Bell, who sent back many suggestions and criticisms.[42] Greene evidently made changes to the manuscript before submitting it to Heinemann, but they refused to publish it. He guessed that they were not interested in a prosecution for obscenity, and even John Hayward, the editor of a limited edition of Rochester's work and later a close friend of Greene, was afraid of being charged himself. Although Greene seems to have tinkered with the manuscript for a couple of years, he did not submit it to another publisher.[43] Vivian de Sola Pinto would scoop him with his biography of Rochester in 1935. Greene's work on Rochester would not see the light of day until the Bodley Head published it in 1973.

Halfway through his three-year deal with the publishers, Greene was alarmed about his finances, so he and Vivien moved out of London in March 1931. For a pound a week they rented Little Orchard Cottage in Chipping Campden, a Gloucestershire market town. Without electricity, it was lit by smouldering Aladdin lamps. On their first night they huddled together in a quiet broken only by the hooting of an owl. Someone then knocked at the door. It turned out to be a woman swinging a dead rat by its tail. She said, 'I thought yu'd be interested.' In fact, the thatched roof was infested with rats until a man with a ferret came to get rid of them.[44] Vivien would later speak of this period as 'hard times'.[45] Of course, they were not the only poor people in Chipping Campden – Greene observed many tramps, as well as gypsies begging from door to door.[46] Graham and Vivien actually hired a maid largely because her father could not find a job.

A rustic Graham Greene is hard to imagine. Twenty years later, he would remark, 'Nature doesn't really interest me – except in so far as it may contain an ambush – that is, something human.'[47] Still, he was an avid rambler. In May he reported to his mother that he had hiked 127 miles that month.[48] He frequently took walks of about fifteen miles – probably best understood as pub crawls – with Vivien's Pekinese.

Charmingly, Graham and Vivien often left messages of affection for each other in a medallion on the dog's collar.[49] All the exercise supposedly caused the beast to go mad, and it had to be put down.

That summer Graham suffered through bad hay fever and asthma. Still he did his best to adjust to country life; he picked apples in the garden, and grew romaine lettuces with the assistance of a gypsy gardener who gathered up snails for his own cooking. The locals would make wine out of almost anything, even parsnips. Vivien threw herself into the life of the place, and was soon organizing the church fête. Their parish priest, Father Henry Bilsborrow, was a far cry from the sophisticates of the Brompton Oratory. He shared his bedroom with an intrusive owl, and rode about on a knock-kneed horse.[50] He struggled in his sermons, sometimes producing spoonerisms, such as 'Jonah in the welly of the bale for three days'.[51] Greene recalled him preaching about the missions, 'What a glorious sight! Seven thousand Zulus coming to communion. We don't see that in England.'[52]

The most memorable of the local characters was Charles Seitz, known in the village as Charlie Sykes. He was born in Bombay, the son of a doctor. In the course of his own medical studies he suffered a mental breakdown, so he went to Canada where he worked as a cattle drover, and to South Africa where he served in the Cape Mounted Police. During the last part of his life, in Chipping Campden, he would often be seen almost hunchbacked under a weight of rags. A hard drinker, he was flea-ridden, and he often tangled with the police. He played up his madness for tourists and would pose for pictures if they paid him. Despite having several hundred pounds in the bank, he was an inveterate beggar, and lived in a cottage of two rooms, which contained only a broken chair, a pile of straw, and sixteen pairs of battered shoes. He froze to death there in a cold snap at the beginning of 1933 and his body had to be lowered down the stairs in a net. Greene was impressed by the extremes of his life, and wrote an article about him for the *Spectator*.[53]

Their new home was isolated, but some visitors made the journey, among them a Norwegian poet and dramatist named Nordahl Grieg.[54] It appears that they were introduced by Nils Lie, the Norwegian translator of *The Man Within*. The son of a Bergen schoolteacher, he signed on at seventeen as a deckhand on a ship bound for China and Australia and afterwards wrote of a shipboard life that was all danger at sea and all prostitutes in port. In 1924 he won a scholarship that allowed him to spend a year at Wadham College, Oxford. He went as a journalist to China during the civil war, and interviewed leaders on both sides. He spent a year and a half in Moscow studying Soviet theory, and remained a supporter of Stalin through the period of the show trials. He also fought in the Spanish Civil War on the Republican side. In the late 1930s, he and his brother Harald, a publisher, cut impressive figures in Norwegian culture. When the Germans occupied Norway he went into exile on a ship that carried the royal family and the national treasure. From England, where Graham met him again, holding court in a roomful of Norwegian exiles, he gave radio talks that were transmitted into Norway, and eventually died in a bombing raid over Berlin. His reputation as a poet faded, but interest revived in the most tragic of circumstances. After the 2011 Norway attacks, one of Grieg's patriotic songs, 'Til Ungdommen' ('To the Youth'), became a source of national consolation and was sung at memorial services and played repeatedly on the radio.[55]

Greene knew almost nothing about Grieg when he trudged up the lane to the cottage in Chipping Campden, and could remember seeing him in person only twice afterwards, but felt an intimacy with him and a freedom to discuss any subject. A skilled debater, Grieg was seldom bothered when his friends disagreed with his ideas. He politely told Greene in a letter that the setting of *Rumour at Nightfall* was botched, and he expected the same degree of honesty in return. It was a deep friendship that sprang up suddenly. When Grieg arrived, he carried hope to the discouraged Greene 'like a glass of akvavit'.[56]

8

THE DEVIL LOOKS AFTER HIS OWN

'That year, 1931, for the first and last time in my life I deliberately set out to write a book to please, one which with luck might be made into a film. The devil looks after his own and in *Stamboul Train* I succeeded in both aims . . .' After his failures, it was imperative that Greene write a popular book.[1] He would later wonder whether the film *Grand Hotel*, which explores the lives of travellers at a Berlin hotel, gave him the idea,[2] but this is not possible as it was released a full year after he began research on his own novel about the Orient Express. The events of the novel are set in April 1932, just as Hitler was narrowly defeated by Paul von Hindenburg for the German presidency and the Nazis were making gains in other elections. Yugoslavia was in the throes of an economic and political crisis – there was a new premier and the police were arbitrarily arresting or executing people who seemed opposed to centralization.[3] Word was reaching the West of grave food shortages in the Soviet Union; it became known a little later that this was a famine caused by the forced collectivization of farms. That portion of the famine which occurred in Ukraine is known as the *Holodomor*, a term meaning extermination by hunger, and it took the lives of 4.5 million people[4] – some estimates are much higher. The European news was alarming, and the public wanted distractions, among them the fantasy of a glamorous journey on the Orient Express.[5]

Greene certainly could not afford it. So he appealed around the end of April 1931 to Wagons-Lits and then to Thomas Cook for free passage to Istanbul. They refused, so he booked a third-class passage as far as the German border and from there took advantage of a generous provision that allowed authors a free pass on the state rail system. Even so, his journey ended at Cologne. He took careful notes and says that readers can be assured, for example, that the allotments he placed near Bruges were in the right place, but in the last stage of the novel he was relying on the inspiration provided by listening over and over to Arthur Honegger's *Pacific 231*, a composition that reproduces the driving rhythms of a locomotive. His description of the key border crossing from Hungary to Serbia at Subotica was cut from whole cloth.[6]

This engaging story is focused on a handful of a strangers thrown together for the journey. Coral Musker is an impoverished dancer headed for a new job in Istanbul. She and Carleton Myatt, a Jewish merchant dealing in raisins, strike up an affair. Dr Czinner, a political exile, is heading back, incognito, to Yugoslavia to lead a leftist uprising. He is spotted by Mabel Warren, an aggressive British journalist whose love for the much younger Janet Pardoe has left her embittered. Among the minor characters are a murderer on the run and a popular novelist.

One difficulty today with the book is the constant reference to Myatt as 'the Jew'. Indeed, occasional uses of the word 'Jew' with a negative or unattractive signification appear in Greene's writing until about the beginning of 1941. In 1988, he observed: 'After the holocaust one couldn't use the word Jew in the loose way one used it before the war. Myatt in fact is one of the nicest characters in *Stamboul Train*, both brave and sympathetic.' Still, he made sure to cut out some instances of the word in new editions, as he did with similar references to Sir Marcus in *A Gun for Sale*, a character based on Sir Basil Zaharoff, chairman of Vickers, and to the gangster Colleoni in *Brighton Rock*.[7]

Greene was alert to the persecution of Jews in Europe and wanted to write about it. Indeed, Myatt is subjected to discrimination which the book plainly deplores. Greene proposed to the editor of the *Graphic* that he go to Munich to report on Hitler's rally of 3 July 1932, but was turned down. Before long, however, his brother Hugh was in a position to tell him anything he needed to know about Nazi Germany. Although an agnostic, Hugh's journalism often focused on Germany's religious groups. For example, Graham obtained introductions for him to Jesuits in south Germany, and this helped him form an impression of Catholic resistance to the Nazis, which became a theme in his reporting.[8] At the beginning of 1934, Hugh became a correspondent for the *Telegraph* in Berlin and promptly made a visit to Dachau, which at that time contained three thousand political prisoners. He made several more trips to the camp and provided the newspaper with unflinching accounts of Nazi brutality, anti-Semitism, and territorial ambition – when other newspapers, notably *The Times*, were trying not to offend the Germans.[9] Graham Greene saw Germany and its treatment of Jews through the eyes of his brother.

In late 1937, Graham Greene and his friend the writer Malcolm Muggeridge, who as a journalist had broken the story of the famine in Ukraine, tried, in vain, to find a publisher for a book about the conflict in Palestine, with Greene to take the 'pro-Jewish' side and Muggeridge the 'pro-Arab'.[10] In the summer of 1939, Greene convinced Heinemann to commission *Refugee Ship*, 'a non-fiction book, describing one of these rather appalling voyages from Constanza in Rumania on old wooden Greek boats carrying 3 or 400 Jews. They try to smuggle them into Palestine and are generally nabbed by British destroyers.'[11] Ruling Palestine under the League of Nations Mandate, Britain had severely restricted immigration and in so doing blocked a route to safety for refugees from the Nazis. Some ships were able to land their passengers at places like Haifa, only for them to be placed in detention camps. Other ships were intercepted or even fired upon and sent back to their ports of origin. Some were redirected to Cyprus where the passengers were interned.[12] With the coming of the war, Greene shelved this project, though perhaps an echo of his concern over Jewish refugees lingers in *The Power and the Glory*, when he describes the whisky priest as 'a man without a passport who is turned away from every harbour'.[13] Few in Britain shared his concern for the Jewish refugees, but attitudes were shifting – he observed with approval in early 1941: 'anti-semitism in this country however moderate has begun to be looked on as fascist'.[14]

Working on the biography of Rochester for most of 1931, he did not actually begin writing *Stamboul Train* until 2 January 1932.[15] By the time he finished it in late July and sent it off to the publisher, he was in a spot. His three-year deal with the publishers was running out – indeed, his annual payment had already been cut by £250. He had a tax bill to pay, and he was, as he told Hugh, approaching bankruptcy.[16] Apart from the payment from the publishers, which was technically an advance on future sales, the amount he earned from books and reviews in the first half of 1932 was just £16 8d.[17] Both Graham and Vivien were entering literary competitions in the hope of prize money. He asked *The Times* to take him back; the assistant editor Robert Barrington-Ward wrote with some asperity: 'Since your day, the tents have been folded and moved on.'[18] Enquiries at the *Observer*, *Spectator*, and *Catholic Herald* came to nothing. He even went as far as to apply for a teaching job at Chulalankarana University in Bangkok.[19]

Then, in mid-August, a letter from Heinemann arrived, which he opened with hands literally trembling. Evans wrote: 'It is beyond doubt the best book, as a whole, which you have written so far ... ' Greene went to St Catharine's Church in Chipping Campden to thank God. While there he decided that an idea he had been considering for a novel about spiritualism and incest was no good and that he should try another story in the vein of *Stamboul Train* – 'a large inclusive picture of a city which should use my experience as much as my imagination'.[20] This was the germ for *It's a Battlefield*. Greene would return to the subject of spiritualism, however fleetingly, in *The Ministry of Fear*. Incest would make its appearance in *England Made Me*.

Evans liked the new work, but Greene was not in the clear. Even a good novel might fail to sell. On 1 September he met with Evans and the representative of Nelson Doubleday, Mary Leonard (later Pritchett), who would become Greene's agent in the United States and a very close friend, but on this day seemed a 'dragon'.[21] With the manuscript on the table, they reviewed his sales record. Evans was willing to extend Heinemann's payment to Greene for one more year, under a new contract for two books with the tough provision that all losses, that is, the difference between the money he had been receiving as advances and the actual amount he was owed from sales, were to be recovered by the publisher before any royalties could be paid. Leonard agreed to no more than a two-month extension while they studied the new novel. Greene realized that he might have to write the two books for no money at all and 'was close to tears'.[22]

Downplaying one of Greene's hopes, they told him that selection by the Book Society was unlikely since the novel included a lesbian character.[23] However, Greene's friend Rupert Hart-Davis had worked for Heinemann until 1932 and was now employed by the Book Society. Hart-Davis was intent on helping Greene and tried discreetly to advance his cause. Moreover, another of Greene's friends, the poet Edmund Blunden, had joined the committee. On 7 October 1932

Hart-Davis sent Greene a telegram of congratulations – his book had been chosen.[24] The success of *Stamboul Train* now seemed assured. Meanwhile, there was every chance of selling film rights. Basil Dean, Metro-Goldwyn-Mayer, Universal, and RKO were are all 'biting'.[25]

However, there was rough water ahead. At the end of November, J. B. Priestley, one of the bestselling novelists of the time, laid hands on a review copy of the book, and concluded, rightly, that Greene had used him as the model for the faux-cockney Q. C. Savory, who styles himself the contemporary Dickens. At one point in the story, the journalist Mabel Warren says that within a few years Savory will be arrested for indecencies in Hyde Park.[26] Priestley threatened Evans with libel action. 'I should laugh if all my hopes did not rest on this book,' Greene wrote in his journal.[27]

Priestley wanted the publication stopped. Evans waved off Greene's suggestion that they fight the action. As a Heinemann author himself, Priestley was more valuable to the firm than Greene was. Greene had to dictate changes from the phone box in Chipping Campden, getting rid of references to Dickens, pipe-smoking, blunt fingers, and other supposedly identifying marks. The thirteen thousand copies already printed had to be cut open and then resewn with the new pages, a process costing £400, of which, evidently, half was added to Greene's debt to Heinemann[28] – a debt not finally cleared until the publication of *Brighton Rock* in 1938.[29] A few days later, he had to listen to Priestley give a speech at a Book Society luncheon and then join a toast to 'Literature coupled with the name of Mr. J. B. Priestley'.[30] Soon he dreamt that he had murdered Priestley at the Times Book Club.[31] Perhaps not quite as satisfying as having him dead, Greene learned at the beginning of March that Priestley was no longer the chief book reviewer for the *Evening Standard* and seized on an erroneous piece of gossip to explain it – he had been sacked because his secretary was writing the reviews.[32]

But his main consolation was that his book was selling – 16,360 by 24 February.[33] Publicity brought certain penalties, including letters from obsessive readers such as Janet Pardoe of Pennsylvania, who had the same name as one of his characters: 'Am considered rather attractive, as was your character, but, hope not the empty-headed, self-centred, parasitical person your Janet was.'[34]

Greene remained anxious about money and was greatly relieved when Derek Verschoyle, the literary editor of the *Spectator*, asked him to review fiction for the magazine once or twice a month. At a rate of five guineas per review, Greene had hopes of bringing in £70 to £130 per year, plus the resale value of his review copies.[35] He worked for Verschoyle for most of the next decade and succeeded him as literary editor when the war came. Jeremy Lewis tells us that according to oral tradition (i.e. Diana Athill's father) Verschoyle 'kept a .22 rifle in the office in Gower Street, and would occasionally fling open his window and, his feet propped up on the desk, take potshots at stray cats lurking in the garden or on the black-bricked wall beyond; but however unpopular he may have been with Bloomsbury cats, his convivial, heavy-drinking ways recommended him to his colleagues.'[36] Greene reviewed hundreds of books for Verschoyle, and from mid-1935 was also the magazine's film reviewer. According to his bibliographers, Greene, over his whole career, reviewed five hundred books and six hundred films.[37] There is no evidence that he shot any cats.

Greene's fortunes were about to turn. His film agent, the influential Elisabeth Marbury in New York, died on 22 January 1933. At the same time, Mary Leonard was leaving Doubleday to set up as an agent. Greene also wanted to distance himself from Doubleday, so threw in his lot with her: she would be his American agent, while David Higham of Curtis Brown would continue to represent him in London. Over cocktails at the Savoy, he blurted out: 'There's nothing like a successful book for getting one free drinks!'[38] By 11 April, she had closed a film deal with Fox for $7500, a huge sum for a young author, it meant that the prospect of real hardship was gone – and just in time. In May, Vivien discovered she was pregnant.

The marriage, though affectionate, was now strained. Graham had been involved with prostitutes, including one named Annette whom he had been seeing for about a year and a half. Vivien knew what was happening: 'I heard a little murmur here, something – I'm very intuitive. And then this prostitute Annette had the nerve to ring up once – and I took the call. And I *knew* – there weren't five syllables before I knew quite well. I think she had a sort of beat in Bond Street. But what could I do?'[39]

Paradoxically, Graham still felt very loving towards Vivien, and was extremely worried about her suffering in pregnancy and childbirth. He regarded their life together as precious and thought of the baby as an 'intrusion' to which he must resign himself.[40] The house at Chipping Campden was unsuitable for a child, and Vivien had already been making enquiries in Oxford. On the day after receiving the cheque for film rights, they headed to Oxford where in the company of a shifty but bonhomous estate agent in plus fours they decided on a recently built third-floor flat at 9 Woodstock Close. It had one bedroom, was reached by a lift and had such luxuries as constant hot water and a fridge. Greene was especially curious about the windows that could be turned right around for cleaning. They agreed to take it from the end of June at a yearly rent of £130.[41]

Two weeks later, Vivien received a postcard from her mother saying that she had broken her leg, and she dropped into a postscript the news that Vivien's father was dead.[42] Long estranged from him, his death seems not to have affected Vivien greatly. On 21 May she and Graham travelled to Horton, near Swansea, for a beach holiday, and on the train she became ill. Once they were settled in Horton, two telegrams were delivered to Graham together, one saying that Vivien's mother was 'extremely ill' and the other that she had died. When Graham broke the news to Vivien she let out 'a horrible high cry' and was desolate. Graham got through to her uncle Vivian Green-Armytage, an obstetrician, who explained that a blood clot had travelled from Marion Dayrell-Browning's leg to her brain and killed her. Graham told him about Vivien's pregnancy and her present state, and he advised she should not travel to London for the funeral, as did a local doctor who came to examine her. After some argument, Vivien decided that she was happier to be represented at the funeral by her husband.[43]

Graham and Vivien moved to Oxford on 23 June, and it was good for both of them. However, moving house is stressful, and in this case it was compounded by Vivien's pregnancy. On 10 July, Greene described his own state of mind on a rainy day when a bus he had been travelling on struck a cyclist – the person was uninjured but there was a long delay: 'My nerves horribly on edge; that feeling of lurking madness, of something swelling in the brain & wanting to burst; every sound, however small, made by anyone else, the chink of a plate on a fork, piercing the brain like a knife. Lay down after lunch but hardly slept at all. Felt a little better with evening. An excess of sexuality.' Greene is describing symptoms consistent with his mood disorder.

There was also work pressure; he was in the last stages of a novel begun the previous September. *It's a Battlefield* follows *Stamboul Train* in looking at a troubled contemporary scene, but this novel was not exactly a page-turner – its virtues were subtler than that. It was unlikely to repeat the success of its predecessor. At the centre of the story is a communist bus driver, Jim Drover, who is awaiting execution for the murder of a policeman, and for whom there is a remote possibility of reprieve. The main character is the Assistant Commissioner of Police. A man of melancholic probity based partly on the Assistant Commissioner in Conrad's *The Secret Agent*[44] and partly on the novelist's uncle, the civil servant Sir Graham Greene, the character seems a dry run for Scobie in *The Heart of the Matter*, though he is not given to anxiety about faith or morals. He does his job, enforces laws, trusts to the courts, distrusts politics, and refuses to think about what might ultimately constitute justice. Much against his will, he has been asked by the Home Secretary to write a report on the likely impact of a reprieve. Greene called on his brief experience of the Communist Party to render a meeting at which an intellectual, Mr Surrogate, modelled on the writer and critic John Middleton Murry, gives a speech about Drover's probable execution as an acceptable sacrifice for the larger cause. Meanwhile, Drover's brother Conrad sleeps with the condemned man's wife, Milly, and is eventually reduced to stalking the Assistant Commissioner with a revolver loaded with blanks. The most effective advocate for Drover is Lady Caroline Bury, the character inspired by Lady Ottoline Morrell.

In this novel, Greene wrote about things he knew or could find out about. Afterwards, he fretted about not knowing enough to render the meeting of communists accurately, but at least he had his experience of the party branch in Oxford and the meeting in Paris in early 1925. He drew on experience to render such places as Battersea, where he had lived, and at one point the action veers north to Berkhamsted. In the course of his research for the book, he received important help from Colonel G. D. Turner, who was married to the Pulitzer Prize-winning novelist Margaret Wilson and whose daughter Comfort would soon marry Rupert Hart-Davis. The couple, whom Greene liked and admired, lived at nearby Blockley, and had come to visit them in Chipping Campden. Both had been Protestant lay missionaries: Margaret Wilson had served in India before becoming a writer, and she was a campaigning pacifist. Greene praised Colonel Turner as an 'ironic humanitarian' with little faith in English law. He had been a reforming prison governor and was now Assistant Prison Commissioner in the Home Office. Among his concerns were the reintegration of released inmates into society and finding alternatives to capital punishment. He arranged for Greene to tour Wormwood Scrubs, which allowed him to describe a very similar prison in the novel.[45] His conversation may have influenced Greene's handling of Conrad Drover, who wonders whether his brother might be better off hanged than left in prison for fifteen years. This was a point Turner made in a public lecture some years later: prisons complete the degeneration of inmates and without major reforms it is hardly a mercy to keep murderers alive.[46] In this sense, the reprieve granted to Drover is by no means a cheerful outcome.

While writing the book, Greene dreamt often about crime – including the murder of Priestley. On one occasion he dreamt that he had murdered someone and left the body in a suitcase at a train station, and wanted to remove the bag before the body began to swell.[47] The novel contains a sub-plot along these lines, with a woman's body found dismembered in a trunk in Paddington Station. Greene represents London as many battlefields – economic, legal, sexual – and, in a flourish of dark metaphor, the trunk-killer turns out to be a mad member of the Salvation Army. Greene's London is summed up by the Assistant Commissioner's housekeeper: '"Them as knows what London is," Mrs Simpson said, "would not be surprised to see their nearest and dearest bleeding."[48]

Finished on 4 August,[49] the book came out in early February 1934. Greene thought that the sales were terrible, but in fact it sold 7500 in Britain and nearly two thousand in the United States.[50] The reviews were respectful, but some expressed a distaste for Greene's sensibility and his refusal to provide a happy ending. The most encouraging response would be private. Greene wrote Ford Madox Ford a fan letter about The Good Soldier, and Ford asked to see some of his work. In December 1934, the older novelist wrote from New York: 'I can hardly express how highly I think of it – construction impeccable: writing very good indeed & atmosphere extraordinarily impressive ... ' It was 'a shaft of sunlight through the gloom that seems to hang over our distant land! I wouldn't have believed that such writing c^d have come out of England.'[51]

9

MINTY STEPPED ON BOARD

Greene was thinking of Sweden. He reviewed a biography of Ivar Kreuger, the Swedish 'Match King' who managed to achieve monopolies on the sale of matches in many countries. Kreuger lied about his assets and lent staggering sums of money he did not possess. He was able to lend $75 million to the government of France and for a time his personal credit stood five points higher than that of the Republic. On another occasion he lent $125 million to Germany. Among those who fell for Kreuger was J. P. Morgan, swindled in an $11 million deal. In the end, Kreuger was brought down by a forgery of £25 million worth of Italian treasury bills.[1] Anticipating disgrace, he shot himself. From the moment he read the biography, Greene could see that this was a brilliant story: 'it can never fail to be exciting, this curve up to success and down to death'.[2]

Shortly after finishing *It's a Battlefield*, which included scenes in a match factory, Greene set off with his younger brother Hugh for three weeks in Scandinavia. For much of the trip they were accompanied by a British magazine writer named Schelling and her two daughters, aged sixteen and twenty, a trio wished on them by their Aunt Helen (one of Charles Greene's sisters). Flirtation ensued. On one occasion when Hugh and the younger daughter had been gone a long time the mother believed they had drowned in a canal. Later, Graham told the elder daughter that he believed she was a virgin and got his face slapped.[3] In Stockholm, Graham met a pacifist who spoke with enthusiasm of a race war involving Russia.[4]

Back home, he got to work on the novel. The fictionalized magnate, whom Greene calls Erik Krogh, is not the main character. Rather he focuses on English twins, Anthony and Kate Farrant, whose love for each other borders on incest. One of Greene's most effective female characters, Kate, is the employee and mistress of Krogh. She tries to rescue the feckless Anthony from his life as a drifter. Anthony is based partly on Greene's cricket-playing brother Herbert, who was always finding new and curious ways to fail in life. For example, he had tried for a time to farm tobacco in Rhodesia. Inevitably, he came back to Charles for cash. According to Vivien, his mother could not bear to be in a room with him. Short of cash himself, Graham offered to pay Herbert a subsidy if it could be concealed from their father, who would certainly disapprove. Marion vetoed the idea as she was not prepared to work behind her husband's back, but as his earnings increased, Graham did pay Herbert an allowance and became his trustee.[5] This was the first of many such regular payments Graham Greene made to members of his family, needy friends, and hard-up writers.

Like Herbert, Anthony cannot hold down a job. For years, he comes back from distant places announcing to his father that he has resigned from his latest position, usually on a matter of principle. But now the father is dead, and Kate wants to bring Anthony into a more conventional way of life by getting him a job at Krogh's – but as she did in their childhood she is trying to tame something in him that ought to be left wild. Oddly enough, he quits this particular job on principle and it costs him everything.

The character is not, however, a simple portrait of Herbert, but contains recognizable traces of Greene himself, such as the appendectomy at the Westminster Hospital, a relationship with a prostitute named Annette, and getting his face slapped when he speculates that a woman is a virgin. This is a tricky point: Greene's characters often begin as portraits of himself or others but travel away from their originals, becoming distinct creations. Anthony Farrant cannot be reduced to a portrait of either Graham or Herbert, though he contains characteristics of both brothers.

The idea of a character taking on a life of his own is nowhere better demonstrated than in *England Made Me*. Greene says that his story was focused on the twins, with Krogh there only to create a narrative. The minor characters were all in place: 'Then suddenly the boat listed because Minty stepped on board.' An Anglo-Catholic frequently invoking obscure saints, the journalist Minty, a remittance man in

Stockholm, was initially needed in the plot to spot Anthony's lies, but then he became a scene-stealer who, among other curious practices, keeps a spider trapped under his toothbrush glass. By far the most vivid character Greene had yet created, he seems to take over the book, including the funeral scene which might otherwise have focused mainly on Kate. Greene had no idea what to do with him: 'Oh yes, I resented Minty, and yet I couldn't keep him down.'[6] Minty appealed to readers as unlike each other as Kim Philby and Evelyn Waugh, both of whom saw something of themselves in him.[7]

While writing the novel, Greene was gathering essays from prominent young authors for a volume published the next summer as *The Old School*. W. H. Auden wrote about his experiences at Gresham's School, Holt; Theodora Benson wrote about Cheltenham Ladies' College; going against the grain of the book, L. P. Hartley wrote fairly respectfully of Harrow, where, as a head of house, he engaged in 'whopping' malefactors.[8] Perhaps the most impressive essay is that of the hardscrabble Salford novelist Walter Greenwood, whose *Love on the Dole* Greene thought 'brilliant';[9] Greenwood, who was nine when his father, a hairdresser, drank himself to death, wrote of a council school where beatings were the normal course: 'To me, the Old School was a place to be avoided, a sort of punishment for being young.'[10] Still at school, Greenwood worked in a pawn shop, and then left school altogether for work at the age of thirteen.

The Old School was published by Jonathan Cape, where Rupert Hart-Davis was now a director. Greene actually tried to leave Heinemann for Cape in November 1933, but when Heinemann raised its advance on *It's a Battlefield* from £200 to £350 he found he no longer had an excuse to move.[11] At much the same time he considered but regretfully turned down an offer to work for the publisher Chatto & Windus because he was committed to his lease in Oxford for another six months and could not manage the commuting to London.[12] So he settled down to his writing, and took on some small practical challenges, such as learning to drive in Raymond's old car – Graham seldom drove in his life and when he did he was always a danger to himself and others.[13]

On the evening of 28 December 1933 Vivien gave birth to a 7 pound 11 ounce daughter. The delivery was especially difficult and Vivien was upset that she could not present a son to Graham, who said he did not care a 'brass farthing' about such things except that they bothered her.[14] The daughter was christened Lucy Caroline, and was referred to as Lucy until the 1950s when she decided that she preferred to go by her middle name. She is now known by her married name Caroline Bourget. Graham Greene was fond of his daughter, but not involved in her upbringing. She says that she did not really know her father until she was an adult, after which they became good friends.

At the time of his daughter's birth, Greene was especially restless and was looking for excitement that was not domestic. In August 1933 he had joined the Independent Labour Party (ILP), which had disaffiliated from the Labour Party the preceding year to take a firmer leftist line. One of the Hall Greenes, Ben, a pacifist, had become an ILP activist and was particularly anxious to see party decisions made at the constituency level in contrast to the operations of the Labour Party's National Executive Committee. By now somewhat ashamed of his role in the General Strike, Graham followed Ben's example and threw himself into the affairs of the ILP, setting up a branch in Oxford. Declaring that 'The growth of Fascism, the new Unemployment Bill, the police repression, all call for action,' Greene and an associate organized a meeting on the foggy, frosty evening of 23 January 1934, addressed by the southern divisional chairman of the party.[15] Characteristically, he hoped for a showdown with some of Oswald Mosley's Fascists to give the branch a good launch. There is no evidence that this happened, but Greene was present at the famous Battle of Cable Street on 4 October 1936, when Mosley led a march, under police protection, through east London and was blocked by Jewish and Irish residents of the area, and other anti-Fascists. The police conducted a mounted baton charge, and as part of the massive crowd Greene experienced panic for the first time in his life, as if by 'contagion'.[16]

Always impatient with political parties, Greene's involvement with socialism was vexed by a number of issues, including a lifelong hatred of the income tax – in 1926, he had asked Vivien to explain whether Catholics were morally obliged to pay it,[17] and his subsequent efforts to resist the tax would come to a climax in 1966 when he became an exile in France. Greene's interest in the ILP did not last long, and, eventually, he settled into what might be loosely described as a social democratic stance.

Fascinated by riots, Greene got the *Spectator* to send him to Paris to report on the Stavisky Affair which rattled the Third Republic, bringing down two governments within a week. A career swindler called Alexandre Stavisky had organized a fraudulent bond issue in Bayonne; he became the subject of a manhunt and shot himself through the temple as the police burst in on him at Chamonix. It was claimed by his wife and various right-wing politicians that the police had shot him so that he could not reveal how members of the centre-left government of Camille Chautemps had been involved in his schemes. At first, the crisis contained an element of farce, as when a member of the Chamber of Deputies and a journalist fought a duel on a football ground, exchanging four shots from twenty-five paces at ninety-second intervals, precisely timed by a metronome. No one was injured and the three surgeons in attendance had to take their bandages and stretchers back home again. However, the royalist Action Française and the fascists organized riots, for which demonstrators came equipped with razors attached to sticks. Mounted police repeatedly charged the rioters and gunshots were exchanged. On 6 February, 150,000 demonstrators staged a pitched battle with police at the Place de la Concorde, resulting in a dozen deaths and many injuries.[18]

Greene flew to Paris in advance of a twenty-four-hour general strike called for 12 February. His trip was organized by his French agent and translator Denyse Clairouin, who would later serve in the resistance and die in Mauthausen concentration camp.[19] Having rejected an invitation to march with the National Front against the communists, Greene, Clairouin, and the American novelist Allan Updegraff drove about Paris looking for signs of trouble. On the day of the strike 150,000 met peacefully in the Place de la Nation. He wrote his article for the *Spectator* having seen 'precious little' violence.[20]

'I've become simply crazy about flying,' Greene wrote to Hugh following his trip to France.[21] He soon pitched a new book to his publishers called 'Zeppelin' about a journey to be taken from Lake Constance to Brazil, where he would write on the civil war that had taken place there two years earlier, presenting it as 'a caricature of patriotism'. For the project to go ahead he needed the Zeppelin firm to give him a half-price fare.[22] The book was never written.

Although he remained devoted to Vivien – in his fashion – Greene was ever more anxious to travel. A fugitive from fatherhood, he started planning a trip to Germany and Eastern Europe. At a cocktail party, he met Baroness (Moura) Budberg, H. G. Wells's 'latest flame'; she recommended that Greene go to Estonia, where she owned an estate, and told him that in Tallinn he could visit a brothel that had been operated by the same family for five hundred years.[23] Delighted by the idea, he also hoped to extend the visit to Moscow, where he could meet with Nordahl Grieg, but this did not happen. Around 5 May, he flew into Berlin and was shocked at the contrast between the beauty of the lighted city seen from the air and, once he had landed, the horror of the swastikas.[24]

In Berlin, he spent time with Hugh and with Albrecht von Bernstorff, both of whom would have briefed him on what to expect in the rest of his journey. The Soviet Union and Germany each wanted to install puppet governments in the Baltic states. The Soviets had recently concluded non-aggression pacts with Finland, Estonia, Latvia, and Lithuania. In March, Estonia had declared martial law in order to purge Nazis from the government, and a major trial was expected to reveal how far they had infiltrated. Greene probably visited Finland and Lithuania, as Malcolm Muggeridge had provided him with introductions to people in these countries,[25] but we do not have a precise itinerary. On 12 May, he left Riga for Tallinn. This was unlucky timing for someone seeking trouble: just after Greene's departure, the Latvian premier Kārlis Ulmanis declared martial law to deal with socialist and Nazi plots – in effect a coup, after which he set himself up as dictator.[26]

On the flight to Tallinn, the only other passenger was a diplomat and spy named Peter Leslie. While reading a novel by Henry James, Greene noticed that his companion was also absorbed in reading *The Ambassadors* in the same edition; as he put it to Vivien, 'we more or less fell into each other's arms'.[27] A lonely vice-consul in Tallinn, Leslie might have been one of Greene's invented characters: an Anglican clergyman, he had converted to Catholicism and become an arms dealer. Moreover, Leslie was a highly regarded MI6 operative holding his own in a city of constant intrigue among Stalinist agents, White Russians, and Nazis. After the war Greene thought about a film script that owed something to his encounter with Leslie: the main character was to be an agent for Singer sewing machines in Tallinn. The idea was laid aside, but eventually came back in a new setting as *Our Man in Havana*. In 1969, the aged Leslie wrote to Greene, reminding him of their encounter and making him a gift of his first editions of Henry James, 'thus', as Greene wrote, 'crowning one of the most pleasant chance encounters of my life'.[28]

As for the brothel, Greene never found it. A waiter in Tallinn's most elegant hotel was puzzled by his enquiries: 'But there is nothing of that kind we cannot arrange for you here.'[29] When they corresponded long after, Leslie told Greene that Budberg had it wrong; the place had been turned into a chemist's.

10

IN ZIGI'S TOWN

'I thought for some reason even then of Africa, not a particular place, but a shape, a strangeness, a wanting to know. The unconscious mind is often sentimental; I have written "a shape", and the shape, of course, is roughly that of the human heart.'[1] Greene had it in mind to do something dangerous: a journey on foot through Liberia to investigate modern slavery.

As he looked back on it, it seemed almost a fashion in the 1930s to do such things: '"young authors" were inclined to make uncomfortable journeys in search of bizarre material – Peter Fleming to Brazil and Manchuria, Evelyn Waugh to British Guiana and Ethiopia. Europe seemed to have the whole future: Europe could wait.'[2] Part of his own motivation was likely a gentle rivalry with the adventurous Raymond, who had recently been involved in a successful ascent of Mount Kamet and a nearly successful one of Mount Everest – he set an extraordinary standard for daring, and the restless Graham was anxious to come out of his shadow. And yet, at its core, the journey to Liberia was, for him, a matter of principle.

This West African state had been founded in 1847 by freed slaves from the United States, who established themselves as an elite living mainly near the coast. Indigenous villagers inland were generally impoverished and powerless. In June 1929, the American government accused the Liberian Frontier Force and various government officials of running a system of forced labour that amounted to slavery.

In 1930, a League of Nations commission led by the physician and zoologist Cuthbert Christy confirmed that while one might not find 'classical' slave markets or traders in Liberia, slavery, as defined by a League of Nations Convention in 1926, was widespread. There was domestic slavery within and among tribes, and the pawning of relatives for the satisfaction of debt was a common practice. Moreover, slaves were used for building roads and military bases, and as porters 'under conditions involving systematic intimidation and ill-treatment on the part of Government officials, messengers, and Frontier Force soldiers'. The government, in a manner 'scarcely distinguishable from slave raiding and slave trading', was sending people at gunpoint into labour on the Spanish island of Fernando Po as well as to Gabon.[3]

In the 1920s, the American tyre manufacturer Firestone, closely associated with the Ford Motor Company, sought to break British dominance of rubber production by leasing a million acres of land for the cultivation of South American rubber trees in Liberia. As part of their deal, they also lent the government $5 million at 7 per cent interest to clear its foreign debts, but payments on the loan soon paralyzed the government – there was no money for anything else. Essentially, the corporation was running the country. As for slavery, the Christie commission could not find evidence that Firestone 'consciously' employed unpaid workers, who were, however, forcibly recruited by the government.[4]

Liberia was, and remains, extremely poor. In the 1930s, it had no inland roads or other infrastructure. There were half a dozen doctors in the whole country, and no public health measures were taken against a variety of grave illnesses including plague and yellow fever. The League of Nations was worried; even so, in June 1934 a proposal for financial relief had failed as Liberia insisted on greater control of the suggested programme and the European powers were unwilling to tolerate what the British Foreign Affairs Minister Anthony Eden called 'gross maladministration' – Eden wanted the Americans to take a greater hand in a country with which it had such a long association.[5]

As well as governments, private organizations were trying to influence events in Liberia. Charles Greene supported the Anti-Slavery and Aborigines' Protection Society, perhaps from a principled regret about his grandfather's ownership of slaves on St Kitts and Monserrat.[6] In any event, Charles seems to have encouraged Graham to become involved with the Society, and Graham volunteered to go as their representative to Liberia and find out what was happening. From late August 1934, he met weekly with Sir John Harris to be briefed for a journey from which he might very well not return. Harris was an extraordinary man.

Inspired by Evangelical beliefs, he had investigated and publicized the Belgian exploitation of the Congo. He then travelled in many other countries, often risking his life, to report on enslavements of colonial peoples. He served a term in Parliament as a Liberal and was knighted in 1933. From 1910 to 1940 he acted as Parliamentary Secretary to the Anti-Slavery and Aborigines' Protection Society.[7] Graham wrote to Hugh that he was being groomed as Harris's 'successor as Parliamentary Secretary to the Anti-Slavery Society. But this in confidence. I have to be stared at and my private life examined by a committee of philanthropists; I'm afraid I shan't get by this.'[8]

Charles Evans liked the sound of this journey and paid Greene an advance of £350 for a travel book later given the title *Journey Without Maps*.[9] *The Times* provided a letter of accreditation, but, disappointingly, no commission. Harris had access to the Foreign Office through his fellow campaigner Dame Kathleen Simon, whose husband, Sir John Simon, was Foreign Secretary.[10] The Foreign Office had an ulterior motive: to make sure that Greene stayed 'on our side' – that is, his eventual book or articles should be in line with British policy.[11] In an effort to do a little freelance espionage, Greene asked Denyse Clarouin whether the French Colonial Office might pay him for a report,[12] though there is no evidence that they hired him.

Having drunk a good deal of champagne at Hugh's wedding on 24 October 1934, Greene asked if 'someone, anyone' among his cousins would join him on his Liberian trek.[13] All the likely candidates, including his childhood companion Edward ('Tooter'), said no, but Barbara, a twenty-three-year-old Hall Greene, said yes, even though she had no idea where Liberia was. At least this is the version of the story that they both told afterwards; however, Hugh had been staying with Barbara in London before the wedding, and already in August Graham was including her in his travel plans. There was a certain amount of flirtation between them, as on one occasion he left a café drunk with his braces in his pocket and her belt around his waist.[14]

On the day after the wedding, when Graham had sobered up, he tried to undo the deal by sending Barbara the League of Nations report. She was unbothered, but said he should not worry – her father would certainly forbid the whole business. Uncle Eppy did nothing of the sort. 'At *last* one of my daughters is showing a little initiative,' he said and wrote a cheque to cover her share of the expenses.[15] Having led an unsettled life and suffering occasionally from depression, Barbara brought one considerable, though unnoticed, qualification to the enterprise: she had trained as a nurse[16] and would be largely responsible for Graham surviving the journey. A good writer, she, like Graham, would produce a travel book, to which she gave the now cringe-inducing title *Land Benighted*, misquoting a phrase from the Liberian national anthem;[17] later editions substituted the title *Too Late to Turn Back*. This book is highly readable, and while it reproduces a number of the stereotypes common at the time, it repeatedly strikes a note of thankfulness to Liberians for their generosity and an appreciation for the beauty of their country.

Sir Graham Greene arranged for a Foreign Office official named G. H. Thompson to meet his nephew in December. Thompson did his best to talk Graham out of the whole business, pointing out how easy it was to pick up a fatal illness in the back country. Clearly, the Foreign Office was not sending Greene as any sort of agent. He did have a vague invitation to meet Thompson again on his return, but was formally advised that the government could take no responsibility for what he was doing.[18]

Thompson sent word ahead to the chargé in Monrovia but Greene suggested that he did not like the idea of a British diplomat, the well-named Mr Yapp, informing the Liberian government of his itinerary for fear they would put a stop to it. Yet the journey was hardly a secret. On 4 January 1935 the *News Chronicle* headline read: 'Beauty of 23 Sets Out for Cannibal Land'. In the article, Barbara looks uneasily at a revolver she now possesses, and muses about the likelihood of contracting yellow fever. The article makes very clear that the Greenes are going to investigate slavery, as Sir John Harris is quoted: 'I should think they ought to get through, and their information, if they do, will be very valuable.' His optimism was restrained, to say the least.

In assembling his gear, Greene had the help of a shipping agent, who scanned the long list of requirements and added one item: a tin opener.[19] Sailing from Liverpool on 5 January 1935 in the Elder Dempster cargo ship *David Livingstone*, they stopped at a number of ports, including Tenerife, where they discovered '*Orient Express* from the novel by Graham Greene' playing at the cinema. At Las Palmas, they returned from a party at 3 a.m. in a rowing boat with a dead-drunk man of 17 stone who had to be got onto the companion-way without being dropped into the harbour.[20]

They reached Freetown on 19 January.[21] Barbara wrote about Graham in her journal: 'His brain frightened me. It was sharp and clear and cruel. I admired him for being unsentimental, but "always remember to rely on yourself," I noted. If you are in a sticky place he will be so interested in noting your reactions that he will probably forget to rescue you.' She saw that he had a shaky hand and would likely miss his shot against any attacking animal. 'He seemed somewhat vague and unpractical, and later I was continually astonished at his efficiency and the care he devoted to every little detail. Apart from three or four people he was really fond of, I felt that the rest of humanity was to him like a heap of insects that he liked to examine, as a scientist might examine his specimens, coldly and clearly. He was always polite. He had a remarkable sense of humour and held few things too sacred to be laughed at ... It was stimulating and exciting, and I wrote down that he was the best kind of companion one could have for a trip of this kind. I was learning far more than he realized.'[22]

In Barbara's view, they were 'two innocents, our ignorance was abysmal'.[23] For Graham, the venture was an opportunity to play Russian roulette with a live round in the chamber. He most certainly knew he was putting his life in danger as he had read the Foreign Office Blue Book and been tutored by Harris. They could be shot by soldiers, poisoned, bitten by snakes, infected by rats, or savaged by larger animals; they might catch elephantiasis, leprosy, yaws, malaria, hookworm, schistosomiasis, dysentery, lassa fever, yellow fever, or an especially cruel thing, the Guinea worm, which grows under the skin and must be gradually spooled out onto a stick or pencil – if it breaks in the process, the remnant may mortify inside the host, causing infection or death.[24] Greene knew all this, and set out in spite, or more likely because, of the risk.

Greene had two maps of Liberia, one from the British General Staff that left large areas white and plotted conjectural courses of rivers, and another from the United States which inserted the word 'CANNIBALS' into the blank space.[25] Maps are a way of imagining nations and peoples: these maps presented nothingness or a kind of fear. In practical terms, this occurred because cartographers had not yet done their job. But the message of emptiness has implications, as if the lives of those in the hidden places did not add up to much. Maps are potent things.

Greene, for his part, was adamantly opposed to imperialism and, at that time, he despised the expats who ran British colonies such as Sierra Leone, though he had no idea how self-rule could be brought about without turmoil and long delay. His journey to Liberia was intended to find out as much as he could about an oppressed population, and he was particularly concerned to investigate how foreigners, notably Firestone, were benefiting from forced labour. While the psychological background to his trip is murky, his attitudes towards Africa were progressive for a white Englishman of his generation. For example, Barbara notes that despite having been advised by white men in Freetown to beat and harangue the men he employed, he spoke to them as he would to an Englishman. In addition to their tribal tongues, the Liberians spoke a distinctive form of English which retained some elements from the American South, and used terms such as 'dash' for payment and 'chop' for food. They sometimes found Greene's bookish syntax impenetrable, but his tone of civility was apparently not, and their occasional disagreements with him were resolved amicably. He readily admitted that they knew far more about some things than he did. Knowing that his accounts would be dismissed by whites, he insisted that he had experienced intelligence, kindness, honesty, and diligence from them. For his part, he wondered whether their loyalty had allowed him to 'victimize' these men.[26]

Tim Butcher has written an engrossing book on his own journey in Greene's footsteps through Sierra Leone and Liberia. He believes that while Greene got a good many things right he was unfair to the Krios or Creoles, the freed slaves and their descendants in Freetown, who were caught between the white colonialists and the indigenous population. Although they were the product of a grim history, Greene saw them as merely corrupted by their contact with white men: 'But one cannot continue long to find the Creole's painful attempt at playing the white man funny; it is rather like the chimpanzee's tea-party, the joke is all on one side. Sometimes, of course, the buffoonery is conscious, and then the degradation is more complete.'.[27]

What Greene saw in the League of Nations report, with its binary emphasis on the conflict between the Americo-Liberians and the indigenous people, was a testing ground for a vision of civilization and of human psychology, a chance for 'a smash and grab raid into the primitive'.[28] Believing that modern culture was overwhelmingly corrupt, he trusted to the primitive as a source of vitality and insight. As a habit of mind, primitivism had been around since the early eighteenth century, but in Greene's case it was mingled with Catholicism, anti-colonialism, and psychoanalysis. For Africans, the whole discussion of the primitive is frequently offensive and exasperating – the novelist Chinua Achebe has famously dismantled *Heart of Darkness* for its presentation of Africa and Africans, and Greene is indebted to Conrad.[29] Coming a generation later, of course, Greene is a little more aware of just how absurd some common notions of Africa were: '... you couldn't talk of darkest Africa with any conviction when you had known Nottingham well'.[30]

Butcher corrects some dates that Greene got wrong, and shows that the journey lasted about two months from their arrival in Freetown on 19 January 1935. It began with a creeping 230-mile train ride across Sierra Leone to the end of the narrow-gauge track and a further 40 miles by truck before crossing by foot into Liberia on 26 January. Graham and Barbara walked east through hill country and cut southeast for 65 miles across a southern protrusion of what was then known as French Guinea. Re-entering Liberia, they travelled south and west, reaching Grand Bassa (now Buchanan) on the coast on 2 March, the trek of about 350 miles having taken nearly twice as long as planned. At Grand Bassa they paid off their servants and carriers, and sailed in a small boat full of drunken politicians to Monrovia, where they boarded a cargo ship that eventually arrived back in Dover on 25 March.

Long before arriving in Freetown, Greene had made arrangements for servants, but nothing had been done. With the assistance of a drunk whom he would later call 'Pa Oakley', he managed to get the services of three excellent 'boys' – a condescending term endemic to imperialism. Indeed, two were older than the Greenes. Their leader was the dignified and reputable Amedoo, who would be Greene's personal servant and act as an intermediary with the carriers. Amedoo selected another experienced man, Souri, a Muslim, as cook and the somewhat younger Lamina Karboh to take care of Barbara; he would scatter blossoms on her bed when she seemed downhearted or their accommodation was especially shabby. Partway through the journey, Amedoo fell ill, to be replaced temporarily by an adolescent named Mark, who had a knowledge of local languages and could interpret. Of the four, at least two had had schooling: they wrote to them after they left Liberia. At the Liberian frontier, Greene hired twenty-five men as carriers, a group with its own leaders who were quick to tell the fast-striding Greene that any given day's objective was too far.

Unexpectedly, his route led him to meetings with some of the principal players in Liberia's drama. It is hard not to think that these were staged, as the Foreign Office had told Mr Yapp, its man in Monrovia, to point out to the president, Edwin Barclay, that the visiting author could exercise great influence on world opinion once he published his articles. Yapp also supplied Greene's itinerary to the government,[31] so Barclay could have rearranged his own travels to include a chat with the Englishman. An educated and generally honest man whose administration was stained by its repression of the Kru people, Barclay was anxious for good publicity.

When Greene reached the village of Kolahun on 3 February,[32] it so happened that Barclay had himself made the hard journey there to investigate complaints about a local official named Reeves, who benefited from slavery and killed a good number of people. Of course, on the day no one took the reckless step of actually saying anything to Barclay against Reeves. Instead, Reeves invited the filthy and dishevelled Greene to a meeting with the president. Greene asked Barclay whether his authority was like that of the American president and received a perfectly candid reply: 'Once elected and in charge of the machine, why then, I'm boss of the whole show.'[33] Greene could see that Barclay was a slick politician, but rather liked him and believed that he would do good for his country.

Later Greene had another supposedly random encounter. Colonel Elwood Davis was a black man from the United States who had served as a soldier in Mexico and the Philippines before coming as a mercenary to Liberia and being given command of the armed forces. Known as the 'Dictator of Grand Bassa', he had been accused of atrocities in the Kru War. As Greene approached the village of Tapee-Ta on 22 February, he discovered that Davis was there as the president's agent, looking into complaints by chiefs against district commissioners. Greene asked for an interview and was offered a few minutes as Davis had had a long day. The conversation went on for several hours and was renewed the next evening.

Swilling Greene's whisky, the talkative Davis presented himself as a patriot and sweet-hearted lover of babies, the national director of the Boy Scouts, who could never do such things as he was accused of, for example the burning alive of women and children – that was a matter of soldiers running amok. Over his long career, Greene was often struck by the charisma of military and political strongmen, among them Fidel Castro of Cuba and Omar Torrijos of Panama. Well-dressed, handsome, and highly capable, Davis fitted the type. Finding his personality difficult to fathom, Greene at first wondered if some of the stories of atrocities had been exaggerated.[34] But by the time he returned to England, he had made up his mind, writing that Davis was responsible for 'horrors',[35] and that the facts had 'been proved to the last degree'.[36]

One of Greene's objectives in Liberia was to discover what Firestone was up to, but he was not able to add much to Christie's findings. The Americans running the rubber plantation did not know on what terms their six thousand workers were recruited so could not be accused of running a system of slavery, but Greene was very sceptical of what would now be called a 'don't ask, don't tell' arrangement.[37]

Along his route Greene encountered a number of 'devils' – a term he found very awkward as it suggests a Christian cosmology. Commonly used throughout Liberia, it refers to religious leaders, figures of power who engage in ritual dances and impart traditional lore to young people. Most of those he saw were benign and generous men who, when not wearing the ceremonial tapia robes and wooden masks, typically worked as blacksmiths. However, arriving in the village of Ganta on 14 February, Greene met a missionary doctor named George Harley, who was also an anthropologist. He judged that some devils were tyrants. As leaders of secret societies such as the Poro, some were guilty of ritual murder and anthropophagy. As Lamina remarked of Ganta, a stronghold of the Poro, 'they chop men' here.[38] Harley believed that his own life was very much at risk as he had pushed his enquiries too far. Barbara thought he suffered from 'persecution mania',[39] but Tim Butcher maintains that ritual atrocities committed in the civil war of

1989 to 1997 indicate that the societies remain active. Graham Greene wanted to see the villagers as pure and wholesome, so did not delve deeply into this aspect of their lives.[40]

Having carefully assembled a medical kit, Greene left it behind in Freetown. On the trek, the carriers looked to him for medical care, and he did his best to dress venereal sores and deal with other illnesses. On one remarkable occasion, a villager came to him with hands badly damaged by leprosy. Greene could offer no real help but went through the motions of giving medicine as a form of consolation.[41] It is possible that in that encounter *A Burnt-Out Case*, Greene's novel about leprosy, began its long gestation.

Leaving Tapee-Ta, Greene received conflicting advice about how long it would take to get to Grand Bassa and the sea – a week seemed likely. Time was pressing, as the rainy season would leave the Greenes and their company stranded. He and Barbara had treated each other cautiously, trying not to allow quarrels to develop. Amusingly, she hated the sight of his sagging socks and he abominated a pair of taffeta shorts she wore, but now nerves were becoming frayed. Graham was ill, and Barbara was having to take command. He insisted on moving quickly but was staggering through a nine-hour walk to Zigi's Town on 24 February. He developed a very serious fever, and there was nothing Barbara could treat it with but Epsom salts and a little whisky.

As a nurse, she knew what she was looking at. She felt calm at the expectation of Graham's death, working out a practical plan: how to bury him, how to get to the coast and send telegrams. 'Only one thing worried me in the most extraordinary way. Graham was a Catholic, and into my muddled, weary brain came the thought that I ought to burn candles for him if he died. I was horribly upset, for we had no candles.' So she stayed up much of the night worrying about candles.[42] Meanwhile, listening to thunderstorms, Graham was racked with yearning to be with Vivien, and his world was reduced to 'Shadow on the mosquito net, the dim hurricane lamp, the empty whisky bottle on the chop box.'[43]

In the morning, Barbara expected to find a corpse, but there he was – up and dressed: 'A kind of horrid death's head grinned at me. His cheeks had sunk in, there were thick black smudges under his eyes, and his scrubby beard added nothing of beauty to the general rather seedy effect.[44] His game of Russian roulette had played out. The round in the chamber had fallen into place but somehow failed to discharge. Indeed, after this, Greene's impulse towards self-destruction would never be the same: 'I had discovered in myself a passionate interest in living. I had always assumed before, as a matter of course, that death was desirable.' He spoke of the experience as a kind of 'conversion', which must fade in time: 'the memory of a conversion may have some force in an emergency; I may be able to strengthen myself with the intellectual idea that once in Zigi's Town I had been completely convinced of the beauty and desirability of the mere act of living'.[45]

   With a temperature now below normal, he renewed the march to Grand Bassa, making some use of a hammock carried on a pole: 'It was too close to using men as animals for me to be happy.'[46] Greene's temperature rose and fell through several more days, as the rains seemed to be overtaking them. Then, a merciful piece of luck. They learned of a lorry in Harlingsville, and sent for it. On 2 March they were driven into Grand Bassa, and the trek was over.

11

RAVEN

L ondon beckoned. Having survived Liberia, Greene returned to the conventional life of an Englishman, and after living for weeks in a tent he now had to look for a house. He and Vivien agreed that they could not stay with a child in the Oxford flat much longer. In April 1935, he found a suitable Queen Anne house for let at 14 Clapham Common North Side. Vivien did not see it but trusted in his decision.[1] They moved there in early May.[2]

Vivien came to love that house, which they eventually purchased. After an unstable childhood, it gave her the certainty of home. Moreover, it was beautiful and historic. Narrow, with a long garden, it was part of a terrace built by the architect John Hutt. In the 1930s, it had an archway leading onto a mews. One of its finest features, their daughter Caroline recalled, was a dramatic staircase. On the third floor, the nursery overlooked the Common.[3]

Vivien began collecting antique furniture, an interest that would grow more specialized as she became the world's authority on doll's houses and would one day set up a private museum for her collection – it would be said that Graham wrote novels and 'she created short storeys'.[4]

Coming to London thrust the Greenes into the 'social whirl'. Graham gave a well-received speech to the League of Nations Union, with the novelist Rose Macaulay in attendance. A missionary priest he had met in Liberia came to lunch on 17 May. On the 24th Denyse Clairouin arrived for dinner with a cheque for serial rights in a translation of *Stamboul Train*. She also brought the intoxicating news that there was soon to be a lecture on his fiction at the Sorbonne. There was a dinner with Rupert Hart-Davis and his wife, and a sherry party where Greene met Antonia White, a Catholic writer whose private life was at least as complicated as his own and who would become a regular visitor to Clapham Common. Meanwhile, the *News Chronicle* agreed to pay £50 for a five-day serial of the 'The Basement Room',[5] a short story that in 1948 was made into a film masterpiece as *The Fallen Idol*. On 18 June he made a report on his travels to the Anti-Slavery Society's annual meeting.[6]

All this notice suggests that Greene's reputation was rising. But Heinemann still could not count on his books to sell. To capitalize on public sentiment around George V's Silver Jubilee that year, the publisher encouraged Greene to switch from his original title, 'The Shipwrecked', to *England Made Me*. The new title was apt only insofar as it referred to the characters as expatriates – Greene eventually reverted to the original title for American editions. As a sales ploy, it did not have much of an effect. Published to rather cautious reviews at the end of June, the book sold 4500 copies in Britain and less than half that in the United States.[7]

Greene told his mother that to meet his new expenses he was going to double his output.[8] He was working not only on his Liberian book but a thriller called *A Gun for Sale*; both were completed and published in just over a year. He continued to review armloads of books for the *Spectator*, and began to write, with amusing savagery and considerable insight, about films.

For the next four and a half years, he went with his gold-coloured cards of invitation to the morning press showings of several new films each week at the Empire and Odeon cinemas, buildings of such 'luxury and bizarre taste' that he thought of them afterwards as the 'pleasure dome' decreed by Kubla Khan. Still distrustful about how directors were using sound and colour, his first *Spectator* review, on 5 July 1935, predicted the emergence of the 'smelly'.[9] Greene's film criticism was sometimes an 'escape' from the rigours of writing fiction, and he was refreshed by it.[10] Indeed, rather like a professional golfer you could not always tell when he was working and when he was playing.

He also looked for a regular job. Once again, there were discussions with *The Times*, but they expected him to write a letter saying he had been wrong to leave. He was not going to return if it meant crawling.[11] He entered into an arrangement with Hamish Hamilton Ltd to read manuscripts, write endorsements, and bring in new books, on which he would get a 2.5 per cent commission on sales with his expenses covered. He hoped that this arrangement might develop into a permanent position and eventual directorship at the firm.[12]

Almost as soon as he began work for the firm, Greene made one of the most significant discoveries of his publishing career. A writer in South India had given the manuscript of his first novel to a friend named Kit Purna, then studying in Oxford, hoping that he would find a publisher for it. Purna received a series of rejections at precise six-week intervals and was instructed by the author to 'weight the manuscript with a stone and drown it in the Thames'. Spotting Graham Greene in Oxford, Purna asked him to read it and shortly after sent off a cable: 'Novel taken. Graham Greene responsible.'[13]

The author was R. K. Narayan, now regarded as one of the leading Indian writers of his generation. Greene was able to convey an offer from Hamish Hamilton on 23 August, along with some suggestions, such as calling the book *Swami and Friends* and allowing Greene himself to do some light editing – as he did with most of Narayan's subsequent books. Until 1935, the author styled himself R. K. Narayanaswami; after consulting Purna on what might be acceptable in India, Greene suggested that he use R. K. Narayan since British librarians tended not to order books if they could not spell the author's name.[14] His new friend's full name was even longer than Greene knew: Rasipuram Krishnaswami Iyer Narayanaswami.

In a career that lasted more than sixty years, Narayan found many admirers, among them E. M. Forster, John Updike, and Anita Desai, but his books were never a commercial proposition. At Greene's suggestion, David Higham took Narayan on as a client and represented him for decades.[15] A series of British and American publishers took him up, usually on Greene's recommendation, and then dropped him. Narayan loved Greene for his loyalty, and wrote in 1954: 'I owe my literary career to Graham Greene's interest in my work. He has encouraged and backed me up for nearly twenty years now, although we have never met. But it seems to make no difference. I consider Graham Greene not only the finest writer, but the finest and most perfect friend a man can have in this world.'[16] For his part, Greene thought Narayan a worthy candidate for the Nobel Prize,[17] and in 1974 wrote: 'Since the death of Evelyn Waugh Narayan is the novelist I most admire in the English language.'[18]

Utterly unlike Greene's, Narayan's sensibility was gentle and melancholic. His stories are rarely political, but based on shrewd observation of the life of a small town to which he gives the name Malgudi. Often, he writes about children, as in *Swami and Friends*. Greene (and many others) believed that Narayan was a superb craftsman who found a way to treat that almost impossible subject, innocence. But there is more to this, and it is necessary to turn here to a discussion of something central to Greene's sensibility and without which no understanding of him is possible.

In his own autobiographies, the ageing Greene performed a cynicism and world-weariness that should not be taken at face value. There is a core of nostalgia, even sentimentality, in him that he worked to conceal and discipline – though it might come out, say, in tears at the cinema. The journey to Liberia was motivated in part by a desire to see human beings in a state of innocence. Greene's characteristically ruinous landscapes, dubbed 'Greeneland' in 1940 by his neighbour on Clapham Common, the novelist Arthur Calder-Marshall,[19] offer a vantage for the backward glance.

Greene writes at the beginning of *Journey Without Maps* that Liberia had a quality that could not be found to the same degree elsewhere: 'seediness has a very deep appeal: even the seediness of civilization, of the sky-signs in Leicester Square, the tarts in Bond Street, the smell of cooking greens off Tottenham Court Road, the motor salesman in Great Portland Street. It seems to satisfy, temporarily, the sense of nostalgia for something lost; it seems to represent a stage further back.'[20] It is a reaching back that dovetails with his experience of psychoanalysis, and even with his Catholicism, which, unlike Anglicanism, had never made its peace with modernity and capitalism. At points in *Journey Without Maps*, he draws a direct comparison between the supposedly primitive character of Liberia and his own yearning for childhood happiness – that is, the world before Carter, Wheeler, and the boarding house. If Narayan was about to become one of his favourite authors, it was because he spoke to something in Greene's imagination and his emotional life that he did his very best to hide.

In 1935, Greene made another great friend, the poet and art historian Herbert Read. It seems that they were brought together by the publication of Read's novel *The Green Child*, which Greene considered rather as a brilliant work of poetry, and in which he would later see affinities with David Jones's *In Parenthesis*. He thought Read the gentlest man he had ever met, but also forthright. Read's wife was a Catholic convert, and Greene thought Read himself lived at the edges of the faith. Perhaps that was part of the bond between the two men.

At the end of the summer he received a letter from Read, inviting him to dinner: 'Eliot is coming, but no one else, and everything very informal.' Greene compared this to receiving an invitation from Coleridge: 'Wordsworth is coming, but no one else.' Rather like a hermit on the run, T. S. Eliot was then hiding from his estranged and mentally ill wife Vivienne, so the Greenes were especially lucky to have this dinner with him. Vivien Greene 'fell for him completely and made the rather grim man positively purr!'[21] Eliot was able 'to unbutton' once conversation turned to detective stories and the adventures of the gentleman burglar Arsène Lupin.[22]

Greene finished his 'shocker' by mid-January 1936.[23] Written in the vein of *Stamboul Train*, it was published in July in Britain as *A Gun for Sale*, having come out in the United States in June as *This Gun for Hire*. His plan was, in future, to publish all such books under the pseudonym Hilary Trench, which he had used occasionally since his Oxford days. He would use his own name for serious fiction. He gave up on this notion once Heinemann told him that as an unknown author he could only have a £50 advance.[24] However, when the book came out, the advertisement page divided his works into 'Novels' and 'Entertainments', a distinction he maintained until the 1960s, when he accepted that a good many of his stories could go into either box.

The story sets the table for *Brighton Rock*. As Greene had first done in *A Man Within*, he put a repulsive character at the heart of the novel and set about making him compelling. With a hare lip, Raven is physically unattractive. He is nervous, boastful, and apparently unbothered by the suffering he causes. Emerging from the racetrack gangs, he becomes an assassin and is hired to kill a politician, with the result that Europe is brought to the edge of a new war, while his real employer, an aged arms-maker, studies the ticker tapes and calculates the money he is about to make. The novel received excellent reviews on both sides of the Atlantic, and Mary Leonard sold the film rights to Paramount for $12,000[25] – which allowed Greene to pay off much of his debt on the house.

Greene's other book, *Journey Without Maps*, suffered a bizarre misfortune. Published in Britain in May and in America in November, it received excellent reviews, but then the lawyers appeared. In the early pages of the book, Greene described a loud-mouthed drunk named 'Pa Oakley', and he later told Hugh this name was invented. However, it turned out that the head of the Sierra Leone Medical Service was named P. D. Oakley, and he initiated a libel action. Heinemann withdrew the book. Luckily for Greene, all but two hundred copies had already been sold,[26] but it remained out of print until 1946, when Pan reissued it with the character renamed.

Meanwhile, Vivien had given birth on 13 September 1936 to a boy christened Francis Charles Bartley Greene – the Bartleys being a branch of Vivien's family. Francis would see even less of his father than Caroline did; the war came when he was just turning three. Raised chiefly by Vivien, he proved a deeply intelligent boy with scientific interests and a quick wit. In time he came to resemble his father in his concern for human rights. He eventually became a photojournalist and a traveller, with particular interests in Eastern Europe and Russia, and in environmental causes. He resembled his father in another important way: a distaste for all the trappings of celebrity, and a strong sense of privacy.

12

MY WORST FILM

An envelope reached Graham Greene at the *Spectator* containing 'a piece of note paper covered with human shit'.[1] This was a reward for one of his film reviews. Indeed, by the mid-1930s Greene was making both enemies and friends in the film world. At the beginning of 1936, John Grierson, a leading figure at the GPO Film Unit, which produced such gems as *Night Mail*, suggested Greene join them as a producer. At the same time, Greene was close to Elizabeth Bowen's husband A. C. Cameron, one of the founders of the British Film Institute, and was serving on an advisory committee on the future of television.[2]

In the summer of 1936, he collaborated with the somewhat testy director Basil Dean on a script of J. B. Priestley's story 'The First and the Last', in which a murderer commits suicide and an innocent man is hanged for the supposed crime. Greene had the treatment done by the end of August, and then wrote a shooting script, having to learn his craft as he went along. He wrote to his mother: 'Every camera angle has to be described, each angle being a scene, the average film having about 550 scenes. A long business. I find it very tiring, as you have to visualise exactly the whole time, not merely what the person is doing, but from what angle you watch him doing it.'[3]

Devoted to films from childhood, Greene's fiction always had a cinematic aspect, and the actual writing of scripts intensified this quality. Many years later he would say in an interview: 'When I describe a scene, I capture it with the moving eye of the cine-camera rather than with the photographer's eye – which leaves it frozen . . . I work with a camera, following my characters and their movements. So the landscape moves. When I turn my head and look at the harbour, my head moves, the houses move, the boats move, don't they?'[4]

Dean persuaded the producer Alexander Korda to put the script into production in 1937. The leads were played by Laurence Olivier and Vivien Leigh, then at the beginning of their affair and in frolicsome mood. The filming was chaotic, with delays occurring, for example, when Dean noticed that in one scene a bowl contained sugar cubes rather than granulated sugar, so everything stopped while an underling went to the shops. That year saw a bad slump for the British film industry, so Korda decided to leave this film, entitled *21 Days*, on the shelf, where it remained until Columbia bought it from him. It was released, or perhaps just escaped, in January 1940.[5] Disclosing his own involvement, Greene gave it a bad review in the *Spectator*, observing that the basic story was 'peculiarly unsuited for film adaptation, as its whole point lay in a double suicide (forbidden by the censor), a burned confession, and an innocent man's conviction for murder (forbidden by the great public)'.[6] Like a convict, he promised never to repeat his crime. In 1987, Greene wrote about the production in an essay entitled 'My Worst Film'.[7]

This project marked the beginning of what became a devoted friendship between Greene and Korda. As a reviewer, Greene had slashed at Korda's films, complaining of their 'slowness, vulgarity, over-emphasis'.[8] You cannot fault Greene for a lack of nerve: he wrote those particular words when, through Basil Dean, he was effectively on Korda's payroll. However, if Korda had never existed, Greene might have had to invent him for one of his novels. Born in Hungary, he did his first film-making there, but after being arrested by the anti-Semitic regime of Miklós Horthy, he left his home for good and pursued a film career in Vienna, Berlin, Paris, and Hollywood, carrying with him a hatred of dictatorship and fascism. In late 1931, he came to Britain to run Paramount's operations, but a few months afterwards, with the assistance of his brothers Vincent and Zoltán, he set up his own company, London Film Productions, which remained closely tied to Paramount.

There was also a confidential side to Korda's operation. At the beginning of the decade, Sir Robert Vansittart, Permanent Under-Secretary at the Foreign Office, had established an intelligence service known as his 'private detective agency' intended to monitor the progress of fascism in Germany and elsewhere via reports from travelling businessmen. In this operation, he worked closely with Colonel Claude

Dansey, a veteran spy famously codenamed 'Z'. As well as being a legitimate firm distributing its products internationally, London Films provided a cover for work done by the detective agency. Indeed, the financing to begin the company came from associates of Vansittart and Dansey. When Korda set up a huge seven-stage studio in 1936, he chose to do so in the village of Denham in Buckinghamshire, where Vansittart owned a large manor house. On occasion the studio was used to train spies. Throughout the 1930s, Vansittart was able to give the government accurate intelligence on German and Italian plans and capabilities – advice that was tragically ignored. One person who did not ignore it was Dansey's old friend Winston Churchill, who, when money was tight, took work as a scriptwriter from Korda. His parliamentary speeches and questions on the Nazi menace often drew on the findings of the detective agency.[9]

Greene wanted more work as a scriptwriter, so met in October 1936 with Alfred Hitchcock about possibly working for British Gaumont, but nothing came of that – indeed, Greene thought Hitchcock 'a silly harmless clown'[10] and always maintained that his work was over-rated. Greene suggests that Korda must have been 'curious' to meet the man who had given him such bad reviews – his 'enemy'.[11] Apart from Greene's potential as a screenwriter, Korda would certainly have known about Hugh Greene's reporting on Germany and about Graham's own reputation as a traveller – he may have looked like a prospect for Z. There is no evidence that Greene was approached, but perhaps his qualifications were noted.

Greene made at least three visits to Denham in mid-November. He met Korda himself on the 17th and was asked if he had an idea for a script. Off the top of his head, he described an opening scene in which a man is standing on a platform at Paddington Station with blood pooling around his feet. When asked what happened next, Greene said it would take too long to explain and still needed to be worked out. It was enough. An agreement was reached.[12] What they really wanted was a character in a series of thrillers, but that did not happen. They gave him £175 to develop something over the next three weeks. If they could use it, he would have four weeks' work on the film at £125 per week. Korda would also have the right to call on Greene for six months of work in each of the next three years, with a salary rising eventually to

£225. During the later part of the contract, Korda could sell Greene's services to Hollywood, and they would split the increase in salary.[13]

Most of Greene's important work for Korda would be done after the war, so the possibilities of this contract were not realized. He did write his script about the bleeding man under the working title 'Four Hours'. It was released in 1940 as *The Green Cockatoo*, with John Mills playing the lead. The critic Quentin Falk observes the film might have served as a trailer for *Brighton Rock*.[14] Here, a man who has been stabbed by racetrack gangsters tells a naive young woman to find his brother at the Green Cockatoo pub, then dies. Holding a bloody knife that has fallen out of his coat, she is accused of murdering him and flees. She finds the brother who shields her from the gangsters and the police, and the film ends with the two in love. The film was panned and forgotten.

13

SHIRLEY TEMPLE

In late 1936, Greene found a job he wanted. Three years earlier, Ian Parsons, a partner at Chatto & Windus, had offered him a position at the publisher and been turned down. Now he sounded him out again, about a sophisticated new magazine. The offer of £600 per annum was one of the reasons Greene postponed a planned visit to Mexico. Drawing its title from Cole Porter's song, *Night and Day* was incorporated on 1 April 1937, publishing its first issue on 1 July and its last on 23 December. Modelled on the *New Yorker*, this astonishing but short-lived magazine was intended to challenge *Punch* as the leading humorous publication in Britain.[1]

Graham Greene was literary editor and John Marks the features editor, but in general they worked together. Marks is otherwise known as the translator of Céline's *Voyage au bout de la nuit*, and Greene recalled him showing up the worse for wear whenever the French writer was in London, as he insisted on late nights watching striptease. The art editor, Selwyn Powell, presided over a group of contributors that included the expressionist artist Feliks Topolski. The travel writer Peter Fleming, writing as 'Slingsby', contributed the 'Minutes' to each issue, describing, for example, the chaos surrounding the first issue: 'our colleagues, haggard and unshaved, were for ever slumping forward on their desks with a groan, we didn't feel too good ourself'. He claimed that one person kept telephoning the office just to answer the receptionist's 'Night and Day' with 'you are the one' and then ring off.[2] A solicitor named Patrick Ransome represented the owners, and he caused a certain anxiety whenever he came out of his office. However, Greene recalled a boozy lunch ending with him pushing Ransome in his wheelchair at top speed along the road, 'while he shrieked at the astonished shoppers with laughter and fear'.[3]

Greene recruited Evelyn Waugh as a book reviewer and Elizabeth Bowen as a drama critic. John Betjeman contributed five instalments of the 'Diary of Percy Progress'. Osbert Lancaster was the art critic and Hugh Casson wrote about architecture. Herbert Read was induced to review detective fiction and, according to Greene, 'his humour streamed suddenly and volcanically out'.[4] Read had devised a comic persona named James Murgatroyd and was proposing a series along the lines of *Diary of a Nobody* just as the shutters went up. On 1 November 1937, Ian Parsons told the board that the magazine could not continue to operate without new capital. The effort to raise it failed, and the magazine was discontinued just before Christmas.

Greene reviewed films for *Night and Day*, writing only on books for the *Spectator* during that time. In the first issue of the new magazine, he discussed a film called *The Frog* in which the plot relies on a gramophone recording of a criminal's voice – presumably that detail leaked directly into *Brighton Rock*, which he was then writing. However, his most famous review was of *Wee Willie Winkie* on 28 October 1937. Refusing to believe that Shirley Temple was supposed to be interesting to other children, he took the position that the film-makers were pimping out her body to perverts: 'Her admirers – middle-aged men and clergymen – respond to her dubious coquetry, to the sight of her well-shaped and desirable little body, packed with enormous vitality, only because the safety curtain of story and dialogue drops between their intelligence and their desire.'[5] Unsurprisingly, the good ship Lollipop cleared the decks for action.[6]

Having earlier had to placate J. B. Priestley and P. D. Oakley, Greene ought to have known libel law. What caused him to say these things? The year before he had written an essay for *Sight and Sound* about the work of the film reviewer, in which he observed that the public did not care about film technicalities, so the only way a reviewer could challenge the cinema to improve was with laughter: 'a flank attack upon the reader, to persuade him to laugh at personalities, stories, ideas, methods, he has previously taken for granted. We need to be rude . . . '[7] That is one explanation: he just overdid it.

The other explanation is somewhat speculative. Although often absent, Greene was a father and seems to have been troubled by what would now be called the sexualization of children. Indeed, he would soon portray a tragically precocious child, the daughter of the whisky priest, in *The Power and the Glory*. It is likely that Greene really did think Temple was being exploited, and he chose to make the point in a disastrously flippant way. Towards the end of his life Greene and Temple, by then an American ambassador, became friends. Her memoir essentially corroborates Greene's view of the studios as full of sexual menace for child actors.[8]

The newsagent W. H. Smith refused to carry the issue. Meanwhile, the dorsal fins of various solicitors could be seen circling the magazine's St Martin's Lane offices. The statement of claim said that Greene had accused Twentieth Century Fox of 'procuring' Shirley Temple 'for immoral purposes'. Greene stuck the document on his bathroom wall, where it remained until a bomb struck during the Blitz.[9] The case came to the High Court on 22 March 1938 with the notoriously hard-nosed Chief Justice in a mood to protect innocence and celebrity. The defendants were Greene, the magazine, Chatto & Windus, and the printing firm. A settlement was announced involving formal apologies and the payment of £3500 in damages. Graham Greene was not in the court and the irate Chief Justice wanted to know where he was, but the barristers had no information for him. He thought this settlement an insufficient response to a 'gross outrage' and notified the Director of Public Prosecutions so that it could be considered for a charge of criminal libel.[10] Greene had wisely removed himself to Mexico.

14

REAL BRIGHTON

I n a year in which so much happened, it is hard to believe that Greene was also working steadily on *Brighton Rock*, one of the most admired novels of the twentieth century. Since returning from Liberia, Greene had completed *A Gun for Sale*. He had also had two false starts. Around May 1936, he wrote several thousand words of 'Fanatic Arabia', set in a town like Berkhamsted and with a partly Jewish main character.

He got much further with 'The Other Side of the Border', which, though unfinished, was published in *Nineteen Stories* in 1947. Despite swearing off the influence of Joseph Conrad in matters of style, Greene constructed his plot along the lines of *Heart of Darkness*: the main character, Hands, has a job interview and is sent to Africa on behalf of a mining company, but, in this case, to Sierra Leone and Liberia rather than to the Congo. One of the reasons Greene abandoned the novel was that Hands resembled Anthony Farrant of *England Made Me*, both characters modelled, to a degree, on Greene's brother Herbert. When the short story was finally published, Greene remarked that he could no longer remember how the proposed novel was supposed to end.[1] However, during his trip to Mexico in early 1938, he had actually put together a short outline for a seventy-thousand-word novel, to be called 'The Leader'. Hands would engage in slavery and set up a fascist state in West Africa. To his surprise, his 'methods' would be approved by a committee of European investigators. Descending into alcoholism and insanity, he would die, but the mining would go on without him, as would the fascist state he established. This promising story was pushed out of the queue by Greene's other work, and he never returned to it.

'*Brighton Rock* I began in 1937 as a detective story and continued, I am sometimes tempted to think, as an error in judgment.'[2] This is one of those intriguingly unhelpful sentences in which Greene's introductions and autobiographies abound. The book was actually begun by the end of the summer of 1936. In the midst of writing it, he discovered one of the great themes in his fiction and seized upon it – the mercy of God, which he would continue to explore in *The Power and the Glory*, *The Heart of the Matter*, and *The End of the Affair*. As he grew older, he wanted to write more earth-bound fiction and especially to shake off the 'Catholic novelist' tag, which first took hold with *Brighton Rock*; Greene would often say that he was 'not a Catholic writer but a writer who happens to be a Catholic'.[3] A memorable phrase, it is more accurate as a description of the second half of his career than of the first. Indeed, it seems that the middle-aged Graham Greene was trying to cover his intellectual and artistic tracks.

In 1934, Greene had reviewed Eliot's *After Strange Gods* and cautiously affirmed the superiority of moral over aesthetic criticism: 'To be a Catholic (in Mr. Eliot's case an Anglo-Catholic) is to believe in the Devil, and why, if the Devil exists, should he not work through contemporary literature, it is hard to understand.'[4] He is not talking in loose secular terms about an ethical approach to literature – he is talking about spiritual warfare on the page.

After about 1948, Greene would occasionally trot out a passage from John Henry Newman's *The Idea of a University*: 'I say, from the nature of the case, if Literature is to be made a study of human nature, you cannot have a Christian Literature. It is a contradiction in terms to attempt a sinless literature of sinful man. You may gather something very great and high, something higher than any literature ever was; and when you have done so, you will find that it is not literature at all.' Newman's comments here and elsewhere contributed to a literary revival among Catholics by giving them leave to render characters who were sinful, even depraved, and by sparing novelists the duty to be relentlessly uplifting.[5] Newman may have also had that liberating effect on Greene, but then Greene was *never* tempted to write uplifting tales about pure men and women, whatever his fellow Catholics may have longed for. As the years went by, Greene would simply quote Newman's words to shut down discussion of the Catholic content of his work, but as one of Newman's biographers, Ian Ker, points out, Greene has entirely distorted Newman's point since the section opens with: 'One

of the special objects which a Catholic University would promote is
that of a Catholic Literature in the English language.'⁶ In the lines that
Greene so often quotes, Newman was merely arguing against the notion
that one could study Catholic writers and exclude pagans. Greene has
badly misread Newman.

And indeed, Greene himself was explicitly struggling with the
problem of how a Catholic sense of the soul and of providence altered
the craft of fiction, specifically in terms of character and plot, and how
a sense of mortal sin required a focus on objective acts performed by
characters rather than on mental process. Greene's sense of craft is
shaped by his faith – the faith and the craft are not separate. To put it
another way, a good writer who happens to be a Catholic is going to be
different from a writer who happens to be something else. Many years
later, Margaret Drabble would have a character in her novel *The Dark
Flood Rises* dismiss Greene's turn of phrase as 'casuistry'.⁷

In 1936, Greene wanted to write another entertainment along
the lines of *A Gun for Sale*, delving again into the world of racetrack
gangsters that formed the background of *The Green Cockatoo*. He liked
writing melodrama, and such a book would make money. Brighton was
a town Greene had known since childhood and continued to visit,
since his parents lived in nearby Crowborough. He had already set
one novel, *The Man Within*, in Sussex – this one, eventually entitled
Brighton Rock, would be set in the present day. His portrait of Brighton
in that book offended local authorities and led him one day to ask,
'Would they have resented the novel even more deeply if they had
known that for me to describe Brighton was really a labour of love, not
hate? No city before the war, not London, Paris or Oxford, had such
a hold on my affections.'⁸ And, in fact, Greene went to Brighton frequently over the years, usually checking quietly into a hotel and setting
to work on whatever novel or film script he had at hand. There were
few places where he found it easier to write.

And yet it had more than its share of troubles. Although it had long
been popular for its pier, beach, and entertainments, Brighton was a
fairly bloody place: in June 1934, the torso of a woman was found in a
trunk in the railway station there and her legs at King's Cross Station;
a few weeks later, in an unrelated crime, a murdered dancer was discovered rotting in a trunk in a house in Brighton. Trunk murders occurred

from time to time in Britain and the United States – Greene had described one in *It's a Battlefield* – but to have two occur in a popular resort in a single summer was shocking. That was not all: at the time of the second discovery, a skull washed up on the beach.[9]

The early pages of *Brighton Rock* are dedicated to the murder of Fred Hale, which Greene recalled, many years later, as being inspired by an actual crime: 'a man was kidnapped on Brighton front in a broad daylight of the thirties, though not in the same circumstances as Hale, and his body was found somewhere out towards the Downs flung from a car'.[10] This would have been the murder in 1928 of Ernest Friend-Smith, a retired chemist, who was attacked near Palace Pier, dragged into a car, robbed, beaten, and dumped on the downs. He managed to find his way home but was so battered his wife did not recognize him, and he died a few weeks later. He had fallen into the hands of a mob that specialized in sexual blackmail, charging victims as much as £500 for their silence about illicit trysts on lonely stretches of the beach – the police knew of their operation but could not persuade victims to come forward. Three men were convicted of murder, and while an appeal was pending their accomplices, very much in the style of Graham Greene's Pinkie, tried to procure alibis for them by blackmail and threats of violence.[11]

Brighton was close enough to London to be drenched in its criminal culture. The races drew tens of thousands of punters; on their approach to the track they might be greeted by the towering Ras Prince Monolulu of Abyssinia in his ostrich-feather headdress – his real name was Peter McKay and he came from the Caribbean island of St Croix – selling sheets of race tips and crying 'I gotta horse!'[12] But the fun was superficial: gangs controlled the betting and they were not to be trifled with.

Their territorial wars were notorious – for example, in 1924–5 a series of 'outrages' culminated in a fight at a tavern on the corner of Aldgate and Middlesex Street in London involving a total of fifty gangsters slashing at each other with razors.[13] These wars continued into the next decade, and there was plenty of violence in the vicinity of Brighton. In the summer of 1936, about thirty men, seeking to avenge a razor attack on one of their own, descended on two bookmakers at Lewes racecourse, beating them nearly to death with hammers, pieces of iron, lead pipes, lengths of wire, and knuckledusters. Sixteen of these men were apprehended by detectives and uniformed constables on the scene.[14] Twenty-nine-year-old James Spinks of Hackney, notionally a 'French polisher' of furniture, led the attack; later, while on bail, he was heard to say menacingly to one of the injured bookmakers, 'You don't recognize me, do you?' That bookmaker tried to disappear before the trial, and when finally brought into the witness box he claimed he did not see Spinks at the scene and had no quarrel with him – this despite Spinks having struck him in the head with a hatchet. The judge and jury could see that the witness had been intimidated. All sixteen were convicted, with Spinks sentenced to five years of penal servitude. Greene began writing his novel just after the trial, and Spinks clearly provided the inspiration for Pinkie.[15]

Of course, the police did not just happen to be present in large numbers at Lewes racecourse. Spinks and his cronies were members of the Hoxton Gang, and their great enemy was Charles 'Darby' Sabini, who is well known to viewers of *Peaky Blinders* as the boss of a large gang in the south of England. It seems that he led the Hoxton Gang to expect a pitched battle, but someone tipped off the police and they were marched away in handcuffs. Having disposed of so many rivals at once, Sabini's own power soon slipped away as he was interned as an enemy alien at the beginning of the war.[16] In its heyday in the 1920s, the gang was a loose alliance of Italian and Jewish criminals, so when Greene created the character of Colleoni, modelled on Sabini, he made him an Italian Jew – a decision he later regretted.[17]

The public had a boundless appetite for stories of gangsters, and the popular newspapers catered to it with lurid tales of beatings and murders. The papers also engaged in stunts to increase their circulation. The *Daily News* sent its '1 £ Note Man' into the streets of various towns to give a pound to anyone who showed him a copy of the paper.[18] For a number of years, the *Westminster Gazette* sent a character called 'Lobby Lud' to various seaside towns to walk along an announced route; a person presenting a copy of the newspaper and saying, 'You are Mr Lobby Lud. I claim the *Westminster Gazette* prize' would receive £50. Greene based his character Fred Hale 'directly' on Lobby Lud – posing as 'Kolly Kibber', the journalist leaves cards along his route which are worth ten shillings each, and there is a £50 prize for anyone who holds up the newspaper and makes such a challenge.[19]

In all of this Greene, was struck by how entertainment, sex, poverty, brutality, and desperation were bound together in Brighton and so searched out the slums around Carlton Hill, where a number of streets were soon to be demolished. From Nelson Place comes the character Rose, and from nearby Paradise Piece the mysterious and despicable Pinkie Brown. In the Brighton of Rose and Pinkie the human heart is open to view. Or, as Pinkie remarks, 'I suppose I'm real Brighton'.[20]

Beginning as genre fiction, the story turns towards something uncategorizable. Pinkie kills Fred Hale for having betrayed the gang's leader and then tries to silence the one person who can break down his alibi, Rose, by marrying her. Meanwhile, a bar singer named Ida, having had a brief encounter with Hale, decides that his death was murder and that she must solve the case since the police seem uninterested. Both Pinkie and Ida are trying to get control of Rose. However, there is a bond between Pinkie and Rose: they are both 'Romans', and see the world not as a matter of right and wrong as the secular and ultimately sentimental Ida does, but as a spiritual battle between good and evil. Pinkie says: 'These atheists, they don't know nothing. Of course, there's hell.'[21] It is the hell that has formed him – the tenements, the violence, the privation, the sound of his parents having sex in the bed beside him.

Greene claims for Catholicism the power of naming truthfully what is worst in life. As an old man he would drop his belief in a Hell beyond this world, but he continued to regard the life we are born to as hellish, or at least purgatorial. Although he yearns for the priesthood, Pinkie commits various mortal sins, including murder, and then in his civil marriage to Rose he is guilty of sacrilege. An embittered virgin, he finds that sex with Rose softens his attitude towards the world and the body; it makes him vulnerable to a pity that nearly leads to repentance 'between the stirrup and the ground'.[22] Still, he continues with a plan to kill Rose and is himself killed. What he may have thought at the end, the reader does not know. Greene refuses to leave us with the sense that Pinkie had a kind heart or that he was simply the victim of circumstance. Earlier in the story, the affectionate Rose had asked him, while they are walking on the pier, to make a gramophone record in a booth, hoping he would speak of his love for her. Instead he whispered a message of hate that she will find after his death. Greene needed to present a life that failed utterly, and came up with Pinkie, who could do great harm even when he is dead.

At the end, Rose makes her confession to an elderly priest. Throughout the novel she has spoken of her 'responsibility' towards Pinkie and is willing to go with him into 'the country of mortal sin'.[23] She is willing to be damned too, if that is his fate, and so believes she should not now ask for forgiveness. The priest tells her the story of the French poet Charles Péguy. Choosing to be on the side of the damned, Péguy refused the sacraments and eventually died at the Front in 1914. The priest adds: 'You can't conceive, my child, nor can I or anyone the ... appalling ... strangeness of the mercy of God.'[24] This is a theme that sentiment could only obscure.

'The novel in its last 5000 words has turned round and bit me,' Greene wrote to his agent David Higham in January 1938, putting the difficulty down to having been unable to work at it without interruption.[25] In the course of writing it, the novel had changed from a topical thriller into something like a morality play, in which the large gestures of melodrama are absorbed into allegory.[26] The original plan for a straightforward detective story can only be seen in the first fifty pages, and Greene wondered whether he ought to have rewritten that section.[27] At the time he was particularly pleased with the title, referring to a stick of rock, in which the words 'Brighton Rock' remain legible right to the end. However, there was no time for further revision. He delivered the manuscript and prepared for Mexico.

15

THE LAWLESS ROADS

G reene's decision to visit Mexico was hardly fashionable. Many writers of his generation had involved themselves in the Spanish Civil War. Even his brother Herbert, who had been deceiving the Japanese intelligence service with false information for pay and would later write a book about it, had gone to Spain. In an episode that is more amusing than probable, Ernest Hemingway is supposed to have pointed to Herbert in Madrid and said he was going to execute him as a spy, but Claud Cockburn intervened: 'Don't shoot him, he's my headmaster's son.'[1]

Graham Greene did not like Franco, but as a Catholic could hardly come out in favour of the Republicans. It is universally acknowledged that the Nationalists were guilty of more atrocities, but the Republicans had on their hands the murders of seven thousand secular priests, monks, and nuns – most of them in the first weeks of fighting.[2] Greene's sympathies were actually with the Basques, who supported the Republicans in exchange for regional autonomy, and in the late spring, at the time of the bombing of Guernica, he had an opportunity to fly into Bilbao as it prepared for a Nationalist assault.

Carrying an introduction from the Basque delegation in London, he flew at short notice to Toulouse, where he was to board a small plane. There are two accounts of what happened next. Greene told his mother that the government had commandeered the plane and that another would not be available before he had to return to London so he spent a short time in Paris with Clarouin and came home.[3] The other, more picturesque, version, written years later, is that he found his contact, a café owner, shaving in the corner of his restaurant at 6 a.m., and despite the ornate letter of introduction he presented the man refused to attempt another flight past Franco's gunners.[4]

Greene's plan to go to Mexico had been on a slow boil for a year and a half. The idea began with the Catholic publisher Frank Sheed, who proposed it to Father Miguel Darío Miranda as head of the Secretariado Social Mexicano and a key figure in the church's struggle against an anticlerical government. He embraced Sheed's plan of sending an important British novelist to write about the persecution and consulted with the apostolic delegate in Mexico City, who was also delighted.[5] So it was that Greene's proposed visit had the support of the highest level of the Mexican church.

Although Sheed commissioned him and promised an advance of £500 in August 1936, the plan languished as Greene went about his other projects. At the end of 1937 Sheed backed out, so Greene pitched the book to Heinemann, but, as he observed, it was not a good fit for a firm that marketed even the Bible as literature.[6] His friend and fellow Catholic Tom Burns was a publisher with Longmans, and, after drinks with Greene, he commissioned *The Lawless Roads*.[7]

The persecution Greene was to investigate had long, tangled roots.[8] In colonial times the church had enormous power, but after independence in 1821 many leaders, including some Catholics, favoured a separation of church and state. The constitution adopted in 1857 took power and property away from the church while Porfirio Díaz, dictator from 1876 to 1911, kept things quiet with the church, paying no attention to the anticlerical constitution so long as the church steered clear of politics. However, Pope Leo XIII's call for social reform in the encyclical *Rerum Novarum* (1891) led to the establishment throughout Mexico of labour and civic organizations with a Catholic identity and this proved a serious provocation. Having been on the side of landowners, Díaz lost power in a peasant uprising that turned into a civil war between 1910 and 1920. Anticlericalism revived among the revolutionaries, especially the constitutionalists, who saw the church as counter-revolutionary and its social organizations as a sham. From 1914 to 1919, there were many attacks on Catholic churches, schools, and institutions, with about five hundred priests, nuns, and bishops driven out of the country.[9]

The new constitution of 1917 was much harder on the church. It denied it legal personality; allowed the government to intervene in its affairs; empowered governors to limit the number of priests in their states; banned religious orders and the taking of vows, church education, and foreign priests; forbade comment by priests on political matters; prohibited religious worship in public places; and nationalized all church property.[10] Even so, harassment remained a local affair; gradually, exiles returned and some Catholic activism resumed. Church piety often focused on the figure of Christ the King, signifying a legitimate authority to set against the claims of the government.

A new president, Plutarco Elías Calles, a hardliner, brought laws into effect on 31 July 1926 stipulating fines and imprisonment for those who violated the constitutional bans. Although divided, the bishops endorsed a national economic boycott, and, surprisingly, a suspension of all religious services in Mexico – a sort of ecclesiastical strike.[11] That autumn saw the beginning of the first Cristero War, which was actually many small uprisings throughout the country, but especially in the states of Jalisco, Guanajuato, and Michoacán to the west of Mexico City.[12] In a conflict that killed ninety thousand combatants and an unknown number of civilians,[13] the Cristeros did battle with federal troops and paramilitaries called *agraristas* (in reference to the cause of land reform). Although the Cristeros were guilty of some excesses, the federal forces were butchers, often forcing suspects to walk on feet that had been flayed and blowtorching bare skin. They took and killed peasant hostages, and there were many mass executions. After battles, they usually killed their prisoners.[14]

The war went on until June 1929, when a peace was agreed between the government and representatives of the Mexican and American churches and the American ambassador, while in the background the Vatican gave its approval. Although they controlled a great deal of territory, the Cristeros were left out of the negotiations; still, they laid down their arms by September. The government then embarked on terrible reprisals, and over the next six years five thousand Cristeros were hunted down and killed.[15] The government renewed its pressure on the church by imposing a specifically anticlerical and revolutionary scheme of education on children, so the Cristeros commenced their second war but it was disorganized and enjoyed less support from the bishops, many of whom were now inclined to conciliation. Indeed, Pope Pius XI issued an encyclical, *Acerba Animi*, in September 1932, affirming that the government had grossly violated the 1929 agreement, but mapping out, nonetheless, how clergy might adapt themselves to evil laws in order to serve their parishes and dioceses.[16] The fighting continued, on and off, until the end of the decade.

Throughout this period, priests were regarded as enemies of the state. In April 1927, all the bishops were expelled, and in total 2500 priests, nuns, monks, bishops, and seminarians took refuge in the United States during the war,[17] but others chose to stand their ground. The uprisings were rural, so priests who remained in Mexico were generally left alone as long as they stayed in the cities. For many years, it was believed that only about a hundred priests remained in the countryside by choice, of whom about forty-five were involved with the Cristeros, with the rest living as fugitives in the rural parishes. Recent research indicates that these numbers grossly underestimate those who kept up a clandestine ministry.

In the course of the rebellion ninety priests were executed,[18] of whom the most famous was the Jesuit Miguel Pro, who figures in both of Greene's books about Mexico, and in fact reminded him of the Elizabethan Jesuit martyr Edmund Campion, the subject of a biography by Evelyn Waugh. Having ingeniously slipped out of several police traps, Padre Pro was even arrested and released without the police realizing whom they had in custody. Finally caught and identified, he was brought to a police station in Mexico City. In revenge for an assassination attempt on the president (in which he had no part) Pro and his brother were to be executed without trial. On 23 November 1927, Pro was called from his cell. Having refused a blindfold, he spread out his arms in the form of a cross and cried '¡Viva Cristo Rey!' He was shot by the firing squad, then finished off by a single bullet at point-blank range. The government published photographs of the execution in the belief that they would discourage the Catholic opposition, but they had the opposite effect: Pro was seen as a martyr and an inspiration.[19] He was eventually beatified by Pope John Paul II in 1988.

Greene's arrangements to visit Mexico came together very quickly in January 1938. Leaving the children with Marion and Charles, he and Vivien boarded the ocean liner SS Normandie on the 29th and spent fifty-six straight hours in bed because of gales in the Atlantic. In New York, Vivien went on 'an orgy of shopping'[20] while Graham consulted representatives of the Mexican church in exile and obtained instructions and introductions. Mary Leonard threw a party for him and brought him to meet his new publishers at Viking Press. After nine days, the Greenes went on to Charlottesville and New Orleans, and from there Vivien headed home at the end of February.

Graham's route took him, by train, to Texas. In San Antonio he visited the College of the Incarnate Word, which was the headquarters for Mexican clergy in Texas,[21] and spoke with an old prelate who received him in a dressing gown. He can be identified as José de Jesús Manríquez y Zárate, the former Bishop of Huejutla who remained in exile until 1948 and was an activist among the emigrant communities.

This stubborn bishop wanted the Cristeros to keep fighting and was enraged by the attitude of the Vatican. He told Greene of another bishop's remark that the pope was 'infallible about faith & morals but not infallible about Mexico'. He even believed that Trotsky, then an exile in Mexico City, was behind everything, including President Cárdenas's present policy of moderation.[22] The sponsors of Greene's visit favoured a degree of accommodation with the government and regarded Manríquez y Zárate as a troublemaker.

The city of San Antonio itself struck Greene as pleasant but symptomatic of America, in that its depths were no different from it surfaces: 'Original sin under the spell of elegance has lost its meaning. Where, I thought, loitering on a bridge above the little tamed river, was there any sign of that "terrible aboriginal calamity" which Newman perceived everywhere.'[23] America, for Greene, was the great spiritual deception – the heresy of well-being.

While in San Antonio, he attended a meeting of pecan workers, whose strike for higher wages had been largely led by a priest and an archbishop – it was an example of how Catholic social teaching rejected both capitalism and communism. As if in rebellion against the superficial rightness of American life, he went to a freak show featuring the preserved bodies of two gangsters, an entertainment meant 'to satisfy some horrifying human need for ugliness'.[24]

Around 1 March 1938, Greene crossed into Mexico at Laredo.[25] He would face some difficulty making himself understood from this point, as after twenty Berlitz lessons in Spanish he could still only manage the present tense.[26] He presented himself at the border as a tourist and a student of antiquities. Once inside the country, he still needed to keep his wits about him as it was always possible to be 'thirty-three'd' – under Clause 33 of the constitution, undesirable foreigners could be expelled from the country on twenty-four hours' notice.[27]

At the time of his visit, gringos were exceedingly unpopular. The international oil companies had just rejected Labour Board rulings on wages and labour practices, so President Cárdenas nationalized the industry.[28] The British government would break off diplomatic ties with Mexico over the episode. Greene refers to the nationalization in *The Lawless Roads*, generally disapproving of the Mexican government's action, but also of the British response – part of his reaction was based on Mexico's subsequent export deals with Italy and Germany.[29] Important as all this was, he was in the country to look at a massive violation of human rights. The oil dispute was not his brief.

Once across the border, he spent the night in a hotel while a thunderstorm rumbled about him. As he would often do while in Mexico, he tried to calm himself by reading Anthony Trollope: 'There is no peace anywhere where there is human life, but there are, I told myself, quiet and active sectors of the line.'[30] The following day, Ash Wednesday, he took a train to Monterrey. The cathedral was open and he was able to attend Mass and receive ashes. By 1938, the worst of the religious repression had ended, and some churches were functioning. Although his real intentions were hard to determine, Cárdenas had stated that the best way to end religion was by socialist education, and he had exiled his old mentor Plutarco Elías Calles. However, there was still a great deal of religious repression in Mexico, especially in the south, and that was where Greene was headed.

From Monterrey he went for a week into the state of San Luis Potosí[31] to interview Saturnino Cedillo at his home in Las Palomas. A general under Calles, Cedillo had played an important role in having him deported, and then served for a time as Secretary of Agriculture, but was now thought of as the possible leader of a rebellion. Cedillo did not believe in religion, but, as the dominant figure in his state, was willing to respect the wishes of those who did. Moreover, he was disgusted by the treachery shown to the Cristeros after the peace of 1929, and allowed many survivors to take refuge in his state. Cedillo welcomed Greene but was evasive, submitting to the arranged interview reluctantly. As it turned out, he was about to go into rebellion himself and would be killed in the mountains in January 1939 – a development Greene had to work into his manuscript at the last minute.[32]

Greene went on to Mexico City, where, in a characteristic pairing, he made visits to a monastery and to a brothel. Also, he met with church leaders. In *The Lawless Roads*, Greene takes the position of the hierarchy even though the idea of witnessing a revolt, perhaps led by Cedillo, excited him. The Vatican did not wish the church to be represented by political parties, let alone armies. During the Cristero War, Rome had offered a very cautious endorsement of armed resistance until it decided that the Cristeros could not win: Catholic theories of the just war require a serious prospect of success. Rome instructed the Mexican church to adopt the methods of Catholic Action, a movement at work in various countries, including Nazi Germany. This meant focusing on education, catechesis, and spiritual formation, and the organization charged with implementing Catholic Action was the Secretariado Social Mexicano, whose leader, Miguel Darío Miranda, now a bishop himself, had originally encouraged Frank Sheed to organize a visit by Graham Greene.

Greene went to the headquarters of the Secretariado, but had the door slammed on him. He was finally let in by a young priest, whom he called 'Father Q' in *The Lawless Roads* but whose real name was Father Ernesto Gomez Tagle. Apart from his work as an administrator with the Secretariado, this man ran a reading group for intellectuals in Mexico City and was involved with a labour federation. He gave Greene information on the Secretariado's educational campaign, including an extremely successful programme that had trained young women in doctrine and prepared them to work as catechists. He was also the first to tell him about a fugitive priest who for ten years had pursued a clandestine ministry in Tabasco.[33]

Shortly after, Greene met the Bishop of Chiapas. A figure of some heft, this man had led a delegation to New York where they met with the Vatican Secretary of State, Cardinal Eugenio Pacelli (the future Pope Pius XII), as he gathered information for a new encyclical published in March 1937, supporting the idea of Catholic Action in Mexico rather than armed struggle.[34] Thirty-five years later, in *The Honorary Consul*, Greene would depict with sympathy a priest fighting in a guerrilla war. His position in Mexico was more cautious and in line with church authority. It is worth noting that Vatican policy on Mexico was largely decided by Cardinal Giuseppe Pizzardo,[35] one of the main promoters of Catholic Action throughout the world and a theological conservative who would try to have *The Power and the Glory* suppressed in 1954 (see pp. 248–50).[36]

As the journey went on, Greene was himself experiencing, as never before in his life, a sense of religious fervour. Just north of Mexico City is the Shrine of Guadalupe, the most famous site of Catholic devotion in the New World. Kneeling before the image of the Virgin imprinted on a peasant's serape, he considered how at the end of journeys it was customary to return and thank her, and he promised to do the same. Yet the fervour went hand in hand with a growing outrage. When his train brought him to Orizaba in Veracruz, he had a yearning to have his confession heard and was impressed by the serenity of his confessor: 'He had lived through so much; what right had an English Catholic to bitterness or horror at human nature when this Mexican priest had none?'[37]

A year later he would find himself mystified at the anger recorded in his journal and offer various inadequate explanations, including the loss of his glasses: ' . . . strained eyes may have been one cause of my growing depression, the almost pathological hatred I began to feel for Mexico. Indeed, when I try to think back to those days, they lie under the entrancing light of chance encounters, small endurances, unfamiliarity, and I cannot remember why at the time they seemed so grim and helpless.'[38] It is normal to be outraged by violence, but his reactions against Mexicans were extreme – afterwards he could not understand them himself, and he generally kept those reactions out of *The Power and the Glory*. It is not unreasonable to suppose that his mood disorder, as yet undiagnosed, had been triggered: excessive irritability is a common symptom of manic depression.[39]

Greene arrived in Veracruz on 20 March 1938 intending to stay for a few days, only to find that there was a vessel sailing for Tabasco the following evening. A humid and marshy state in the extreme south of the country, part of which borders on Guatemala, Tabasco was where the persecution was at its worst and Greene was anxious to see it. He spent forty-one fearful hours in a tiny, rolling boat on the Atlantic.[40]

Coming to port in Frontera, he made another boat trip, of ten hours, up the Grijalva River to Villahermosa, the capital, where he spent the next week.[41]

'The Godless State'[42] had been the preserve of the local dictator, Tomás Garrido y Canabal. A Marxist and an atheist, he required all priests to marry. Those who did not comply he killed, imprisoned, or drove into exile. He operated a group of 'Red Shirt' paramilitaries, who were guilty of many atrocities. In addition to stamping out the church in the state, he banned liquor and corsets,[43] so Greene referred to him scathingly as an 'incorruptible' man.[44] When Cárdenas became president in 1934, Garrido was appointed Secretary of Agriculture and brought his Red Shirts with him to Mexico City. Just after Christmas that year they killed five church-goers in the suburb of Coyoacan[45] and frequently harassed Catholics with a connection to Tabasco. By June 1935, Cárdenas had had enough and replaced him with Saturnino Cedillo, to the relief of Catholics throughout the country. Garrido returned to Tabasco, where he was immediately responsible for the machine-gunning of student demonstrators. A popular uprising then drove him into exile in Costa Rica.[46]

Even with the dictator gone, Tabasco was a desolate place. The old policies continued and the surviving priests did not dare to return. There were no Masses and no absolutions, which led Greene to think of Rilke's description of 'a town where nothing is forgiven',[47] and he remained curious about the fugitive priest: he 'existed for ten years in the forests and the swamps, venturing out only at night; his few letters, I was told, recorded an awful sense of impotence – to live in constant danger and yet to be able to do so little . . . ' A doctor told Greene, '"he was just what we call a whisky priest"'. The doctor had taken one of his sons to him for baptism, and the drunken priest insisted on naming the boy Brigitta.[48]

A strange mixture of weakness and strength, this alcoholic priest, Father Macario Fernández Aguado, was born in Michoácan and by 1912 was ordained and living in Tabasco. Around 1919, he was assigned to a parish in the city of Jalpa, where he can hardly have been an effective pastor, and yet, when the persecution came, he continued his ministry even though all the other priests left the state. He did, of course, have help: people of the Chol, the Zoque, and especially the Chontal aboriginal communities kept him safe in a hiding place near the border of Chiapas, and he ventured out from there.

For a time there was a second notable fugitive, a Chontal catechist, Gabriel García, whose heroism was more straightforward. Advocating resistance by peaceful means, García had kept the faith alive in the mainly aboriginal town of San Carlos by preaching, singing, teaching, and even playing a gramophone record of the Mass. Garrido tolerated this influential catechist for political reasons until August 1929, when a 'defanaticization' fair ended in the slaughter of seventeen Catholics and one or two policemen. Soon there was an effort to blame Father Macario and Gabriel García for the killings.

García fled to Mexico City, then returned to Tabasco and hid in the mountains and swamps, eventually locating Father Macario, but at the end of September 1930 he was betrayed and caught. It is believed that Garrido's henchmen followed their usual procedure of carving up the body and dumping it in a river to avoid identification. Father Macario continued his lonely work until 1935, when he too was captured. His supporters tried to rescue him but failed, and he was deported to Guatemala.[49] Garrido was driven from power the same year, and this may explain the priest's comparatively mild fate. Greene supposed that he was still at large, and was apparently unaware that a great many other priests had carried on clandestine ministries elsewhere in Mexico.

While in Villahermosa, Greene was afflicted with the company of an American dentist, who was married to Garrido's niece and seemed always to be hiding from her. The falling peso trapped him in Mexico, so he spent his days moaning about family life and the state of his stomach. Homesick, Greene spent the evening of 28 March, his last in Villahermosa, in a hotel room crushing large beetles and reading Anthony Trollope. In the morning he walked to the airport past a pockmarked cemetery wall that Garrido's firing squads had used for executions. From a six-seater plane, he looked down on 'the landscape of a hunted man's terror and captivity', beyond which the mountains of Chiapas looked 'like a prison wall'.[50]

The plane landed just beyond the state border, in the town of Salto de Agua. The situation in Chiapas was oppressive, but not like that in Tabasco. Greene wanted to travel to the village of Yajalón and then quickly on to the old state capital of San Cristóbal de las Casas, and so to start slowly back towards Mexico City. No guide was available, so he accepted an alternative – a long mule ride to see some Mayan ruins. During this side trip, Greene became exhausted and feverish, and was brought to a *finca* run by a brother and sister, Lutherans of German descent, where he rested, and even bathed in a stream among fish the size of sardines that tugged at his nipples. The siblings, with their odd mixture of tolerance and Protestant rectitude, would serve as models for characters in *The Power and the Glory*.[51]

Travelling by mule back to Salto, Greene stayed for a night as the guest of some indigenous people in a hut on the plain. Always terrified by birds, he was tormented by turkeys and chickens, as well as by the pigs. Lightning struck within a hundred yards of where he was sleeping, and he spent the night saying 'Hail Marys' and shivering. Back in Salto, he boarded another tiny plane and, flying between the mountains rather than above them, reached the village of Yajalón. There he met another Lutheran, a sorrowful Norwegian woman named Rasmussen who had lost both her husband and her eldest daughter. She had sent her sons to the United States for education and her two surviving daughters got their schooling by correspondence – they would later give Greene the idea for the Fellows family. One of the most memorable characters in the novel is the young Coral Fellows, who assists the priest and whose mysterious death occurs, Greene later explained, when she is accidentally shot by the gringo as he is trying to make his escape from the police.[52]

In the village, he met a mestizo, a man of combined indigenous and European descent; he had ugly teeth and a strange laugh, and worked as a typist clerk. Many years later, the biographer Norman Sherry encountered this man, Don Porfirio Masariegos.[53] A character modelled on him would dog the whisky priest's tracks and eventually hand him over to the police lieutenant.

Yajalón was meant to be merely a stage on his journey, but Greene was stuck there for almost a week waiting for a plane. He eventually gave up hoping for it to arrive, so set out with a guide in torrential rain for another three-day journey by mule through the mountains. On the first night they were welcomed into a gathering of huts by people who had no interest in being paid for hospitality. They took just a swig of his brandy for fellowship: 'I felt myself back with the population of heaven.'[54] At dusk on the second day, he saw a grove of tall black crosses tilted in various directions, an expression of the syncretistic forms of Christianity to be found among the indigenous people: ' . . . a dark tormented & magic cult. But what harm in that? We are too inclined to forget that Christianity *is* magic – the man raised from the dead, the devils cast out, water turned into wine, an earth religion – the clay mixed with spittle, the body raised again. Perhaps those dark crosses had more in them of original Christianity than our aseptic rational variety.'[55]

In San Cristóbal de las Casas, Chiapas's old state capital among the mountains, he had again the luxury of a hotel room and bedsheets. He had begun his travels in Mexico on Ash Wednesday, and was now wondering whether there might be a Catholic uprising during Holy Week.[56] Exploring the cobbled streets, he found five churches open but without priests; following the example of other worshippers he tried to pray kneeling on the stone floor with his arms extended in the form of a cross, but found it hard to bear after a few minutes.[57] He was directed to a 'Mass house' where on 13 April he attended his first 'bootleg' Mass, the priest appearing 'in a natty motoring coat & a tweed cap' and the woman of the house very proud: 'she had sheltered God in her house'.[58]

The next day, Holy Thursday, Greene went again to this house and the priest spoke of sacrifice. Emerging from Mass, he found there had been an 'invasion' of indigenous people who had come into the city to venerate the statues of the crucified Christ in the churches, some bringing flowers and lemon blossoms. He was seized by a longing for God, and wrote in his journal: 'To be a saint is the only happiness. O Christ, if one could set one's ambition at goodness – so that financial worry meant nothing more than failure at tennis, cricket, something on which one had not set one's heart.'[59] It is an extraordinary statement for the usually ironic Greene; he is perhaps recalling the saying of Léon Bloy: 'There is but one grief in the world – not to be a saint.'[60]

He spent the rest of Holy Week in San Cristóbal de las Casas before going by crowded bus to the new capital of Tuxtla and then by plane out of Chiapas to Oaxaca, where he found it strange to see a functioning church with Mass notices and exposition of the Blessed Sacrament. The rest of the journey was miserable as he had contracted dysentery. Greene travelled to Puebla by train, and then back to Mexico City on 21 April 1938, where after five weeks out of touch he picked up his letters, including news of the Shirley Temple action and a solicitor's bill.

Father Tagle from the Secretariado brought him to meet Bishop Miranda and they went for a drive, during which Miranda told Greene stories about Padre Pro, how he himself had been imprisoned at the time of the execution and how others had been killed at the hands of the government. In a shrewd piece of staging, he had chosen for their driver a man whose sister, María de la Luz Camacho, a twenty-seven-year-old lay catechist, had been killed in Garrido's raid on the church in Coyoacan in 1934; at her funeral the Archbishop of Mexico City, indicating that the church had moved beyond the methods of the Cristeros, declared her the first martyr of Catholic Action.[61]

Amid fears of a European war, Mexico was old news. The bishops knew this, and so treated Greene with kindness and respect as someone who could tell their story to a distracted world. Before leaving Mexico City he was invited to the jubilee celebration of the former apostolic delegate, where he met more of the church leadership. But Greene needed to return to England, so with the rains falling he began his voyage back to Europe in a German liner. Many of his fellow passengers were on their way to Spain to fight for Franco.

16

DOLL

Having desired in Mexico to become a saint, back in England Greene was anxious not to be prosecuted as a criminal. Thankfully, there was no further libel charge, and the matter of Shirley Temple receded into anecdote. *Brighton Rock* was released in June in New York and in July in London. In October, Greene told Narayan that it had sold six thousand copies, and later recalled a total sale of eight thousand.[1] In the long run, it proved the best-selling of all Greene's books.[2]

Brighton Rock certainly raised his profile in the United States, as Viking put a good deal of effort into advance publicity for its new author. The *New York Times* declared the novel 'as elegant a nightmare as you will find in a book this season . . . a revival of the Poe manner – modernized with streamlined abnormal psychology and lit by neon'.[3] In England, the book was enough of a hit for a Sloane Square department store, part of John Lewis, to take notice; Greene wrote to his brother Hugh: 'A new shade for knickers and nightdresses has been named Brighton Rock by Peter Jones. Is this fame?'[4]

Greene could see that war was not far off. On 13–14 March 1938 came the Anschluss, Hitler's annexation of Austria. In May the Czechoslovakian army mobilized against a German threat to the Sudetenland, where there was a large German population. This crisis passed, but with negotiations ongoing through the summer, Hitler sent three-quarters of a million men on manoeuvres in August, to which Britain responded by a mobilization of the fleet. On 24 September, Czechoslovakia mobilized again, and war was imminent. The Munich Agreement of 29 September allowed Hitler to absorb large swathes of territory into the Reich, and purchased for Great Britain and France, at the cost of betraying their obligations to Czechoslovakia, an illusory promise of peace. Like many others in Britain, Graham Greene was opposed to the deal. When on 3 October Duff Cooper resigned as First Lord of the Admiralty in protest, Greene thought his action 'magnificent'.[5]

In the days before the agreement, he saw that his family collected their gas masks, and he prepared them for the prospect of a long stay in relative safety outside London. He told his mother that he expected either to be conscripted and have almost no income or to go into a job in the Ministry of Information or Propaganda with a modest salary, in which case he would rent out the house and take cheaper lodgings.[6] From October 1938, Greene viewed the war as merely postponed and urgently set about earning money that might ease the circumstances of Vivien and the children in his absence.

He finished *The Lawless Roads* in January – the death of Cedillo occurred on the 11th and is referred to in the book. It was published by Longmans, Green in March and by Viking under the title *Another Mexico* in June. Apart from his usual reviewing, he wrote a radio play, *The Great Jowett*, about the Victorian sage Benjamin Jowett who became Master of Balliol – one of the rare occasions Greene wrote about Oxford. Produced and narrated by Stephen Potter, it was broadcast on 6 May.[7]

At much the same time, he was juggling two novels. Thinking *The Power and the Glory* unlikely to be a bestseller, he began an entertainment, *The Confidential Agent*, which was completed in just six weeks, during which he would work in the mornings on the thriller and in the afternoons on the story of the whisky priest, which proceeded more slowly. On 18 June, he told his mother that he had written a quarter of million words in the last year and was exhausted; however, the thriller was finished.

The cost of all this productivity was terrible. Going beyond his usual resource of manic energy, he took Benzedrine – a tablet at breakfast and another at midday. He would leave Clapham Common in the morning to do his writing at a studio he had rented in Bloomsbury. The effects of the amphetamine wearing off in the late afternoon, a depression would set in; with a tremor in his hand, he would return home primed for quarrels. Long after the entertainment was finished, he had to wean himself slowly off the drug, and later believed that his conduct towards Vivien under the influence of Benzedrine did more to destroy their marriage even than his infidelities.[8]

Perhaps. As far as we know, Greene's liaisons with other women in the 1930s were transitory – until he met Dorothy Glover. He rented the studio in Mecklenburgh Square, later bombed, from her mother. An affair between Greene and Dorothy was evidently under way by 7 April 1939, when he told Hugh, 'In confidence, life at the moment is devil-ishly involved, psychologically.' The affair was a serious one: 'War offers the only possible solution.' The relationship may even have begun some months earlier, as in October 1942 he told his sister Elisabeth that it had been going on for four years,[9] but he was never accurate about dates.

Surprisingly little is known about Dorothy Glover. Although as an old man Greene disposed of his papers in major sales to three American universities, he included few letters from women with whom he had been involved, apparently thinking it his duty to destroy them. Since Dorothy did not deposit his letters in an archive either, the two have kept many of their secrets.

Born in 1901 in Wandsworth, Dorothy Mary Glover was the daugh-ter of Thomas Craigie Glover, an electrical engineer from Glasgow, and his wife Annie.[10] Dorothy was evidently married, though the relationship broke up; it is not certain who her husband was, as there is more than one Dorothy Glover in the public registers. Theatrical records afford occasional glimpses of her. At the age of fourteen, she and her younger sister Eileen appeared as the boy princes in a production of *Richard III* at His Majesty's Theatre in London.[11] In 1931, she took small roles in three plays at the Grafton Theatre.[12] In 1932–3, she was in a Bristol production of *The Barretts of Wimpole Street*;[13] records for provincial theatre are more difficult to trace than those for London, so it is entirely possibly that she had other parts of this kind. She may also have worked as an accompanist,[14] and possibly as a dancer.

When Greene met Dorothy, she was a designer of sets and costumes. By early 1940 she had written a play, described by Greene as a 'farcical-thriller', which was not staged,[15] and she would later make her living as an illustrator and children's author. Greene collaborated with her on at least four children's books, of which the first, *The Little Train*, appeared in 1946 under her pseudonym, Dorothy Craigie, but was republished in 1957 with Greene named as author and Craigie as illustrator.[16] It has been argued that Greene may have written or contributed to three other books for young people published under her name: *Summersalts Circus* (1947), *The Voyage of the Luna I* (1948), and *Dark Atlantis* (1952).[17] With regard to at least two of these titles, the claim is impossible. Greene read *The Voyage of the Luna I* only when it was in typescript and *Dark Atlantis* after it had been printed.[18]

Contrary to what has been written about her, Dorothy or 'Doll' was short and slim, and Greene thought she was like 'Peter Pan' when he met her.[19] Surviving photographs are from a later time, when she had grown stout. There was an intense physical attraction between them. Moreover, her forceful, outgoing personality and her conviviality – she 'could down her pint and Irish'[20] – offered a contrast to Vivien's reserved, intellectual, and sometimes feline manner. Greene's interest in this woman surprised some friends, but not Hugh, who may have had his own affair with her a few years later. Graham Greene's love affair with Dorothy Glover had run its course by about 1947, but she rather clung to him. The following year, he gave her the revenues from the film of *Brighton Rock*,[21] and later provided her with a pension.[22] In 1952 she became a Catholic,[23] doubtless under his influence.

Throughout 1939, Vivien could see that her marriage was in danger. She worked out that Graham was involved with someone else. With war coming and evacuation almost certain, she believed that if she was sent to the United States she might never be brought back. Although the marriage staggered on for another decade, and was never formally dissolved, it is reasonable to say that it was little more than a shell after 1939. That summer she and the children were evacuated, but only as far as her in-laws' house at Crowborough – not a comfortable arrangement, as she was never very popular with Graham's family. She later moved in with Stella and John Weaver in the President's Lodgings at Trinity College, Oxford, and made some visits to the Turners, who still lived at Blockley.[24] Although Graham wrote to her affectionately, he was now much more interested in Dorothy.

Having registered with the Army Officers' Emergency Reserve, he was awaiting call-up as a second lieutenant, and wrote to Vivien about how he found 'London very odd. Dim lighting, pillar boxes turned into white zebras in some parts. The common a mass of tents, and nobody about on North Side.'[25] Hitler invaded Poland on 1 September, and Britain and France declared war two days later. By the 4th, Greene had experienced two air-raid warnings, which, though false, offered a foretaste of the aerial war. He watched barrage balloons going up – these were meant to obstruct bombing runs with long cables. He walked through central London in the blackout, and its seediness appealed to him: 'Very lovely and impressive with all the sky signs gone and little blue phosphorescent milk bars and a hurdy-gurdy invisibly playing – rather like a Paris back-street. Newspaperman calling, "'Ave a paper tonight", plaintively. Another one very conversational, "Reminds me of the trenches. Never knew which way you was going."'[26]

That September *The Confidential Agent* was published, with the American release a month later. The newspapers were full of war news, so it was difficult for a new title to get much notice, but the public was also yearning for distraction. The two factors probably balanced each other out, and the book sold a respectable five thousand copies in Britain.[27] The background of the story is not specified, but it is obviously the Spanish Civil War, the outcome of which will be decided by the arrival of enough imported coal to warm houses and revive industry. A widowed academic and translator identified only as 'D' goes to Britain to negotiate the purchase of this coal on behalf of the socialist government. His credentials are stolen and he becomes a hunted man, framed by fascist agents for a series of crimes, including murder. He is grieved by all the trouble he causes, and the narrator remarks of him, 'To live was like perjury'[28] – possibly a glimpse into the author's own state of mind. Wherever 'D' goes he spreads suffering like contagion. However, he falls in love with the daughter of a coal magnate, and even as his mission fails he is helped to escape by the generous acts of the girl's Jewish fiancé, who enables them to sail away to an uncertain fate – the first edition offers more hope for their future than did subsequent ones, which he revised.[29]

The book appeared with a dedication to Dorothy Craigie, and some episodes occur in a flat belonging to a woman named Glover. There is also a gesture to Greene's new friend Alexander Korda, whose name is used in an invented language, rather like Esperanto, to represent the heart.[30] *The Confidential Agent* was made into a film in 1945, with Charles

Boyer and a young Lauren Bacall playing the leads, and was one of the rare occasions that Greene liked a Hollywood adaptation of his work.[31]

On 13 September, Greene finished his draft of *The Power and the Glory*. In what most readers regard as his finest work, and one of his strangest, he attempted for the only time in his career a story based on a thesis: that the sacramental work of a priest is effective regardless of his own moral state.[32] Theologians express this idea by the phrase *ex opere operato*: the sacrament is valid because the work is performed by Christ. It is surprising that a novel built on this abstract notion could ever succeed, and yet as Greene writes of the whisky priest, 'Curious pedantries moved him.'[33] For Greene, this particular idea cannot stay abstract – it almost forces its way into the material world. In Greene's most Catholic novels, there is a remarkable fleshiness, with characters belching and hiccupping, as if the idea of Incarnation were being probed to the last unsettling degree. Of course, the version of Catholicism that Greene adopted in the 1920s *was* fleshy; it was based on the teachings of the Council of Trent, which affirmed the true presence in the Eucharist, the earthly institutions of the church, and the necessity of charitable works against the Lutheran idea that salvation was by faith alone.

Just as in San Antonio Greene distrusted the comforts of America, in Mexico he sees piety as a distraction from human reality. The once-pampered priest understands himself more as his clerical garments wear out and his shoes lose their soles so that his feet are exposed to dirt, stones, and snakes. His descent into the common poverty of being is nowhere better illustrated than in the jail scene where he feels at home in the company of a couple having sex, a pious but embittered woman, a senile man crying out for his daughter, and others who exist only as voices in the dark: 'This place was very like the world . . .'[34]

Greene tells us that the police lieutenant was more of an invention than the other characters. A true-believing atheist and communist, he is described as a 'priest' and a 'mystic' who perceives the coldness of the universe. In his view, simoniac priests are pillaging the poor – a position with which Greene has some sympathy. However, Greene found no such principled police or paramilitaries in Tabasco: 'I had to invent him as a counter to the failed priest: the idealistic police officer who stifled life from the best possible motives: the drunken priest who continued to pass life on.'[35]

The priest and the lieutenant are not treated as equivalent. By the end of the book, it is clear that he prefers the failures of the priest to those of the policeman. However, once the priest has been arrested, the two sit together beside the corpse of the bank robber in a hut and speak amicably while outside there is hard rain – a scene which for the first time crystallizes the dialogue between Catholicism and communism that would be so much a part of Greene's later work.

The measure of the priest's failure is Padre Miguel Pro. Although he is not named, a mother reads a story of martyrdom very like his to her children. The episode in which the whisky priest spends a night in police custody without being identified resembles one in the life of Pro. At the end of the novel, some pamphleteer transforms the priest's death into a heroic martyrdom, a tale which seems to win a young boy to the faith even though he had earlier been drawn to the lieutenant as a man of action. And yet for all that, the priest goes to his death with a sense of failure. He has no idea how to repent – perhaps a reflection of the author's own reality. He expresses his sense of failure in terms that again seem to echo Léon Bloy: 'He felt like someone who has missed happiness by seconds at an appointed place. He knew now that at the end there was only one thing that counted – to be a saint.'[36]

Heinemann was more hopeful of the book's success than was Greene. Published in early March 1940, its original print run was 12,600 copies and it sold five thousand in the first five weeks.[37] In the United States, it was published under the title *Labyrinthine Ways*, a phrase from Francis Thompson's poem 'The Hound of Heaven', since another author had recently used 'The Power and the Glory' as a book title. A visually impressive but rather pious film, directed by John Ford, was released in 1947 as *The Fugitive*. In time, Viking removed the confusion over titles by adopting 'The Power and the Glory' for its editions.

The publication of this novel was a landmark in Greene's career. It was very well reviewed on both sides of the Atlantic. Indeed, American reviewers were now looking upon Graham Greene as one of the most important writers of his generation. For example, the influential *Saturday Review of Literature* made these claims: ' ... the atmosphere and detail of this book are convincing. So are the variegated people. So are the squalor and the heat and the venality of man, the sloth and the violence. And Mr. Greene has told the story of a truly spiritual struggle, in the breast of a miserable sinner, who can yet do brave things, in a fashion that sets this novel of his a little above and apart from his others. Also, he has now proved himself one of the finest craftsmen of story-telling in our time.'[38]

In June 1942, Greene, by then serving abroad, learned by telegraph that he had received the Hawthornden Prize for his novel – an award delayed by the circumstances of the war. He wrote to his mother that even though the prize had gone in the past to writers he despised, it pleased him: 'I suppose at the bottom of every human mind is the rather degraded love of success – any kind of success. One feels ashamed of one's own pleasure.'[39]

17

BOMBS AND BOOKS

'He was staying near the Ministry [of Information] in a little mews flat where I spent an occasional evening with him, the invariable supper dish being sausages, then still available. Whatever his circumstances, he had this facility for seeming always to be in lodgings, and living from hand to mouth. Spiritually, and even physically, he is one of nature's displaced persons.'[1] That was how Malcolm Muggeridge recalled Graham Greene's way of life in the second year of the war. He was trying to get some money together to support Vivien and the children once he was called up, so having signed a £2000 scriptwriting contract with Korda, he took a job as head of the writers' section in the Ministry of Information, which allowed him to leave the Officers' Reserve. Located in the University of London Senate House, the ministry set up a huge bureaucracy to manage awkward facts and expound useful falsehoods. Famously, George Orwell drew from it his inspiration for the Ministry of Truth in *Nineteen Eighty-Four*. Greene saw it as trivial, and his short story 'Men at Work', published in 1941, satirized it as a self-contained universe of committee meetings. Mainly, he commissioned patriotic books and pamphlets, and suppressed some others deemed harmful to the war effort.

According to Muggeridge, also employed at the ministry, Greene took a 'professional' approach to his job, 'coolly exploring the possibility of throwing stigmata and other miraculous occurrences into the battle for the mind in Latin America to sway it in our favour'.[2] Greene was only a little ahead of his superiors in thinking his work useless. At the end of September, the Director-General of the Ministry of Information, Frank Pick, a former transport administrator responsible for, among other things, London's Tube map, 'Pick-axed' him – his position was eliminated.³ The following year Greene was invited to return but refused.

The Germans had been bombing Britain through the summer, with the objectives of strangling the war economy and eliminating the RAF, so to force a negotiated peace or to facilitate an invasion. In a change of tactics, they began heavy bombing of London on 7 September. The assault continued for fifty-seven nights, and in its first two months caused thirteen thousand fires. By the time the Blitz ended on 11 May 1941, 28,556 Londoners had been killed.⁴

Greene was spending his nights with Dorothy in a shelter accommodating two dozen people off Gower Street. Walking about after the all-clear at 5:45 in the morning, he was excited by the scenes of wreckage, though shocked by the worst of the destruction. A little later he would remark flippantly to Anthony Powell: 'London is extraordinarily pleasant these days with all the new open spaces, and the rather Mexican effect of ruined churches.'⁵

Graham and Vivien knew that the Clapham Common house was likely to be hit, as this had already happened to at least one house in their row, so they made plans to remove the contents to Oxford. But they were too slow. At 1:30 a.m. on 18 October the back of the house was hit either by a group of bombs or by a parachute mine. Vivien would remark that because Graham was with Dorothy on the night of the bombing his life had been saved by his adultery. He arrived at the house at 8:30 a.m. to find it roped off. The structure was still standing, but it was impossible to move beyond the hallway because of debris. He decided to tell Vivien in person, but she was furious with him for breaking the news in front of the children. Hearing of this long after, Muggeridge supposed that her reproach, though reasonable, arose from the knowledge that when the house went the marriage was likely to go as well.⁶

Greene wrote to his mother: 'Rather heartbreaking that so lovely a house that has survived so much should go like that. And I feel over-awed without my books.'⁷ With the help of two labourers, he was able to salvage many of his books, sending them down a makeshift chute, but most of the fine furniture that Vivien had collected was lost. He was able to pull out of the wreckage a set of Victorian chairs made of rope in commemoration of Trafalgar, a gas refrigerator, some china, and a few other household objects.[8]

After the initial shock, the destruction of the house had a strange effect on him, as if he had been paroled. Muggeridge noticed this: 'Soon after his house on Clapham Common had been totally demolished in the Blitz, I happened to run into him . . . and he gave an impression of being well content with its disappearance. Now, at last, he seemed to be saying, he was homeless, *de facto* as well as *de jure*.'[9] Greene would later tell Muggeridge that his sense of relief had come from getting rid of a heavy mortgage, but Muggeridge thought that Greene actually felt relieved of a moral burden.[10]

Derek Verschoyle had gone into service so Greene took over as literary editor of the *Spectator*, a 'reserved occupation' that kept him out of military service until the following summer. By the end of 1940, he was offered five jobs doing propaganda, including one in Lisbon, but turned them all down, preferring to stay with the magazine. He actually hoped to go to West Africa to do propaganda for the Free French.

In his Bloomsbury studio, Greene slept on a sofa directly beneath a skylight; at times it was necessary to take refuge in the basement. One evening the house next door was hit, and he had to flee a possible gas explosion.[11] Soon, both he and Dorothy were working as ARP (Air Raid Precautions) wardens. For him, this meant patrolling three nights a week, from ten until two, or later, depending on the severity of the raids. He and his fellow wardens worked from Holborn Post Number 1 under the School of Tropical Medicine in Gower Street, and he kept a journal of his experiences, publishing sections of it in *Ways of Escape*.[12]

He was on duty during the enormous raid of 16 April 1941, launched in retaliation for an RAF attack on Berlin a week before. Eight hospitals and several churches were hit.[13] A parachute mine destroyed the King George and Queen Elizabeth Victoria League building in Malet Street where 350 Canadian airmen were sleeping. This huge explosion blew out a plate glass window directly above where Greene and two other wardens were standing in Tottenham Court Road – a distance of at least 300 yards from the main impact. They had just enough time to crouch as the shards rained on their helmets. Running to Gower Street, he and three others helped rescue an injured woman in the Royal Academy of Dramatic Arts building.

Although the sight of wreckage often excited him, Greene found this night unbearable, with salvos falling about every three minutes. Sent to the Victoria League building to rescue a trapped man, he spotted a head and shoulders resting in the debris. He later wrote about this to his mother: 'One's first corpse in the Canadian place was not nearly as bad as one expected. It seemed just a bit of the rubble. What remains as nastiest were the crowds of people who were cut by glass, in rather squalid bloodstained pyjamas grey with debris waiting about for help.'[14]

Back outside, more bombs fell and Greene dropped to the ground, a sailor on top of him. This time his hand was cut by glass so he went to the dressing station, and while being bandaged another stick of three bombs landed near by, and there was nothing for him to do but utter an Act of Contrition. As the night wore on he assisted in the rescue of other people, including an old man just out of hospital and still fitted with a catheter tube; he had been told that he would never walk again, but the bombing proved otherwise. The wretchedness of people caught in the bombing was 'disquieting' to Greene, as it 'supplied images for what one day would probably happen to oneself'.[15]

It was an extraordinary night, affecting everyone who lived in the city. One of Greene's friends, the Dominican priest Gervase Mathews, to whom he dedicated *The Power and the Glory*, was called to administer conditional absolution to people injured in the bombing and was asked by a soldier, who had been away from the sacrament for forty years, to hear his confession. Mathews told Greene that another priest had gone to a pub and crawled under a billiard table to hear the confessions of the landlord, his wife and daughter, all trapped in rubble. When challenged about what he was doing, he said, rather stiffly, 'I am a Catholic priest and I am under the billiard table hearing confessions,' to which came the response, 'Stay where you are a moment, Father, and hear mine too.' It was a Catholic among the rescue crew.[16]

The fires, the parachute bombs, the flying glass, and the corpses provided an improbable backdrop for discussions of the antiquarian book trade. Among Greene's fellow ARP wardens at Gower Street was David Low, who for many years kept a bookshop at 17 Cecil Court. Since his sojourn with Kenneth Richmond, Greene had been a frequent visitor to the bookshops on and near Charing Cross Road, and Low had become

a friend. Both Dorothy and Hugh shared Graham's particular interest
in collecting detective fiction, spy stories, and thrillers.[17] Over many
years Graham and Hugh would go on long marches across the English
countryside in search of bookshops and beer.[18] Graham collected,
among other things, seventeenth-century plays and Thomas Nelson's
red seven-penny editions of Victorian classics. In his introduction to
Low's memoir 'with all faults' (1973) he remarked: 'Secondhand book-
sellers are the most friendly and most eccentric of all the characters
I have known. If I had not been a writer, theirs would have been the
profession I would most happily have chosen.'[19]

Another warden, known as 'Little' Cole, was a 'runner' in the book
trade, buying low and selling high between one bookshop and another.
On one occasion, he and Greene were sent out to investigate a reported
landmine, but did not find it; instead, he took Greene to his room
and showed him his treasures. Given Greene's knowledge of writers
and Cole's of books, they seemed a natural pair, and they discussed
setting up a shop to be called Cole and Greene. But as the summer
passed, Greene went on to other duties and the idea of the shop came
to nothing.[20]

18

THE HOUSE IN THE SWAMP

I t was time to fulfil an old ambition. Graham's sister Elisabeth had joined MI6 (also known as the Secret Intelligence Service (SIS)) in 1938, and by the beginning of the war was working in G Section, which controlled overseas posts. Having been born a decade apart, she and Graham were not close, although they did become so after the war. Elisabeth's superior at MI6 was the dashing and influential Captain Cuthbert Bowlby, and she believed that through him she could help her brother and Muggeridge come into the Service.

It took a long time for the string to get pulled, but it was. Graham said that he was invited to a series of parties hosted by a 'Mr Smith', at which everyone seemed to know each other and there was unlimited liquor – this constituted part of his vetting. Scotland Yard looked into his background and noted the Shirley Temple affair as a black mark, but it was not enough to disqualify him. Greene's knowledge of Sierra Leone and Liberia made him a compelling candidate for service in West Africa. He told his mother that he would be working for the Colonial Office – he could not say exactly what he was doing, at least not in a letter.

SIS still had no standard training programme for its officers, so the Chief of Staff, Reginald 'Rex' Howard, devised an individual course for Greene, elements of which would serve him in good stead when he wrote *Our Man in Havana* and *The Human Factor*. He was to visit Section I: Political, Section II: Air, Section III: Naval, Section IV: Army, Section V: Counter-Espionage, and Section VI: Economic in order to learn about the work of each and to find out what information they wanted him to gather in West Africa. Counter-Espionage was to brief him on their general approach, the methods used by the enemy, and how to maintain security. He was instructed in the use of codes, the wireless, and secret inks. Howard himself gave him an overview of objectives, the relations of SIS with government and other branches of service, methods for establishing and maintaining personal cover, as well as such pieces of tradecraft as the use of 'postboxes' (caches for messages), 'cut-outs' (communication by intermediary), and the use of double agents and provocateurs. His next instructor was Frank Foley, a remarkable man who had served as head of station in Berlin just before the war under the guise of a passport officer and arranged for thousands of Jews to receive British visas, to learn about the training of agents, and then to other experts for information on censorship and the secure use of telephones. At the end of this programme he was to meet the deputy chief, Valentine Vivian.[1]

As part of his cover, Greene needed to look the part of a soldier, so Howard sent him to Oriel College, Oxford, for four weeks of training in the autumn of 1941, but he made only a slightly better show than he had with the OTC at school. There were battle-dress drills at dawn,[2] and he learned, more or less, to salute while marching with a swagger stick under one arm. He was taken out to Shotover to learn how to ride a motorcycle, but crashed the machines. Finally, he came down with flu and was moved to a nursing home in north Oxford, where he con-tracted bronchitis. While there, he saw himself in a mirror looking like a character in Dostoevsky, bundled up in an old overcoat and 'pursuing the scent of a samovar into somebody else's flat'.[3]

Greene shipped out from Liverpool on 9 December 1941 in a 5000-ton Elder Dempster cargo vessel. Along with the dozen other passengers, he was required to assist in its defence. Each day, he served a one-hour shift on the machine guns above the boat deck, watching for enemy aircraft, and another shift on the machine guns below the bridge watching for U-boats. The mood in the ship turned dark on their second day out with news that the Japanese had sunk the warships HMS *Repulse* and HMS *Prince of Wales* in the South China Sea[4] – this disaster, of course, followed on the heels of Pearl Harbor. There was a certain amount of gallows humour on board, as, apart from aeroplanes, their own vessel was carrying a cargo of TNT.[5]

The ship stopped first in Belfast, where Greene went to a presbytery to have his confession heard, only to have the housekeeper try to close the door on him – 'This is no time for Confession' – an experience he

would later work into his second play, *The Potting Shed*. Perhaps thinking of all that TNT, Greene stood his ground against the woman. He
was received by a simple-minded young priest, who called him 'son' and
asked what Greene felt were unnecessary questions about the convoy.[6]

The voyage was slow and anxious; they were near Iceland before
turning south, and by the tenth day out of Belfast were just at the
latitude of Land's End. During these days, Greene was able to finish a
short book called *British Dramatists*, a competent history of the theatre
in Britain from the Middle Ages to the present. Later, he wondered if
the cold watches and the conditions of the voyage were responsible for
his somewhat harsh account of William Congreve. The book appeared
in Collins's much-loved Britain in Pictures series, a morale-raising
enterprise celebrating the national heritage, featuring such authors as
George Orwell, Edith Sitwell, Elizabeth Bowen, John Betjeman, and
Cecil Beaton writing on an array of topics from birds to boxing.

Arriving in Freetown on 3 January 1942, Greene was seen off by
the other passengers forming a makeshift orchestra with frying pans
and forks as he boarded a launch. He was sent on to Lagos, where his
immediate superior was located, for further training. Greene's work
there consisted chiefly of coding and decoding cables, a subject that
fascinated him. He later found that in a historical throwback his code
books contained a symbol for eunuch, which he then employed in a
message to an intelligence officer in the Gambia: 'As the chief eunuch
said I cannot repeat cannot come.'[7]

Greene was somewhat surprised, even disquieted, by how comfortable his life was in Lagos. He reported to his mother that he had access
to safe running water and lavatories, and that he shared a bungalow
near the edge of the lagoon and could watch ships coming into port.
The house was actually swarming with mosquitoes, and at night Greene
and the colleague with whom he shared it used electric torches to
hunt cockroaches, an entertainment that reappears in *The Heart of
the Matter*. Yet, in contrast to wartime Britain, the food was excellent,
including bacon, eggs, coffee, oranges, grapefruits, even Bourbon
biscuits. On the night of Friday 13 February 1942, he thought he had
escaped the day's bad luck when he fell six feet into an open drain and
came out of it badly scratched and covered in turds. He treated his
injuries with a cold bath, Dettol, and whisky.[8]

Greene left Lagos at the end of March, stopping first in Accra, then at Roberts Field, an American air force base in Liberia, where the meals consisted mainly of foot-long overcooked steaks. The Americans had all of their food flown in, and although the barbecuing went on almost non-stop the meat was never shared with the local people who, as Tim Butcher learned, still refer to the place as 'Smell-No-Taste'.[9]

Back in Freetown, Greene found a small house in the Brookfield flats below Hill Station, the European area. He wrote to his mother: 'It's terribly difficult to get anywhere to live alone in these days, so one can't look a gift horse in the mouth. All the same I wish I was not just across the road from a transport camp in process of erection with two steam shovels going all day. And there's no water although there are taps. Freetown has 147 inches a year, but distribution is so bad that there won't be any water in my part till the rains six weeks hence. Drinking water I have to fetch in empty bottles from Freetown and then of course boil it, and bath water is fetched from a water hole.'[10]

The house had two bedrooms upstairs, a living room, and a dining room that served as his office. Rats swung from the curtains, while vultures loitered on the tin roof waiting for things to die. The house had been condemned on medical grounds since it stood in what was essentially an open latrine for the extremely poor neighborhood near by – when the rains came the ground turned into a fecal marsh. Greene advocated successfully to get lavatories for his neighbours, though they distrusted the angry man who came out at night in his pyjamas to throw rocks and swear at the howling pye-dogs. Greene hired a capable cook who then went insane and chased another servant with a hatchet.[11] Austerity had certain involuntary benefits, of course – liquor was rationed, and during the war years Greene gave up smoking.[12]

However much he grumbled, Greene was in love with Sierra Leone: '... in those first six months I was a happy man'.[13] He had a history here, and in April he was visited by Aminah, the youngest of his personal servants from the Liberian trek who reported that the old cook was well but Amedoo was 'under the ground'.[14] Freetown also offered Greene a refuge from trouble back home, as he wrote to Elisabeth: 'Things can be hell, I know. The peculiar form it's taken with me the last four years has been in loving two people as equally as makes no difference, the awful struggle to have your cake and eat it, the inability to throw over one for the sake of the other . . . '[15] His time abroad post-poned that reckoning.

Through the 1940s Greene was haunted by the question of whether his life was of use to anyone, especially as he was doing harm to his family and to Dorothy – a consideration that later brought him close to suicide. While in Sierra Leone, he told Raymond that he regarded his work in the service as having no value, but wrote to his mother: 'Tomorrow's Good Friday . . . Good Friday four years ago I went to a secret illegal Mass in Chiapas. I've had an odd life when I come to think of it. Useless and sometimes miserable, but bizarre and on the whole not boring.'[16]

Boredom did catch up with him from time to time, even in Freetown, and one day he stood on the stairs of his bungalow for half an hour watching two flies copulate.[17] Still, daily life was generally stimulating and distracting, something London offered only when the bombs were falling. Greene's passion for West Africa is not reducible, however, to a flight from marital troubles or an effort to stave off depression. As we have seen, he distrusted the veneers of a comfortable life and felt that reality was only knowable under conditions of privation. His quest for absolutes required such conditions, and if Greeneland, a term he disliked, has a central place it may just be the little house in Freetown, which he came to regard as home.[18]

Greene's career as agent 59200 got off to an awkward start as he was first told that his ostensible position would be that of inspector for the Department of Overseas Trade, but this cover was withdrawn. Then the British Council refused him a nominal appointment in Freetown, and so too the navy and air force both refused to grant him a rank. Finally, he was made an officer in the CID Special Branch.[19]

Greene was a minor figure in British intelligence, but Freetown was not an insignificant posting. At the time of his appointment there was rivalry between SIS and the rapidly expanding Special Operations Executive (SOE), which specialized in subversion and sabotage: although they collaborated in many theatres of the war, their interests were not the same, as SIS found it difficult to pursue the quiet work of gathering intelligence in places where SOE was blowing up trains and factories. SOE wanted to take control of intelligence gathering in West Africa,

something SIS strongly resisted.[20] With the Mediterranean closed to shipping, convoys to Egypt and North Africa had to sail south towards the
Cape of Good Hope, with Freetown the main port of call. At the same
time, there was some threat of attack by Vichy forces across the border
in French Guinea. So Greene's job required him to monitor shipping
and, through a very small network of agents, to keep track of any French
troop movements inland. He searched Portuguese ships for commercial
diamonds, and watched for enemy agents and evidence of espionage.
He interrogated a suspected spy just once, and hated it. He also discovered among the papers of another suspected spy the name of his friend,
translator, and French literary agent Denyse Clarouin – her work for the
resistance was evidently known to the Nazis and Greene assumed she
had already been arrested.[21] Deported in 1943, she was held first at the
concentration camp at Ravensbrück, then died at Mauthausen in 1945.[22]

A great many ships docked at Freetown, often carrying officers to distant postings, among them Nicholas Elliott who, in late May, was on his
way to Cairo. A very close friend of the double agent Kim Philby, whom
he long supposed a patriot, he would later be sorely embarrassed when
Philby defected. On the quay in Freetown, he met Greene, 'who had
the unrewarding task of trying to find out what was going on in Dakar'.
Presently Greene became worked up on the subject of contraceptives
in Sierra Leone – he could not get any – so Elliott obligingly took up
a collection of French letters among passengers of his ship and handed
them over. When reminded of this episode later, Greene 'retorted that
when I came ashore I was the tattiest Army officer he had ever seen. I
had even, he said, omitted to put on my badges of rank.'[23] It is curious
to think of Greene caring much about such things

Greene was kept busy. A young woman came to help him with coding
but he recalled that she was not particularly competent and the cables
often had to be repeated. Greene's relations with his superior at Lagos
deteriorated, and in the late summer the two quarrelled openly about an
occasion when Greene wanted to go inland to a meeting with an English
commissioner and the superior wanted him to search a ship. Greene
obeyed his orders, but complained vociferously, only to find his pay cut
off. London intervened, removing Greene from the control of Lagos so
that henceforth, without knowing it, he got his orders from Kim Philby,
who was then a senior figure in the counter-intelligence section of SIS.

Greene proposed two schemes to his superiors. He suggested black-mailing an imprisoned African intellectual to provide information on French Guinea, but the man, a socialist, had influential friends such as the publisher Victor Gollancz, and Greene's superiors feared that a question might be asked in Parliament. He also proposed setting up a brothel on a Portuguese island near Dakar to gather information, especially from the officers and men of the battleship *Richelieu* stationed near by. He found a cooperative Portuguese madam ready to set up shop, but, according to Greene, London nixed the idea on the grounds that all brothels were under the control of French intelligence.[24] Philby recalls that they took the idea seriously but said no because it was 'unlikely to be productive of hard intelligence'.[25]

Never very sociable, Greene made just a few friends in Freetown, going from time to time for drinks at the City Hotel, a gathering place for Europeans described in the opening pages of *The Heart of the Matter*. He found the company of expatriates tiresome as they spent their time complaining about the blacks and seemed immune to the horror of war; he wrote to Raymond: 'As far as I can see their contribution [to the war effort] has been confined to cowardice, complacency, inefficiency, illiteracy and thirst . . . Of course one is referring only to the Europeans. The Africans at least contribute grace ... People say the African is not yet ready for self-government. God knows whether he is or not: the Englishman here certainly isn't.' He added that it all amounted to 'copy' – he knew he would one day write about this place.[26]

Greene did become very friendly with Father Michael Mackey, an Irish missionary of the Congregation of the Holy Spirit (the 'Spiritans') known to his confreres as 'Mick'. Born in Waterford, he was sent in 1934 to teach at St Edward's Secondary School in Freetown. In 1938, he was made vicar-general of the diocese and pastor of St Anthony's Church, near the house in the Brookfield flats that the novelist would occupy in 1942. Mackey would regularly preach in the Sierra Leonean creole called Krio. A fine raconteur, he possessed a superb tenor voice, and was usually the centre of attention at parties – in fact, a profile of him preserved by his order remarks that sometimes he could be 'over rumbustious' but that he 'mellowed'. He was also rather 'abrasive' for mission work and was sent on to other assignments after 1946, and was successful at almost everything he turned his hand to. In his later years, he lived in California and was popular with celebrities, including Bing Crosby, with whom he played golf.[27] The character of Father Rank in *The Heart of the Matter* owes a good deal to Father Mackey.

Greene's closest friend in Sierra Leone was Patrick Tait Brodie.[28] The child of an Inverness wine merchant who died young, Brodie had earned his living as a 'mechanical dentist'[29] – he made dentures. In 1908 he went to South Africa as a labourer,[30] and in the following year he joined the British South African Mounted Police, serving until 1912 when he took to hunting elephants and other big game. In the Great War, he served in the 2nd Rhodesia Regiment and then the King's African Rifles, rising to the rank of captain; he was wounded twice and named in despatches three times, winning the Military Cross and the Distinguished Service Order.[31] He remained with his regiment until 1923, when he became Police Commissioner in Sierra Leone, running a force of about three hundred men.[32] In 1941, he was awarded an OBE.[33]

When Greene met him, Brodie was also working on behalf of MI5 (the branch of intelligence that investigates subversion and threats to internal security, in contrast to MI6 which gathers foreign intelligence). Each day Greene would bring his outgoing cables to Brodie for transmission and pick up those that had come in – all in code. The two men became close, and Brodie lent Greene money when his salary was cut off in the dispute with Lagos. Eighteen years older than the novelist, Brodie was worn out by his job, especially the ongoing struggle against corruption among his officers and continual demands and instructions from MI5 officials back in England.

According to Greene, one day during the rains, evidently in the autumn of 1942, Brodie went 'out of his mind'.[34] His career in Sierra Leone was over, and he was replaced within months.[35] Greene insisted that Scobie was not a portrait of Brodie,[36] and yet in addition to the similar-sounding names, the broad outlines of an upright police officer disintegrating under pressure are undeniably similar. However, the inner life of Scobie and his final act of self-destruction have little to do with Brodie, who lived another twenty years and eventually died in Wiltshire. Indeed, the dilemmas of Scobie are, in some respects, Greene's own, and in other ways they are purely imaginary. As is often the case, Greene's fictional character developed in the writing and became very different from the person who had been the initial inspiration.

Through his months in West Africa, Greene had written some of his most lyrical and evocative letters to his parents, as if he could speak more freely now that he was away from England. It is assumed that the letters, addressed to Marion, were actually written to both parents and that she would read them aloud to Charles,[37] who spent much of his time in his study with the curtains drawn. A passionate chess player, he taught the rudiments of the game to Lucy Caroline when Vivien brought the children to visit.[38] He had had the benefit of insulin, but diabetes gradually ruined his health, and he died on 4 November 1942.[39] Rather as had happened with the death of Vivien's mother, Graham received first a telegram informing him of his father's death and then a second advising of his serious illness.

Stricken with regret for arguing with his father about politics and morals,[40] he arranged for Father Mackey to say a Mass for him and the priest suggested a useful memorial tribute, which Graham described to his mother: 'This may seem Popish superstition to you, or it may please you, that prayers are being said every day for Da in a West African church, & that rice is being distributed here in his name among people who live on rice & find it very hard to get.'[41]

Naturally restless, he wrote to Hugh: 'This place will be most amusing to look back on, I daresay, but it's extraordinary how dull and boring the bizarre can be at the time.'[42] After his row with Lagos, he was offered another appointment but did not have the languages necessary to take it up, and yet in the last months of 1942 he wanted and expected a transfer.[43] The intelligence situation changed on 8 November when the Allies commenced Operation Torch, a series of successful assaults on Morocco and Algeria, after which there was less need for the information officers further south could provide. In February, he sailed back to England for a new assignment. He later wrote: '"Those days" – I am glad to have had them; my love of Africa deepened there, in particular for what is called, the whole world over, the Coast, this world of tin roofs, of vultures clanging down, of laterite paths turning rose in the evening light.'[44]

19

THE MINISTRY OF FEAR

Greene had little time for British detective stories – too many country houses, too many Bradshaw's timetables – but while sailing from Liverpool to West Africa he had read a book by Michael Innes, which prompted him to write a 'funny and fantastic thriller' of his own, *The Ministry of Fear*. As Greene observed, this book did not turn out to be particularly funny though it had, in his understated phrase, 'other merits'.[1] Many years later, L. Ron Hubbard, the founder of the Church of Scientology, claimed through a publicist that Greene had stolen the idea for the novel from him and then proposed, as a remedy, that they collaborate on new stories. Finally nagged into a response, Greene dismissed both suggestions with polite scorn.[2]

Greene began writing the book once he had settled in Freetown in April 1942, worked quickly despite the burden of his official tasks, and finished around the beginning of August. Getting the manuscript home was a problem, as so many of the ships were sinking and he did not want to lose it – indeed, he valued it at £600. Working in the evenings and typing with one finger, it took him almost as long to produce a typescript as it did to write the story.[3]

He regarded *The Ministry of Fear* as the best of his 'entertainments', but this novel seems ill-served by that term. Although it is a story of spies, bombs, abductions, and killings, it is also a subtle exploration of memory, selfhood, politics, psychoanalysis, and the growth of pity. The main character, Arthur Rowe, has served a brief detention for the mercy killing of his sick wife. The story opens with him attending a church fête in bombed-out Bloomsbury, where some fifth columnists mistake his identity and arrange for him to win a cake containing microfilm. They try to get it back it from him, then to silence him by making him believe he has committed another murder. Trying to uncover the facts, he encounters two of the spies, a brother and sister named Hilfe, refugees from Austria; Rowe and Anna Hilfe fall in love, but the brother remains true to the cause. A bomb in a suitcase wipes out Rowe's memory of his adult life and leaves him temporarily happy. Under the name Richard Digby, he is placed in a sanitorium, resembling Berkhamsted School even down to the green baize door, run by a blackmailed psychiatrist who refuses to help Rowe recover his memories. The plot plays out with several killings and a suicide, in the course of which Rowe does recover his memories, especially that of killing his wife. He and Anna come together but have much to conceal from one another. Greene ends on a chilling note: 'after all one could exaggerate the value of happiness'.

The book is built around dream-logic; the daily round of bombs, politics and treachery are understandable only by a larger form of psychoanalysis. A Special Branch investigator, Mr Prentice, based on one of the men who trained Greene for intelligence, is said to be 'the surrealist round here'. In anticipation of *The Heart of the Matter*, the book is fundamentally concerned with the errors of pity that might lead one to kill, but also with the possibility of pity as a 'mature passion' – in Greene's lexicon 'pity' is usually, but not always, inferior to 'compassion'.

In its way, this book is nearly as concerned with theology as *Brighton Rock* or *The Power and the Glory*. Pity forces one into fellowship with wretched humanity: 'Wasn't it better to take part even in the crimes of people you loved, if it was necessary hate as they did, and if that were the end of everything suffer damnation with them, rather than be saved alone?' This is a variation on the thinking of Charles Péguy, and it is also reminiscent of the whisky priest at home in the prison cell.

The novel was released in London and New York in May 1943. Many reviewers were confused by the ambition of the book – they thought it too complex, but book-buyers had no such reservations: in Britain alone it sold eighteen thousand copies.[4] Paramount British Productions bought the film rights just on the strength of the title.[5] Decades later Greene recalled that he was 'overjoyed' to receive £10,000 for the rights. According to the contract, the price was £2,250.[6] Presumably, he confused currencies – the pound was worth about four dollars in 1943.[7]

And perhaps the event loomed so large in memory that it *felt* like he had received £10,000.

At the beginning of March 1943, Greene had returned to England and was thrust back into the old dilemmas. He visited Vivien and the children in Oxford, but spent little time there.[8] He was often at the flats in Gower Mews and, from November 1943, at 18 Gordon Square, which he shared with Dorothy Glover. Vivien knew what was going on, but wanted the marriage to continue. They were certainly quarreling, and shortly after his return from Freetown a drunken Greene wrote to her from a pub that he had told many lies in his life and that he wished to die: 'I hate life & I hate myself & I love you.' In May he responded to a sad letter of hers by saying that he felt he had 'fooled' her: 'I really feel that it would have been better for you if I'd been torpedoed or plane crashed'.[9] This line of reasoning, that a bad husband's death could be good for his wife, would re-emerge in *The Heart of the Matter*.

Greene's return from Africa triggered a number of extreme moods. Having seen a stage production of *Brighton Rock* in Oxford on 2 March, he was still incandescent two days later when he wrote a letter to his agent, Laurence Pollinger, saying he 'was horrified by certain changes: these seemed to me to ruin the play for the sake of allowing Hermione Baddeley [as Ida] to fling a heart throb to the back of the gallery. She is a very bad piece of miscasting: her performance is on the overacted level of a revue sketch & her grotesqueness is all wrong for the part.' The story itself had been stripped of its Catholic elements, including the priest's closing speech about the 'the appalling strangeness of the mercy of God'. This change violated his agreement with the producer, so Greene was prepared to seek an injunction and insisted that his name be removed from all advertising.[10] When confronted by Pollinger with Greene's demands, the producer backed down. The script was revised according to Greene's wishes, and Hermione Baddeley reined in.

The play, the novel, and the troubles in his marriage all mattered greatly to him and had to be dealt with after his long absence, but the return to England landed him in the middle of even greater complexities, which he seemed not to detect. Having often written about betrayal, he was now going to work beside men who turned out to be traitors.

20

CANARIES AND DEFECTORS

G reene's intelligence work in 1943–4 has been widely discussed, but the evidence concerning it is by its nature scant. He had been recalled from Freetown to work in the Iberian subsection of SIS Section V, which was dedicated to counter-intelligence. Since the summer of 1941 this subsection was headed by the penetration agent Kim Philby, who had been sending Greene his orders and had generally taken his side in the dispute with Lagos.

Greene was put in charge of the Portugal desk in the Section V headquarters, first at Glenalmond House, an Edwardian mansion in St Albans in Hertfordshire, and then from late July 1943 at 14 Ryder Street, off St James's Street, in London.[1] Greene's subsection had been expanded from two to six officers, each with his own territory; among them was a fellow Catholic, Arthur George Trevor-Wilson,[2] who would later become Greene's most trusted associate in Indochina.

The key point about Greene's work was that the supposedly neutral Salazar regime in Portugal, like that of Franco in Spain, was sympathetic to the Axis powers and allowed the Abwehr, the German intelligence service, to operate on its soil.[3] However, the Salazar regime was not as openly pro-Nazi as the Spanish government, so Section V had to conduct itself more cautiously there for fear of driving them further into the Nazi camp.[4] Spies being sent to Britain would often come via Portugal or Spain, and in theory MI6 would identify these people while still abroad and pass the information to MI5, which would pick them up once they arrived in Britain. The difference between counter-intelligence conducted by MI6 and the work of MI5 often boiled down to a question of territory. Hampered by rivalries with MI5, MI6 expanded its operations in Spain and Portugal.[5]

What did Greene's job involve? His first, very tiresome task was to produce a large index, known as a 'Purple Primer', of enemy intelligence officers, agents, and contacts in Portugal; Philby wrote an introduction; his deputy Tim Milne (nephew of A. A. Milne) updated and enlarged it, and later wrote in his memoir: 'Perhaps this entitles me to go down in history as the co-author, with Graham Greene and H. A. R. Philby, of a volume privately published, in limited edition, with numbered copies.'[6]

Much of Greene's work would have involved signals intelligence, now called SIGINT.[7] He would have processed two kinds of material from the codebreakers at Bletchley Park: ISK ('Intelligence Services Knox', named after Dilly Knox, who led the Enigma codebreakers); and ISOS ('Intelligence Services Oliver Strachey', named after the leader of the section breaking Abwehr hand ciphers).[8] Whereas in Sierra Leone Greene was searching ships and making forays to the border, at St Albans he was tied to a desk, poring over intercepts, as well as a certain amount of intelligence from human sources – what is now referred to as HUMINT.

In Milne's recollection, Greene was not all that interested in intelligence work, especially as the Allies were becoming so dominant in the field. What got his attention was the plight of agents who suffered as a consequence of serving in SIS. For weeks, he 'bombarded' his colleagues with pleas for a man jailed in Lisbon and was also known for entertaining marginal comments on documents, as on a letter from an officer in Lisbon: 'Poor old —, bashing about like a bull in a china shop, letting in great glimpses of the obvious.'[9]

One man whom the subsection tracked carefully was Admiral Wilhelm Canaris, head of the Abwehr. Philby proposed tossing a couple of grenades into his hotel room, but his superiors rejected this plan since they knew that Canaris was secretly opposed to Hitler, wanted an early peace, and might be counted on to lead a coup. Indeed, Philby's desire to get rid of Canaris was precisely in line with Soviet plans to come as far west into Europe as possible, something a negotiated peace would prevent.[10] As Philby's subordinate, Greene harassed Canaris personally by sending word of his whereabouts to the Portuguese police.[11] Arrested as part of von Stauffenberg's plot against Hitler, Canaris was executed by garroting in April 1945.

Greene was involved with running some double agents, among them one codenamed 'Josef', a Russian seaman who had been trained as a spy by the Soviets but then lost touch with them. MI6 ran him against the Japanese in Lisbon for two years, with Greene handling and inter-preting much of the ISOS traffic relating to him. In the intelligence file for this case there is a curious correspondence between Greene and Richmond Stopford, one of Josef's case officers, about a suspected spy aboard a ship headed to Britain who could be identified by the four canaries he had with him. In his letter of 29 December 1943, Greene, perhaps thinking of his children, added, 'Your secretary has promised to reserve me one canary.'[12] Tim Butcher wonders whether these canaries might have something to do with an effort by Greene and others to get around Philby and make contact with Canaris.[13] The historian of intelligence Nigel West, however, thinks not.[14] His view is, essentially, that even in the secret world sometimes the canaries are real.

The Iberian subsection had some involvement in one of the war's most important pieces of strategic deception – the 'Garbo' case. Greene's own involvement in this affair was slight, but the story, and some others similar to it, remained with him and helped to shape the plot of *Our Man in Havana*. This complicated tale was unravelled by West.[15] In January 1941, a Spaniard named Juan Pujol García, who hated Hitler, offered himself to the British embassy in Madrid as a willing spy against the Germans. Under orders to be discreet and to create no incidents, they sent him packing. Undaunted, he went to the German embassy and volunteered to go to Britain as a journal-ist and spy on *their* behalf. By October, he was in Portugal sending the Germans bogus reports, concocted with the aid of a Baedeker, a Bradshaw, and an Ordnance Survey map. In his first message, he claimed the assistance of a pilot with KLM – in fact, a KLM pilot was known to the British as a spy. In another message, his description of a convoy of ships from Liverpool to Malta bore a freakish resemblance to one that actually sailed. Intercepting these reports, British intelligence at first believed that an expert spy was at work. Pujol then contacted an American official in Lisbon who took him seriously, just as the British worked out that he was really operating from Portugal. He was taken by ship to Gibraltar then flown to England in April 1942. Having been originally codenamed 'Bovril', he was renamed 'Garbo' in tribute to his acting skills.

Handled by Tomás Harris of MI5, he fed a great deal of false information to the Germans, and convinced them of the reality of his twenty-six invented sub-agents. He was a prized asset of German intelligence. Just before D-Day a message of his had great influence on the High Command, helping to convince them that landings at Normandy were a diversion and that the real attack would come at Pas de Calais. Indeed, that message, initialled by Field Marshal Jodl and presented to Hitler, helped to muddle German thinking at a key moment and so buy time for the invasion force. A hero to both sides, Juan Pujol García was secretly awarded both an MBE and an Iron Cross.

During his time in Section V Greene struck up friendships with two of the five members of the Cambridge spy ring. His friendship with John Cairncross began in June 1943 with them taking the same train to St Albans. Greene asked the Scotsman what he was reading; it turned out to be *England Made Me*, which he was enjoying very much. Pleased, Greene described it as not bad. Cairncross kept talking and said there were better books by this author, such as *The Power and the Glory*. Getting the sense that his travelling companion was himself a writer, he asked whether he actually knew Graham Greene, to which came the reply, 'I am Graham Greene.'[16]

At St Albans, Cairncross was technically Greene's subordinate but was shunted off to other work.[17] A fondness developed between them, and Greene dubbed him 'Claymore'. However, having been recruited by the Soviets in 1937, Cairncross was not a benign figure. Fluent in German, he was sent in 1942 to work on Ultra decrypts at Bletchley and provided the Soviets with thousands of documents, some of which contributed to their victory at the Battle of Kursk in the summer of 1943. After about a year at Bletchley, he suffered eye strain and was moved to a job in SIS Section V. When the war was over, he entered the civil service and provided the Soviets with an array of sensitive military information, including nuclear secrets. Once Burgess and Maclean defected in 1951, Cairncross was suspected of treason and forced out of the civil service; he confessed to MI5 in 1964.[18] Shortly after Anthony Blunt's exposure in 1979, Cairncross was publicly identified as the fifth man in the Cambridge spy ring.[19] In the 1980s he turned to Greene for help with a memoir and his problems of residency in France, sending him many long letters. Always sympathetic to outcasts and underdogs, Greene tried to help.

On a day-to-day basis in 1943–4, Greene saw much more of Kim Philby than of John Cairncross. At first glance, Greene and the Cambridge spies seem to belong to the same class and generation, but Greene felt there were subtle differences: 'All the five concerned were at Cambridge long after I was at Oxford. Generations at university go in three years. I belong to the 1922 generation and Kim and the others belonged to a much later one – at the beginning of the thirties. It was then apparent that Germany was the main threat and the hunger marchers were busy. It was more natural in the early thirties to side with our possible ally Russia.'[20]

Convinced of the truth of Marxism at university, Philby was recruited by the NKVD in 1934. At the instruction of his controllers he reinvented himself as a man of the right, in 1937 going to Spain for *The Times*, where he wrote admiringly about Franco. Brought into the intelligence services by Guy Burgess, he moved to Section V in 1941, where he was given charge of the Iberian subsection. In the following year, he was also made responsible for Italy and North Africa, including Sierra Leone. While at St Albans he scoured the archives, especially the two-volume 'Source Book' detailing all SIS agents in the Soviet Union.[21]

Intelligent and charismatic, Philby was popular with his colleagues. Greene enjoyed his company, recalling long boozy pub lunches on Sundays in St Albans, and other drinking sessions around St James's. According to Greene, Philby went out of his way to hide the errors of his subordinates.[22] Of course, his loyalty was strictly superficial, as he had laid bare the workings of Section V to his Soviet controllers; in their archives, even Greene has a codename, LORAN.[23] A high-functioning alcoholic, Philby still managed to keep his own secrets, exercising an aloof charm that sometimes looked like intimacy. He could, however, be severe. A secretary walked into Greene's office one day to find him in a fury. Asked what had happened, he replied, 'I've just had a caning from the headmaster.'[24]

With the war ending, German espionage was fading, and it was necessary to refocus counter-intelligence on the Soviets. Beginning on a small scale, with a retired MI5 officer in charge, a new unit, Section IX, was established for this purpose. Philby told his controllers what was going on, and they insisted that he get himself appointed head of this new section, a job that would ordinarily have gone to Felix Cowgill, the capable but sometimes cantankerous head of Section V.[25] Philby began manoeuvring in March and finally got the appointment in September, while Cowgill was travelling in Italy. On his return, Cowgill protested in vain to 'C' (the chief of MI6, Stewart Menzies) and resigned shortly after. Philby was now in control of the efforts of MI6 against Soviet spies.

In the midst of this plotting, Graham Greene left MI6. Indeed, his resignation coincided with D-Day, and it is difficult to understand how a trusted intelligence officer could leave the service at a crucial moment in the war. Twenty-four years later, Greene offered this account in his preface to Philby's memoir, *My Silent War*:

> I saw the beginning of this affair [Section IX] – indeed I resigned rather than accept the promotion which was one tiny cog in the machinery of his intrigue. I attributed it then to a personal drive for power, the only characteristic in Philby I thought disagreeable. I am now glad that I was wrong. He was serving a cause and not himself, and so my old liking for him comes back.[26]

Greene liked to deal in provocations – here he suggests that an ambitious bureaucrat is morally worse than a mole who sent many people to their deaths in the service of Stalin. Why *did* Greene leave at such an unlikely moment?

One might speculate that Philby tried to recruit him as an agent, and Greene decided that he should quit rather than turn Philby in – or perhaps he reported Philby and was then removed from Section V to prevent word getting out. The problem with this suggestion, as Nigel West observes, is that Philby was highly unlikely to have attempted independent recruitment, having tried it once and been rebuked by the NKVD. And, indeed, he made no independent approach to Tim Milne, who would have been a more likely target.[27] Philby was himself an intelligence asset of unsurpassed value and his controllers did not want him taking large risks for small rewards; Greene possessed no knowledge that was not available to Philby.

Milne maintains that it is wrong to see Philby as trying to take over Section V in early 1944.[28] In September 1943, Cowgill promoted Philby to a position from which he controlled much of Section V anyway, and Milne was made head of the Iberian subsection. By late winter Philby was focused on Section IX. A routine promotion was offered to Greene at about this time, and he took Philby, Milne, and an administrative officer to a pleasant lunch at the Café Royal to persuade them to leave him in his current post. In June, he resigned altogether.

Two of Greene's biographers have suggested that he somehow saw into Philby's mind and intuited betrayal.[29] This is a sentimental, even fantastical, reading of the situation in an attempt to set up an interpretation of the character of Harry Lime in *The Third Man* – Greene had actually been describing betrayals of mentors and dominant friends since *The Man Within*, and having experienced Carter at school he did not need Philby to inspire that sort of fiction.

For Tim Milne, the memory of those years became a very raw point. In his last interrogation by Nicholas Elliott before defecting in 1962, Philby said that he had suggested Milne to his controllers as a possible recruit but they rejected the idea. Although cleared and allowed to continue working in sensitive posts, Milne was mortified. He wrote a memoir of Philby, which was accepted for publication in 1979, but SIS refused its permission; Milne died in 2010 at the age of ninety-seven, and his family arranged for its publication four years later. In it he says that after seeing Greene's account of his resignation, he took the matter up with him, and asked for details to substantiate the comments. Greene said he could remember nothing specific, just an impression of ambition and intrigue on the part of Philby.[30] It is entirely possible, then, that Greene had read subsequent revelations about Philby into his memories of 1944.

Simpler answers present themselves. Greene was a man easily bored. He had been doing desk work for a year at a very modest salary and was tired of it. Indeed, he never held a desk job for very long, always craving change, distraction, and stimulation. By 1 May 1944 the Political Intelligence Department of the Foreign Office offered him a job with a promise to send him to France following the invasion.[31] Accepting promotion at Section V would have increased the demands on his time and likely set up a post-war career in MI6, but, as we shall see in the next chapter, he already had a job waiting for him at the publishing firm Eyre & Spottiswoode.

The most likely explanation of Greene's desire to leave MI6 for a less demanding position lies in a scriptwriting contract he signed with MGM on 3 February 1944, providing him with twelve weeks of work in each of two years at the handsome rate of £250 per week. The studio would have an option on Greene's services on similar terms for a third year. There was also an elaborate set of options on the screen rights of any literary works Greene might produce during the term of the con-tract – these would prove to be a separate source of trouble. However, the key point here is that MGM wanted to get Greene working as soon as possible, so included a requirement that once hostilities ended he 'will use his best endeavours to obtain his release and discharge from compulsory national service at the earliest possible date'. He was also required to keep MGM apprised of the steps he was taking to obtain release and act on any suggestions they might give.[32]

It seems that Kim Philby's conduct played, at most, a minor part in Greene's departure from Section V. Greene did take the job offered by the Foreign Office, but they reneged on the promise of sending him to France. Working from their Editorial Unit at 43 Grosvenor Street, he assembled an anthology of English writers to be distributed in France, and returned to his old duties of fire-watching.

On the whole, Greene's work in MI6 broadened his imagination, even though he was never a significant figure in the intelligence ser-vices. David Cornwell, the former MI6 officer who writes as John le Carré, was a friend and protégé of Greene's; they fell out over Greene's public remarks on Philby's defection, but he remains grateful and sym-pathetic to him. In an interview for this book, he explains that some writers, notably Somerset Maugham, have made a considerable contri-bution to intelligence work but Greene was not among them: he was probably 'quite effective' in Africa, but on the whole, the secret world mattered more to him than he did to it. In Cornwell's view, intelligence work appeals to writers as it is close to their own process, and they find it has a lasting hold on them:

> ... watchfulness, the secrecy of your perceptions – you keep them to yourself – and the sense of alienation, of being an observer within society rather than a member of it. And I think that was very much in Graham. There are people, I count myself among them, who are writers first and everything else second, who go through these

strange corridors of the secret world and find an affinity with them and it never leaves them. There's a kind of inside-out thinking that never leaves you. It has to do with the manipulation of people, and with self-examination – so if I am constantly wondering what will procure you as my friend, my informant: what do you eat? What are your appetites? How can I get hold of you? – then by the same token I am asking the same questions of myself: what will I actually fall for? I think it invests you, while you are in this mode, with a superior power which is thoroughly unhealthy. And I don't think Graham ever shook it off. Even when he was being oppositional, he imagined he was changing world history.[33]

Cornwell believes that service in MI6 affected Greene's way of seeing the world and himself, and that he later tended to confuse his pre-eminence as a writer with a degree of political standing that he did not really possess. It is an interesting point, though difficult to prove. One day Greene would look back on his childhood flight to Berkhamsted Common and claim that his hope had been to live in concealment, 'an invisible watcher, a spy on all that went on'.[34] His early life and reading disposed him to believe such personal narratives. His time in the secret world may have made them indelible.

21

MRS MONTGOMERY

Separated only by office furniture and some piles of paper, Graham Greene and Douglas Jerrold worked together at Eyre & Spottiswoode for three years. It was said that Jerrold had a large body and small head, causing him to resemble 'an inflated *hors d'oeuvre*'.[1] A fairly prolific author, Jerrold's books were unreadable. As a publisher he was irascible, but in fairness, he was in constant pain from an arm wounded at the Somme.[2] According to Malcolm Muggeridge, one of the firm's authors, Greene and Jerrold did manage to inhabit the same office in Bedford Street without quarrelling.[3]

The two had made a gentleman's agreement in 1942 for Greene to join the firm, and they confirmed it by contract the following year, giving him then a director's annual fee of £100 even if he was called up, and an entertainment budget for the same amount so long as he was present in London. In the summer of 1944, with the war's end in sight, they made a new agreement for him to receive an annual salary of £1000, rising by annual increments to £1500, and Jerrold, who wanted to retire, told him that he would be in sole charge in about eighteen months.[4] The firm had been the King's Printer with a lucrative monopoly on publication of the King James Bible and the Book of Common Prayer. It was Greene's job to develop the fiction list, while Jerrold handled non-fiction.

Greene and Jerrold were both Catholics, but, as Muggeridge observed, very different sorts of Catholic. Jerrold had admired Mussolini, considered Franco a living saint, and been a supporter of the British Union of Fascists – however, he did not support Hitler or espouse racist theories. He edited the *English Review* and later the *New English Review Magazine* as platforms for very conservative ideas on faith and politics.[5] For his part,

Greene, though a centrist, was interested in the left and would eventually claim that Catholicism and communism had much in common.

Jerrold regarded Graham Greene with a mixture of respect, amusement, and scepticism. He thought that Greene was at pains to conceal being 'an absolutely first-class man of business'. Indeed, as Jerrold later wrote, he would come into the office early and behave as if he had a hangover which he had to dispel with a trip to the pub as soon as possible. When asked how some engagement had gone the previous evening, 'he always replied with a look of intense pleasure, "It was perfectly ghastly."' His bearing would then change: 'he would settle down to the serious business of the day, telephoning with rapid succession to his bank, to his stockbroker, to his insurance agent, to his literary agent, to a film company or two, and, if it was really a busy morning, to two or three editors'. Jerrold thought there was a great deal of 'play-acting' about Greene, what another generation would call schtick: 'His club must be what he calls the "the seedy club"; if he goes to a party it must be "simply appalling" or "perfectly ghastly"; even a quiet cocktail with two or three friends becomes, on leaving, "a dreary little drink."'[6]

The play-acting included practical jokes executed on a grand scale, especially the one about Mrs Montgomery: 'Who is this "Mrs Montgomery"?' wrote Jerrold. 'The answer must be that there is no such person.' Greene invented her. An irate author whose manuscript had been lost in the office, she demanded meetings 'at impossible times in inconvenient places'. A biographer came forward with a request in the *Spectator* for letters of hers. She then disowned the biography as unauthorized and intrusive. Greene kept Mrs Montgomery in action for quite some time: 'Here for once the whole of Graham Greene was at work in a harmonious universe of his own choosing – the mischievous child, the brilliant man of affairs, the creator of entertainments, the writer of film scripts, and the psychological analyst. Only the power and the glory were ephemeral.' The last sentence captures Jerrold's severe opinion that despite being 'the finest living novelist' in terms of skill, Greene was trivial in that his preoccupation with doubt and failure caused him to miss the essence of a Catholic life.[7]

Before joining full time, Greene had brought a new author of enormous talent to the firm, and in so doing proved that Greeneland is not that far from Gormenghast. In the spring of 1943, Graham Greene met Mervyn Peake in Chelsea. In June, Chatto & Windus turned down the unfinished *Titus Groan* when Peake refused to make cuts, so Greene, having read a portion, urged him to meet Jerrold to discuss the novel and an illustration project. Peake kept writing and at the end of August sent the completed manuscript to Greene, who took some weeks to wade through it. Peake cannot have expected the response he received:

> I'm going to be mercilessly frank – I was very disappointed in a lot of it & frequently wanted to wring your neck because it seemed to me you were spoiling a first-class book by laziness. The part I had seen before I of course still liked immensely – though I'm not sure that it's gained by the loss of the prologue. Then it seemed to me one entered a long patch of really bad writing, redundant adjectives, a kind of facetiousness, a terrible prolixity in the dialogue of such characters as the Nurse & Prunesquallor, & sentimentality too in the case of [Keda] & to some extent in Titus's sister. In fact – frankly again – I began to despair of the book altogether, until suddenly in the last third you pulled yourself together & ended splendidly. But even here you were so damned lazy that you called Barquentine by his predecessor's name for whole chapters.[8]

Oddly enough, this was an acceptance letter. Greene was willing to publish if Peake would sort out the manuscript. At the end of the letter he suggested that they conduct their duel over glasses of whisky in a bar. Greene got through to Peake in a way that Chatto could not, convincing him of the importance of the 'blue pencil method'. It took a long time to revise, and there were further delays owing to the post-war paper shortage, but the novel finally appeared in March 1946.[9]

Greene remarked to his mother that the whole company was paid for by the sale of books by the American popular novelist Frances Parkinson Keyes, whose appeal mystified him.[10] They could not publish enough copies of her books, which, in his view, weren't exciting or sexy, though one might learn from them how to run a sugar plantation.[11] Such bestsellers allowed him to publish authors whose appeal was more limited, among them R. K. Narayan, whose novel *The English*

Teacher he accepted in October 1944. During his employment at Eyre & Spottiswoode, the firm published three new books by Narayan, but soon after Greene's departure in 1948 the firm dropped the Indian novelist.

One of Greene's main responsibilities was the Century Library, a reprint series of modern fiction that allowed him to revive many of his old favourites that had fallen into neglect, among them Herbert Read's *The Green Child*, which had been first published in 1935 and now appeared with an introduction by Greene. In choosing the titles for this series, Greene took advice from a number of writers, including George Orwell. Another advantage of his position was that he could commission Dorothy to design book covers, as she certainly needed the work.[12]

It was also time for Greene himself to start writing again. The liberation of France brought with it steady news about the resistance, collaborators, and Nazi atrocities, so Greene pitched a story called *The Tenth Man* to Alexander Korda for development into a film script. On 6 November 1944 he signed a contract with MGM, separate from the agreement of the preceding February; it would pay him £1500 and assign the copyright in the work to MGM.[13]

The story opens in a prison where the Nazis are planning to shoot one man in ten as a reprisal for killings by the local resistance. A group of thirty is told by a German officer to choose three from among themselves for execution at dawn. One of those chosen by lot, a lawyer named Louis Chavel, offers all he has to anyone who will take his place. A young man accepts the offer, documents are hastily drawn up, and he goes to the firing squad. Upon release, the disgraced Chavel returns, in disguise, to his own home, as he has nowhere else to go, where the young man's mother and sister have taken up an uneasy residence. The sister thinks her brother did a stupid thing and wishes to spit in the face of the man who offered him the deal. Having false papers that might lead to his execution as a collaborator, Chavel stays on in the house as a manservant and falls in love with the sister. His end comes when a down-at-heel actor appears on the doorstep in the character of Chavel, with a scheme to recover his property. In a confrontation with the false Chavel, the true one is shot.

Greene wrote the story as the basis for a script. The style is stripped down, though there are some finely written passages about the ownership of time. It is tightly constructed and well paced. He delivered the story to MGM, where it vanished into an archive or perhaps an oubliette. When it came to light in the 1980s Greene claimed to have forgotten it.[14] It is hard to know what to make of this – perhaps his memory did fail him by that time.[15] MGM made a number of copies of the typescript, and occasionally these made their way to the open market and Greene would snap them up – at least two came into his possession in 1966–7.[16] He often referred to his main agreement with MGM as a 'slave contract'. According to one of several side agreements, *The Tenth Man* belonged entirely to MGM, and its publication would not return another penny to Greene. In 1983, the publisher Anthony Blond acquired the rights to the lost novella from MGM. At first Greene dug in and said he would declare publicly that the story was written solely for film work and was being published now against his wishes.[17] However, Blond had no intention of causing Greene harm and entered into an agreement with his then publisher, the Bodley Head, for a joint publication in 1985, an arrangement that paid Greene about £22,000 in royalties in the following year[18] – a handsome profit on a title he had sold long before. Despite his efforts to suppress it, Greene felt that this 'child I don't recognize' was 'very readable', and he preferred it to the novel of *The Third Man*.[19]

There was to be more trouble with MGM. Under an agreement from 1946, the studio had an option on three of Greene's books within five years. Greene wanted to work with Alexander Korda, not MGM. In March 1947, they were persuaded not to consider *Nineteen Stories* an option work – this allowed Korda to buy the rights to 'The Basement Room' as the basis for *The Fallen Idol*. In 1947, Greene submitted *The Heart of the Matter*, which MGM declined. Next, he submitted part of the treatment of 'The Stranger's Hand' and a synopsis of the remainder; since it was not a completed work, MGM refused to regard it as one of the works it was owed. In early 1951, Greene came up with the extraordinary notion of submitting *The Little Fire Engine*, a children's book he had written in collaboration with Dorothy, to be the basis of a cartoon; Pollinger's solicitor advised him not to try it, and, indeed, when the studio heard of it they threatened to sue. Greene then sent them 'The Point of Departure' (*The End of the Affair*) in a messy typescript, with many handwritten notes and revisions, to curb their enthusiasm – by the end of May it, too, was rejected. He finished off his obligation to the studio with his play *The Living Room*, which it turned down the following year.[20]

22

HOT IRONS

B y the war's end, Greene's visits to Oxford were infrequent. His family had spent several years as guests of the Weavers at Trinity College, so in September 1944 he installed them in 6 Ship Street, a rented house near Cornmarket, where they remained until the end of May 1945, when they moved to 15 Beaumont Street, a house owned by St John's College.[1] Aside from the chasm between himself and Vivien, the children were growing older and he hardly knew them. When he did appear, he would bring small curiosities, such as an early Biro (the pen known in North America as a Bic) which fascinated the children because the ink did not need blotting.

In adolescence, his daughter was developing a strong personality. She loved riding, but despised school. She was sent to Rye St Antony, a solemn Catholic establishment in Headington, first as a day girl, then a boarder for the sake of discipline. She wrote to her father saying she did not like the place just as the women who ran it were complaining to him about her behaviour. Greene came to sort things out, but his daughter told him, 'I want to be expelled.' He withdrew her from that school and sent her to one in north Oxford, before enrolling her at a convent school in the Cotswolds. Caroline describes herself as 'not studious', learning 'more after school than during'.[2] Although widely read, she was more practical than either of her parents and would even-tually run her own ranch in western Canada. Three years younger than Caroline, Francis Greene was a reserved, bookish child, with interests in poetry, science, carpentry, and photography; he was educated by the Benedictines at Ampleforth College in Yorkshire, and then read physics at Christ Church, Oxford.

In the last year of the war, Graham would usually rush back from

Oxford to Dorothy and volunteering with the ARP. Life in London was infinitely more stimulating for him, and some of the atmosphere of the Blitz had returned. After D-Day, the Germans unleashed thousands of V-1s against England. As the launch sites were overrun by Allied forces, they turned in September to the longer-range V-2 rockets. By March 1945, the two weapons had caused about nine thousand deaths, most of them in or near London.[3] Greene's fire-watching duties were in Mayfair; at one point he was so upset by the disorganization of a 'death-trap' post in Mount Street that he invited an administrator to come to his office: 'I will be delighted to tell you what you can do with your fire-guard duties.'[4] Despite this threat, he continued to do the work.

On Sunday 18 March 1945, he was lying in bed at Gordon Square when he heard an enormous crash and rumble, then the sound of broken glass. Through his window, he could see smoke going up from an impact that was actually as far away as Marble Arch. Had the explosion occurred a little later, when the usual crowds had converged on Speakers' Corner, the casualties would have been catastrophic. Greene hurried over and saw the crater near the arch and the damage to the Regal Cinema and Cumberland Hotel. He was annoyed with well-fed American GIs taking pictures, so 'wandered around making anti-American cracks!'[5] A week later, the last of the V-2s killed or injured thirty-five people at Whitefield's Tabernacle in Tottenham Court Road, a little over 300 yards from Gordon Square. Graham had gone for a walk with Hugh so did not witness the calamity. Surprisingly, his flat was undamaged apart from a coating of dust and a cupboard door knocked loose.[6]

VE day came on 8 May – Hitler was dead and Germany surrendered. The long-postponed general election in July produced an unexpected victory for Clement Attlee and the Labour Party. Graham Greene went against that tide, telling his mother that he would vote Conservative in his constituency. He wished that there were a suitable Liberal candidate but could not abide socialist 'bores'. He was not sentimental about Churchill and looked forward to him going, taking his ministers Lord Beaverbrook and Brendan Bracken with him.[7] Throughout the rest of his life, Greene's party preferences are difficult to pin down. In the 1960s, he made an annual donation of £10 to the Liberal Party.[8] In later years, he lived abroad and appears not to have voted in British elections, but he said that in 1979 he would have voted for Margaret Thatcher for her 'integrity', as the Labour leaders seemed to be liars – he later objected to her policies, sometimes very strongly. In an interview in 1984, he said that he would vote as a Social Democrat, adding that he was not Marxist and disapproved of the hard left in the Labour Party but approved of some things that then leader Neil Kinnock said about Central America.[9] In truth, Greene had little time for political parties.

With the war over, Greene soon returned to regular reviewing. The *Evening Standard* asked him to write a weekly book article, but he did not want the work, so demanded thirty-five guineas per week, assuming the amount would be impossible. They agreed and he was cornered into taking it on. By October, he got into a convenient row with the editors and resigned, but according to their agreement he continued to be paid for three more months.[10]

At about this time, he began a novel set in Sierra Leone. *The Heart of the Matter* took two years to write and lifted Greene into a degree of literary and religious celebrity that could never have been foreseen. He would come to hate what the book did to his life and did not want it to be seen as his masterpiece, so argued, not very convincingly, that it was technically flawed owing to the 'rustiness of my long inaction' as a novelist. This claim is nonsense, as he began the novel within months of completing *The Tenth Man*. He was not rusty at all. Nonetheless, having started the novel with Wilson looking down at Scobie from the hotel balcony, he faced a period of indecision – should this be an entertainment in which, as a twist, the criminal is known and the detective unknown, or should he try for a serious novel about Scobie. It took months to resolve: ' . . . when I left Wilson on the balcony and joined Scobie, I plumped for the novel'.[11]

He also had scriptwriting projects. Through their firm Charter Film Productions, John Boulting and his twin brother Roy had purchased the rights to *Brighton Rock*. The playwright Terence Rattigan produced a treatment, but this was not used, and the film play was exclusively Greene's work.[12] The censor required that Pinkie's references to the Mass be cut as these, coming from a killer, might offend Catholics. Greene had admired nothing about the stage production of 1943, so the return of Hermione Baddeley as Ida and of the young Richard

Attenborough, now under contract to Charter, as Pinkie filled him with unease. The Boultings insisted, however politely, on their casting decisions, and once Greene saw the film he assured John Boulting that the choice of Attenborough could not be improved upon.[13]

At much the same time Attenborough also appeared as Francis Andrews, alongside Michael Redgrave, in a film of *The Man Within*. Decades later, Greene recalled transferring the rights for the nominal sum of £200–300 to his friend Ralph Keene, a documentary-maker who wished to make his first feature film. Keene could not finance the production so sold the rights at a profit to a producer named Sydney Box, who made the film released in 1947.[14]

However, there is something wrong with this account. A contract survives, dated 7 February 1944, between Box's firm, Theatrecraft Limited, and Graham Greene, paying him £400 for the film rights, of which he, not Keene, is identified as the beneficial owner.[15] Greene must never have formalized the sale to Keene, leaving it at a handshake. Perhaps, once Keene and Box made their agreement, they realized that it was necessary to approach Greene, offering him some money to confirm the sale. While some critics have made claims for the film as an innovative historical drama,[16] Greene despised the work Box then produced, especially its portrayal of torture with hot irons as part of the British justice system in the nineteenth century. He later told Quentin Falk that he was more pained by the 'treachery' towards his 'first-born' novel than by the political distortions in the 1958 production of *The Quiet American* – Michael Redgrave appeared in that film too. Greene made it a point to include in subsequent film contracts a clause forbidding resale of rights to Sydney Box,[17] and yet Box did manage to obtain the rights to one more of his stories, 'Across the Bridge',[18] which he sold. Greene remembered him as purely a scoundrel and a bungler.

23

MOTHER OF SIX

The story of Catherine Walston has been told by several writers, however, the most detailed and accurate information is contained in an unpublished family history by her son Oliver Walston.[1] Born on 12 February 1916, she was one of four children of Lillian Crompton (née Sheridan) and David Crompton, a solemn New York shipping executive who never really recovered from the deaths of his brother and all his brother's family aboard the *Lusitania*, torpedoed in 1915. Known as 'Bobs', Catherine was intelligent and literary, but lazy at school. Unusually beautiful, she had brown hair and blue eyes, and her height in adulthood, according to her passports, was 5′ 7″.[2] Following a visit to the dentist when she was thirteen, the family's nanny advised her parents, 'Mr and Mrs Crompton, I must tell you that I am worried about Bobs. As she walks down the train every man looks at her. She is going to need a great deal of supervision.'[3]

In a biography of this sort, there is a danger of presenting a complex and intelligent person as just a combination of good looks and sexual appetites. Indeed, a similar danger exists in describing Graham Greene himself, whose life is sometimes boiled down to sex, books, and depression. In writing about Catherine Walston there is also the problem of misogyny, as a highly promiscuous man is sometimes presented as an entertaining rogue, while a woman can be rendered a carnal monster.

Just before her nineteenth birthday, Catherine met an Englishman named Harry Walston, a Cambridge graduate studying bacteriology at Harvard. He came from a well-to-do Jewish family, known as Waldstein until the First World War, whose original fortune was derived from the manufacture of optical instruments. A restless character, Catherine decided that marriage would get her away from home. Five months after meeting, they were married. Later, Catherine claimed to have crossed her fingers during the vows, and she maintained that the marriage was not valid as she had never believed the words she was saying. Perhaps it was her intention to dump Harry once she had got the freedom she yearned for, but as it turned out, they had a curiously durable connection, while both pursued numerous extramarital affairs. Sometimes, Harry is understood as an extreme cuckold and the victim of Catherine's infidelities – in fact, he lived in a similar manner but apparently with fewer partners. The term 'open marriage' did not yet exist, but that is what they had.

Returning to his family's estate in Cambridgeshire, Harry gave up his academic work and turned to farming. Always an adventurer, Catherine took flying lessons and earned her private pilot's licence in 1936 – this at a time when Amelia Earhart was a heroine of the newsreels. The Walstons raised six children, though the parentage of two is doubtful. According to Oliver Walston, his brother David, born in 1940, was probably fathered by Daniel Pettiward, Catherine's lover for some years before and after the marriage. A more bizarre set of facts surrounds James Walston (born 1949), who was, apparently, not the child of either Catherine or Harry. The family believes that he was the son of Harry's girlfriend at the time, by another man. Too embarrassed to reveal the pregnancy to her parents, she needed to have the child adopted. For some reason this appealed to Catherine, so she travelled to Dublin, where the child was to be born, went about with a pillow under her clothes until the delivery, and was then certified as the mother.

A letter from John Hayward, who became her close friend, offers a modicum of proof for this tale by addressing her as 'Mother of Six', then joking about how Harry has informed him of an error in arithmetic and how she showed no sign of pregnancy two months before.[4] Greene worked an episode like this into *Travels with My Aunt*, and it is sometimes claimed that this must have been based on the child of Catherine and Graham Greene, but the family is doubtful of this and no documents have come to light supporting the suggestion. Graham Greene's non-involvement in this peculiar episode is worth recording, even as doing so brings to mind an inscrutable headline from a British newspaper in 1986: 'Body Found, Boy George Not Involved.'

During the war, Catherine became a friend of John Rothenstein, the director of the Tate Gallery, and his American wife Elizabeth, author of a noted study of the painter Stanley Spencer. The Rothensteins were both Catholics. Having considered becoming an Anglican, Catherine was particularly influenced by her conversations with Elizabeth and concluded that the Catholic attitude towards truth, that it cannot change between one age and another, was a decisive difference between the churches. Indeed, Elizabeth was a very fervent woman and could see that Catherine was struggling to find meaning in her life. She introduced her to the Jesuit intellectual Father Martin D'Arcy, whose rigorous manner of thinking she found impressive. Elizabeth also introduced her to the writings of C. S. Lewis and to the novels of Graham Greene.

Contrary to some accounts of Catherine simply parachuting into Greene's life with a request that he be her godfather in late 1946, she was, in fact, already acquainted with him and, indeed, with Vivien. For a time, John Rothenstein, whose home was near Oxford, lodged on weekdays with the Walstons in their flat at 6 St James's Street in London; in the autumn of 1945 he held a small party there at which Catherine met Graham Greene and spoke also with his friend the artist and politician John Hastings (16th Earl of Huntingdon, and father of the author Selina Hastings). On Good Friday 1946 Walston travelled from Cambridge to Oxford with the Rothensteins and the young Vincent Turner, SJ, who was giving her religious instruction, to spend the afternoon with the Greene family. On the way, she made her firm decision to become a Catholic.

In September 1946, Elizabeth Rothenstein wrote to Greene asking him to be Catherine's godfather. He was slow to respond, perhaps because he had gone to Paris for a romantic liaison with a French literary critic named Claudette Monde – Greene later told Walston about this affair, but no French critic of that name seems to have existed; either he was boasting to Walston or the woman was using a false name, as many did in the days of reprisals against *collabos*.[5] According to Catherine, the situation caused him to feel guilty so he delayed a response to Rothenstein's letter. It seems, also, that he regarded Catherine as a bit of Catholic business that Vivien could take care of. Greene did not attend her baptism and first communion, sending Vivien to represent him. He sent a delayed note of congratulations to Catherine on Eyre & Spottiswoode headed paper.[6]

With Elizabeth Rothenstein and the IRA man Ernie O'Malley, who was one of her lovers, Catherine visited the Greenes again in November: 'V was nervous and giggled ... G hardly spoke. Francis stood completely silent behind his head. V and I talked of Poland. G looked haunted and very sad. Left after 30 minutes. V asked if I knew a house near Cambridge. I promised to look.'[7] That Christmas, she sent the Greenes a turkey,[8] and in February called Vivien to tell her about a Queen Anne house in the village of Linton. The next day, with snow falling, Graham went with Catherine to look at it. He made the purchase soon after, but sold the house again without occupying it. Vivien resented the suddenness of his decision to buy this house without her seeing it too.[9] More important was what passed between Graham and Catherine. Having seen the house he faced a long journey back to Oxford, so she proposed an alternative, 'Why not fly? I'll come over with you & fly back.' It was just a forty-five-minute flight to Kidlington aerodrome, but something happened: 'A lock of hair touches one's eyes in a plane with East Anglia under snow, & one is in love ... '[10]

Greene's life was now knotted in the most extraordinary way. He was married to Vivien, living with Dorothy, purportedly involved with a possibly non-existent Claudette Monde, and in love with Catherine Walston. At the beginning of March he went to Amsterdam to buy paper for Eyre & Spottiswoode, and sent a cryptic postcard to Catherine: 'I love onion sandwiches. G.' The image would re-emerge in *The End of the Affair*: 'Is it possible to fall in love over a dish of onions? It seems improbable and yet I could swear it was just then that I fell in love. It wasn't, of course, simply the onions – it was that sudden sense of an individual woman, of a frankness that was so often later to make me happy and miserable. I put my hand under the cloth and laid it on her knee, and her hand came down and held mine in place.' In April, Greene went to Walston's cottage on Achill Island in County Mayo. He cut turf and worked on his novel, storing up idyllic memories of her whistling as she worked in the kitchen and of her tending the fire at night.[11] Their relationship would rarely be more happy.

Vivien was worried. She told Greene he had changed during his time in Ireland, but he thought she did not realize he was having an affair with Catherine Walston. He told Evelyn Waugh that he would like to find a house in Ireland, but that Vivien had a 'phobia' about the

Irish[12] – perhaps she was just wary of Graham living anywhere near Achill Island. He made a trip to Dublin in May, apparently accompanied by Vivien, to consider houses, and again in July when he stayed with Catherine at Achill. At about this time, he described himself as 'a cornered rat' and was talking about whether life insurance policies covered suicide.[13]

Greene's relationship with Dorothy was crumbling. She wanted to be the only woman in his life, and he would not agree to that. In August, their quarrels sometimes went late into the night, and Greene hoped she would just leave him. In September he arranged for her to take a three-month voyage along the West African coast where, in one of the ports, was a sea captain who carried a torch for her. However, the situation was not resolved until the following May when Graham and Dorothy took a short, hellish trip to Morocco, during which peace was obtained only from pipes of kif and watching naked dancers, and they finally agreed that he should no longer live at Gordon Square.[14]

Graham and Vivien took a comparably gloomy trip to New York in September, where he was negotiating, unsuccessfully, with *Life* magazine for a commission that would send to him to recently partitioned India – he hoped to be joined there by Catherine. In November, an amorous letter he had written to Catherine was returned to Beaumont Street. Vivien opened it and had final proof of the affair. She confronted Graham, and revealed all to his mother who took her side unreservedly.[15] Some months later Graham wrote to Vivien: ' . . . the fact that has to be faced, dear, is that by my nature, my selfishness, even in some degree by my profession, I should always, & with anyone, have been a bad husband. I think, you see, my restlessness, moods, melancholia, even my outside relationships, are symptoms of a disease & not the disease itself, & the disease, which has been going on ever since my childhood & was only temporarily alleviated by psycho-analysis, lies in a character profoundly antagonistic to ordinary domestic life. Unfortunately the disease is also one's material. Cure the disease & I doubt whether a writer would remain. I daresay that would be all to the good.'[16]

While formal terms of separation were being agreed, Vivien offered a divorce which Graham refused on the grounds that he would lose contact with the children.[17] Afterwards, she refused his requests for a divorce and an ecclesiastical annulment. In later years, the Jesuit literary scholar Father Alberto Huerta reportedly asked why she had done so and elicited the response, 'to punish him'.[18] Until her death in 2003, at the age of ninety-nine, Vivien continued to style herself 'Mrs Graham Greene'.

24

BANNED IN THE REPUBLIC OF IRELAND

With his private life in chaos, Greene was about to experience a string of professional triumphs. In July 1947, Heinemann published *Nineteen Stories*, including 'The Basement Room', which had first appeared in 1935. Korda paid £1000 for the rights to that story, conditional upon Greene working on the script, employment that would bring him another £2100 – his earnings on the film were double his annual salary as a publisher.[1] Eventually entitled *The Fallen Idol*, this was his first collaboration with Carol Reed,[2] one of the few directors whose work he had raved about when he was a film critic. Reed's most recent film was *Odd Man Out*, an atmospheric production about the last twenty-four hours in the life of a wounded IRA man. The penny-pinching executives at the Rank Organisation caused Reed so many problems that at the beginning of 1947 he bolted for Korda's London Film Productions, where he enjoyed large budgets and an unusual degree of artistic freedom. For his part, Reed treated Greene as a collaborator with perfect respect, doing everything he could to bring the author's intentions to the screen.[3]

At Korda's suggestion, Reed and Greene had met for lunch in May to discuss the possibility of making a film from the story. Initially, Greene thought it unlikely for film development because it was so bleak: a little boy admires a butler named Baines, who has a horrible marriage and becomes involved with a young woman; the butler eventually kills his wife and is caught because of a comment the boy makes to the police; in later life, the boy accomplishes nothing and eventually dies still haunted by the arrest of Baines. This was a characteristic plot for Graham Greene, since it involves the betrayal of a mentor or dominant friend. In their subsequent discussions they reworked the plot so that the death of Mrs Baines really is an accident, and the boy's remark to the police leads them rather to falsely suspect the butler, who is eventually cleared.

Around the end of July, the two men took connecting rooms at a hotel in Brighton, brought in a typist, and put the script together. Although Greene was on the payroll for six weeks, the most important work was done in about ten days. Not everything was to Greene's taste, of course: the overblown title was chosen by the distributor. He had to work hard to convince Reed to work into the script the boy's pet snake MacGregor, whom Mrs Baines destroys in a symbolic castration. With a handsome budget of £400,000 and a cast led by Ralph Richardson, Michèle Morgan, and the boy actor Bobby Henrey, Reed took advantage of the freedom given to him by Korda to create a quiet but enduring masterpiece of British cinema. The film won the British Academy Film Award for Best Picture,[4] and for his effort Graham Greene won the prize for best screenplay at the 1948 Venice Film Festival.

Having completed his draft of The Heart of the Matter in June 1947, he described it to his mother as 'a long and gloomy book. It depresses me even to write it! I don't know whether it comes off or not.'[5] He did some revision but was not ready to let it go. He told Catherine Walston that the last third was good, but that the whole book would have been if he had gone with her to Ireland two years earlier.[6]

Greene turned to John Hayward, whom Eliot had relied on for criticism when writing the Four Quartets, to judge whether the novel should be published.[7] An acquaintance from the 1930s, when Greene had first consulted him about the Earl of Rochester, Hayward became a much closer friend in the late 1940s. Greene had once been warned that Hayward's appearance was 'ugly' – muscular dystrophy confined him to a wheelchair, and he rejected the notion entirely: 'That powerful head ugly? that twist of the half paralysed arm, as the agile hand seized a cup or procured itself a cigarette? the wicked intelligence of the eyes? A cripple yes, but there are few men I can remember with greater vitality and with a greater appreciation of physical love.'[8] Hayward had fallen in love with Catherine Walston when he met her in 1941, calling her 'one of those tantalisingly beautiful American brunettes with a poise that would make a performing sea-lion jealous'.[9] From 1948, he became an occasional visitor to the Walstons' home in Cambridgeshire, where both Graham and Catherine helped him navigate the house and to perform personal tasks such as dressing – he described Graham as 'an admirable valet'.[10] Greene became devoted to Hayward, relishing his witty, sexy talk and his supply of gossip. In 1957, Greene took his side when Eliot abruptly left the flat the two men had shared for many years to marry Valerie Fletcher, seeing in it 'the moral cowardice of a sensitive man . . . '[11] Of course, that was a weakness he was well acquainted with, and it is the essence of Scobie, who accepts his own corruption to avoid giving pain.

As it turned out, John Hayward loved *The Heart of the Matter*,[12] and publication went ahead. Determined to avoid an old trap, Greene had it read for libel by a man who had been a senior administrator in Sierra Leone and afterwards maintained that none of the characters was based on living people, apart from an illiterate Syrian trader who was unlikely to sue.[13] This was not really true. We have seen how both Scobie and Father Rank were initially inspired by real people, even as Greene departed from those models as he went more deeply into the work. 'Literary Louise' refers to Scobie as 'Ticki' just as Vivien, a cat-lover, called Graham 'Tyg', though in this case the parallels between the person and the character are more complicated. Whether the harrowing accounts of night-time conversations between Scobie and Louise, compared to passing into and out of an emotional cyclone at the centre of which terrible truths are told, are close to any that passed between Graham and Vivien is a question that can no longer be answered. Indeed, Graham and Dorothy had some nocturnal quarrels and these may be part of the mix. Malcolm Muggeridge and Anthony Powell, who also served in intelligence during the war, felt confident that they could identify most of the minor characters in the book.[14] One measure Greene took to frustrate libel actions was to avoid naming the colony in which the novel was set.[15]

The Heart of the Matter was released in Britain on 27 May 1948 and in the United States two months later. A selection of the Book of the Month Club, a Book Society Choice, the *Evening Standard* Book of the Month, and winner of the James Tait Black Prize, it sold on a scale far beyond any of his earlier works – three hundred thousand copies within three years.[16] In a heaven-sent boost to international sales, it was briefly banned in the Republic of Ireland.

The reviews were spectacular. Typical among them was Richard Church's claim that Greene had a 'Dante-esque ... genius': 'Think of El Greco's long, emaciated and twisted figures, with their leper-white faces and agate eyes. They could walk into Graham Greene's books and be at home there.'[17] One review was decidedly and memorably negative. Writing for the *New Yorker*, George Orwell felt that Greene, who had written 'admirably' about Africa elsewhere, had made too little of the local people, their political concerns, colonial conflicts, and the context of war; he felt that Greene might as well have set the book in a 'London suburb'. Moreover, he felt that there was a spiritual 'snobbishness' in Greene's Catholicism: 'Hell is a sort of high-class night club, entry to which is reserved for Catholics only', since everyone else is invincibly ignorant and so spared. He found that Scobie's motivations are contradictory and improbable. Showing a snobbishness of his own, he complained that ordinary characters like Pinkie and Scobie were unlikely to be so focused on the possibility of their damnation: it is the result of 'foisting theological preoccupations upon simple people anywhere'.[18]

The theological foisting was actually occurring across the aisle. Many Catholic readers were asking whether Scobie is saved or damned. Having committed the mortal sin of adultery, compounded by sacrilege when he receives the Eucharist, and finally the supposedly unforgivable sin of suicide, the struggles of Scobie lifted the lid on an aspect of Catholic life. Many millions of Catholics lived with profound guilt and fear, owing to the 'sin of impurity', which included not just extramarital intercourse, but masturbation, and even sexual thoughts. A person who died in a state of mortal sin was understood to be literally damned. This was bad enough, but to commit sacrilege was utterly terrifying, so a great many church-going Catholics remained in their pews at communion, except after their occasional visits to the confessional. Anglicans sometimes wonder what all the fuss was about, but their Eucharist has a 'general absolution', which offers a quick scrub for the repentant. For Catholics, it was a different story.

In 1905, Pope Pius X, known otherwise for his suppression of 'modernist' theologians, issued a teaching that frequent, even daily, communion was desirable for Catholics. So there was nowhere to hide – if one did not go to the rail there was a reason for it. Late in the

The young Graham Greene, an outsider at school and a manic depressive, attempted suicide, spent six months undergoing psychoanalysis, then tried a form of Russian roulette.

Charles Greene, father of Graham and headmaster of Berkhamsted School. Young Graham was torn between his loyalty to his father and loyalty to the boys in his dormitory, and was traumatized.

Intellectual, elegant and remote, Marion Greene encouraged her son through a life he once described to her as 'Useless and sometimes miserable, but bizarre and on the whole not boring.'

The Greene siblings *c.* 1916 (from left to right): Graham, Raymond, Herbert (in uniform), Hugh, Molly and Elisabeth.

Graham and his brother Hugh, c. 1912.

Graham, at about twelve, in the greenhouses where his father grew rare orchids.

Berkhamsted School: Graham sits in the centre of the front row; Charles Greene sits in the centre of the second row, with Marion to his left.

Graham in a Balliol College blazer. He went up to Oxford at the age of eighteen and spent much of his time there 'in a general haze of drink'.

Graham's younger brother and closest friend, Hugh Carleton Greene, knighted in 1964, was a reforming Director-General of the BBC.

A physician and mountaineer, Graham's elder brother Raymond was part of a nearly successful attempt on Mount Everest in 1933.

Graham Greene, on the far right, with colleagues at *The Times* during the General Strike of 1926. When it was over, he lamented the end of free beer at the office.

Graham and his cousin Barbara Greene on their way to investigate slavery in Liberia in 1935. As a nurse, she was largely responsible for his surviving the jungle trek.

With money scarce in 1931, Graham and his wife Vivien rented Little Orchard Cottage in Chipping Campden, a house with no electricity and rats in the thatch.

In 1935, the Greenes moved to this Queen Anne house at 14 Clapham Common North Side. It was bombed during the Blitz.

Vivien Dayrell-Browning married Graham Greene on 15 October 1927. The marriage failed, largely owing to his repeated infidelities.

Graham and Vivien's daughter Lucy Caroline at her ranch in Alberta during the 1950s.

Graham and Vivien's son Francis at play, c. 1940.

Graham Greene and his lover Catherine Walston visiting the dressing room of Noël Coward at the Theatre Royal, Brighton, in May 1953. Coward was starring in Shaw's *The Apple Cart*.

Pouring drinks for John Hayward, Jocelyn Rickards and a friend

Anita Björk starred with Gregory Peck in the thriller *Night People* (1954) but then abandoned Hollywood and returned to Sweden, where she and Graham Greene had a three-year relationship.

novel Louise wants to know what is going on in Scobie's conscience so presses him to go with her to communion. '"Aren't you coming, dear?" Louise asked, and again the hand touched him: the kindly firm detective hand.' Failure to do it would indicate that he was in a state of mortal sin and so confirm her suspicions of adultery. When Seán O'Faoláin suggested that the situation of the novel was 'rigged' against Scobie, Greene seemed surprised and insisted that he had known such situations among many of his acquaintances.[19] The novel brought into the open an extraordinary desolation at work in the lives of Catholics. Many rather damaged priests and laypeople came to regard Graham Greene as someone who could help them with their personal problems; he hated this reputation and wished they would seek psychiatrists.

Some reviewers, such as Raymond Mortimer and Edward Sackville-West, considered whether Scobie might actually be a saint. Evelyn Waugh proposed that the conclusion of the book affirms the mystery that 'no one knows the secrets of the human heart or the nature of God's mercy'. He suggests that Greene regards him as a saint, but insists this does not matter, as what passes between Scobie and God is necessarily hidden.[20] In a letter to Waugh, Greene denied that he thought Scobie a saint, but there can be no doubt that he implicitly planted the question in the novel. The book's epigraph, taken from Péguy, claims that the sinner is at the heart of Christianity and that only the saint knows more about Christianity. Following Péguy, Greene has narrowed the gap between sinner and saint. Curiously enough, at his death, Scobie drops a medal of 'the saint whose name nobody could remember'. This gesture could indicate either that he has lost the protection of heaven or that he himself has become one of the blest, another of the anonymous saints. After its publication, Greene spent a good deal of time pretending that he had written an altogether different book from the one his very best readers were drawing obvious conclusions about. He was covering his tracks.

Traditional moralists smelt sulphur. Responding to Waugh, Canon Joseph Cartmell agreed that no one knows whether a person is damned, but speaks of Scobie as 'a very bad moral coward'. He said that the only good that came of Scobie's death 'was a negative one, the removal of himself as a source of sin'.[21] Another theologian, Father John P. Murphy, concluded that Scobie feared two women more than he feared God.[22]

William Brown, the Bishop of Southwark, denounced the book on the grounds that 'adultery is adultery' and endorsed the actions of the Irish censors.[23] Greene had able defenders, among them the author and broadcaster Father C. C. Martindale, SJ, and Christopher Butler, OSB, the Abbot of Downside, who would later be a leading figure at the Second Vatican Council. Both made the case that the book was consistent with good theology, and Greene thanked them for their efforts. The exchanges rumbled on all summer in the pages of various Catholic magazines and newspapers, after which the question of whether Scobie is a saint finally migrated to scholarly journals.

Of course, there can be many grounds on which to fault a book other than moral theology. In September, Heinemann forwarded to Greene a letter from the makers of Elastoplast, complaining that the novel referred to their product with a lower-case e, which was bad for business. Also, since the book presents Elastoplast as somehow inferior to an ordinary bandage, they volunteered a member of their medical department to explain to the author the superior merits of their product.[24] Greene ignored this golden opportunity to stretch his mind.

25

LIME

One evening in late September 1947, Greene went out for a solitary dinner and drink, and then restlessly walked along Piccadilly and into a public lavatory in Brick Street, where he suddenly had the idea for what would become *The Third Man*.[1] He wrote a single sentence on the flap of an envelope: 'I had paid my last farewell to Harry a week ago, when his coffin was lowered into the frozen February ground, so that it was with incredulity that I saw him pass by, without a sign of recognition, among the host of strangers in the Strand.'[2]

At a dinner soon after, Korda asked him to write a new film for Carol Reed to direct, so he suggested a story begun along these lines. Korda was actually thinking of a comedy-thriller, but was content for the two men to work on Greene's idea. However, he wanted the film set not in London but Vienna, which was then divided into four zones occupied by the British, French, American, and Russian armies.[3] He had money in Austria which he could not get out owing to currency regulations but which could be used to pay for a production there.[4]

Korda paid Greene £1000, and would later pay him £3000 more for his work on this project.[5] He sent him to Vienna in mid-February, arranging a room for him at the Sacher Hotel, which was then exclusively reserved for officers of the occupation – the excellent kitchen was largely supplied with meat and vegetables by young women working the black market.[6] On his first day, he saw the enormous central cemetery and knew that it should be used in the opening of the film. The city itself was in a desperate state, with piles of rubble everywhere and people struggling to find the basics of life. It was a setting perfectly suited to Greene's imagination.

Unable to organize his plot beyond the phoney funeral, he explored night clubs, strip joints, the Josefstadt theatre, the Prater amusement park with its great Ferris wheel, and many other spots that might be suitable for filming, but more than anything he needed to decide exactly what Harry Lime's racket was and how he was pursuing it. He says that he found the solution after a lunchtime conversation with Colonel Charles Beauclerk, the future Duke of St Albans, a contact from SIS and now an official in the British zone, who told the novelist an amusing story about the 'underground police': when he learned of their existence he assumed they were secret police and ordered them to be shut down. Finding later that they were still operating, he was annoyed that his orders had been disobeyed. It was explained to him that these men really did work underground, patrolling the large system of sewers through which spies and criminals could move between the zones. Beauclerk also told Greene that there was an illicit trade in penicillin, often diluted or adulterated, and potentially causing great harm to those who received it. Greene says that Beauclerk took him on a tour of the sewers, and it was then that he worked out the final shape of his story.[7]

However, there was another source for Greene's information on sewers and penicillin. One of Korda's employees, Elizabeth Montagu, who had worked in American intelligence, arranged for Greene to speak with *The Times* correspondent Peter Smollett. Born Hans Smolka in Austria, he changed his name in England, and became a highly regarded journalist, once considered by David Astor as a possible editor of the *Observer*.[8] During the war he served in the Russian department of the Ministry of Information, where he may have crossed paths with Graham Greene. He was, however, a Russian spy and a close associate of Philby and Burgess.[9] Greene read some pieces Smollett had written about the sewers, police patrols, and the penicillin trade. When she read Greene's early draft, Montagu was concerned that there might be a claim of plagiarism so she pressed to have Smollett signed to a contract. Although not credited, he was paid about £200 and was satisfied.[10]

Elizabeth Bowen came to Vienna to deliver a lecture on the English novel, so Greene invited her out to dinner at the very seedy Oriental night club, and once there predicted that there would be a police raid at midnight, something he had learned through his 'contacts'. Loving practical jokes, he had, in fact, made an arrangement with Beauclerk for just such a raid to occur. At exactly midnight, a British sergeant, accompanied by representatives of each of the other three powers, came into the night club; the sergeant went straight to Bowen demanding to see her passport. Greene later wrote: 'She looked at me with respect . . .'[11]

Greene was supposed to begin writing immediately, but that month there was a new European crisis, this time in Czechoslovakia, and, perhaps prompted by MI6, he wanted to see it.[12] Surprisingly, his brief foray there became in 2017 the subject of an engaging, though fanciful, graphic novel.[13] Despite a snow storm, he flew on 23 February 1948 to Prague, where the Communist Party under Prime Minister Klement Gottwald was carrying out a coup in order to avoid scheduled elections. The police force had been purged of non-communists and was arresting opponents of the party. Demonstrations and a strike put pressure on the president, Edvard Beneš, so he accepted the resignations of a group of non-communist cabinet ministers, giving full control of the government to Gottwald and his party on 25 May, a landmark event in the Soviet takeover of Eastern Europe.

Greene witnessed some of the demonstrations, visited his publishers and agents, and on one occasion found the office of his Catholic publisher under armed guard. Egon Hostovský, one of whose novels he had published in translation at Eyre & Spottiswoode,[14] worked in the Foreign Ministry, and spoke of how the minister, Jan Masaryk, the last non-communist in the cabinet, had said farewell to his staff. Two weeks later, on 10 March, Masaryk was thrown to his death from a high window in the ministry.[15] Czechoslovakia would remain close to Greene's heart, and he eventually numbered among his friends the novelist Josef Škvorecký and the playwright and future president Václav Havel.

Making his way to Antibes, Greene boarded Korda's yacht, the *Elsewhere*, for a journey down the coast of Italy. This craft was a converted Royal Fairmile torpedo boat, lengthened to about 120 feet and given a rounded stern[16] – Greene would sail on it often in the years to come. Among the passengers for this excursion were Carol Reed, Randolph and Pamela Churchill, and Vivien Leigh.

Vincent Korda's fifteen-year-old son, Michael, was overwhelmed by the company until a tall, sandy-haired man handed him a pre-lunch cocktail. "'Go on,' he said. "It's a martini. It can do you no possible harm. I'm Graham Greene, by the way.'"[17] There grew up an alliance between the two, as if in opposition to the world of adults, which at that moment was manifesting itself especially in the noisy, drunken talk of Randolph Churchill. Greene fixed his eyes on Churchill as on a zoo animal, and said, 'The great advantage of being a writer is that you can *spy* on people. *Everything* is useful to a writer, you see, every scrap . . .'[18] Young Korda was in awe and shortly after decided that he too must become a writer, and so he did – a novelist, memoirist, biographer, historian, and publisher. Greene offered him advice on sex, and took him to a brothel in Nice and to a bar in Genoa where sailors wore drag and one sang in creditable imitation of the American comedian Sophie Tucker.[19]

Michael Korda witnessed the early work on the script, with his uncle Alex, Reed, and Greene holding laborious conferences on deck – and getting nowhere. There was that first sentence and not much else. They reached Capri, once the resort of the emperors Augustus and Tiberius and now an enclave of artists, writers, and intellectuals. Sipping his drink and watching the sun set over the island, Greene remarked within Alex's hearing, 'I should give anything to own a villa there'. The next morning at breakfast, the novelist unfolded his napkin and a large rusty skeleton key fell out. Greene asked what it was, and Alex replied, 'It's the key to a villa in Anacapri. Quite a nice one. I had myself taken ashore late last night in the motor launch. I bought a villa. It's in your name, dear boy. Now the rest of my story, please!' Not surprisingly, things came together very quickly after that.[20]

Korda had problems with currency regulations and Greene hated income tax, so some of their transactions, such as this one, were in kind. The compact Villa Rosaio on Via Ceselle in Anacapri, a commune in the upper part of the island, had been occupied at different times by the novelists Francis Brett Young and Compton Mackenzie.[21] It was, in fact, two tiny peasant houses renovated and turned into one by the town's enterprising former mayor Edwin Cerio, an engineer and author who became a friend of Greene's, as did his daughter, the artist Laetitia Cerio. With its vaulted construction, it is a notable example of the vernacular architecture of the island.[22] Each of the little houses had a double and a single bedroom, and a bathroom; one had a kitchen, dining room, and living room.[23] The villa also had a small rooftop patio, where the novelist often sat. It offered him a quiet place to write, as well as privacy in which to entertain Catherine. Under the imprint 'Rosaio Press', he soon printed, in only twenty-five copies, a collection of love poems for her, *After Two Years*.[24] For each of the next forty years he would spend a month or two on Capri, and was named an honorary citizen of Anacapri.

While in Capri in March 1948, Greene and Korda had discussions with the travel writer Norman Douglas about making a film of his novel *South Wind*, a hedonistic satire set in a fictionalized version of the island. When it came out in 1917, it had been a scandalous bestseller, admired by Greene and many of his generation.[25] A friend of Joseph Conrad and many other writers, Douglas had a history of paedophilia which forced him to stay away from Britain for fear of the law. The film project went no further than a first treatment,[26] but Greene, with characteristic sympathy for the disgraced, grew fond, even protective, of the eighty-year-old Douglas, as well as of the novelist Kenneth Macpherson and the photographer Islay de Courcy Lyons who lived with him. Suffering from a painful skin disease, Douglas hastened his own death in 1952 with an overdose. As final attempts were made to keep him alive, he reportedly muttered, 'Get those fucking nuns away from me.'[27]

Greene was not usually able to sit down and simply write a script. His own writing process required him first to create the story as a short novel – just as *The Tenth Man* was supposed to be the basis of a script. Many years later he wrote: 'My film story, *The Third Man*, was never written to be read but only to be seen.'[28] This is just wrong. In early January 1948, he told Mary Pritchett, his American agent, that he planned an entertainment of the sort he had written in the past, perhaps thirty or forty thousand words, and asked what would be an ideal length for serial publication. He told her he would write it as 'straight fiction', to be turned into a script only 'if approved' by the film-makers.[29] It was always intended to be a book, which he finished on 2 June 1948. It then went through four revisions as a script by the autumn.[30] Published in 1950, the novella of *The Third Man* represented an early version of the story. Greene had control of the story throughout, and felt that the contribution of Carol Reed was wholly positive so that the story was better finally on the screen than it was on the page.[31]

After his difficult holiday in Morocco with Dorothy, and a short visit to New York to sort out contracts, Greene returned to Vienna around 20 June 1948, this time with Carol Reed and other members of Korda's organization to scout locations. The city had been tidied up since February. Restaurants were beginning to offer more than gruel, and a pile of rubble in front of the Café Mozart ('Old Vienna' in the film) had been carted away. He said to Reed: 'But I assure you Vienna was really like that – three months ago.'[32] It was as if Greeneland were being erased by the Marshall Plan.

Back in London, Greene and Reed continued their script conferences, which involved Greene walking endlessly about the room and the two men, from time to time, acting out scenes. Not even Korda was allowed to take part in the work. They did, however, have to face David O. Selznick, best known as the producer of *Gone with the Wind*. Korda's business had fallen apart during the war, and his co-production and American distribution agreements with Selznick kept his firm afloat. To meet his obligations to Selznick, he sent Greene and Reed to California in mid-August for script conferences.[33] Greene first told Catherine that he liked him 'enormously'[34] – that would change. Some of his suggestions made sense, such as making both Holly Martins and Harry Lime American. Indeed, he was anxious that the film should appeal to American taste and not provoke the censor. But his efforts to modify, and in fact seize control of, the film were relentless. He disliked the title, and in a memorable exchange he attacked the probability of the story, asking why did Martins stay in Vienna after learning of Lime's (first) death? Greene pointed out that he had fallen in love with a woman and been punched by a policeman, but Selznick dismissed this, judging instead that the film's narrative was based on one man's affection for another: 'It won't do, boys, it won't do. It's sheer buggery.'[35]

Graham Greene had a Homeric tolerance for liquor. He could, and regularly did, drink vast quantities without evident effect. However, drinking, some drug use, exhaustion, and extreme stress caught up with him on 21 August 1948, on the way back from California. An hour before he was to board his flight from New York to London, he suffered a haemorrhage in his urinary tract. Admitted to the Medical Arts Center, he remained very ill for twenty-four hours and wondered whether he would become impotent. After various tests, the doctors merely forbade him to drink for ten days and gave him a barbiturate for the flight home. The actor Ralph Bellamy, who wanted to do a stage production of *The Heart of the Matter*, brought him a copy of Aldous Huxley's latest novel, *Ape and Essence*, to read on his flight. Greene despised the book, after which the sedative must have come as a blessing.[36]

Through the rest of the film project, Korda deflected Selznick's many suggestions and then protests. Selznick did agree to the casting of Joseph Cotten and Alida Valli, but objected to Reed's choice of Orson Welles, suggesting, instead, Noël Coward. Korda politely insisted on Welles, who was annoyed with Korda for cancelling other projects so had his own fun by dodging from one Italian city to another with Korda's brother Vincent on his heels with instructions to get him back to London. At some risk to his own business, Alexander Korda allowed Greene and Reed to make the film largely as they wanted to.[37]

The film brought together some extraordinary artists, among them the Australian cinematographer Robert Krasker, who was responsible for the tilted camera angles and shadowy effects. Reed discovered the zither player Anton Karas, whose Harry Lime theme became an international hit and popularized an instrument most people had never heard of. The cast included a group of distinguished Austrian actors, including Hedwig Bleibreu as the landlady. Joseph Cotton, Alida Valli, and Trevor Howard all turned in superb performances.

But there was something miraculous about Welles. From the moment a cat toys with his shoelace and the light from an open window catches his face, he dominates the film. Martin Scorsese thinks this scene 'might be the best revelation – or the best reveal, as they say – in all of cinema'.[38] Some words Orson Welles contributed were among the most memorable in a script where everything is memorable: 'After all it's not that awful. You know what the fellow says – in Italy, for thirty years under the Borgias, they had warfare, terror, murder, and bloodshed, but they produced Michelangelo, Leonardo da Vinci, and the Renaissance. In Switzerland, they had brotherly love, they had five hundred years of democracy and peace – and what did that produce? The cuckoo clock. So long, Holly!' This extraordinary speech caused Welles some awkwardness, as he explained to Peter Bogdanovich: '... the Swiss very nicely pointed out that they've never made any cuckoo clocks!' It was the Germans who invented them.[39]

Greene finished his script by the end of September, and location filming in Vienna ran from late October until December, followed by studio shooting in England, which finished in March.[40] The film opened in London on 2 September 1949, and almost immediately after took the Grand Prix du Festival at Cannes. An American version re-edited by Selznick was released in February 1950. With its predilection for honouring the second best, the Academy could only scrape up three Oscar nominations for the film: Reed for best director, Oswald Hafenrichter for editing, and Krasker, the sole winner, for black-and-white cinematography. In May, The Third Man won the British Film Academy Award for Best British Film. It remains one of the finest films ever made.

26

A PIECE OF GRIT

Three years was about as long as Graham Greene could bear a desk job, and he no longer needed the one he had at Eyre & Spottiswoode. Douglas Jerrold had reneged on the arrangement for him to retire and leave full control of the firm to Greene. The pot called the kettle black when Greene complained to his mother in June 1947 of Jerrold being unstable. At the end of that year, Greene told Catherine Walston that he would like to leave in six months.[1] He stayed longer and the departure was messy.

In early 1946, Greene had bid high for Anthony Powell's *John Aubrey and His Friends*, a biography, in order to get a further deal for three novels. At a lunch at the Authors' Club in mid-September 1948, Powell complained that the biography was still not published, and the two got into a row. Greene dismissed the book as boring, and immediately accepted Powell's request to cancel the fiction contract. Malcolm Muggeridge was present at the lunch and remarked in his journal on Greene's appetite for conflict. Indeed, Greene had once told Muggeridge that rows were nearly a 'physical necessity' for him.[2] Jerrold rejected the notion that Greene could simply cancel the contract, as it was one of the firm's assets, so Greene resigned. He casually invited Powell for drinks shortly after, but Powell, not so easily assuaged, did not speak to him again for twelve years.[3]

Money was no longer an issue. He was able to establish Vivien and the children in the spacious Grove House at Iffley Turn in Oxford, a Regency villa which, though it needed initial repairs, served as Vivien's home for the rest of her life. Graham himself moved into a flat at 5 St James's Street, directly adjoining one occupied by Catherine and Harry Walston, and this was his London residence until 1953. Although this sounds like they were all together in a lovers' commune, in fact Greene and the Walstons were seldom in residence at the same time. In 1948 he purchased – or perhaps it was again payment in kind from Korda – the *Nausikaa*, a 32-foot double-ended cutter which he docked at Lymington in Hampshire, in the mistaken hope that he and Catherine might use it often. He took Francis and Caroline sailing, and on a few occasions friends such as the Dominican priest Thomas Gilby, then sold it in late 1949.[4]

His ties to England were gradually being loosened. Frequently visiting Paris, he basked in a new kind of glory. He wrote to Catherine in late January 1949: 'It's all too fantastic. My books in every shop – a whole display in the Rue de Rivoli. Three different people writing books on me for three different publishers. The Professor of English at the Sorbonne has asked me to lecture & says that he can fill the hall twice over.' Priests were fussing over him. Magazines were looking for interviews. Graduate students were parsing his world view: 'I'd really be rather enjoying it if I believed it, but I don't, quite . . . commonsense tells me it's all a joke that will soon pass. But I wish you could see the joke too. I'd love to preen my feathers in front of you.'[5]

With the death of Denyse Clairouin at Mauthausen in 1945, Greene's business in France had been taken over by her younger colleague, Marie Schebeko (later Biche), a Russian with command of many languages. She became an important, if hitherto little-known, figure in Greene's life. Her manner was formidable, even disconcerting, possibly owing to a blue-eyed gaze that was off-centre.

She was warm-hearted, discreet, and extremely devoted to those closest to her. Although a private person, she became one of Greene's closest friends, and, surprisingly, an intimate of Harry Walston. She remained Greene's French agent until about 1977, managing most of his business on the Continent.

Greene's most important admirer in France was François Mauriac, who would win the Nobel Prize in Literature in 1952. While at Eyre & Spottiswoode, Greene had arranged for Muggeridge to negotiate with Mauriac so that they became his English publishers.[6] Greene's own standing in France owed a great deal to a tribute Mauriac paid to his work in *Le Figaro* in October 1948. After they had both appeared at a conference the following May, Greene wrote to him: 'Please believe that though I am no longer your English publisher, I am your admirer, your disciple & your friend.'[7] Both novelists had found their best subject in the agonized Catholic conscience,[8] but they saw things differently. Privately, Greene thought himself the better novelist – he was probably right. Moreover, Mauriac dreaded that his work might glamorize sin; he thought that the writer's dilemma was to show the evil in human nature without causing the reader to be tempted. Greene could not care less about this.

In a friendly debate about the writing of novels with Elizabeth Bowen and V. S. Pritchett, broadcast on the BBC Third Programme in 1948 and then published as a pamphlet, Greene specifically distanced himself from Mauriac's position, saying that although he did feel pressure from the church to be edifying, he was saved from this by his 'disloyalty'.[9] His views were obviously shaped by the battering he was taking from priests and theologians over the morality of *The Heart of the Matter*. In 1969, he would return to this topic in a famous lecture entitled 'The Virtue of Disloyalty', delivered upon receiving the Shakespeare Prize from the University of Hamburg. In it, he argues that writers must often be disloyal to their countries or to the prevailing systems of belief in order to 'enlarge the bounds of sympathy in our readers'. It suited Greene intellectually and temperamentally to be a 'piece of grit' in the machine.[10]

27

POINTS OF DEPARTURE

'Mass at 12 at Farm Street where I met the shambling, unshaven and as it happened quite penniless figure of Graham Greene. Took him to the Ritz for a cocktail and gave him 6d for his hat. He had suddenly been moved by love of Africa and emptied his pockets into the box for African missions.'[1] Evelyn Waugh had known Greene since Oxford, though they had moved in different circles there. They had contact from time to time in the thirties, and Waugh had been a contributor to *Night and Day*. The friendship grew much closer after the war, when both Waugh, with *Brideshead Revisited*, and Greene, with *The Heart of the Matter*, found themselves lofted into literary and religious celebrity. Greene's attitude towards Waugh was strikingly humble: he always spoke of him as the best writer of their generation. He commented to James Salter in 1975: 'In the Mediterranean you can see a pebble fifteen feet down. His style was like that.'[2]

Just as Greene grew uncomfortable with *The Heart of the Matter*, Waugh told Greene in 1950 that although he liked the plot of *Brideshead Revisited*, the book, in its original form, was the product of 'spam, Nissen huts, black-out' and not suitable for peacetime.[3] After initial admiration, Greene wavered in his view of this novel, but many years later decided firmly that it was an outstanding work, and indeed Waugh's finest.[4] For his part, Waugh looked to Greene as the one person who might produce a decent screenplay of the novel. In the summer of 1950, Greene tentatively agreed with David O. Selznick, whom he now regarded as a fool, to take on the job.[5] However, Waugh lost heart about the whole business.

Along with respect for each other's craft, the two converts had a damaged Catholicism in common. Apart from his own complicated sexual history, Waugh had needed an ecclesiastical annulment of his marriage to Evelyn Gardner ('she-Evelyn' to his 'he-Evelyn') before he could marry Laura Herbert in 1937. He seems to have believed that more dangerous than sexual sins were his own lapses of charity, and some of these achieved Olympic standards, as when he wrote to Laura in 1945 about their first son: 'I have regretfully come to the conclusion that the boy Auberon is not yet a suitable companion for me.'[6] Although a very conservative Catholic, he refused to sit in judgement on Greene and Walston, inviting them to stay at his home, Piers Court.[7]

Harry Walston did not like Waugh, but Catherine invited him to their home at Thriplow in Cambridgeshire, where he was astonished by the profusion of the place and recalled seeing Picassos on the wall, though, in fact, the Walstons did not possess any. He also marvelled at the freewheeling conversation, in which, for example, the children's nanny Beatrice Ball, known as 'Twinkle',[8] might discuss masturbation and incest with her employers and their guests at the dinner table.[9] Waugh found the unaffected Catherine entertaining, but he was not accustomed to hostesses going barefoot and it may have been on account of this that he questioned her sanity.[10]

Waugh thought there was something that set Graham Greene apart – that he had an 'apostolic mission' that many Catholics might fail to understand because of the sexual content of his books.[11] He did not mean that in some vague secular sense Greene had a writer's vocation, but that he had been literally sent out in the manner of the apostles. Despite leading a 'disordered' life, Greene had a surprising effect on Catholics. Hovering on the edges of the church, his old friend Edith Sitwell, who converted some years later, wrote to him in 1945: 'I said before, but I repeat it, what a great priest you would have made. But you are better as you are.'[12] She felt that he understood sin and redemption in a way the clergy did not. In May 1948, she read *The Heart of the Matter* and wrote to a Catholic friend: 'Have you read Graham Greene's new book? It may prevent me from committing suicide!!'[13]

Greene continued to go to confession occasionally and entertained an agonized hope that one day he might live a faithful and orderly life married to Catherine – indeed, the two privately exchanged marriage vows during a Mass at Tunbridge Wells.[14] He took advice from canon lawyers and concluded that he had grounds for an annulment from

Vivien, but was stymied as she was now even more opposed to an annulment than to a divorce.[15] In the early days of Graham's affair with Catherine, there had been a wild hopefulness mixed in with all the guilt, but by mid-1949 Catherine showed no real signs of leaving Harry. In her correspondence with Graham she wanted him to speak of 'liking' rather than 'loving' her. Despite having got along well with him for two years, Harry was beginning to find the novelist a pest and a threat to his household. There was a crisis in July, when Harry told Graham he must not speak to Catherine any more. At the same time, Greene received a letter from the outspoken Twinkle, advising him that he was too demanding of Catherine's time.[16] The row was smoothed over, but he was very unhappy.

There was plenty of gossip about Graham and Catherine. A wise-crack went around that they had made love behind all the high altars of Europe. Father Vincent Turner, SJ, who had instructed Catherine for reception into the church, remarked at the end of the summer that her personality was 'corrupting'. When he heard of this Graham wrote to her, 'Can't these people get it into their heads, after all this time, that we aren't having a flippant thoughtless fuck, that we love each other sufficiently seriously for it to be a problem that deserves their sympathy?'[17]

Greene's yearning for Walston found little relief, except in liquor and in work. While in Paris in mid-December, he went for a walk after Mass and found himself sobbing in the Tuileries Gardens.[18] A month later, she conveyed to him the details of a shattering quarrel she had had with Harry, so he wrote up a detailed plan for her to leave England and join him in Capri while divorces, annulments, and child custody were settled.[19] Though her feelings for Graham were very strong, Catherine was not going to risk running off with him. His pleas forced her into a firm and devastating refusal.

Over the past two years, Greene had at least enjoyed professional tri-umphs to set against private frustration. But now, in the autumn and winter of 1949–50, he was involved in a failure. Basil Dean, the pro-ducer with whom he had worked on the film *Twenty-One Days* in 1936, collaborated with him on a dramatization of *The Heart of the Matter*, with Dean working mainly on structure and Greene on dialogue.[20]

From the earliest stage of the work, he was driving himself with Benzedrine and then looking for sleep with the barbiturate Nembutal. In early December, the two men visited Freetown to gather images for sets, and Graham wrote to Catherine about how, if he could not have her, he would like to live and work in West Africa. In February, Rodgers and Hammerstein put together a production of the play in Boston, with plans to take it to New York, but there were problems with the script and, according to Greene, Basil Dean was arguing with everyone. Although swarmed by sympathetic press who might have skewered the play, Greene had little hope for the production.[21] At the beginning of March Rodgers and Hammerstein withdrew the play for revision and it was never brought back to the stage.

In the meantime, Greene was going through a crisis, worse than the one in Paris before Christmas. On 28 February he wrote to Catherine that he was 'desperate', and had been crying in bed. He required pills to sleep even as little as three or four hours. He was close to taking his own life, but he could not go out a failure: 'I'd raise the price for anybody with a gun now to 5000. I look at the Nembutal with such longing, but people would say it was because I'd written a flop.'[22] At some point in his adult life, probably in the 1950s, he did attempt suicide, mixing three-quarters of a pint of whisky with a quarter-bottle of gin and ten aspirins. With his usual flippancy, he claimed to have slept it off with pleasant dreams.[23]

Greene returned briefly to England before going for two weeks to Goslar in Lower Saxony, a town near the border of East and West Germany. With the help of a British intelligence officer,[24] he was researching a story he had pitched to Korda in January, and was evidently accompanied for part of the time by Carol Reed.[25] To be called 'No Man's Land', the proposed film would follow *The Third Man* by setting events in zones of occupation along a dangerous frontier. The Russians were particularly watchful of the Harz Mountains in northern Germany as they were thought to contain deposits of uranium.[26]

In the story, Catholic pilgrims are coming in large numbers to a grotto in the mountains to see a holy woman modelled on the German mystic and stigmatic Therese Neumann.[27] An Englishman named Richard Brown slips into the Russian zone, posing as a pilgrim but actually searching for his half-brother, a vanished spy named Kramer.

He falls in love with the woman who, under torture, is responsible for the capture and death of Kramer. By betraying the trust of a lenient Russian official they escape, having recovered a microfilm about the mines which Kramer had hidden in a candle in the grotto. The couple return to the West and get married, but the place of pilgrimage is deemed a threat to security and shut down.[28] Greene wrote a fifteen-thousand-word version of the story that spring,[29] but he and Korda agreed in September that it needed much more work before going into production[30] – it was eventually abandoned.

While in Goslar, he remained desolate, writing to Catherine, 'I pray every night for you or death – I'd prefer the first, but the second would be a good second-best.'[31] He prayed repeatedly each day to St Thérèse that his true vocation to love Catherine not be lost and also sought comfort in reading the works of the eighteenth-century Jesuit Jean-Pierre de Caussade, who is best remembered for his teachings on resignation to providence. In these years he often read spiritual masters, among them Baron von Hügel, author of *The Mystical Element of Religion* (1908). Although he later changed his mind about Thomas Merton, he read the Trappist's autobiography *The Seven Storey Mountain* (1948) with great admiration and wrote a cover endorsement for it. He shared such reading with Catherine, who was strongly attracted to the Catholic mystical tradition, and made the case to her that all of the great events of their relationship were part of God's plan.[32]

One friend thought Greene was missing the point about his own vocation. Father C. C. Martindale, SJ, was fifteen years older than the novelist and a calming influence. Like his friend Teilhard de Chardin, SJ, who brought the theory of evolution into theology, Martindale was, by the standards of the time, a bold thinker, and so regarded with some suspicion by church authorities.[33] He had publicly tangled with theologians denouncing *The Heart of the Matter* in the summer of 1948. Knowing what kinds of personal trouble the novelist got himself into, Martindale nonetheless thought he discerned a calling in Graham Greene's life: to write about what is present in the lives of most saints, 'a black tunnel, in which he/she experiences terrific interior hate, lust, above all dis-belief – or something equivalent'. The job for Greene was 'to show how *real* holiness can coexist with real imperfection (e.g. greed; cowardice; snobbishness), and perhaps to do so is your vocation'.

Perceptively, he urged Greene not to be 'seduced by money' from the cinema.[34] He urged him to put order into his existence, live more simply, and look for the real meaning of his life in his writing.

Raymond Greene spoke with Catherine in early April, and concluded that she would never leave Harry for Graham, even though she felt a 'responsibility' towards him. Graham was causing trouble for her with Harry and she found that his physical demands were overwhelming. Graham asked her if all this was accurate, and she told him plainly that she could not begin a new life with him by abandoning her children.[35] At this point, they declared a 'sabbatical' in their relationship.[36] Although things were strained, they came together again in Paris before the month was out.

Greene knew that he suffered from a mental illness – he had said so to Vivien after the break-up of their marriage (see p. 171, above). Most of those who knew him well thought so too. When asked to predict what Greene might be writing in twenty years' time, his old friend the novelist Edward Sackville-West (later 5th Baron Sackville) replied: 'Oh, Graham will have committed suicide by then.'[37] With Catherine herself embarking on a course of psychoanalysis,[38] Greene agreed to meet with a psychiatrist named Eric Strauss. This was an inspired choice, and Strauss was essential to keeping Greene alive through the next hellish decade.

A Jew of Austrian descent who converted to Catholicism, Strauss was one of Britain's leading psychiatrists and a therapist of unfailing practicality. Having attained the rank of captain in the Middlesex Regiment in the First World War, he read modern languages at New College, Oxford, with a view to becoming a diplomat, but then switched to medicine. He was particularly influenced by time spent in Marburg studying under the psychiatrist Ernst Kretschmer, some of whose work he translated into English. A man of broad culture, Strauss composed music and was an amateur actor. Most of his medical career was spent at St Bartholomew's Hospital in London, where he became a pioneer in the use of electro-shock therapy.[39] His frequent collaborator, the wonderfully named neurologist Russell Brain (eventually created Baron Brain), wrote of Strauss: 'He stressed "the principle of multiple causality", by which he meant that no explanation of a psychological disorder is adequate which does not take into account the part played in its causation by the mind, the body, the inherited constitution, and the social environment of the sufferer; and he criticized the Freudians for laying undue stress on the psychological compared with other causal factors. He found support for his holistic approach in the Thomistic teaching on the nature of man, and he applied it in his practice . . .[40] Strauss hated easy answers. Although a fervent Catholic, he believed that spirituality had a good deal to learn from psychiatry; at the end of his life, according to Philip Caraman, SJ, he was working on a study of the fifteenth-century mystic Margery Kempe as an authentic saint afflicted with mental illness, and hoped also to write a psychiatric interpretation of St Paul.[41]

Greene was initially reluctant to see Strauss, suggesting that what he really needed was 'deep analysis', but he was also desperate, praying, at a friend's suggestion, to St Jude, the patron of lost causes.[42] Greene met Strauss twice in the first week of May and three times in the second. It was not what he expected. Straightaway, Greene asked for shock therapy. Despite being its main advocate in Britain, Strauss refused: 'Bear with your depression another fortnight. Meanwhile start writing down what you remember of your childhood.' Greene did so and his depression lightened. After twenty years in his drawer, this long 'screed' provided him with the opening pages of A Sort of Life.[43] Although lithium was used to relieve bipolar illness from the 1950s,[44] there is no evidence that Greene received that treatment. In fact, nothing ever worked better for Greene than laying pen to paper, as he put it in 1980: 'Writing is a form of therapy; sometimes I wonder how all those who do not write, compose or paint can manage to escape the madness, the melancholia, the panic fear which is inherent in the human situation.'[45]

Greene soon came to think of Strauss as a kind of a 'saint', even though he found the sessions with him difficult.[46] Strauss evidently diagnosed manic depression, a term that Greene then used to describe himself.[47] By the end of June, Strauss told him that his love for Catherine was unreasonably intense, and would thereafter hold to the view that the relationship should end.[48] Greene was annoyed by this, and sometimes put Strauss's opposition to the affair down to his being homosexual,[49] but he continued to consult the psychiatrist for another decade, their therapeutic relationship and close friendship ending only with Strauss's death in 1961.

Greene and Walston spent about four weeks together in France in the early summer of 1950. It seems that she also came later to visit Greene in Anacapri, leaving in early July.[50] In August, Greene sailed with Alex Korda on the *Elsewhere* in the Adriatic, then to Athens, and finally up the Rhône. Among those on board, again, was Michael Korda, for whom Greene now had a great affection. Michael Korda recalls how Greene worked: sitting on deck, he would write a precisely counted five hundred words, and stop wherever he was, even in the middle of a sentence, until the next day. Korda supposed that this discipline gave Greene something he could govern amidst the chaos of life.[51] A bad typist, Greene wrote his stories in longhand, usually in a notebook with a Parker 51 fountain pen. By the early 1950s, he used a Dictaphone for all but his most personal correspondence; when abroad, he would post the Dictabelts to his secretary, Doris Young, in the St James's flats where she worked for both Greene and Harry Walston. Young (and her successors) would type the contents of the belts onto already-signed sheets of letterhead. This practice led to the creation of carbon copies of the tens of thousands of letters Greene wrote over four decades, now preserved in an archive at Boston College. At some point, Greene took to reading the longhand versions of his novels into the Dictaphone as well.

During the 1950 cruise, Greene was trying to finish his new manuscript. Before the publication of *The Heart of the Matter*, Greene decided he wanted to write what he called 'the great sex novel'.[52] Until fairly late in the day it bore the title 'The Point of Departure', before being published as *The End of the Affair* in 1951. He started on it in earnest at the end of 1948 while on Capri,[53] and by mid-August 1950, with just a few days' work left to do, he had completed sixty-one thousand words.[54] Greene re-read *Great Expectations* just before beginning his novel and was struck by how Dickens, despite operating under the constraint of first-person narration, managed always to vary his tone. Apart from *The Third Man*, Greene had made little use of first-person narrators and worried that Bendrix's opening declaration might be a trap: '... this is a record far more of hate than of love ...'. The rest of the novel might take on a tone of unrelieved rancour. At times, he was tempted to rewrite everything from his accustomed third-person perspective, but part of what makes the novel work is that Bendrix's claims about what he thinks and feels are always suspect – the reader learns quickly to question what he says and how he says it, just as the sections of Sarah's journal provide a contrasting voice to set against that of Bendrix. Moreover, by choosing first-person narration Greene puts the whole notion of 'I' on trial.

There is no doubt that the book's basic situation was drawn from Greene's affair with Catherine and his dealings with her husband. Bendrix is a novelist in love with the wife of a senior civil servant, to whom he gives the name Henry. However, it is almost as important to emphasize the ways in which this novel is *not* a transcript of Greene's affair with Catherine. Beginning in 1939, the book describes a love affair in the Blitz, something Greene experienced with Dorothy Glover. The setting is Clapham Common, a place Greene shared with Vivien. His personal letters and journals rarely sound in any way like the snarling Bendrix. Catherine was a far edgier and more playful figure than Sarah, and by no means was Harry as downtrodden as Henry. So while the novel is correctly called a *roman à clef*, the elements drawn from life merely mark out the broad territory in which the act of imagination occurs.

In another sense, treating it as a who's who of Greene's sex life is a precise denial of what the book is about. The epigraph is taken from Léon Bloy: 'Man has places in his heart which do not yet exist, and into them enters suffering in order that they may have existence.' The characters that are so easily equated with Graham, Catherine, and Harry actually have no being at all, even in the fictional world Greene has created, except as they approach Golgotha. Greene felt that a disaster had set in for the English novel after the death of Henry James; whereas traditional novelists had always conceived of their characters as being somehow under the eye of God, where their actions had an eternal consequence, Virginia Woolf and E. M. Forster had produced characters who seemed nothing more than the sum of their drifting perceptions. This is a problem philosophers have worried about since the days of John Locke, whether identity is a matter of 'substance' or 'consciousness'.[55] Although he does not use the term, Greene believed in identity of substance, in there being an essential self. Greene saw *Mrs Dalloway*, for example, not as a novel with realized characters but as a mere 'prose poem'.[56] In his view, this was not only an intellectual difference between Woolf's beliefs and his, but a failure of craft – her characters are defective because ontologically adrift. Of course, in pursuing such a point, Greene undermined his claim to be a novelist who happened to be a Catholic: his Catholicism was here shaping his sense of the novel. As a side note, it is worth observing that Greene did not simply dismiss Woolf – he thought highly of *To the Lighthouse*.[57]

Once finished, Greene was slow to deliver his manuscript, causing some anxiety to A. S. Frere at Heinemann, who wanted to get it into print. Greene sent it first to Edward Sackville-West, a recent convert to Catholicism, who said he did not especially like it but believed Greene should go ahead and publish.[58] That autumn he worked with Sackville-West to simplify the chronology of the journal section, and began to feel that it was indeed a good novel.

At forty-six, he was young for the honour, but Greene discovered that he had a realistic chance of being awarded the Nobel Prize in Literature. He heard that Hemingway, whom he admired, had put himself out of the running with a bad book, *Across the River and into the Trees*, and that his real competition was William Faulkner and the Swedish writer Pär Lagerkvist, author of *Barabbas*, which would be made into film starring Anthony Quinn in 1961.

Greene headed to Stockholm, where he had dinner with the permanent secretary of the committee and one of its members on 19 October.[59] No prize was awarded in 1949, so two were available in 1950. They went to Faulkner and Bertrand Russell. Enjoying home advantage, Lagerkvist won it in 1951, and then in 1952 it went to Greene's friend Mauriac. It was the one honour Greene longed for and there was every reason to believe he would one day receive it. This was merely the first page of a saga of frustration and disappointment – the prize was never granted. In old age, Greene said, melodramatically, that he now longed for a prize bigger than the Nobel – 'Death.'[60]

28

MALAYA

'Malaya was the first of my escapes.'[1] Distressed over Catherine, Graham decided to follow his brother to Malaya, then in the midst of the Emergency – essentially a war, though overshadowed by the one in Korea. Some of Greene's most memorable journeys in the next decade would be to countries breaking from the colonial control of Britain, France, and Belgium. His way to Malaya was paid for by *Life* magazine, for whom he had written an article on the recently proclaimed dogma of the Assumption.

As a group of British colonies and protectorates federated in 1948 in preparation for independence, Malaya was ethnically diverse, with large Chinese, Malay, Indian, and aboriginal populations. The Communist Party drew its strength chiefly from the Chinese population, and its military wing, the Malayan Races Liberation Army (MRLA), retained a great many weapons from the war against the Japanese and was extremely violent. The ethnic Malays generally opposed communism, and Graham Greene's sympathies were with them. About four-fifths of the country was ancient rainforest and mangrove swamps;[2] the insurgents struck out from such terrain in a campaign of terror that especially targeted British rubber planters and those who worked for them.

The response to the insurgents, however, was heavy-handed: hundreds of thousands of Chinese were resettled from their smallholdings to new fenced-in villages so that they could not supply the communists, an approach anticipating the 'strategic hamlets' used in Vietnam. There is evidence that in December 1948 Scots Guards shot twenty-four unarmed rubber workers in cold blood at Batang Kali,[3] an event which, as late as 2015, was the subject of unsuccessful court proceedings in Britain aimed at forcing an inquiry.[4]

Having worked for most of the Second World War with the BBC, Hugh Greene was a good choice to oversee psychological warfare in Malaya. Arriving in mid-September 1950, he had two main tasks: to alienate soldiers from their officers and civilians from the cause. Following BBC practice, he maintained that, to be effective, propaganda must be truthful and positive. He knew that they needed to make a sound case to intelligent people fighting for, or supporting, the MRLA. One of the practical difficulties he faced was that in a very rainy country leaflets would turn to pulp as soon as they were scattered, so he ordered them to be waterproofed and vastly increased their effect. Most importantly, he sought out able Chinese assistants who took over the campaign when he left a year later.[5]

Graham arrived in Singapore on 27 November 1950 and when he saw Hugh was 'over-joyed'[6] – a term he almost never uses to describe his own feelings. Presumably at the request of Alex Korda, he met right away with the film-producer brothers Run Run and Run Me Shaw,[7] who controlled a chain of cinemas. Run Run Shaw, who was to live to 106, was later known for developing the kung fu genre, and when asked what were his favourite films famously responded, 'I particularly like films that make money'.[8]

Greene soon found a new friend in Kuala Lumpur, Noël Ross, the 'Resident' or chief British adviser to the Sultan. Ross had been a Dominican novice and was sensitive to Greene's struggles – the two attended Mass together. In Malacca, Greene prayed at the original burial site of St Francis Xavier. Visiting a dance hall, he met a young blue-eyed Englishman named Jolly who was enraptured by one of the taxi dancers, saw her home in the evenings, claimed she was a virgin, and hoped to marry her. When Greene returned to the hall on a later occasion, he saw the girl taxi dancing again and was told that Jolly had been shot to death in his car; he found the story pitiable and agonizing.[9]

The thrill of seeing a new place subsided, and his own prayers reverted to the request for Catherine or death. On a train, he saw that officers travelled with their revolvers unholstered in case of attack, and he wished that one might happen. While much of his time was spent visiting besieged planters, the centrepiece of his visit was a trek with Gurkhas through the jungle in search of MRLA fighters. Equipped with anti-leech boots, a heavy pack, and a revolver – a rifle being too much for him to carry – Greene joined a fourteen-man patrol that moved not by path but by compass line, so as to cross many tracks looking for evidence of guerrillas. This meant facing the full density of the vege-tation, getting slashed by branches, and sliding down steep hills slick with mud from the almost daily rainstorms.

A march of nine miles took two and a half days. There was a stench of decay and the ceaseless buzz of insects. By the end of the first day, Greene was barely upright. Afraid of slowing the patrol, he hoped to be hit by a bullet.[10] Sleeping on a bed of logs and leaves, Greene woke cramped, and on the second night dreamt that he was at the Ritz with Catherine, only to find that his rough bed was shared by Major Joey MacGregor-Cheers, a man who lived up to his benign name by listen-ing for bird-calls at dawn and dusk. On the third morning Greene was retching as he marched. He had had leeches removed from a buttock and from his neck[11] and was almost at the end of endurance when the Gurkhas spotted a squatter's shack, and they emerged from the jungle at last. All they had found were two abandoned camps. It was a 'rou-tine' patrol.[12]

Routine soon brought Graham Greene face to face with a private enemy. On 23 December 1950, while buying drinks at a cold-storage depot he was approached by a man who introduced himself as Wheeler, and spoke of how at Berkhamsted School Greene had helped him with his Latin. This was his sometime friend and Carter's sidekick, Augustus Henry Wheeler, who recalled their companionship wistfully, 'What inseparables we were – you and me and old Carter.'[13]

Graham wrote to Catherine: 'What a lot began with Wheeler & Carter – suspicion, mental pain, loneliness, this damned desire to be successful that comes from a sense of inferiority, & here he was back again, after thirty-five years, in a shop in Kuala Lumpur, rather flash, an ardent polo player. And instead of saying "What hell you made my life 30 years ago," one arranged to meet for drinks!'[14] Always raw, those school memories had recently been dredged up in sessions with Strauss, so this sudden appearance of Wheeler must have been unspeakably strange. Greene says he forgot about the appointment for drinks, as if forgetting was a kind of revenge[15] – more likely he chose to avoid the company of Wheeler, as one might forgo a night on the town with Judas Iscariot.

Greene often fell in love with the troubled countries he visited, but not Malaya. The British soldiers seemed grim and graceless, and it was impossible to romanticize the rebels – especially, for example, when he had to photograph the naked body of a Malay constable bayoneted through the heart.[16] He also learned that some of their victims, including children, had been trussed up and disembowelled.[17] He spent a melancholy Christmas in Malacca, where at least he had the company of Hugh, who then went on to Singapore.

In Kelantan, on the north-east side of the Malay Peninsula, Greene caught up with Noël Ross. In a celebration of the visit, he witnessed Thai boxing and was, after many drinks, induced to join in the Joget and Ronggeng traditional dances.[18] While there he also had a long drinking session with a couple of British priests, one of whom denounced the church's position on birth control; the three of them ended up in agreement that mortal sin was practically impossible as no one could really reject God with full understanding apart from a saint, who would cling to God in any event.[19] Afterwards, he spent several more days with the Gurkhas in the dangerous region of Bentong, north-east of Kuala Lumpur, and travelled through the state of Negeri Sembilan, north of Malacca, using a train system notorious for derailments.[20] He came safely through it all.

29

SHOULDER FLASH

Greene's hankering for risk ought to have been satisfied by the Malayan Emergency, but his eye was now on a different war. Since the late nineteenth century, the French had ruled what we now call Vietnam as three territories: Tonkin in the north, Annam in the centre, and Cochinchina in the south. During the Second World War, the Axis-aligned Vichy government administered policies determined by the Japanese, who took direct control in the last months of the war. The actions of Vichy France and the Japanese led to a famine killing not less than a million people in 1944–5.[1] The strongest of a number of nationalist groups, the Viet Minh under Ho Chi Minh, fought against the Japanese, with the ultimate goals of independence and socialist revolution. On 30 August 1945, the Annamite emperor Bao Dai, who served as an equal-opportunity puppet for the French and Japanese, abdicated, and Ho declared the independence of a unified Vietnam.

However, colonialism dies hard. The British promptly transported a contingent of Frenchmen re-armed after their release from Japanese prisoner-of-war camps and some Gurkhas to Saigon and reclaimed Vietnam on behalf of France. After some arm-twisting from the French, the United States, notionally opposed to colonialism, not only acquiesced in the French claim to Vietnam but transported thousands of French soldiers there by sea.

In the north, there was an army of 180,000 Nationalist Chinese, the forces of Chiang Kai-shek. An agreement in March 1946 got the Chinese out and provided for the independence of Vietnam within the French Union, but this arrangement did not last. In November, a dispute over customs led to the French shelling the port city of Haiphong, near Hanoi, with many civilian casualties. Throughout the following year, the better trained and equipped French army sought to defeat the Viet Minh in a single decisive battle, but they chose not to engage on such terms. A guerrilla army skilled at ambush, its numbers increased rapidly, and despite the best efforts of the French, Ho and the other leaders eluded capture.

In the Chinese Civil War, the Communists defeated the Nationalists in 1949 and became, along with the Soviets, a steady supplier of materiel to the Viet Minh. Meanwhile, the Americans, who provided the French with money and weaponry, were hardening into a Cold War frame of mind: they saw the Viet Minh as just another kind of communist and failed to understand the degree to which they were inspired by nationalism and open to friendship with them. The French controlled the cities and were strong in the south, while the Viet Minh were powerful in the countryside and in the north. The ineffectual Bao Dai was brought back from exile as a non-communist leader for Vietnam. In October 1950, at the Battle of Route Coloniale 4, in the northern part of Tonkin, near the Chinese border, the French were humiliated and it became evident that they might lose this war.

While still in Kelantan, Greene had spent about two days with Sir William Jenkin, the Director of Intelligence Services in Malaya.[2] Presumably, he also met James Fulton, who ran SIS operations in the Far East, or his deputy Maurice Oldfield, who later became head of the service – Fulton and Oldfield were stationed in Singapore.[3] Their discussions almost certainly dealt with the situation in Vietnam. It is worth noting that, like Graham and Elisabeth, Hugh Greene was also recruited by MI6 and, even late in his life, continued to be debriefed about his journeys, especially to Greece and Germany.[4] He may have been part of the consultations in Singapore.

After these meetings, Graham arranged a visit to his friend Trevor Wilson in Vietnam. Also a Catholic and something of a womanizer, he had worked with Greene in Section V of MI6, handling Morocco and Tangier, and was described by Tim Milne as 'admirably unorthodox'. He had a contrary streak and would deliberately wear incorrect or mixed uniforms to annoy the authorities and the police.[5] He went on to work in Paris with Malcolm Muggeridge and then in the Pacific under Mountbatten. Now British Consul in Hanoi, he was in the middle of the crisis. While Greene maintained somewhat evasively that he first went to Vietnam just to visit Wilson, it was hardly a social call: he was headed to one of the most dangerous places in the world.

While Greene was in Malaya, the French government appointed Jean de Lattre de Tassigny, the charismatic sixty-one-year-old Commander-in-Chief of Western Union ground forces in Europe, to take over supreme military and civilian authority in Indochina. His immediate task was to protect Tonkin's Red River Delta, which included Hanoi, Haiphong, and important rice-growing areas, from imminent encirclement and a possible seaborne invasion by Chinese and Viet Minh forces. At the time of his appointment, French women and children were about to be evacuated.[6]

General de Lattre had star power. Whereas most French generals observed strict practice about uniforms and kepis and wound up looking like lesser versions of Charles de Gaulle, de Lattre had recently met with correspondents in white trousers and an open-necked shirt, projecting himself, especially to Americans, as a man of energy.[7] He was photogenic, with a gaze that could be construed as either kind-hearted or calculating.

In his first month of command he held the Red River Delta in a series of bloody engagements that lifted the morale of his forces – happily for the French, the feared invasion by the Chinese did not materialize. Two days before Greene's arrival, de Lattre thanked the United States for providing nearly all the shells, artillery, and aeroplanes used by the French forces in recent fighting.[8] He and his aides recognized that, as a representative of *Life* magazine, Graham Greene could have wide influence over American opinion. Moreover, as a Catholic with connections to France he might see things the French way.

Greene was ready to be impressed. He wrote to Hugh, 'This is the country, not Malaya.'[9] He was dazzled by the sophistication of the women, and the air of 'Gaiety in spite of grenades'[10] – indeed, the restaurants were protected against grenades by wire mesh since, by Greene's estimate, about a quarter of the city turned Viet Minh at night. The French army had a swagger that Greene liked, taking 'war so much less seriously than the British – "'La vie sportive."'[11]

He had no sooner arrived in Saigon on 25 January 1951 than a car was put at his disposal and he was invited to an 'informal' dinner with de Lattre the following evening – it was as informal as a dinner in a palace where two hundred men are engaged in a musical changing of the guard can be. In any event, Greene did not have to wear black tie. Presumably from prior intelligence briefings, he took an immediate interest in areas controlled by Catholic bishops and by new religious sects. He visited a territory in the south controlled by the Cao Dai; a group founded in the 1920s, they mingled spiritualist, Catholic, Confucian, and Buddhist beliefs, and had their own pope and female cardinals, while venerating among their saints Sun Yat Sen and Victor Hugo. Their membership was estimated at two million and they had an army of twenty-five thousand supporting the French. Another group that Greene visited was the Hoa Hao, a recent Buddhist offshoot, numbering about eight hundred thousand, with a tougher fighting force than the Cao Dai. At this time, the Hoa Hao, too, were allied with the French.

Greene went to Ben Tre in the Mekong Delta, south-west of Saigon, and met there with Colonel Jean Leroy, a fiercely anti-communist former paratrooper of mixed Vietnamese and French ancestry; he had put together the Unités Mobiles de Défense de la Chrétienté (UMDC), nominally Catholic paramilitary units, numbering about two thousand all told. Greene toured Leroy's marshy fiefdom in an armoured boat with machine guns at the ready, and retained a good impression of the man who, though lapsed himself, seemed to inspire Catholics to fight in a way that no else could. Years later Greene contributed a foreword to Leroy's memoirs. In his travels out from Saigon, Greene saw guard towers erected about every kilometre, reminding him of the structures erected along the Welsh border in the Middle Ages.

He flew to Hanoi with de Lattre on 30 January 1951, and the general gave him the use of a small plane, a Morane-Saulnier, assuming he would use it to view the defence perimeter his forces had established in the Red River Delta. At this point, Greene did something the general did not expect. He and Trevor Wilson flew 120 kilometres south to Phat Diem, near the coast, where Bishop Le Huu Tu maintained a private army of two thousand to guard his Catholic diocese. Although Greene did not meet him yet, the bishop of the adjoining see of Bui-Chu, Pham Ngoc Chi, was also something of a prince-bishop. Both prelates regarded themselves as independent of, but allied to, the French.

The historian Kevin Ruane has researched Foreign Office documents to find out what Wilson and Greene were doing.[12] Although de Lattre and other French officials spoke of Vietnam eventually achieving full independence, Bao Dai was not a plausible leader – he would always appear a mere figurehead for a government still dominated by the old colonial master – so the French promises were suspect. It is well known that the Americans were searching, however ham-fistedly, for a 'third way' between colonialism and communism. The British too were looking for a non-communist path for Vietnam, giving special attention to the Catholic leadership of the country. This included not just the bishops, but local strongmen like Colonel Leroy. Wilson was extremely enthusiastic about this project, but it had the potential to outrage the French, as it meant undermining a policy for which their soldiers were dying.

When they flew back to Hanoi, Greene and Wilson were shot at from within the defence perimeter. Unwisely, at dinner Greene joked about this to de Lattre, who was somewhat put out, since it suggested that Viet Minh fighters could easily cross through and conduct operations in a supposedly secure zone. De Lattre continued to treat Greene well, and gave him a shoulder flash of the First French Army, which, under his command, had liberated Strasbourg in November 1944. He took the novelist to a reunion of old comrades, where he said that while he must himself return to Saigon his wife would remain in Hanoi as a sign of French commitment never to abandon the city.[13] It was a typically grand gesture, but even at his most inspiring de Lattre did not erase doubts as to the ultimate success of French arms in Indochina. Assured of his good will, Greene left on 5 February 1951.

Back in Paris, where Catherine met him with warm clothes for a European winter,[14] he received a telegram from *Life* asking whether he would be interested in writing not just on Malaya, but on Indochina as well, and he said that he would be glad to go back and do more research, especially if the fighting intensified.[15] By the early summer, the magazine was pressing to make firm plans, and he finally went back in October. While sailing with Korda in mid-June, Greene wrote to Catherine from Epidaurus, en route to Athens, that while listening to the Jupiter Symphony at a night-time open-air concert, he had had an idea for a novel set in Indochina.[16]

30

THE CARDS IN HIS WALLET

For the moment, Greene was the darling of *Life* magazine. His article on Malaya came out at the end of July. He wrote another, appearing in September, on Pope Pius XII (Eugenio Pacelli), who would one day be described by John Cornwell as 'Hitler's pope' – unfairly, according to Sir Martin Gilbert who maintains that the pope did in fact stand up against German persecution of Jews and saved a great many lives.[1] The matter continues to be debated, albeit with caution as documents released from the Vatican archives are examined and assessed. Greene would have been surprised by the controversy: he had no doubt about the pope's attitude. He recounted a story told by his friend the Marchese Bernardo Patrizi, whose father approached the then Cardinal Pacelli at a party and said that it was good for Germany to have a strong leader to deal with the communists. Having served in Germany as papal nuncio, Pacelli replied: 'For goodness sake, Joseph, don't talk nonsense. The Nazis are infinitely worse.'[2]

Greene wrote of the austere Pacelli with a nuanced admiration, observing that while his encyclicals were a bore he was possibly a great pope. He was impressed by how a career as a papal diplomat had not erased the instincts of a parish priest and a manner of life that was essentially 'Franciscan'. In 1950, Greene had made a visit to the Vatican and was shown the excavations of the putative tomb of St Peter. He had a private audience with the pope, and committed what he thought was a faux pas. In answer to a question from Pius, he said that two Masses had moved him profoundly. One was said by the pope himself on the jubilee of his ordination, which occurred on 2 April 1949; in his article Greene described the pope on that occasion passing up the nave of St Peter's amid cheers and hats thrown in the air, his 'fine transparent features like those on a coin'. When the other clerics withdrew and left the pope alone at the altar to go through the actions of the liturgy, Greene wondered if he was looking at a saint.

Having recounted this experience to a doubtless gratified pontiff, Greene made, as he believed, the mistake of saying that the other Mass was said by the stigmatic Padre Pio at San Giovanni Rotondo in Apulia. It seemed to Greene that the pope was a little miffed at the comparison to this peasant whom many in the Vatican believed a fraud.[3] Perhaps Greene read too much into the conversation: Pius was not himself especially opposed to Padre Pio. The pope gave some thought to Greene's visit and then read *The End of the Affair*, saying to Bishop John Heenan (later Cardinal Archbishop of Westminster), 'I think this man is in trouble. If he ever comes to you, you must help him.'[4]

In the long run, Padre Pio, a Capuchin friar canonized in 2002, mattered more to Greene than did Pope Pius XII. Just as he had been inspired by the popular piety of Mexicans, here too was a holiness on the borders of magic.[5] When Graham Greene and Catherine Walston had arrived in Apulia, Pio invited them to speak with him, but Greene refused, fearing that a conversation with a saint might force him to change his life.

Early the next morning, they attended Pio's Mass. Standing about six feet away, Greene watched him pulling down his sleeves to hide the black wounds of his stigmata. Having been warned that Pio's Masses went on for some time, Greene became so absorbed that afterwards he was surprised to find that it had taken not the half-hour he supposed but a full two hours. For the rest of his life, through years when he struggled to remain a Catholic, Greene carried two pictures of Padre Pio in his wallet, and as he put it to John Cornwell, this encounter in 1949 'introduced a *doubt* in my *disbelief*'.[6] This is an important phrase, echoing one he used of the Earl of Rochester so many years before (see p. 60). Greene regarded most atheists, including his friend the logical positivist philosopher A. J. Ayer, as far too assured of themselves. Had he lived a little longer Greene would almost certainly have regarded the scientism of Richard Dawkins and the new atheists as just another brittle orthodoxy.

31

'C'

B y the summer of 1951, Greene's desire to sustain his relationship with Catherine Walston against all comers, among them a saint and a psychiatrist, was facing very long odds. With *The End of the Affair* soon to be released, Harry Walston had had enough. The British edition was dedicated 'To C.' and the American 'TO CATHERINE *with love*'. Even though he himself had had mistresses, this relationship of Catherine's was taking on a public character, and he did not like to be seen in his horns. In August, he insisted that she break off with the novelist, and threatened to divorce her. Graham proposed that he delete the American dedication but was not taken up on the offer; and he tried, unsuccessfully, to have her come and see him in Paris.[1]

Later in the month, while travelling in Austria with the troubled priest Thomas Gilby, he organized an invitation for himself and Catherine, then at Achill, to Piers Court. Waugh tried to wriggle out of it by saying that they were most welcome but his butler was ill, so they would have to bear up like the Swiss Family Robinson. Catherine wrote privately to Waugh, saying that Graham was often happier without her. Waugh left the invitation open, and remarked that he had read about the Walstons getting public money and planning to grow groundnuts at the farm, 'But, dear Catherine, I don't listen to gossip about you.' She could see friendship in that oblique phrase and accepted the invitation. Waugh later reported to Nancy Mitford that Greene had been on his best behaviour, and had even worn a dinner jacket; having never witnessed such a thing previously, Catherine announced that she would make him always do it. During the days, Greene, in whimsical mood, discussed with Waugh such matters as the sex life of Perry Mason and went for long walks, collecting licence-plate numbers,[2] a superstitious practice that he would later work into *Our Man in Havana.*

After this visit, Greene wrote to Catherine proposing that they have a child and devote their lives to Catholic Action, promising her that he would go to communion weekly if they were together.[3] They saw each other in September, but she refused to come to him in Paris in October, at which point their affair was understood to be over. But, as will be seen in the following chapters, they would reconcile and break up again and again through the next decade, a pattern that created sorrow for both of them.

Apart from gloom about Catherine, Greene was anxious about the novel – that it was aesthetically flawed and religiously wrongheaded. He took comfort from a letter written by the Dominican friar Father Gervase Mathew, who had served as Francis's godfather, just as his brother David, an archbishop, had served as Caroline's. He wrote: 'How much I disagree with your judgement of the End of the Affair. Now that I have finished it I think that you have never dived to a more real level and I think that the conception of God that underlies that reality is the truest of those in all your books – and you said so much that I have seen so often in life but never before in print. Love Gervase.'[4]

Greene's spirits usually improved in the company of Alex Korda. At the end of September 1951, they set sail from Athens for Istanbul, where Elisabeth was then living, her husband Rodney, a senior SIS officer, having been posted there. The weather was against them, so they sheltered on the island of Skiathos for three days spent mostly in a pub drinking retsina. Their shipmates were Margot Fonteyn, Laurence Olivier, and Vivien Leigh, who had been mobbed by paparazzi in Athens. In the course of many games of canasta, large meals, and much drink, Greene decided that Leigh was more intelligent than Olivier. He flirted with Fonteyn and they decided that he should write a ballet for her.[5] He considered the project during his sojourn in Indochina and in March pitched it to Alex, who thought that Peter Brook might be a suitable director. However, the idea faded away.[6]

Greene arrived in Paris around 21 October 1951, and saw Father Martindale. He had hoped Catherine would meet him in Paris; she telephoned and confirmed that while she wanted the relationship, she could not be separated from her children. On his way to Indochina Greene took some comfort in that statement but said that if the break were absolute he would remain in Indochina and die there.

The End of the Affair had come out in Britain in early September and drew a wide range of opinions from reviewers, some of whom were taken aback by his decision to carry the story beyond Sarah's death into a period when she seems to bring about miracles of healing through saintly intercession. While this was consistent with his taste for a religion that openly embraced something close to magic, the gesture took him outside the traditions of the realist novel and alienated readers who did not share his faith, so he revised later editions of the novel to make the healings more ambiguous.[7]

But there was great praise too. *Time* magazine ran a picture of him on its cover with the caption: 'NOVELIST GRAHAM GREENE *Adultery can lead to sainthood*',[8] and devoted six pages to a biographical and critical piece that judged him as accomplished a craftsman as William Faulkner, Ernest Hemingway, or Evelyn Waugh. The praise Greene most valued, however, came not in a review: Faulkner himself wrote in a letter to his British publisher, the contents of which were soon passed on, 'I have also read Mr Greene's THE END OF THE AFFAIR; not one of yours, but for me one of the best, most true and moving novels of my time, in anybody's language.'[9]

32

THE BELL TOWER

On 30 October 1951, Graham Greene found himself at a dinner in Hanoi where General Jean de Lattre de Tassigny was giving a speech aimed at one of his guests, the Bishop of Bui Chu, Pham Ngoc Chi, whose commitment to the French cause was no sure thing.[1] Indeed, the general spent as much time managing allies as he did fighting the enemy. He had just returned to Vietnam after three months of travel. Having been in Washington to get military aid speeded up, he had appeared on *Meet the Press* and other television programmes, selling the war to the American people not as the last gasp of colonialism but as a heroic stand against communism.[2] The general's charisma attracted the interest of American politicians, among them the young congressman John F. Kennedy, who briefly toured Vietnam.[3]

De Lattre also visited London to secure cooperation with British forces in Malaya. Having won a series of battles through the past year, he convinced much of the world's press that the war was rounding a corner. For example, an article appeared in *The Times* on 5 October, based on sources no closer to Tonkin than Paris, declaring that in Vietnamese public opinion the cause of the Viet Minh was 'virtually lost'. That was the kind of coverage the general was looking for, but it was nonsense.

Greene expected the same welcome he had received on his earlier visit, but the atmosphere had changed.[4] Trevor Wilson had continued his search for a Catholic third force without much discretion. Having been decorated for his work in Paris at the end of the European war, he was now told to get out of French Indochina. Allowed back in mid-November and given about four weeks' reprieve to sort out his affairs, he was *persona non grata*. This was not simply a local matter, involving one consul who happened to be a loose cannon. On his visit to London de Lattre had urged the British to work with his forces in Indochina, for example in the matter of naval patrols, but he would hardly want them to meddle in military or political affairs, even as he was opening the door to this. Expelling Wilson sent a message to the British government about the limits of cooperation. In the meantime, Greene's choice of company was unfortunate – when he first landed in Saigon, he was met at the airport by, among others, Donald Lancaster, a British diplomat and MI6 representative.[5] He wrote to his mother that he met in Saigon with two members of 'the old firm'.[6]

French patience was wearing thin. Over the summer the Catholic militias had collapsed: they were encircled by the Viet Minh and had had to be rescued by French paratroopers. At the end of May, the general's son, Lieutenant Bernard de Lattre, had been trapped in an outpost not far from Phat Diem. Having signalled for reinforcements, he was hit by an artillery shell.[7] Greene maintained that the general blamed Catholics for his loss and was embittered against them, and perhaps he was.

At the level of policy, the general was frustrated by the bishops' failure to accept the French as their true allies, but he did not really grasp what he was dealing with. Even today, it is commonly assumed that Catholicism in Indochina was a foreign imposition and that Catholics were stooges of the French. In fact, the faith had been present in the region for about four hundred years; by 1945, Catholics represented something like a tenth of the population. There were six times as many indigenous priests as there were missionaries, as well as four bishops of Vietnamese descent, whose ordination the Vatican had insisted upon. Many of the Vietnamese clergy were involved in Catholic Action and so had a qualified sympathy with progressive causes. Unlike the French missionaries, the indigenous clergy strongly supported independence, so much so that in 1909 three priests had been jailed for nationalist activities. Nor were the foreign missionaries all of one mind: some from Belgium actually supported independence.

Although the Vatican dreaded communism, it had long foreseen the end of European empires and was encouraging the transition to indigenous church leadership in soon-to-be-independent territories. Pope Benedict XV and Pope Pius XI had both written encyclicals on the subject.[8] As the war progressed, the leading Catholic intellectual in Vietnam, Nguyen Manh Ha, was trying to find a path to peace that avoided both communism and colonialism, so de Lattre had him exiled too.[9] The Bishop of Phat Diem, Le Huu Tu, loathed the French and in 1945 accepted a role as adviser to Ho Chi Minh but withdrew as the Viet Minh became more openly committed to communism. He wanted to keep his diocese out of the fighting, but Phat Diem was in a strategically important area in the lower Gulf of Tonkin, so the war came to him. The French rescue in the summer of 1951 humiliated the bishop.

De Lattre wanted help from the Vatican. During his visit to the United States, he met with Cardinal Spellman of New York, an ecclesiastical power-broker convinced of the threat of communism. De Lattre went on to Rome for a private audience with Pius XII in mid-October[10] and discussed the status of the Catholic church in Indochina. What he wanted was for the pope to pressure the Vietnamese-born bishops into a full alliance. The pope, a career diplomat, expressed concern, but then did a peculiar thing. In an evident concession to the general, he immediately appointed a new apostolic delegate to Vietnam, but chose an Irishman, Archbishop John Dooley, to take the post which had for a generation been held only by Frenchmen – what the pope gave to the French with one hand he took away with the other.[11] Having made very limited progress on his Catholic problem, the general returned to Vietnam at about the same time as Greene in late October 1951.[12]

Tainted by association with Trevor Wilson, Greene's movements were now scrutinized by the Sûreté Fédérale – the police and security service. He would afterwards satirize his minders in the character of a hapless Monsieur Dupont, whom he and Wilson, during the time of his reprieve, teased mercilessly, crushing him in games of chance and sending him home drunk to a sceptical wife. They brought him to *fumeries* and a bathhouse, where an erotic massage caused him to pass out and need reviving with whisky. Greene put it about that he was writing a *roman policier* to be called *Voilà, Monsieur Dupont*.[13] In the end, he did something rather like that, as the frame of *The Quiet American* is the investigation conducted by Inspector Vigot into the death of Alden Pyle. Of course, Vigot is no buffoon; he is portrayed as something of a priest, reading Pascal and listening to men's confessions.

Greene could not stand having his movements supervised. But being penned in with journalists in Hanoi and Saigon had a benefit which he would recognize later. *The Quiet American* is dedicated to a couple named

René and Phuong, and Greene insisted that he had only borrowed the woman's name and the location of their flat in Saigon for the story. René de Berval, a journalist and cultural writer living in Saigon, edited the journal *France-Asie* and wrote books on Buddhism and the kingdom of Laos; he was extremely fond of Greene. Not a great deal is known about Phuong, except that, like her namesake in the novel, she had a sister who was anxious to see her married.[14] He had met the couple on his first visit, and looked to de Berval for advice on when to come back.[15] During his sojourns in Vietnam, Greene spent many evenings with this couple and they were probably his closest friends there once Wilson left the scene. He was also attracted to Phuong, as on one occasion he kissed her through the grille, 'like Pyramus and Thisbe', at the airport.[16]

Inter-racial couples were common in French Indochina, so the situation in the novel is most likely an amalgam of several relationships Greene observed, and, of course, the result of a good deal of invention. The married Trevor Wilson had a Vietnamese girlfriend named Tuan.[17] Greene had other friends, such as the police officer Paul Boucarut[18] and his wife Hô, who come back into the story a little later.[19] A memoir by Danielle Flood describes how she was the child of a French-Vietnamese woman and an Englishman but her paternity was ascribed to an American – this series of events may have been known to Graham Greene.[20] There had even been a novel by the little-known Harry Hervey entitled *Congaï: Mistress of Indochine* (1925), in which the half-Annamite protagonist chooses among relationships with European men.[21] Greene may have come across that book, but the idea of a triangle involving two foreigners and a local woman in a war zone was not new for him. It was precisely what he had portrayed in *Rumour at Nightfall*, where the journalists Crane and Chase compete for the love of Eulelia Monti, and the matter is decided by a betrayal. *The Quiet American* is partly constructed out of the rubble of that book.

Greene spent some time with the Reuters correspondent, an Australian named Graham Jenkins, and with the somewhat traumatized Associated Press representative Larry Allen, who had won a Pulitzer Prize in 1942 for war reporting. Allen had been aboard at least three ships (eight by some accounts) that were sunk, including a destroyer off Tobruk, then imprisoned for many months in Poland and elsewhere, escaping and being recaptured several times. After the war, he reported from Moscow, Tel Aviv, and Singapore. He moved on to Indochina, where the French liked his reports and awarded him the Croix de Guerre in 1952.[22] Bernard Diederich, a journalist from New Zealand who will become a central figure later in this book, knew Allen: 'He told me about covering a riot in Singapore, and the UPI fellow traveling with him was killed while he was saved in a ditch by a couple to whom he gave 2000 dollars he said he always carried with him.' Diederich believes that all these brushes with death left Allen somewhat 'gun shy' in later life, and the quality of his reporting fell off.[23] Greene disliked Allen; he told Diederich that he based the character of the journalist Granger on him and that a press conference in which Granger badgers the briefing officers into divulging casualty figures was based on an actual event;[24] of course, one might observe, that in playing rough with the officers Allen was just doing his job.

With a Viet Minh assault anticipated, Greene was taken by car to see the improved defences at Haiphong. He had a French commissioner as escort, who showed him what the French wanted him to see. On All Saints' Day (1 November), he went in a destroyer to an uninhabited island where soldiers were buried and then found himself playing confessor to a naval chaplain, who poured out his moral and spiritual troubles. It was the sort of thing Greene hated, as he felt he had nothing to give these 'victims of religion'.[25] By 10 November, he was travelling with American medical aid workers – an experience that he later worked into the novel: Pyle is supposedly treating the bacterial eye disease trachoma. Greene met the young Dr Warren Winkelstein, an epidemiologist with the United States Public Health Service, who was doing precisely that.[26] Greene photographed 'Wink's' team in the field and exchanged letters with him.[27] Although Pyle's medical work is a cover for political and military activity, Dr Winkelstein was an admirable character, who went on in later years to prove in a pioneering study that unprotected sex between men led to the transmission of HIV and AIDS.[28]

Slipping his leash, Greene found a pilot willing to disobey orders and take him for a couple of days of dive-bombing – Greene was allowed to fly, but only on horizontal missions above the range of enemy fire. They flew out in a B-26, which the pilots called a 'prostitute' as with its short wings it lacked a 'visible means of support'.[29] With just room enough in the cockpit for the pilot, the navigator, and the long-legged novelist, they began with a series of fourteen dives from 9000 to 3000 feet.[30] The plane was sent out again, and dropping to 200 feet above the Red River, targeted a sampan. Greene wrote about this sortie in *The Quiet American*: 'Down we went again, away from the gnarled and fissured forest towards the river, flattening out over the neglected ricefields, aimed like a bullet at one small sampan on the yellow stream. The cannon gave a single burst of tracer, and the sampan blew apart in a shower of sparks; we didn't even wait to see our victims struggling to survive, but climbed and made for home ... There had been something so shocking in our sudden fortuitous choice of a prey – we had just happened to be passing, one burst only was required, there was no one to return our fire, we were gone again, adding our little quota to the world's dead.'[31]

Greene's difficulties with the French came to a head on 18 November 1951. At lunch de Lattre asked 'le pauvre Graham Greene' to return for a cocktail party that evening. The general was off on his travels again, but word had got around that he would not be coming back. There was an air of discouragement, and by now senior officers felt free to criticize him, even to an Englishman. With the much-decorated General Raoul Salan and two others making a show of not listening, de Lattre asked, 'And now, Graham Greene, why are you here?' Greene gave the obvious answer that he was writing an article for *Life* magazine, so de Lattre asked him point-blank whether he was in the Secret Service and associated with Trevor Wilson.[32] Nonplussed, Greene offered another unconvincing denial, and was left feeling he had not spoken up enough for Wilson.

After a meal in which Greene was observed disapprovingly by the general's wife, the bereaved mother of one soldier and the soon-to-be widow of another, he asked the general if they could meet in private. When everyone had left after midnight, he explained his work again, including the amount he was being paid by *Life*, and the general responded with what sounds like regret for a friendship lost, though Greene saw it as 'grandiloquence': 'I have told the Sûreté, Graham Greene is my friend. I do not believe what you say about him. Then they come again and tell me you have been here or here and I say, I do not believe. Graham Greene is my friend. And then again they come ...'

They shook hands warmly, but the general's doubts returned immediately; Greene claimed it was over an innocent but unsigned telegram he received from Marie Biche. The next day the general remarked that he knew Greene must be a spy: 'Who would come to this war for four hundred dollars?' His English was weak, and he had 'mislaid a zero'.[33]

One of those dominant, charismatic men who so often fascinated Greene, the sixty-two-year-old Jean de Lattre de Tassigny was at the end. Having fallen ill during his visit to the Vatican, he delayed treatment for bone cancer because of his obligations in Indochina. *Le roi Jean* went home to two operations, and died at a nursing home in Paris on 11 January. Despite his reported anti-Catholicism, he received the last rites of the church.[34] He was posthumously named Marshal of France and, following a state funeral, buried beside his son in the Vendée.[35]

'My friendship with Trevor has mucked things up for me here completely. The French imagine all kinds of sinister motives, & very politely all doors are closed. I shall probably go back to Saigon in a few days, visit Angkor & then leave the blasted country. But as one was really looking for a bullet, it's unsatisfactory.'[36] So Greene wrote to Catherine. He had had enough of Wilson's project, but the damage to his reputation had already been done.

And yet in the months since his first visit, Greene had thought a good deal about Phat Diem, and it had grown in significance for him. In the last week of November he made his return, from the north by jeep, 'heaving along at evening between the uncountable churches by the canal sides, the fresh green of the new rice shoots washed in a flat gold light as the sun sank, a landscape like Holland ... It was then I had the delight of the half remembered, the half forgotten. To return to a place is always happier than a first visit, and though the bishop in the months past had lost his private army (all except the band) it was a contented town, war had reached the outposts but had passed on again out of earshot ...'[37]

No place in Greeneland is truly safe or content. On about 13 December 1951 he heard a rumour in Hanoi that Phat Diem had been overrun by the Viet Minh.[38] The new Commander-in-Chief Raoul Salan allowed Greene, whom he liked, to go where he pleased without the Sûreté and gave him specific permission to go to Nam Dinh, a city on the Red River. Once he got there, he made his way thirty kilometres south to his real destination of Phat Diem. He arrived in a landing craft in the company of Lieutenant Roger Vandenberghe, a highly decorated killer with 'animal face and dangling hangman's hands', who in June had been entrusted with the recovery of Bernard de Lattre's body; his Tigres Noirs commandos, extremely violent ex-Viet Minh who typically operated in disguise behind enemy lines, mutinied about a month later and killed him.[39]

The nightmare that Greene came across in Phat Diem – including a mother and child dead in a ditch – is described in the opening paragraphs of this book. He was a journalist at a small but very ugly battle that the French did not want the world to know about, so with an offer of him spending a day with the navy they persuaded him to board a boat back upriver to Nam Dinh, where his escort simply abandoned him. But he had seen what he had seen.

At Christmas, Greene left Vietnam for a few weeks in Hong Kong, Macau, and Malaya, mostly in the company of Wilson, who finally boarded a ship for Naples. Greene returned to Saigon by about 20 January 1952, and went on to interview the Emperor Bao Dai on the 24th, but the emperor had almost nothing to say.[40] Almost a year after his first visit, Greene returned at the beginning of February to the small Catholic stronghold at Ben Tre in the Mekong Delta. By now, Colonel Leroy had built a lake with a pagoda, modelled on the ancient one in Hanoi, and opened a zoo for the entertainment of local people. On Greene's earlier visit, he and Leroy had travelled about in an armoured gunboat. This time they went on a barge with dancing girls and a gramophone playing, among other things, the Harry Lime theme.

Greene's travelling companion was the American journalist Leo Hochstetter,[41] then serving as press spokesmen for the Special Technical and Economic Mission. Believed to represent the CIA, this outfit was dispensing about $23,500,000 per year in aid. The French feared that it was encouraging extreme nationalism (conceivably in the person of the future president Ngo Dinh Diem), and de Lattre had offered its head, Robert Blum, an academic from Yale, a backhanded compliment: 'Mr Blum, you are the most dangerous man in Indochina.[42] Greene listened to Hochstetter's harangue on the necessity for a 'third force', and although he had decided some months before to write a novel set in Indochina, he now realized that it could be written specifically about American meddling. He later said that The Quiet American had its origins in this conversation.[43] Greene denied that Hochstetter was the model for the idealistic Pyle, and various efforts to see that character as a portrait of someone present in Vietnam, such as the cold warrior Edward Lansdale, have proved unconvincing.[44] Although Greene did once say, perhaps jokingly, to the novelist Mike Mewshaw that the character was based on an American diplomat whose wife he had seduced, Pyle, for the most part, is a product of Greene's imagination.

Greene went the next day to interview Pham Cong Tac, the chain-smoking pope of the Caodai, at the Holy See at Tay Ninh on the Cambodian border, north-west of Saigon. Although the religion has endured, Greene could not take it seriously except in its military aspect. He regarded it as something close to a cartoon, with its iconography drawn discordantly from half a dozen different traditions, mingling, for example, a papal throne and the tail of a dragon.[45]

During the Second World War, the French had imprisoned this pope in Madagascar because of his links to the Japanese. After the war, the group, though opposed to communism, was briefly aligned with the Democratic Republic of Vietnam, so the French attacked their head-quarters, killing some of their leaders and torturing others, until they agreed in 1946 to switch their allegiance to the French and in exchange their pope was allowed to return to the country.[46] By early 1952, General de Lattre had given great offence to the Cao Dai by demanding that their twenty thousand-strong army be absorbed into that of the Associated State of Vietnam; two months after Greene's visit they finally broke with the French, while continuing to oppose the communists.[47]

Perhaps with Hochstetter's voice ringing in his ears, Greene wanted to know about a rogue Caodai named Trinh Minh Thé, a colonel in the French army who deserted in June 1951. He took two thousand men with him, declared himself a brigadier-general, and was responsible for the assassination of a young French general and the planting of bombs in Saigon.[48] This was not Greene's idea of a third force, but he suspected that for the Americans the shadowy Thé represented the future of Vietnam. He would be made responsible for the bomb blast in the centre of Saigon that is a key event in The Quiet American.

*

During these months in Vietnam, Greene was happiest when smoking opium, the pleasure of which he initially described as 'intellectual' – whatever that meant.[49] He had his first pipes in Haiphong around the beginning of November: he was brought to a *fumerie* in a back street, where the madame spotted him as a 'debutante'. He lay down on a hard couch and watched the pipe-maker in the light of a tiny lamp kneading the brown gum into a ball and plunging it on a needle into the flame, where it bubbled and its smoke rose into the pipe's inverted cup. With a little experience, he would learn to take all the smoke in one breath. Sleepy after two pipes, his fourth left him calm and alert, and his perpetual anxieties became like memories. Despite his 'execrable' French, he felt free to recite a poem by Baudelaire. Going back to his room, he experienced for the first time the 'white night' of opium, lying awake, watchful and untroubled before going into a deep sleep seeming to last all night but in fact only twenty minutes, then returning to the first state, repeating the process over and over.[50]

He wrote of his new pleasure to Catherine, who worried that he might get addicted, though she too would eventually try it. Greene insisted that he limited himself to five pipes, only once exceeding that number, while a true addict required a hundred per day.[51] On one occasion, having smoked his five, he had a dream about a man at the Nativity who could not see anything. The Magi presented their gifts to what seemed an emptiness. The shepherds listened to what seemed no sound. The man had a gold coin with which he planned to pay a prostitute, but he followed the example of the Magi and presented it to what appeared to be a vacancy. Long afterwards, this man, who becomes Greene himself, tells the story but cannot remember whether he gave the money to the Blessed Virgin or to a prostitute, '"but it doesn't really matter," he says'.[52] This dream oddly anticipates the conclusion of Greene's late novel *Monsignor Quixote* where, just before his death, the old priest says Mass without actual bread and wine, consecrating a vacancy. Greene found it easiest to believe when in the company of fervent Catholics – Vivien, Catherine, his priest friends, or for that matter the indigenous people in Mexico. Deprived of their witness, he inclined to doubt, though he continued to make the gestures of worship, sometimes to what seemed an emptiness, until the end of his life.

33

VISAS

J ust before he left Vietnam, Greene had a skirmish with American consular officials obstructing his plans to visit California and New York in February 1952. The McCarran Act of 1950, passed over Harry Truman's veto, attempted to keep people who had been communists or fascists out of the country. In the belief that it would be a useful example of the absurdity of such measures, Greene had disclosed to a sympathetic American diplomat in Brussels that while at Oxford he had been a member of the Communist Party for a period. He then repeated the disclosure to a *Time* magazine reporter, and a 'plastic curtain fell'. To enter the country he required the special permission of the Attorney General, a process taking three weeks, and his visits were limited to four weeks.[1]

He was being stonewalled by consular officials in the Far East, so he arranged for the *New York Times* to run a front-page story on his difficulties on 2 February. Two days later his visa was approved,[2] though with prohibitions on political activity and speeches. For the rest of the decade, Greene's efforts to get into the United States were similarly obstructed, but he enjoyed fighting back in the press and causing embarrassment to the American government – although he was acting on principle, it became for him a hobby, just as an habitual protestor might join any march.

Greene arrived in Los Angeles on 13 February 1952[3] for meetings with the producer David Lewis, to whom he sold the rights in *The End of the Affair* for $50,000 – a very indifferent film starring Deborah Kerr and Van Johnson was released in 1955.[4] While in Los Angeles, Greene went out for drinks with Charlie Chaplin.[5] Having once advocated American friendship with the Soviet Union, Chaplin was being watched by the FBI. Greene did not like what he was hearing about blacklists in the film industry, and would soon make common cause with Chaplin over the McCarran Act. In the midst of a tax dispute, Chaplin, who had never become an American citizen, went to London in September for the premiere of *Limelight*, with plans to remain in Europe for six months. While still at sea, he learned that the Attorney General was refusing him re-entry to the United States because of his communist associations.

Greene wrote a robust public letter to Chaplin, published in the *New Statesman*,[6] describing him as the finest of all screen artists, savaging Senator Joseph McCarthy, and upbraiding the American Catholic church, including Cardinal Spellman, for encouraging a persecution of the sort Catholics themselves had suffered in the past. Chaplin did not go back to the United States, settling instead in Switzerland, where Greene visited him. Their friendship was close, and Greene had a hand in Chaplin's 1964 bestseller *My Autobiography*, both as editor of the manuscript and as a director of the Bodley Head, which published it.[7]

From California, Greene went to New York mainly for a rapprochement with Catherine, but he was also hankering for another brawl with the American government, so held a news conference at the offices of Viking Press on 19 February, in which he lamented the role of the 'informer' in American life. Senator McCarthy, he said, had induced a 'reign of terror' in the film industry: 'if a man said yes, he had been a member of the communist party, he is expected to give the names of his friends in the party'. He said that he was indeed apprehensive of the effects of international communism, but also of the 'second effects whipped up by your own countrymen'. With an actor's timing, he hesitated, smiled, and added, 'You may be prepared to take on Stalin, but not McCarthyism.'[8]

Still in a pugilistic frame of mind, Greene proceeded to a reception at the Roosevelt Hotel, where he was given the Catholic Literary Award for *The End of the Affair*. After a short speech from the president of Hunter College on his achievements as a Catholic writer, Greene responded drily, 'I think of myself as an author who happens to be a Catholic. I think that by order of the Attorney General of the United States [my talk] will be even shorter.' Greene had managed to turn a non-speech into a news story.[9] It was a trick he would use for the rest

of his life, frequently teasing journalists with his refusals to be interviewed, and they would then, often enough, write about this reclusive
author and his silences.

Back in London, Greene wrote up an impressive article about
Indochina that was a poor fit for the magazine that had commissioned
it. The publisher of *Time* and *Life* was Henry Luce, whose wife, the
playwright and politician Clare Boothe Luce, was a recent convert to
Catholicism. The magazines' interest in Greene had mainly to do with
his standing as a Catholic author, and *Time* had, of course, lavished
a cover story on *The End of the Affair*. However, the Luces were also
Republicans and cold warriors, and that set the editorial tone.

Since his time in Malaya, Greene had grown doubtful about the
wars in south-east Asia. He opened his article on Indochina with a
summary of what President Eisenhower would soon call the 'falling
domino' effect, referring to the vulnerability of Tonkin, Malaya, Korea,
and Hong Kong to the menace of communism. Greene wrote: 'This
is the simple truth: war can sometimes appear to be simple.' He then
described how 'simple' matters seemed when he watched the fighting
from the bell tower in Phat Diem, but this simplicity was an 'illusion'.
Not always sensitive to other people's ironies, Christopher Hitchens in
an essay published in 2005 misread Greene's statements here as somehow endorsing the domino theory,[10] when he was clearly rejecting it.

Greene went on to describe the splintered alliances and complex
motivations on both sides of the fight. While he spoke respectfully of
the sacrifice of the French, and portrayed Ho Chi Minh as being pulled
along by communist hardliners, the best that could be hoped for, in
his view, was an armistice comparable to the arrangement in Korea.
The French would then get on with their withdrawal. The communists would probably persecute Catholics in Tonkin, but even so he
did not believe there could be a general victory against communism
in this war.[11]

In early March, Greene submitted a version of the article to his editor
at *Life*, Emmet Hughes, who did not like it. Over the next two months,
he submitted a series of updates as new information came to him, and
in early May obtained permission to publish a French version in *Paris
Match*. However, the English version languished on Hughes's desk, and
by June he knew it was being spiked.[12] Long afterwards, he incorporated

portions of it into the memoir *Ways of Escape*, and it appears in full in a late collection of his prose entitled *Reflections*.

Greene spent most of that spring in Anacapri, in the company, first, of his sister Elisabeth and then of Catherine. He wrote to Catherine that he wished they could go together to Ravello in July to witness the miraculous liquefaction of the blood of St Pantaleon[13] – about as Catholic a tryst as can be imagined.

In the meantime, he was becoming more at home on the island of Capri. He usually dined at a restaurant run by a woman named Gemma near the cathedral and a couple, Aniello and Carmelina maintained his house. That summer an old German, Baron von Schack, an impoverished pederast who repaid hospitality with wild flowers, died in Anacapri. Over the objections of the carabinieri who wanted to seal up his little flat until his estranged wife arrived, the novelist made sure that his pickelhaube, his spiked helmet from the First World War, was placed on his coffin,[14] just as Wormold does for Dr Hasselbacher in *Our Man in Havana*.

Greene became friends with the uninhibited Elisabeth Moor, an Austrian doctor whose practice was mainly among the poor of the island, and twenty years later he ghosted her lusty memoir *An Impossible Woman*, which contains amusing, and evidently authoritative, anecdotes about Greene himself. For example, her boxer dog, likely the inspiration for 'Buller' in *The Human Factor*, frequently shook to death cats that came into her garden; rather than have this known and the dog put down, she stealthily got rid of the corpses, once with Greene's help – they each took one handle of a bag containing an enormous dead cat – and he complained about the weight all the way to her secret burial ground.[15] He admired the sheer intensity with which she lived and her refusal to regret a carnal past – she eventually provided the inspiration for Aunt Augusta in *Travels with My Aunt*.

34

THE SPLINTER

Long ago, Greene's family had staged skits, and as a schoolboy he had written historical plays. As a mature writer, he had written film scripts and radio plays, but *The Living Room* was his first full stage play. He had begun it five years earlier on Achill,[1] the first notes written inside the back cover of the anthology *Devotional Poets of the XVII Century*, which he often carried when travelling.[2] He had worked on the play from time to time, and now learned that the producer Donald Albery wanted to stage it at Wyndham's Theatre in the spring of 1953. The director would be the young Peter Glenville,[3] later best known as director of the films *Becket* (1964) and Graham Greene's *The Comedians* (1967).

The story of an affair between a married psychologist and a young Catholic woman who commits suicide, *The Living Room* reflects Greene's sense that Catholic marriage doctrine, regardless of its ultimate validity, left couples and families in misery. The house in which the play is set becomes a metaphor for repression: as each room in which a person dies is closed off there is less and less room for the living. Important parts of the play are conducted as a dialectic between the psychologist and the girl's uncle, a priest in a wheelchair. Among the many changes to the script was one necessitated by the Lord Chamberlain's objection to the sounds of a lavatory.[4] By September 1952 Greene provided Albery and Glenville with at least three revised versions of the play.[5]

As the British production was gearing up, the Royal Dramatic Theatre in Stockholm put on a production, which was immediately acclaimed by Swedish critics.[6] Greene went to Stockholm, and while there met with Pär Lagerkvist, who had taken the Nobel Prize in 1951 – doubtless, he hoped that a good word from him would sway the committee for a future award. He also met, in passing, Stig Dagerman, the most highly regarded Swedish writer of the younger generation, and his wife the actor Anita Björk, then appearing in Shaw's *Pygmalion*.[7]

The British production was a great success. The cast was led by the young Dorothy Tutin, whom Greene regarded as 'the making of the play',[8] and Eric Portman in the role of the priest. It had its first performance in Glasgow before opening in London on 16 April 1953, for a run of 310 performances at Wyndham's, earning Greene about £5000.[9] The play opened at Henry Miller's Theatre in New York on 17 November 1954, with Barbara Bel Geddes playing the part of the young woman.[10] One of Greene's most durable plays, *The Living Room* has been successfully staged on various occasions, including a revival at the Jermyn Street Theatre in London in 2013.

Meanwhile, Korda had put *The Heart of the Matter* into production, with much of the filming in Freetown. Having invested a great deal of time in Basil Dean's failed stage version, Greene did not want to write this script. The director George More O'Ferrall and the scriptwriter Ian Dalrymple came up with a version that evaded Scobie's actual suicide by having him on the verge of shooting himself, but then being called away on police business, in the course of which he is killed. Their version also made little of the priest's comments on the mercy of God. While Greene accepted that there would be trouble from the censors, he proposed slight changes, which would clarify Scobie's intent to commit suicide, and give the priest the last word again, something he regarded, as few other people might, 'a happy ending'.[11] The director tried to accommodate his wishes with some reshooting, but the film's structure was not altered. Released in November 1953, it disappointed Greene, though he could not fail to admire Trevor Howard's performance as Scobie.[12]

As usual, he went sailing that summer with Alex Korda aboard the *Elsewhere*. Leaving Venice around 2 August, they sailed to the Croatian island of Rab, and then to Split, before leaving the yacht in Brindisi around 11 August. This particular voyage had a touch of derring-do as British intelligence had given them a large currency allowance to photograph the coastline of Yugoslavia[13] – if challenged by Tito's men, no one would have a better excuse for taking pictures than a film producer.

And yet, this was not the deepest secret among those making the cruise. That actually belonged to Thomas Gilby, a Dominican priest two years older than Greene. A former naval chaplain who lived at Blackfriars priory in Cambridge, and a regular visitor at Thriplow, he had written books on literature, Thomas Aquinas, and, somewhat ironically, the morals of married life. Another who confessed to a reluctant Graham Greene, he disclosed that he was having an affair. After leaving the *Elsewhere*, the two went briefly to Anacapri before taking a further holiday in Salzburg. Greene shared some of his sleeping pills with the disconsolate priest, and poured him many glasses of liquor. Greene wrote to Catherine that it would probably be best for Gilby to leave the priesthood.[14]

Though disturbed by Gilby's revelations, he could understand his feelings, and sometimes wrote about how falling in love was like being ambushed – his mind was still full of the Viet Minh. Embarrassment over *Babbling April* had not quite killed off the poet in Graham Greene, and from time to time he still wrote poems, many of them highly accomplished. In November 1952 he produced what may be the most memorable of them all, 'On the Road from Strasbourg to Paris', later retitled 'I Do Not Believe':

> I believe only in love that strikes suddenly,
> out of a clear sky:
> I do not believe in the slow germination of friendship
> or one that asks 'why?'
>
> Because your love came savagely, suddenly,
> like an act of war,
> I cannot conceive a love that rises gently
> or subsides without a scar.[15]

The scar was on its way. Philip Caraman, a Jesuit priest, soon told Greene that Thomas Gilby's affair was with Catherine Walston. However, Greene had suspected it already and wrote to her: 'I hadn't realised that other people were wondering too what I wonder – I thought I was crazy & manic-depressive.'[16] Whatever relationship there was between Gilby and Walston ended by January, but the breach between Greene and Walston never quite healed. The officious Caraman had made it a project to separate Greene and Walston, and on another occasion told Walston that Graham had women in Paris.[17] Editor of *The Month* and the author of middlebrow histories and biographies, Caraman was much loved by Evelyn Waugh, Edith Sitwell, and Alec Guinness, but after this episode, Graham Greene grew to resent him, and near the end of his life judged his priesthood 'very suspect'.[18]

'I can't get you out of my heart, you've splintered inside it & surgeons are useless. They say one day I may die of the splinter, but it can't be removed.'[19] Greene's letters to Walston in early 1953 varied in tone between bitterness and studied resignation, but the splinter was not coming out. The problem was not that she had been involved with someone else – they both had other lovers – but the choice of Gilby, whom he regarded as a close friend, seemed a complicated betrayal of love, friendship, and the shared faith that was the backdrop for their relationship. Things improved enough for him to join her for a chaste holiday in Jamaica in March, where they were entertained by the Bond creator Ian Fleming, whose wife Ann wrote to Evelyn Waugh about Greene: 'Is he living in sin? Is he tortured? He remained remote from all, totally polite and holding the cocktail shaker as a kind of defensive weapon.'[20]

The perfect moment for Graham and Catherine to untangle themselves came in February, when their landlord gave them four months' notice to vacate their adjacent flats in St James's Street. Instead, they maintained their arrangements by taking two sets of chambers at Albany, an historic and exclusive enclave off Piccadilly which had numbered among its residents Lord Byron, Lord Palmerston, Aldous Huxley, and J. B. Priestley.[21] According to an unpublished essay of his, Greene once enlivened this rather sober place by smoking opium there, though it was so old it had dried up and crumbled away.[22] He and the Walstons were seldom in London at the same time, and for him his flat was as much a business address as a home. Doris Young, the secretary he shared with Harry, did her typing there. What time Graham had with Catherine was now usually spent abroad, as, for example, in May of that year when they had a happy time together at Anacapri. Indeed, Anacapri was also where he was able to write most productively.

In the summer of 1953 Greene was often in the company of the Australian Jocelyn Rickards, a small woman with black hair and astonishing green eyes who went on to become a leading costume designer in British cinema. She said that she met Greene at an exhibition in 1951, and experienced an instant chemistry – she says they fell in love. They did not begin an affair for about two years, as Catherine Walston was always in the way. Rickards had already begun a much longer-term open relationship with A. J. Ayer, whose sexual wanderings were prodigious. She recalled: 'Progressively, I became part of a trio, a quartet, a quintet and sextet.' Still, her relationship with Ayer endured, as did another with the playwright John Osborne. As for Greene, she recalled, 'His skin was always faintly sunburned and the texture of fine dry silk.'[23] Their relationship was reckless and exuberant, involving on one occasion intercourse in the first-class carriage of a train from Southend, observable to those on each platform where the train stopped. She said that Greene was full of guilt and spoke of himself as a manic depressive, and yet the man she knew was 'full of gaiety, wit, immense charm and perfect manners. According to some of his so-called friends, you'd think he was never off his knees.'[24] When Rickards came to write a memoir many years later, she had his approval: 'I'm no more ashamed of our affair than you are.'[25]

Greene was seldom a happy man, if often an amusing one. His practical jokes included from time to time ringing up a retired solicitor in Golders Green who happened also to be named Graham Greene and berating him, in various accents, for writing 'these filthy novels'. To get down off this particular cross, the solicitor changed to an ex-directory telephone number. Greene (the novelist, not the solicitor) would carry with him other people's business cards, and when he spotted a friend in a restaurant he would write lewd or inscrutable proposals on the back of a card, send it across, and watch the friend's reaction.[26]

From time to time, Greene entered competitions in which, under pseudonyms, he imitated his own writing style.[27] The first time he did it led to the making of a new film in 1953. Four years earlier, the New Statesman had offered a six-guinea prize for the best opening or conclusion to a novel in the manner of a contemporary author named Greene or Green. Graham Greene submitted three entries; one of them, 'The Stranger's Hand' by M. Wilkerson, managed to pick up a guinea, as the prize was divided six ways. Other entrants, including Kingsley Amis and Philip Larkin, had to settle for honorable mentions.[28] In a letter to the editor, Greene identified M. Wilkerson as 'yours truly', and lamented the failure of D. R. Cook and N. Wilkinson (his other pseudonyms) to win prizes, as the money would be, in a phrase reminiscent of Harry Lime, 'free of Income Tax'.[29]

That guinea was the first of thousands that the story earned for its author. One of his best friends in Italy was the novelist and film-maker Mario Soldati, a flamboyant, womanizing, high-living genius, whom he had met in the late 1940s. Soldati had had an affair with Gillian Sutro, whose husband John was a film producer and a contemporary of Greene's at Oxford. In Italy, Greene and Soldati kept glamorous company, dining with the likes of Roberto Rossellini and Ingrid Bergman. When Soldati learned of the 'The Stranger's Hand' caper, he loved it.[30]

At his prompting, Greene expanded the two paragraphs into a story before handing off the writing of the script itself to Guy Elwes and Giorgio Bassani. Working for Korda's firm British Lion, Soldati served as the director, with John Stafford and Peter Moore the producers. Looking to retain some control of the script, Greene took on a new role as associate producer, and this may have also appealed to him as a way of continuing to have a career if he ever reached an end as a writer. However, he found the financial side of producing films dreary and soon gave up on it.[31]

Filming began in Venice in April 1953, and he hurried there as soon as *The Living Room* had opened in London. The new film rather grafted *The Fallen Idol* onto *The Third Man* – with some success. Strange as it now seems, Venice was, as the opening narration puts it, 'a border city'. As Churchill defined it in 1946, nearby Trieste marked one end of the Iron Curtain. Yugoslavia, on which Greene and Korda had done some spying the previous summer, was a communist country, and the story turns on a pair of kidnappings by Yugoslav agents in Venice.

The production brought back Trevor Howard as Major Court, an MI5 officer, and Alida Valli, who had played Anna in *The Third Man*, as a refugee and hotel receptionist. Major Court witnesses the kidnapping of a Yugoslavian and gives chase only to be abducted himself and held captive by the very complicated Doctor Vivaldi, played by Eduardo Ciannelli, who injects the two men with various drugs to aid interrogation – they are to be taken across the Adriatic in a cargo ship. Court's young son Roger sounds the alarm and a search begins. Like Philippe in *The Fallen Idol*, Roger wanders the streets; by chance, he encounters Doctor Vivaldi, a surprisingly sentimental torturer, who befriends him and buys him a gelato. The doctor later remarks to Major Court, 'Aren't we all fond of children?'

Valli's character, Roberta, wants to help the boy and persuades her American boyfriend, played by Richard Basehart, to rescue Major Court from the ship, which the authorities may not search without causing an international incident. He does so by setting the ship alight, so that a waterborne fire brigade must board the ship in what becomes a Trafalgar of firehoses. Meanwhile, one of the Yugoslav agents shoots at Major Court, only to have Vivaldi block the bullet with his own body out of loyalty to Roger. Towards the end of the movie, Greene makes a cameo – his hand is seen untying the knot of one of the fireboats.[32]

If not quite as good as *The Third Man*, it was an excellent thriller, despite being outflanked by political changes. At the end of the Second World War, the Yugoslav leader Josip Broz Tito was an ally of Stalin and unquestionably a threat to his neighbours. By the time the film was released in 1954, he had fallen out with the Russians and was regarded, despite the repressiveness of his regime, as the sort of communist the West could live with. It was no longer plausible to think of his agents as truly dangerous or of Venice as threatened, and the film lacked the air of menace that hung over Harry Lime's Vienna. Though fairly well received, it fell short of the hopes of Korda, Soldati, and Greene.[33]

35

MAU MAU

For half a century, Kenya had seemed the most secure of British possessions in Africa – white settlers could obtain large, fertile farms in the highlands, with an orderly and submissive workforce of local people. Although her own farm failed, Karen Blixen's memoir *Out of Africa* presents an eloquent and nostalgic account of the settler project. In the 'Happy Valley' of the Wanjohi, aristocratic expatriates contrived a privileged, gin-soaked, and sexually freewheeling way of life, which, again, was founded on the availability of land and labour and the illusion of racial harmony.

The end of colonialism in Africa was not in all places the same as the end of white power. In South Africa, apartheid kept the black population in subjugation, as did white minority rule in Rhodesia. Many whites in Kenya approved of these arrangements and expected to entrench their own power by similar means.

The Mau Mau uprising referred to by the British as an 'Emergency', the same term used of the fighting in Malaya, lasted from 1952 to 1960. It had its origins in numerous local conflicts and grew into a civil war, often portrayed as a regression from civilization to savagery. Though they were thrown into panic at the thought that their servants were now probably bound by oaths to kill them, the white settlers were not the real victims of the violence. According to the most accurate numbers available, only thirty-two European settlers died in the uprising, while casualties among the police and the British military amounted to fewer than two hundred. However, eighteen hundred African civilians were killed and many more disappeared, while about twenty thousand Mau Mau died in combat. Colonial authorities conducted a harsh anti-insurgency campaign, which at one point saw seventy thousand

Africans in detention camps. Over the course of the whole Emergency, 150,000 were rounded up. Detainees were frequently tortured or sexually assaulted. Moreover, in an extraordinary piece of repression, about two thousand were condemned to death, of whom 1090 were actually executed.[1] Greene found the mass hangings repugnant, and later proposed feeding information to sympathetic Members of Parliament so that they could raise a protest.[2]

He pitched articles on Kenya to the *Sunday Times*, but without waiting for their answer flew to Nairobi on 25 August 1953. By that time, the trial of Jomo Kenyatta as a supposed leader of the uprising – he actually rejected Mau Mau violence – had been going on for almost a year. Greene wrote to his mother that with every passing day he was more in favour of the Kikuyu and against the Europeans: 'The settlers make such a howl & yet only about 20 have been murdered: they ought to try Malaya for a change – or Indo-China.'[3]

In the first of the four weeks he spent in the country, Greene met with the deputy governor, the archbishop, various generals, the commissioner of police, and some politicians and journalists. He met more than once with a legislator named Michael Blundell, who, though liberal by the standards of his community, wanted to crush the revolt; in a 1954 meeting with Winston Churchill this man rejected the Prime Minister's long-held and strongly expressed opinion that the whites should just sit down and negotiate. In Blundell's view, the uprising had no basis in legitimate grievances but arose from a mental illness producing atavism – he wanted the rebels strung up. His opinions did evolve, and in 1960 he was part of the negotiations that brought majority rule and an open franchise to Kenya. Many whites saw him as a traitor, and one threw a bag of silver coins at his feet.[4]

Greene's complaints about settlers probably arose from conversations with Blundell and his ilk. Someone tried to win Greene over to a hardline view of the conflict by showing him photographs of victims of the Mau Mau, including the charred, disembowelled corpse of a woman; a child chopped in half; and a policeman who somehow survived losing a foot and a hand and having his lower jaw nearly hacked off with a panga (machete). This material gave Greene a sense of the extreme violence of the conflict, which had seen, for example, 120 people, mostly the wives and children of local loyalists, burned or hacked to death by Mau Mau in the village of Lari in March. This was followed by a little-known second massacre, in which the Home Guard, seeking vengeance, killed a comparable number of people thought associated with the Mau Mau.[5] Greene abhorred what the Mau Mau were doing, but was under no illusion about 'trigger-happy units' assigned to quell the revolt.[6] The excesses of the counter-insurgency were well known: General George Erskine, recently appointed commander of East African Forces and one of the more sensible officials with whom Greene met, had issued orders forbidding 'Football League Competition' among units engaged in an obscene rivalry over the killing of Mau Mau.[7]

In his second week in Kenya, Greene visited the Kikuyu reserves, for a time in the company of James Hardie Candler, the thirty-four-year-old District Officer for Kangema Division in the Fort Hall District. The weather was cold and wet and their Land Rover was sliding from side to side on a hilly track south of Nyeri when Candler remarked in a steady voice, 'Now we've had it.' The vehicle lurched over a bank and stuck there with a front wheel hanging over a ravine. Shortly after, Greene himself drove a hired car into another Land Rover. He and Candler stayed for a night in a small house in the company of two prisoners and two guards who had formerly belonged to the Mau Mau. As a demonstration of trust, Candler did not carry a gun that night, but he did lay a grenade between his bed and Greene's, just in case they were attacked.[8] Seven months later, Candler was shot and killed by the Mau Mau in a roadside ambush.[9]

Greene himself did not carry a gun while in Kenya, causing a young Kikuyu to remark, 'You trust in the goodness of God.'[10] Conversations of this sort caused him to become very fond of the Kikuyu. As he did throughout his life, he courted danger and one day, driving to a remote military camp, he was confronted by a rhinoceros which, thankfully, did not charge his car but just stood near and shook its enormous head. Afterwards, he wrote that he was more afraid of an encounter with another rhino than of an ambush by the Mau Mau. Greene also arranged to go on a bombing run, but it was not on the scale of what he had experienced in Vietnam – it involved a tiny Piper Pacer dropping four bombs – and yet there was always the risk of being shot down.[11]

As in Vietnam, he turned to missionaries for an alternative to the official narratives – even as he recognized that they, too, had blind spots. The hardliners in the colonial administration, perhaps remembering the Irish uprising, distrusted Catholics, thinking they were assisting the insurgents, feeding and sheltering them, and tending their wounds.[12] Whereas many of the settlers had been surprised by a uprising among their supposedly contented servants and labourers as if 'Jeeves had taken to the jungle',[13] the missionaries had seen trouble brewing for some time.

In Kikuyu territory, Greene was sometimes accompanied by the Bishop of Nyeri, Carlo Maria Cavallera, who had lost two missions and two schools, but whose priests had been unharmed apart from one shot in the shoulder[14] – though later there were deaths. Greene made a particular friend of an Irish priest named P. J. McGill, stationed in Ruiru, with whom he debated the nature of love. Together they played a practical joke on an elderly priest from Alsace, making him appear an alcoholic before his bishop by loading his vehicle with wine bottles that rattled when he drove off. This prank became the basis of the short story 'Church Militant',[15] a work of greater interest than it seems, as in it Greene makes clear his view that not only is the settlers' land stolen from the Africans, but so too is that taken by the church despite the certainty of the bishop (closely modelled on Cavallera) that it is God's will to establish a new religious house for nuns.

This story was written in a single day, 13 October 1954,[16] so Greene had had time to reflect on his experiences in Kenya. While there, he had to digest atrocities committed on both sides, and to make some sense of them. He consulted with the Attorney General, John Whyatt, who was trying to maintain due process as the number of capital cases multiplied, and saved a good many lives by a dogged insistence on legal niceties.

No one exercised more influence on Greene's thinking than Sir John Barclay Nihill, a fellow Catholic who had been Chief Justice of Kenya and was now the President of the Court of Appeal for East Africa. Although obliged to enforce the laws as they existed, he was alarmed at the abrogation of human rights. In one instance he overturned fifty convictions from a mass trial related to the Lari massacre.[17] It was probably Nihill who sent Greene to observe a mass trial at Githenguri early in his visit. Later, Greene attended a sitting of the Court of Appeal. Nihill was unhappy about the extension of the death penalty to include, for example, the mere possession of ammunition, as the police seemed to be planting their own .303 rounds on people they wanted to arrest. When, after the publication of his articles, Greene wrote a further letter to *The Times*[18] describing the cruel behaviour of forces fighting the Mau Mau, killing people for not having appropriate papers and then leaving their bodies to rot in the open to terrify others, Nihill wrote that he was 'heartened ... by your fearless letter' and agreed with it entirely: 'I feel sure that a terrible harvest of hate is being sown out here.'[19]

Greene found the British farmers repugnant and annoying, with one very notable exception. About twelve years older than the novelist, Maria Newall, a Catholic, had settled in Kenya around 1949. She was about six feet tall, and Graham's sister Elisabeth recalled her as devastatingly beautiful.[20] She was running a 500-acre farm on the edge of the forest without a guard and without the assistance of other Europeans. Greene was impressed by her good looks and her courage, dubbing her 'Pistol Mary'. Possibly amorous at first, their relationship evolved into a sincere friendship that lasted several decades. Greene's Kenyan journal records what she told him of her life. Her first, sacramental marriage ended in divorce, so she remarried outside the church, but her second husband was swindled and committed suicide. During the war she had operated her own ambulance unit and gone out to Cairo, being torpedoed en route. In Cairo, which was presumably where she encountered Elisabeth, she fell in love with the future cabinet minister Sir Walter Monckton (later Viscount Monckton) and had an affair with him, only to be unceremoniously dumped when he married another woman; Newall still loved him and followed his speeches in *Hansard*. Newall and Greene spent several days together in the latter part of his visit to Kenya. They remained in touch, and twenty-five years later Greene and Father Leopoldo Durán would sometimes visit her in Sintra during the journeys through Spain and Portugal that gave birth to *Monsignor Quixote*.

Greene's reading of the situation in Kenya may strike the contemporary reader as unconventional. In his articles for the *Sunday Times*,[21] he followed the same approach that he had used in writing about Indochina, emphasizing complexity and competing interests. He was somewhat more generous about the settlers than he was in private correspondence and maintained that Kenyatta, if freed, would have to be exiled. Despite a note of paternalism in the articles, he was having no truck with the argument that the revolt pitted the civilization of whites against the savagery of Africans. Whereas the oaths and rituals of the Mau Mau were commonly seen as expressions of something mad and brutish, Greene saw them, as he saw, for example, the spiritual practices of the indigenous people of Mexico, as the expression of an authentic religious consciousness that was comprehensible from a Catholic viewpoint, but not from a Protestant or a secular one: it was otherworldly and implicitly sacramental. He did object to some practices, such as clitorectomies (now referred to as female genital mutilation), and, of course, he approved of conversions to Catholicism.

Drawing on his visit to a prison and his conversation with the chaplain to the condemned in Nairobi, a Father Fuller, who was a friend of Nihill, he claimed that the vast majority of condemned Mau Mau converted to the Catholic faith before execution, and, as the priest put it, 'They die like angels.' It is rather strange to think that Greene would see the conflict as a problem of theology, but he did. And the essence of his position was that by despising the traditional beliefs and rituals of the Africans, the British ensured that they would have no lasting part in the life of the place they had colonized.

Although the events of the Mau Mau uprising are now remote in time, their consequences are still being felt. In 2013, the British government settled a mass claim by 5200 elderly Kenyans concerning human rights abuses arising from the counter-insurgency with a payout of £19.9 million, and this has been followed by a much larger class action, still before the courts, on behalf of forty thousand people who seek damages for a wider range of abuses.[22] As part of the first settlement, the then Foreign Secretary, William Hague, gave a statement to the House of Commons, which included this apology: 'I would like to make clear now and for the first time, on behalf of Her Majesty's Government, that we understand the pain and grievance felt by those who were involved in the events of the Emergency in Kenya. The British Government recognises that Kenyans were subject to torture and other forms of ill treatment at the hands of the colonial administration. The British government sincerely regrets that these abuses took place, and that they marred Kenya's progress towards independence.'[23]

36

DIEN BIEN PHU

The commandant in the Catholic enclave of Bui-Chu was a confident and thoughtful Buddhist. His famous guest was only a few minutes away, approaching in a jeep through a series of narrow causeways between canals. He was to show the visitor Thui-nhai, a fortified village where the whole population had drawn together in the fight against the Viet Minh – a remarkable thing in the uneasy days of January 1954 and a sign of the enclave's near-independence from the French. Best to be safe, he decided, and at the last moment sent a team ahead to scout the road to the village. Sure enough, they found a landmine in a box buried in the ground with a piece of wood covering the detonator. The instructions in Chinese for its deployment were still there.[1]

Just as another person might grow addicted to blackjack or slot machines, Graham Greene wagered his life again and again and just could not lose it. His most engrained habit was survival. Following his brush with the landmine, he wrote in his journal: 'After lunch lay down & haunted by unpleasant thoughts of C. How strange that one feels no gratitude that the mine was found.'[2]

This was Greene's third winter sojourn in Vietnam – there would be one more. In the autumn he had corresponded with Trevor Wilson, now working, as Hugh had, in the Information Service in Malaya. He learned that Wilson had been granted, with no difficulty, a fifteen-day visa to Vietnam. They plotted a return, with Greene flying into Saigon and Wilson into Hanoi, in order to avert or at least delay suspicion on the part of the authorities. Arriving on 30 December,[3] Greene hoped for a better reception from the French than on his last visit as he came with the blessing of their high command and carried a message from the chief of staff to the latest commander-in-chief in Indochina, Lieutenant-General Henri Navarre. Indeed, he told his son Francis that he had had a long interview with the chief of staff in Paris in March 1952 with the objective of getting himself off 'the list of suspects' and had evidently succeeded.[4]

On this visit, he would pursue leads in the south, while Wilson, who even in exile stayed in touch with officials in Hanoi, would lay 'a few trails' in the north.[5] Representing the *Sunday Times*, Greene's objectives on this trip appear to have been mainly journalistic, but he needed Wilson's contacts. His friend was indeed making a report to 'the old firm', but only as a means of making some money – he was usually hard up.[6] Greene's journal shows that he spent a good deal of time in the company of 'Donald', presumably Donald Lancaster, the MI6 representative who met him at the airport on his earlier visit. However, this does not, in itself, indicate that Greene had undertaken any significant task for the service on this occasion, beyond keeping his eyes open.[7] Greene's relations with the Sûreté seem also to have improved – he visited André Moret, head of the Tonkin section,[8] who had clearly become a friend and may even have provided the inspiration for the character of Inspector Vigot in *The Quiet American*.

On his first evening, Greene wrote in his journal: 'Is there any solution here the West can offer? But the bar tonight was loud with innocent American voices and that was the worst disquiet. There weren't so many Americans in 1951 and 1952.' When he observed to a member of the American Economic Mission that the French might give up on the war soon, he was told, 'Oh no, they can't do that. They'd have to pay us back . . .' and a sum in the thousands of millions was named.[9] That money was the deposit on a war the Americans would soon own.

Of his presence there, Greene wrote: 'I always have a sense of guilt when I am a civilian tourist in the regions of death: after all one does not visit a disaster except to give aid – one feels a *voyeur* of violence . . .'[10] His reaction, common to war correspondents, is understandable. But whatever his psychological motivations, the search for stimulation and for escape, even the side employment for MI6, the task of observing and making known the truths of a place like Vietnam was of such magnitude that any other consideration seems trivial.

Greene arrived at a time when both the French and the Viet Minh were hungry for a major victory that would strengthen their hand in the Geneva peace talks. On 3 January 1954, Greene travelled to the strategic airbase at Seno in the Savannakhet province of Laos and could see that the place would fall if attacked in force. The following day, he met General René Cogny, commander of the French forces in the north, in Hanoi. A tall, handsome officer, he had nearly starved to death at Buchenwald and was left with a permanent limp from his treatment there.

They discussed the huge encampment at Dien Bien Phu, intended to control the approaches to Luang Prabang. Navarre wanted to lure the enemy into a set-piece battle and to repeat, on a larger scale, the victory at Na San on the Laotian border at the beginning of December 1952. There, the French set up artillery, entrenched their position, and constructed an airfield, so that they had a fortress. The forces of General Vo Nguyen Giap attacked in waves, and were shelled and bombed mercilessly. After their victory, the French abandoned the Na San camp, in favour of Dien Bien Phu. Cogny had doubts about the plan, and tended to speak his mind on the subject. He felt the French should concentrate forces on the Red River Delta to ensure that Hanoi was not cut off.[11]

Cogny arranged for Greene to go to Dien Bien Phu[12] on 5 January 1954, and he was disturbed by what he saw. The French had indeed assembled a great many men, guns, and aeroplanes, and could point to locations where the approaching Viet Minh would be subject to enfilade or flanking fire. The camp was set in the middle of a plain where human-wave tactics could only end in slaughter. It was ringed by hills that the French had fortified and given names as if they were girlfriends or mistresses: Anne-Marie, Beatrice, Claudine, Dominique, Eliane, Gabrielle, Huguette, and Isabelle.

Further off, other hills were held by the Viet Minh, who could see every movement within the compound but were themselves hidden from view. General Giap had studied the abandoned camp at Na San and changed his tactics. Motivated by a popular land reform recently begun in the countryside that promised to give freedom from traditional landlords, two hundred thousand civilian porters dragged artillery and anti-aircraft guns over great distances to the heights above the French camp. They also brought a huge amount of rice to sustain the army of fifty thousand Giap had assembled.[13] The French had sent out scouts and knew that the Viet Minh were massing for attack. Shells fell intermittently on Dien Bien Phu as the Viet Minh worked out the exact range. The French, however, could not locate the enemy guns, which were dug in and camouflaged by trees and vegetation.

Greene witnessed a curious display of nerves among the French when the commander, Colonel Christian de Castries, lost his temper in the officers' mess. The chief of artillery mentioned the withdrawal from Na San and de Castries angrily declared that that was a defensive position and that this was intended for counter-attack. He ordered that no one mention the withdrawal again in the mess. When Greene later asked what the colonel had meant, an officer waved at the hills and said that to take the offensive they would need not a squadron of tanks but a thousand mules.[14]

Greene toured the hilltop outposts and slept in a dugout beside an intelligence officer, then returned to Hanoi the next day for a further meeting with General Cogny.[15] Greene had no training in field tactics, but common sense, and perhaps the remarks of Cogny, made him afraid of what would happen at Dien Bien Phu.

He could see that the great dilemma was that without independence the Vietnamese had no incentive to fight the communists, and yet if the French left the communists would likely seize a quick and permanent victory. What was possible? To pursue this point he went to Bui Chu, the Catholic enclave adjoining Phat Diem, where the French had experimented by allowing the Vietnamese to conduct their own defence. At first, it was a disaster, as two battalions deserted to the Viet Minh, taking their new American weapons with them, and the French had to rush back, but given time and training the local forces were certainly up to the job.

Greene was taken to see Thui-nhai, and it was on the road to this village that the landmine was found and disarmed. He referred to Thui-nhai as 'the most impressive thing' he had seen during the war. Everyone who could walk served in the militia, with girls as young as twelve armed with knives and grenades, other villagers with Sten guns or merely old rifles. Mud ramparts had been built, extending even inside the church, as that was an apt place for a final stand. This village had survived nine attacks and received the surrenders of Viet Minh who had had enough of the war – one officer brought with him plans for the capture of Bui Chu. Taken for a flyover in a small plane, Greene saw a French flag on just one artillery position and felt that he was looking at 'a bird's eye view of independence'.[16]

This was a village with one culture – nearly everyone, apart from the Buddhist commandant, was Catholic – so the model might not apply easily everywhere, but for Greene this was the best possible way forward: the Vietnamese, given the means, could look after themselves. Moreover, he seems to have been proud that Catholics could lead the way. On his earlier visits, he had been fascinated by the Bishop of Phat Diem, mistakenly referring to him as a Trappist – he was actually a member of a similar and equally austere branch of the Cistercian Order.[17] As Greene saw it, he had only one ambition: to build new churches, even though he did not have enough priests to operate them. He was left with an image of the gaunt bishop riding stiffly in a jeep with his fingers raised in benediction. The Bishop of Bui Chu, Pham Ngoc Chi, was a very different sort of person. He could see that while his people needed churches, they also needed schools and hospitals, and they needed a functioning economy. Greene thought of him as a much-needed modernizer; however, he regarded both men as compromised by their military activities.[18]

Certainly, the church in Bui Chu had endured a great deal. Seven months earlier, the Viet Minh had abducted four priests; among them were two Belgians whom Greene had met in 1952 and with whom he had discussed English literature. The Viet Minh had fired into a chapel, killing four nuns, one of whom fell dead beneath a statue of Mary. And yet Greene, in the midst of his own depression, found the liturgies in Bui Chu cheerful, utterly unlike those of 'bourgeois' Europe: 'The Bishop was robed to the music of violins, gay tinkly music like an eighteenth-century gavotte. The altar boys carried the vestments with a ballet grace: even the candles on the altar seemed to dance ... This was a Mass to be enjoyed, and why not? The sacrament is too serious for us to compete in seriousness. Under the enormous shadow of the cross it is better to be gay.'[19]

Greene returned to Hanoi, where he heard that the Viet Minh had initiated pincer movements in Laos, and through the evening of 11 January 1954 listened to helicopters bringing in the wounded.[20] The next morning he flew to Vientiane, where he attended an audience with the crown prince and tried to find out what was going on. In the latter days of his visit to Indochina, he had meetings with a series of leaders, among them the regent of Laos, General Fernand Gambiez, and King Norodom Sihanouk of Cambodia, but no records of the conversations have come to light.[21] Greene did record a very illuminating discussion he had on a flight to Luang Prabang, when an unnamed French colonel, one of nine who were travelling together, complained that they needed 250 more planes in this part of Indochina, but had nowhere to put them, as all the landing strips were full. He also spoke uneasily about Dien Bien Phu, confirming for Greene that the Viet Minh were moving artillery there, though he spoke with scorn of the prospects of a massed assault.[22]

The colonel was right to worry about those guns. On 13 March 1954, the Viet Minh began a massive bombardment that knocked out unprotected French artillery pieces and destroyed the airstrip. The camp was besieged, relying on the Americans to airdrop supplies. Having dismissed the capabilities of the Viet Minh, the artillery commander at Dien Bien Phu, the man whom Greene had heard rebuked in the mess for speaking of Na San, went to his bunker, held a grenade to his chest, and blew himself up.[23]

Under heavy rainfall that created misery for the thousands of wounded on both sides, the Viet Minh expanded a system of trenches allowing them to mount ground attacks against the hills controlled by the French. As the situation unfolded, it became clear that only American airpower could relieve the camp. In the end, President Eisenhower, having been refused British support, decided there would be no bombing, as it might provoke China. On 7 May 1954 the camp fell. About ten thousand Viet Minh and two thousand French had been killed.[24] Nearly eleven thousand French soldiers were marched off to a grim captivity, from which only a third ever returned.[25]

This battle still lay a few weeks in the future, but the atmosphere was gloomy, and Greene spent a great deal of time among soldiers, who always made him nervous.[26] In Hong Kong, just after Christmas, he had dabbled in heroin and did not like it.[27] In Vietnam he smoked opium almost every day, sometimes as many as eight pipes. Between the mood disorder and the countless objective reasons to be depressed in Vietnam in 1954, he was particularly troubled.

Over the next month or so he engaged in some erratic behaviour. Going to Bangkok to meet Catherine on 22 January, he was at the same time conducting a liaison with Mercia Ryhiner, a strikingly beautiful young woman of Eurasian descent. She had been briefly married to a man who trapped exotic animals by the thousands for European zoos, and became herself an expert trapper who would, without the protection of a gun, take on apes, leopards, tigers, elephants, and king cobras. She became something of a celebrity when the couple came ashore in Genoa with a shipment of rhinoceroses for the zoo in Basel and the press pursued a 'beauty and the beasts' storyline.[28]

Unhappy with Catherine and feeling strongly about Mercia, Greene found ways to spend time with both women in Bangkok at the end of January. He went to Saigon with Catherine from 6 to 17 February,[29] and made arrangements to see Mercia in Singapore at the end of the month, spending a total of three weeks with her. They quarrelled, something Greene blamed on himself. As there was now no likelihood of a marriage to Catherine, Greene wished that something more might come of his connection with Mercia, but she felt uneasy about his not being divorced,[30] so released him back into the wild. The two remained friends, and in later years she struck up a friendship with Greene's daughter. In 1978, she married the actor Rex Harrison.[31]

While in Singapore and then Penang, Greene worked on his articles, which he feared might close a door for him in Indochina. He wrote to Catherine: 'I don't know how the papers will take them because they are very anti-American & anti-Emperor. I'm afraid so much they won't let me back again which means the end of opium.'[32] He was wrong about the newspapers. He arrived back in Europe just as Dien Bien Phu was taking over the headlines, and his first-hand knowledge was exactly what the editors needed. The *Sunday Times* published two pieces (21 and 28 March 1954), as did the *New Republic* (5 and 12 April 1954), with single articles appearing in the *Spectator* (16 April 1954) and *The Tablet* (17 April 1954)[33] Greene wrote politely to General Cogny to thank him for his help and to express the hope that his articles did not give offence. Cogny seems to have taken it all graciously and the two remained in touch.[34]

37

NO ONE EXPECTS THE INQUISITION

I n Vietnam, Greene had been working in a soldiers' world of orders, duty, and obedience; on his return to England he found himself unexpectedly caught up in another chain of command. On 9 April 1954, Greene was summoned to meet Bernard Griffin, the Cardinal Archbishop of Westminster, who read to him a letter from Cardinal Giuseppe Pizzardo, the arch-conservative head of the Holy Office, once known as the Inquisition. Addressing Griffin, Pizzardo wrote that *The Power and the Glory* had been denounced to the Holy Office, and while he made a show of gentleness in referring to Graham Greene as a convert, he maintained that in the book the human condition seems insuperably wretched and that the work caused harm to the priesthood: '[it] portrays a state of affairs so paradoxical, so extraordinary and so erroneous as to disconcert unenlightened persons, who form the majority of the readers'. Greene was instructed to stop publication and translation of the book until its errors were corrected.[1]

Greene almost always treated priests and prelates with respect – the notable exception coming late in his life with Pope John Paul II, whom he thought a vastly over-rated bully – and he was not sure how to proceed. Evelyn Waugh, who had also had brushes with censorship, volunteered to join any public demonstration that Greene wished to make but assumed he would not wish to do so.[2] This was a generous offer: a key difference between the two novelists was that whereas Greene was a rebel and a Catholic, the great rebellion of Waugh's life was, in fact, just being a Catholic. He hated confrontations with the church; in particular, he disapproved of Greene's public letter of protest, shortly after, concerning the church's refusal to provide a funeral or even prayers at the graveside of the French author Colette, who was divorced.[3]

Greene believed that his problem with the Holy Office had actually originated with Griffin, who in his Pastoral Letter for Advent 1953 had implicitly condemned *The Power and the Glory* and other works by Catholic writers for their treatment of adultery.[4] In fact, the complaint had come from a priest in Switzerland, and Griffin was merely articulating the views of Cardinal Pizzardo.[5]

There was, however, a hidden dynamic. If Pope Pius XII had read *The End of the Affair* and only expressed concern for its author, and *The Heart of the Matter* had outraged conservative clerics throughout the world, why did the Holy Office turn its guns on the *The Power and the Glory*? Years later, Greene remarked to Anthony Burgess that it was an odd choice.[6] As a matter of theology, it reads as a thought experiment conducted within a very orthodox understanding of the priesthood. Moreover, the Holy Office sent the novel to three theological consultants, none of whom recommended it be condemned. The most negative said the book was terribly sad and ought not to have been written, and that Greene's bishop should admonish him to write differently.[7] So why did the Holy Office ignore this advice?

The answer probably lay in the 1930s. Pizzardo had been the architect of Vatican policy towards Mexico and the Cristeros, advocating Catholic Action rather than armed struggle, and he was anxious about the reputation of the church in that country.[8] Insofar as Greene portrayed the moral inadequacy of a certain kind of priest, he inadvertently gave support to anticlericalism. In portraying simony as a cornerstone of parish life, he was confirming part of the claim that the Mexican church exploited the poor. It is very likely that Pizzardo's difficulty with the book had little to do with sex and that he was really attempting to control the historical narrative.

Taking the advice of his old friend, the papal diplomat Archbishop David Mathew, and a copyright lawyer, Greene composed a 'casuistical' letter to Pizzardo that began by apologizing for a delay in answering the Holy Office as he had been in Indochina, trying to mobilize world opinion on behalf of persecuted Catholics. He then pointed out that the licences for publication and translation of *The Power and the Glory* had long since passed to various publishers and he no longer had the power to suppress the book. At Mathew's suggestion, a copy of this letter was sent to the very cultured Monsignor Giovanni Battista Montini, Pro-Secretary of State at the Vatican, in the hope that he would get involved.[9]

In fact, Montini had already intervened, advising Pizzardo that he had read the book long ago as one of 'singular literary value'. He went on to accept that it was sad but insisted that it showed the priest's spiritual fidelity to his mission.[10] It was at his suggestion that the book was sent to the third consultant, who thought the investigation was pure nonsense. Pizzardo could see he was playing a weak hand and allowed the complaint against *The Power and the Glory* just to fade away.

After his election as Pope Paul VI, Giovanni Battista Montini met in July 1965 with Greene and told him, to his delight, that he had read *The Power and the Glory, Brighton Rock, Stamboul Train,* and *The Heart of the Matter*.[11] Greene brought up Pizzardo's attempt to suppress his Mexican novel; the pope seemed not to remember the case, but said to Greene, 'Parts of all your books will always offend some Catholics and you shouldn't pay any attention to that.'[12] Canonized in 2018, Paul VI is the first saint known to have been a fan of Graham Greene.

Pizzardo used up the last of Greene's patience with Catholic interference with his work. Not long after, Greene read Ralph Ellison's 'wonderful' novel *Invisible Man*: 'One's own books seem tight & narrow by comparison.' Meanwhile complaints about his work continued to emanate from Rome. He felt that, like Ellison, he should be bolder in just saying what he thought: 'What fun is there in writing if one doesn't go too far? What makes me a "small" writer is that I never do. There's a damned cautiousness in what I write, & therefore one has a "damned" success.'[13] From the mid-1950s, Greene became more willing to write about doubt as the counterpart of belief – something he had certainly experienced but had rather shied away from in his fiction.

He was making little progress on *The Quiet American*. As usual, in the middle of a major work, Greene felt confused and uncertain, telling his mother at one point: 'I still don't know what the book's about.'[14] In May 1954, he was seized by the idea for a novella, *Loser Takes All*, which he wrote in a matter of weeks while staying at a hotel in Monte Carlo and conducting his research at the gaming tables.[15] He later recalled, in error, that the book was written in 1955.[16] It was serialized in August and September 1954, then published as a book in January 1955.[17]

It is the story of an accountant named Bertram whose employer, Mr Dreuther, offers him and his fiancée, Cary, a honeymoon cruise in his yacht, beginning at Monte Carlo. The employer then forgets all about it. The couple have to live by their wits in the casinos, quarrelling, and reconciling. Mr Dreuther eventually appears and remembers the arrangement. In writing the 'sentimental' *Loser Takes All*, Greene wanted to break out of old habits: 'A reputation is like a death mask. I wanted to smash the mask.'[18] This novella anticipates the comic fiction he would write over the next decade, and, in particular, it introduces numbers as a leitmotif, which reappears especially in *Our Man in Havana*. In *Loser Takes All*, Bertram becomes enslaved by a mathematical gambling 'system' and recovers his humanity only when he gets rid of it – it stands for any system of thought that is too sure of itself.

The situation was drawn from an occasion in June 1951 when Greene and Walston were left waiting in Athens for the *Elsewhere*.[19] Mr Dreuther is closely modelled on Korda and given many of his catchphrases. Korda was not at all offended by the portrait, but he and Greene had a rare quarrel over the casting of the part when it was made into a film. Greene wanted Alec Guinness, but Korda refused, and it went to the lugubrious Robert Morley.[20] There was more to this than Greene was willing to make public. Korda's distribution company, British Lion, went into receivership in the late spring of 1955;[21] Greene heard that the film of *Loser Takes All*, for which he wrote the script, would be cancelled. He was livid and thought the friendship finished – but they sorted out their differences.[22] The project went ahead with John Stafford as producer, Ken Annakin as director, and Rossano Brazzi and Glynis Johns playing the leads. Released in Britain in September 1956, the film was a pleasant but decidedly minor production.

Unfortunately, Greene's friendship with Alex Korda was nearer to the end than either realized. With his business on the ropes and auditors identifying improprieties, especially in his Italian operation, the producer suffered a heart attack in July 1955 and withdrew for three weeks to a nursing home. That autumn, he sold the *Elsewhere* and bought a house in Cannes. In November, he learned from his doctors that he could not live long, and on 23 January 1956 died of a massive heart attack.[23] Greene, who had two very friendly meetings with Korda just before his death, would later write lovingly of this man and recall his lament for lost hopes: 'When my friends and I were young in Hungary, we all dreamed of being poets. And what did we become? We became politicians and advertisement men and film producers.'[24]

38

A REFORMED CHARACTER

G reene spent much of the early summer of 1954 in Anacapri.
Then, after Catherine left in mid-June, he went to Florence and stayed with Allegra Sander, the very beautiful French author of *Les Hommes: ces demi-dieux*, a witty dialogue between two women on their dealings with men; Greene contributed a preface to the English edition, which was illustrated by Mervyn Peake. They visited the memoirist and aesthete Harold Acton, once Greene's foe at Oxford but now a dear friend, living at the Villa La Pietra, just outside Florence. Acton managed to spill chianti over Sander's dress.[1] She took Greene to the Calcio Storico, the war-like football matches played in historical garb in the Piazza Santa Croce, where they saw a man killed by an exploding cannon. They then went to Siena for the July running of Il Palio, the bareback horse race likewise known for period garb, pageantry, and accidental death. It seems that Catherine remarked on the 'ambiguity' of Greene's connection with Sander, so in one letter he made a point of how she was bringing her boyfriend (and future husband), a Venetian lawyer, with her when they were next to meet in Rome.[2] Sander did, however, have enough influence over Greene in those weeks to put him on a regimen of no martinis and just two whiskies before dinner – he remarked with a certain wistfulness that he was 'a reformed character'.[3]

On a whim he went to Haiti that August in the company of the director Peter Brook, his wife the actor Natasha (née Parry), and Truman Capote. Greene was overwhelmed by Capote, whom he liked very much, seeing him as a psychic. He predicted that Greene would marry a younger woman, have another child, live by the sea, begin his best book, and remain sexually active in his eighth decade. How much Capote knew about Greene's private life is unclear, but he told his fortune in such a way as to touch on all the raw nerves – his frustration about women, a fear of sexual decline, guilt over his children, and a sense of unfulfilled potential as a writer. Doubtless hoping to make her jealous, Greene reported the prognostications to Catherine, claiming that it depressed him as he really wanted to be with her.[4]

What Capote did not foresee was that Haiti itself would play a part in Greene's future. Occupying the eastern portion of the island of Hispaniola, it had a democratic legacy going back to 1791 when Toussaint L'Ouverture led the slaves in a successful revolt. The country's subsequent history included an American occupation from 1915 to 1934 and the notorious massacre in 1937 of twenty thousand Haitians living in the Dominican Republic.[5] By the 1950s Haiti was independent and under the relatively benign rule of President Paul Magloire, a former police chief. The island was poor but peaceful and law abiding. It was also experiencing a cultural revival, notably the emergence of a local painting style, of which the outstanding example, the biblical murals in Cathédrale Sainte-Trinité featuring solely black figures, was destroyed in the earthquake of 2010. Haiti was also producing writers, poets, and intellectuals.

In the years before the emergence of François Duvalier, the dictator known as 'Papa Doc', there was also every reason to hope for prosperity based on the tourist trade. After 1957, this physician would transform the island into what Greene dubbed 'The Nightmare Republic' through the operations of paramilitaries called the Tontons Macoutes and a distortion of the Vodou religion. Greene would eventually write a novel, *The Comedians*, with the intention of focusing the world's gaze on this psychopathic regime.

In the summer of 1954, Greene travelled about the island mainly in the company of Natasha Brook, while her husband and Capote were trying to work out sets for a musical based on Capote's short story 'The House of Flowers', set in a Port-au-Prince brothel – it would open on Broadway at the end of the year.

Greene had a lifetime phobia of birds, and it was tested by seeing a cockfight and then a Vodou ceremony in which a participant bit the head off a hen and squeezed blood from its still-moving body. This was followed by an initiation rite, in which a man was carried into the gathering wrapped in a sheet and a hand and a foot held briefly in a fire to the sounds of drums and singing. There was then a possession in which the god of war arrived from Africa and entered the body of a worshipper, who went about the room spitting rum and menacing the crowd with a panga. The possession ended and the person collapsed with a shriek.

What stood out for Greene was how very much Catholic imagery was involved in the ceremony: a banner of St Jacques, the kissing of crosses and vestments, and water for asperges. The ceremony was authentic, but it was also tailored for tourists;[6] even so, he detected something here of what had so impressed him in Mexico and Kenya, a faith on the margins of Catholicism, a spiritual intensity expressed in rituals akin to sacraments. The next day he described the evening in detail for Catherine and wrote at the top: '*Will you keep this letter in case I need it to refresh my mind?*' He would later incorporate much of that description into a major article on Haiti, and into *The Comedians* itself.[7]

While in Haiti, he met, just in passing, a journalist who would become indispensable to him and to his work in the coming decades, and who would eventually write an important memoir of him. Bernard Diederich was born in New Zealand in 1926. A tall, handsome youth with skill as a boxer, he served in the American merchant marine during the Second World War, afterwards continuing for several years as a sailor in one of the last square-rigged ships in regular service. In 1949, he settled in Port-au-Prince, where he established a newspaper, the *Haiti Sun*, and served also as a resident correspondent for the *New York Times* and other news agencies. Once the Duvalier repression began in earnest, his reporting – often without a byline – kept the world aware of conditions within Haiti.

Diederich watched one of Greene's best-known tangles with American immigration authorities. The two men had only exchanged a few words in the bar of the El Rancho Hotel before Greene set off for Britain by what would be the most convenient route, changing planes in Puerto Rico, but there he was turned back. He did not have an American visa, and when asked the question, so typical of the McCarthy era, about having belonged to the Communist Party, he gave his usual answer: 'Yes, for about four weeks at the age of nineteen.' The startled officer told him to wait for his boss to deal with the matter, so Greene, perhaps foreseeing a bit of fun, sat down contentedly and read some P. G. Wodehouse. After about two hours, the boss appeared and told Greene he would have to go back to Haiti; Greene warned him to expect publicity. The immigration officers did not believe him, so he sent a telegram and got the story out on Reuters, followed a day or two later by a shorter piece on the INS newswire, and soon the British newspapers picked up on it. Those were a bad few days for the McCarran Act.[8]

Greene was returned to Port-au-Prince. Bernard Diederich happened to be at Bowen Field airport and witnessed a stand-off between the novelist and the irate Delta Air Lines manager, a white Southerner who was refusing to let him on a plane to Havana for lack of a Cuban visa and insisting that he wait several days for a flight to the British colony of Jamaica. Greene barked, 'What? I am going on this plane.' The pilot then got involved, as Diederich recalled: 'Like a boxing referee, he raised his hand to separate them. We heard the pilot tell the Delta man, "Thank you, I am taking this gentleman on my plane."' When Greene had boarded, the manager turned to the bystanders and kept repeating, 'I was just trying to help him.'[9]

Greene is thought to have made about twelve visits to Cuba over the years. On this occasion, Greene simply skipped immigration formalities and, with the police searching for him, spent two days in what he described to Peter and Natasha Brook as 'quite the most vicious city' he had ever been in. He was approached by prostitutes, attended blue films, found pornographic books, and smoked his first marijuana.[10]

39

ACCIDENTS CAN ALWAYS HAPPEN

The battle of Dien Bien Phu was followed by negotiations over Vietnam at the Geneva Conference in the late spring and early summer of 1954. The participants agreed to a temporary division of the country at the 17th parallel and then democratic elections in 1956. The division actually remained until the final victory of North Vietnam in 1975. Catholics generally opposed the Geneva Accords as most of them lived in territory to be ceded to the Viet Minh. Before the agreement, about eight hundred thousand Catholics lived in the Red River Valley; of those, about half a million left their homes for the south in what became known as the 'Northern Migration'.[1] It was the end of the Catholic enclaves ruled by warrior bishops, and it profoundly altered the south as there were now, as one historian notes, more practising Catholics in Saigon than in Paris or Rome.[2]

Graham Greene believed in an independent Vietnam, but not a divided one. Partition was the blunt tool of twentieth-century diplomacy, leaving terrible wounds in Ireland, India, Pakistan, and Korea. He felt that those who proposed it for Indochina had little understanding of the human cost involved.[3] On the other hand, the French could not keep fighting, and abandoning the country to the Viet Minh was still unthinkable.

The leader who emerged in the south was indeed a Catholic, but Greene disapproved of him. Ngo Dinh Diem was the son of an imperial mandarin and brother of the reactionary Archbishop of Hué. A fervent Catholic with Confucian sympathies, he had been regarded for about a decade as a potential leader, but he had refused various proposals as they did not involve real independence for the country. In June 1954, he became prime minister, and in the following year, having rigged the referendum that ended the reign of Bao Dai, made himself president of the new republic. He rejected the Geneva Accords and cancelled the elections scheduled for 1956, which Ho Chi Minh would have won. A complicated figure, Diem has been condemned for corruption, authoritarianism, and repression of Buddhists. He trusted almost no one outside his family, giving another brother, the scholarly Ngo Dinh Nhu, control of the security services. After widespread protests, including Buddhist monks setting themselves on fire, Ngo Dinh Diem and Ngo Dinh Nhu were killed in 1963 in a *coup d'état* authorized by an ill-briefed John F. Kennedy.

Greene arrived in Saigon on 14 February 1955. Early in his visit he saw a good deal of Colonel Leroy, who showed him two camps of migrants or 'déracinés'. One morning he woke to see from his hotel window a ship full of evacuees from the north, and thought of the assurance they had been given, 'Here is freedom to work', and wrote in his journal 'what work?' When he saw lorries queueing to transfer the new arrivals, he added, 'Happy the very poor who have such a little way to fall.' In the face of all this suffering, he was struck by the remark of an Indian member of the International Commission overseeing the implementation of the Geneva Accords: 'You in the West never realize the power for sacrifice in the East. There is no possibility of a Gandhi in the West – or of a Ho Chi Minh.'[4]

Greene learned that some priests had told their parishioners God had gone south and they should follow Him. Certainly, the Americans wanted as many anti-communists as possible to move south, and the American expert in subversion Edward Lansdale was responsible for the distribution of leaflets on the whereabouts of God and the Blessed Virgin.[5] The Vietnamese church was divided over whether the migration should have been encouraged, and the bishops of Bui Chu and Phat Diem were criticized for leaving their dioceses. Greene heard of two Dominican friars who, despite belonging to an anti-colonial order, had died in captivity, and he was worried about the fate of his friend Father Willichs, who had heard his confession in the bell tower during the assault on Phat Diem three years before.[6]

Greene himself was in some danger. Colonel Leroy sent word that he must not go outside the city, and, especially, he must turn down any invitation from General Tran Van Soai of the Hoa Hao, who was offended by a reference to himself in one of Greene's articles. The Hoa Hao now had a dossier on Greene, and as Leroy put it, 'Accidents can always happen.' Greene thought of how reality was following the plot of his unfinished novel.[7]

He was invited to the Cabinet Office for what turned out to be a reception in honour of himself and Father Georges Naidenoff, SJ, an ecclesiastical journalist. Here he met Diem, his brother Nhu, and the flamboyant Madame Nhu, who served as the country's first lady since Diem was unmarried – later very unpopular, she struck Greene as 'lovely', though he did not take to the brothers. Greene got directly to the point and asked Diem about General Thé's bombings – Greene believed that the Americans had helped Thé mount the attack on the Continental Hotel in Saigon in January 1952, which he made a central event in his novel. Diem merely 'laughed & continued to laugh for a long time'.[8] That month he was under pressure to bring Thé and other generals into his government as the Americans wanted, or to face them in battle as the generals themselves seemed to want.[9] He was not going to talk to Greene about this.

The novelist dined at Nhu's house and witnessed a sharp exchange between Diem and the American General Joseph Lawton Collins, who had recently negotiated an agreement with the French to take over the training of Vietnamese forces. Although not as well known as his nephew Michael Collins, who flew the lunar module while Neil Armstrong and Buzz Aldrin walked on the Moon, 'Lightning Joe' did his best to prevent a religious war within South Vietnam. He reported back favourably to Washington on the prospects of the new republic but followed the French line in counselling against support for Diem, in favour of some more conciliatory figure who would share power.[10]

The conversation grew hot. Diem declared, 'We are an independent country.' Collins returned, 'Thanks to American aid.' And Diem concluded, 'So much the worse.'[11] While this was another instance of a foreigner trying to dictate to the Vietnamese, Greene had a surprising sympathy for Collins – a sometime Catholic, the general admitted to embarrassment at a recent visit to Vietnam by the ubiquitous Cardinal Spellman, whose episcopal warmongering would one day win him a rebuke from the Vatican.[12] On this visit, Spellman had brandished a large cheque for the relief of refugees and brought out tens of thousands

of Catholics at public events – his performance drawing attention to
the exclusively Catholic character of Diem's regime at the very moment
it should have been open to broad representation of religious groups.[13]

At this dinner, there was also discussion of General Thé's role – he
had accepted a large bribe, but if he did not like the government Diem
put together, he was prepared to fight against it as a 'maquis'.[14]

Greene and Leroy were among the guests at a dinner at the house
of Tran Van Huu, who had been head of government under Bao Dai.
Opposing Diem, he soon went into exile and came to favour the north.[15]
At this dinner, Greene was struck by the general anti-Americanism
and contempt for Diem.[16] He also met on more than one occasion the
former minister of economics, Tran Van Van, who maintained that it
was essential to bring together the various religious groups and create
a solid army. This man, too, would eventually go into public opposition
to Diem, who had him arrested in 1961.[17]

At about the time of Greene's visit, Diem discontinued subsidies that
had been paid to the religious groups as allies in the fight against the
Viet Minh and instead bribed individual generals, among them Thé.
He also had a confrontation with the Binh Xuyen; a criminal gang
based in Cholon, on the west side of the Saigon River, they specialized
in gambling and prostitution, and had purchased control of the local
Sûreté from Bao Dai as a kind of franchise. This stand-off broke out
into a full-scale battle in the streets of Saigon in April, killing five
hundred civilians and leaving twenty thousand homeless. General Thé
joined in the fight against the Binh Xuyen, and his conflict of loyalties
was resolved when he was killed by a sniper's bullet. The battle was
almost pointless, except to raise Diem's profile in the United States as
a leader of courage and rectitude, with Senate Majority Leader Lyndon
B. Johnson proclaiming him 'the Churchill of Asia'.[18]

Greene wished to visit Singapore, but found that his request for a re-
entry permit was just sitting on Diem's desk – it was a sign of the prime
minister's paranoia that he personally issued visas and travel permits.
An application for a permit to go north was also held up.[19] For much
of his time in Saigon, Greene was obliged to cool his heels between
meetings, so apart from photographing refugees, he got to work on 'The
Potting Shed', the play he had begun in the early summer of 1953.[20]

He was bothered by how few letters Catherine wrote and commented tellingly in his journal, 'If only one could be free of this affair and its continual frustrations', and yet felt better about it when an affectionate letter arrived. He briefly reduced his drinking, but increased his consumption of opium, tallying it up at the end of his stay at 144 pipes over a period of thirty-five days.[21]

He met almost daily with Fergus Dempster, an entertaining character from the Elder Dempster shipping family; a former head of station in London, 'Fergie' succeeded Maurice Oldfield as Head of Security Intelligence Far East in 1953.[22] It is difficult to know what they were doing, but Greene's visit to Vietnam had a purpose apart from journalism. On 4 March, Fergie hand-delivered a letter from Trevor Wilson, who had had many meetings with Ho Chi Minh,[23] and four days later Greene decided to go north. Diem had finally approved his visa.[24]

Haiphong had not yet been handed over to the Viet Minh, and when he arrived on 12 March Greene had to threaten both the Viet Minh and the International Commission with bad publicity in order to get a visa to go into Hanoi.[25] While waiting for it to be issued, he met old friends, among them André Moret of the Sûreté, who held a dinner party for him. He had a chance meeting with Father Willichs, whom he had supposed imprisoned.

In this port city, Greene encountered a young American who would soon become, like himself, a Catholic celebrity. Dr Tom Dooley was struggling to meet the medical needs of refugees; he told Greene that about 350 people were still arriving every day, and among them he would usually find two 'atrocity cases'[26] – these included mutilated thumbs and castrations.[27] Dooley wrote several books about his work as a medical missionary in Haiphong and Laos, which sold in the millions, before he died of cancer in 1961 at the age of thirty-four. A Gallup poll in 1960 found him one of America's ten most admired men, and the press followed each stage of his illness.[28] After his death there was a groundswell for his canonization, but this faded as his ardent anti-communism and involvement with the CIA were seen by progressive Catholics to have helped bring on the American war in Indochina, while the revelation that he was gay and sexually active offended conservatives.[29]

Greene met Father Willichs on 15 March 1955 and had lunch with

General Cogny before going by car to Hanoi. He caught sight of Ho's portrait hanging from a bridge, and entered a city that seemed nearly deserted. The trishaws were empty and the shops and cafés shuttered. Over the next three days, Greene was idle. The apostolic delegate refused to receive him, and his visits to the shabby press office accomplished nothing. He watched a film about Dien Bien Phu and drank what he believed was the last bottle of beer in Hanoi.[30] Then, on the morning of the 19th, he received the invitation he had been waiting for; after lunch and two opium pipes he headed to what had been Bao Dai's palace for a meeting with Ho Chi Minh.

What happened at the meeting is something of a mystery. He met the Minister of Information, who pretended not to be able to speak French, and was escorted into Ho's presence. Greene concluded that Ho, dressed in khaki with socks hanging down over his ankles, must still be more than a figurehead as the minister was afraid to say anything in the old man's presence. Having heard him described as 'un homme pur comme Lucifer', Greene saw in him not a fanatic, but one who had 'solved an equation' – a mathematical metaphor for destructive certainty that had appeared in *Loser Takes All*. He reminded Greene of the schoolmaster 'Mr Chips', but he was too old himself to attend such a school or to imbibe his lesson.

The three drank tea, and Greene carried out his mission: he handed Ho a letter. Greene would never reveal the nature of the letter or the content of their conversation – they would probably have been covered by the Official Secrets Act. His journal records that Ho expressed 'Curiosity about French Catholic reactions' and added, perhaps to encourage Greene to speak freely, '"We are in the family."'[31] It is likely that the letter was a proposal for the relief of Vietnamese Catholics, but a full understanding of this episode depends on further documents coming to light. He watched Ho, socks sagging, wave as he left the room.

Greene flew back to Saigon, and following a discussion of 'next moves' with Fergie, left Vietnam on 22 March for Hong Kong and Singapore.[32] His three articles for the *Sunday Times* appeared just over a month later in successive issues as 'Last Drama of Indo China'.[33] The first, 'The Dilemma of the South', offered a general view of the situation and concluded that Diem was running an 'inefficient dictatorship'. The second, 'Refugees and Victors', described the lot of the migrants, and quoted Tom Dooley, without naming him, while the final part, 'The Man as Pure as Lucifer', described the meeting with Ho Chi Minh but not what was said.

40

ANITA

The Graham Greene who had come back from Vietnam was not well. Opium had quelled his appetite, so he ate less than he should and was even leaner than usual. Despite regular contact with the psychiatrist Eric Strauss, a frequent visitor to Anacapri, he remained in a melancholic and irritable state. The 'dottoressa', Elisabeth Moor, diagnosed a liver ailment, and suggested to his dismay that he might need to give up drinking. Blood tests came back negative, but Greene lamented that there was not a medical explanation for how he felt and acted.[1]

Meanwhile, some of his personal relationships showed signs of neglect. Both as a journalist and a parent, Graham Greene could fairly be described as a foreign correspondent. His children, Caroline and Francis, saw little of him but received interesting letters from far-off places, and occasionally ones which revealed how distant a father he was; for example, he wrote in the mid-1950s:

Dear Francis,

I wish I had seen more of you the other day – I was too busy with 'affairs of no earthly importance' & now it looks as if I shall see nothing of you this holidays. Remember to send me your blue card for next term, & let's see also – if you feel like it – whether we can plan a small trip together somewhere queer or interesting on the Continent in the summer holidays. I mean two males together! Have you any views?

In any case a lot of love,

G.

Now eighteen, Francis had finished at Ampleforth College and gone up to Christ Church, Oxford, where he read physics and learned to speak Russian. Francis himself wrote amusing letters, including one in which he described how someone had poured Tide detergent into the Mercury fountain in Tom Quad, with predictable consequences. Something of a wit, he won national magazine competitions for light verse. In early 1955, he was reading through his father's works and enjoying them, and announced, whimsically, that he would become a collector, so Graham had Doris Young send him a full set.[2]

Caroline had recently turned twenty-one, and a party her father held for her at Albany was a bit discouraging as many of those invited were his friends rather than hers.[3] Having worked as a model and found it unpleasant, indeed predatory, she conceived a surprising ambition to become a rancher in western Canada. After consultations with Vivien, in August Graham travelled with his daughter to Alberta to look at properties, and remarked, 'The women are all sympathetic to Lucy's ambition: the men pour cold water.'[4] He strongly approved of his daughter's unconventional plan and provided the capital for a ranch near Calgary, to be operated in partnership with a couple named Parker who provided the livestock and equipment. It was not the kind of life the novelist could enjoy, but he knew it was right for his daughter.[5]

As a journalist, Graham Greene's special subject was faith under conditions of oppression. He spent the second half of November in Poland, and then wrote two articles for the *Sunday Times*.[6] On 17 November, he went to Auschwitz and afterwards maintained that no one should go to the country without seeing this site of annihilation – he drew special attention to a display of tons of women's hair and another of tiny shoes. He felt that an awareness of the horror forced one to be cautious in making judgements about contemporary Poland. A few days later, after he had seen both Warsaw and Kraków, he remarked, 'My goodness, how I love these people. Their kindness has been beyond belief.'[7]

Initially, he was impressed by how far the country had come since 1945. He believed that the Russians had done the Poles less harm than the Nazis had, but then considered how in the late summer of 1944 the Russians halted their advance so that the Germans could wipe out the partisans of the Warsaw Uprising and leave the country ripe for occupation. The church, which had stood up to tsars and Nazis, was now at the heart of resistance to the puppet government installed by the Soviets. Despite the incarceration of Cardinal Stefan Wyszyński in 1953, the church continued to function, perhaps aided by the Virgin of Częstochowa, whom Greene referred to in Hilaire Belloc's phrase as 'help of the half-defeated'.

Greene rejected another kind of Catholic response to the occupation of Poland, perhaps as wholly defeated. He had been invited to the country by the PAX Association, which had relaunched an old Catholic newspaper on pro-Soviet lines and was permitted to publish foreign literature, and he reported on this group to MI6.[8] He was met at the airport by one of its principal members, the novelist Jan Dobraczyński, and had meetings with its leader Bolesław Piasecki, who had been a right-wing nationalist and Jew-baiter before the war, then a brave figure in the Uprising; he was taken to Moscow for execution, spared, and returned to Warsaw to start the PAX Association, which was intended to sever the Polish church from Rome.[9] Opposed by most Catholics, it supported death sentences handed down against priests as well as the cardinal's imprisonment and then house arrest. Greene attended at least one large meeting of the group and several small gatherings, and fell out with them by enquiring at what point PAX would actually stand up to Moscow as the incarceration of Cardinal Wyszyński was not enough of an offence for them to do so. At one dinner, a publisher became so annoyed with him that she had to be escorted from the table.[10] Greene presented Piasecki with an open letter to the cardinal, requesting an audience and offering to keep such a meeting out of the news, but heard nothing more about it.

At the University of Lublin, among mainstream Catholics, Greene was impressed by a production of *Murder in the Cathedral*[11] which spoke to the yearning of Polish believers for the return of their own archbishop. When the professor who organized the production came to England in 1956, Greene arranged for T. S. Eliot to meet him.[12]

Cardinal Wyszyński's place in history is not a simple matter. A mentor of the future Pope John Paul II, he is well on his way to canonization, but his legacy of courage in the face of oppression is tainted. In 1945–6, after the Germans had gone and when Poland was in a state approaching civil war, Catholics carried out pogroms in Kraków and

Kielce, killing about fifteen hundred Jews. When a delegation of Jews approached Wyszyński, asking him to denounce the ancient 'blood libel' that Jews murdered Christian children and used their blood to make matzo, a notion that had animated the attackers especially in Kielce, the newly installed Bishop of Lublin commented on how many Poles were being killed and said that all murder was wrong, but as for the matter of blood, it was 'not definitively settled'. One historian notes that as long ago as 1247 there had been a papal bull dismissing the blood story as a fraud. Seven centuries later, Wyszyński thought it deserved further consideration.[13]

Greene's visit to Poland had begun with a four-day visit to Stockholm that would transform his personal life. On the first evening, his Swedish publisher, Ragnar Svanström, held a dinner for him attended by the permanent secretary of the Swedish Academy, Anders Österling – the man who usually announced the winners of the Nobel Prize. Also present were Harald Grieg (the brother of Greene's old friend Nordahl Grieg), the literary Prince Wilhelm of Sweden, and the translator Michael Meyer.[14] After many drinks, Greene asked Meyer to join the Svanströms and himself for another dinner the next night, but Meyer said he had a date. Greene told him, 'Bring the girl.' He added, 'Perhaps you could find one for me', then backtracked: 'No, I was joking.'

Jocelyn Rickards, Mercia Ryhiner, and Allegra Sander were all remarkable women. Greene's interest in them may have been partly owing to the waywardness of his mood disorder, which he recalled as being at its worst in the 1950s, but he also knew by now that nothing would ever come of his relationship with Catherine Walston and was searching for an alternative. He was about to find one.

Graham Greene had met Anita Björk in passing almost exactly two years earlier, when *The Living Room* was produced in Stockholm. He had actually had a clearer impression of her husband, the playwright and novelist Stig Dagerman, widely believed to be one of the most promising figures in European literature – Greene certainly admired his works. Following Anita's success in the film adaptation of Strindberg's *Miss Julie*, which shared the Grand Prix at Cannes in 1951, she went to Hollywood, where Alfred Hitchcock wanted her for the lead in *I Confess* (1953).[15] Since at the time she was living with Stig without being married to him and had a child from an earlier relationship, a studio boss, whose own adulteries would have led to remarks in Gomorrah, told her that she was falling short of the moral standards of Hollywood and the couple went home. They did marry the following year, and she gave Hollywood another try – in June 1952 she was the subject of a long article in the *New York Times*, comparing her skills and appearance to those of Greta Garbo and Ingrid Bergman.[16] She appeared with Gregory Peck in the unremarkable Cold War thriller *Night People* (1954), but gave up on the American film industry as she preferred to live and work in Sweden. She had a long and accomplished career in European theatre and film.

'Our Need for Consolation is Insatiable' is the title of one of Stig Dagerman's best-known works. Suffering from bipolar illness and burdened by debt from his efforts to support the children of his first marriage, he took his own life on 4 November 1954.[17] By the time she met Graham Greene again, Anita Björk had been a widow for almost exactly a year.

Hoping to cheer her up, both Meyer and Svanström invited her to the dinner. When Meyer told Greene what they had arranged, the novelist felt very awkward and said, 'I didn't mean it seriously. I hate blind dates, they're always a disappointment.' The party met in an old restaurant in Djurgården, the island in central Stockholm dedicated to gardens, amusements, and museums, including, nowadays, one devoted to ABBA. After dinner, Meyer invited Greene and Björk back to his apartment, where it was obvious that there was an attraction between the two.[18] Just before Greene left Stockholm, Björk had lunch with him between rehearsals, and afterwards sent him a single rose.[19]

At Christmas Anita was able to come to London for a day, and the relationship began. Graham went to Stockholm on New Year's Day 1956 and stayed for about two weeks, and in early March they took a holiday together in Portugal. On his return, Greene composed a bibulous letter to Catherine, in which, without referring to Anita, he suggested, yet again, that they consider ending their affair. In fact, he did not tell Catherine about Anita until December, although she had picked up rumours well before.

As ever, Greene's private life was a mess; much as he loved Anita, he could not get Catherine out of his system, and their affair revived from time to time into the 1960s, when he finally distanced himself from her. It is perhaps in the character of Greene's relationship with Anita Björk that less is known of it. She was a discreet person, and deposited none of her correspondence with Greene from the 1950s in an archive. Her work was centred on the Royal Dramatic Theatre in Stockholm and she wanted to raise her children there, so Greene became a frequent visitor. Near the end of his life Greene wrote to her: 'Some of the happiest days of my life were spent with you in Stockholm.'[20]

41

OUR MAN ON THE POTOMAC

The most interesting bad review that Greene received in his career was doled out to him by A. J. Liebling, a distinguished war reporter who shared with E. B. White the role of main essayist at the *New Yorker*. He is the author of at least one quiet masterpiece, *Between Meals: An Appetite for Paris* (1963), and his essays on boxing are unsurpassed. Though almost forgotten nowadays, Liebling was one of the best American prose stylists of the mid-twentieth century, and in a title-shot against Graham Greene he was by no means over-matched. His article was as much a parody as a review, in which he describes the experience of reading *The Quiet American* between naps while flying across the Atlantic.

He claimed that the book was the product of one dominant culture succeeding another, as might have happened with the Greeks and the Romans or the French and the English. The gist of his position is that the senior culture treats the junior as a whippersnapper. He proposed first of all that 'Fowler-Bogart' was actually a poor imitation of a Hemingway hero and that Greene himself was a 'minor American author'. He then considered whether some (slight) errors in idiom and cultural references to the United States showed that Pyle was really an Englishman. He called the book an 'Eastern Western' and made fun of Greene's startling metaphors, before referring to the novel as 'Mr Greene's nasty little plastic bomb'. He concluded: 'There is a difference, after all, between calling your over-successful off-shoot a silly ass and accusing him of murder.'[1] Liebling's essay is funny, but it is hardly fair, as its closing indignation implies that American foreign policy would never engage in what we now know as black ops. Even as Liebling was writing, Edward Lansdale and his ilk were at work in Indochina.

Others were at work in Hollywood. Claiming that the British edition of *The Quiet American* had sold a breath-taking two hundred thousand copies within a month, gossip columnist Louella Parsons revealed that the four-time Oscar winner Joseph L. Mankiewicz had 'scooped' the rights and planned to write, produce, and direct the film himself.[2] Greene was giving Caroline the rights so that she could sell them and pay for the ranch, and it took several months to do all the paperwork, but Mankiewicz closed the deal for about $50,000.[3] By the beginning of 1957, it became evident that he was doing something disgraceful. Even though the book was effectively banned in South Vietnam, Mankiewicz, in search of 'local colour' – though not perhaps red – was permitted to film there, something Diem himself would have decided. A journalist in Saigon learned that the film would be a 'travesty', heralding 'the triumphant emergence of the democratic forces in the young and independent state of Viet Nam backed by the United States'.[4] With Michael Redgrave and war hero Audie Murphy playing the leads, the film, released in February 1958, showed the innocence of Pyle and the gullibility of Fowler. Greene regarded the whole business as a betrayal, but his immediate reaction was rather mild: 'I am vain enough to believe that the book will survive a few years longer than Mr. Mankiewicz's incoherent picture.'[5]

With the rockets' red glare of patriotism and outrage contributing to his American book sales in the spring of 1956, Graham Greene was busy with auditions and then rehearsals for a new play. *The Power and the Glory* ran for a week in Brighton, then from 4 April to 2 June at the Phoenix Theatre in London. Directed by Peter Brook, with whom Greene had travelled to Haiti, the play worked from a script that Denis Cannan and Pierre Bost had rewritten several times since 1951, with revisions from Greene. The whisky priest was played by Paul Scofield, who would also appear in Greene's *The Complaisant Husband* (1959); in *When Greek Meets Greek* (1975), the first episode of Thames Television's *Shades of Greene* series; and in a Yorkshire Television production of *The Potting Shed* (1981). The Lieutenant was played by Harry H. Corbett, a capable actor who became popular in the comedy series *Steptoe and Son*.

With Scofield playing Hamlet at night and rehearsing the whisky priest during the day, Greene was afraid that he was making the part too 'romantic', and both he and Brook thought the play was in trouble.

A breakthrough came at the dress rehearsal, once Scofield had finished with Hamlet and cut off the long hair that went with that part; he then found himself entering the downtrodden character in a new way. Laurence Olivier seldom went to any play more than once but saw this one several times and said later that it was the best performance he could remember: 'The evilly catalystic Peasant, digging into the Priest's inner life, asks him if he has any children and in his fascinatingly chosen Birmingham accent Paul, in a way I have never been able to forget in twenty-five years, replied, "Ovva daw-taw."'[6] Olivier himself would act the part on American television in 1961, but could not outdo Scofield's stage version.

42

THE FILTHIEST BOOK
I HAVE EVER READ

I t was never quite enough in Graham Greene's life to have a single controversy running. As one of his three books of the year for the *Sunday Times*, he chose the little-known Vladimir Nabokov's *Lolita*,[1] which had been published in Paris by Maurice Girodias, who specialized in sexually explicit books, among them works by Anaïs Nin and Henry Miller. A reporter gave a copy of the book to John Gordon, editor-in-chief of the *Sunday Express*, who denounced it as 'the filthiest book I have ever read' and commenced a campaign against Graham Greene and the *Sunday Times*.[2]

In his own right, Gordon was a fairly amusing, if illiberal, character. As a young reporter, he had taken carrier pigeons to football games to get the results to his office without delay. As an editor, he had introduced horoscopes into his newspaper, with the result that he and his astrologer were prosecuted as rogues, vagabonds, and fortune-tellers, but acquitted when it was decided that the Vagrancy Act did not quite cover this new kind of wickedness.[3] Greene saw in Gordon's outburst an opportunity to ridicule British censorship, which still involved the confiscation and burning of proscribed works. Just at the moment he needed a guide through the historical and legal niceties of the issue, he came upon the young Norman St John-Stevas's book *Obscenity and the Law*, which he reviewed favourably[4] and afterwards mined for comical quotations on censorship and pornography.

With the help of the film producer John Sutro and Ian Gilmour, the owner of the *Spectator*, Greene set up the John Gordon Society in honour of the journalist's efforts to protect British homes from filth. Its first meeting, at Greene's flat in Albany, was attended by about sixty grandees, among them A. S. Frere, Freddie Ayer, Christopher Isherwood, Lady Bridget Parsons, and Lord Kinross. The Home Secretary and Director of Public Prosecutions were invited but sent their regrets. A public meeting was held at the Horseshoe Hotel in Bloomsbury on 25 July 1956, and Gordon himself was invited to speak on pornography. A tall, grey figure, he asked, 'Am I in the right room for the John Gordon Society Dinner?' Upon hearing that he was, he added, 'I am John Gordon.' Making the *obligato* reference to Greene's libel against Shirley Temple, he found the large crowd, which included Lady Antonia Fraser, Lilian Gish, and Anita Loos, generally set against him; however, badgering interruptions from a shirt-sleeved Randolph Churchill, who was sweating heavily and probably drunk, won him a little sympathy. As a consequence of these shenanigans, Nabokov's book found an American publisher and became a sensation.

Greene and the equally manic Sutro had done this sort of thing before. In the late summer of 1953, they met two young American women at the bar of the Caledonian Hotel in Edinburgh and spent the next day with them. Sutro recalled, 'I must say those Texan girls really enlivened our stay in Edinburgh and taught us quite a lot about Texas.'[5] On the train back to London, Greene drank a good many black velvets and proposed, 'Le's found an Anglo-Texan Sh-Society'.[6] The two composed a letter to *The Times*,[7] announcing its birth and inviting those interested to contact them. Greene signed as president and Sutro as vice-president. With Greene in Kenya, Sutro received sixty letters from British Texophiles, among them the MP and architect Sir Alfred Bossom and the banker Samuel Guinness, both of whom got the joke but essentially took over the society and ran it with a straight face.

On 6 March 1954, in honour of the anniversary of Texan independence from Mexico, the society held a barbecue at Denham Film Studios, where more than fifteen hundred guests, many of them American airmen, consumed 2800 pounds of beef and dozens of barrels of cider; there were three country bands; and London buses hired to shuttle guests had as their destination signs 'TEXAS From Piccadilly Circus'. Unfortunately, Greene missed the event as he was in Vietnam dealing with somewhat quieter Americans.

The society later hosted many political, cultural, and commercial delegations. In 1959 the Governor of Texas revived, without launching any ships, the Texas Navy, which had been disbanded for well over a century, just so that he could name honorary admirals. Twenty-five Britons, including Prince Philip, were commissioned Texas admirals, and the society became responsible for entertaining them. Greene resigned as president on April Fool's Day 1955, pleading the demands of travel. Sutro stayed a member until 1972, when he and his wife Gillian moved to Monaco. In its last days, one member remarked that 'the society was a little top-hatted instead of ten-galloned', and despite efforts to rescue it, the Anglo-Texan Society rode into the sunset in 1979.[8]

The madcap Sutros were among Greene's closest friends in London, especially after they moved in 1953 to 26 Belgrave Square, where he was a frequent guest for dinner. The invariable dish was shepherd's pie, which he prized; Greene contributed bottles of Château Cheval Blanc. At Oxford, John, a big man and an accomplished mimic, had been close to Evelyn Waugh and Harold Acton, and was known for taking his friends motoring in a hired Daimler followed by a more humble vehicle carrying champagne, caviar, and foie gras, which might not be available in country shops.[9]

Somewhat younger than her lumbering and very amiable husband, Gillian, who had grown up in France, was a small, dark-haired woman often mistaken for Vivien Leigh.[10] At different times she aspired to be an artist, an actor, and a writer, being moderately talented in each of these areas. One evening, the Sutros held a cocktail party to which Greene came very early, saying he was in a nervous state and could not bear meeting the guests, and so would have to leave again shortly. Gillian, dressed in tangerine silk Gucci trousers, was upset, and Greene pondered what to do. He said that he would stay if she let him spank her, so she turned around and said, 'Spank!' The novelist gave her two slaps and pronounced himself fit to attend the party.[11] While there was undoubtedly an attraction between them – Greene said he envied John nothing but Gillian – she denied there was ever an affair and no evidence to the contrary has come to light. The Sutros, of course, had an unconventional marriage, with both taking numerous lovers. Gillian's included Mario Soldati, Arthur Koestler, Carol Reed, and the Hungarian artist Marcel Vertès. John was involved with the writer Barbara Skelton and various actresses.

Like Greene, John Sutro suffered from manic depression; Gillian was extremely grateful for the novelist's assistance when, heavily indebted, John suffered a breakdown in late 1965, tried to kill himself, and had to be hospitalized. While recovering, he sent Greene a very sad letter and was told, 'stop flagellating yourself. We all make mistakes, we all make people we love suffer in one way or another – c'est la vie, & luckily people don't love us for our virtues or we'd be in a bad way … So do forgive yourself because then we can all be at ease again & laugh again over a shepherd's pie.'[12]

Greene was involved in John's production business and served as a director on at least two of his companies, and Sutro performed a similar role for Greene. Their friendship nearly disintegrated over a long and fruitless effort to make a film of *The Living Room*, and they quarrelled about Kim Philby. John died in 1985, and Gillian wondered whether Greene retained any affection or respect for him. Gillian herself will take on a large and somewhat ambiguous role in the rest of this book. Much of her life story has been told by Nicholas Shakespeare in the greatly admired *Priscilla*, a book about his aunt, Priscilla Mais, Gillian's closest friend, who was caught in Paris during the war and, apart from a period of internment, managed to survive as the mistress of Germans and black marketeers. After many years of nursing a grudge against the deceased Priscilla over one of her lovers, Gillian unearthed the facts about her life in Paris and wanted to write a book exposing her. Of herself, Gillian once wrote, 'I possess the capacity to hide rancour behind a mask of indifference.'[13] Any effort to think well of Gillian ends up as all benefit and no doubt.

In the late 1980s, she wanted to complete a memoir John had begun, but her focus soon shifted to Greene. As a memoirist, she took no prisoners: 'I made great efforts to like Catherine although I thought she was a destructive character, a lion hunter & fundamentally tough as an army boot.'[14] Assuming that she would write mainly about John, Greene submitted to many interviews with her. Meanwhile, she surreptitiously taped conversations and transcribed telephone calls with him and with his last mistress, Yvonne Cloetta, who was shocked to discover, after Greene's death, that Gillian was planning to write a book. Among her papers is a letter from Kim Philby to Graham Greene, which she must have snatched from the copy of *My Silent War* in which Greene kept

Philby's letters. Her book was never completed, but her large archive of letters, documents, cassette tapes, and transcriptions has made its way to the Bodleian Library, where scholars may study it. It is a disturbing example of intimate espionage.

43

6½ RAVES

I n the autumn of 1956, Greene took a holiday in Portugal with Anita Björk, during which he finished off his work on a film script of George Bernard Shaw's *St Joan* – the script turned out well, but the production itself was a fiasco, owing to a miscast lead. That visit to Portugal also entailed research for a story, the proposed setting of which shifted three times. Just after the war, the director Alberto Cavalcanti had asked him to come up with a script, so Greene sketched out one to be set in 1938 in Tallinn, the capital of Estonia and a hive for spies of all the great powers, which he had visited in 1934 (see above, pp. 78–9). The story was to have had a representative of Singer sewing machines peddling false intelligence to London in order to maintain an extravagant wife.[1] Cavalcanti checked with the censors and was told that no film could make fun of the Secret Service, so it was shelved, but Greene wondered whether the director simply did not like the idea.

In 1956 Greene was encouraged by the producer John Stafford to go ahead and write such a script. Stafford was then working on a very competent, if minor, film of Greene's short story 'Across the Bridge', in which a fugitive swindler, played by Rod Steiger, is killed trying to rescue his dog. At the time, Greene believed that he should write the new script about a husband who invents sub-agents and his wife who invents lovers and that it should be set in Portugal, then under the dictatorship of António de Oliveira Salazar. After all, for a couple of years Greene had known all there was to know about espionage in Portugal and Spain, and it was in these countries that the agent Garbo, inventor of two-dozen imaginary agents, had actually operated (see above, pp. 151–2). Greene had not yet considered placing his man in Havana.

That idea may have grown on him during a Caribbean holiday in

November and early December, with an itinerary that included Jamaica, Haiti, and Cuba. His companion for most of the time was Catherine Walston, and in Port-au-Prince Greene's fleeting acquaintance with Bernard Diederich developed into a close friendship.[2] Diederich recalls coming upon Graham and Catherine playing Scrabble, and the novelist being forced to consult a dictionary as he struggled to work out spellings that came naturally to her. Diederich took Greene's picture and agreed not to run a story about their visit in his newspaper until after they had left. Greene wanted to go to a 'house of flowers', so Diederich took the couple to brothels where they watched erotic dance acts. Even though she enjoyed such shows and often went to them with Greene in Paris, Walston remarked teasingly that all writers are interested in brothels: 'It allows them to see and sometimes feel humanity in the raw.' And when a surprised Greene looked at her, she added, 'You know it's the male oppressor's workplace!'[3]

During their visit, they attended vernissages with Diederich, and got to know the primitive and modernist schools of Haitian art. Greene acquired two paintings, one by Rigaud Benoit of a priest and parishioners on their knees as a flash flood sweeps away everything in its path. He later acquired other Haitian artworks; they remained precious to him and were hanging on the wall in his flat in Switzerland at the time of his death.

Unlike most tourists, Greene and Walston travelled aboard taptaps, the vividly decorated pick-up trucks that carried ordinary Haitians about for a tiny fare. At Diederich's suggestion, they switched from the El Rancho Hotel to the Oloffson, owned by Roger and Laura Coster. Once a maternity hospital for the wives of American Marines, this hotel allowed Greene more privacy, and it also employed Haiti's best bartender, a smiling man named Cesar who specialized in rum punches. Some years later, Greene would make an almost undisguised version of the Oloffson, a gingerbread structure with prominent balconies, the setting for *The Comedians*.

Graham and Catherine then made a short visit to Cuba in late November, about which little is known – their presence there is recorded mainly by passport stamps.[4] It was a fraught moment for the island, then ruled by the corrupt Fulgencio Batista, who led a successful Sergeants' Revolt in 1933, served as elected president from 1940 to 1944, sought election again in 1952, then seized power in a coup when he saw that he was not going to win. Allowing mobsters such as Meyer Lansky and Lucky Luciano to run an enormous business in drugs, prostitution, and gambling, Batista clung to power by arbitrary detention, torture, and murder of his opponents. His best-known henchman was Colonel Esteban Ventura, commander of the police in Havana's fifth precinct; this torturer and killer was often seen in a linen suit, and served as the model for Captain Segura in Our Man in Havana.[5]

At the time of Greene's visit, localized revolts were taking place, notably in Santiago de Cuba, so Batista immediately rounded up five hundred people, and suspended constitutional guarantees in four of the island's six provinces.[6] This coincided with the return of Fidel Castro. Having led a failed attack on the Moncada Barracks on 26 July 1953, he had been briefly imprisoned before going into exile in Mexico. On 2 December 1956, he and eighty-two men landed from the yacht Granma in Oriente Province; battling Batista's men, many were killed and others scattered. Although revolutionary myth put the number at a biblical twelve, perhaps as many as eighteen of the force, among them Raúl Castro, Che Guevara, and Camilo Cienfuegos, reached sanctuary in the Sierra Maestra mountains, from which they conducted a guerrilla war.[7] There is no certainty that Greene was investigating the troubles in Cuba in late 1956, but if not, he picked an extraordinary time merely to change planes in Havana.

Leaving the Caribbean, Greene went to New York to put what he thought were the final touches on The Potting Shed before going to Canada in late December. He stopped in Montreal to set up a holding company related to the ranch, and met his friend in that city, Karl Stern, a German-born psychiatrist and author who had recovered a belief in God through psychoanalysis and eventually converted from Judaism to Roman Catholicism; he is now best remembered for his autobiography The Pillar of Fire.

Greene took a restful two-day journey by train through a wintry landscape to Alberta. Caroline, clad in blue jeans, met his train and took him to the ranch, where he saw her beloved new horse, Silence, who would serve as the model for Seraphina in Our Man in Havana. He was alarmed by his daughter handling two Percherons, one unbroken, but she knew what she was doing.[8] The beauty of the place astonished him. He could look over a valley to the foothills and at the end of the vista see the Rocky Mountains. Caroline had transformed a 23-foot cabin into a comfortable home, complete with bookshelves of her own construction and furniture acquired from shops in Calgary. At night, coyotes howled near by and the horses leaned against the cabin for warmth. He wrote to his mother: 'It's a strange feeling looking round at the country, hill & valley & stream, & knowing that Lucy is the owner. It makes one feel there's some point in writing books after all.'[9]

It was not all easy for him that Christmas, as Caroline had a candid conversation with him about how his conduct had injured the family. Greene was stung by her words, but there was no lasting breach, and he was amused to receive her Christmas gift: a Geiger counter – something that he soon worked into his fiction.

Greene was never likely to write a novel about Canada – not an obvious trouble-spot, at least not for the settler population – but he did set a story in Calgary. In 'Dear Dr Falkenheim' (1963), a man writes to his young son's psychiatrist about a traumatic experience the boy has had. He and the boy's mother planned to get rid of, indeed 'liquidate', the notion of Father Christmas in their household but to continue with seasonal gifts to their son, including the Geiger counter he has asked for. Things go further than expected, and at an outdoor celebration Father Christmas arrives by helicopter, only to be decapitated by the rear blade. The son, 'a bit like an early Christian', continues to believe Father Christmas is real because he has seen him die. The father writes, 'Please do what you can, Doctor.'[10] The question of who is most sane is left unanswered.

It may be that this apparently cruel story represents one pole of Greene's religious thinking at the time: that the only possible basis for faith is trauma, or at least an intimacy with suffering. For him, the most authentic believers had always been in the trouble spots, the ones who had no comfort to deceive them.

In 1956, Greene had written a short story exploring the other side of the question, what he saw as the weakness of intellectual Catholicism. In 'A Visit to Morin' a wine merchant curious about the church encounters a novelist named Morin whose works had once been very popular among Catholics and finds that the man's views have shifted – he seems to be poised between doubt and affirmation. Even though he does not receive the sacraments, Morin reacts angrily to the suggestion that he has lost his faith: 'I told you I had lost my belief. That's quite a different thing.'[11] This distinction between belief – intellectual conviction – and faith – an intuitive or experiential assent – would remain with Greene for the rest of his life. In 1975, he reassured a concerned stranger who believed Greene had lost his faith and so prayed for him every day, 'I once wrote a short story A Visit to Morin in which I distinguished between the loss of belief and the loss of faith. I think I still have faith, even though the belief is a bit ragged.'[12] He found the Thomistic arguments for the existence of God tiresome and unconvincing, yet, like Morin, he continued to go to Mass and at night he said his prayers.[13]

After Christmas, Greene was suddenly called back to New York to revise The Potting Shed, which was set to open at the Bijou Theatre on 28 January 1957. The director was the young Carmen Capalbo, then best known for a 1954 production of Bertolt Brecht's The Threepenny Opera. Robert Flemyng was cast as James Callifer, the main character who as a boy hanged himself and was mysteriously revived – Greene referred to this as his first attempt to create a 'hollow man', a forerunner of Querry in A Burnt-Out Case, whom he thought the more successful character.[14]

It is often observed that Greene had difficulty creating interesting female characters; one of his most subtle is the ageing Mrs Callifer, who had concealed the miracle to protect her atheist husband from what would have been a crisis of disbelief; she was played on this occasion by Dame Sybil Thorndike, who especially loved the first two acts of the play, but wondered whether Greene had a sense of dramatic form. There were artistic clashes on the set, as Thorndike and especially her husband, Sir Lewis Casson, playing Fred Baston, grew tired of Capalbo's 'Method' approach to rehearsal – in their view, all talk and no acting.[15]

The script was changing almost every day, as Capalbo wanted Greene to enlarge the part in the third act of Sara Callifer, played by Leueen MacGrath. Greene threw himself into the task and even proposed changing the title to 'A Lion on the Path',[16] which would have been a nightmare for publicists who had been advertising The Potting Shed for months. In the midst of this frenzy, he reported to Catherine: 'I'm pretty tired & exist & work on dry Martinis, Scotch &

Benzedrine.'[17] Still Greene enjoyed the companionship of the theatre, loved the actors, and felt a pang when he left New York at the end of January. Despite his usual misgivings, the play did well: Capalbo telegraphed to him in Paris: '6½ raves out of 7 notices.'[18] Receiving one Tony nomination as best play and another for Thorndike as best actress, the production moved to the Golden Theatre and had a run of 119 performances before packed houses.[19]

John Gielgud had turned down *The Potting Shed* as it seemed to him too poetic and hard to grasp, but seeing its triumph in New York he changed his mind and accepted the part of Callifer in the London production.[20] He thought the play 'morbid and gloomy but very sparely and concisely written and the first two acts are really fine in an Ibsenesque way'.[21] Directed by Michael Macowan, this cast included Gwen Ffrangcon-Davies as Mrs Callifer and Irene Davies as Sara. After a week's run in Brighton, it opened at the Globe on 5 February 1958; despite large audiences, it closed prematurely on 3 May 1958, as Gielgud was committed to appear in another play.[22] The London notices were favourable, though more reserved than those in New York.

Gielgud was not the only one to change his mind about the play, as Greene scrubbed out the alterations he had made to the third act in the weeks before the New York opening. According to Gielgud, Capalbo wanted the changes without even having the company give the first version a full reading.[23] For the London production, Greene cut out a discussion among rationalists of abandoning Christmas festivities in favour of 'Children's Day', a notion he also treated in 'Dear Dr Falkenheim'. Published by Viking in 1957, the American version suffers by comparison with the tighter one included in Greene's *Collected Plays*. Looking back years later, Greene was fond of the first act but remained unsatisfied with the ending in both versions, and he may be echoing a conversation with Thorndike when he discusses the problem of dramatic unities in *Ways of Escape*.[24] Even so, the third act, in either version, has some extraordinary touches in it, not least Callifer's claim that he knew his uncle the priest no longer believed in the miracle merely by looking at his room: 'Have you ever seen a room from which faith has gone? A room without faith – oh that can be pretty and full of flowers, you can fill it with Regency furniture and the best modern pictures. But a room from which faith is gone is quite different. Like a marriage from which love has gone, and all that's left are habits and pet names and sentimental objects, picked up on beaches and in foreign towns that don't mean anything any more. And patience, patience everywhere like a fog.'[25]

44

A MIXTURE OF PETROL AND VODKA

I t is not just the loss of faith that resembles an empty room in *The Potting Shed*, but the loss of love, something Greene knew a good deal about. During 1956 and 1957, Greene could not choose between Anita and Catherine, so made a mess of both relationships. He decided to go to Portugal with Anita only after Harry had forbidden Catherine to visit him in Paris. Then, as described above, he travelled with Catherine to the Caribbean. At the end of that trip, they quarrelled, evidently about the presence of another woman in his life.

In early December 1956, Catherine sent a conciliatory letter and he at last explained to her his year-old relationship with Anita.[1] She responded in such a way that he then stated plainly his willingness to leave Anita for her. He also said that he regretted having told her the truth about Anita, rather than just letting that relationship run its course, and said that it had been a mistake for her to tell him about her other lovers.[2] In June, they took a holiday together in Rome and it ended in another row. Their bleak correspondence continued through 1957, and around the beginning of November she broke up with him in a telephone call.[3]

Greene made repeated visits to Stockholm in 1957 but found it lonely as, apart from Anita, he had just two friends there, Michael Meyer and the publisher Ragnar Svanström. Greene's humour seemed to alienate Swedes, and he was certainly doing himself no good in his campaign for the Nobel Prize. With Anita, he was trying family life again, but dealing with small children was, for him, purgatorial. He and Anita considered buying a house in Versailles, but this would have ended Anita's career at the Royal Dramatic Theatre in Stockholm, and Greene, to his credit, felt this was too much to ask of an artist.

It appears that at some point he asked her to marry him, as he had repeatedly asked Catherine.[4]

For her part, Anita was aware that she faced competition from Catherine and that this was eating away at their relationship. In late June, they travelled to Martinique and remained in the West Indies until the beginning of August. While there, Greene believed they would break up, but the crisis passed, or at least it was postponed. Shortly afterwards, he was obliged to look happy when Anita announced she might be pregnant, but Greene promised God that if he were spared this child he would *consider* making a long retreat at a religious house. There was no baby, so he considered the matter and left it at that.[5]

Greene accepted an invitation to go as part of a delegation to the People's Republic of China in April 1957. This month-long trip was paid for by the Chinese government, who doubtless saw in the author of *The Quiet American* a possible sympathizer; in fact, he thoroughly disliked the regime. Greene agreed to the trip in a brief period of relatively free expression in China, encouraged by Mao Zedong's slogan 'Let a hundred flowers bloom and a hundred schools of thought contend', which was promptly followed by new repression of intellectuals and opponents of the government.[6]

The Foreign Office briefed Greene about priests and writers who had been imprisoned, and once he got to China he tried, with limited success, to make contact with Catholics. He was forced to spend most of his time with the lawyer and Labour peer Robert Chorley; with Professor Joseph Lauwerys, an expert on comparative education and an advisor to UNESCO;[7] and a Mrs Brown, who was an orthodox communist from Hampstead.[8] Greene had expected to travel with Margaret and John Hastings, who were friends of his and of the Walstons, but he discovered at the airport that there were two British groups who would travel separately and meet in China. At Greene's urging his group went from Beijing to the old imperial city of Xi'an, then to Chongqing, followed by a four-day journey down the Yangtze to Hankou, and a return to Beijing.

Among the British visitors was the poet Hugh MacDiarmid, the guest of honour at that most unlikely thing, a Robert Burns festival in Chongqing. In Greene's recollection, the Scot was displeased to encounter an Englishman at the event and warmed to him only after he displayed a knowledge of Scotch whisky. MacDiarmid recalled their encounter as very friendly, with Greene giving him a small stoneware jar of the sorghum-based spirit Maotai, which the poet thought tasted like 'a mixture of petrol and vodka'. Greene would not take it on the plane for fear it would explode.[9]

On this trip, Greene himself exploded several times – something consistent with his mood disorder. He took against Lauwerys, who liked to explain things and spoke in full paragraphs. Greene gave him such a hard time that while they were on the boat the professor threatened to throw him into the Yangtze. That night, Greene heard strange sounds and imagined that Lauwerys was strangling someone, perhaps their guide, so beat on his door, 'Stop that fucking noise, you bugger.' As it turned out, the noise was merely the conversation of cooks in the galley.

During the journey, Greene and his party visited universities, factories, a collective farm, and at his request a cinema school. At a May Day celebration in Beijing, he saw Chairman Mao from a distance and shook hands with Zhou Enlai.[10] However, the most memorable event occurred in Chongqing. At a dinner with the mayor Greene asked about the case of the art theorist Hu Feng. In a long report to the cultural bureaucracy, this man had rejected Mao's belief that the purpose of art was objective and political, and instead emphasized the importance of the individual mind. Arrested in July 1955 as a counterrevolutionary and Taiwanese spy, he would spend the next twenty-five years in prison, with his whereabouts concealed for the first decade. In a broader purge of intellectuals, the government also imprisoned Hu's friend the novelist Lu Ling, and a 'Hu Feng clique' of two hundred writers and artists, some whom had never met the man.[11]

At first avoiding Greene's question, the mayor merely confirmed that Hu Feng lived in Chongqing. Greene pressed the point and suggested that the mayor, once a friend of Hu Feng, would be relieved to see him brought to trial and his guilt or innocence decided. The mayor responded that he must be guilty or he would not have been arrested. Lord Chorley then decided to get their host off the hook and said that he had been studying the case: 'All of us here realize the special difficulties you suffer from in the People's Republic, overrun as you are by spies from Taiwan.' Greene was on his feet again instantly, saying he was outraged to hear an English lawyer speak in such terms: 'Was a man considered in his eyes to be guilty without being tried?' If that was so, Greene could no longer travel in Lord Chorley's company. With that, the dinner broke up. Although the two shook hands that night, the events overshadowed the rest of their stay in China, and led to a public exchange in the *Daily Telegraph* once they got back home.[12] Regretting the Maotai and the irritability, Greene later described his own behaviour as abominable,[13] but it is hard not to see it as also magnificent.

45

HANDSHAKES AND CONTRACTS

Greene worried about money. Since he had left *The Times* at the end of 1929 and sunk within three years to near-bankruptcy, he had never trusted writing as a profession. Having so often failed in his relationships, he felt strongly that he should at least help people out financially, a concern that animates some of his characters, notably Scobie in *The Heart of the Matter* and Wormold in *Our Man in Havana*. Reasonably enough, he supported Vivien and his children in comfort: Vivien complained about money, but she did have a substantial house in Oxford, along with a sufficient income to travel and to pursue her scholarly interests – in the 1960s she set up a private museum dedicated to antique doll's houses, which her husband paid for.

He also contributed handsomely to the support of his mother and of his brother Herbert, and established financial covenants for his sister Elisabeth's children. He paid a steady allowance to Dorothy Glover, and frequently made open-ended loans or gifts of money to Trevor Wilson, Elisabeth Moor, Claud Cockburn, and other friends who were down on their luck. Even aristocrats looked to him for loans or handouts – a Catholic friend, Sherman Stonor (6th Baron Camoys), whose ancient house near Henley-on-Thames resembled Greene's fiction in that it had once harboured fugitive priests, asked him to pay his son's school fees at Downside, and Greene was very surprised when the money was eventually repaid; he was fond of Sherman Stonor and would have forgiven the debt.[1]

At Greene's memorial service in 1991, Muriel Spark recounted how when she was very poor in the 1950s, he had sent her £20 each month, often with a few bottles of red wine, 'which took the edge off cold charity'.[2] He also urged her to use his name when seeking employment with publishers, and made various small, helpful gifts such as a typewriter. He contributed constantly to charitable, ecclesiastical, and political appeals. He made his flat in Albany and his house in Anacapri available to family and friends who wished to use them in his absence. In later years, he handed over a flat he rented in Paris to an ailing Marie Biche.

Helping so many people was a matter of conscience for him, but it caused him great anxiety. His financial juggling would create problems in the early 1960s, but for now he thought there might be security in a return to publishing. A rising figure in the business, Max Reinhardt, had acquired the Bodley Head, a venerable firm in need of new blood, and in June 1957 he made Graham Greene a director.

Reinhardt would become one of Greene's most devoted friends, in many ways replacing Alex Korda, who had once advised him on how to borrow money from banks: always ask for more than you need, then the decision will be made by someone at the top.[3] Of course, Reinhardt was more cautious than the swashbuckling Korda, especially about tax law and currency regulations. A secular Jew, he was born in 1915 in Constantinople, his father an Austrian military officer and his mother belonging to an Italian-Ukrainian family in the shipping business. Reinhardt was educated chiefly in English but spoke a number of languages. In the late 1930s, he worked with an uncle, Richard Darr, in the Paris office of the family firm – Darr remained his closest business associate for over forty years and took care of numerous transactions involving Graham Greene. At the beginning of the war, they left Paris for London, where, after a brief internment, Reinhardt served in RAF intelligence and studied at the London School of Economics. He became close friends with the actors Ralph Richardson and Anthony Quayle, and with Louis Albert 'Boy' Hart, who became the head of the Ansbacher bank, financing many of Reinhardt's ventures and handling some transactions for Greene. Reinhardt's early publishing efforts in London concentrated on textbooks and theatrical works. He had a set of rooms at Albany, so crossed paths with the novelist.[4]

Greene proved a very active director at the Bodley Head, asking right away about publishing some of the authors he had handled at Eyre & Spottiswoode, among them Barbara Comyns, whose books he described as 'crazy but interesting'. He urged Reinhardt to keep an eye on young authors such as Muriel Spark and Brian Moore, and was curious about the sales of George Bernanos's *The Diary of a Country Priest*. He argued for a reprint of the works of Ford Madox Ford, something opposed by another new director, J. B. Priestley, but Greene eventually had his way, editing a multi-volume series. Entirely at Greene's suggestion, the firm published a selection of Stig Dagerman's work.[5]

Greene cabled Charlie Chaplin to tell him of his joining the firm and to let him know that they would make an offer on his autobiography: the pursuit of Chaplin, who preferred handshakes to contracts, went on for years, but Greene eventually edited the manuscript and it became a worldwide bestseller in 1964. One that got away was Nabokov. Having largely created his fame through the John Gordon Society, Greene urged the firm to make an offer for the British rights in *Lolita* and proposed that, if successful, he should sign the contract since that would make him the one to appear in court if there was an obscenity charge.[6] Priestley objected to *Lolita* and resigned. By the time Reinhardt made his offer it was too late: Weidenfeld & Nicolson had acquired the British rights. In later years, Greene persuaded Reinhardt to publish many books he admired, including some by his old friend R. K. Narayan, whom he believed likely to win the Nobel Prize.[7]

How deeply Greene wanted to go into publishing again was put to the test in early 1958, when Oliver Crosthwaite-Eyre asked him to come back to a much-expanded Eyre & Spottiswoode as managing director on an annual salary of £6000.[8] At first, he simply dismissed the proposal, but then saw its attractions – financial certainty and the opportunity to promote the authors he most admired. However, he felt the risk of 'claustrophobia' as he would need two or three months each year to travel.[9] Also, he believed he was nearly finished as a novelist and feared that too steady an income might finally destroy his motivation to write, and so refused the offer: 'I am first and last a writer even though the vein may be running thin and I cannot help fearing that without the necessity of writing I might abandon it altogether. This is a psychological problem for me alone ... '[10]

46

BOMBS AND DAIQUIRIS

'Two days ago in NY the story began to grow & I even thought it might grow into something good & funny & sad & exciting, but now the feeling has slipped away.'[1] It was the morning of 8 November 1957, and Greene was in Cuba for a three-week visit.[2] Having written out some of his discouragement in a letter to Catherine, he took a sheet of foolscap, wrote the first sentence, then the first paragraph, and was satisfied.[3] He gave his main character the name Wormold, based on that of the Cambridge historian Brian Wormald, an Anglican clergyman who converted to Catholicism, and along the way had had an affair with Catherine.[4] This was to be a novella, an entertainment, just something to make up for the money he had lent to Sherman Stonor.[5] *Our Man in Havana* would turn out to be much more than that.

On the flight south the day before, he had sat beside an engineer who showed him an issue of *Gun Digest*; seeing the huge prices, Greene, after three whiskies, fantasized about buying up antique guns in France and selling them in the United States. That would settle his money problems. Once he had checked in at the Seville-Biltmore, which had a mobbed-up casino, he went for a walk; prostitutes whistled at him, but he was not interested, as the city seemed to stifle his desires. In the morning he went into an American bank to cash a cheque from Viking Press, and stood around waiting for a clerk to finish his matey conversation with an executive who had it in mind to borrow $150,000; in a passage written shortly after, Jim Wormold would stand in just such a queue.

Greene then visited the hapless British ambassador, Stanley Fordham, who described for him an attack on Batista's palace on 13 March 1957 by the Directorio Revolucionario Estudiantil, one of several groups fighting against Batista; they had come close to killing the dictator. Fordham had watched part of the attack from the typists' room in the embassy, before drawing a burst of machine-gun fire and having to take cover. For matters which he did not witness with his own eyes, Fordham was a far less reliable source of information, as he would continue to report to London that Batista was defeating the rebels, and on the basis of what he said the British government proceeded with arm sales to Batista, even after the United States had turned its back on him.[6]

Havana was a dangerous place. While Greene, hoping to revive his appetites, attended a sex show at the Shanghai Theatre on 8 November, sixty bombs had gone off around the city in just fifteen minutes – they had been positioned to create a disturbance rather than a bloodbath, but even so eight people were hurt.[7] Greene walked the streets, and suffered nothing worse than pursuit by bootblacks wanting to find him a girl. He generally ate at the old Floridita restaurant, which he loved for its crab, crawfish, and daiquiris.

With just a few hundred words written, he was not certain whether his new book was actually a comedy. He may have thought of the wartime case of Heinz Lüning, a spy for the Abwehr in Havana so incompetent that he could not construct his radio or even attach its antenna, so he sent reports to his superiors in invisible ink, which the British intercepted. The Americans and Cubans thought they were on to a master spy, who was directing U-boats to their kills. Lüning's capture and execution by firing squad were trumpeted as a great victory for the intelligence services, but, in fact, he was a nobody.[8] On Sunday morning Greene went to Mass and his attention fell on 'a honey coloured girl with a pony tail', and the next day he experienced a breakthrough in his writing: he could see Milly.[9]

There was still a good deal that he had not seen. In his earlier visits, Greene had not ventured outside the city, and he had met few ordinary Cubans. He tracked down a taxi driver named Rocky[10] who, on an earlier visit, had obtained suspiciously cheap cocaine which turned out to be boracic powder. The man apologized for the earlier swindle, blamed the newsagent from whom he had procured it, and offered a refund. Untroubled by all this, Greene asked Rocky to find some opium, and then arranged for him to drive him to Cienfuegos and Trinidad on the south coast.[11]

'There was one place in Cuba to which we were unable to drive – Santiago, the second city of the island.'[12] Located in the south-east, this was the centre of Batista's operations against Castro's *26 de Julio* organization, whose stronghold was in the mountains of the region. It was necessary to fly there, as a foreigner approaching by car would be stopped at a roadblock and face an ugly interrogation. Once in the city, he would need to contact the *Fidelistas*, and this required a fairly long chain of intermediaries. Through Stonor, he had met the Cuban ambassador to the Court of St James's, Roberto González de Mendoza, who provided an introduction to his brother Nicolas, a lawyer in Havana, as someone to drink with.[13] There is no strong evidence that Nicolas was deeply involved with the opposition to Batista, but he did connect the novelist with one of his relatives,[14] Natalia Bolívar, who became a distinguished cultural anthropologist after the revolution; she had participated in the *Directoria*'s storming of the presidential palace, and specialized in smuggling people and arms. Soon after meeting Greene, she had all her ribs broken and lost the hearing in one ear as the result of interrogation – she was even shown the bag of cement that would be used to make her overshoes, but was spared because her family did business with Batista.

Bolívar wanted to send Greene to meet the *Directoria* in the Escambray Mountains in the central part of the island, but found that some new leaders were not receptive to the idea, so she put him in contact with a courier for the *26 de Julio*, Nydia Sarabia, whom Greene knew only by her *nom de guerre*, Lidia Hernández. Subsequently a historian, Sarabia recalled Greene saying at the time that he intended to write two books, one set in Havana and the other in Santiago, and that he would like to interview Castro.

Greene and Sarabia took a commercial flight to Santiago, the novelist carrying a suitcase full of warm clothes for fighters in the mountains – an Englishman was unlikely to be searched. He checked into the Casa Granda Hotel in Santiago on a humid night after the unofficial curfew and found that the desk clerk made no pretence of welcoming a foreigner. Anyone walking the streets after dark was liable to be arrested, and, as Greene put it, the lucky ones were found in the morning hanging from lamp-posts. By day, the city reminded him of Villahermosa in Tabasco during the persecution: 'I was back in what my critics imagine to be Greeneland.'[15]

In Santiago, he witnessed an uprising of schoolchildren. In the middle of the night soldiers took as hostages the three young daughters of a man fighting in the mountains for Castro: 'The news reached the schools. In the secondary schools the children made their own decision – they left their schools and went on the streets. The news spread. To the infants' schools came the parents and took away their children. The streets were full of them. The shops began to put up their shutters in expectation of the worst. The army gave way and released the three little girls. They could not turn fire-hoses on the children in the streets as they had turned them on their mothers or hang them from lamp-posts as they would have hanged their fathers.'[16]

Having been warned against phone taps and impostors, Greene became uneasy about his friend the *Time* journalist Jay Mallin, who had flown to Santiago on the same plane, with a plan to help Greene arrange his meetings and perhaps get a few paragraphs for the magazine.[17] His presence made it necessary for Greene and Sarabia to sit apart and not make eye contact on the flight. He came to Greene's hotel room with a man in a gabardine suit claiming to be Fidel's public relations man – he has since been identified as Fernando Ojeda, a businessman allied with Fidel.[18] The phone then rang: it was Sarabia, who told Greene to go to an address in Calle San Francisco. She thought Mallin and the other man were spies, just as Ojeda insisted that whoever was on the phone was a spy. Greene made the two men leave, but was now very worried about being detected by Batista's agents.

Clutching the suitcase full of sweaters and leather jackets, he dared not give the address to a taxi driver so gambled on there being an Iglesia de San Francisco on a street with the saint's name and was right – he told the driver he wanted to pray. Once he got out of the taxi he found that it was a long street, and while searching for the house he was overtaken by a car containing Mallin and Ojeda, who said that he had confirmed that the call in the hotel room was from their organization. As Bernard Diederich points out, almost the entire American press corps opposed Batista, and a number of journalists, such as Mallin, had highly placed contacts in the rebel groups.[19] Sarabia and Ojeda were on the same side without knowing it. Afterwards, Greene trusted Mallin fully, and a year later told his brother Hugh, just appointed Director of News and Current Affairs at the BBC, that Mallin had the right contacts to get a film crew into Santiago.[20]

Once inside the house on Calle San Francisco, Greene found Sarabia, her mother, a priest, and a young man disguising himself by having his hair dyed[21] – this was Armando Hart, a lawyer who had just made a daring escape from police custody at the law courts in Havana; he later became Fidel's minister of education and then minister of culture and served on the Cuban politburo. His wife, Haydée Santamaria, was also there; an important figure in the revolution, this tragic woman had participated in the attack on Moncada Barracks in 1953, been captured, and shown the castrated corpse of her then-fiancé. Together they discussed whether Greene should come into the Sierra Maestra to meet Fidel, but with the fighting growing more intense, the rebels were not allowing outsiders into their camps.[22] For his part, Greene saw that he was running short of time and that he was not equipped for such a trek as he didn't even have boots. With evident regret, he decided against it. However, the rebels still wanted his help on an important matter. Even though most countries saw Batista as entirely discredited, Britain was still selling him fighter planes. They explained what was going on and asked Greene to put pressure on the government.

He left Cuba on 21 November 1957, and after short stays in New York and Montreal went to Greene-Park Ranch for Christmas with Caroline. He was making terrific progress with the book, and less than a month later he could report to Gillian Sutro that he had completed twenty-one thousand words. He kept up the pace, and by late February had written forty-one thousand; what had begun as a novella was turning into one of his longest books.

However, he was headed into a period that was tumultuous even by his standards. After Christmas, he had a sharp disagreement with Vivien. Then, in London for rehearsals of *The Potting Shed*, he received a phone call from Catherine that caused him to weep in the bath over the loss of her. He sent her a letter saying that he expected he would next fail Anita, and concluded, 'The death wish is very strong.'[23]

In Stockholm, he and Anita suddenly agreed in mid-February that they were finished. He told Catherine, assuming she would want to start again, but she hesitated. After six weeks, Anita sent him a conciliatory letter and he flew back to Stockholm straight away. Over the years, Catherine had sent her share of mixed messages, but now she was confused, and she put Marie Biche on the spot by asking whether somehow she now bored Graham, and had he been play-acting? After a long delay, Biche wrote that while Dorothy did bore him, he had said that could never be the case with Catherine. Biche also said she had put it to him that in life you just can't make returns, but he had said 'one knows one could, like that, with Catherine'.[24]

Our Man in Havana, delivered to the publisher on 2 June 1958,[25] ends with Wormold and Beatrice finding private happiness in a mad world. Graham went to Sweden, only to see that there was nothing of the sort in store for himself and Anita. After a miserable holiday on an island in the Stockholm archipelago, they agreed in early July to make a final break, as he remarked to Catherine: 'This should have been an affair – just as ours should have been marriage.'[26] He judged that it was partly his fault and 'a lot just Sweden & circumstances'. In a characteristic gesture, he bought a house for Anita: 'I do want her to come out of this episode better than she went in.'[27]

47

THE WHOLE TROUBLE

Graham Greene came close to being tried at the Old Bailey. A young MI5 officer named David Cornwell was drinking coffee with a 'benign' lawyer who worked for the service, and the lawyer was unhappy. Halfway through an advance copy of *Our Man in Havana*, he was convinced that Graham Greene must go to prison as he had given a precise account of the dealings of a head of station with an agent in the field: '"And it's a good book," he complained. "It's a *damned* good book. And that's the whole trouble."'[1]

Of course, Wormold is not prosecuted for his crimes – rather he gets an OBE and is made an instructor in spycraft. 'C' – Sir Dick White, the chief of MI6 – was not such a fool as to let anyone lay charges against Greene; a little later, the novelist heard that when the head of MI5 proposed a prosecution under the Official Secrets Act, White just laughed.[2] The service hired many writers, and an indiscretion from time to time was merely the cost of doing business. If nothing else, a charge would be an admission that *Our Man in Havana* had some truth in it.

When the book was released around the beginning of October, some critics chided Greene for the unreality of his portrayal of intelligence work. Ian Fleming, for example, loved the novel but thought the 'Wodehousian' presentation of the service its single fault.[3] Reviewers had no idea how clearly Greene had read the situation in Cuba, and in the midst of the Cold War few were willing to think of spies as bunglers and fantasists. However, it would soon become clear that he had, at a stroke, remade the genre of the spy novel.

He had not forgotten the request of Armando Hart's group that he should pressure the British government about arms sales. With its fragile post-war economy, Britain was desperate for export markets, while the Cubans were trying to sell sugar, cigars, and rum, so the two countries entered into a trade agreement in 1953, granting the British tariff concessions; after much negotiation it was extended in late 1958. Although military allies, the British and the Americans were trade rivals in Cuba, and on three occasions British Leyland outbid General Motors for large contracts to sell buses to the island. With American sales of arms to Batista drying up – Congress passed a formal embargo in March 1958 – the British government saw another opportunity.[4]

Greene passed information about the sales to his friend Hugh Delargy, a Catholic from Antrim and the Labour MP for Thurrock, who rose in the House of Commons on 17 March 1958 and asked whether Britain was selling arms or aeroplanes to the government of Cuba. Ian Harvey, a junior minister in the Foreign Office, issued a categorical denial and so lied to the House.[5] In *Ways of Escape* Greene recalled incorrectly that the denial was made by the Foreign Secretary, Selwyn Lloyd.[6]

Greene returned to Cuba for two weeks in October 1958 to scout film locations. He could see that the rebels were gaining recruits and territory, so urged Delargy to keep after the government. On 19 November, Delargy asked Lloyd whether the government had supplied jets and tanks to the Cuban government, eliciting an admission that the government had some months ago approved a sale by a private firm of seventeen piston-engine planes and fifteen Comet tanks from surplus stocks. On 15 December, Delargy got rough, asking another junior minister, Allan Noble, whether the government had licensed the sale of rockets, and the slippery Noble took refuge in the ministe-rial passive voice as he confirmed that 'the sale of seventeen Sea Fury aircraft to the Cuban government was authorised some months ago. These aircraft are equipped to carry rockets and a normal complement for each aircraft was authorised in the usual way.' Delargy then asked whether he was aware that a ship named the *Sarmiento* carrying a cargo of more than a hundred tons of rockets was waiting to set sail from a British port. He asked for an assurance that this ship would not sail and called it a 'a dirty deal done behind the backs of the British people and of Parliament'. With the support of Nye Bevan as Shadow Foreign Secretary, he demanded that the Speaker allow an adjournment debate and, in a splendid piece of unparliamentary behaviour, challenged the impartiality of the Speaker, William Shepherd Morrison, and called him 'frivolous' for choosing to hold a debate on 'Scottish horticulture' over one on the killing of Cubans.[7] He had made his point, and the red-faced British government stopped selling weapons to Batista.

The historian Christopher Hull believes that Greene and Delargy may have contributed modestly to Batista's downfall by adding, at the last moment, to his international isolation – a straw for the camel's back.[8] With his regime simply falling apart and Fidel's forces marching on both Havana and Santiago, the dictator decided that it was time to flee to the Dominican Republic, where he would have to scrape by on a few hundred million dollars. He boarded a plane early on 1 January 1959, taking his family and some supporters, but not, initially, Colonel Ventura, who forced his way onto the plane at gunpoint. According to Greene, Ventura became a fixture at the fruit machines in Ciudad Trujillo.[9] The man in the linen suit eventually set up a private security firm in Miami, and he died there in 2001.[10] Unwelcome in the United States, Batista moved on to Portugal and then Spain. He hired body-guards to keep assassins at bay and died of a heart attack in 1973 – he was, of course, a wealthy man, so death by natural causes was within his means.

On 3 January 1959 Greene wrote to *The Times* about the 'welcome' victory of Fidel Castro's forces: Greene understood, correctly at the time, that Castro was not a communist but a nationalist. Greene castigated the British government and, without naming him, the ambassador Stanley Fordham, for remaining unaware of ubiquitous atrocities and not recognizing that Cuba was in the midst of a civil war *before* the weapons were sold – something obvious to a private travel-ler such as himself. He lamented that the bombing of the old city of Trinidad had probably been done with British planes. He followed this letter with another three days later expressing wonder that the British government had not known that by the autumn three-quarters of Cuba was out of Batista's control. There is another irony here. Whereas Jim Wormold had convinced his superiors of an imaginary threat of war, Fordham had failed to notice a real one.

Predictably, *Our Man in Havana* excited film producers, and Monica McCall, Greene's American agent, thought she could get $125,000 for the rights. Alfred Hitchcock was the main early bidder and would go as high as £25,000 (about $70,000), but the idea of working with Hitchcock had no attraction for Greene. His old friend Carol Reed, backed by Columbia, then pushed Hitchcock aside with an offer of $100,000, which was accepted. After Mankiewicz's betrayal of *The Quiet American*, Greene decided that he should write this script himself, a task for which he would receive another £6000 – the combined amounts coming fairly close to the original asking price.[11] Moreover, he trusted no film-maker more than Reed, with whom he was now working for the third time. In mid-October, they flew to Cuba for two weeks to scout locations, and it was during this time that Greene garnered the new information which he passed on to Hugh Delargy. Reed was afraid that the regime would stop the filming, but Greene remarked, 'Don't worry, they'll all be washed up by the time we're ready to come back here for production.'[12] He could see that Batista and his gang were into injury time.

Returning to England, they checked into adjoining rooms at the Hotel Metropole in Brighton and fell into their old pattern of collaboration. Greene woke early and wrote; he would hand what he had done to a typist working in their shared sitting room. Once she was finished, Reed, still lying in bed, would pore over it; they would confer during lunch, go back to work in the afternoon, and carouse in the evening. Greene had a revised version of the script ready around 22 November. Reed was still worried about conditions in Cuba, so they travelled to Seville and Cadiz to look for alternatives to Havana. On 7 December, Greene finished another version, with which Reed was 'delighted', but Greene was too exhausted to know whether it was any good.[13] He continued tinkering, especially with the last scene, but the job was done.

48

TAXIDERMY EVERYWHERE

G reene had begun a new novel, to be entitled 'Lucius'. It is hard to pin down the exact dates, but a typescript of his autobiography prepared near the beginning of 1971 has a note placing 'Lucius' twelve years earlier, and Greene's bibliographers judge that it came shortly after *Our Man in Havana*.[1] Set in a version of Berkhamsted School, the story is perhaps loosely based on a recollection of how a young master named F. 'Dicker' Dale, appointed in September 1915, married the matron.[2]

Greene had tried before to write fiction about his school days – notably in the unpublished 'Anthony Sant' – and would approach the subject again in his last novel, *The Captain and the Enemy*. 'Lucius' revis-its the plotline of 'The Basement Room' and *The Man Within* where a young person betrays a mentor. The schoolmaster in the story is named Stonier; he is separated from his wife but not divorced and is secretly conducting an affair with the matron. He protects a boy named Lucius Darling from bullies modelled on Wheeler and Carter, but Darling steals a sexy photograph of the matron from Stonier's rooms and black-mails him. Stonier resigns from his post and commits suicide. Decades later, Darling, an unpleasant boy grown to unpleasant manhood, has become Foreign Secretary, and he learns of the suicide when he returns to the school for a prize-giving. Greene gave up on the project after about twenty thousand words, either because he thought the story a failure or because he could not bear thinking about his school days.

With a great deal of work on hand – he was, at the same time, finishing the script of *The Complaisant Lover* – Greene had a health scare. For many months, Elisabeth Moor had been doubtful of his liver. Raymond took a different view. He thought the abdominal pains from which his brother was suffering were not related to the liver or duodenum and might be entirely psychosomatic, owing to stress, so he ordered a barium X-ray. When the results came back negative, Graham wrote to Catherine: 'Raymond had told me frankly that it would be either nothing or cancer. I didn't much mind about the cancer, but the ten days of waiting were a bit of a strain with nobody much to talk to.'[3] Cancer would become rife in the Greene family, with the novelist himself requiring a colectomy in 1979.

In the midst of all this, Sherman Stonor's wife made some unwelcome moves. The hyper-Catholic Jeanne Stonor (née Stourton), the daughter of a Spanish diplomat and an Englishwoman, was an inveterate lion-chaser, with a long string of famous lovers. In late 1958, she decided to pursue Greene, who had no interest: 'It's so difficult to explain without rudeness that I like her but could no more go to bed with her than with her husband.'[4] Years later, he was extremely annoyed to hear that she boasted of having had an affair with him.

Meanwhile, Carol Reed was able to assemble what was nearly a great cast for the film. Alec Guinness took the part of Jim Wormold, with Noël Coward as an inspired Hawthorne, Burl Ives as Hasselbacher, Maureen O'Hara as Beatrice, and Ralph Richardson as 'C'. The part of Captain Segura went to the American comedian Ernie Kovacs. The choice of Jo Morrow for Milly is probably a flaw in the film, but it doesn't amount to much – in the second half of the film she appears on screen for mere seconds at a time.

Greene was present in Cuba for the early part of the filming in mid-April. The revolutionary government had objections to a film that found comedy in their recent history, and was dubious of the claim that it was a satire not on Cuba but on British intelligence. On set, officials demanded changes in dialogue, so that, for example, Segura could only be seen as a villain. They spoke up when burlesque dancers showed too much flesh, and required that a bootblack be given clean trousers.

Cuba's most famous foreigner, Ernest Hemingway, put in an appearance when filming moved to Sloppy Joe's Bar in Havana, which Greene found a little awkward: 'we shook hands & exchanged wry glances: I was muscling in to his territory'.[5] Guinness later wrote that Greene and others attended a dinner at Hemingway's house, but Greene did not actually go to the dinner.[6] And yet, Hemingway was Greene's favourite American novelist: he rated him even more highly than he did Faulkner.[7] In the early 1960s, Gillian Sutro asked Greene's opinion of him, and he said, 'All writers of my generation owe a debt to Hemingway. After him, one just can't write dialogue as before.'[8] Although he dismissed the 'hairy-chested romanticism' of *For Whom the Bell Tolls*, he so admired *A Farewell to Arms* that he dared not go back to it in later years for fear of discovering its faults. Of course, it is perhaps as well that Greene did not have dinner at Hemingway's that night, as the atmosphere might have brought out the worst in him. He did visit the house in August 1963, two years after Hemingway's death: 'Taxidermy everywhere, buffalo heads, antlers ... such carnage.'[9]

He left Reed and the actors to their work and so missed a visit to the set by Castro. Greene had to get to London for rehearsals of *The Complaisant Lover*, a play focused on three main characters. Victor Rhodes is a dentist who loves tedious practical jokes – as exemplars of middle-class banality, dentists are to Graham Greene what accountants are to *Monty Python*. Victor's wife, Mary, is somewhat younger than he is, an intelligent, slightly nervous woman having an affair with a supercilious antiquarian bookseller named Clive Root. Ultimately, their secrets come out and the three accept an arrangement in which both marriage and affair continue. The title reverses the usual situation of a complaisant husband bearing his wife's infidelity, and presents a lover adapting himself to the continuation of the marriage. This triangle, in which nobody is happy and nobody is rejected, is remarkably bleak, even by Greene's standards.

The play burnt a bridge for him, and this was unexpected. After their break-up, he had given a copy of it to Anita Björk, who then fell silent, acknowledging neither the play nor the payments on her house. Greene missed her terribly and wanted to reconcile with her, and in mid-November he asked Michael Meyer to let her know this.[10] He also sent John Sutro to Stockholm as an ambassador; he brought back word that a scene in the play had caused Anita pain. When the affair is revealed, Victor goes to the garage and runs the car engine with a view to killing himself. As a method of suicide, this was once very common – and chosen by Stig Dagerman in 1954, so Anita thought it 'unfeeling' of Greene to work such a scene into the play.[11] Although she forgave him and maintained a quietly affectionate relationship with him until the end of his life, there was no way back.

The play was a great success, but how it happened surprised every-one. John Gielgud, the director, had other commitments and was a week late for rehearsals, so the play went on stage after a mere two weeks of work. It had a brief provincial tour beginning in Manchester, and then opened at the Globe in London on 18 June 1959, with Phyllis Calvert appearing as Mary, Paul Scofield as Clive, and Ralph Richardson as Victor – for a number of days Richardson was acting both as 'C' in studio filming for *Our Man in Havana* and as Victor on stage. Greene and Richardson had an argument, and the actor nearly quit, over the question of how long it had been since Victor and Mary had sex.[12] This problem was sorted out, but it set the table for a more terrible row over Richardson's performance in the lead of *Carving the Statue* (1964). Oddly enough, Gielgud and his cast understood *The Complaisant Lover* as a tragedy, and yet the audiences responded to it, with its trick cushions and other practical jokes, as a grim comedy.[13] It was extremely popular and ran for almost a year.[14]

The play was in one respect a victim of its own success. The New York producer Irene Mayer Selznick had optioned the work, expecting to bring the whole production over from London, but it was doing too well to close. The daughter of Louis B. Mayer, Selznick had once been married to David O. Selznick, and she terrified most directors and actors. She admitted to being intimidated by Graham Greene. In the summer of 1959 she proposed to Greene that the spelling of 'complaisant' should be changed to 'complacent'. Greene sent her an explanation of how the two words differed, and his letter was leaked to the press.[15]

Nonetheless, they developed a pleasant relationship, with her remem-bering him as 'cozy' and 'delightful' to work with, even as problems piled up. A planned production for the autumn of 1960 was one of forty-three postponed owing to a labour dispute between the producers and Actors' Equity.[16] Moreover, they had a difficult time coming up with a suitable cast. At a certain point, Greene despaired and suggested they give up on his 'ragbag' of a play.[17] In 1961, Selznick did finally launch a production at the Barrymore Theatre, directed by Gielgud's friend and collaborator Glen Byam Shaw. Cast as Victor Rhodes, Michael Redgrave, not an obvious choice for the role, finally appeared in a faithful production of a work by Graham Greene. It started badly, with him drinking and unable to learn his lines, but in due course he was able to give his part tragic depth. Googie Withers appeared as Mary and was required for a time to wear a rubber body suit so as to look her age. Richard Johnson as Clive was sacked and then rehired. A young Gene Wilder was aptly cast as the hotel valet.[18] Opening on 1 November 1961, the play did well, if not as well as in London, and with many productions queued up from the preceding year and awaiting theatre space, it closed after a three-month run.[19] It was the last theatrical success Greene would enjoy for many years.

49

THE SEPARATING SICKNESS

Hansi Lambert had once astonished Graham Greene by splashing Guerlain perfume on a roaring fire.[1] Born Johanna von Reininghaus, she was an Austrian Catholic and the widow of Baron Henri Lambert, a member of the Belgian branch of the Rothschild family and founder of the Banque Lambert. Following her husband's death, she ran the bank for some years. She also established a literary and artistic salon, where she numbered among her friends the poet Stephen Spender, the philosopher Isaiah Berlin, and the composer Nicolas Nabokov. Graham Greene had met her by January 1948, probably in connection with a large Catholic congress held annually in Brussels. They remained in touch, and when he came to Brussels, he usually stayed at her grand house at 24 Avenue Marnix. Lambert was used to helping authors and artists with strange requests, and so she helped Graham Greene find his way to some leproseries in the Congo.

Why did he want to go to such places? The answer is complicated and perhaps melodramatic. Since biblical times, leprosy has been seen as a curse, and those suffering from it treated as outcasts. In Greene's fiction, he often depicted his protagonists spreading sorrow like a contagious disease – 'D' in *The Confidential Agent*, the whisky priest, and Scobie are all described as carriers of illness. Moreover, Greene often employed specific images of leprosy: Richard Smyth in *The End of the Affair* is healed of a skin ailment, and Father Rank in *The Heart of the Matter* indiscreetly remarks on having seen Scobie visit Yusef and is suddenly embarrassed: ' . . . he swung his great empty-sounding bell to and fro, Ho, ho, ho, like a leper proclaiming his misery'.[2]

It will come as no surprise that Graham Greene often expressed self-loathing: 'I wish I could stop being a bastard,' he once wrote to

Catherine.[3] He was fully convinced that anyone he touched would suffer. He could not easily sustain normal relationships so thought of himself as effectively unclean and separate. A reader of Greene's next novel, *A Burnt-Out Case* (1961), will immediately see it as a work responding to Conrad's *Heart of Darkness* because of its setting and long journey by river, but the book's initial conception owed more to that other early influence on Greene's writings, his distant cousin Robert Louis Stevenson who wrote about the Belgian missionary Father Damien (or St Damien of Molokai as he is known since his canonization in 2009).

In 1873, Father Damien went to serve eight hundred people on the Hawaiian island of Molokai who suffered from leprosy, known there as the 'separating sickness'.[4] A difficult man in some ways, he nonetheless made many practical reforms in the treatment of those he lived among, and decided it was necessary to touch them in the normal course of things. By the late nineteenth century, it was known that leprosy does not spread easily and that the centuries-old notion of almost instant transmission was entirely wrong, though its epidemiology remains a difficult question even today. However, in time, Father Damien did contract the disease, and he continued to live and work on the island. His story became widely known and many regarded him as a saint.

A month after the priest's death in early 1889, Robert Louis Stevenson, in his Pacific travels, came to Molokai and saw the settlement. He had no fear of the people and wanted to be of use, but there was nothing for him to do apart from teach some young women how to play croquet. Some months later he read a published letter by the Presbyterian missionary Dr Charles McEwen Hyde, making several claims about Damien, among them that he had a history of immorality – he assumed this because some scientists believed, erroneously, that leprosy was a stage of syphilis. Stevenson came down on Hyde as with a scimitar: he wrote an open letter defending Damien, which was republished many times throughout the world and helped to cement the priest's reputation as a saint.[5] As the foiled biographer of Stevenson, Greene knew all about this episode and had a fascination with Father Damien.

Greene's initial sense of leprosy was probably mythic or metaphoric, even though he had seen an actual case during his trek through Liberia – a person with the disease asked him for medicine, and he gave him what he had even though it was not going to do any good (see above, p. 89). He probably saw other cases in his travels. Still, he needed to learn what the disease actually is.

It is certainly not the skin ailment that Moses legislated for, and we do not know what Jesus was healing. Leprosy is thought to have come to Europe with Alexander the Great's soldiers returning from Asia.[6] In a paradox that appealed to Greene, the disease does its harm by removing pain. Peripheral nerves are damaged, and the patients injure themselves without knowing it. Subsequent infections can lead to the loss of fingers, toes, hands, and feet, all for the lack of warnings that pain gives. Some patients lose the ability to blink and so go blind. The only animal apart from humans to harbour the leprosy bacillus is the nine-banded armadillo, whose low body temperature makes it a suitable host; this is important for research as scientists have had scant success reproducing the bacillus in vitro.[7]

For many centuries, there was no treatment for leprosy except segregation. In about 1940, the antibacterial sulfone drugs, particularly Dapsone, known as DDS, made it possible to cure the disease, and nowadays a superior multi-drug treatment is available.[8] The disease often eludes early diagnosis and mutilations continue to occur. The World Health Organization reports that by the end of 2016, there were still about two hundred thousand new cases each year.[9]

In September 1958, Greene told Hansi Lambert that he was looking for a 'hospital of the Schweitzer kind' but run by a Catholic religious order, preferably in West or Central Africa. In Vietnam, Greene had come to know and respect Belgian missionaries, so he was especially interested in going to the Congo. Lambert knew just the person for him to contact, and, in fact, he had already met him. In 1950, the young medical student Michel Lechat had attended a dinner she gave in Greene's honour, though he and the novelist exchanged just a few words. Lechat came from a literary family and in his youth aspired to be a poet, so was in awe of the company at Lambert's gatherings. Something of an adventurer, he travelled in Turkey and managed to get himself jailed there for three days without having committed a crime. In 1951, he joined a group of health workers bicycling through the jungle distributing sulfones to people with the disease. When asked about this remarkable work, he confirmed that it occurred, but downplayed it: 'Quite poetic. Yes and no. Probably more funny! The creation of a myth.'[10]

He went to the Congo on a six-month fellowship towards the end of his medical studies, in 1951–2: 'There, I studied with Dr Hemerijckx, one of the greatest figures of leprosy in the forties and fifties, a widower – he had lost his wife on the spot during the very first years after his arrival, in the twenties. A hybrid of Schweitzer and Father Damien, so to speak, living in the complete bush, he was in charge of organizing the ambulatory treatment of leprosy in the remote villages of central Congo. Nurses distributing the new drugs, often travelling on bicycles, paths permitting. Hence the story of "yours truly" on bicycle.'[11]

Lechat returned to Belgium to finish his training, and in 1953 went to the Congo again for the first of a series of three-year terms. By 1958, accompanied by his wife, the artist Édith Dasnoy, he was running a leprosy clinic in the village of Iyonda in the province of Équateur in the north-west of the country. About 15 kilometres from the provincial capital of Coquilhatville (now Mbandaka), it was off the beaten track, but not utterly isolated. There he had the care of many patients and began the research he would continue in the 1960s at Johns Hopkins University as he became the world's pre-eminent expert on the disease, and then pursued a distinguished career as an epidemiologist in Louvain. When it was proposed to him in an interview for this book that he had 'worked like a dog' at Iyonda, this self-effacing man was induced finally to express wonder: 'how did I succeed to spare time to do research in Iyonda with 1200 patients on my [hands]'.[12]

Lechat was not keen to have the novelist visit the leproserie, fearing that his presence might unsettle his own relations, as a government employee, with the priests and nuns with whom he worked. It might also further expose his vulnerable patients to the world's curiosity, as if they were 'giraffes'.[13] Since the leproserie was a 'show piece' for the modern treatment of the disease, there had been other visitors, including an eminent ornithologist, a doctor, a saxophonist, a diplomat, the manager of a travelling circus, and an official from the American State Department.[14] Lechat extended a very qualified welcome to Greene, but sent him a list of two dozen other leproseries that might be more suited to his purpose. However, he noted that Iyonda was situated in the area Conrad described in *Heart of Darkness*,[15] and that detail may have ensured that he would choose Lechat's leproserie.

As part of his journey to Havana in October 1958, Greene met in

New York, at Lechat's suggestion, Frederick Franck, an oral surgeon and artist who had visited Iyonda in 1958. Subsequently known as an authority on Buddhism, Franck worked with Albert Schweitzer and wrote a book about him, which Greene reviewed warmly. Greene went to two exhibitions of his drawings and was surprised by how very good they were, and later wrote an introduction to his *African Sketchbook*. After talking with Franck, he felt sure that Iyonda was the right place for him to learn about leprosy.[16]

Even though there were still demands on his time from the productions of *Our Man in Havana* and *The Complaisant Lover*, Greene needed to spend not less than five or six weeks in the Congo, which was then approaching independence. He was not there as a political or military reporter on this occasion, but the context is important as just ahead lay the Congo Crisis of 1960–65. The Belgian approach to decolonization was gradual, to say the least, and they did essentially nothing to prepare the Congo for what turned out to be an abrupt change in government followed by a five-year bloodbath.

The Belgians did not want to let go of their colony – it was worth too much. In the Second World War, the exiled leaders of occupied Belgium had made heavy demands on the territory, including a Kurtz-like requirement of up to 120 days per year of forced labour from rural workers. The colony contributed large supplies of copper, tin, lumber, rubber, even uranium to the war effort, while about forty thousand Congolese fought for the Allies, some serving in Africa and some in Europe. In contrast to British and French practice, which would see a white officer court-martialled for striking an African soldier, floggings were an almost daily occurrence in the Congo regiments. Returning from the war, many veterans had no patience with European claims of racial superiority. Moreover, as Belgians working in the colony had themselves gone to war, many Congolese took over skilled jobs and administrative positions, creating a new upwardly mobile class known as *évolués*.[17]

The 1950s, especially the early years, were a time of prosperity in the Congo, but with the benefits going mainly to the white settlers and to Belgium itself. There was, nonetheless, an expansion of infrastructure, with roads, electrical generators, hospitals, and clinics springing up throughout the colony. The Congo had a high rate of literacy, but university education was extremely restricted, and at the time of independence there was not a single Congolese lawyer, doctor, engineer, or economist – a void that would have terrible consequences when it came time to govern the country.[18]

Still, in the 1950s supporters of independence found ways to inform themselves of the changes occurring throughout the world. Many belonged to political clubs, and others engaged in galvanizing discussions at the Brussels Expo and the Accra All-African People's Conference, both in 1958. An array of new parties emerged, the largest being the Mouvement National Congolais (MNC) led by Patrice Lamumba, later the country's first prime minister – this party favoured immediate independence and a unitary state. The Alliance des Bakango (ABAKO), led by Joseph Kasavubu, who became the country's first president, had its roots in the Bakango ethnic group and was less radical in its demands. Among the emerging leaders was Joseph Désiré Mobutu (later Mobutu Sese Seko), who served as head of the military in the new government.[19]

Independence came on 30 June 1960. In the ensuing administrative vacuum, there was a mutiny in the army, a mass departure of Belgian civilians, a military invasion by Belgium, an intervention by the UN, and large-scale secessions. Over the objections of Kasavubu, Lamumba looked to the Soviet Union for assistance in controlling the country, a decision that brought the new republic into the front line of the Cold War. Barely six months after independence, Mobutu, with American approval, arranged for the execution of his former friend Lamumba. Until 1965, a civil war was fought along ideological and ethnic lines, with the Americans and Soviets backing certain groups as proxies. Already the dominant figure in the country, Mobutu made an outright seizure of power in 1965 and ruled as a repressive and corrupt dictator until 1997.[20]

Greene made his arrangements to visit the leproseries in late 1958, when these events could not possibly have been foreseen, and yet even before he reached the Congo the situation was changing. On 4 January 1959, just as Greene was getting the good news that he did not have cancer, the white mayor of Léopoldville cancelled a large political meeting organized by ABAKO. Thousands of frustrated supporters turned on the police, looted shops and businesses owned by whites, and attacked government institutions, as well as missionary churches and schools. The police shot many rioters, and after four days there were not less than forty-seven Congolese dead and 330 injured. Forty-nine Europeans were injured but none killed. On 13 January, King Baudouin released a recorded address, played throughout the colony, in which he assured the Congolese that within a reasonable time they would have independence. The announcement caused great excitement, and even though some violence continued, this was understood as a break-through.[21] It was a moment of hope.

Nonetheless, when Greene arrived in Léopoldville on 31 January 1959 he found the city still on a war footing. The streets were patrolled by tanks, lorries, and soldiers moving in single file – much as he had seen in Vietnam. A series of journalists came to Greene's hotel room, assuming he was there to report on the riots.[22]

As in Mexico, where he paid little attention to the nationalization of the oil industry and focused on the abrogation of religious rights, Greene was in the Congo to learn about leprosy. Having already written extensively about forced labour in Liberia and about the Mau Mau uprising in Kenya, he would continue to investigate African politics, as for example in his treatment of apartheid in The Human Factor. At the time, there were about a hundred thousand people in the Congo suffering from the disease,[23] almost all of them condemned to misery, destitution, and segregation. The disease was a perfectly legitimate focus for research, even if there was something close to a revolution going on at the same time.

On 2 February 1959 Greene went to Coquilhatville, where Lechat picked him up and took him to Iyonda. A village of small brick houses arranged in avenues bordered by mango trees on the edge of the equatorial forest, it was home to just over a thousand people with the disease. Greene was given a room in the priests' house, with just a few sticks of furniture and a container of brownish water. Once alone, he had sudden misgivings: 'Why was I here?' It was not a question to which he had much of an answer. He was, as usual, in flight from the disappointments of his personal life. He was also following an obscure hunch that he could write a book that involved leprosy: 'All I know about the story is a man "who turns up" ... the place where he emerges into my semi-consciousness is a leper station, many hundred miles up the Congo.'[24]

Semi-consciousness is one thing, experience is another. Having come with what was probably a stereotype of 'the leper', Greene now watched Lechat at work with his patients – real people with an often devastating disease. Lechat recalled him as particularly observant, making note, for example, of a man with no fingers who became an expert knitter, and people with damaged feet who were given special shoes that some chose to wear only on Sundays.[25] A patient named Deo Gratias caught his attention,[26] and a character based on him plays an important part in Greene's novel. He took an interest in medical technology, including a device that could measure the reactions of nerves to one twenty-thousandth of a second, and another that measured the temperature of the skin in twenty places at once, allowing the doctor to prevent the formation of a leprous patch. Indeed, Lechat, and all leprologists, sought to treat the disease at an early stage and so avoid mutilations. Nonetheless, Greene saw some terrible sights, among them numerous cases of tuberculosis, a common cause of death among people with leprosy. There were also cases of elephantiasis: one man whose legs and feet had swollen like tree trunks and another whose testes were the size of footballs.

After a week at Iyonda, Greene discerned a connection between his imagined character and the patients he was meeting: 'Leprosy cases whose disease has been arrested and cured only after the loss of fingers or toes are known as burnt-out cases. This is the parallel I have been seeking between my character X and the lepers. Psychologically and morally he has been burnt-out. Is it at that point that the cure is effected? Perhaps the novel should begin not at the leproserie but on the mission boat.'[27] Knowledge of these things imposed an ethical and technical challenge for Greene: the novel was to be focused on a physically sound European, whose psychological troubles had some parallels with leprosy but hardly bore comparison with the real thing. Although he often hinted that he was washed up as a writer, his eventual approach to this problem would be surprising and inventive. In the meantime, his visit to the Congo had a different outcome from the one he made to Kenya. He reported on Kenya as journalist, but produced no novel. His visit to the Congo led him to write a novel, but no journalism; towards the end of his time in the leproseries, he told Marie Biche that he would not be writing articles on the Congo as his experience there was 'too limited & specialised'.[28]

Still, he formed views on the political situation. He met the local governor and had a discussion with his *adjoint*, a man of twenty years' experience, about the future of the Congo: 'He spoke with emotion of the gentleness of life in the villages, but he too feels – as I cannot – that the tribal framework must be broken and material incentives be given for that purpose. Doesn't this lead straight to the gadget world of the States? He spoke of the necessity for a mystique, but is there any mystique in America today, even inside the Catholic church?'[29] As in Kenya, Greene felt that the departing colonial power should not meddle with traditional values and social arrangements.

Greene did his best not to disturb the life of the mission, which was then a place of great activity as a hospital was being erected to replace the four-room dispensary where Lechat did much of his work. The novelist would spend part of his day lying in a disused pirogue (a form of canoe) by the bank of the Congo River, reading there until the heat became too intense. He would usually eat his lunch with the four priests,[30] members of a congregation called the Missionaires du Sacré-Cœur de Jésus. Perhaps spoiled by his experience of saintly and bookish Belgian missionaries in Vietnam, Greene did not especially enjoy the company of these men, as their concerns were decidedly practical – they were building a hospital. Like the superior in *A Burnt-Out Case*, Father Pierre Wijnants smoked cheroots constantly, but he was a quiet man and seemed unlikely at the time to give any such sermon as that which appears in the novel, and was so unworldly as to mistake bidets in a catalogue for footbaths and proposed to order a dozen for the use of the patients.[31] Nonetheless, he later proved himself an able archbishop.[32]

In the evenings, Greene typically joined the Lechats and their children for dinner, and his manner was reserved but polite. Édith Dasnoy owned an 8mm movie camera, and on 5 March 1959 Père Paul Van Molle made a brief film of Greene. He can be seen dancing with the very whimsical Père Hendrik Vanderslaghmolen (known as Henri or Rik), who then gets on a tricycle belonging to Lechat's three-year-old son. The film also catches some cheerful footage of Greene dining with the family,[33] and although he was doubtless performing for the camera, he does not appear gloomy, let alone as prodigiously grim as his character Querry. Still, he did not reveal much to Lechat about his observations at Iyonda, nor did Lechat question him.[34]

His journal does record irritation at would-be authors approaching him either to get tips on writing, or, worse, to give them. Such authors would show up by around five o'clock, supposedly to have a beer. According to a plan worked out with Lechat, whose sense of humour he greatly appreciated, the approach of a car was the signal for the novelist to climb out of a back window of Lechat's house and vanish into the forest.[35] One of these authors, the schoolmaster R. Van den Brandt, first asked Greene for help finding an agent, and the novelist gave him some names; then he asked for a meeting to discuss 'religion' as he had lost his faith because of a bankruptcy, but Greene refused to do this, telling him to look to the priests for advice.[36] This man was almost certainly the model for the character named Rycker. For a short while, the novelist tried to stay incognito as 'Mr Graham', but that did not succeed, and one woman, the much younger wife of a veterinary surgeon, recognized him from the cover of a magazine, as does Marie Rycker in the novel.[37]

At Iyonda, Greene was observing a fairly modern leproserie, operated on scientific principles, even if it was very short of resources. He also wanted to learn about old-fashioned leprosy settlements, run on 'sentimental' lines, so arranged to travel on the bishop's steamboat, the *Theresita*, along the Ruki-Momboyu, a tributary of the Congo. He was given the bishop's cabin where, in equatorial heat, he slept under a picture of a church surrounded by snow.[38] A battered paddle-steamer, the boat itself would not have been out of place in the pages of *Huckleberry Finn*, except perhaps for the folding altar in the deckhouse.

Apart from the crew, Greene's companions were three missionary priests, including Rik Vanderslaghmolen, 'tall & cadaverous & a joker',[39] who could speak some English. The captain, Père Georges, reminded Greene of an officer of the Foreign Legion and seems to have been easily bored, firing off his rifle at monkeys, a cormorant, an eagle, and a crocodile – at one meal Greene ate a heron the priest had shot and supposed it rabbit.[40] The priests' innocent jokes in Flemish left him a little confused, and he decided that his novel's hollowed-out character should be surrounded by a humour he cannot participate in, and a sign of his eventual healing is that he 'perpetrated a joke'.[41] He was glad to encounter a young man named Lipscomb, who had served as a military officer in India and was now the manager of a palm oil factory at Flandria; finding their conversation relaxing and intelligent, he visited the Lipscomb family on the journey upriver and then again on his return.[42] In the novel, the far less amiable Rycker is made the manager of just such a factory.

Having sworn off Joseph Conrad since 1932, Greene at last re-read the collection *Youth* while on the *Theresita*: 'The heavy hypnotic style falls around me again, and I am aware of the poverty of my own. Perhaps now I have lived long enough with my poverty to be safe from corruption.' He was chiefly interested in *Heart of Darkness*, which he still believed an excellent story though it had its flaws, the language 'inflated' and the character of Kurtz not coming to life: 'It is as if Conrad had taken an episode in his own life and tried to lend it, for the sake of "literature", a greater significance than it will hold.' Greene was curious about Conrad's habit of comparing concrete objects to abstractions and wondered whether he had himself picked it up[43] – this is true, though Greene also does the reverse, frequently comparing an abstraction to an unlikely physical object, just flirting with bathos, for an effect that can be startling, amusing, or ironic. It is a stylistic mannerism he shares with W. H. Auden, whom he admired more than any living poet apart from Robert Frost.[44]

As the boat passed into more remote territory, along a narrowing and meandering river course, Greene grew melancholic, feeling the pang of his estrangement from Anita, dreaming about Catherine and her lovers, and pondering a brief liaison that had just concluded in Brussels – the woman's name is blotted out in his journal and replaced with 'Tony'. She was married to a man serving in Cyprus, and while Greene had some strong feelings for her, he did not want to fall in love. He described the affair as lifting him from the 'broken backed state' of his emotions following the loss of Anita.[45]

On 16 February, at a place called Imbonga, Greene was led by a guide on a quick hour-long walk into the forest towards a leproserie, but as soon as the guide left him he was disconcerted to find a large red monkey obstructing his path. The leproserie itself consisted of three villages, laid out in an orderly fashion, one having a 'wide alley of palm trees' down the middle. The mentality of the missionaries in such places was rather different from what he had encountered in Iyonda. He came across nuns so devoted to the old ways of treating the patients that they resented the sulfone cure: one even remarked, 'It's a terrible thing – there are no lepers left here' – evidence of an obsessional or 'leprophilic' attachment to people with the disease.

There was, in fact, an enormous amount of suffering. In one hut, he could just discern the outlines of a pot and heard sounds of movement as an old woman crawled towards the voices of her visitors on the remnants of her hands and knees. She could not lift her head, and all he could do was address her with a local greeting: 'Ouané'. He came across an old man in good spirits who waved to him with the stumps of his arms and raised his mutilated feet. It was hard to find a more obscure place, but even here Greene was known – 'a regional officer and a doctor suddenly appeared out of a rainstorm with a copy of *The Third Man*.[46] During his days on the river, he would also be asked to sign copies of *The Power and the Glory* and *Stamboul Train*.[47]

On 20 February, he reached Lombolomba, where he found a wide, airy leproserie. By necessity, children were separated from their mothers at birth in order to prevent infections. He saw a room with tables where the mothers could clean their babies, but also saw one tragic child in a fetal position, evidently wasting to death. The settlement was run by some nuns and one very lonely priest, a Father Octave, who was glad to have Greene's company and that of the priests from the boat. Greene noticed that here much more attention was paid to the psychological well-being of the patients than at Iyonda, where the medical facilities were so much better. The school band put on a show for him, complete with torches. Father Octave was asked again and again who was this visitor and he replied, memorably, 'a big fetishist'.[48]

Delayed by a bent rudder, the boat, with three goats in the bow, eventually headed back down river. At night Greene watched the stars come out and listened to the vampire bats passing over the forest. Rain fell and he played the dice game 421 with the priests. He made an important note for inclusion in the novel: 'I am alive because I feel discomfort.' When Querry has become psychologically numbed, he is, in the logic of the novel, closest to the condition of leprosy, injuring himself and those around him. The return of first discomfort, then actual pain, marks the beginnings of health, and as the phrase echoes Descartes's *cogito*, it offers a paradoxical assurance that he actually exists.

He also decided that the doctor would not be the embittered figure he had first planned; a widower, Dr Colin was inspired as much by Lechat's mentor Dr Hemerijckx as by Lechat himself, and the character would be objective and fair-minded, while Querry's problems would be caused mainly by a plantation owner and his wife. Colin is more complicated still, as Greene later remarked that the evolutionary theology of the Jesuit Teilhard de Chardin, whose best-known work *The Phenomenon of Man* impressed him 'more than any other book for many, many years',[49] was essential to his conception of this character. Late one night on the river, Greene wrote some sentences that might serve as a conclusion to the novel but wondered whether he would ever reach them.[50]

Arriving back at Iyonda, where he remained for another week, on 26 February Greene found from his accumulated post that the journey to the Congo had caused him to miss an invitation to Buckingham Palace; 'thank God', he wrote in his journal. 'The trouble is it may occur again.'[51]

Many of the observations in his journal at the time pertain to the psychological condition of those cured of leprosy, the burnt-out cases. He also noted what he called 'the virtual enslavement of women' owing to the lack of education.[52]

In the Congo, he had seen his share of brave people, those who bore leprosy and those who cared for them. One was particularly famous: he met Andrée de Jongh on three occasions. A hero of the Belgian resistance, she had escorted many Allied airmen along what was known as the Comet Line into Spain. In 1943, she was betrayed and sent to Ravensbrück concentration camp. After the war she decided to lead a celibate life and work among those suffering from leprosy. Although his own relationship to the church was vexed, Greene was proud to learn that her decision to become a Catholic in 1947 had been strongly influenced by a reading of *The Power and the Glory*. Having received a number of honours for her wartime service, she was the subject of a popular book by Airey Neave, *Little Cyclone*. When Greene asked her how she came to be working in the Congo, she said, 'Because from the age of 15 I wanted to cure the lepers. If I delayed any longer it would be too late.'[53]

50

ALONE IN A LIFT

O ne can hardly plan for a volcano. Mount Cameroon was erupt-
ing for the fourth time in fifty years. A formation with two
peaks, it rose 13,000 feet above sea level and had a base of 600 square
miles. On its eastern slopes there were four craters and three flows
of lava. The main stream was a mile wide and 50 feet high, pouring
from two vents in what had been a wooded area; it consumed banana
and cocoyam farms, then stopped just short of an oil-palm plantation
and the only road to the interior of the South Cameroons.[1] Bouncing
through updraughts and clouds of ash in a three-seater plane, Greene
sat beside Hô Boucarut, an old friend from Vietnam, and watched the
outpouring.[2]

The volcano was not the only thing that Greene did not plan for –
his personal landscape was also about to change beyond recognition.
He had left Iyonda on 5 March 1959, travelling via Léopoldville,
Brazzaville, and Libreville for the port city of Douala in Cameroon,
where he stayed from 8 to 13 March. There he visited an old-fashioned
leproserie at Dibamba. When interviewed by a priest about what he
saw, he apparently said that he preferred it to Iyonda, with its scientific advantages, as its approach was more compassionate. When
those remarks, consistent with what he wrote in his journal about
Lombolomba, appeared in a newspaper, an embarrassed Greene told
Lechat that he had been misquoted.[3]

Part of the attraction of Douala was old friends. He planned to meet
André Moret, formerly commandant of the Sûreté in Tonkin, now
serving in Cameroon; however, immediately before Greene's arrival he
was injured in a road accident and had had to be transported back to
France, so another old friend from the Sûreté, Paul Boucarut, met him

at the airport and that night took him to a dance hall where he watched sailors buy drinks for the prostitutes. Paul's Tonkinese wife Hô, a tiny woman of great beauty who usually wore garments of peacock-coloured silk, wanted to introduce him to a few of her friends, especially a thirty-six-year-old French woman named Yvonne Cloetta.

Born in Pontrieux in Brittany on 17 January 1923, Yvonne (née Guével) grew up in a devout family and was educated at the lycée in Quimper. Her father worked for the French national rail firm SNCF and was involved in the construction of the Niger–Benin railway – indeed, from the year of her birth he spent most of his time in Africa. During the German occupation, Yvonne lived with her aunt and uncle at Carhaix-Plouguer. Her uncle wept at the arrival of the Germans and expected them to rape the young women as he recalled the French doing when they occupied Germany in 1918. The town was spared such horrors, though other places were less fortunate. Yvonne observed the 'putes' receiving German soldiers and sensed a sadness among the young women of the town when Germans were transferred to the Eastern Front, where they would likely be killed. Gillian Sutro gathered from one conversation that Yvonne, or someone close to her, had witnessed the shooting of two suspected maquisards as they had a drink, along with the café owner who served them.[4]

At the end of the Second World War, Yvonne and her mother, a station master, joined her father in Dakar, where Yvonne took a secretarial job with the United African Company, a large subsidiary of Unilever, dealing especially in peanut oil and palm oil. She soon married her boss, the Swiss Jacques Cloetta, and they lived in some luxury in Dahomey (now Benin), Mali, Togo, and French Cameroon.[5] By the time she met Graham Greene, the marriage to Jacques had dried up, though they remained together for the sake of their two young daughters.

Cloetta knew exactly who Graham Greene was – she had seen The Third Man and had read some of his books. She regretted not being able to take up Hô's invitation to dinner with the author of The Power and Glory, which she thought a masterpiece. However, Hô then invited them both to her house for a drink, where the awkwardness of new acquaintance was relieved by Hô's recounting of the flight over the volcano.

That night they went to the Chantaco, the one night club open to Europeans, and stayed till four. It was probably on this night that

Greene met Jacques Cloetta – they did not meet again for about six years. Greene did not enjoy dancing, so Yvonne and Hô kept him company by turns, but after his weeks in the leproseries, he could not unwind. Of course, the Boucaruts were match-making. Yvonne said goodbye at the night club, but the next afternoon Paul asked her to come to Greene's hotel, as the novelist wanted to say goodbye again. She made Paul swear not to leave her alone with him. They went to his room, where he was packing his suitcase, and, to Paul's great disappointment, the two fell into a serious discussion of love and mortality. It was an odd flirtation, but Greene's interest in this petite, blue-eyed woman was piqued. Since Yvonne and Hô would be in the South of France in the summer, he suggested that they meet for drinks in Saint-Jean-Cap-Ferrat, where he would be visiting the Reinhardts.

That proposed meeting was a long way off. In the meantime, Cameroon was in the midst of a rebellion in the run-up to independence at the beginning of 1960, so Yvonne and Jacques agreed that she should return with their daughters to France, while he remained working in Africa, an arrangement that implied liberty to pursue other relationships.[6] She then went through something of an ordeal. She was having an affair with a young diplomat and was devoted to him. However, his father disapproved of this involvement and so arranged a suitable marriage for him. After a night in a hotel with Yvonne, the young man got up early, settled the bill, and vanished, leaving Yvonne humiliated.

When Greene saw her again on 29 July,[7] he could see something was wrong. While they were having drinks with Hô, he quietly asked Yvonne to have dinner with him the next evening at Le Réserve in Beaulieu. She found it easy to confide in him, since he was like a priest, so she told him all that had happened.[8] They then sat in her car looking at the boats in the harbour and talked till dawn. He was leaving for London the next day, so they had lunch at the airport, and when it was time for him to check in they stepped into a lift. He embraced her and asked, 'Est-ce que tu m'aimes?' Startled, she said it was too early to know. After ten days he came back and pretended that he had confused his verbs in the lift, having meant to ask whether she liked him, and yet over the next thirty-two years he would always embrace her when they were alone in a lift.[9]

51

CHANGES

The arrival of Yvonne Cloetta was the most important change in Greene's life in 1959, but other things were changing too, and it is helpful at this point to survey them.

Marion Greene had a sometimes frosty manner, and while it is said that she would leave the room whenever her son Herbert came into it,[1] she was consistently kind and encouraging to her other children, especially Graham, whose achievements and adventures she followed closely.[2] Having been incapacitated by a fall, she lost interest in life. After a period of decline, she spent about two weeks in a coma and died peacefully on 22 September 1959 at the age of eighty-seven.[3]

In her last years, Graham and Raymond provided her with a pension, while she, for her part, helped out her younger sister Nora, or Nono, who also lived in Crowborough. Learning of his mother's death, Graham immediately wrote to Nono from Paris: 'Perhaps as a Catholic I am more "cold-blooded" because I believe there is a future & that she is probably happier at this moment than any of us ... What I want to say now is hard to phrase. I want to be of any help I can & I want you to feel that anything I was able to do for Mumma at the end, I would like to transfer to you. Please between us of the School House days, between the favourite aunt & the most difficult nephew, don't let's have any shyness ... I know how much she depended on you & worried about you, so you *must* let me help.'[4] Marion had consistently loved and encouraged Graham as he went about his utterly unconventional life. She did reproach him for leaving Vivien, but there had been no lasting rift even then between mother and son. Grief for her was likely a factor in his mental state in the following months.

There were yet more changes in his family life. Caroline would soon marry a man named Jean Bourget and leave the ranch for Montreal and there start a family. Francis, having completed his degree in physics at Christ Church, Oxford, began National Service in October 1957 and was given a position in the Atomic Weapons Research Establishment at Aldermaston. He visited Russia whenever he could, including a journey there with his father in 1957 and other longer stays to strengthen his grasp on the language. He became a producer on the BBC television series *Tomorrow's World*, where he put together programmes on contemporary science, among them one in which he thoughtfully debunked a purported sighting of a UFO.

The BBC was, of course, Hugh Greene's territory. Having been appointed Director of News and Current Affairs, he was being groomed by Sir Ian Jacob to succeed him as Director-General. Perhaps resenting his youngest brother's success, Herbert Greene bombarded Jacob with letters and telegrams protesting at Hugh's programming decisions. Trying to put a stop to this nonsense, Graham threatened to cut off the allowance he was paying him,[5] but Herbert was not to be bullied. He went on to lead a public protest against the cancellation of the *Nine O'Clock News*, which featured the chiming of Big Ben,[6] claiming that his dispute was not with Hugh but with the corporation. Strange as all this is, Herbert had very pleasant qualities, which were discovered by Caroline when she went to visit this uncle about whom she knew nothing, and the two got on surprisingly well.[7] Afflicted with Parkinson's disease, Herbert died in 1969, and Graham remarked that he had had little luck in life except to have found a loving wife.[8]

Herbert's shenanigans caused no real harm to Hugh, who was indeed appointed Director-General of the BBC in the summer of 1959. He remained Graham's closest male friend, and they sometimes went on long rambles, looking for pubs and bookshops in the countryside.[9] Avid book collectors, they assembled an anthology of vintage tales of espionage, *The Spy's Bedside Book*, with numerous pieces by John Buchan and William Le Queux, and even an odd effusion from Herbert on his involvement with the Japanese intelligence services in the 1930s. Neither Graham nor Hugh was particularly demonstrative, but Hugh's fourth wife, Sarah Greene, suggests that they were both shy, and so understood each other.[10]

Having returned from postings in Turkey and Paris, Elisabeth and

Rodney Dennys became increasingly important to Graham from about 1957, and he grew fond of their children Amanda, Louise, and Nick. Indeed, Nick recalled him as an affectionate and playful uncle.[11] In 1961, Graham set up a financial covenant to assist with their education.

Apart from the family bond, he could speak freely with Elisabeth and Rodney about intelligence. Having been a senior figure in SIS, Rodney retired from the service in 1958, and began to look for a new career. Graham tried to set him up as a literary agent, but that did not work out. Ultimately, he took on a surprising and very colourful line of work. A learned man with a sense of protocol, he joined the College of Arms, where he was involved in the organisation of Winston Churchill's state funeral and the Investiture of the Prince of Wales. He was appointed Rouge Croix Pursuivant, then Somerset Herald, and when he retired he became Arundel Herald Extraordinary and wrote two engaging books about heraldry. The separate strands of Rodney's working life came together in 1968 when he advised the makers of the film *On Her Majesty's Secret Service*, in which James Bond poses as a herald.[12]

One figure who disappeared early from the story was Graham's eldest sister Molly, who had once tracked him down on Berkhamsted Common. With the ranks of young men so thinned by the Great War, she had decided to marry Lionel Walker, a sedentary man more than twenty years her senior, and Charles Greene had settled some money on her. Seldom travelling, the couple lived in semi-retirement in a rural cottage without electricity. When their son John, of whom Graham was particularly fond, built himself a house many years later he refused to have a chimney or a hearth in it as he never again wanted to see solid fuel. At 6' 1", Molly had something of her mother's impressive bearing. At her funeral in 1963 her eleven-year-old grandson, Peter Walker, could not spot his father John, who was a mere six feet tall, among his towering aunts and uncles.[13]

An important change was coming to Graham's business affairs. He had been a client of the literary agency Pearn Pollinger and Higham since it was formed in 1935. Indeed, he had been a client of David Higham since 1928. When Higham went into service during the war, Laurence Pollinger, who specialized in film rights, took over Greene's business. The partnership split up in 1958 and Greene followed Pollinger rather than Higham, who was rather taken aback as he saw

Greene as a friend – the two had even gone birdwatching together. Higham gathered that Greene chose Pollinger because he was the underdog in the split; Greene told him that he would return as a client once Pollinger retired or died.[14]

In 1959, Greene hired a new secretary, Josephine Reid, who would handle his correspondence and type most of his manuscripts until 1975, continuing such work on an occasional basis until 1991. In addition to her secretarial skills, she had a Foreign Office background and understood how to work on a confidential basis. She did not pry into his business and she revealed nothing. Long after Greene's death, she continued to refuse requests for interviews and rebuffed all enquiries.

Graham Greene turned fifty-five on 2 October 1959 and was feeling his age. The affair that had begun with Yvonne Cloetta was a slow burn: although sexually driven at other times, he now needed coaxing and encouragement, a grim experience that led somewhat later to the writing of 'Cheap in August', a short story about an older man's sexual failures. In a book of interviews with Cloetta, Marie-Françoise Allain asked how it was that in 1959 Graham began a satisfying new relationship but was also in perhaps the deepest depression of his life. Cloetta accepted the paradox but did not herself understand it.

When she met him, Greene had almost finished believing in either religion or love, and he was living with his burnt-out case, the architect Querry, whose emotional emptiness and despair were based on his own feelings but were then concentrated and magnified. Long afterwards he remarked, 'When you live for two years with a character one is apt to catch his depression.'[15] He and his character passed the illness back and forth like a virus in a boarding school. Cloetta recalled that one evening he stayed up working on the novel and found it so distressing that he vomited.[16] And perhaps the time he spent with Querry felt like two years, but, driving himself with Dexedrine, he had a draft of the novel finished by 24 March 1960, a little over a year after his visit to the leproseries.[17]

If his mood disorder predisposed him to extremes and the amphetamine was encouraging anxiety and restlessness, there was still the longstanding issue of Catherine Walston to trigger his depressions. From time to time Graham and Catherine still took holidays together – they went to the Caribbean in the autumn of 1959 and again in 1960, but by 1961 she was complaining in her letters that he found her boring, was uncommunicative, and wanted to 'dislodge' her from his heart.[18]

Although Yvonne remained married to Jacques, she urged Graham to make a firm break with Catherine. He did so very slowly, and there were painful moments, such as when Yvonne discovered a picture of Catherine beside his bed in Albany. Yvonne's tastes and sensibilities were different from Catherine's, and Graham tended to discover this the hard way. In the late summer of 1959, he took her and a friend to a brothel in Paris's louche Rue de Douai and arranged the sort of erotic entertainment that Catherine had shared with him. Yvonne got up and left.[19] In the contest with his older mistress, however, time was on Yvonne's side. Catherine was now lamed by arthritis, and in the coming years endured two not very successful operations to repair a broken hip. She took heavy medication for pain, and tended to drink too much. The sheer vitality that had once characterized her was draining away.

Immediately after his mother's death, Greene travelled to New York for business, and Irene Selznick threw a small, but doubtless distracting, party for his birthday, attended by Claudette Colbert, Lauren Bacall, Ingrid Bergman, Margaret Leighton, and Janet Gaynor. He went then to Alberta to see Caroline, and along the way was tempted to lay aside the leprosy novel in favour of a sadly comic play to be called 'May We Borrow Your Husband?', which he later wrote as a short story.

He spent November in Jamaica with Catherine, and after a brief return to London in December headed to the Pacific with Michael Meyer, experiencing Christmas Eves on either side of the International Date Line, one in Fiji and the other in Samoa. They stayed for a month in Tahiti, where he grew increasingly irritable over things as trivial as games of Scrabble. At the same time, he was working at the hated novel, writing twenty thousand words in twenty-five days, bringing the total manuscript close to fifty thousand words by the time they left.

On the way back, he discovered a part of the United States that he loved – San Francisco – and went to a party where 'the beatnik poet who is half negro, half Jew & half Catholic & very very drunk paid me his highest compliment by saying that I was the only true beat in English literature!'[20] This must have been Bob Kaufman, who came from New Orleans and whose father was a German Jew and mother a black Catholic. He would now be called a performance poet, reciting his compositions wherever he was welcomed. When John F. Kennedy was shot, he took a vow of silence which he observed until the end of the Vietnam War.[21]

Driving a Chevy half-ton about 1300 miles from Alberta, Caroline picked up her father and Michael Meyer in San Francisco at the beginning of February, with a plan to go back to the ranch on a route through Nevada and Utah. They ground their way through snow to Reno, where Graham won enough money at the slot machines to pay for their night's lodging,[22] but that was not their best stroke of luck. They got under way again, and the truck's driveshaft broke within sight of the only garage for fifty miles in the Great Salt Lake Desert – it had then to be towed to another service station further down the road to be fixed.[23] Waiting in a hotel in 'claustrophobic' Salt Lake City, Greene could find nothing better to listen to on the radio there in the Mormon heartlands than a lecture on the health benefits of chewing gum. He had left all his luggage in the truck, but clung 'like grim death' to a briefcase containing his manuscript.[24]

52

DEATH AND TAXES

G uy Burgess was knocking at his door. Greene was in Moscow: he had flown there for a short visit on 1 April 1960 as the guest of British European Airways on the inaugural flight of its new Comet service. The ambassador to the Soviet Union, Sir Patrick Reilly, once chairman of the Joint Intelligence Committee, was on that plane along with a contingent of the Scots Guards who piped the passengers on and off and later went skirling in Red Square.[1]

This junket gave Greene the chance to see a Russian play of *The Quiet American* – 'very bad', he reported to his daughter. He politely endured the speeches made from the stage and gave one himself when called upon. This play and his books were earning him some roubles he could not take home, so he opened a bank account, which struck him as a very capitalist thing to do. He took long walks with Tanya Lanina, who worked for the Writers' Union and was the main translator of his books. He went to the Bolshoi Ballet and to the circus, and had dinner with a Russian family which left him feeling 'quite accepted', but after an embassy party on his last evening in Moscow he began to feel very ill.[2]

Guy Burgess worked, in his desultory way, for the state-run Foreign Languages Publishing House, so caught wind of his visit to Moscow. He called Greene and asked to see him. Despite having an early flight, the novelist was curious, so said yes, but, hoping to keep the meeting short, told him that he had been up for sixty-five of the last seventy-two hours.

It may be that Greene was actually meeting Burgess at the behest of MI6, if only to keep tabs on the defector and perhaps profit by an indiscretion. However, there is no hint of such an assignment in his descriptions of the meeting, although he would certainly have reported even an unexpected contact with Burgess to the service. He had met him just once before, during the war, with David Footman, a novelist and an MI6 officer specializing in Eastern Europe.[3] Greene did not like him – certainly not as he liked Kim Philby. At the time of their defection in May 1951, Guy Burgess and Donald Maclean had been working in Washington, and Philby tipped them off that they were about to be questioned, so they had fled.

In Moscow, Burgess's material needs were taken care of, but his lifestyle was cramped and isolating, since Communist Party discipline was surprisingly prim and Burgess's homosexuality was disapproved of. He was also desperate for conversation, so stayed late with Greene, whose sickness was taking hold so that he really did feel like 'grim death'. Burgess rehearsed his old cover story that in 1951 it had been his intention to accompany Maclean only as far as Paris, and then to go to Ischia to stay with W. H. Auden, but became caught up in the arrangements that had been made for them so went on to Prague and finally to Moscow. He was portraying himself as an accidental defector. He asked Greene to thank Harold Nicolson for a letter he had sent, to carry a message to his mother, and to give Moura Budberg, the woman who had once advised Greene on what to see in Tallinn and who was now under scrutiny by MI5, a consolatory bottle of gin. Burgess was drinking himself to death in Moscow – and succeeded in doing so two years later. If he had a serious purpose in talking to Greene, it was likely to send a signal to MI6 that he wanted to come home.[4]

Greene flew back to London on the morning of 5 April 1960, and was promptly laid on a stretcher and taken to hospital in an ambulance. He had pneumonia. In his usual way of concealing illnesses, it was two weeks before he informed his daughter in Canada, but not Francis or Vivien in Britain, saying that the matter was 'TOP SECRET'. His cough persisted and his doctors became concerned that he was actually suffering from lung cancer. He did not get the all-clear until July. He afterwards incorporated his experience of bronchoscopy into 'Under the Garden', a long, dream-like short story which he particularly favoured. The worry of lung cancer hung over him, especially in the following year when his psychiatrist and friend Eric Strauss underwent surgery for the disease and died.

Greene understood from his doctors that England's climate was bad

for his lungs. He wanted to be near Yvonne, and now his health provided him with a second reason to spend much of his time in France.
That spring he acquired a small flat at 130 Boulevard Malesherbes
in Paris's seventeenth arrondissement, a neighbourhood noted for its
embassies, museums, and academic institutions, and for its association
with writers, musicians, and artists, such as Gabriel Fauré and Marcel
Proust.[5] The flat's best feature was a room with two fireplaces and a
window looking out onto large chestnut trees. Marie Biche arranged for
renovations, and Greene began using it late in 1960. He kept it secret
for a time as he did not want to lend it to friends or family as he did
the house in Anacapri.[6] There was a business problem about the transaction, as he could not use the holding company that owned Caroline's
ranch for this purpose, but he told Catherine he would work around
the difficulty: 'Luckily I have got a lot of bankers & crooks among my
friends.'[7]

These words were more true than he realised, and what followed over
the next few years would provide him with a third reason to become a
permanent resident in France – as a tax exile.[8] It all began straightfor-
wardly. Harbottle & Lewis were, and remain, a reputable law firm in
London, specializing in entertainment and media. In good faith, this
firm strongly recommended the services of the solicitor and financial
adviser Thomas Roe to John Sutro, who in turn recommended him to
Graham Greene.[9] Roe would also add Noël Coward, Charlie Chaplin,
Robert Mitchum, and William Holden to his list of clients. He had various points in his favour: an upbeat manner, an air of competence, an
excellent war record, and a CBE. He worked mainly in Lausanne, where
his company Co-Productions Roturman helped British individuals and
firms – most wanting to avoid British taxes – to establish themselves.
Roe solved Greene's problem about the purchase of the Paris flat by
setting up a new holding company in Switzerland, to be called Verdant,
on which he had signing powers. By the summer of 1960, Roe had more
or less taken over Greene's finances and was making investments.

His years as a publisher had made Greene a far better businessman
than many other writers, but by 1960 he was acting out of despair – a
sometimes costly state of mind. He believed that A Burnt-Out Case
might be his last novel, and he had to find a new way to make a living.
Although he had made a great deal of money over the years, he had

saved relatively little, and his main asset was his copyrights. He saw some prospects in his arrangement with Max Reinhardt, but they were not sufficient to take care of himself, his family, and the various people who depended on him – his kindness being a matter for the debit column. A plan to have the Bodley Head publish a collected edition of his novels required the cooperation of Heinemann, which was highly resistant to the idea of losing its most famous author.

Roe moved quickly to have Greene's royalties, other than those from the United Kingdom and Commonwealth, paid into Verdant. A more important plan was to grant paperback rights in ten of Greene's novels to Penguin for an advance of £33,750, to be paid to Roe's firm in Lausanne, which would agree to pay Greene an annuity of between £1500 and £2000 – a solid pension at a time when the average annual salary in Britain was about £600 – no matter what happened, he would have enough to live on.[10] Roe would then transfer these rights and obligations to Verdant, putting Greene back in control. As the situation unfolded, Verdant took over the copyrights of all Greene's books, apart from *The Quiet American*, which he had given to Francis.[11] His London company, Graham Greene Productions, now about a decade old, was mainly concerned with film and stage rights, and any profits went not to him but chiefly to Vivien and Francis. Another company, called Pasture, was set up in Liechtenstein, and Greene signed service agreements with both Verdant and Pasture – he was essentially employed as a writer by these two companies, the more important being Verdant.

The goal was to minimize taxes, and avoid the surtax on dividends altogether. It is difficult now to credit how high British income tax was in the 1960s. The Beatles found out when they began to make money; George Harrison wrote, 'Let me tell you how it will be, there's one for you nineteen for me – 'cause I'm the taxman'.[12] He was describing a situation where between income tax and surtax, he was paying 95 per cent on investment income. In the 1967–8 tax year, there was actually a special charge on investment income over £8000 of 45 per cent plus income tax at 41.25 per cent and surtax at 50 per cent – for a total of 136.25 per cent.[13] Successive governments, still dealing with the financial consequences of the war, were trying to support the NHS and the welfare state, so needed a great deal of revenue. Meanwhile, those who paid the top rates felt they were being pillaged, and many decided to live abroad. In Greene's case, the simple course of investing the Penguin advance, say, on the London stock exchange and receiving dividends was highly unattractive owing to the surtax.

On 31 October 1961, Greene lamented to Catherine that the paper-back plan could not work as tax would be deducted at source.[14] A long struggle then began with the Inland Revenue, as Greene hoped to be granted a particular form of exemption, allowing his advance to be paid to Roturman and then to Verdant without tax. Laurence Pollinger, who was sceptical of the plan, reserved just over £11,000 in escrow in case the exemption was not granted.[15] Discussions went on literally for years. At first Roe wanted all the money sent to Switzerland, without worrying a great deal about the exemption – Pollinger refused. Later Greene himself would make periodic enquiries about the sum in escrow. No exemption was granted, and Greene's London accountants decided that it belonged to the Inland Revenue even if they were slow to collect it. He had to be resigned to that. He was able to obtain exemptions only for royalties earned after 1 January 1966[16] – that is, once he had become a resident of France.

Behind this rather dry narrative of tax rates and holding companies lies a story about pigs, sausages, and counterfeit banknotes.[17] When Greene met him, Roe had just built a villa overlooking Lake Geneva at a cost of £130,000. To make ends meet, he took £27,000 belonging to his clients, among them Graham Greene, and made himself a temporary loan. In time his debts would amount to £480,000. A boundlessly opti-mistic man, Roe saw a path to salvation in his dealings with a sinister figure named Denis Loraine, who in 1959 had established the Royal Victoria Sausage Company – so named on the basis of a fictitious claim that King Edward VII had once enjoyed its products. In fact, Loraine had gone into the sausage business as a way of settling the very large bill his wife had run up with a butcher in Hove, East Sussex – rather than pay it, he became the man's partner.

Roe and Loraine soon founded another company, Cadco Dev-elopments, to build a huge piggery in Glenrothes, one of the 'new towns' in Fife, and were promising to create about two thousand jobs. They received substantial funding from the Royal Bank of Scotland and from various government agencies, of which £83,000 simply disappeared from the country, much of it in the form of travellers' cheques. More money was squandered on a Jaguar and an Aston Martin, trips abroad, and perks for board members. One of the directors resigned and reported irregularities to the Board of Trade. George Sanders, a once-famous actor who won an Oscar for his part in *All About Eve*, was a client of Tom Roe; he served as a director of Cadco, perhaps without knowledge of the frauds, but was nonetheless disgraced. The piggery project collapsed in November 1964, with total liabilities of £828,000 and assets of £195,000. The MP for West Fife, Willie Hamilton, demanded an investigation in the House of Commons: 'At the best, this has been a story of unexampled negligence and incompetence; at the worst, a tale of fraud and corruption on a gigantic scale.'[18]

Roe had put most of Greene's Penguin advance, apart from the sum in escrow, into Cadco – he may have invested other money belonging to Greene in the same project – and it was gone. Greene estimated that he had lost half his savings. Roe had also invested funds from his other clients, who were, likewise, fleeced. He became desperate and tried to raise money by selling bogus stocks obtained from the mafia; he later admitted with some understatement that these stocks were 'doubtful'.

Roe met with mobsters in Los Angeles and agreed to buy counterfeit $100 bills for $25 each. Roe was warned that if he did not keep up his end of the bargain he would be killed. A courier delivered the bills with a total face value of $375,000 to Switzerland in July 1965, and Roe passed some of them at a bank, only to be detected. Police found the rest of the notes in his car and at his office. Meanwhile, Loraine and others were arrested in the United States. A Swiss court convicted Roe of fraud, misappropriation of £183,000 belonging to his clients, and possessing counterfeit notes, sentencing him to six years in prison and other penalties.

At Charlie Chaplin's recommendation, Greene retained as his Swiss lawyer the scrupulous and learned Jean-Felix Paschoud, who walked into the offices of Roturman and seized all the files pertaining to Graham Greene and Verdant. He also terminated Greene's original 1960 agreement with Roturman.[19] However, Greene made nothing in the 1960s from the Penguin deal in which he had placed so much hope – as late as 1971 the paperbacks had still not sold out the advance, so there were not even any royalties.[20]

After his release, Tom Roe, stripped of his CBE, returned to a version of his old business. He made the rounds of literary agents with a scheme to help authors avoid British taxes by buying their rights and employing them through companies set up, apparently, in Liechtenstein. He visited Bruce Hunter, who would later become Graham Greene's agent, and proposed all this as highly beneficial for authors, indeed foolproof. Sceptical, Hunter asked how people could trust him given his history, but Roe swept aside the objection.[21] This was in character. He was, after all, an optimistic man.

In a curious way, the swindler Tom Roe did literature a service. Graham Greene wanted to stop writing in 1960. By depriving him of his pension, he created a financial incentive for Greene to keep his Parker 51 in hand. Samuel Johnson said in a memorable half-truth that 'No man but a blockhead ever wrote, except for money.' Money mattered. It was part of Greene's motivation to write, though his aesthetic, religious, and political concerns mattered more. By the time the various frauds were exposed, his creative energies had revived and he had begun a new novel, *The Comedians*, and over the next twenty years he would write six more.

53

THE END OF A LONG ROPE

'I think it is his best book at least since "The Power and the Glory", and perhaps the best book he has ever written', wrote Philip Toynbee of *A Burnt-Out Case*.[1] So went the reviews. Of course, Greene knew this book would also cause trouble, but some of it surprised him. He had had Michel Lechat vet it for technical errors concerning leprosy, but one of the leading specialists in the disease, Robert Cochrane, assailed him for using the terms 'leprosy' and 'lepers', which had been abandoned by a round-table agreement of leprologists long before. Greene responded, cogently, that if these terms were so offensive why did Cochrane persist in calling himself a 'leprologist'?

Cochrane's outburst does raise the question of how Greene deals with leprosy in the novel. Certainly, the book has a documentary aspect, providing a wealth of practical detail about the disease, the patients, and the treatment. A bestseller, *A Burnt-Out Case* did as much as any book possibly could to shed light on the facts of a misunderstood illness. At the heart of the book is the idea that since leprosy, now curable, persists in its psychological effects, the conditions of those with the disease and someone like Querry actually converge: both come to loathe themselves. There is merit in the observation, but it requires an obvious caveat. With his background of privilege, his money, his race, and his physical health, Querry's state is not equivalent to that of people with the disease.

Greene built a recognition of this fact into the structure of the novel. At the end, one of the priests says, 'What I mean is that it's a little like one of those Palais Royal farces that one has read ...'[2] In one of the jokes that signal his cure, Querry remarks on the absurdity of the supposed triangle involving Rycker and his wife, 'The innocent adulterer.

Not a bad title for a comedy.'[3] Greene had written three successful plays, and was shaping his novel in dramatic terms. Querry, his depression, recovery, and absurd death are only part of a larger story – it is a 'farce' contained within the tragedy of infection and mutilation. The experiences of the white man are at best a play within a play – which, like 'The Murder of Gonzago' in *Hamlet*, touches the conscience on just a particular point. His next novel, *The Comedians*, would rely even more heavily on this structural device. That Querry and his problems are not all that important is seen when he is telling the doctor about his loss of vocation while a little boy awaits treatment: 'The boy's four toes wriggled impatiently on the cement floor, waiting for the meaningless conversation between the white men to reach a conclusion'[4] – meaningless indeed. In the last paragraph of the novel, once Querry is dead, the narrative focuses again on a child – one whom the doctor, now very angry, hopes to cure without mutilations.

Evelyn Waugh sensed something 'melodramatic' in the ending but missed its significance – he dismissed it as merely absurd.[5] Waugh thought that in this novel, as in the short story 'A Visit to Morin', which Greene distributed in a special edition to friends at Christmas 1960, the author was publicly abandoning the faith. Moreover, he felt himself criticized in the character of Rycker, since he had given lectures in the United States on Greene as a Catholic writer. The *Daily Mail* asked him to review the book and he refused. Instead, he sent Greene a letter praising some aspects of the book, then apologizing for his decision not to review and for any behaviour of his that resembled Rycker's.[6]

Greene was pained by this letter and wrote a lengthy response, entirely rejecting the idea that Waugh had ever behaved like Rycker. Whether Querry was a self-portrait was a more complicated question: 'With a writer of your genius and insight I certainly would not attempt to hide behind the time old gag that an author can never be identified with his characters. Of course in some of Querry's reactions there are reactions of mine, just as in some of Fowler's reactions in *The Quiet American* there were reactions of mine. I suppose the points where an author is in agreement with his character lend what force or warmth there is to the expression. At the same time I think one can say that the parallel must not be drawn all down the line and not necessarily to the conclusion of the line. Fowler, I hope, was a more jealous man than I am, and Querry, I fear, was a better man than I am. I wanted to give expression to various states or moods of belief and unbelief. The doctor, whom I like best as a realized character, represents a settled and easy atheism; the Father Superior a settled and easy belief (I use "easy" as a term of praise and not as a term of reproach); Father Thomas an unsettled form of belief and Querry an unsettled form of disbelief. One could probably dig a little of the author also out of the doctor and Father Thomas!'[7]

Waugh was having none of this, and in his next letter dismissed the notion of 'a settled and easy atheism' as an impossibility. He took the view that an atheist rejects the real purpose of his life – union with God – and so can never be settled. Waugh's position was out of touch with Catholic theology of the time, which made much of what the Jesuit Karl Rahner called the 'anonymous Christian', one who might live a graced life without believing church doctrine. In any event, Waugh lamented Greene's departure from faith and spoke of him as a 'lost leader'.[8] Greene responded: 'I suggest that if you read the book again you will find in the dialogue between the doctor and Querry at the end the suggestion that Querry's lack of faith was a very superficial one – far more superficial than the doctor's atheism. If people are so impetuous as to regard this book as a recantation of faith, I cannot help it. Perhaps they will be surprised to see me at Mass.'[9]

Greene seems to have been troubled by this correspondence, and he wrote soon after to Catherine Walston about the novel and the state of his beliefs: 'I'll probably never succeed in getting any *further* from the Church. It's like, when one was younger, taking a long walk in the country & at a certain tree or a certain gate or the top of one more hill one stopped & thought "Now I must start returning home." One probably went on another mile to another hill or another tree, but all the same . . . '[10]

About a year later, Greene was very pleased with a letter from a Benedictine monk, Ralph Wright, who detected hope in the last pages of the novel. Greene wrote to him: 'You have disinterred my intention – you notice that Querry even makes a joke at the last moment which is also a sign of returning health. However the first hundred and seventy four pages were not intended in any way as a debunking. One must remember that technically the book is written through

the eyes of Querry and it is Querry's irritation with the facile Father
Thomas and the bogus Rycker. These two are intended as a contrast
to the really selfless and practical work of the fathers in the mission.
I think you would find that if these two characters had been left out
the book would suddenly have become extraordinarily sentimental. On
the one side Querry rediscovering a bit of life, on the other a group of
noble priests. To make even their nobility plausible one has to put in
the shadows. After all even the everyday life of a Catholic is haunted
by the *corruptio optimi*.' Originally a monk of Ampleforth Abbey in
North Yorkshire, and now at St Louis Abbey in Missouri, Father Ralph
Wright is a gifted but little-known poet. Greene was nearly incapable
of praising books he did not admire, and he praised the poetry of
Ralph Wright.[11]

After the publication of A *Burnt-Out Case*, Greene decided to put
together a volume called *In Search of a Character: Two African Journals*,
combining the notes he kept while sailing in convoy to Freetown at the
end of 1941 with the longer record of his stay in the leproseries. Before
publication he again sent proofs to Michel Lechat to check for technical errors. Lechat was dismayed by what he read. Greene was about
to publish his unfiltered impressions of the archbishop, various priests,
aspiring authors, local officials, and others who would be crushed by
his comments and who would hold it against him that he had brought
this man into their midst. Lechat wrote at length to Greene, pointing
out all the harmful passages, and let him know that if the book was
published as it stood their friendship was over. At once, Greene wrote
to him with apologies and assurances that changes would be made – he
made more besides. In the end, the short book that was published in
October 1961 contains a vastly more genial account of his time in the
Congo than is recorded in the original journal.

In Search of a Character was the first of Greene's books published
by Max Reinhardt at the Bodley Head. He decided to leave William
Heinemann in June 1961.[12] The background to this is very complicated
and can only be summarized here.[13] After thirty-two years with the
firm, Greene had seen a new generation of directors and editors take the
place of those he had once worked with. Short of capital, Heinemann
was taken over in April 1961 by the conglomerate Thomas Tilling
Ltd, headed by Lionel Fraser, formerly chairman of Heinemann. There

followed in May a tentative agreement for a merger with the Bodley Head, which would see Greene and Reinhardt on the board of the new entity. But then it all fell apart. The directors of Heinemann disliked the deal when they saw it, and they disliked the idea of Graham Greene being a member of the board. Under the new arrangements, Greene's close friend A. S. Frere would serve in the symbolic position of president, without real contact with authors, and so he left altogether. A little later, Frere joined the Bodley Head as an adviser. The bestselling authors Georgette Heyer and Eric Ambler also moved to the Bodley Head. Heinemann retained the rights to Greene's earlier books, and only after a protracted, sometimes contentious, negotiation did the two firms collaborate on a collection edition, of which the first volume, *Brighton Rock*, finally appeared in 1970. One of the benefits to Greene of moving to the Bodley Head was that Reinhardt was willing to ease his tax burden by spreading out payments to him over time so that he received something like a salary, and generally relieved him of the detailed management of his financial affairs.[14]

In the early 1960s, Greene probably believed that he had more of a future as a publisher than as a novelist. *A Burnt-Out Case* had shaken his confidence, and he did not think he could produce another work on that scale. In late 1961, he turned his hand to short stories, even though some of them hardly qualified as 'short', such as 'Under the Garden', which drew on childhood visits to Harston and on his recent brush with cancer. Completed by the beginning of January 1962, it stretched to about twenty-two thousand words, which can be compared to thirty-one thousand for *Loser Takes All*, published as a novel or novella.[15]

He followed it with 'May We Borrow Your Husband?', a skilful work which has not aged well. Readers often feel its portrayal of two gay men as predators is harsh, although this effect is softened towards the end when the older of the two, Stephen, is revealed as a tragic figure. The plot turns on the men borrowing a honeymooning husband from his new wife; she takes comfort and counsel of a sort from an older man who is writing a book, as Greene himself once did, on the Earl of Rochester and who falls in love with her. Initially, Greene conceived of it as a play, then dwelt on the plot for some time before deciding it should be 'a very short novel'.[16] Once he started it in January 1962, he found that it became 'sadder and sadder';[17] it seems that he was finding sexual misunderstanding and deception not nearly as amusing as he had supposed.

'May We Borrow Your Husband?' belongs to a key moment in his life. He was in a hotel in Antibes, suffering from flu and reading John Henry Newman's letters – almost certainly the just-published volume which covers the buoyant years right after the future cardinal's conversion in 1845.[18] Greene was moved by what he read and wrote to Catherine that he was 'at the end of the long rope which has been allowed me. There seems to be little left except a blind leap back into faith or what I haven't the courage to do.' Reading Newman put the question into relief: faith or suicide. He pondered a break with Yvonne in order to complete his return to an orderly Catholic life,[19] but he never went that far. Still, he would later be able to say that it was only faith that kept him from committing suicide.[20] It is another paradox, so characteristic of Graham Greene, that at the very moment he was writing perhaps his most cynical story he was deciding that his life probably had a meaning.

54

PLASTIQUES

Writing short stories may have restored some of Greene's confidence, but there was nothing like a couple of bombs to get him thinking of a novel. The French fought a very ugly war against the Algerian National Liberation Front (FLN) from 1954 until the signing of the Evian Accords on 19 March 1962. In the course of that war twenty-five thousand French were killed and three hundred thousand Muslims.[1] The war caused the collapse of the Fourth Republic in 1958, bringing Charles de Gaulle out of retirement to serve briefly as prime minister, then as president of the Fifth Republic. His willingness to compromise with the FLN outraged the French in Algeria, the so-called *pieds-noirs*, and led to the formation of the paramilitary Organisation armée secrète (OAS) intent on keeping Algeria French, and then to a failed putsch in April 1961, led by four generals, among them Raoul Salan, whom Greene had known and liked in Indochina. France's most decorated soldier, Salan was sentenced to face a firing squad but was eventually pardoned.

Like everyone in France, Greene followed the events in Algeria. In 1957, he made tentative plans to visit Colonel Jean Leroy, who was serving there, but had to cancel as the dates conflicted with his visit to China.[2] In the summer of 1960, he addressed a long open letter in *Le Monde* to André Malraux, then Minister of Cultural Affairs, to protest against the torture and secret trial of the Algerian journalist Henri Alleg, whose book about his experiences was banned. Alleg had become a cause célèbre among writers and intellectuals. Greene had had some brief contact with Malraux when they had both served as judges for a translation prize set up in honour of Denyse Clairouin. When younger, Greene had admired Malraux's writing, especially

La condition humaine, but when he re-read it with a view to writing a film script he was disappointed, and he later complained of Malraux's rhetoric and 'mythomania' – that is, his habit of exaggerating aspects of his life and career.[3] Greene was perfectly content to make trouble for him.

Meanwhile, Evelyn Waugh had an offbeat response to Greene's protest on behalf of Alleg, which Greene thought utterly revealing of how his friend's mind worked. In an interview with Gaia Servado, Greene remarked: 'He was a rebel. Politically, he couldn't stand anybody, the Tories included. It is a mistake to label him a right-wing writer. He did not reason in political terms. To give you an example, one evening we went to see Ionesco's *The Rhinoceros* with Laurence Olivier. On the following day a letter of mine appeared in *The Times* in which I denounced tortures in Algeria. And then I got a little note from Evelyn: "I see that you send letters to The Times about tortures in Africa. Why don't you mention the torture inflicted upon us by Laurence Olivier last night?"'[4]

In early February 1962, Greene rushed to Paris, since news reports described the city as torn apart. He did not want to miss the eruption of a civil war, and, in the event, he did not even have to leave his flat to witness the violence. Following large demonstrations in opposition to the OAS, *plastique* bombs (plastic explosives) were planted in districts sympathetic to the political left. One went off in a street thirty yards from Greene's flat on Boulevard Malesherbes and blew out one of his windows. He ran to another window to look out and saw a flash and heard a great bang – a second bomb had gone off two doors away. Both were aimed at left-wing publishers. The experience left Greene feeling 'close to history'.[5] He was sorely tempted to write an entertainment, to be called 'The Last Time I Saw the General', but it was not really possible. He would have to spend a week in Algiers doing research[6] and that would be playing Russian roulette with all the chambers loaded.

55

MASKS

Graham Greene may have hated his life, but others thought it a good thing to be him and so borrowed his identity. Beginning in the 1950s, he tracked the activities of what he called 'the other' – actually several men who impersonated him on different occasions, among them an escaped prisoner named John Skinner, and one whose name, Meredith de Varg, might have suited a minor villain in *The Maltese Falcon*. A third impersonator got himself jailed in Assam, so Greene proposed to interview him for *Picture Post*, but this fellow skipped bail, and while he was at large the real Graham Greene could not easily go to India for fear of arrest. There was word of an attempt in Paris to blackmail Greene over sexy photographs – at a time when Greene was not in Paris.[1] As late as the mid-1980s, a man posing as Graham Greene turned up at a reading by Joseph Heller in Newcastle upon Tyne, conducted himself with Greene-like diffidence, and then fielded questions, including one about the difficulty of creating female characters.[2]

Greene thought he was close to catching 'the other' once, at a hotel in Rome. Then, in late 1959, a man thought to be named Peters approached a young woman at the Hôtel Prince des Galles in Paris and offered her a job as secretary to Graham Greene, supposedly his friend and business partner. She worked in a bookshop and knew all about Graham Greene. She could not quite believe her luck so got in touch with Marie Biche, who told her the offer was indeed a fraud but suggested that she keep her appointment with Peters and so find out what was going on. The young woman refused, fearing that she was about to fall into the hands of white slavers.[3] And so, again, 'the other' slipped away.

There were, of course, moments when the real Graham Greene was himself required to assume implausible identities, as for example on 14 June 1962, when he donned a gown of scarlet cloth with a lining of scarlet silk to receive an honorary doctorate from the University of Cambridge. Greene walked in procession with Wilmarth Sheldon 'Lefty' Lewis, an almost insanely dedicated scholar who edited forty-eight volumes, each one Bible-thick, of the letters of Horace Walpole – Greene thought of him as a character out of Damon Runyon.[4] Also receiving a degree was Lord Coggan, then Archbishop of York, later Archbishop of Canterbury, whose presence required Greene to conduct himself ecumenically. The sole representative of any world Greene actually belonged to was Dame Margot Fonteyn, who, by the logic of the ancient university, was honoured for her accomplishment as a dancer with a doctorate of laws.[5]

It is difficult, likewise, to imagine Graham Greene in a top hat, but he wore one – under conditions of strict obedience. Caroline's wedding to Jean Bourget took place at St Mary's Cathedral in Calgary on 29 April 1961. Photographs of the extremely beautiful bride, her new husband, and the wedding party appeared in the local newspaper. Caroline and Vivien had overruled his objections, so Graham wore morning dress.[6] In the photographs, he looks happy though a little confused. The new couple went to Quebec for a reception with the Bourget family, which Graham did not attend, and then on to their honeymoon.

The story, so cheerfully begun, took a sorrowful turn. On 10 May 1962, Caroline gave birth to a boy named Richard Jean Graham Bourget. Delighted to have a grandson, Graham ordered copies of books by Dr Spock for Caroline, since they encouraged new mothers not to worry.[7] However, Richard was found to have a heart defect, and his best hope lay in experimental surgery, to be performed in Oxford. He made it through the operation, but, shortly after, on 19 July 1962, he died. The parents were heartbroken. Afterwards, the doctors told them that owing to Richard's surgery they could improve the procedure and save many other children – this was something of a comfort.[8] Having returned to England at the time of the operation, Graham was also disconsolate. He dictated a letter addressed to Marie Biche, asking her to organize a holiday for Caroline and Jean, and his secretary added at the bottom: 'How sad for Graham – he has taken it very, very much to heart.'[9] Although he did not speak of it often, he was haunted by his grandson's death, and in 1986 wrote that he was still 'tormented' by the tragedy.[10] Caroline had a second child, Andrew, in 1963, then moved from Alberta to Montreal, where her third son, Jonathan, was born in 1964.

The beginning of 1963 marked the unmasking of an old friend. Following the escape of Burgess and Maclean, Kim Philby, who had warned them in Washington that they were about to be questioned, had been brought to a form of trial by MI5 in November 1951. Although he used his stammer to frustrate the rhythm of the questions, those who listened to him were certain of his guilt; however, there was just not enough evidence for a charge. He was forced to resign from the Foreign Office, but MI5 felt he had got off lightly. He later said that he ended his friendship with Graham Greene at this time in order to spare him trouble.[11]

It does not seem that the two had actually had much contact since the war. During the 1950s, they both had connections to Crowborough: Marion Greene still lived there, as did Philby's mentally ill wife Aileen, from whom he was increasingly estranged, along with their children. Greene met her only once and that was during the war. At first, Philby came to Crowborough at weekends, but not after 1956, when he moved to the Middle East. Elisabeth and Rodney Dennys knew Philby well from the war years and from their posting in Istanbul, and they too moved to Crowborough in the 1950s. Their daughter, Amanda Saunders, later Greene's secretary, recalls: 'My father and mother had also thought of Philby as a close friend. Before his cover was blown we had good times together with the Philbys and their children. I was at the same school as one of the children, who was around my age, and I remember Philby as being very charming and charismatic. But, unlike Graham, my father never forgave him – when Philby defected my father was still working closely with him, whereas Graham was by this time much distanced from it all.'[12]

Aileen Philby, who had realized that Philby was a traitor and so become a threat to him and to his controllers,[13] was found dead in her Crowborough house in late 1957. When Graham and Malcolm Muggeridge went to have a look,[14] they found the garden overgrown, the post uncollected, everything like 'a gypsy encampment'. They looked in the windows and saw scattered advertising brochures, unwashed dishes, and empty milk bottles.[15] There was talk that Aileen had died of an overdose – however, the official cause of death was congestive heart failure, myocardial degeneration, respiratory infection, and pulmonary tuberculosis,[16] and there is no basis on which to dispute that. Nonetheless, the circumstances are at least suspicious.

It was the job of MI5 to catch traitors. SIS (MI6) had a different culture, and, according to Philip Knightley, there were within it three different attitudes towards Philby after 1952: a small group thought him guilty; a larger group thought him probably innocent but felt it best to have no more to do with him; and another small but influential group thought that he had been hard done by and should be helped out until an eventual restoration to the service. His most notable friends in SIS at this time were Nicholas Elliott and Tim Milne.[17]

In 1955, J. Edgar Hoover of the FBI leaked information to journalists that Philby had tipped off Maclean and Burgess in 1951, allowing them to escape to Moscow, and so Philby became known to the world as 'the third man' of the spy ring. The Foreign Secretary, Harold Macmillan, disliked the intelligence services and was not much interested in the case. In exchange for Philby's sacking (he technically remained on the books of SIS) and a re-organization of the service, Macmillan made a statement to the House of Commons on 7 November 1955 clearing him of suspicion. Philby followed with a circus-like press conference from his mother's flat, in which, with a smirk and a tongue rolling inside his cheek, he answered many of the questions with 'No comment' and made solemn references to the Official Secrets Act. With the help of Elliott, Philby became a correspondent in Beirut for the *Observer* and *The Economist* in mid-1956. In 1960, Elliott, by then head of station in Beirut, brought him back as an agent, perhaps in order to have him feed traceable information to the Soviets and thus expose him as a traitor.[18]

In any event, evidence against him was mounting, and even Elliott finally agreed that his friend must be guilty. A highly placed KGB figure, Anatoliy Golitsyn, brought clues concerning the identity of Soviet agents when he defected to the West in 1961, and an old friend of Philby's named Flora Solomon revealed his early communist sympathies.[19] Elliott was sent to confront Philby in January 1963, and their meetings have been much written about. At first, Philby remarked, 'I rather thought it would be you' – this troubling comment contained a hint that some other mole still active in the service had warned him to expect an inquisitor. Elliott offered immunity if he told all he knew. Philby confirmed that he had been a Soviet agent and provided a two-page confession, which Elliott took back to London.[20]

Philby then turned to his controllers, who got him onto a freighter bound for Odessa, and by the end of the month he was in Moscow. The sudden disappearance of a long-suspected traitor became international news and, indeed, part of a huge controversy concerning spies. It coincided with the Profumo affair, in which the Secretary of State for War, John Profumo, was forced to resign on 5 June 1963 over his affair with Christine Keeler, who was at the same time involved with a Soviet diplomat. On 1 July 1963, Edward Heath, as Lord Privy Seal, confirmed in the House of Commons that Philby had indeed spied for the Soviet Union and that he was now likely in an Eastern Bloc country.[21]

Greene's response to all this was surprising, but entirely in character. What he had to say about Philby was connected to his views of the Cold War, which was at its most perilous in these months. The Cuban Missile Crisis of October 1962 had brought the world close to nuclear war. Greene wanted to go back to the island, but first he decided to inspect for himself what was going on in Germany, the other place of confrontation between the great powers. With the country divided after the war, millions of people had been able to make their way to the West, especially through Berlin. In 1958, the Russians began to take a harder line against such defections, but they continued. On the night of 13 August 1961, a makeshift wall was erected, with construction continuing for years until it became a system of barriers, with hundreds of watch towers, as well as dog-runs and a 'death-strip' in which the guards had an open field of fire.

Some people were killed trying to get past the Berlin Wall, and others made it, occasionally by strange means. Their efforts were in the news in early 1963. In February, an acrobat crawled across a disused electrical cable over the heads of guards armed with sub-machine guns; eventually his arms tired so he straddled the now swinging cable and slid along before tumbling at last to the bank of a canal – though injured, he survived.[22] Just after Greene's visit in April, a mechanic drove an armoured car into the wall and made a hole, but he could not get through it, so, assisted by people on the other side, he climbed over the top; in the process, he was shot twice by the guards, but he too survived. As he made his escape, the guards' bullets threw up stone chips that wounded a policeman on the West side, so other police briefly returned fire. The guards on the East side then used water cannon for two hours to disperse the crowd on the West side, which included cameramen.[23] Such border incidents – and there were many of them – could have escalated into a new war.

Greene arrived in Hamburg on 7 April 1963 for a visit organized by Rudolf Walter Leonhardt, a journalist with *Die Zeit* who had worked in England for a number of years.[24] The two flew to Berlin the next day, where Leonhardt had tried, unsuccessfully, to arrange a meeting for Greene with the mayor Willy Brandt, soon to be chancellor of West Germany. Leonhardt took Greene for a close-up look at one side of the wall. The novelist was struck by its shabbiness, and he thought there was something mean-spirited in the way it had divided streets and neighbourhoods, and run straight across the only entrance to a church.[25]

Around noon on 10 April 1963, Greene walked, unaccompanied, past the famous white shed at Checkpoint Charlie, and went to a meeting with his East German publishers. The next day, he asked his driver to take him to Dresden by side roads. Returning via Potsdam he visited Arnold Zweig, best remembered for his novel *The Case of Sergeant Grischa*. In East Berlin, he went to look at the wall from the other side and was given a half-hour propaganda lecture by a young army captain. Greene had tried to keep his visit quiet, but encountered cameramen at the wall, so the best he could do was to refuse interviews. Then, after a mere two and a half days, he was back in the West. Whether his trip involved an errand for SIS is not known.

Leonhardt had not been able to accompany Greene east but later asked him to write something not in the manner of a leader writer, but as Fowler would – that is, as a reporter. Having spent such a short time in Germany, and not speaking the language, he did not feel competent to write in that way. Instead, he wrote a 'Letter to a West German Friend' describing for Leonhardt and his readers his own fleeting impressions. In it he compared his thoughts when he first passed Checkpoint Charlie to those of someone converting to Catholicism, accepting all the dogma and being left with one more – say, the infallibility of the pope – beyond which the commitment would be complete. For one who could accept the doctrines of Marxism, and was willing to be converted, this wall, when all you could see was the wall, would serve as the last obstacle.

Problems of belief were the lens through which Greene interpreted new places. It had served him well at times – especially in Mexico, Vietnam, and Kenya. But as a means to interpret the monolith of the Soviet empire, one could carry the metaphor only so far before it became reductive, or even a category error. Nonetheless, he found in his short visit that communists, too, could inhabit the world of Morin; a formerly observant Jew remarked: 'I gave up my faith when I was eighteen and joined the party. Now at fifty one realizes that everything is not known.'[26] Whether Greene intended it or not, this article set up the terms of his response to Philby's defection.

'In the lost boyhood of Judas / Christ was betrayed.' Graham Greene often quoted these lines from the Irish poet 'A.E.' (George William Russell), and they may have guided his first public comment on Philby's defection. In an article called 'A Third Man Entertainment on Security in Room 51',[27] just after Edward Heath's statement to the House of Commons, Greene declared a 'great affection' for the man now universally condemned in the West. He spoke of their working together during the war in an Edwardian house in Ryder Street that their service shared with the OSS, the forerunner of the CIA, and of security arrangements that allowed Greene to play practical jokes on the Americans. When on fire watch in the building, he would pull top-secret documents from a damaged cupboard and stack them on the duty officer's desk as if they had been found in the open, and in the morning some bemused American would be fined for a security breach. Greene asked: 'Which of us then were betraying secrets to our American allies? Which of us in the far past at Oxford and Cambridge had become corrupted by the capitalist way of life?'

In a sense, Greene's defence of Philby began in the dormitory at Berkhamsted School where he had been caught between loyalty to the other boys and loyalty to his father, out of which emerged a personal mythology concerning trust and betrayal. Growing up under the shadow of the Great War, he found nationalism distasteful, and preferred loyalty to individuals over loyalty to states. He absorbed a longstanding Catholic disdain for American forms of culture and government as one of the soulless outcomes of the Enlightenment – an idea which seems odd nowadays, when conservative, often wealthy, American Catholics lead the opposition to a reformist pope, but Greene was influenced by these ideas, especially in the 1930s. However, his anti-Americanism grew most acute after his sojourns in Vietnam. He felt that American meddling in foreign countries was as bad as that of the Russians, so he was not going to be sanctimonious if an old friend happened to have looked east when most Britons were looking west. In addition to all this, Greene liked fights and he liked underdogs. He was going to stand up for Kim Philby.

Greene's view of Philby's defection was more than eccentric. Even during the Khrushchev interlude, the Soviet Union was being run by Stalin's protégés. Francis Greene understood Russia more deeply than his father did and rejected all sympathy with Philby, whom he thought a scoundrel. Quarrels about Philby nearly destroyed Greene's friendship with John Sutro.[28] Rodney Dennys was outraged about Philby, as around 1950 Dennys had had a part in training Albanian partisans to fight as *maquis* against the regime of Enver Hoxha – on the strength of Philby's revelations, almost all these men had been slaughtered. No one in Greene's circle shared his sympathy with Kim Philby, but that did not bother him.

56

THE REAL END OF THE WORLD

'I was quite converted to Castro without any effort on their part,' wrote Graham Greene to Marie Biche in August 1963.[1] A great deal had changed since his last visit to Cuba. In 1960, Castro, sensing a threat from the Americans, had entered into trade agreements and then a political alliance with Moscow. In April 1961, Cuban exiles sponsored by the United States invaded and were repulsed in the Bay of Pigs operation. On 31 August 1962, Senator Kenneth Keating announced that the Russians were putting together missiles in Cuba, and, shortly after, the Soviet Foreign Minister, Andrei Gromyko, warned the Americans of war if they invaded the island. U2 spy-plane photographs soon provided a clear view of the suspected sites, and on 22 October 1962 John F. Kennedy declared a naval blockade and promised retaliation if any missile was fired. On 28 October 1962, Nikita Khrushchev agreed to remove the weapons while Kennedy made a secret concession to withdraw American missiles from Turkey, and so the Cuban Missile Crisis came to an end.

Given that the world was not going be incinerated after all, there was still work for roving journalists. Graham Greene quickly acquired an undeserved reputation for having predicted the crisis in *Our Man in Havana*; those who said so had forgotten that Wormold's missiles were a hoax. Still, Greene had a knowledge of Cuba that few outsiders could rival. Around the beginning of 1963 the *Sunday Telegraph* commissioned him to go to back to Cuba and to Haiti, though, because of other commitments, he could not do it before late July. The new embargo made travel to Cuba difficult, roundabout, and time-consuming. He decided that he should go via Mexico, which he had not visited for twenty-five years. It proved a useful stop, as he later wrote: 'For Mexico is a warning to revolutionaries: it presents a remarkable tableau of a revolution that failed.'[2] Indeed, so completely had the business ethic reasserted itself that within ten minutes of getting off the aeroplane he was pickpocketed. His real point was that a socialist revolution had withered in Mexico without trade sanctions by the Americans.

He reached Mexico in a depression, which, oddly enough, the pickpocket helped rouse him from: 'he acted & I reacted'.[3] Greene attended Mass in an old church, where everyone carried a pink flower and sang beautifully. He was moved by the devotion of the crowd, which included many indigenous people, and then spent a long time in prayer to the recently deceased Pope John XXIII, whom he regarded as a saint, so that Yvonne could be spared an operation – and she was. Greene teasingly wrote to her that he was going to see his 'favourite virgin' – the black Madonna in Guadalupe.[4] His time in Mexico was darkened by news from home that his sister Molly had died but he regarded this as a mercy, since she had been in great pain. He noted in his journal: 'I always seem to be out of England for all our deaths.'[5] He wrote to Jeanne Stonor asking for a Mass to be said for Molly in the chapel at Stonor.[6] While in Mexico, he began work on his next play, Carving a Statue.[7]

Contending with flight cancellations, he arrived in Havana on 25 July 1963, remaining there until 8 August. Shortly after his arrival, he listened to a three-hour speech by Castro, an event that seemed a family outing for those who attended. Greene found Castro's style utterly unlike that of Hitler, as he seemed to be thinking aloud, and when he repeated himself it was to modify or give nuance to something he had said before.

That night, Greene went to the Tropicana with the British chargé and some others. Owing to the holiday, the place was nearly empty, and they found themselves sitting at the next table to the Soviet ambassador and Alexei Adzhubei, a jovial journalist who happened to be Khrushchev's son-in-law and a powerbroker in the Kremlin.[8] Adzhubei asked a woman in the British party to dance, and while he was two-stepping Greene shouted to him, 'How did you get on with Pope John?' The man 'made a long nose' and kept dancing. A little later Greene got a straight answer: 'The Pope told me we were following different paths to the same end.' Greene replied, 'Yes. To death, I suppose.'[9]

As always, Greene liked Havana – it had an air of fun that reminded him of Brighton[10] – but consumer goods were hard to come by owing to the embargo. At the Floridita, daiquiris ran out because there were no more limes – in his journal Greene referred to this as 'The real end of the world'.[11] Most of the louche night clubs had been closed down, and the roulette tables were gone, but then so too was Meyer Lansky.

Greene could see that Ché Guevara was running his economic ministry on Soviet lines, and this was at odds with what the novelist admired in post-revolutionary Cuba – its air of constant debate that reminded him of Ancient Greece. Greene's article 'Return to Cuba' came out in the *Sunday Telegraph*,[12] and it contained no reference to the hundreds of political executions that had taken place there, or to other human rights abuses – by 1963 it was no longer only the former henchmen of Batista who were facing the people's justice. As his father Evelyn had done from time to time, the young Auberon Waugh promptly challenged Greene about this gap in his thinking and pointed out that thousands of people were even then imprisoned in Cuba on purely political grounds. An admirer of the younger Waugh, Greene accepted the criticism, and in later visits to the island made private appeals for the release of dissidents.[13]

Cuba was in the headlines in 1963, but so too was Haiti, a country Greene had known in better days. In 1957, the rural physician François Duvalier had emerged as Haiti's president after the exile of the relatively benign dictator, Paul Magloire.[14] The self-styled 'Papa Doc' spoke vaguely and in rather mystical terms, and the military thought he might be a useful puppet. Following a murderous election campaign, which involved a coup against the brief-serving interim president Daniel Fignolé, Duvalier, who had his own thugs and bomb-makers, won a six-year term on 22 September 1957 – the army obliged by stuffing the ballot boxes. In a country where small differences of skin colour had social meaning, Duvalier, a dark-skinned man, appealed to the black majority, in particular the lower middle class. He won without the usually decisive support of the Americans, who stood behind one of his opponents, the dapper Louis Déjoie, a representative of the lighter-skinned elite.[15]

Both Déjoie and Fignolé went into exile, and another of Duvalier's opponents in the 1957 election, the accomplished Clément Jumelle, an economist who might have modernized Haiti, went to ground. His two brothers were hunted down and shot. Extremely ill, Jumelle sought refuge in the Cuban embassy in early 1959 and died there. Learning that the government was going to seize the body, the ambassador had it dressed in a suit and placed upright in his car; making a show of conversation with the corpse, he drove past Duvalier's men and conveyed it to Jumelle's mother. A large funeral was planned, with a number of Haitian writers and intellectuals in attendance, but the police put a stop to that. Brandishing Tommy guns, they blocked the hearse and made off with the corpse, burying it without ceremony in a distant graveyard.[16] In *The Comedians*, Greene describes just such a scene, with Duvalier's enforcers seizing the coffin of the fallen cabinet minister, Dr Philipot. The death of Jumelle caused the final disillusionment of some senators and other honourable public figures who had once supported Papa Doc.[17]

Although the regular army had helped him gain power, Duvalier did not trust the officer class, so surrounded himself with militias, a presidential guard, and especially the paramilitary group known as the Tontons Macoutes after a figure of fear from Vodou tradition.[18] The Tontons Macoutes, usually wearing dark glasses, swaggered about Haiti, menacing or killing supposed dissidents and collecting on lucrative protection rackets. Duvalier's security was overseen by a particularly efficient torturer and killer named Clément Barbot.

Duvalier's relations with his neighbours could, at different times, resemble a flirtation or a knife fight. Early in his presidency, he particularly wanted American Marines to be in Haiti as a sign of favour that would discourage his rivals, and he proposed that the navy set up a base there. In Bernard Diederich's view, the conduct of the commander of the American Marines in Haiti was disastrous: this man, Colonel Robert Heinl, persuaded Washington to provide training and weaponry to the Haitian military, then he permitted their old weapons to be passed on to paramilitaries.[19]

Obviously, the Americans faced a problem in Haiti. They knew Duvalier's election was a sham and that he was killing off his enemies. They sent a good deal of aid, most of which disappeared into the pockets of the president and his cronies. Jobs on American-supported construction projects went strictly to Duvalierists. Corruption on all building sites stored up horror for the future – in the earthquake of

2010, many sub-standard buildings from the period collapsed, adding to the vast death toll. The Americans demanded control of how the money was being spent, but Papa Doc insisted that this was an interference with Haitian sovereignty. Once Castro took power in Cuba and moved into the Soviet orbit, the Americans feared Haiti going the same way, so Duvalier dabbled in blackmail, meeting with representatives of Czechoslovakia and other Eastern Bloc countries.[20] However, Duvalier and Castro found themselves at odds as opponents of Papa Doc attempted small-scale invasions from Cuba.

In May 1961, Duvalier, already ruling by decree, did yet another extraordinary thing. On the strength of an assembly election in which he was not a candidate, he claimed a second six-year term in office.[21] His first mandate, itself fraudulent, would have expired in May 1963. As that date approached, there was increasing resistance to his rule, something he tried to conceal, but Bernard Diederich's sometimes unsigned articles in major American newspapers ensured that the world knew what was going on. There were at least two mass resignations from the otherwise docile cabinet, one of them believed to be caused by his refusal to admit to the country a group of human rights investigators from the Organization of American States.[22] Papa Doc simply rejected the resignations. Later in 1963, the International Commission of Jurists concluded that Duvalier was indeed running a 'tyranny' and that his operatives were arresting, torturing, and killing large numbers of people without any form of legal process.[23]

Despite purges of the officer corps, the army still posed a threat to Duvalier. With American encouragement, some officers began plotting to remove Papa Doc. Getting wind of this, he summoned all colonels to the presidential palace on 10 April 1963. Some fled or sought asylum. One, Charles Turnier, refused to hide and was arrested, beaten, and then shot repeatedly. His corpse was dumped on a parade ground to send a message to the rest of the army. This was followed by the purging of another seventy-two officers. Duvalier himself helped prepare lists of men to be arrested and sent to Fort Dimanche, his place of torture and execution.[24]

Meanwhile, other threats emerged. In late 1961, Clément Barbot, Duvalier's security chief, had fallen from favour and been sent to Fort Dimanche without explanation. In the same arbitrary manner, Papa

Doc released him and gave him a new car, believing he would devote himself to prayer and penitence. With a claim on the loyalty of many Tontons Macoutes, Barbot had the potential to turn the dictators' guards into assassins. Resenting injuries done to himself and his family, Barbot went into open and highly publicized rebellion. It was a vulnerable moment, as Papa Doc had also to watch the activities of small groups of exiles undergoing military training in the Dominican Republic, where another dictator, the notorious Rafael Trujillo, had been assassinated two years earlier. One exile group dropped leaflets on Port-au-Prince promising to wipe out the Duvalierists by 15 May – Papa Doc's response was to declare a national month of gratitude to himself.[25]

A crisis came on the morning of 26 April 1963. Barbot's men tried to kidnap the young Jean-Claude Duvalier, later to rule as 'Baby Doc', and his sister Simone as they were being brought to school. Their driver and two bodyguards were shot, but the children themselves escaped harm. Bernard Diederich came upon the scene on the way to work and was told to leave or be shot. He hurriedly wrote up the story and then ran to a telegraph office to get it out to the New York Times and the Associated Press before the censors could stop him.

He had been warned repeatedly about how his news stories were damaging the government's reputation, so he expected trouble. The next morning the Tontons Macoutes came to his house, arrested him, and placed him in a prison cell. The killing of a journalist with a New Zealand passport entailed tiresome complications, so after two days' detention he was put on a plane to the Dominican Republic with four cents in his pocket. Still vulnerable to the Tontons Macoutes, his Haitian-born wife Ginette and their baby went into hiding and it took an agonizing three weeks for them to reach safety.[26]

Not knowing that the attack was Barbot's doing, Papa Doc decided to kill all former army officers, beginning with the young Lieutenant François Benoit, a national sporting hero who had competed against American Marines in marksmanship. It was supposed that only he could have taken the shots that brought down the three men. In fact, he had fled from his parents' house to the Dominican embassy two days before and had nothing to do with the attempted kidnapping. Nonetheless, palace guards and Tontons Macoutes conducted a full-scale assault against that house. They shot his parents, a servant, and a visitor. What remained of the house was set on fire, and the lieutenant's infant son was lost in the flames.

The Benoit massacre, which Graham Greene recounted in the first chapter of *The Comedians*, marked the opening of several days of reprisals against army officers and their families. Scores died, and in many cases funerals were impossible.[27] Fifty years later, on 26 April 2013, the Archbishop of Port-au-Prince said a Mass for the disappeared at the Église St Pierre in Pétionville. It was attended by the aged survivors of that bloodbath, and in the midst of them was the tall figure of François Benoit, who had gone on to oppose Duvalier in exile, prospered in business, and entered Haitian politics. He was there with his wife Jacqueline, the mother of the lost child. Bernard Diederich, too, was there – eighty-seven, hunched, white-bearded, and leaning on a carved Maori stick, himself an honoured figure in Haiti. He shook Benoit's hand with great warmth – they were old friends and something close to comrades.

The events of late April 1963 nearly led to war on the island of Hispaniola, as some of Papa Doc's men barged into the Dominican embassy, where twenty-two people had taken asylum. Above all, they wanted to get their hands on Benoit. The new Dominican leader, Juan Bosch, possessed a much stronger army than Duvalier, and he issued an ultimatum. Meanwhile, the Kennedy administration briefly suspended diplomatic relations with Haiti, and sent warships close to shore with Marines at the ready to ensure the safety of American citizens.[28] These threats gradually subsided, as neither the Dominican Republic nor the United States had the stomach for invasion.

For a time, Barbot carried out small attacks and publicly taunted Duvalier. In mid-July he was about to launch an audacious attack on the palace when his hiding place became known. He and his followers were chased into a sugar-cane field which was then set on fire. Those who ran from the flames were gunned down, among them Barbot and his brother. Photographs were taken of the corpses.[29]

Graham Greene arrived in Port-au-Prince on 13 August 1963 and he stayed nine days.[30] By that time the regime had weathered its most recent troubles. There was still, however, the threat of exiles coming across the Dominican border towards the north, and Greene hoped to witness an attack. He told Yvonne Cloetta that he felt fear going to the country.[31] Arriving at night, he found the Grand Hotel Oloffson lit only by oil lamps as a result of frequent power outages. He had known the place as a thriving centre of literary and artistic culture, but now it had just three guests, including an old couple from the United States who sought to help Haiti by teaching its artists the silk-screen process – they probably gave him the idea for the Smiths, a pair of crusading vegetarians in *The Comedians*. Greene went with them to an entertainment at a brothel, which he recreated in the novel as 'Mère Catherine's'. The old man began to sketch the girls, who flocked around him 'like excited schoolchildren', while a couple of Tontons Macoutes 'glared through their dark glasses at this strange spectacle of a fearless happiness and an innocence they couldn't understand'.[32]

There had recently been a change of management at the Oloffson, and with tourism drying up the place was nearly bankrupt. Most of the staff had been let go, though the barman Cesar, the model for Joseph, was still making his famous rum punches.[33] This three-storey hotel, with its wooden turrets and balconies and its air of abandonment, would be the setting of Greene's novel.

Greene received daily visits from the local gossip writer Aubelin Jolicoeur,[34] whom he had first met with Truman Capote in 1954. Often dressed in a white suit and silk ascot, and sporting a gold-topped cane, he wrote on many subjects but typically reported on social life in Port-au-Prince.[35] Greene found him entertaining, but believed him a spy for the Tontons Macoutes – Diederich thought him merely a 'survivor'.[36] He appears in the novel under the thinnest disguise as 'Petit Pierre'. He is thought to have given Greene the title for his book when he described Haitians as story-tellers or 'comedians'.[37]

Greene's efforts to arrange an interview with Papa Doc were stymied by the Foreign Minister, René Chalmers, who reminded him of a frog and whom he would later mimic for Diederich: 'I regret, Monsieur Greene, the President is not receiving the foreign press at this time.' With similar expressions of regret he told him that for his own safety it would not be possible for him to go to the northern part of the country, but then he denied that any rebel incursions were happening there. On his way out of the office, Greene was told by an indiscreet aide that Chalmers was about to prepare a protest to the United Nations concerning just such an incursion.[38]

Chalmers was willing to permit a trip south to the seaport of Les Cayes, where Greene wished to visit some Canadian missionaries. To do it, he needed a *laissez-passer* to get him past the innumerable road-blocks. At a police station that stank like a urinal, he found himself sitting near a photograph of the bullet-riddled corpses of the Barbot brothers and being stared at by an officer in mirrored glasses – it was at that moment his character Captain Concasseur was born.[39] After two days of waiting, Greene was given a permit for two days of travel, but even so he was searched four times while still near the capital. He was frisked one night at a roadblock near the hotel and was particularly annoyed at how the man put his hand under his testicles. Diederich later determined that Greene was shadowed for almost every moment of his visit.

He went to see Duvalierville, a supposed showcase for the regime undoubtedly inspired by the construction of Brasilia. A small village had been demolished to accommodate a new one made of concrete. It was paid for largely by road tolls, but relatively little of the money received was spent on building. The plan was to house two thousand peasants in one-room houses. When Greene saw it, there were a few concrete structures and nothing really complete except a stadium for cockfights. He heard of another curious project on Kenscoff, the moun-tain that rises beyond the capital – an officer of the Tontons Macoutes was building an ice rink; in the novel, Captain Concasseur loses money on such a project.

Over drinks at the Oloffson, Greene gave an interview to the journalist Richard Eder, and while most of his comments were about the antics of the 'other' Graham Greene back in Europe, he said he was thinking of writing an entertainment set in Haiti, beginning with a hotel owner returning to find his premises empty.[40] In fact, he had begun that book some months before but had made no progress since May as he needed to see for himself what was going on in the country.[41] Having lost confidence while writing *A Burnt-Out Case*, he initially proposed nothing more than an entertainment. One can see the possibility of sad humour in the situation of the hotel owner, but Greene soon decided that to do justice to what he had seen he needed to write a full-scale novel, a thing he had almost despaired of ever doing again. The moral and political urgency of Haiti required him to become ambitious about his art once again.

Greene sought out troubled places as an escape from boredom, but some of these journeys left him shaken. He knew that at any moment the Tontons Macoutes could knock at his door or prove trigger-happy at a roadblock. Although he often wrote about desiring death, he did experience fear, never more so than on this visit to what he would soon describe as 'The Nightmare Republic'.[42] As he was boarding his plane to Santo Domingo, a stranger asked him to carry a letter to the exiled presidential candidate Louis Déjeoie. Thinking it a trap, he refused.[43]

Across the Dominican border, Diederich had learned of Greene's visit to Haiti from Jolicoeur's column. He had not actually seen the novelist in about seven years, and was surprised to get a visit from him. Greene appeared at the airport with little luggage, but he was carrying a painting by the Haitian artist Philippe-Auguste, which he had purchased with his winnings from the nearly deserted casino. That picture of a religious procession illustrated his article, 'The Nightmare Republic', for the *Sunday Telegraph*, and indeed he treasured it for the rest of his life. He recounted for Diederich what had happened while he was in Haiti, and spoke of his frustration at not seeing the border. Diederich proposed a journey there which they took in January 1965. For years afterwards, Greene dreamt about the terrors of Haiti. As he put it to Diederich on this occasion, 'I thought I was doomed to stay . . . I felt something was going to happen. I was so sure of it.'[44]

57

STATUES AND PIGEONS

'Graham Greene's new play at the *Haymarket* is possibly the worst play by a reputable dramatist that I have ever seen. I cannot think why H. M. Tennent and Donald Albery wanted to put it on, why Sir Ralph Richardson and Roland Culver were prepared to appear in it, why Peter Wood wanted to direct it or why Mr Greene ever let it loose outside his study. The story is banal, the development inept, the characterisation is perfunctory and the observations about God (the play is about God) are more excruciatingly naïve than I would have thought possible this side of the Arian heresy. The play is called *Carving a Statue . . .*'[1]

That was one way of putting it. It is the story of a very bad sculptor who has spent fifteen years carving a mammoth statue of God. He sacrifices to his meagre talent all human intimacy and warmth – ignoring his son and debauching the boy's girlfriend. For the most part he just hangs in the air from a harness, worrying about his statue. Greene meant the play to be funny – another farce – even though the jokes were so grim and subtle as to escape notice. His sculptor was conceived as a modern version of Benjamin Robert Haydon, who specialized in grandiose historical and religious subjects, such as his 12′ 6″ × 15′ rendering of *Christ's Entry into Jerusalem* – it required a 600-pound frame and now hangs in a seminary in Ohio. Haydon eventually killed himself.[2]

Begun in Mexico while he waited for a long-delayed flight to Cuba, Greene worked on the play through the autumn and had a draft completed by 13 December 1963,[3] after which he made a two-week journey to report for the *Sunday Times* on the formerly Portuguese territory of Goa, a Catholic enclave annexed by India in 1961. On his return, he made some improvements and waited to see if a producer was interested.

Binkie Beaumont of H. M. Tennent read the script by 12 March 1963 and decided to put it into production.⁴ Greene and Beaumont initially hoped that John Gielgud would direct Paul Scofield as the sculptor. Neither was available, so Peter Wood directed Ralph Richardson, with the part of the boy played by Dennis Waterman.

As the rehearsals progressed that summer, Greene and Richardson disagreed about the play, as they had disagreed about *The Complaisant Lover*. Richardson thought *Carving a Statue* was about the nature of God, while Greene thought it should be played for laughs. Sensing in it something of Ibsen's *The Master Builder*, Richardson did not see any irony in the profusion of overblown symbols of Father, Son, and Blessed Virgin. It opened in Brighton and the local theatre critics tore it apart. Greene immediately wrote a letter to Richardson, essentially a rant into his Dictaphone, accusing the actor of laziness, obstinacy, and the 'vanity of an ageing "star"'.⁵ Richardson himself could be bloody-minded: he had recently punched Alec Guinness in the jaw without obvious provocation during the filming of *Doctor Zhivago*.⁶ He stuck with his interpretation of the sculptor's part, and when the play opened at the Theatre Royal Haymarket on 17 September 1964, most reviewers dismissed it as wordy, portentous, and tiresome. It closed at the end of October. Although they made peace for the sake of the play, Greene and Richardson never worked together again.

If the play proved a 'nightmare',⁷ Greene was confident about his new novel. The writing took off in April 1964, and at that time he gave it the title 'Les Comédiens' – other working titles were 'The Dissemblers' and 'A Man of Extremes';⁸ he finally settled on *The Comedians*. Just as the crushing reviews of the play came in, he was able to report to Marie Biche that the novel, approaching fifty thousand words, was about half finished.⁹

It was, however, difficult for him to undertake further research for the novel. Now a known enemy of the regime in Haiti, he could no longer go there, so he decided instead to visit the Dominican Republic. He spent Christmas with Caroline in Montreal and then went on to New York. His flight to Santo Domingo on 1 January 1965 made a stop in Port-au-Prince, which caused him some unease¹⁰ since there was a remote chance that the Tontons Macoutes would pull him off the plane and exact their revenge for what he had said in 'The Nightmare

Republic'. Nothing happened, and he was met in Santo Domingo by Diederich, who now assumed a key role for Greene; as he has described in his memoir of the novelist, for the next twenty-six years he served as Greene's guide to Central America.

Diederich's life had changed. Having lost his newspaper, he could no longer report from within Haiti, though he had sources there and continued to write for American news agencies.[11] He sympathized with the rebel bands training in the Dominican Republic, preparing for forays into Haiti, so gave what supplies he could, including an expensive handgun, to one group called the Kamoken, led by Fred Baptiste, a former schoolmaster from Jacmel, and his brother Renel. Diederich took Greene to their training camp in a disused insane asylum, which had recently been inhabited by goats. In an adjoining pasture was a herd of zebras once owned by the dictator Trujillo. Fred Baptiste was desperate for weapons and supplies, and hoped that Greene could help obtain them. All the novelist could do was leave a small cash donation, which was spent on the purchase of some chickens. A rebel band modelled on this one makes a gallant attack on the Tontons Macoutes at the end of *The Comedians*. Greene remained in touch with the Baptiste brothers for several years and continued to seek news of them after they were captured in 1970 and taken to Fort Dimanche. Eventually, he issued a public appeal on their behalf,[12] sponsored by Amnesty International and composed by the journalist Greg Chamberlain, only to learn a little later that both brothers had died of tuberculosis in prison, and that by the end Fred had gone insane.[13]

The main purpose of Greene's visit in January 1965 was to see the long, dangerous border between the two countries, which generally followed the track of rivers or wound among mountains. Over two days, they travelled in Diederich's chartreuse Volkswagen Beetle along with Jean-Claude Bajeux, an exiled priest and activist whose family had recently disappeared at the hands of the Tontons Macoutes; this heartsore man provided the model for the priest who, in the novel, preaches against indifference at the funeral of Jones and the other rebels, taking as his text the saying of Thomas the Doubter: 'Let us go up to Jerusalem and die with him.'

Travelling from the north, their first important stop was at the frontier bridge over the Rio Dajabón, known as the Massacre River after a seventeenth-century bloodbath. Greene and Diederich went out towards the yellow line at the centre of the bridge, snapping photographs, but were warned by Dominican soldiers that Haitians hidden on the other side had their weapons trained on them. There had been a significant skirmish here in September 1963, when a band of rebels retreating from their attack on a barracks came under heavy fire as they crossed back into Dominican territory. The place had an even uglier history. Along this river in 1937, soldiers under orders from Trujillo had killed what some have estimated as up to twenty thousand Haitians; they were rounded up and required to pronounce the Spanish word for parsley, 'perejil', and if they had the wrong accent and were black they were killed.

In the middle part of the journey, they drove on the neglected International Road, a place where some of Papa Doc's most violent henchmen operated, and where the Volkswagen was the sole target in the landscape. At several points, Greene thought he had spotted Tontons Macoutes, but he was wrong, and one of his sightings turned out to be no more than a guinea hen. At Las Matas de Fanfan, they went to a house of American Redemptorists, the order that once specialized in Hell sermons. Greene wanted to avoid theological discussion with such men, so it was agreed that he be introduced as 'Mr White'. It didn't work. He was instantly recognized, either from a photograph on a book jacket or because word of his visit had reached the priests on the ecclesiastical grapevine, which Greene often compared to an intelligence service. The priests greeted them warmly but had no room for them, so they went to a nearby hotel, where they were obliged by a Trujillo-era regulation to specify their skin colour in order to check in. Greene was outraged, so wrote 'pink' on the card. Diederich followed suit with 'black' and Bajeux with 'purple'.

Their journey then took them along tracks in the mountains, where the car was in frequent danger of sliding off precipices. Diederich recalls that Greene grew very affable as the trip went on, though unhelpful as he ignored requests to get out of the car whenever it needed to be lightened to get past a particularly rough patch.

At the southern end of the border, near Pedernales, Diederich had a supposed friend who managed a bauxite facility for Alcoa and who had often invited him to visit. However, when they got to the gates, the man tried at first to get rid of them, before grudgingly allowing them in. He found them some dry sandwiches, and when Greene enquired about whisky he grimly provided each with a single shot. Greene got his revenge by portraying him as the miserable Schuyler Wilson, who refuses to give the exile Brown a job.

Greene went back to Europe and had a draft of a novel just about finished by the end of April 1965, when a violent coup took place in the Dominican Republic. Forces loyal to the deposed president Juan Bosch, a socialist, sought to restore him to office. President Lyndon Johnson sent in thousands of Marines to protect American citizens and property, and to support the junta opposed to Bosch. After much killing, the conservative Joaquín Balaguer took power with Johnson's blessing. Greene judged that the Americans wanted to preserve the Dominican Republic as a place from which Cuban exiles could conduct raids like 'pin-pricks' when larger operations against Castro were impossible.[14] He had planned his novel to have a peaceful last chapter set in the Dominican Republican, but had to reshape his ending in May to account for the violence.[15]

Greene did not often create major characters who were wholly admirable – Dr Colin in *A Burnt-Out Case* is a rare example – but he did so again in *The Comedians*. The Marxist Dr Magiot, a cardiologist and patriot, becomes a father figure to the hotel owner Brown, whose adult life has been a succession of scams, and he encourages him to make a new commitment. Greene later told Diederich that the character was based on Camille Lhérisson, Haiti's most distinguished physician, who had been educated at McGill and Harvard. He served, briefly, as a cabinet minister during the Magloire administration and later as a representative to UNESCO. He was also a philosopher and had once hosted a conference in Haiti, which attracted the pre-eminent Catholic philosopher of the time, Jacques Maritain, who then encouraged Greene to meet Lhérisson on one of his visits to Haiti in the 1950s. Greene admired his bearing, dignity, and intelligence. According to Diederich, there were some things that he did not understand about Lhérisson – he was not, as he thought, a 'noir', but belonged to the mixed-race elite of Haiti, something he prided himself on, and his views were right wing.[16] Lhérisson died at sixty-two, as an exile in New York on 31 December 1965,[17] just before the novel was released. Had he lived, he would doubtless have been annoyed at what Greene's imagination had made of him.

For the first time in his career, Greene, in *The Comedians*, had portrayed the intelligentsia of a formerly colonial society. The existence of such groups is implicit in *The Power and the Glory*, *The Quiet American*, and *Our Man in Havana*, but they are marginal. In this book, Greene figured out how to make them central to the story – not only is Magiot a man of learning, but the young rebel Philipot is a poet, and the book is replete with sadness at how the days (and nights) of Duvalier have crushed a Haitian renaissance. As Philipot remarks, 'Our novelists are published in Paris – and now they live there too.'[18] Again, Greene faced the ethical and aesthetic challenge that lies behind *A Burnt-Out Case*. If he wrote in the character of Magiot or Philipot, he would be out of his depth, and indeed guilty of what is now called appropriation of voice. He would have to begin with what he knew.

The book opens with four white characters, who are presented as little more than masks: Brown, Jones, and the two Smiths in a ship called the *Medea*. The narrator, Brown, is a crook – he has been involved in forging art. Returning to Haiti after a visit to New York, he thinks of little but his affair with Martha, the wife of a diplomat, and his failing hotel, where a former cabinet minister, the uncle of the rebel leader, has killed himself: ' . . . the corpse in the pool seemed to turn our preoccupations into comedy. The corpse of Doctor Philipot belonged to a more tragic theme; we were only a sub-plot affording a little light relief.'[19] As the story unfolds, it becomes clear that the troubles of the white people simply don't matter in comparison to the oppression all around them. To make this point, Greene again uses the technique of a play within a play. Even the title of the book points to this structural element: the French word *comédien* has a broader reference than its English cognate and means an actor:[20] to become authentic, one must risk involvement. Brown thinks of his mother's lover Marcel who hangs himself once she has died, ' . . . perhaps he was no comédien after all. Death is a proof of sincerity.'[21]

One of the main characters, Jones, is an amiable con man, and Greene afterwards maintained that he was based on the financial adviser Tom Roe, something that would have required him to have very early misgivings about the man.[22] The piggery business in Fife collapsed in November 1964; Greene told Francis that he feared his savings had been wiped out, but Roe sent him a soothing letter that briefly relieved his worries.[23] The book was half finished by then. A draft of the novel was completed in May,[24] and Roe's arrest did not occur until July. The character of Jones must have existed before Greene knew the whole truth about Roe; however, it is perfectly reasonable to believe that while writing the second half of the book he feared he was dealing with a thief.

Although Greene hoped that his book would injure the regime, he was under no illusion that it would topple a dictator. Indeed, one theme in the book is whether art can ever bring about political change, as so many of the rebels in the book begin as poets and artists. In the first paragraph, Brown speaks of statues raised in London to politicians who stood for free trade or perhaps the Ashanti War, while to the pigeons none of it makes any difference. Brown considers what memorial can be raised to Jones and the rebels. He quotes a phrase from the Odes of Horace, *'Exegi monumentum'* – translated, the whole sentence would be 'I have raised a monument more lasting than bronze.'

At the end of the story, Brown becomes involved in the struggle, not as a soldier, but as an undertaker – that is, an agent of memory. Auden famously wrote that 'Poetry makes nothing happen'.[25] For Greene, however, remembrance is a political act: the revolutionary work of this novel is to remember the obscure dead and name truthfully what killed them.

58

THE NEW LIFE

'Today I have been cleaning drawers, destroying letters, preparing for the new life ... So many letters have shown me how good & sweet & patient people have been to me. If only I'd been as good to other people.'[1] So wrote Graham Greene to Yvonne Cloetta on 6 November 1965. He had made a firm decision to become a resident of France, where he was already spending most of his time. His move was motivated by a desire to be near to her, by exasperation with the British tax regime, and by worries about his health. Other things contributed to his willingness to leave England, including the death from cancer of his much-loved 'daily', Mrs Cordery, which Greene felt keenly; she made breakfast for him and he was attached to her company.

He held a farewell dinner for the Sutros, the Reinhardts, and his secretary Josephine Reid at the Connaught Hotel in Mayfair. It was a melancholy evening, and while he was away from the table Reid broke down in tears and left, saying 'Tell [him] I'll be at the station tomorrow morning.'[2]

Greene's residency in France took effect from 1 January 1966, just as he was being named a Companion of Honour in the New Year Honours List. He had turned down a CBE in 1956,[3] but this more significant honour he accepted. In a peculiar irony, the distinction was being conferred by a country which, for tax reasons, he was not supposed to put his foot in for at least a year. His visit to Buckingham Palace on 11 March 1966 to be invested with the insignia was an exception, as even the Inland Revenue knew better than to tangle with the Queen.

In France, Greene went first to his flat in Paris, but then spent much of the following months at the Hôtel de la Mer in Antibes,[4] as Yvonne lived near by in Juan-les-Pins. The affair had assumed something like permanence. In 1964, there had been a crisis in Yvonne's marriage and she considered breaking with the often-absent Jacques, and at the time Graham wrote a letter to Jacques explaining the situation between himself and Yvonne, but it is not known whether he ever sent it. She was worried about the effect of a separation on her two daughters, so Greene told her he wanted her to live with him but only if she could do so without regrets.[5] It never came to that and the marriage continued; however, Jacques seems to have accepted Graham's role in Yvonne's life and the two men occasionally socialized together.

Graham remained in touch with Catherine but was much more distant. Her health was poor, with surgeries on her hip, and then electro-shock therapy for depression. Towards the end of 1965, Marie Biche conveyed Catherine's complaints about his attitude and suggested he was neglecting her; he wrote a long letter saying this was not so,[6] but it was true. He had made his choice. Yvonne was confident enough about their relationship to accept that Graham and Catherine might spend some time together. In May 1965, Catherine was hospitalized with an inflamed pancreas, a dangerous condition that left her very weak, so with Yvonne's consent he invited her to recuperate at Anacapri,[7] but the days of passion were over.

Graham Greene could never be described as a happy man, and there would be low points in future, mainly as he fretted from time to time over whether Yvonne might break with him, but the horrific, sustained depressions of the 1950s would not be repeated. One factor must have been that there was just less drama in his dealings with Yvonne than there had been with Catherine; his daughter suggests that he was generally more even-tempered and courteous after the 1950s. It is also possible that there was some change in the way his mood disorder affected him. Greene made some loose claims about entering a long manic period in the mid-1960s;[8] this may be so, but it is hard to assess. In any event, he was, very simply, doing better. The leprologist Michel Lechat wrote him a sad letter in February 1966, and Greene responded: 'I'm so sorry that you are feeling empty. Perhaps your menopause has come a little early. I went through a year or two of that in the 1950s, but I seem to have emerged and my melancholy now when it does rear its ugly head is quite bearable. I suppose that is one of the consolations of age.'[9] This vastly understates Greene's earlier depression but is accurate in claiming that his troubles were now more manageable.

Of course, he would never again worry about money. Since the arrest of Tom Roe in the summer of 1965, his fortunes had been almost entirely and unexpectedly restored. *The Comedians* was set to appear on both sides of the Atlantic on 27 January 1966. It had already been made a first choice of the Literary Guild, so a great deal of money was coming from the United States. Meanwhile, Truman Capote's *In Cold Blood* had set a new standard for the sale of film rights, at $500,000.[10] 'A baker's dozen' of producers swarmed Laurence Pollinger for proofs of Greene's new novel, the very first being Sir Carol Reed,[11] but the bidding went too high for him. Monica McCall believed they could get $250,000, though Pollinger thought, at first, that she was dreaming. As it turned out, Peter Glenville, who had directed *The Living Room* in 1953, had the backing of MGM and made a complicated bid, with a calculation partly based on book sales, which added up to precisely a quarter of a million dollars. They offered Greene an additional $50,000 to write the script, plus expenses.[12] This all came as a pleasant surprise, as the rights to *A Burnt-Out Case*, though optioned, had never sold at all. He asked Yvonne: 'You'll go on loving me if I become rich, won't you?'[13]

Immediately upon its release *The Comedians* was given superb reviews and became the number-one bestseller in Britain;[14] by 24 March it had sold forty-four thousand copies.[15] In New York, Viking released the book a few days earlier than expected, just when Peter Glenville was in Haiti, making an incognito tour in order to meet people like Jolicoeur and to get a visual sense of the hotel and the other locations described in the novel. The director saw his project as deeply political, and likely to have more immediate effect on the Duvalier government than the bullets of the partisans. It was a blessing that the Tontons Macoutes did not read book reviews, or the director might have been found dead in a ditch.[16]

Greene was becoming dissatisfied with his American publisher for other reasons, particularly their delay in passing on the payment from the Literary Guild.[17] Although his financial picture was very good now, he had not yet received the various large sums he was owed, and in early 1967 was briefly reduced to borrowing money from Marie Biche.[18] A disaffected Greene finally left Viking in 1970 for Simon & Schuster, where Michael Korda, whom he had befriended twenty years earlier on the *Elsewhere*, would be his editor until the mid-1980s, when he returned to Viking..

Although Malcolm Muggeridge had once called him 'one of nature's displaced persons', Greene could not live in a hotel for ever. In May 1966 he used some of the money from *The Comedians* to buy a flat in Antibes, at 51 La Résidence des Fleurs in Avenue Pasteur. He liked it for its view of the town, the harbour, and the distant mountains.[19] He retained the flat in Paris and the house in Anacapri, but Antibes became his permanent home. He filled it with perhaps two thousand books and some artworks, but it was otherwise unremarkable. About a decade later, V. S. Pritchett came to interview Greene there and wrote: 'I had imagined that the novelist who had lived in Albany would be living now in one of those fine and rosy old houses on the ramparts of old Antibes looking down at the sea and the gardens where the sly old men of the town play boules all day. It was strange to find him in this huge modern block, flaunting its bombastic concrete balconies.'[20] Greene generally worked in the sitting room at a table beside a tall window overlooking the harbour. His enjoyment of the place was lessened when a large marina was developed in the 1970s: the view was changed and the noise increased, but he was content to remain there. At about that time, Greene gave a lecture at the Anglo-Argentine Society, after which the journalist Julian Evans asked him why he was living in France; he said: 'The bread is very good, and occasionally the wine is good.'[21]

The new life in France generally lifted Greene's spirits, but back in England one of his most valued friends was in trouble. The bond between Graham Greene and Evelyn Waugh had certainly revived after their exchange over *A Burnt-Out Case*, but perhaps not completely. Their correspondence continued, and at the beginning of 1966 Waugh wrote: 'I greatly admire *The Comedians*. What staying power you have. It might have been written 30 years ago and could be by no one but you.' He still rather disapproved of what Greene was up to, as he wrote to Ann Fleming: 'Graham Greene has fled the country with the CH and a work of communist propaganda.'[22] At the same time, Greene received a gloomy letter from Father Philip Caraman, saying that according to Margaret Waugh her father was seriously ill and refusing help; Caraman suggested that Waugh's melancholy was 'incurable'.[23] Greene wrote back, expressing regret that Eric Strauss, who could have helped Waugh, was dead. Surprisingly, he took the view that no depression was beyond treatment, especially as he had seen how John Sutro had been helped by electro-shock therapy. Since Caraman was then in Norway and unable to do it himself, Greene asked him to send some priest in England whom Waugh would trust to check on him,[24] but it was probably too late for anyone to help Evelyn Waugh.

Waugh was devastated by the changes brought about by the Second Vatican Council, in particular the demise of the Latin liturgy, which made it much more difficult to claim great differences between Roman Catholic worship and that of Anglicans. Greene actually shared Waugh's view, though for rather more practical reasons: as a traveller, he had been able to attend the same Mass, more or less, in any country of the world. Now, with vernacular liturgies, he had to accept often not knowing what was being said at the altar.[25] Waugh's concern was much deeper and more agonized: he felt that something at the heart of his own life was being erased. Apart from the question of the Latin Mass, Greene was in favour of the reforms of the Council, and his own opinions on birth control, ecumenism, social justice, and papal infallibility would soon go far beyond what the bishops espoused.

Waugh collapsed and died on Easter Sunday 1966 in a lavatory in his home in Somerset just after hearing Caraman celebrate a Mass in Latin. Upon hearing of his death, Greene wrote to Laura Waugh: 'I was shocked more than I can find it possible to write by the news of Evelyn's death. As a writer I admired him more than any other living novelist, & as a man I loved him.'[26]

59

FIDEL AT NIGHT

A nervous aide laid a copy of *The Comedians* on Papa Doc's desk and assured him that it was a piece of shit. It lay there for some time beside a Bible and a loaded pistol. Although he could not read English well, Papa Doc soon decided that the book posed a huge threat.[1] Surprisingly, his first known response was an attempt at literary criticism. When asked about it at a news conference in May, he said mildly: '*Le livre n'est pas bien écrit. Comme l'oeuvre d'un écrivain et d'un journaliste, le livre n'a aucune valeur.*'[2]

Papa Doc was actually obsessed with the book and the movie project as part of a plot against him. Since he wanted to rebuild the tourist industry and needed to avoid bad publicity, he chose not to send out his assassins, though an article in a Duvalierist newspaper later declared openly that Greene and his accomplices were lucky to be alive, as Papa Doc could have had them shot no matter where they hid.[3] From the beginning of 1966, Greene was on the lookout for strangers hanging about his flat in Paris.[4]

Despite the danger, there was little difficulty assembling a cast for the film. Having been approached by both Glenville and Greene, Richard Burton wrote to the novelist at the end of March, saying that he 'loved' the book and was anxious to see the script.[5] He was perfectly suited to play the gamecock Brown, who constantly challenges the Tontons Macoutes but stands for nothing and has no way of backing up what he says. He had recently played just such a hollow man, also under Peter Glenville's direction; in the title role of *Becket*, his character is nothing until forced to become archbishop and make a stand, almost against his will, for 'the honour of God'. Although there are different versions of the story, Greene understood that the price of getting Richard Burton as Brown was that they had to give the part of Martha to Elizabeth Taylor, and this caused Greene a pang as he had hoped to see it played by Anita Björk.[6] Alec Guinness, who took the part of Jones, wrote to Greene in July that it was the best script he had ever read. James Earl Jones was cast as Magiot, Peter Ustinov as Ambassador Pineda, Roscoe Lee Brown as Petit Pierre, Lillian Gish as Mrs Smith, Paul Ford as Mr Smith, and Raymond St Jacques as Concasseur.

With the production taking shape, Greene visited Cuba from 28 August to 19 September for the *Daily Telegraph*. While there, he spent much of his time in the company of the novelist and poet Pablo Armando Fernández, who had once worked at the Cuban embassy in London and was acquainted with Francis Greene. Later regarded as one of the island's most important writers, Fernández largely organized Greene's visits in 1963 and 1966, and a genuine respect and friendship sprang up between the two writers. Some years later Graham Greene asked Max Reinhardt to publish a novel by Fernández, but nothing came of the idea.[7]

Greene was a guest of the government and they wanted to put him up in a grand house usually reserved for visiting heads of state with a butler, a guard, servants, and a swimming pool.[8] He felt that this was a bit much for an independent journalist, so he checked in to a hotel, but he did make use of an ancient Packard and a French-speaking driver, for excursions about the country in the company of Pablo Fernández, the writer Lisandro Otero, and the photographer Ernesto Fernández. He met with many political and cultural figures, among them Haydée Santamaria, a survivor of the 1953 Moncada Barracks attack, whom he had first encountered at the safe house in Santiago in 1957; she was now in charge of Latin American relations and the publishing house Casa de las Americas. He visited René Portocarrera and Raúl Milian, a gay couple who were among Cuba's leading artists, and he enjoyed their company very much.

Greene remained enthusiastic about the Cuban experiment, finding it infinitely preferable to the 'Stalinist capitalism' of the United States,[9] but he had also learned a good deal about the mistreatment of dissidents. Raúl Castro arranged a military flight for him to the Isle of Pines, the site of an enormous panopticon prison where the Castro brothers had themselves been incarcerated following the attack on Moncada

Barracks. After the revolution it remained the harshest Cuban prison, with several thousand inmates, many of them opponents of the new regime. In 1963, the Organization of American States' Interamerican Commission on Human Rights issued a report on Cuba, drawing particular attention to abuses occurring at this facility; Fidel initially disregarded the report, but the prison was becoming an international embarrassment and in 1967 he shut it down.[10]

Greene had first met Armando Hart, Santamaria's husband, at the same Santiago safe house in 1957, and watched him having his hair dyed. A very cultured man, he was now a cabinet minister, and Greene challenged him about the persecution of homosexuals, finding his answers 'less than satisfactory'.[11] The novelist wanted to know about the UMAP (Unidades Militares de Ayuda a la Producción) camps run by the army. Theoretically, they provided an alternative form of service for conscientious objectors, but were in fact hard labour camps, where homosexuals, supposed layabouts, and members of certain Protestant groups were sent for years at a time, with almost no contact from their families. Given that there were three priests currently in such camps, Greene judged that the position of the Catholic church had deteriorated since his last visit.

Seeing that the revolution was very much a project of the young who would one day become set in their ways, Greene remarked, 'I do not wish to live long enough to see this revolution middle-aged.'[12] Some of those he met in Cuba were already wavering, among them the poet Carlos Franqui, a journalist and spokesman for the government, who went into exile in 1968 when Fidel endorsed the Soviet invasion of Czechoslovakia.

During his three weeks in Cuba, Greene was kept waiting for a meeting with Fidel, who travelled about the country according to no very fixed schedule, a practice that wrongfooted would-be assassins. Raúl was far less elusive, and Greene was even able to watch him and other cabinet ministers play a 2 a.m. game of basketball: Cuban revolutionaries tended to be night owls. One day, Greene, who was shown several agricultural projects during his visit, arrived late at the Isla Turiguano, a state farm specializing in cattle, horses, and pigs, and found that Fidel had already been there and left. They reached Morón, to find that he had spent the night there and moved on. Fidel showed up in Camaguey – after Greene had left. So it continued, until the last evening of Greene's visit, when he was having dinner with the British ambassador, only to be called away by Carlos Franqui for his long-delayed meeting with the leader. The ambassador was envious of Greene as he had never had such a meeting with Fidel.

Franqui took him to a house outside Havana, watched over by many guards. Inside he found Fidel, his top aide and physician René Vallejo, who acted as interpreter, and the minister of education José Llanusa. The meeting lasted from about 11 p.m. until 2 a.m. For the first forty-five minutes or so, Fidel held forth on farming and country life, telling Greene a practised anecdote of how he had gone into a pueblo at night and found two men playing dominoes, so he joined them. As word of his presence spread, a crowd gathered and demanded a speech. Instead he had asked them about the minute details of their lives, and decided to try an experiment in the town, a bolder kind of communism where everything would be provided and the results could be judged by economists and sociologists.

Greene drew Fidel into a discussion of how Catholicism and communism have much in common, making the case not just for coexistence but for cooperation. Castro then praised the papal nuncio to Cuba. They agreed that right-wing American clerics like Cardinal Spellman and the television preacher Bishop Fulton Sheen posed a threat to Cuba. Greene gathered that since Castro hoped to export his style of revolution to South America he could not appear to the peasants in other countries as a persecutor of the church. When it was over, Greene noted 'He plays Communism by ear & not by books.'[13] As a parting gift, Fidel gave him a painting of flowers by Portacarrero, and signed the back of it. Franqui gave him one by Milian. The artists themselves had already each given Greene a picture, so he returned to France with four Cuban artworks.

Apart from political discussions, Greene and Fidel struck up a friendship. Indeed, it was common for visitors, among them the Canadian prime minister Pierre Elliott Trudeau and his wife Margaret, to find the Cuban leader affable and in many ways admirable – the Trudeaus and their sons regarded Fidel as nearly a family member. By a fluke, the British ambassador encountered Fidel on the beach the day after Greene had met him and reported back to Whitehall that the Cuban leader had 'waxed eloquent in Graham Greene's praise. Of course it must be gratifying to him that an eminent author from the capitalist world – and a Roman Catholic to boot – should take this benevolent interest in the Cuban revolution, but Graham Greene evidently struck a personal note.' He also judged Greene's view of the revolution as 'sympathetic but not wholly uncritical'.[14]

60

PAPA DOC HONOURED ME

At their late-night meeting, Fidel Castro offered Graham Greene all facilities free of charge for the filming of *The Comedians*.[1] It was, perhaps, not a serious offer as MGM was hardly going to ignore the embargo. However, the problem of where to shoot the film was real. In the end, Glenville decided to re-create scenes from Port-au-Prince in the coastal city of Cotonou in Dahomey, among them a replica of the Oloffson Hotel. When he reached the country in early February 1967, Greene saw the sign 'Welcome to Haiti' and had an irrational moment of fear, thinking he was back there. The guerrilla leader Fred Baptiste came to Cotonou during the filming and liked what he saw: 'But this is Haiti.'[2]

About two months later, an American journalist asked Greene, then making another visit to the set, what he wanted the film to accomplish. Mixing a Scotch and soda, he commented, 'I'd like it to help isolate Duvalier. And I would hope it might have some influence on your State Department. Duvalier has brought the country to the verge of economic disaster, and the only thing that props him up is outside aid and the dwindling tourist trade. *Any* aid to Haiti only ends in keeping the *tontons* happy. It never reaches the poor.' He added, 'These are, of course, ideal objectives for the film's impact. I'm afraid it's a little like David flinging the pebble . . .'[3]

News coverage focused on Burton and Taylor, their drinking, fighting, and love-making, but there were other things happening on the set. James Earl Jones remarked: 'You know, if Hollywood were doing *The Comedians*, all the Negroes would have been type-cast. The girls would have been fair-skinned so the American male could warm to them. I think I have a very good part. The doctor's a Communist. But Greene made him a sympathetic character and Mr Glenville is going to play me as Greene wrote it. I don't portray the sinister Marxist. In Hollywood, they'd have turned me into a bastard.'[4] Various explanations have been offered for the indifference of audiences to this film, which had had the promise of greatness about it when it was released in October 1967. Greene blamed Elizabeth Taylor, Guinness blamed Peter Glenville for a slightly 'mechanical' way of directing,[5] others claimed it was too long, but Jones may have put his finger on the problem. American movie-goers were not all that interested in the problems of very black people in a country they could not find on a map.

The book and the film did matter – very much – to Haitian exiles. Throughout 1966, Greene hosted a number of them in Paris. Fred Baptiste's visit to the film set was intended to raise $80,000 to help pay for a new invasion. Greene was uncomfortable about his companion, a former Duvalierist army officer, who seemed to be a spy. Nonetheless, he made a small donation and wrote personal letters to the leading actors asking them to do likewise, but there was no response. Unfortunately, Peter Glenville had already wasted a large donation, and they probably had heard about this. He had just given $50,000 to another former Duvalierist, Father Jean-Baptiste Georges, who tried to organize a small invasion from Florida. Georges sought to enlarge his war chest by selling documentary rights for the expedition to CBS, and so his plans became known. In early 1967, customs officials seized their equipment and arrested the priest. The episode was afterwards known as 'The Bay of Piglets'.[6]

The film premiered in New York on 31 October 1967, to a certain amount of fist-waving from the Haitian regime. The ambassador to the United States called it 'a character assassination of an entire nation' presenting Haiti as a country of 'Voodoo worshippers and killers'. Its intention, he claimed, was 'disgusting and scaring the American tourist at the beginning of the season. Haiti is one of the most beautiful, peaceful, and safe countries in the Caribbean.'[7] When Glenville looked to Greene for a response, he wired back: 'Suggest following: The ruler of Haiti, responsible for murder and exile of thousands of his countrymen, is really protesting against his own image in the looking glass. Like the ugly queen in Snow White he will have to destroy all the mirrors. But perhaps someone with a sense of humour drafted the official protest with its reference to "one of the most peaceful and safe countries in the Caribbean" from which even his own family has fled. I would like to challenge Duvalier to take a fortnight's holiday in the outside world away from the security of his Tonton. Love Graham.'[8] Presumably, the love was directed towards Glenville and not Papa Doc.

Duvalier's diplomats conducted a panicky campaign against the film, and tried to get it banned in various countries. Their main success was a court action in France claiming that the film insulted Duvalier. In 1970 a judge ruled that some scenes should be cut before the film could be shown, with the effect that it no longer made sense, but while Papa Doc claimed ten million francs in damages she awarded him just a single franc. In October 1968, Haitian embassies around the world issued a glossy volume entitled *Graham Greene Demasqué/Finally Exposed*, a collection of essays in English and French by various officials in the foreign ministry.[9] In it, Greene was described as an opium addict, a spy, a racist, a pervert, a swindler, and a torturer. Haiti, under Duvalier, was portrayed as a kind of paradise – a claim supported by futuristic images of Duvalierville, the concrete wasteland that figures in the novel. Greene spoke of the book as one of the greatest compliments he had ever received, telling Bernard Diederich: 'Papa Doc honoured me.'[10]

61

MORSE CODE ON THE WATER PIPES

W hile Peter Glenville was filming and the Burtons were quarrelling, Graham Greene was working on a new novel. The first
notes for what in early 1967 he called 'Sense of Security' were scribbled
inside the back cover of Victor Canning's *The Limbo Line*, a thriller
about the abduction and return to the Soviet Union of defectors who
have taken asylum in England. The hero of Canning's book, a retired
spy recalled to service, is instructed by his superiors to allow the anticipated abduction of a ballerina to occur so that the ring and the route
can be traced, but he falls in love with the woman who is being used
as bait. This conflict between loyalty to a national purpose and loyalty
to an individual evidently gave Greene the idea for his own story.

Despite being the story of an MI6 officer who is working for the
KGB, *The Human Factor* is decidedly *not* the story of Kim Philby. The
defector, Maurice Castle, is a conservative character and opposed to
Marxism. He leads a rather grey life in Berkhamsted, with a mortgage,
a dog, and a bicycle. Formerly stationed in South Africa, he fell in love
with a black woman named Sarah and so was blackmailed by the security services there. He returned to London, protected by a diplomatic
passport, but she had to escape with the aid of communist rebels. Out
of love for her and gratitude to her protectors, Castle begins leaking
material to the KGB, culminating in the revelation of an appalling
plan to back the apartheid regime with American nuclear weapons.
Once that document is leaked, he must take refuge in Moscow and so
is separated from Sarah. Although a version of the book was almost
finished in late 1967, Greene spoke of it then to V. S. Naipaul as one
he might write in the future: 'I am hoping, when the present spy vogue
is over, to write a book in which the villain is M.I.5, not the Russians

or the Chinese. It will be set in England right until the end. A sympathetic study of treachery.'[1]

This 'spy vogue' included a book by Philby's third wife, Eleanor, *Kim Philby: The Spy I Loved*, which appeared in January 1968. That book recounted, just as Greene's did, the ruin of a defector's marriage. He had been consulted about the book, and later relied on it for a description of Castle's flat in Moscow.[2] After it came out he laid his own manuscript aside for about seven years. *The Human Factor* was finally published in early 1978, more than eleven years after he had written those notes inside the cover of *The Limbo Line*.

He appears to have had almost no contact with Philby himself for a good many years, and it was not until 1977 that an occasional correspondence started up between them. Nonetheless, he was known to be a defender of Kim Philby. He published a ferocious, almost incoherent, review of two new books on Philby in February 1968,[3] claiming that the real purpose of intelligence work was not to gather scientific or military information but to sow distrust on the other side, and to this end MI5's revelation of Philby as a traitor was a mistake as it created distrust between Britain and America. He speculated on how interesting it would have been if Philby had become 'C' and had access only to the 'vacuous' minutes of high-level meetings; his eventual flight to Russia would have caused widespread laughter. Indeed, he dismissed the whole phenomenon of defection: 'No harm done by Philby, Burgess, and Maclean can outweigh the entertainment they have all given us.' In the article he argued very dubiously for the moral equivalence of crimes committed by East and West. Even allowing for the outrages of American foreign policy, it is hard to equate them with those of Stalin and his successors.

The same review contained a comment that the 'distinguished' John le Carré (David Cornwell) must not really be the author of a 'vulgar and untrue' account of Philby contained in one of the books. Five years earlier, Greene endorsed *The Spy Who Came in from the Cold* as 'The best spy story I have ever read' – a phrase which still appears on reprints – and the two writers struck up a pleasant connection. After 1968, Greene always found fault with le Carré's novels, saying they were too long, and on one occasion compared his style to 'bad Kipling'.[4] He probably had a special dislike for the character of Bill Haydon, the treacherous penetration agent modelled on Philby. Although the two authors did subsequently exchange letters with expressions of good will, Greene was not very interested in renewing the connection, and this was a source of pain to Cornwell as he admired Greene and felt indebted to him.[5] For his part, Greene may have been influenced by the younger writer in the mid-1960s; in *The Human Factor*, the bureaucratic world of MI6, with its melancholic functionaries and its obsession with files and pieces of paper rather resembles the one inhabited by George Smiley. Indeed, the broadcaster and journalist Robin Lustig maintains that in this novel Greene 'does le Carré better than le Carré does'[6] – high praise indeed.

Doubtless as a consequence of the *Observer* review, Philby's London publisher asked Greene to write a short introduction to the defector's autobiography, *My Silent War*.[7] In it, Greene asked the rhetorical question, 'Who among us has not betrayed something or someone more important than his country?' It was an article of faith for Greene that relationships with individuals were more important than those with countries or societies or groups. This was the same stance E. M. Forster took: ' . . . if I had to choose between betraying my country and betraying my friend I hope I should have the guts to betray my country'.[8] It is an attractive thought, as nations have a lot to answer for, especially after two world wars. And yet as a moral principle it falls apart: it hints at tribalism and tends to justify indifference to strangers, things Greene abhorred. In a rather different sense, it suggests a failure of imagination; one cannot put a value on the pains of people one has never met, and that is precisely what novelists claim to do in their art. Of course, in reality, Greene was acutely sensitive to suffering and was constantly helping out strangers. Characteristically, he interpreted Philby's career as a problem of belief, and compared him to Catholic zealots in the days of Elizabeth I awaiting the triumph of Philip of Spain. At the end of the introduction, he remarked of Philby's defection: 'After thirty years in the underground surely he had earned his right to a rest.'[9]

Greene's own relationship with the Soviet Union could hardly be characterized as 'rest'. He condemned both sides in the Cold War, and his attitude towards the Soviet Union, especially after the accession of Leonid Brezhnev in 1964, was highly critical. He took a particular interest in the cases of Andrei Sinyavsky and Yuliy Daniel, a pair of satirists whose works were smuggled abroad and published. In 1965, they were arrested for anti-Soviet activities. They were tried in the following year and sentenced to hard labour. In September 1967, Greene wrote to the Secretary of the Union of Writers and asked that any royalties owed to him and any money being held for him be paid to the wives of the two imprisoned writers.[10]

Greene wrote a letter to *The Times* about Daniel and Sinyavsky, remarking that if he had sent it to *Pravda* or *Izvestia*, it would not have been published.[11] He outlined his decision concerning the royalties and stated that he could no longer visit the Soviet Union, of which he had such happy memories, while these men were in jail. Greene specifically wanted to make a protest over human rights, nothing more, so he added this wildly provocative declaration: 'There are many agencies, such as Radio Free Europe, which specialize in propaganda against the Soviet Union. I would say to these agencies that this letter must in no way be regarded as an attack upon the Union. If I had to choose between life in the Soviet Union and life in the United States of America, I would certainly choose the Soviet Union, just as I would choose life in Cuba to life in those southern American republics, like Bolivia, dominated by their northern neighbour, or life in North Vietnam to life in South Vietnam. But the greater the affection one feels for any country the more one is driven to protest against any failure of justice there.'[12] This statement was made while in his fiction he was working out what he took to be the wholly moral grounds for Maurice Castle's defection. Even so, it is unreasonable. If Graham Greene had been a Russian writer, he would long since have been declared an unperson. He could not live and work in Russia without the protections of international celebrity, money, and a foreign passport, and he knew this. His remarks had a more straightforward rhetorical purpose. He wanted to make sure that his protest on behalf of Daniel and Sinyavsky was useless for American propaganda. He was poisoning the well.

Greene was as good as his word and refused to visit the Soviet Union until the Gorbachev years owing to the treatment of dissidents. In July 1969, the novelist Anatoly Kuznetsov, author of *Babi Yar*, left the Soviet Union and sought asylum in England. Greene wrote to *The Times* on 6 August 1969 asking his fellow novelists to join him in refusing permission for their works to be published in the Soviet Union 'so long as work by Solzhenitsyn is suppressed and Daniel and Sinyavsky remain in their prison camps'. The secret police soon claimed to have found letters from foreign authors including Greene in Kuznetsov's apartment; Greene denied this and took it as a sign that the authorities no longer trusted him.[13]

He made many such protests. In late 1956, the Russians had crushed the revolution in Hungary and killed or imprisoned many dissidents. Greene made a plea to the new Interior Minister for the release of Tibor Déry, an anti-Stalinist writer who had been spokesman for the now deposed government.[14] In 1958 Greene had privately urged the Soviet Union of Writers to allow Boris Pasternak to accept the Nobel Prize: at first he did accept it, but was pressured to decline, and was then persecuted until his death two years later.[15] Alexander Solzhenitsyn won the prize in 1970 but was unable to travel to Stockholm, for fear of not being allowed to return home; however, his undelivered lecture was eventually published in a pamphlet by Max Reinhardt and then printed in the *Listener*; Greene issued a statement through the BBC World Service about his 'excitement and admiration' upon reading it.[16] Reinhardt was actually Solzhenitsyn's British publisher, and Greene certainly approved of this.[17] As late as 1981, Greene turned down an invitation to Russia and Georgia because of the continued imprisonment of the mathematician Anatoly (Natan) Scharansky; Greene did not care to offer the Soviet government even a minor propaganda victory.[18]

He was especially involved with dissidents in Czechoslovakia. The emergence of Alexander Dubček as leader in January 1968 initiated the Prague Spring, a brief, lighted time in which it seemed possible for an Eastern Bloc country to reform its government and embrace human rights and free speech. However, the Kremlin was having none of it, and on 20–21 August 1968 sent in half a million troops.

Greene had visited Czechoslovakia before, notably at the time of the revolution in 1948, and had friends there. Since early 1966 he had been in contact with Josef Škvorecký, a novelist who was helping to translate some of his works. Škvorecký feared that he or his wife would soon be arrested, so the couple fled just before the invasion. He wrote to Greene asking for advice about political asylum and opportunities for work, but then he and his wife decided to risk a return to Czechoslovakia. They established a code phrase: if Škvorecký was arrested, his wife would send a message asking for permission to translate *The Man Within* and Greene would know it was time to go to the newspapers and begin agitating for his release.[19]

Škvorecký organized an invitation from the Union of Writers for Greene to visit Prague, but then finally decided the country was not safe and left for Canada. Greene arrived for his 'visit of protest' at the beginning of February and did all the things he normally refused to do in the West – met reporters, gave interviews, spoke on the radio. He met a good many of Škvorecký's friends, including the playwright Václav Havel, who would later become president of the Czech Republic. On the evening they met, Havel had just discovered a listening device in his ceiling and was suffering from the company of someone Greene believed to be a spy. Havel was afraid that Greene was not meeting 'representative' people so introduced him to some of his friends.[20]

Just before Greene's arrival, a young philosophy student had set himself on fire in the centre of Prague to protest the Soviet occupation. In an interview with the television journalist Karel Kyncl, Greene called this act 'courageous' and so gave offence to the government. His works soon ceased to be available in Czechoslovakia.[21] In 1972, Kyncl was sentenced to twenty months in prison for speaking out at the Union of Writers in defence of a dissident chess grandmaster and writer named Luděk Pachman. Kyncl fell seriously ill in prison, so Pachman approached Greene, who sent a letter to *The Times* in February 1973, urging the authorities to release the journalist.[22] Nothing happened, but word of Greene's appeal made its way to Kyncl and he immediately spread the news to fifty other political prisoners by tapping the novelist's name in Morse code on the water pipes. He later wrote to Greene: 'only a person who has spent at least a few weeks in prison can really perceive how we felt about the fact that the great author, whom we all highly respect and whose books we love, spoke out in our name'.[23]

With the help of Rodney Dennys, Greene was able to assist Kyncl's son, a photographer, to come to Britain in 1980 and start a new life.[24] However, Karel Kyncl himself remained in Czechoslovakia, eking out a living by selling ice cream and other such employments; he was eventually arrested again, for his work with the Charter 77 human rights group. Greene was a leading figure in protests that eventually secured his release in 1983, after which Kyncl took asylum in Britain.[25]

Although exiled, Josef Škvorecký remained Greene's main source of information about Czechoslovakia, writing him long letters full of news he picked up from his contacts over a period of twenty years, some of which Greene passed on to MI6. However, there was more to Škvorecký than a source of political intelligence. In the autumn of 1968, Greene read his novel *The Legend of Emöke* and was astounded, calling it a 'master work' and comparing it to Chekov.[26] When Škvorecký applied for a teaching position at the University of Toronto, Greene provided a reference that made similar claims. When Greene's niece Louise Dennys became a publisher in Toronto, he suggested that they work together. One of his novels, *The Engineer of Human Souls*, published by her firm Lester & Orpen Dennys, won Canada's highest literary prize, the Governor General's Literary Award, in 1984, and he was nominated for the Nobel Prize. He received many honours, of which the greatest may have come when a Czech astronomer discovered a very large piece of rock orbiting between Mars and Jupiter, and it was officially named Asteroid (26314) Škvorecký.[27]

62

BEHIND THE SAND DUNE

'I came back from a battle! I do seem to have a nose because I stumbled on the worst point of the worst incident in two months. For more than two and a half hours in the sun I had to lie with my companion & our driver on the side of a sand dune with artillery (anti-tank guns), mortars, & small arms fire. Alas. I'd only had lemonade for two days – I could have done with a whisky. As we were within a hundred yards of the Israelite artillery who didn't know we were there & which was the Egyptian objective, I really thought I'd had my last game of roulette.'[1]

It was 27 September 1967 and Graham Greene was experiencing the fourth month of the Six Day War – the violence continued long after the official ceasefire. In June, Israel had routed the forces of Egypt, Jordan, and Syria, and seized control of the Sinai, the Gaza Strip, the West Bank, and the Golan Heights. Greene was commissioned by the *Sunday Telegraph* to write about the aftermath of the war, and so arrived in Israel on 17 September 1967 and stayed for three weeks.[2]

Early in the visit he had dinner at an Arab restaurant in Jaffa with the architect of Israel's victory, the eye-patched defence minister Moshe Dayan. Also at the meal were his wife, who spoke in praise of Arabs, their daughter the novelist and future politician Yael Dayan, and her new husband. Greene stayed in touch with the younger couple throughout his visit. Much of the time, he was in the company of Israeli documentary-makers as he travelled throughout the country and the newly occupied territories. He spent a couple of nights in a kibbutz in Galilee and looked at fortifications in the Golan Heights. It was all fascinating, but he could find no fresh angle to write about. Then came the shelling.

Following the road taken into the northern Sinai by General Israel

Tal and his forces to the city of El Arish, Greene saw the burnt-out hulks of Egyptian tanks and trucks. After staying the night at Kantara on the east side of the Suez Canal, he travelled south with United Nations observers to four observation posts. At each, the officers made the ritual declaration, 'All peaceful'. At Bitter Lakes, Greene saw the so-called 'Yellow Fleet', fifteen ships trapped in the closed canal. They drove as far as Port Tewfik at the southern end and headed back, only to be warned of an 'incident' in the vicinity of Ismailia. With the traffic stopped, they were slow to take cover behind sand dunes, but then a shell flew overhead, landing close by, followed by two more, one landing close enough that a tiny piece of shrapnel hit an observer's face. Once they were behind a sand dune, he saw the man dabbing his cheek.

He had been told that 'incidents' were usually resolved within forty-five minutes, and a ceasefire arranged. Not this time. After a long delay, an Israeli artillery post almost directly behind their position returned fire, with the likelihood that the Egyptian artillery would now shorten its range and drop a shell on their hiding place. Greene took off his sunglasses so they would not break into his eyes, and thought of the Blitz, 'but the blitz had one great advantage – the pubs remained open'.[3]

Greene felt something close to panic, as he had felt when charged by the police at the Battle of Cable Street in 1936 and again at Phat Diem, when he momentarily wandered into the gap between French and Viet Minh fighters. He thought of the effect his death would have on Yvonne, and said 'Hail Marys' while trying to appear blasé and accustomed to battlefields.[4] There were five men hiding behind the dune; two drivers had run for the truck and made their escape. Too slow to join them, the rest stayed put, and when the firing died down they ran for a jeep and drove off at a speed that 'would have been reckless if it had not been prudent'.[5] And prudent it was, as shelling along the canal that day was reported to have killed a total of sixty-two Israelis and Egyptians.[6]

Malcolm Muggeridge was in the country with a BBC film crew; though old friends, he and Greene had had some quarrels and regarded each other as fairly treacherous. At this time Muggeridge was recovering a Christian faith; largely influenced by Mother Teresa, whom he made famous in the West through a 1969 documentary, he would later become a Catholic. Greene remarked with some asperity in a letter to

Yvonne that Muggeridge was 'giving absurd interviews about himself & Christ'.[7] They did, however, meet very amicably, and Muggeridge had an idea for the future: they should appear together on television when Greene turned eighty. Reminded of the plan years later Greene said no, as he nearly always refused to go on television and he hadn't expected to live so long.[8] When the day came for Muggeridge himself to be received into the Roman Catholic church, Greene wrote: 'I don't know whether to congratulate you or to commiserate with you on making your decision, but I can sincerely wish you good luck & I can also hope that you will make a better Catholic than I have done.'[9]

After his conversation with Muggeridge in Jerusalem, Greene was left to wonder what he himself made of being in the Holy Land. In his hotel room he wrote: 'Out of the window the lights of Bethany. One feels closer here, & in the Holy Sepulchre, to the man Jesus, the builder from Nazareth, but no closer to the God. The particulars, this landscape, the exposed rocky fragment of Golgotha belong to the man like the house where Tolstoy lived. But God seems no more connected with this place than with one of the innumerable stars.'[10]

Greene did feel connected to Israel. He felt that it had been entirely justified in the pre-emptive attacks that began the war, as the soldiers of Egypt were preparing to overrun the tiny state. He admired Dayan and a number of other leaders, especially the tolerant and pragmatic mayor of Jerusalem, Teddy Kollek. He remained a supporter of Israel for many years, and was proud to receive the Jerusalem Prize for the Freedom of the Individual in Society in 1981, but the people he admired generally belonged to the Labour Party. The Likud Party, under Menachem Begin, was elected in 1977, and after agreeing to the Camp David Accords of 1978 and the subsequent treaty with Egypt, it held to hard-line policies on permanent settlements in occupied areas and resisted significant concessions to its neighbours, so Greene's views changed. He remarked in 1988, when the party now led by Yitzhak Shamir was sharing power with Labour under Shimon Peres, that, proud as he was of the award, if it had been granted to him at that time he would have had to refuse it.[11] Also in 1988, he lent his name to protests on behalf of Mordechai Vanunu, the nuclear technician who provided the *Sunday Times* with firm evidence of Israel's nuclear arms programme; following a 'honey-pot' abduction scheme, this whistle-blower was brought back to Israel to stand trial and sentenced to eighteen years' imprisonment. In a telegram to the anti-nuclear campaigner Monsignor Bruce Kent, Greene described this as 'a disgrace to the government of Israel'.[12] Indeed, Amnesty International remains concerned about Vanunu's case; after he served his whole sentence, eleven years of it in solitary confinement, he was subject to bizarre restrictions on where he might live and whom he might talk to.[13] As late as 2017, he was convicted, for the third time, of an obscure violation of his terms of release.[14]

Graham Greene's visit to Israel put his life at risk, and over the years his travels to the dangerous places of the world caused enormous worry to his family and friends. In 1967, what went around came around, and Greene was himself the worrier. Working now as a freelance reporter, photographer and documentary-maker, thirty-one-year-old Francis Greene had been in Israel for the Six Day War itself. Immediately before the fighting began, he went to a sad feast in Tel Aviv attended by young people, some in uniform – they expected their country to be invaded and believed that in a few days most of those present would be dead. Francis went with the army in its storming of the Golan Heights and witnessed Israeli units moving quickly through minefields, without regard for their horrific casualties. One of the first reporters to reach the top of the Heights, he could hear Russian being spoken and worked out that some prisoners were Russian artillery instructors; they were soon permitted to leave via a secret rendezvous with a submarine. This was a major story, but as a freelancer he did not have the means to get it out in time. He then followed retreating Arab forces through Gaza, and went on foot into the Negev, where he briefly became lost.[15]

Francis also reported on the Vietnam War in 1967–8, and this led him into even greater peril. From October 1967, Graham was in frequent contact with Trevor Wilson, then posted in the Laotian city of Vientiane, seeking news of his son. Moving in remote parts of Laos, Francis was first arrested in November by CIA operatives in a helicopter, who confiscated his film.[16] Back in Vientiane, he was found to be suffering from 'malignant malaria' – an often fatal disease. Trevor Wilson reported to Graham that his fever reached 105°.[17] Writing to his father, Francis described himself 'as weak as a smoke ring',[18] but soon returned to his work. He was photographing in the old Imperial capital of Hué at the end of January, and was, again, lucky to escape with his life. He was on one of the last flights out before the Vietcong launched the Tet Offensive. During the three-week occupation of Hué, they executed any Westerners they could find, and any local person suspected of collaboration.

For much of the next month, Francis was out of contact in the Mekong Delta – Graham 'could hardly sleep at night'[19] and had to content himself with scraps of news from diplomats as he and Wilson fired off telegrams to anyone they could think of who might have seen him. Then, in early March, Francis and another journalist were detained by the Royal Laotian Army at the much-bombed Boloven Plateau at the southern end of the Ho Chi Minh Trail, where they had witnessed covert American military activity. Supposedly a 'protective arrest',[20] it was anything but: they were held naked in a cage and were likely to have been shot, except that Trevor Wilson was tipped off by a midnight telephone call from an anonymous American radio operator and then agitated for their release. As it was, Francis's exposure to the elements brought back symptoms of the illness he had suffered in December.[21] These troubles he accepted as part of his profession and so regarded Graham's search for him as somewhat tiresome, especially when he had to reimburse people for all the return telegrams. He wrote to his father and asked him to 'call off the hounds'.[22]

While Graham Greene could no longer undertake such arduous journeys himself, he followed developments in Vietnam and had even hoped to make a trip there in 1965, but was frustrated by visa difficulties. In the meantime, he was an inspiration to the new generation of reporters who wrote about the war, even if he did not always admire their work. When, some years later, a publisher sent him a copy of Michael Herr's memoir *Dispatches*, composed in driving rhythms like rock music, he wrote: 'I read *Dispatches* naturally with great interest. I was rather put off by the opening part which seemed to me too excitable, but Herr calmed down a bit later. I think when one is dealing with horrors one should write very coldly. Otherwise it reads like hidden boasting – "just see what a brave chap I am to have voluntarily put myself in the way of such experiences." To adapt Wordsworth, horror should be remembered in tranquility.'[23]

He frequently wrote letters to the newspapers about the conflict and thought that American policy was fundamentally unrealistic, since they failed to accept that much of the rural south was already in the hands of the communists. In his view, the only sensible course was for the Americans to negotiate with them – something that began fitfully in 1968. Apart from an extensive correspondence with opponents of the war, Greene made various public gestures. Most memorably, he tried in 1970 to organize a mass resignation of foreign members of the American Academy of Arts and Letters since it had not come out against the war. He could not persuade anyone to join him, so made his own stand: 'I have tried to put myself in the position of a foreign honorary member of a German Academy of Arts and Letters at the time when Hitler was democratically elected Chancellor. Could I have continued to consider as an honour a membership conferred in happier days?'[24] Of course, it changed nothing, and yet he did it. He was, after all, a reader of Cervantes.

63

A HOUSE SURROUNDED
BY ORANGE TREES

When *The Human Factor* went into a drawer towards the end of 1968, Greene began thinking of a banker named Henry Pulling who goes down a rabbit hole into the world inhabited by his Aunt Augusta. *Travels with My Aunt* was partly inspired by Greene's long friendship with the dottoressa Elisabeth Moor, the Austrian woman whose stories of a rackety life had captivated him whenever he went to Capri. The Australian-American writer Shirley Hazzard, a regular visitor to the island, recalled her: 'A squat, categorical figure, formless in winter bundling, the Dottoressa had the rugged, russet complexion of northerners long weathered in the hot south, prominent paleolithic teeth, and memorably pale blue eyes.'[1] In the mid-1970s, the photographer Islay de Courcy Lyons had attempted to write up Moor's tape-recorded memoirs; then Greene took over the job, added passages of his own in her style, and saw it into print as *An Impossible Woman* in 1975, figuring she would earn a much-needed £5000 from the book.[2] He described the dottoressa to Michael Korda as 'a combination of Chaucer's Good Wife of Bath and Mrs Bloom'.[3] This would also be an apt description of Aunt Augusta.

Greene could not decide whether this was to be a novel or an entertainment: 'I found more and more that the distinction was a bad one and that the two types of book came closer and closer to each other. I abandoned the distinction altogether in the case of *Travels with My Aunt*, which I thought was on one side quite a funny book and could be described as an entertainment but on the other hand it was a book that described old age and death.'[4]

Old age and death were on his mind, but so too were youth and memory. At the same time, he was working on his autobiography, something he had pursued in fits and starts for nearly twenty years. He had written an autobiographical 'screed' for Eric Strauss, and tried later to shape his life's story in terms of the many airports he had landed at, and on turning sixty in 1964 had produced a rather gloomy meditation, 'The Last Decade', on what his life had been and what he might yet expect, but as it turned out he had the better part of three decades still ahead of him. His uncertainty about autobiography as a form, and about the nature of his own experiences, came together in the title he finally decided on: *A Sort of Life.*

Relying on his often-mistaken memory, he confirmed few of the details, at times treated fact and personal myth in much the same manner, and exaggerated dramatic elements – a common flaw in the memoirs of novelists, whose craft is always to improve a story. Nonetheless, the outcome was an elegant and haunting account of sheltered early years, Judas-time in the dormitory, self-harm and attempts at suicide, and then growth into a novelist. By December 1967, the manuscript was forty-five thousand words long and he had reached the age of twenty-two in his account,[5] but he held this book back, perhaps to coordinate the launch with the first volumes of his new collected edition. Released in 1971, *A Sort of Life* was received, as Walter Clemons described it, as 'one of Graham Greene's best books'.[6]

With the past so much on his mind in late 1967, he went with Mario Soldati back to one of the great scenes of his earlier life – Sierra Leone – and wrote an article called 'The Soupsweet Land', which was an open-hearted love letter to West Africa.[7] Thinking of himself as a ghost, he was surprised to be recognized right away on the street and drawn into the company of old 'coasters'. The day after their arrival, he went to the little house in the flats he had occupied in 1942–3. It was still there, rats and all, but the swamp had been cleaned up and new buildings had improved the neighbourhood. He went to the Catholic church in Brookfield with the statue of St Anthony above the altar: 'What had I lost for him to find? The whole past.'[8]

It was not all nostalgia: Greene had picked, as he often did, a delicate moment for his journey, perhaps acting on a prompt from MI6. His journal shows that during the two-week visit he did some research on diamond mining. For many years this industry was dominated by

De Beers' Sierra Leone Selection Trust, but at times the firm was in conflict with many thousands of unlicensed indigenous miners whose stones were smuggled out of the country, mainly through Liberia, leading to tensions across the border. In 1967, there was an election in Sierra Leone, but the winner, Siaka Stevens, was immediately thrown into jail and the country experienced months of political crisis. Stevens took power again in early 1968 and turned diamonds into a political issue, encouraging the illicit miners. He nationalized the industry in 1971,[9] and he and his associates subsequently grew fat on the sale of diamonds. Stevens's legacy is complicated, as for some he is a pioneer of democracy and for others a killer and a thief.[10] 'Blood diamonds' or 'conflict diamonds' were a key factor in the hideous war that broke out in Sierra Leone in 1991, with different factions using them to pay for the fighting.[11] During his visit, Greene observed the De Beers mining sites and noted their elaborate security arrangements, and he also watched the work of some unlicensed miners. What he made of it all is not certain, as he did not turn his scattered observations into the proposed article on 'Post Colonialism'.[12]

Going back to Sierra Leone caused Greene to burrow even more deeply into distant memories. Among other things, it brought back to mind two brothers named Wordsworth he had met on his trek through Liberia. One was the district commissioner of Tappa Tee, a man of ferocious aspect, accused by local chiefs of oppression, though Barbara Greene discovered that he was actually 'shy and timid' and she could not believe the accusations. The younger Wordsworth asked for brandy and affected a swagger but yearned for affection. Speaking in the local dialect of English, he told the Greenes they were his best friends and begged them to write letters: 'He stood, a pathetic little figure, by the gateway of the compound, and watched us till we disappeared into the forest.'[13] Thirty-two years later, Greene created a character from Sierra Leone named Wordsworth, who is Aunt Augusta's lover. He begs cigarettes and is a drug smuggler, but by the end of the story lives up to his name as a pure romantic; although much of what he does is amusing, his death takes on dignity as he refuses a pay-off (or 'dash') to leave Aunt Augusta and return to Europe.

Greene's own return to Europe from Sierra Leone led him to break a cardinal rule: he submitted to a television interview. The documentary-maker Christopher Burstall proposed a clever format in which the camera might play on the novelist's hands but never on his face. Leaving from the Gare de Lyon on 4 April 1968,[14] they retraced the route of *Stamboul Train* from Paris to Istanbul, and Burstall recorded Greene's conversation over two days and three nights. Broadcast on the BBC's *Omnibus* on 17 November 1968, Burstall used old photographs and dramatizations of the novels to provide the visual element. The absence of the novelist's face added a man-of-mystery quirk to the production. When asked why he wanted to be interviewed this way, he said he was afraid of 'playing the part of a writer – part of a Catholic. I don't know, but I think it would be a little bit of a part. And I would cease to be a writer, and I would become a comedian. I feel myself infinitely corruptible. It is just possible that it might be successful and then I'd be tempted to do it again. Like a successful first night with a woman . . . '

Although he gave many interviews to print journalists, there was nothing in his career quite like this. He quoted a passage from Browning's poem 'Bishop Blougram's Apology' that he thought might serve as an epigram for all his works:

> Our interest's on the dangerous edge of things,
> The honest thief, the tender murderer,
> The superstitious atheist, demirep
> That loves and saves her soul in new French books –
> We watch while these in equilibrium keep,
> The giddy line midway . . .[15]

When asked about his attraction to seediness, he said, 'I think it's the same draw that a child has towards making a mud pie. Perhaps it's a certain remaining infantility in one's character. The seedy is nearer the beginning, isn't it – or nearer the end, I suppose.' Burstall asked why his books were set so far from England: 'It's a restlessness that I've always had to move around, and perhaps to see English characters in a setting which is not protective to them'[16] – a statement which hints at why it is difficult to fit Greene into standard academic arguments about the colonial impulse in literature. There was one more very surprising thing: Burstall asked him to speculate on what a heaven might be like – he obliged, and what he said will come up again later in this book.

The Orient Express was no longer so glamorous as in the 1930s, and Greene brought the modern, more workaday train service into *Travels with My Aunt*; it is a challenge for his characters even to get meals as they roll towards Istanbul, and at one point Henry counts himself lucky to get six ham rolls off a trolley. On the train, Henry encounters the uninhibited young wanderer Tooley and unwittingly smokes some pot she has obtained from the in-all-places-at-once Wordsworth. They talk about travel, love, religion, sex, and the CIA, and she eventually discloses the fear that she is pregnant by a hitchhiking boyfriend (whereabouts unknown). Inevitably, Henry falls a little in love with her.

The novel proceeds according to a strange logic, which at times is dream-like, and, indeed, Greene had resumed recording his own dreams systematically in a diary in the 1960s. This may have affected his way of telling a story, as many of his late narratives are similarly enigmatic. Aunt Augusta belongs to the lawless world of dreams, and for Henry Pulling to find himself he needs a little lawlessness. He also needs to be made vulnerable. As Greene told Burstall, he liked to see his English characters in settings that did not protect them; so, it was necessary to bring Henry to 'the dangerous edge of things'.

At about this time, Greene was considering a visit to Paraguay, a repressive country with no industry to speak of, apart from smuggling. One of its distinctions was that its primary language was not Spanish or Portuguese, but Guaraní. He had been interested in this place for almost forty years, as around 1929 he had met the social reformer and historian R. B. Cunninghame Graham,[17] who wrote of the Jesuit *reducciones* in Paraguay, a religious and social experiment that survives in modern memory through the film *The Mission*.

In the early seventeenth century, the Society of Jesus attempted to create what amounted to an indigenous republic among the Guaraní of north-east Paraguay. By 1732, about 140,000 people lived in communes with shared ownership of most possessions. The Jesuits assigned just two priests to each of thirty missions, which would have had an average population of 4500, so they had little power of compulsion – the Guaraní lived in these places by choice. The Jesuits, of course, worked to make Catholics of the Guaraní; they also encouraged the development of a rich musical, artistic, and technical culture.[18] For a time they were successful in protecting the Guaraní against slavers, but were finally overmatched, as many thousands were abducted and forced to work in Brazil. The priests were expelled and the *reducciones* destroyed; Cunninghame Graham called it, rather romantically, 'A Vanished Arcadia'.[19] Having made an enemy of the Portuguese government, the Jesuit order was suppressed by Rome in 1773, although it continued to exist vestigially in Russia and a few other places, before being revived in 1814. The history of the *reducciones* took on an enormous importance in the evolution of Catholic social thought, and Graham Greene in particular gave a good deal of consideration to it. He longed for a non-Marxist alternative to capitalism that would be respectful of indigenous peoples, and the *reducciones* contained the seed of such a thing.

In 1938, he had pitched a book about Paraguay to his agent. From 1932 to 1935, the country had fought its neighbour Bolivia, another landlocked country, over possession of the desolate Chaco region, thought to have oil reserves, and over control of rivers that would, with Argentina's cooperation, give access to the sea. It was a dire conflict in which nearly a hundred thousand people died.[20] Paraguay won, partly owing to the support of Argentina, but was internally riven with coups and revolutions. At the time, Greene saw in Paraguay 'the totalitarian state transported to the center of South America'.[21]

And he was right. A civil war fought in 1947 saw the deaths of another fifty thousand people and the emergence of the right-wing Colorado Party as the dominant force in the country.[22] In 1954, General Alfredo Stroessner, afterwards known as 'El Excelentísimo',[23] seized control and ruled as dictator for thirty-four years. His regime was nationalist, corrupt, and repressive, and it maintained a large force of paramilitary killers. Since it had democratic pretensions and hunted down possible communists, the regime enjoyed American support. He had no real policy platform, and ran the country on the basis of what one historian has called 'neo-sultanism'[24] – he gave orders and expected them to be obeyed.

From the mid-1970s, Paraguay was a very active participant in 'Operation Condor' along with Chile, Argentina, Uruguay, Bolivia, Brazil, and later Peru and Ecuador. This secret cross-border arrangement, backed by the CIA, facilitated the pursuit, torture, and killing of supposed subversives. In 1992, an enormous cache of records now known as the 'Archives of Terror' was discovered in Asunción, the

Paraguayan capital, documenting the deaths, disappearances, illegal detention, or torture of hundreds of thousands of people throughout Latin America.[25] Some of these documents were later used in the prosecution of Augusto Pinochet, dictator of Chile from 1973 to 1990. The Truth and Justice Commission/Commission for Historical Memory of Paraguay found that under Stroessner 19,862 people were detained illegally, 19,722 tortured, and 459 murdered or disappeared. It is hard to deny the dictator's close involvement in all of this, as his summer residence near Ciudad del Este, known as the 'house of horrors', was understood to be a centre for torture; human remains were discovered there, under the floor of a bathroom, in 2019.[26]

Greene arrived in Buenos Aires in mid-July 1968 and found himself treated like a film star, pursued by the press and by amorous women.[27] He planned to travel up the Paraná River, which formed a boundary between the countries, to Asunción, but was delayed two weeks trying to organize his passage.

His main contact in Argentina was his publisher and translator, Victoria Ocampo, whom he had first met in 1938 and for whom he had a considerable fondness though they seldom saw each other. A leading figure in South American letters, she owned two houses, now UNESCO sites, one in San Isidro outside Buenos Aires and the other in Mar del Plato, to which she welcomed many authors and intellectuals, including Rabindranath Tagore and Albert Camus. She had a mystical bent, with interest in the Gospels, Dante, Buddhism, and the teachings of Mahatma Gandhi, and this combination led her to pursue social justice and, especially, women's rights.[28] An opponent of Juan Perón, whom she regarded as a fascist, she had been imprisoned for a month in 1953 as the police tried, without evidence, to connect her to a bomb attack on the leader.[29]

At the time of Greene's visit in 1968, Argentina was under the authoritarian rule of General Juan Carlos Onganía, and there was unrest in the country. The northern state of Tucumán was near insurrection, largely over wages in the sugar industry; in the absence of labour leaders, parish priests led the protests.[30] At the same time, the Montonero rebel group, consisting of Catholics, socialists, and left-wing Peronistas, pursued a small-scale urban insurgency, and would make international headlines two years later by kidnapping and killing a

Carol Reed was Graham Greene's favourite director. They worked together on three films, including *The Third Man*.

Max Reinhardt became one of Graham Greene's closest friends and his publisher at the Bodley Head.

Graham Greene often sailed the Mediterranean and Adriatic with his friend Alexander Korda, on the film producer's 120-foot yacht *Elsewhere*.

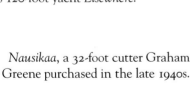

Nausikaa, a 32-foot cutter Graham Greene purchased in the late 1940s.

'All I know about the story is a man "who turns up" . . . the place where he emerges into my semi-consciousness is a leper station, many hundred miles up the Congo.' Researching *A Burnt-Out Case*, Greene travelled on a paddle-steamer to visit church-run leproseries.

'What an extraordinary thing it was that a tiny country like Panama produced one of the great men of our time': Graham Greene and the country's leader Omar Torrijos, who renegotiated the Canal Treaty.

A former schoolteacher, Fred Baptiste led a tiny rebel band against the forces of the Haitian dictator 'Papa Doc'. Greene modelled a fighting force on them in *The Comedians*.

'¡Viva Cristo Rey!': Padre Miguel Pro, executed in 1927, was regarded as a martyr by the persecuted Mexican church, and was part of the inspiration for *Lawless Roads* and *The Power and the Glory*.

Travelling along the border of the Dominican Republic and Haiti in 1965, Greene, a known enemy of the Haitian regime, daringly stepped a few feet across the border while soldiers had weapons trained on him.

'President for Life' François 'Papa Doc' Duvalier kept a copy of *The Comedians* on his desk along with a Bible and a revolver. He was tempted to have Graham Greene assassinated for portraying repression in Haiti.

In 1956, in the peaceful days before Papa Doc took power, Graham Greene and Catherine Walston visited Haiti and spent time with some of the country's leading artists, finding their works extraordinary.

Greene and his Panamanian friend Chuchu Martínez in the cockpit of a single-engine Cessna, which Chuchu used to run arms to Nicaraguan rebels. Greene describes such a plane in his last novel, *The Captain and the Enemy*.

Planter's punch on the island of Contadora: the Panamanian power-broker Rory Gonzalez, Graham Greene, and the journalist Bernard Diederich who guided the novelist through Haiti and Central America.

Father Robert Willichs, a Belgian missionary to Vietnam, heard Graham Greene's confession in a bell-tower during a battle at Phat Diem in 1951.

A leading figure in South American letters, Victoria Ocampo was Graham Greene's publisher in Argentina and one of his closest friends. She was briefly imprisoned for her opposition to Juan Perón.

The penetration agent Kim Philby and his fourth wife, Rufina. Greene had been his subordinate at MI6 and defended him staunchly after his defection in 1963.

Graham Greene and Bernard Diederich at their last meeting in Antibes in 1989.

Greene's lover for thirty-two years, Yvonne Cloetta, stands
beside his grave in Corseaux, Switzerland.

In 1966, Greene purchased a small flat in Antibes overlooking the harbour, and it remained his home until the last months of his life.

former president, Pedro Eugenio Aramburu; this group became a special target of right-wing Peronistas once the Dirty War started in 1974.[31]

Ocampo arranged for Greene to spend an evening with a 'clandestine' group of young Catholic revolutionaries, whom he thought naive and in love with theories. However, some of what they said did get his attention. They told him that in Paraguay opponents of the regime had been flung from planes and that their bodies, with hands bound, had been known to wash up on the Argentine bank of the Paraná – he did not know whether to believe them.[32] This was early evidence of the death flights which were later common practice in several South American countries. The best-known victim of a death flight was the Argentine chemist Esther Ballestrino, a very close friend of Jorge Bergoglio, the future Pope Francis.

Greene was struck by the young people's devotion to Camilo Torres, a Colombian priest and sociologist who had joined a group of rebels and been killed in a skirmish in 1966. He is now regarded as one of the pioneers of liberation theology, which sought to reconcile the demands of the Gospel with a Marxist critique of class relations, but it is actually a very loose term, and can include quite traditional thinking about doctrine, a gradual approach to social reform, and a commitment to non-violence. Because Father Torres took up arms, his legacy is controversial. There were many other priests who joined revolutionary movements or endorsed them, but Torres stands out partly because he could turn a phrase: 'I took off my cassock to be more truly a priest'; 'The duty of every Catholic is to be a revolutionary. The duty of every revolutionary is to make the revolution'; 'The Catholic who is not a revolutionary is living in mortal sin.'[33] Greene spoke of him as the 'Catholic equivalent of Che Guevara',[34] but he had little hope for the struggle such men were waging. Torres lodged in Greene's imagination and was part of the inspiration for the rebel priest Father Rivas in his next novel, *The Honorary Consul*, also set largely in Paraguay. Greene later told Bernard Diederich that Torres was a 'romantic' figure and so somewhat different from Father Rivas.[35] Nonetheless, had there been no Torres, there would have been no Rivas.

Greene finally got on a steamboat on 1 August 1968 for the 1300-kilometre river voyage north to Asunción, a journey with its absurd aspects: among the passengers was a Hungarian plastics manufacturer trying to find a buyer for two million drinking straws.[36] Greene worked him into the story. The five-day journey provided the background for an encounter between Henry and Tooley's father, a CIA operative obsessed with his own bladder. Indeed, the comic and pathetic elements of his novel at times mask an underlying horror at the political situation of Paraguay. Sailing north, he looked upon the fallen walls of the *reducciones* on either side of the river as if they contained the lost promise of justice and peace.

Arriving in Asunción for a three-week stay, he had a brief encounter with the press but was then left alone. He met the British ambassador, who told him that artists accepted certain rules of censorship here and must not openly criticize the United States.[37] Greene noted that such constraints were intolerable to the leading Paraguayan writer, Augusto Roa Bastos, a magic realist who spent most of his career in exile. Greene received a letter from Stroessner saying he was 'gratified' that the novelist was there in time for his inauguration to a new term as president and offering him any help he could[38] – he had no idea the Englishman was about to embarrass him much as he had recently embarrassed the President for Life of Haiti.

Greene did meet members of the government but was more interested in the activities of the Jesuits, who were trying to create a new kind of Catholicism in Paraguay, peacefully emphasizing the rights and dignity of the Guaraní and encouraging the formation of peasant cooperatives. He admired these priests, but again had little hope of them succeeding. It was dangerous work in a right-wing dictatorship; as the Brazilian Archbishop Dom Hélder Câmara put it: 'When I give food to the poor, they call me a saint. When I ask why they're poor, they call me a communist.'[39] In 1969, the police invaded a church in Asunción in search of radical Jesuits and beat up some elderly priests, an act for which the Minister of the Interior was excommunicated.[40] For obvious reasons, the regime preferred the traditional clergy of monsignors and army chaplains, who, in the midst of a malnourished country, specialized in grace after meals.

Paraguay had a superficial air of peace, which would suit the dreamlike but menacing conclusion of his novel. The flowers of the capital alone were intoxicating. He came upon a large old house, which later provided the setting for the last section of his novel. It had a garden, sweet-smelling with jasmine and roses. Oranges fell to the ground and lay ungathered. There were also lemon, grapefruit, and palm trees in this Eden of privileges. It could be purchased for £3000 and the necessary servants employed for just £40 per month. Greene later framed his article on Paraguay with descriptions of this house. It stood as a temptation. One could end one's life as a lotus eater in a country without income tax and in such a house. The additional cost would be bearable – just living in a military dictatorship: 'Only 150 men in the police station cells to forget and the children dying of malnutrition – no evil comparable at all to the wholesale massacres in Biafra and Vietnam. Perhaps if one were sufficiently fond of beef . . . '[41]

64

NO ONE'S POODLE

'W ould rather change publisher than title. Graham Greene.'[1] So the novelist cabled his New York agent Monica McCall when Viking Press asked that he make a switch; they also published John Steinbeck's *Travels with Charley* and did not wish to introduce confusion into their list by the addition of an aunt.[2] No one's poodle, Greene stuck by *Travels with My Aunt* and, and in August 1969 asked Michael Korda, to whom he had once handed a first martini in the *Elsewhere*, and whom he had introduced to a brothel in Nice and a sailors' drag bar in Genoa, to become his new publisher in the United States. By then a senior figure at Simon & Schuster, Korda answered 'yes yes yes'.[3]

Greene had no more patience with Viking. He had been furious when they refused to make a quick pay-out of the money from *The Comedians* in early 1967 (see p. 370), and this request for a change of title merely proved, to him at least, that they were not only skinflints but had no clue about his work. As it played out, Viking did publish *Travels with My Aunt*, and Greene worked with them on other books, but Michael Korda became his main publisher in the United States.

Travels with My Aunt was released in the United Kingdom in November 1969, and in the United States two months later. The novelist and playwright Nigel Dennis was mightily amused and wrote that the book was about sin – the almost unforgivable sin of respectability – and that Greene, as ever, wanted to 'to get our goat, to tread on our Bunyans'.[4] On the whole, however, Greene was disappointed that British reviewers would not, as he put it, allow him to be funny.[5]

He had a good time writing this story and assumed it would soon be made into a film. The producer Robert Fryer, backed by MGM, bought the rights for about $110,000,[6] but that was all the pleasure Greene got out of it. The script abandoned much of the plot, including the ending. Maggie Smith played the lead in a very weak film, released in December 1972, and Greene found it unwatchable.[7] In fact, in the coming years, he would have little to do with the films made from his novels. When *England Made Me* was finally filmed in 1972, he attended a viewing and left a note for the director, Peter Duffell: 'Pleased enough.' He was far less pleased with nearly bankrupt Otto Preminger's version of *The Human Factor*, which despite a solid script by Tom Stoppard moved at a glacial pace and had lost all the intensity of the original. After years of struggle to find financing and arrive at a final script, a fairly flat production of *The Honorary Consul* came to the screen in 1983 under the title *Beyond the Limit*, with Michael Caine and Richard Gere the leads. Greene is reputed to have approached Caine in a restaurant and said that he hated the film, but liked his performance.[8]

At the end of 1969 Greene felt that he had more to say about South America. There had recently been at least half a dozen high-profile kidnappings; most notably, the American ambassador to Guatemala had been killed in an attempted abduction, and the American ambassador to Brazil had been kidnapped and released after three days.[9] Usually, the captors sought to exchange their hostages for political prisoners, of whom there were a vast number in South American dictatorships.

He was thinking of a new novel[10] to be set, possibly, in a river port on the Paraná, about a botched abduction. The rebel group would be seeking to capture the American ambassador, but instead end up with the tiniest of diplomatic fish, a British honorary consul. Greene had already named the consul Charlie Fortnum, after the Piccadilly grocer, and his friend the physician Eduardo Plarr, and put together an outline of chapters.[11]

Colombia was 'the classic country of guerrillas', where Camilo Torres had been killed and where the new theology was springing up, so he gave some thought to setting the book there. He was particularly interested in an organization of about fifty left-wing priests there called the Golconda Group: politicians denounced it as subversive, and conservative prelates tried to stamp it out.[12] He wanted to observe the Colombian elections to be held in April, the results of which he understood to be fixed in advance in favour of the country's traditional rulers,[13] but it turned out that Argentina and Paraguay could offer him more than enough material for his story.

'Overtaken by events', he wrote in his journal on 26 March 1970.[14] He had flown to Buenos Aires a week before, and then spent a few rainy days with Victoria Ocampo at Mar del Plato, before flying on to Corrientes, a border city on the Argentine side of the Paraná, which he had observed briefly on his earlier voyage upriver to Asunción, and stayed there for eight days. As he put it to Catherine: 'Nobody could understand why I was going there. It's very hot and humid, they said (and that was true) and nothing ever happens there. (That wasn't). I flew up in the same plane as the governor who passed a decree making me the guest of the province so I paid for nothing ... hotel, drinks all free.'[15] He encountered a community of British expatriates, and visited a brothel and a camp outside the city – all of these featured in the novel.

But then came news that a Paraguayan consul named Waldemar Sánchez had been kidnapped by the Argentine Liberation Front. He had been in Buenos Aires, trying to sell his just-imported Mercedes-Benz to prospective buyers who turned out to be rebels – this detail prompted Greene to have Fortnum importing and selling a Cadillac from time to time as a matter of diplomatic privilege. In their communiqués, the captors described Sánchez as a CIA operative and said he would be shot if two men held by the Argentine government were not released. The government took a hard line and refused these terms, and, without interrupting his fishing holiday in Argentina, General Stroessner announced that he could accept the death of the consul. After eighty hours in captivity and an extension of the deadline, the blindfolded Sánchez was released near a train station in Corrientes. Greene heard that the rebels had probably abducted the wrong man: 'More & more like my own story.'[16]

Greene cut out a long article on the abduction from a Corrientes newspaper and had it translated for further study.[17] Meanwhile, he and his guide, an airport manager, came upon the scene of a murder. The police were going about their work and Greene, seeing the corpse covered by a long sheet of paper with only its toes showing, asked if he might photograph it; he was taken aback when they actually peeled away the sheet to reveal the body with its knife wounds, and yet, to Greene's mind, the man looked 'peaceful'. The killing was not political, but just something between friends – a matter of smuggling, or merely of *machismo*.[18] Indeed, some male characters in *The Honorary Consul*, notably the novelist Saavedra, are obsessed with this sense of sexual honour, which Greene himself found unfathomable. Also, during Greene's visit, a man locked the doors of his car and drove with his family into the river, killing them all.[19]

In this city where nothing was supposed to happen, there was yet more trouble. Greene met with and liked Father Raúl Oscar Marturet, a member of the 'Third World Movement' of priests, which had the support of perhaps 10 per cent of Argentine clergy, including a few bishops. Their views were progressive but diverse,[20] and in many cases no more radical than those of Pope Paul himself, whose 1967 encyclical, *Populorum Progressio*, espoused many points of social justice. Even so, Monsignor Francisco Vicentín, the old-school Archbishop of Corrientes, had encouraged the police to harass Marturet, who finally went to court and had Vicentín arrested. Vicentín then excommunicated Marturet, a measure that was rescinded by Rome in 2016, by which time the priest was long dead.[21] Vicentín tried to replace him with a more pliant priest, who showed up with some supporters to take over the church, only to be fought off by the parishioners who were stalwarts of Marturet. In a series of such confrontations Vicentín closed four churches with the backing not only of the police but of an infantry brigade. Just before returning to Europe, Greene made a statement to the press supporting Marturet, saying that the Third World organization was doing 'great work'.[22]

He got down to writing the novel in Anacapri at the beginning of June 1970. It made good progress, though he recalled the writing as difficult; he had about forty thousand words written by September, and reported to Marie Biche in July 1971 that he had completed seventy thousand, but it took until June 1972 for him to complete his typescript, at 91,500 words.[23] He revised it extensively and the result was a novel he particularly favoured. He conceived *Travels with My Aunt* as loosely structured and so wrote on ordinary-sized paper, but *The Honorary Consul* was to be tightly plotted so he used foolscap.[24] It was an odd discipline, but it may have reminded him of how each word he wrote must fit a larger design.

Part of the challenge of this book was to weave in ideas he had about the compassion of God. For many years he had had an offbeat interest in Manichaeism; an ancient religion that once rivalled Christianity, it imagined God to have a dual nature, good and evil in perpetual struggle. In 1947, Greene had read *The Medieval Manichee* by Steven Runciman, and wrote to Catherine Walston: 'I've almost come to the conclusion that I'm a good Gnostic instead of a bad Catholic. It's much more convenient. Even *The Power & the Glory* is a Gnostic phrase & not a Catholic one.'[25]

The problem for Greene was that he could not take the idea of a devil very seriously, and if there was evil in the world God must be in some sense answerable for it; neither free will nor Original Sin offered a serious explanation for the way an omnipotent God had placed human beings in unbearable circumstances.

Seeing poverty and repression all around him, in the novel Father Rivas agonizes over this question and offers a tentative solution: 'He has to be a God made in our image with a night-side as well as a day-side. When you speak of the horror, Eduardo, you are speaking to the night-side of God. I believe the time will come when the night-side will wither away ... It is a long struggle and a long suffering, evolution, and I believe God is suffering the same evolution that we are, but perhaps with more pain.'[26] In addition to Manichaeism, Rivas is espousing what is called 'process theology'. Sometimes Teilhard de Chardin is claimed as a process theologian, but the names most commonly associated with this wide-ranging school of thought are Alfred Whitehead and Charles Hartshorne, and not all theologians of this school are Christian. They regard God not as a psychological construct, but as really existing. Their essential claim is that God is Himself subject to the sorrows and flux of time, and is evolving. According to process theology, God cannot force final outcomes in the material order, though he may create possibilities for free beings to accept or reject.[27]

There was no reason to rush into print with *The Honorary Consul*, as *A Sort of Life* came out in September 1971 and the volumes of his *Collected Edition* were being released at intervals. His introductions to the individual novels, drafted in the early 1960s for a German edition,[28] appeared in the *Daily Telegraph Magazine* from 1970 to 1974, and Greene thought that together they could form a second volume of autobiography. In the late 1970s, his niece, the publisher Louise Dennys, did the necessary editorial work, stitching together the introductions and some other articles Greene had written over the years. It was published as *Ways of Escape* in 1980.

The delay with *The Honorary Consul* also allowed Greene to find out more about South America – and he did owe the *Observer* an article, having accepted payment some time before to write a piece about Finland, which never materialized. He wanted to meet Salvador Allende, the socialist president of Chile, who took power in November 1970. Allende saw foreign exploitation of Chilean resources as a major cause of poverty, so he nationalized copper mines owned by the huge American firm Anaconda, later offering minimal compensation from which the company's 'excess profits' were deducted. He took similar steps against other companies, causing outrage among foreign investors.[29] As is well known, the Nixon administration saw him as a communist enemy of the United States, and worked first to prevent his election and then to bring about his downfall. Allende died during a CIA-assisted coup on 11 September 1973 which brought to power the junta dominated by General Augusto Pinochet.

The Prague Spring had taught Greene that democratic socialists would always be playing a weak hand, and he was discouraged by recent events. In March 1971, Fidel Castro unveiled a new forced labour scheme for 'vagrants' and 'parasites'[30] – all too reminiscent of the UMAP camps that Greene had objected to on his last visit. Greene wrote to Victoria Ocampo: ' . . . the situation in Cuba seems to be turning sour so that I am beginning to despair of a human face to communism!'[31]

In May 1971, Ocampo arranged for Greene to meet the poet Pablo Neruda, now Allende's ambassador to France. It was, perhaps, just chance that the two writers had not met before. In 1952, Neruda, then exiled, spent a year on Capri in a house owned by Greene's friend, the engineer and sometime mayor of Capri, Edwin Cerio – this time in Neruda's life would later inspire the film *Il Postino*. Greene wrote to Ocampo: ' . . . I went and had lunch with Neruda and to my astonishment found myself rather liking him. Perhaps he was showing his best side. Within half an hour we were Graham and Pablo to each other. He has sent a telegram to Doctor Allende asking him to receive me . . .'[32] Neruda lived only two more years. Supposedly suffering from prostate cancer, he died in a Santiago hospital two weeks after the coup, and evidence has since emerged suggesting that the Nobel laureate was poisoned.[33]

Arriving in Buenos Aires on the heels of a tornado on 11 September 1971, Greene again stayed with Ocampo, who set up a meeting for him with the short-story writer Jorge Luis Borges. Perennial contenders, both writers failed to win the Nobel Prize. In 1967, they were under consideration until the very end of the process. That year, Greene had the support of the permanent secretary of the Swedish Academy, Anders Österling, but three other members disagreed and the prize went to Guatemala's Miguel Angel Asturias.[34] Of course, since Leo Tolstoy, Henry James, and James Joyce were also denied the prize, it is possible that by being snubbed Greene and Borges were in better company than if they had won.

Meeting Borges proved a delight for Greene. It was explained to him that as an enemy of the former president Juan Perón, who was exiled in 1955 but would return to power in 1973, Borges was in some danger from his followers. He lived with his ancient and unflappable mother, who picked up the telephone one day only to be told they would both be killed. She answered: 'As my son is blind you will find that easy – as for me you had better do it soon since I am over 90.'[35] Greene was impressed.

Sent to fetch Borges from the National Library, he immediately liked the man, and was dazzled by his ability to quote poetry, even in Old English, which he had memorized as his sight failed: 'I wasn't going to trumpet my self-pity. My mother wanted me to learn Greek, but so many people know Greek.' They spoke of G. K. Chesterton and Robert Louis Stevenson: Greene could only remember a few words from Stevenson's poem 'Say not of me that weakly I declined', and as they were about to cross a street Borges paused on the pavement and quoted it perfectly.

At lunch Greene observed his 'angelic' expression while gazing into the corner of the room. Of course, Greene thought his politics 'very conservative'. When Greene said that he had found Paraguay 'beautiful' but disliked its leaders, Borges remarked, 'It's better than here. A Dictator should know his own mind, not like the one we have here.'[36] Presumably, he was referring to the Argentine General Alejandro

Lanusse's cautious movement towards elections and a compromise with the Peronistas. Greene did not share his views about Lanusse, and believed that an unsuccessful plot to overthrow him about a month later, while he was meeting Allende at the Chilean port of Antofagasta, was a very dangerous matter.[37]

Greene flew to Santiago on 17 September 1971 and had his first meeting with Salvador Allende that afternoon; they briefly discussed aspects of his political programme. He struck Greene as a technocrat, and this was a 'refreshing change from charisma. At my age charisma begins to lose appeal. One prefers a doctor for one's sickness.'[38] Throughout his life Greene had been intrigued by charismatic leaders, but this remark may specifically indicate his disappointment with Fidel Castro. He heard that one of the right-wing newspapers had published a report that this was not the real Graham Greene in Chile, but an impostor[39] – he had been confused again for the 'other'.

Allende thought this Greene was real enough, and lavished attention on him. At a lunch on 21 September he assembled the most important members of his government to meet the visiting novelist, among them Chief Economic Minister Pedro Vukovic, David Baytelman, who was in charge of land reform, and the Finance Minister Américo Zorillo. Conversation ranged over the possibility of rationing, a blockade, and the military threat from Bolivia and Brazil as proxies of the United States. Rather bluntly, Greene questioned Baytelman about whether land reform in Chile might fail as collectivisation had failed in Cuba.[40] During his visit, there was constant unease about a possible coup, and he took it as ominous when Radomiro Tomic, the leader of the opposition Christian Democrats, was uncertain whether the next presidential election would take place at all: he wondered if they might instead have a government of 'colonels'.[41]

Greene spoke little Spanish, so Luis Poirot, known as 'Lucho', a photographer and theatrical director whom Allende trusted, translated their conversations into French; he also served as Greene's main guide, driving him about in in his mother-in-law's red Austin Mini. When he first met him at Santiago's Hotel Carrera, he saw that he had already unpacked a teddy bear, his companion on many journeys, and placed him in the middle of the bed. He had also placed a bottle of Cutty Sark on the nightstand. Discovering that Greene disliked being photographed, he took no pictures, but listened carefully to his conversation and learned that the novelist distrusted the Christian Democrats, especially one of their leaders Patricio Aylwin,[42] who went on to support the coup but eventually became an opponent of Pinochet and succeeded him as the country's leader in 1989.

He visited copper and nitrate mines and a large textile mill, trying to find out how the workers were treated, and he spent time at Valparaiso, where he met with university students. He witnessed a good deal of misery: those who did best were copper miners who took good wages in exchange for the risk of silicosis, of which many were dying. He also met some priests who had allied themselves with Allende, and for whom the glory of God was in the barrios, and he approved of them.

Leaving the country on 11 October, he set to work on 'Chile: The Dangerous Edge', describing the regime, the economy, the church, and the threat of a coup, and sent it to the *Observer*. Over the years, Greene had had several spats with the editor, David Astor, and for a time would not write for the newspaper at all. When another of the editors, Richard Hall, showed Astor the list of forthcoming articles on a clipboard, Astor said: 'I should not like that. Greene is mischievous. He is anti-American. He is a fellow-traveller.' Hall was himself deeply moved by the article and waited until Astor was on holiday to slip the feature into print on 2 January 1972. When Astor returned, he made no comment, but soon ran another article as what Hall called a 'counter-blast', but its purpose failed since the author took much the same line as Greene. Hall spoke of Greene's article as 'terribly prescient': 'Of all the many pieces of writing I have steered into print over the years, that is the one of which I am most proud . . . '[43]

65

LIGHT BULBS

Dorothy Glover once claimed that her diet consistently solely of avocado pears.[1] In the 1960s, she was not especially well, ate poorly, and seems to have drunk a good deal. She had ceased to publish new children's works and had little to do that was satisfying. While she could rouse herself and be pleasant at parties, she was inclined to melancholia, which she poured out to Graham – so much so that he once dreamt of reproaching her for this and was told in the dream that it was just her nature.[2] As he had bought a house for Anita Björk, so he provided Dorothy with a pension and contributed to her purchase of a cottage, where she lived with her mother, in Crowborough, the same town where Charles and Marion Greene, Elisabeth and Rodney Dennys, and indeed the Philbys, had all lived at various times.

Around the end of November 1971, Graham noticed that she had not drawn her pension from the bank and thought something must be wrong. He soon found out that on 23 November the seventy-year-old Dorothy had died suddenly while sitting at the dining-room table. In a macabre touch, her infirm mother, still very much alive, was sitting beside her. Yvonne Cloetta said that she only saw him cry twice in their relationship, and one of them was upon hearing of Dorothy's death, when he shed 'bitter tears'.[3] He made a depressing journey from Antibes to organize her funeral. She had made him her executor, so there were many details to take care of with regard to her books and papers and, of course, her mother.[4] One aspect of her small legacy as a writer and illustrator vanished in 1973–4, when the Bodley Head republished Graham's four children's books with new illustrations by Edward Ardizzone.[5]

Although something of a burden, Dorothy had always been precious to Graham. It seems that the year that followed her death was a low time for him, and that he relied very heavily on Yvonne, but he was afraid she might end their relationship as Jacques was making a stand against the affair, and there was talk of the family moving to Switzerland.[6]

These worries passed, and he had the novel to absorb his attention, but he felt lonely. In the late winter, he wrote to the South African novelist Etienne Leroux (pseudonym of Stephanus le Roux), who had visited him not long before, about the state of things in Antibes: 'I can't remember whether the new port had been started when you were here last. It's now nearly finished except for the gardens which are going to be planted outside my windows. I hope the value of the apartment has risen to atone for all the dust and noise we have suffered for more than a year … I am not sure whether the whores are still in the Hotel Metropole. The bar has changed completely and become clean and a pizzeria … The mysterious man with the Mercedes who used to turn up in the old days is now wanted by the police both in Italy and in France and is rumoured to have escaped to Morocco. We have our dramas. I expect you read about the boat which was chased and shot at from Villefranche nearly to Marseilles which was over-loaded with heroin.'[7]

'We have our dramas.' Indeed. He still suffered from a mood disorder and Yvonne saw that he would be absorbed in 'violent urges' for a time, only to emerge and curse himself for what he had said or done.[8] But in his private life the dramas became fewer and fewer. Although they had quarrels from time to time, Graham and Yvonne had a calmer and more durable relationship than any he had had in the past, and this was partly owing to his improved state of mind.

The journalist Julian Evans knew Yvonne well and thought her intuitive, generous, and 'bloody intelligent'.[9] The Canadian scholar Judith Adamson witnessed a flash of her insight in a conversation between Graham and Yvonne about *Brighton Rock*. Graham remarked: 'It's going into its 50th printing. It's very popular. Who can identify with Pinkie?' Yvonne answered that women would see something of their husbands in him, to which he replied, 'I hope not.'[10]

Her attitude was practical, and she had no time for myths about Graham: 'People often called him "the hunted man", but he was only ever hunted by himself, a victim of the traps that, unconsciously or not, he had set up around himself.'[11] It would be hard to improve on that insight. Elisabeth Dennys thought that Yvonne was 'wonderful' in how she coped with Graham's harsh moods.[12] A frequent visitor to Antibes, the publisher A. S. Frere dubbed Yvonne a 'happy, healthy kitten', and Graham adopted that nickname for her, dedicating *Travels with My Aunt* to 'HHK'.[13]

Graham believed that one of the most important things he could do for Yvonne was to help out her daughters. In October 1972, one daughter, then in her early twenties, was trying to launch an acting career and hoped to get a part in François Truffaut's *La Nuit américaine*, then being filmed in Nice. To put in a good word for her, Greene needed first to meet Truffaut, and as it turned out it was he, and not Yvonne's daughter, who appeared in the film.[14] Michael Meyer's girlfriend was in the cast, so he went to the set, and found out that they needed an Englishman to play the tiny part of an insurance salesman. Truffaut rejected Meyer at a glance because his face was too 'intellectual'.

Meyer thought that maybe Graham Greene was the answer, but Greene's only experience as a film actor had come in *The Stranger's Hand*, when just his hand was seen grappling with some mooring ropes. They went to a party where the novelist, posing as 'Henry Graham', a retired businessman, was pointed out to Truffaut, who thought him perfect, and Greene agreed to take the part. But before his scene was to be shot, Greene decided there was a chance that journalists might notice what he was doing and perhaps pry into his relationship with Yvonne; he tried to back out, but Meyer coaxed him into appearing in the film.

After a lifetime of writing and rewriting scripts, Greene took a pen to his own lines, explaining to Meyer that he could not pronounce the letter 'r' so was changing 'three-quarters of an hour' to 'half an hour'. The inconsequential scene required many takes. Truffaut was known to explode if he found himself lied to, and he was soon on to this 'Henry Graham', asking if he was an actor: his face was familiar – had he appeared in a documentary? Looking through the camera viewfinder, he felt he recognized that face. Finally, his assistant whispered in his ear, and after an uncertain moment in which he might have erupted, Truffaut laughed, and the two men became friends, emerging from the studio with their arms around each other.[15]

Even as he tried to be helpful to Yvonne's children, Graham was never going to be a family man. Although generous and friendly towards his own children and grandchildren, he remained distant. He particularly liked Francis's wife Anne (née Cucksey); in the mid-1970s they settled in Devon, where he visited them from time to time. Caroline and her sons were now living in Vevey, Switzerland, and Graham made a good many brief visits there. She had decided to move there once her marriage ended, because the climate would suit her younger son, Jonathan, who suffered from asthma.[16]

On a couple of occasions, Caroline took her father to the ancient Abbey of St Maurice not far from her home. These visits made a surprising impression on him. He wrote in his journal on 30 January 1977: 'Last Easter (?) there was the sermon of the Abbot & the passage from John describing like an eye-witness the race to the empty tomb – & he came second. This time a private Mass in Latin for Lucy & me in a chapel by Father Fox – the gospel & the epistle – the epistle most striking – you can have faith & hope & it doesn't count compared with charity. I haven't faith & not much hope – can I claim to have charity? Doubtful. Being burnt at the stake counts too for nothing. How many martyrs have falsely been nominated as saints. Thomas Becket? And what does it matter anyway?'[17]

Greene's body caused him nearly as much trouble as his spirit. He was awkward, and practical details sometimes muddled him. After a visit to Vevey he wrote to Caroline: 'I've lost all my keys. I expect they fell out of my sack when I broke a bottle of whisky in it at Orly airport and tried to pour the liquid into an almost closed pot for cigarette ends, but it's just possible it fell out in the boot of your car. You remember my passport slipped out and we recovered it. Could you have a look?'[18] Some years later, Caroline was surprised when her father proposed calling an electrician to his flat to replace a light bulb; she reached up and dealt with it herself.[19]

Light bulbs were one problem, spotlights another. Greene suffered from a certain amount of sloppy journalism, but he also tended to recoil once he saw even the most accurate interviews in print. In June 1973, the publisher Weidenfeld & Nicolson proposed to commission a short biography of him, and he rejected the notion out of hand, but here was a problem he had to think about.

One way or another, his story would be told, either during his life-time or soon after his death. Already many scholars were writing about Graham Greene and his books, not least among them the poet and editor Philip Stratford and the novelist and critic David Lodge. In the early 1970s Greene received some letters from a professor of English at Lancaster University named Norman Sherry, who had written books on various nineteenth-century authors and then a major biography of Joseph Conrad, which Greene admired. A common friend, the drama critic and Catholic journalist Bill Igoe, wrote to Greene in 1973–4, suggesting first that he meet with Sherry and then that he should allow Sherry to get on with a book.[20]

Greene disliked Christopher Sykes's biography of Evelyn Waugh, and wanted his own story to be told only by a stranger and a non-Catholic.[21] Sherry assured him that he was himself a lapsed Catholic, and that it would not be a hagiography. Also Sherry proposed to look primarily at his involvement in trouble spots, and as their relationship unfolded gave this assurance: 'Understanding your fears, I will try to keep away from the personal, where this is irrelevant to my work. I will try to work in the manner of my Conrad but if the work begins to move in a biographical direction you will be free to censor it ... If I seem to be moving into the more private sphere I'll consult with you hurriedly.'[22] On the strength of this undertaking, which would protect Yvonne and the other women in his life, Greene allowed him to proceed.

Contrary to what is believed, Greene saw little of his authorized biographer, remarking in 1987: ' ... he's left me alone. An occasional written question – we haven't, since the first meeting, spent ten min-utes together.'[23] He saw somewhat more of Sherry than this suggests, but generally kept him at arm's length. After much travel in Greene's footsteps, some of it arduous, as in Paraguay where he lost a portion of an intestine to gangrene, Sherry eventually published a first volume in 1989, which Greene disliked because of its great length and its intrusion into his sexual life, something contrary to their original agreement. After a couple of sharp confrontations, Sherry was allowed to continue his work, only to face a different sort of trouble: in the later stages of his project he was developing dementia. His third and final volume, published in 2004, was strangely incoherent, so received many negative reviews. It is difficult for one biographer to write graciously of such a predecessor, not least because of the problem of glass houses. It is, however, necessary to state that the common view of Sherry's work is that it was a lost opportunity.

66

ABOUT MY BEST

S ome people really did read *Playboy* for the articles. The magazine had paid Greene $20,000 for a section of *Travels with My Aunt* that appeared in the November 1969 issue,[1] and in early 1973 asked him to write about South Africa. They were especially interested in soldiers of fortune who lived there, such as the famous Mike Hoare, an Irish-born accountant turned mercenary. In the Congolese civil war he led a group of anti-communist commandos and there was blood all over his adding machine. In the 1970s, he was still a celebrity, but that would fade by 1982, when he and his men, disguised as a drinking club called the Ancient Order of Froth-Blowers, were apprehended on their way to overthrow the government of the Seychelles. Hoare then spent three years in prison.[2]

Greene did not commit to an article specifically about mercenaries, but he was willing to do the research – and to get a free trip to South Africa. For about five years, he had been in correspondence with Etienne Leroux, whose darkly funny novels delighted Greene. He was part of the *Sestigers* ('sixties') movement of Afrikaans writers, a counter-cultural group who generally worked in exile, wrote in a some-what experimental manner, and set themselves against the apartheid system.[3] He was best known for *Seven Days at the Silbersteins*, a satire on sex, courtship, and marriage, which was denounced in South Africa as morally subversive and yet won the country's highest literary prize. When it appeared in English, Greene named it his book of the year,[4] and he gave another of his novels, *One For the Devil*, an enthusiastic review.[5] For his part, the younger novelist had been strongly influenced first by *Brighton Rock* and then Greene's other novels,[6] and he grew devoted to Greene as a friend and mentor.

Following an itinerary laid out by Leroux,[7] Greene spent a little over a month in South Africa. Arriving on 20 July 1973, he was met in Johannesburg by Leroux and his friend Kowie Marais, a judge from the Transvaal and a leading figure in the Progressive Party, of which the anti-apartheid campaigner Helen Suzman was the best-known member.[8] Greene spent much of his time at Marais's house in Pretoria, and the two talked about the politics of the country and the use of torture by the security services.[9] He spent some very pleasant days at Leroux's 60,000-acre sheep farm near Koffiefontein in the Orange Free State – a place he found idyllic. At Leroux's urging, he turned down an invitation to go to a war zone in Angola as he might be blown up by a landmine; in the past, landmines might have attracted him. Sadly, Leroux could not contact Hoare, who was, apparently, pursuing murderous business opportunities in the Far East.

Greene visited several universities, where he was keen to learn about the relative representations of the races among students and faculty. He met an array of Afrikaner intellectuals, and attended a party at the Cape Town home of the tobacco and liquor magnate Anton Rupert, a contradictory figure who though a member of the ruling National Party opposed many of its hardline positions and was one of the founders of the World Wildlife Fund.[10]

Greene met the Foreign Minister Hilgard Muller on 30 July 1973, and they discussed Rhodesia; the UN, which was then pressing the South Africans about the status of Namibia; relations with Paraguay; and the possibility of back-channel contacts with African leaders.[11] Although Greene did visit some black homelands, his itinerary generally kept him in the company of Afrikaners, among whom he found many reform-minded people. A proposed meeting with Mangosuthu Buthelezi, founder of the Inkatha Freedom Party and ruler of the KwaZulu territory, seems not to have taken place. Greene was able to report to Caroline about a rather vivid encounter with the Rain Queen in Limpopo Province: a matrilinear ruler with numerous wives as a form of property, she was believed to have powers over the weather. Greene knew of her as the inspiration for Ayesha in Rider Haggard's novel *She*.[12]

In August, after three weeks in South Africa, Greene suffered an attack of lumbago and was taken to hospital. He was given an injection, which left him groggy, and he lost 'the coloured tablets to which I'm condemned for life'; for years he had suffered from digestive trouble, and this medication, Celevac, allowed for the correct functioning of his bowels.[13] He went on to Lesotho, then flew to Paris around the 28th, exhausted and miserable.[14]

He was very fond of Leroux and treasured their time together on the farm, but the trip had failed. As he told John Anstey of the *Telegraph*, he had 'been dragged about 6000 miles in four weeks'. He had not been able to get off by himself to pursue separate lines of enquiry, and felt incapable of writing about the country.[15] The readers of *Playboy* would have to do without an article from Graham Greene. In the long run, however, the trip did have a value as it gave him plenty of new material for *The Human Factor*, which had been waiting in the drawer since 1968.

Though tired and sick at the beginning of September 1973, Greene soon had cause to rejoice. *The Honorary Consul* was a hit even by his standards. The critic Michael Ratcliffe called it 'exemplary' and said of Eduardo Plarr: '. . . he is one of the most haunting of all the Greene heroes who have cut down desolation and put their hand in the fire'.[16] Peter Lewis described it as 'perhaps the most enduring novel that even he has given us'.[17] And so it went on in both Britain and the United States.

Although he often feigned indifference about such things, Greene was thrilled. He wrote to Bill Igoe: 'The book was hell to do and never seemed to get off the ground, but finally after seven revisions it does seem to me to be about my best. I was getting tired of having to say that *The Power and the Glory* was the best – published in 1940!'[18]

67

LONG SPOONS

It was 1974, and the dentists were getting their revenge for all that Graham Greene had written about them. It was an orgy of grinding, drilling, and tugging. They got rid of four teeth and recapped others. They installed a bridge that might have done nicely at the River Kwai, and relieved him of something like £5000 in a string of appointments that went on for the whole year.[1] In the summer, his doctors worried, yet again, that he was suffering from cancer – thankfully he was not. In December, he suffered an electric shock from a defective lamp that might have killed him.[2]

In the midst of all this, he needed some diversion, so while in Anacapri in August and September[3] he wrote a lighthearted play based on the A. J. Raffles stories of E. W. Hornung, the brother-in-law of Sir Arthur Conan Doyle. When they appeared in the early years of the century, these stories of a gentleman thief and cricketer and his dim sidekick Bunny were hugely popular. After David Niven played the part in the 1939 film of the same name, Raffles rather slipped from view.

The Return of A. J. Raffles was staged by the Royal Shakespeare Company at the Aldwych Theatre in December 1975. The director, David Jones, said that Greene had seen their production of *Sherlock Holmes*, which premiered in January 1974 with Denholm Elliott in the lead, and decided to bring back Raffles from the grave at the South African battlefield of Spion Kop, to which Hornung had consigned him.[4] In Greene's pastiche, the burglar, using a top hat as a dark lantern, helps Lord Alfred Douglas get revenge on his father, the Marquess of Queensberry, for his hand in the imprisonment of Oscar Wilde and for withholding his allowance. The Prince of Wales comes into the story, and by the end preserves Raffles from imprisonment. The play,

Greene's first in eleven years, was pure fun – something to get his mind off his teeth.

Apart from *Raffles*, it was a time of entrances and exits in Greene's world. After seventeen years of service, his secretary Josephine Reid resigned, saying she could no longer bear the weight of the job, though she did continue to take on occasional tasks for him. Reid had been able to keep private things private, and Greene was not happy about losing her,[5] but her replacement was even better placed to enjoy his confidence. From the end of August 1975, his sister Elisabeth took over, working from her home in Crowborough. She was someone Graham could rely on absolutely, and she remained in the position until suffering a stroke in 1989, when the job was taken on by her daughter Amanda, who had been a stills photographer for the BBC.

Other important changes were in the works. For many years, Laurence Pollinger had been Greene's main literary agent. Although Greene and Pollinger never seem to have been close friends, the agent was steady and methodical, and so a good counter to the author's impulsiveness. He died in April 1976,[6] leaving the business to his sons Gerald and Murray. Greene remained a client of the firm for about fourteen years, but never regarded the younger Pollingers as he had their father. Near the end of his life, he left the firm altogether. He went back to David Higham Associates, whose founder, of course, had been his primary agent until the 1940s.

In Paris, Marie Biche had been indispensable to Greene: her efforts over about thirty years went far beyond those usual for a literary agent as she became essentially a personal manager for him. She was also one of his most dedicated friends. In June 1976, her husband Jean suffered a cerebral haemorrhage[7] that would eventually lead to his death. Greene observed Marie's troubles with some frustration that he could not really assist her, but in late 1977 he made a gesture. He wrote her a whimsical letter begging her to 'be reasonable & do something – which will hurt you – to please me. I'm scared of your reaction & afraid you'll disappoint me, but please say Yes & allow me this year for Christmas to give you instead of a classic shirt from the Faubourg unsuitable for country wear, allow me – I ask it with trembling voice – to give you a small car – Volkswagen or what you like . . . ' She wrote back 'no present could make me happier! It makes me sad tho' to realize what a bitch I am that you should have to go to such verbal pains to offer me this precious gift.' She compared her excitement to that which she felt on getting her first bicycle. With his next letter, Graham enclosed a cheque to pay for a new Citroën.[8] Biche's career was winding down and before long Greene's account was taken over by another leading French agent, Michelle Lapautre. However, he remained close to Biche for the rest of his life.

Greene had some important unfinished business. By the beginning of 1975 he had taken up *The Human Factor* again, but progress was slow, as he was then navigating his root canals. He wrote to Leroux in January 1976: 'God knows whether the book will ever be finished. I have now done 43,000 words and it should run to more than 70,000.'[9] It took another full year to complete and even then he wondered whether it was a dud. He decided finally to do what he always had done in the early years: he turned to A. S. Frere, who by then was living near by in Monte Carlo. Having read the manuscript, Frere wanted to talk about it in person, so the novelist assumed that he would be told, however kindly, that it was just not fit for publication. In fact, Frere told him it was one of the best books he had written and predicted a great success.[10] Greene wrote to his American agent: 'To my surprise Frere is enthusiastic about the novel, so published it will be.'[11]

Many of the reviewers thought the same thing when it came out in March 1978, with Anthony Burgess, for example, writing: 'Let me say at once that *The Human Factor* is as fine a novel as he has ever written – concise, ironic, acutely observant of contemporary life, funny, shocking, above all compassionate.'[12] Two months after publication, the book was still top of the *Sunday Times* bestseller list.[13]

Meanwhile, Greene's imaginary defector, Maurice Castle, was of great interest to a real one. When *My Silent War* was published in 1968, he had received a letter of thanks from Kim Philby and nothing more for almost a decade. In the autumn of 1975 Greene was in Budapest for a few days to assist the Hungarian film-maker László Róbért with a documentary about the novelist's time in Vietnam. László was a nasty piece of work. An officer in Hungarian intelligence, he was usually assigned to Catholic targets, including the Vatican.

Philby had recently been quoted in a newspaper as saying that the one thing he would like in life would be to share a bottle of wine with

Graham Greene. While Greene waited at the airport for his flight home, he reportedly told László that he longed to see his old friend Philby again, so László called the Soviet embassy, and in the thirty-five minutes before take-off put in a request for a meeting to be arranged between the two, but it could not be arranged on such short notice.[14]

In August 1977, Hugh's son, the publisher Graham C. Greene, went to Moscow for a book fair and sent a letter to Philby, asking him to meet for drinks. His reply was dated 30 October, and he blamed the delay on the slow postal service and his being in the Carpathians at the time 'chivying the local trout'. Undoubtedly, Philby's response was vetted by his superiors and this took time. The letter was very friendly, and included greetings to 'your respected uncle', and this odd sentence: 'Incidentally, if you should come here again, I shall always be able to locate you wherever you are.'[15] He was warning Graham C. Greene that the KGB would be watching him whenever he returned to Russia. The letter was passed on to Graham, to Elisabeth and Rodney Dennys, and then to Maurice Oldfield ('C').

In late 1977, László Róbért visited Greene in Antibes and brought word from a 'friend' enrolled in a Soviet school of espionage that Philby, still amiable though drinking heavily, was now an instructor there. This too was passed on to Oldfield, who thought he recognized László Róbért's name – that is to say, MI6 had already taken note of him.[16] Thirty years later, Lászlo appeared at the Graham Greene International Festival and was asked whether he still believed in communism. He replied, 'Until tomorrow.'

In early 1978, a very occasional correspondence began between Greene and Philby. Greene sent a copy of *The Human Factor* to Moscow; Philby read the novel twice and planned to read it a third time. He admired it and confessed to wry amusement. He thought the treatment of Castle at the end somewhat 'shabby and most un-Russian', as he himself had been provided with all he might need, even a shoe-horn.[17] Greene's description of the flat was based on Eleanor Philby's book, but even so, he changed a few details for future printings in light of what Philby told him.[18]

They both wanted to meet, but the problem was that Philby could not come to a Western capital, and Greene refused to go to Russia while dissidents were being ill treated; this left as possibilities such places as

Budapest, Havana, or Hanoi.[19] There is no solid evidence that Greene and Philby met in person before Greene's visit to Moscow in 1986, once glasnost and perestroika were under way.

During those years, however, they continued to write occasional letters. However, a question hangs over their closely vetted correspondence: who is talking to whom? It is perfectly possible to see some of what was said, especially by Philby, as rather impersonal, as if one intelligence agency was addressing another by a back channel. Apart from distant reminiscences and talk of books, their letters chiefly discuss international relations. The most startling comments in their correspondence came at the end of 1979: Greene suggested that having signed the SALT II agreement, the Russians and Americans would do well to act jointly against Iran, with defined spheres of influence, and stand face to face across a frontier rather than engage in brinksmanship in neutral territory. In his response on 2 January 1980, Philby mused about the Ayatollah's irrationality and then said he had passed the suggestion on 'to the competent authorities'.

But then, in the same letter, Philby introduced the topic of 'this infernal Afghan business' – the Soviets had invaded the country a week before and overthrown the government: 'I need hardly tell you that I am very unhappy about it; what may surprise you is that I have met no one here who *is* happy about it.'[20] Philby was talking about the mood of the KGB, a most indiscreet thing to do except with the approval of his superiors. When Rodney Dennys forwarded the letter to Sir Dick Franks, Oldfield's successor as head of MI6, he drew attention to this statement and remarked: 'I have felt, for some time, that the K.G.B. were probably doves rather than hawks and this seems to bear it out. Is it, do you think, a tentative feeler for the initiation of a dialogue between the K.G.B. and S.I.S.? No doubt you possess a canteen of long spoons.' Remarking on Philby's 'flair for strategic deception', he nonetheless believed he was telling the truth.[21] So did Greene.[22] Sadly, this tantalizing story stops there – what may have happened next is unknown. For the rest, if there is anything more, we must await the release of secret files.

As Greene would explain soon after to his great friend in Panama, Omar Torrijos, he had a 'favourite theory' that in time the KGB would take control of the Soviet Union: 'it would prove more easy to deal with pragmatists than ideologists. The KGB recruited the brightest students from the universities, they learnt foreign languages, they saw the outer world, Marx meant little to them. They could be instruments of a measure of reform at home.'[23]

This was one of Greene's odd predictions that came true, but hardly as he had hoped. It was well known that Yuri Andropov, after fifteen years in charge of the KGB, was positioning himself to succeed a declining Leonid Brezhnev as General Secretary of the Communist Party, and he was cultivating his image abroad. He took over in November 1982, and enacted some internal reforms but continued the war in Afghanistan and engaged in a diplomatic stand-off with the Reagan administration.[24] He was dead by February 1984, and after thirteen months of retrenchment under Konstantin Chernenko, Mikhail Gorbachev, a serious reformer and not KGB, came to power. In the long term, however, Greene was sadly right to foresee the KGB ruling Russia – this happened with the accession in 2000 of Vladimir Putin, once a lieutenant-colonel in Soviet intelligence. Greene's faith in the pragmatism of the KGB as inclining towards reform was misplaced. What the novelist did not foresee was the territorial ambition, the repression, and the greed.

68

EFFERVESCENCE AND VIBRATION

The old firm was a good place to get a briefing. In late June 1975, Graham Greene emerged from a 'most interesting' private lunch with Maurice Oldfield ready to pack his bags for Portugal.[1] Thirty years before, Greene had run the Portugal desk in Section V of MI6. In 1956, he had thought of setting in Lisbon the story eventually written as *Our Man in Havana*. Recent events, however, had transformed the country.

The dictator António de Oliveira Salazar had died in 1970, having been enfeebled by a stroke and replaced by Marcelo Caetano two years earlier. For almost forty years Salazar had ruled the one-party *Estado Novo* (New State), maintaining control through a security apparatus, which spied relentlessly on the citizens and made short work of opposition. Caetano adopted cautiously liberalizing policies, but did not address the roots of disaffection with the regime. Over the years, what protests there were had come mainly from university students – protests officially referred to by the security forces as 'student effervescence'. After 1968, students became decidedly more effervescent, some advocating Eastern Bloc forms of communism, Maoism, or terrorism.[2]

At the same time, almost every family in the country of ten million had sent a son to fight in pointless wars in Angola, Mozambique, Guinea Bissau, and other colonies that were demanding independence. University students were conscripted, so the lower officer ranks included many leftist opponents of the regime. Disputes over seniority, pay, and training magnified the discontent, and on 25 April 1974 the army conducted a nearly bloodless coup, afterwards referred to as the 'Carnation Revolution' since many citizens placed carnations in the barrels of the soldiers' rifles.[3]

There followed a messy period of attempted counter-coups, and then elections for an assembly in the spring of 1975. At the time of Greene's meeting with Oldfield, it was not certain whether Portugal would become a Western satellite of the Soviet Union or lurch back towards fascism. As it turned out, Portugal followed a third path, largely under the leadership of Mário Soares, a democratic socialist who brought the country into the European Economic Community.

Greene wanted to make a discreet visit to Portugal, and considered going to see his old friend Maria Newall,[4] 'Pistol Mary', whom he had known in Kenya (see p. 239) and who was now living in Sintra. With General Franco looking corpse-like, Greene also wanted to see Spain that summer. ETA had struck hard in their campaign to establish an independent Basque state in southern France and northern Spain. In December 1973, they killed Franco's likely successor, Luis Carrero Blanco, in Madrid: a bomb tossed his car 35 metres into the air and over a building into the courtyard beyond.[5] In April 1975 they carried out less spectacular killings of two policemen, and the government placed much of the Basque territory under a state of emergency.[6] *Monsignor Quixote* captures this atmosphere of menace with the protagonists being dogged by the Guardia Civil, who suspect that they are dealing with a disguised terrorist, not a monsignor authentic down to his purple socks.

That priest, of course, was loosely modelled on a real one. Before his meeting with Oldfield, Greene had already contacted Father Leopoldo Durán, a literary scholar in Madrid, proposing to make a visit there.[7] A perfectly orthodox priest who spoke of Franco with veneration and had no great devotion to democracy, Leopoldo Durán offered an ideal travelling companion for an author known all over the world as a leftish troublemaker. Greene could look at what he wanted in Spain and Portugal, and it would always be assumed that they had a pious, or at least respectable, purpose for what turned out to be fifteen journeys of about a fortnight each through Spain and Portugal between 1976 and 1989.[8]

And for the most part they did have respectable purposes. Greene doubtless kept his eyes open for things that would interest Oldfield or his successors, but over the years his travels through the Iberian peninsula seem to have been mainly personal and pleasant – especially as the countries grew more stable. They stayed in small hotels or in religious houses, and the always restless Greene wanted to linger no more than a day or two in any place. For each journey, Durán found a 'third man' to do the driving, so he and Greene could stop for picnics and drink Manchegan wine. At a certain hour of the day they turned to something stronger, so Greene dubbed his friend 'the whisky priest'.[9] All this gave him the idea for his gently comic novel published in 1982.

Born in Galicia and for a time a member of the Vincentian Order, Durán had first contacted Greene in 1964; he was then writing a thesis at the University of Madrid on the theological background of Greene's novels.[10] From 1968 to 1972 he was a doctoral student at King's College London, where he wrote another thesis focused on priests in Greene's fiction;[11] he later turned this into a book. Greene did not get to Spain or Portugal right away – that took another year to arrange – but he did meet Leopoldo Durán in the flesh in London on 20 August 1975. Durán's anecdotes are sometimes unreliable, and he got this date wrong by two years in his memoir of Greene.[12] As Durán recalled, the novelist put on a jacket and tie and met him for a meal at the Ritz, where they talked about fiction, films, theology, and the conservative Catholic group Opus Dei, which Greene hated for its political activities. At a certain point Greene asked Durán, as a person who had studied his works, whether he thought he had 'true faith'. Durán responded that the fiction 'hinged' on the existence of God and that he believed Greene's faith greater than his own, and it appears that this answer got Greene's attention even as most pious responses to his work merely bored him: 'Thank you very much indeed. Your answer is very comforting.' When Greene asked Durán about his own belief, he received an extraordinary – and very Catholic – answer: 'I do not believe in God, I touch him.'[13] In his search for a plausible travelling companion, Greene had stumbled onto something resembling sanctity.

That autumn, Franco fell into a coma and eventually died on 20 November 1975, so Greene tried right away to organize a visit to Durán at Christmas, but work on *The Return of A. J. Raffles* and the television series *Shades of Greene* got in the way.[14] He did finally get to Spain on 16 July 1976, having requested to see Toledo, Salamanca, and the Basque territory.[15] He stayed for about two weeks.

In his first night at a Madrid hotel, he had a piece of luck. There was a box beside the bed, which Durán could not figure out, so the novelist explained that if you inserted a 25-peseta coin the bed would vibrate, giving its occupant a massage to induce sleep. The next morning, a very rested Graham Greene reported that the machine was broken and a single coin had purchased a whole night of vibration: 'Strange things happen to me in hotel rooms.'[16]

On their way to Salamanca, they passed the Valle de los Caídos, or Valley of the Fallen, where thirty-three thousand Civil War dead are buried. It features a 500-foot-high cross, and an enormous basilica, where Franco was buried. Out of respect for his victims, Spain enacted a law of historical memory in 2007, removing fascist statues throughout the country and forbidding political ceremonies at this shrine. After a long controversy, the socialist government moved Franco's remains to another site in 2019. Greene thought the Valle de los Caídos disgusting – something the pharaohs might have gone in for. Durán would later write, somewhat wistfully, 'Graham never understood Franco's political and spiritual ideology.'[17]

Greene soon saw something he did like. In the university city of Salamanca they visited, at his request, the grave of Miguel de Unamuno, a writer best known for his essay 'The Tragic Sense of Life' and for his retelling of the story of Don Quixote. His writings presented doubt and belief as almost inseparable, and Greene admired him greatly. At the cemetery, they asked where the grave was and were told that it was marked '340' – that was all. They stood in silence by the grave for about fifteen minutes, and it was then, Durán believed, that the novel began stirring. In the story, Sancho, the communist mayor, is a former student of Unamuno, and it was by his example that Sancho was able to retain for some years a degree of belief in Catholicism; just as Monsignor Quixote's belief is challenged by the events of the novel, so too is Sancho's disbelief.

They travelled north-west into the Galician province of Ourense, and made their first visit to the large Trappist monastery of Oseira in a river valley among the Martiñá mountains. Founded in 1137, it was abandoned and looted in the time of Napoleon, then re-established in 1929.[18] When Greene first saw the monastery in 1976, it was undergoing a slow restoration, but even so, he was impressed by its austerity, and wrote in the guest book: 'Thank you very much for these moments of peace and silence. Please pray for me. Graham Greene.'[19] Each year, the novelist and priest returned to this monastery, and it is where, in the novel, Monsignor Quixote meets his end.

By comparison with these silent monks in their silent home, Santiago de Compostela was hard to bear. They arrived on the eve of the feast of St James and found the cathedral overrun with pilgrims and tourists. In the afternoon the liturgical hours would be marked by the firing of cannons. Greene declared himself willing to forgo the Indulgences – Purgatory was preferable to all that noise – so they got back on the road. In Coruña they visited the tomb of Greene's distant relative Sir John Moore, who died there in battle against Napoleon's forces in 1809; Greene had first visited the site with his Aunt Eva and cousin Ave in 1921. He recited for Father Leopoldo a little of Charles Wolfe's famous poem on Moore:

> Not a drum was heard, not a funeral note,
>   As his corse to the rampart we hurried;
> Not a soldier discharged his farewell shot
>   O'er the grave where our hero we buried.[20]

Greene and Durán then entered Basque country, the only time they did so in their many journeys. They crossed Asturias and stayed overnight in Vitoria, the chief city in what after 1978 would be known under the Spanish constitution as the Basque Autonomous Community, an act of devolution intended to put a stop to separatism. It was only with some reluctance that the priest revealed their identities to a young hotel desk clerk, who then asked for the novelist to autograph her copies of his books. By this stage in his life, Greene could not stay incognito for long.

According to Durán, Greene had visited Vitoria before and was very fond of it. The north-eastern limit of their first journey was San Sebastián, on the seashore not far from Biarritz, and this was not a place Greene liked – all those bodies on the beach slowly roasting.[21]

They returned to Madrid and then to the walled city of Avila, where at the Convent of the Incarnation they saw the preserved right index finger of St Teresa, from the hand with which she wrote her books[22] – an object which Franco had kept in his possession. Despite this unsavoury association, Greene was a great enthusiast for St Teresa, with her exalted visions of God, her boundless energy, and her common sense. He was an even greater admirer of her contemporary, the poet St John of the Cross. Fundamentally, Greene trusted mystics far more than he did theologians: they were on the side of faith, whereas theologians stood for mere belief.

In July 1977 – that is, a year later – Greene came back and this time, after their visit to the Abbey of Oseira, they made the long drive to Sintra in Portugal to see Maria Newall. Eighty-five now, she was still a formidable figure, even though she relied on walking sticks and soon a wheelchair. Her house was filled with books and flowers, and surrounded by a large garden. The travellers stayed with her for three days. As a young woman she had had trouble in her marriages and in a failed love affair, and was grieved by exclusion from the church. In old age, she was very fervent, and she was knowledgeable about theology – enough to engage her visitors in debate. But piety did not diminish her sense of humour. She and Greene started spouting wild heresies which Durán tried in vain to correct, and he grew increasingly angry until he realized that they were teasing him.

Sintra became a regular destination for the priest and the novelist; Newall was glad to see them, and their stays lengthened to about a week. Although a forceful character, she was fragile, suffering a heart attack in 1978, and broken bones owing to osteoporosis. Greene played draughts with her and treated her very solicitously. Durán, who seemed to have a crush on her, remarked on her beauty and sanctity, and said Mass in her drawing room. She died in the early summer of 1984, just before Greene and Durán were to make one of their visits.[23]

After their first visit to Newall in 1977, Greene and Durán went on to Cuenca in central Spain, a city famous for its cathedral and its hanging houses perched on stony outcrops – Greene thought it 'spectacular'. They went also to El Taboso, the supposed home town of Don Quixote, which Greene had thought fictional until he read about it in Unamuno. There, as he reported to Newall, they visited a small museum which featured copies of *Don Quixote* signed by national leaders, including Ramsay MacDonald and Hitler; the one signed by Stalin had vanished.[24]

As they drove, Greene had an idea for a new story. He remarked: 'So it's agreed: I'm Sancho, you're the Monsignor.'[25] He described what they had seen and done in a letter to Newall and added: 'Father Durán was delighted by the story I started writing in my head – asking for his aid in technical matters – of a book to be called *Monsignor Don Quixote*. We added to the adventures of the Monsignor as we went along the road.' By this time, Greene was also working on a novel about Panama, featuring a character based on the head of state's bodyguard who happened to be a professor of mathematics, but Father Quixote had now seized centre stage: 'Chuchu in Panama is going to be worried as I have now got another character to play with.'[26]

By the spring of 1978, Greene had an opening chapter to show Durán.[27] In November he contacted Tom Burns at *The Tablet*, the progressive Catholic magazine of which Greene was a trustee, offering him, for no charge, 'the first chapter of a novel which probably will never be completed'. That excerpt, 'How Father Quixote Became a Monsignor', appeared in that year's Christmas issue, and later sections in those of 1980 and 1981.[28] The writing of this short novel was not easy, and at one point he believed he had the ending wrong – that the mayor should die rather than the priest, who, excommunicated, would then live out his years at the Abbey of Oseira, saying Masses in private for the souls of Sancho and Karl Marx.[29] He reverted to the original plan, but all this took time, and it was not until December 1981 that he could tell Father Leopoldo that he had completed a draft.[30]

As their friendship grew closer Greene spoke with the priest about his experience of writing a novel, how at times he could only shut down the urge to write by taking sleeping pills.[31] He also described the sheer intuitiveness of his work:

A novel is a work in which characters interrelate. It doesn't need a plot. The novelist's own intervention must be very limited. What happens to the author of a novel is rather like the pilot of a plane. The pilot needs to get the plane off the ground. It takes off with the help of the pilot. Once it is in the air, the pilot does virtually nothing. Once everything has started working, the characters begin to impose themselves on the author, who no longer controls them. They have a life of their own. The author has to go on writing. Sometimes he writes things which appear to have no raison d'être. Only at the end is the reason apparent. The author intervenes to allow the plane to land. It is time for the novel to end.[32]

Monsignor Quixote touched down in mid-September 1982. William Trevor wrote: 'Father Quixote benefits greatly from his travels but his companion benefits more, and we most of all. Mr Greene, who has travelled long and far himself, has rarely done so as remarkably as in this profound and funny novel'.[33] American reviewers tended to express similar opinions: a few felt that Greene had overdone the parallels with Cervantes, but most applauded an almost hypnotically attractive book. As Frederick Busch put it: 'He is at his best in this novel, and he knows it.'[34]

69

THE DIPLOMATIC PASSPORT

'I thought that I had lost for ever the excitement of a long plane journey to an unknown place ... Now after the drinks the old sense of
adventure returns.'[1] It was 3 December 1976, that is, about five months
after the first of his Quixotic journeys in Spain and Portugal, and now
Greene was flying towards Panama in the first of five visits. This would
prove the last great international 'involvement' of his long life, and
would form the basis of some major articles, a memoir, an abandoned
novel, and a completed one. It would also gain for him, however briefly,
a diplomatic passport.

The tiny country of Panama, through which much of the world's
shipping passes, was created by President Theodore Roosevelt in 1903
out of what had been a province of Colombia. He fomented a secession
movement there, and set up a new country, in the middle of which was
the Panama Canal Zone, fifty miles long and ten wide controlled by the
United States as if it were a sovereign territory. Possession of the Zone
was governed by a treaty signed by the United States and France, but
not by Panama. The Americans bought out French interest in a failed
project to build a canal and brought it to completion in 1914.

The Americans paid almost nothing to the new republic – a pittance
in shipping tolls – for what amounted to a colony, and relations between
the two countries were never easy. Indeed, when American forces
overthrew the regime of Manuel Noriega in December 1989 it was
actually their twentieth military intervention in Panama since 1856.
Over the years, the Zone assumed aspects of American life, including
a 'Jim Crow' segregation of the majority of black workers from whites.
American stewardship of the Zone was poor; construction damaged the
environment, as did secret testing of chemical weapons and storage of

depleted uranium.[2] The Canal Zone was also home to the School of the Americas, which taught advanced anti-insurgency techniques to soldiers from some of the most repressive regimes in Latin America.

Possession of the canal offered obvious mercantile and strategic advantages to the United States, which they were loath to surrender, and Americans living in the Zone took a particularly hard line against negotiations. Meanwhile, it became a point of national pride among Panamanians to reclaim the Zone, and on 9 January 1964 university students tried to raise the Panamanian flag there. Riots broke out, and American forces killed twenty-one people and wounded more than five hundred.[3] The Johnson administration could see that a new treaty was required that would maintain American control of the canal and satisfy the nationalist strivings of Panamanians – a difficult objective. Nonetheless, agreements were drafted with the Panamanian government led by President Marco Robles; while abrogating the 1903 treaty with its perpetuity clause, they established the neutrality of the canal but allowed for American forces to remain on the isthmus and for the Panamanians to take a hand in management of the canal. Nationalists did not like these terms, and Johnson faced opposition in the Senate, so the agreements withered on the vine.[4]

Meanwhile, Panama was about to produce an extraordinary, if flawed, leader. Political leadership was generally restricted to a small number of rich families. In October 1968, the conservative Arnulfo Arias Madrid, belonging to such a clan, managed to manoeuvre himself into the presidency of Panama, and while few doubted that he was a crook, his accession was more or less constitutional.

A warhorse of Panamanian politics who in his youth had supported Mussolini and Hitler,[5] he had held the post twice before, and immediately tried to solidify his position. Within days of taking office he sought to purge the National Guard, which the Americans had supported and equipped as a guarantor of stability in country. The National Guard had interfered in politics in the past and its officers tended to be nepotistic and greedy for kickbacks.[6] Arias was promptly overthrown in a coup led by the right-wing Colonel Boris Martínez and the pragmatist Colonel Omar Torrijos. Soon after, Martínez was exiled and Torrijos took charge.

In late 1969, Torrijos was visiting Mexico when a counter-coup took place at home, and it was assumed that he would remain abroad. Not for the last time, he defied expectations. He boarded a plane and headed home. A military commander in Chiriquí Province near the border with Costa Rica took the risky step of permitting him to land in the city of David – that commander was Manuel Noriega.[7] Joined by other loyalists, Torrijos began a celebratory motorcade down the isthmus to the capital, and in a surge of popular support took back power. Those who had attempted the coup were imprisoned, but escaped to the Canal Zone. Torrijos went on to consolidate a broad coalition that included the military, student groups, and many rural workers; he brought about impressive reforms in healthcare and education, and embarked on an ambitious programme of public works. He was also responsible for the growth of international banking in the country,[8] and as the Panama Papers scandal of 2016 demonstrated, the country became a good place to hide money.

In 1971, Torrijos put Noriega in charge of G-2, the country's intelligence service. In the following year or so some branches of American intelligence decided that Noriega was very trustworthy, just as they dropped plans to kill or overthrow Torrijos and to have his brother Moisés Torrijos prosecuted for drug trafficking.[9] Despite their earlier support for the counter-coup, the CIA decided that Torrijos, for all his revolutionary rhetoric, was actually a force for stability. The KGB courted him especially from 1977, referring to him by the codename RODOM. He accepted the presents they gave him, such as a hunting rifle and a selection of vodkas, but he seems to have done almost nothing for the Soviets apart from complain about Americans. He was using the contacts, which he took little trouble to conceal, to scare the Carter administration into concluding a new treaty.[10]

Panama had a far better human rights record than most Latin American countries at the time, but there was repression, and it was typically carried out by G-2. An international commission determined that by 1977 thirty-four murders were attributable to the regime, mostly in its turbulent first four years, and that torture had sometimes been employed against its enemies.[11] As the 'chief of the revolution', Torrijos was ultimately responsible for this, and it is a scar on his record. Moreover, his manner of taking power and holding it was illegitimate. He did permit elections to a weak assembly, but banned political parties and hand-picked government ministers. Although a maverick with notable accomplishments, he was very much a strongman or *caudillo*.

Bernard Diederich, Greene's old friend from Haiti, was now based in Mexico City as *Time* magazine's Central American correspondent. On 11 October 1971, the third anniversary of the Panamanian revolution, he attended what was possibly the largest demonstration ever held in the country. Never comfortable at a podium or indeed in his formal white uniform, Torrijos still lit a fire with his speech, declaring that his country would not go down on its knees: 'What people can bear the humiliation of seeing a foreign flag planted in the very heart of its nation?' While the elites generally dismissed him as uneducated and unsophisticated, the handsome and charismatic Torrijos was clearly loved by the ordinary people, and he had stirred them up, just hinting at an armed seizure of the canal. He had, however, shrewdly forestalled any repetition of the 1964 riots by posting guards to turn back the crowds from the Zone.[12] Over the years, he observed, even as it went against his temperament, the advice of Fidel Castro to remain moderate in his confrontations with the United States.[13]

No one was killed that day, so Diederich's story on this pivotal demonstration was spiked, but he could see that Torrijos was a new kind of leader. He soon wrote a letter to Greene endorsing Torrijos's stand with regard to the canal,[14] and the novelist began to study the history and politics of the country, with a view to going there. At a meeting with Diederich, Torrijos spoke of his love of the novels of Gabriel García Márquez, so the journalist mentioned Graham Greene, whom the General had not heard of, as a leading writer who would be sympathetic to his cause. He described how *The Comedians* had damaged Papa Doc far more than if he had faced an army of exiles. Torrijos was intrigued to hear of Greene's encounters with Salvador Allende, and decided he wanted to meet this 'Viejo Ingles'.[15]

As early as March 1973, Greene asked Diederich to help him arrange a visit,[16] but it took three years for it to happen, by which time Ronald Reagan's tough talk about Panama in the Republican primaries had put the country in the headlines. Long after, Greene wrote that he had been 'mystified' by the invitation he received in 1976. This was not actually true: he had asked Diederich to help him organize a visit, but the two agreed that Greene should not write about his efforts as

Diederich did not want to be seen as part of the stories that he had to cover as a journalist.[17]

Now seventy-two, Greene relied a good deal on Bernard Diederich. The jet-lagged novelist arrived first in Panama, and was 'gloomy' until his friend arrived at the hotel: 'Why had I left my home in Antibes and my friends and come to Panama where the hours moved so slowly, even though they no longer moved backward.'[18] It had been about a decade since he had seen Diederich; Greene wrote in his journal, 'We drank whisky & gossiped. The years seemed to have changed neither of us.'[19] Diederich was fluent in Spanish, and knew all the people Greene would need to meet. When Greene was invited to go to the interior of the country with Torrijos, he insisted that Diederich accompany him – Torrijos overruled his subordinates, especially a PR man named Fabian Velarde, who wanted to control how his visit was reported: 'Señor Greene is our guest. He can bring whom he likes.'[20] The General later told him to do the opposite of whatever Velarde wanted. Already ill, this PR man died of a heart attack almost immediately after Greene's departure, causing the novelist to muse on whether his visit had been too much for him.[21]

The next day, a driver picked them up, assuming he was some other man named Greene – always there was that 'other'. Once returned to the hotel, Greene and Diederich were fetched by the right car to see the General. Their driver was a hot-headed polymath who in a novel – and Greene did try to put him in one – might seem improbable. Sergeant José de Jesús Martínez, generally known as 'Chuchu' (a diminutive for Jesús), was born in Nicaragua, had studied at the Sorbonne, and was a professor of mathematics and philosophy, as well as a poet and playwright. A Marxist and an atheist who claimed to believe in the devil, he spoke five languages, and had joined the military after being greatly moved by hearing recruits singing patriotic songs. Against the odds, he got through his training, and became a member of Torrijos's security detail while continuing to teach part time.[22] His rank was only that of sergeant because he preferred it that way; some years later he accepted promotion.

Torrijos liked to surround himself with advisers representing the whole political spectrum, and Chuchu acted, in Diederich's phrase, as his 'left-hand man'.[23] He undertook many delicate tasks for Torrijos, and operated a 'pigeon house', a refuge for political exiles from other Latin American countries that would have been unthinkable in the days of Arias. On this occasion, Chuchu served as Greene's chauffeur and, when Diederich was absent, translator. Often drunk and frequently disappearing in pursuit of estranged wives and mistresses – and, on one occasion, a lost dog – he endeared himself to the novelist, who found him lovable, exasperating, and altogether brilliant.

Chuchu drove them to a small suburban house owned by Rory González, an old friend of the General and something of a power-broker. He was the head of a group of newspapers that had been seized by a bank from the Arias clan after their downfall.[24] He was also the director of a huge copper mine in a remote area north of the capital, which was expected to make Panama wealthy. Changing hands several times, it did not produce any copper until 2019; the slow development of the open-pit mine did create thousands of jobs, but also led to claims by critics of environmental damage.[25] The forty-seven-year-old General liked to move about the country impulsively, and regarded this house as a safe and discreet stopping place. He certainly relaxed there. He and González met Greene in their bathrobes and underwear, and Diederich guessed that the General was struggling with a hangover.[26] Once dressed, Torrijos took them to an airfield where a propeller plane was waiting to take them to the island of Contadora.

Conversation was slow starting, and perhaps out of a certain unease Torrijos challenged Greene: 'Intellectuals are like fine glass, crystal glass, which can be cracked by a sound. Panama is made of rock and earth.' Despite his standing as a writer, Greene would never let himself be called an intellectual, which to him meant a purveyor of abstractions and a bore – it was as bad as being called a sociologist. But he could see that there was more to Torrijos than the plain man of action; with Diederich translating, Greene won his first smile by remarking that the General had only been saved from being an intellectual by running away from school in time.[27] Torrijos met constantly with groups of ordinary people, and encouraged them to speak about their concerns; he had a gift for listening much as Castro had one for oratory. Torrijos had a deep fund of peasant wisdom and proverbs. He felt, for example, that if the grass was uncut in a village cemetery it was a bad village: 'If you don't look after the dead you won't look after the living.'[28]

In the following days, Greene and Diederich took a train through the Canal Zone and attended a small demonstration of hardliners who felt that all negotiations with the Panamanians were a betrayal. Greene was amused that they referred to the American president merely as 'Gerry' and the Secretary of State as 'Henry'.[29] Since 1971, the Nixon and then Ford administrations had shown themselves open to a new arrangement for the Canal Zone; the discussions had been energized when Panama hosted a meeting of the United Nations Security Council in March 1973 and won international support for its position. In 1975, Kissinger advised Ford: 'If these negotiations fail, we will be beaten to death in every international forum and there will be riots all over Latin America.' But Kissinger also insisted on the right of the United States to defend the Zone indefinitely. The presidential primaries saw Ford supporting a new treaty and his opponent Ronald Reagan opposing it, while the Democrat Jimmy Carter seemed likely also to oppose it.[30]

In December 1976, while Greene was visiting the country, the diplomat Ellsworth Bunker came to Contadora to conduct another round of negotiations. Greene distrusted Bunker owing to his having been American ambassador to South Vietnam through much of the war. Greene learned that the least Torrijos would settle for was neutralization of the canal, control of it by 2000, a fairly prompt adoption of Panamanian law in the Zone, and a reduction of the American military presence[31] – terms that would barely satisfy the demands of Panamanian nationalism, but might just secure an agreement. Bunker did not stay long, and Greene could see that there had been no breakthrough.[32]

The General gradually became more confidential with Greene, revealing to him the troubles of his marriage and private life, and describing his nightmares and premonitions of death. He even remarked that the two of them had in common a 'self-destructive' quality. Greene accepted this, but added that he was not himself suicidal,[33] which by this time in his life was a fair claim. Greene began to see in this man, in whom he discerned the 'charisma of near despair',[34] a kindred spirit.

Torrijos was unquestionably self-destructive – successfully so, as it turned out. Some journalists thought him impulsive to the point of madness: Diederich had once described him as 'a delightful madhatter-type modern caudillo'.[35] A part of Torrijos yearned to launch a guerrilla war against the Americans. Like Greene, he could not sit still, so he flew about the country in small planes and helicopters. He preferred pilots who were young and easily cowed, as they would attempt to fly through storms, fog, and high winds if he gave the order.[36] Greene somehow survived all the risks he took. Torrijos did not.

Diederich left Panama on 8 December 1976, and Greene remained until the 21st, mainly in the company of Chuchu. They spent a good deal of time on the road, and even made three visits to a supposedly haunted house, which was locked. On his visit the following year, Greene finally got into the vacant house by posing as a medium, and found it not haunted by a ghost but full of objects and photographs from another age.[37]

Of course, there was nothing amusing about most of what Chuchu showed Greene. Indeed, Greene visited the slums and saw some terrible poverty. They met a group of indigenous people whose village had been flooded by the recent construction of the Bayano hydroelectric dam in the eastern part of the country. They told Greene that the government had not kept its promises of compensation and aid after their resettlement. The next day, he took their concerns to Torrijos, who assured the novelist that the problem would be seen to.[38]

Chuchu was getting as much of a grip on Greene's imagination as had the General. After a week in the country, and a reading of *Heart of Darkness* for the first time since his sojourn in the leproseries, Greene suddenly had an idea for a novel to be entitled 'On the Way Back'. He asked Chuchu's permission to make a character of him, and to have him killed. Delighted, Chuchu agreed. In the story, a French journalist is commissioned to write about Panama. She travels about with the Chuchu character, much as Greene was doing, and they come to a series of things such as the haunted house to which they cannot get access, so they speak of seeing them on the way back. The Chuchu character is given some real phrases from his conversation, such as 'a revolver is no defence'. It is not a standard love story, but by the end they are about to go to bed together. However, Chuchu's character dies in a car bombing[39] – just before Greene's arrival, Chuchu's car had actually been bombed.[40] What the couple hoped to do on the return journey proves an illusion, a metaphor for the failure of a revolution. At times Greene considered having the General die instead, or merely having Chuchu disappear in pursuit of a lost dog.

The novel proved impossible to finish. Greene felt the problem was that by basing the story so closely on real people and places his imagination could not get airborne. Meanwhile, he wrote a similarly structured *Monsignor Quixote*, a road novel in which two characters set out through dangerous territory and one is eventually killed. In the end, he abandoned 'On the Way Back', publishing only the first chapter, 'An Appointment with the General', as a short story. One of the reasons to regret his not finishing this novel is that it portrayed a woman pursuing her profession in the face of toxic masculinity among both editors and soldiers – not a subject Greene had ventured on before.

Leaving Panama just before Christmas 1976, Greene got to work on 'The Country with Five Frontiers', a long article in which he claimed that the country's real importance had not to do with the canal itself, as the tonnage of freight that passed through it was steadily diminishing, but 'as a symbol of colonialism'. He dismissed the deposed Arias, not unreasonably, as an oligarch, but made a weaker case that 'other forms of democracy even under a military chief of state' could be made to work in an adequate way, especially with a leader, like Torrijos, so dedicated to consultation. He spoke of 1977 as the decisive year, after which there might be a turn to guerrilla warfare. Even though the General was 'bored with prudence', he stood between the hard left and a group of corrupt military officers who might overthrow him simply for greater opportunities of graft. Accordingly, the United States should see him as someone to deal with.[41]

The article appeared in the *New York Review of Books* on 17 February 1977, and created a sensation: here was arguably the most important writer in the English language explaining the perniciousness of American involvement in Panama. Of course, many people disputed his views, including one of his closest friends. Victoria Ocampo wrote him a somewhat angry letter, pointing out that Torrijos had had a longstanding personal connection with the now deceased Juan Perón, whom she knew to be a tyrant. This took Greene rather by surprise; he suggested that Torrijos was more like Tito than Perón, and promised to go into the matter with him whenever he saw him next.[42] Hugh Greene was more conservative than his brother and thought Graham was being naive about Torrijos, musing on one occasion: 'How can he like him?'[43] Oddly enough, Chuchu was against the writing of the article on imaginative grounds, thinking it might damage the novel Greene was hoping to write. Greene thought this a very 'sensitive' observation, but felt he needed to get something on paper right away.[44]

Working in Capri, Greene got about six thousand words of the novel written, and despite the urging of both Diederich and Chuchu, did not want to go to Panama again, as he had already committed part of the summer to a second journey with Father Durán.[45] A telegram from Torrijos in early July broke down his resistance. The situation there was coming to a boil. Jimmy Carter had taken advice from Cyrus Vance, his Secretary of State, and others before deciding to press for a new treaty. Rather than insisting on language about a guaranteed military presence in the Zone, Carter accepted 'an assured capacity or capability' to keep the Zone neutral and open once it was in Panamanian control. Moreover, the United States was prepared to grant new revenues from the canal to Panama, and to provide a great deal of direct financial aid to the country, which had experienced an economic downturn.[46]

On 10 August 1977, negotiators for both countries held a news conference at the Holiday Inn in Panama City. They announced an agreement allowing for the transfer of the canal to Panama by 2000. What they had come up with was actually two treaties. The Panama Canal Treaty abolished the Zone and allowed for a transition to Panamanian control. The Neutrality Treaty gave the United States its military assurances. Carter faced a grim struggle to get two-thirds of the Senate to vote for ratification, with the likes of Strom Thurmond of South Carolina digging their heels in against the supposed communist Torrijos, who did have one unlikely supporter on the American right; the actor John Wayne was a personal friend and came out in favour of the treaty, but since he had never auditioned for the Senate he could not really help the cause.[47] In his own country, Torrijos had to assuage nationalists who wanted an immediate transfer; in particular, he was likely to lose the support of students and the left. He said 'the treaty is like a small stone in a shoe which one must suffer for 23 years in order to remove a nail from one's heart'.[48]

Greene arrived in Panama on 21 August 1977, just as Diederich was leaving, since he had a rare opportunity to visit his old home in Haiti. Chuchu met Greene at the airport and soon told him that the General was unhappy about the terms of the treaty; he was not sleeping and had stopped drinking at weekends, 'a bad sign'. Greene wrote in his journal: '*The big question* – is the General moving to the right?' If so, there was a risk of him becoming just another military dictator like all the others in the region.

The next day, he had lunch with the General and learned that he was very happy with 'The Country with Five Frontiers'. They travelled to the General's home town and met his family and childhood friends. The next day they went by helicopter to David and then to some villages. In each place Greene asked whether the treaty should be ratified, and learned that it did have support. He asked what should happen if the treaty failed and received everywhere the answer that they should fight.

Chuchu introduced him to some of the people who sheltered in his 'pigeon house' for political refugees. One couple had been present in Chile at the time of the coup against Allende, and the husband had recently been detained by Noriega's G-2 as an 'ultra' left-winger. What happened next demonstrates how divided the regime actually was. With the connivance of Torrijos, Chuchu got this man out and went through a pretence of house arrest to save him from torture. Greene and a very drunk Chuchu went with the couple to a restaurant and learned that Noriega was actually there too, in a private dining room. Chuchu proposed, as a joke, to introduce Greene to him, but this terrified the couple, who had had quite enough of G-2.[49]

Chuchu also introduced Greene to a woman who had been tortured with electric shocks to her legs and another who had been sexually assaulted with a bayonet – both by the security forces in Argentina.[50] These sobering conversations, and others like them, led Greene to consider writing an article solely about the pigeon house, and he would later describe it in *Getting to Know the General*.[51]

Part of Chuchu's work for Torrijos was to harbour fugitives and to give discreet aid to rebels in neighbouring countries. He took Greene to meet some Nicaraguan exiles, including Dr Ramiro Contreras, who swore to drink the blood of Anastasio Somoza, the Nicaraguan dictator, in revenge for the death of his brother.[52] That brother, Eduardo

Contreras, was the original Commander 'Cero' or 'Zero', who in a spectacular raid on the house of a cabinet minister on 27 December 1974 had taken many politicians and relatives of Somoza hostage, so winning the release of Daniel Ortega and other political prisoners, and many political concessions. Commander 'Cero' was later killed in action, and his widow had married Ramiro.[53]

Meanwhile, Chuchu's drunkenness was becoming a problem. He vanished entirely for a day, leaving Greene to cool his heels. The novelist wrote in his journal: 'Counting the days before I could escape from Panama.'[54] He was in a bad mood when Chuchu then presented him with a request from the General that he should come to Washington for the signing of the treaty. He said no because it would complicate his route back to France, but accepted after Chuchu proposed to send him home from Washington on Concorde. As his humour returned, he also put in a joking request for a diplomatic passport, only to discover later that Chuchu had taken him seriously and obtained one – they were fairly easy to come by. Within a few days Greene found that he 'cherished' it.[55]

There was another famous addition to the Panamanian delegation: the Colombian novelist Gabriel García Márquez, whom Greene found 'very cordial, very vain' over glasses of whisky.[56] 'Gabo' later claimed that their presence in Washington was part of a joke Torrijos wanted to play on Carter, bringing into the country two authors who had, in the past, been forbidden entry.[57] However pleasant these ironies – the Secretary of State and a Marine Honor Guard met their plane at Andrews Air Force Base[58] – the General's purpose was to borrow the prestige of the great authors and to set his delegation apart from all the bemedalled dictators coming north for the signing, among whom he felt vastly outnumbered.

Once asked about what place he wanted in history, Omar Torrijos had replied: 'I don't want to go down in history, I just want to go into the Canal Zone.'[59] He was now on the verge of doing both, and he found it daunting. He would have to speak at the signing, so he asked Greene for help. The novelist added a sentence to the text of his five-minute address and slightly reorganized it, and both men were content. Torrijos told Greene he did not like having all the tyrants at the ceremony, and said he was nervous, 'but Carter's more nervous & that comforts me'. He then spoke of a Bolivian officer who found his feet trembling before he went into action and said: 'You sons of bitches, this is nothing to what you are going into later.'[60]

Carter had invited all the heads of state in the Organization of American States and each one had a private meeting with him. Fidel Castro was the only leader denied an invitation to Washington. Carter needed this show of unity in the Americas to help with ratification, but even so, he was welcoming some monsters to the White House. Worst of all was the presence of Augusto Pinochet, and in a sign that the Carter administration actually saw him as a criminal the Department of Justice leaked information from the FBI linking him to the murder by car bomb of Orlando Letelier, a former member of the Allende government, and his secretary in Massachusetts the year before.[61] Back in Panama, left-wing students, once supporters of Torrijos, were rioting against the treaty; being seen in such company would cost him support on the left and make him more vulnerable to a coup by ambitious military officers.

As Torrijos had hoped, Graham Greene cut a considerable figure in Washington. At a large reception at the OAS headquarters for heads of state and their delegations, Greene spent much of his time giving autographs; many guests came over to him specifically to praise *The Honorary Consul*. He could see in the room General Jorge Rafael Videla, the military ruler who was then presiding over the killings of tens of thousands of people in Argentina's Dirty War. Greene was standing close to Alfredo Stroessner of Paraguay, but could not actually approach him as he was surrounded by flunkies. When he was introduced to a Paraguayan minister, the man withdrew his hand and glared, before saying: 'You once passed through Paraguay.' Greene was 'pleased'.[62]

The treaty was signed the next day in the Hall of the Organization of American States. Greene saw it all as theatrical and wrote of it in 'The Great Spectacular' for the *New York Review of Books*, remarking on how it was attended by all the 'actors' – Henry Kissinger and Lady Bird Johnson and Nelson Rockefeller. Some of the actors were torturers and dictators, notably Pinochet looking like 'Boris Karloff'. Greene found Carter's speech 'banal' and 'inaudible'. Torrijos spoke in a clearer voice, and without preliminaries began, 'The treaty is very satisfactory, vastly advantageous to the United States, and we must confess not so advantageous to Panama.' He paused and added, 'Secretary of State Hay, 1903'. Greene enjoyed the joke, but then, he may have been responsible for it being there.[63]

70

STORMING THE PALACE

'If shit was worth money the poor would be born without arses,'[1] said Chuchu in August 1978. In his patched-up single-engine Cessna he was flying arms to leftist rebels in Nicaragua and El Salvador, and his gun-running would inspire the conclusion of Greene's last novel, *The Captain and the Enemy*. Meanwhile, Torrijos, having won a plebiscite in favour of the treaty in his own country, had cooperated with Jimmy Carter to see it ratified in Washington. It squeaked through the Senate in April, but legislation needed for its implementation was delayed. To promote the treaty, Torrijos had allowed for the return of political exiles, among them the former president Arnulfo Arias, and the re-establishment of political parties. He also received a parade of about fifty American senators and listened to their lectures on how to run a country.[2] He doubtless enjoyed the irony of watching them puff cigars with his name on the label – they were a gift from Fidel Castro.

Graham Greene arrived in Panama for his third visit on 19 August 1978 and would stay for two weeks. He hoped to interview Arias for *Time*, but the old politician, who was giving speeches comparing Torrijos to Satan, ignored the invitation.[3] Greene spent his first evening with Chuchu and Diederich drinking Planter's punch. Chuchu was worried: he thought the General was drifting from a quiet sympathy with the radical left to a form of social democracy. Greene teased him a little[4] – whatever he may have said in certain extreme moments, his own preference was for social democracy; he had looked for its emergence in Czechoslovakia, Cuba, and Chile, and now hoped that Panama, and indeed the whole of Central America, might evolve towards that elusive ideal. Chuchu, the Marxist, wanted politics with more teeth.

The next day Greene and Diederich flew in Chuchu's Cessna to the General's house at Farallon on the Pacific coast. They found him fighting off a fever, but otherwise relaxed. Lying in a hammock, rocking it with one leg, he spoke of his desire to be done with public life; the work on the treaty had tired him. He thought he should set up his own political party and use it to perpetuate his policies, while he himself could retire: 'What I need is a house, rum and a girl.'[5] He was not one to boss his guests around, but on this occasion he did. He believed, correctly, that the civil war in Nicaragua was about to heat up. The rebels had been trying to meet him, and he was keeping them at a distance, since any public sign of his involvement there could derail the legislation for implementing the treaty. He believed the rebels were likely to ask Graham Greene to come on campaign with them in the mountains. The General forbade him to do so, as he did not want him to become a 'propaganda martyr'.[6]

The invitation did come, from Father Ernesto Cardenal. Greene was not at all impressed by the Trappist monk and poet turned revolutionary, whom he met that night at dinner and again at a party the next day. With his flowing white hair, beard, and beret, Cardenal struck Greene as a 'foolish old priest' and the very 'caricature' of a revolutionary.[7] His sense of 'old' was off the mark – Cardenal was just fifty-three. According to Diederich, Greene thought little of the Sandinista leadership upon first acquaintance, but gradually warmed to them.[8] He did come to respect Cardenal, and took his side when he fell foul of the Vatican: in a visit to Nicaragua in 1983, Pope John Paul II publicly wagged his finger at the kneeling Cardenal, who was by then the Minister of Culture. Greene wrote that the pope was behaving as a politician rather than a priest, precisely the thing for which he was rebuking Cardenal.[9] The pope suspended Cardenal's faculties as a priest, and those of others, over their refusal to resign from the government. His suspension remained in place until Francis I lifted it in February 2019, just a year before his death at the age of ninety-five.[10]

The party on 21 August 1978 was held at the house of Ramiro Contreras, the brother of the original Commander 'Cero', and it was attended by some leading Sandinistas. If Greene did not initially respect Cardenal, he was impressed by another Nicaraguan, German Pomares Ordoñez – indeed, the party was in honour of his birthday.

Sizing him up, Greene remarked that he would trust *this* man to take him to Nicaragua. A tough, stolid fighter recently released by Honduran authorities at the request of Torrijos, Pomares said that it was not enough to depose Anastasio Somoza if his system remained in place. He believed that the FSLN (Frente Sandinista de Liberación Nacional) must achieve a revolution or win a great victory. Even as he was speaking, such a thing was in the works.[11]

When it happened the next day, Graham Greene was looking into pirates. As a child, he had been wild about Long John Silver and Henry Morgan, and throughout his adult life he had tried to walk one plank after another. On this occasion, he went off briefly with Diederich and Chuchu in search of Sir Francis Drake, who had died of dysentery in 1596 after his failure to capture Portobelo, and was buried at sea in full armour inside a lead coffin, further weighted with round-shot so the Spanish would never find his body. A bemused Torrijos provided the requisite helicopter but could make no sense of a grown man going on a quest for 'El Draque'.

Had he lived long enough, Greene would have been ecstatic to see the eventual discovery of two of Drake's scuttled ships in waters off Panama.[12] The novelist's own search took him to Nombre de Dios on the Atlantic side, where the now-overgrown Camino Real or Royal Road across the isthmus had ended and where mules carrying Inca gold shipped from Peru had once trudged. Without the aid of scuba gear or sonar, Greene was relying on old poems and a little research to guide him; when they reached what he supposed was a spot not far from the submerged coffin, he announced to Chuchu and Diederich, in an uncharacteristic expression, that he was feeling mystical 'vibes', but the pilots then discovered that they had misread their map and deposited the searchers in entirely the wrong place, so alas the vibes were contradicted. It was in the end a failed search, but a happy one, to which Planter's punch made all the difference.[13] This bit of skylarking might not merit retelling, except that imagery of pirates and of mules transporting gold in Panama is at the heart of *The Captain and the Enemy*. The little plane running guns to Nicaragua is even called 'one of the mules'.[14]

While Greene was having a siesta after this search, Diederich received a call from his editor telling him to go straight to Managua.

Leaving Greene asleep, he went off to cover a huge hostage-taking: the day before (22 August 1978) twenty-four FSLN fighters, under a new Commander Cero, Edén Pastora, had seized the National Palace, which housed the Congress and many government offices, and taken fifteen hundred hostages, including forty-nine deputies. Anastasio Somoza typically did not work at this location, preferring a nearby bunker, so he was not among the captives; however, it was a disaster for him. The guerrillas obtained the release of fifty-nine political prisoners, as well as a cash ransom, and their 'War Communiqué Number One', which took 105 minutes to read aloud, was broadcast half a dozen times and published in newspapers.[15] A general strike followed, with local uprisings throughout the country. Somoza turned aircraft and tanks on rebellious towns and cities, killing about two thousand people, mostly civilians, by the end of September.[16]

Chuchu celebrated the news from Managua by getting drunk, but in so doing cost Greene an extraordinary opportunity. Torrijos had told them to fly to Managua and help evacuate Pastora, his fighters, the freed political prisoners, and some remaining hostages. Chuchu got the arrangements wrong and they missed the flight. The two spent a miserable day drinking rum, but soon the General, himself in a mood to rejoice, sent for them. At a military base Greene met some of those who had flown from Managua, including Edén Pastora, a complicated figure who later turned against the Sandinistas but was eventually reconciled to them, and Tomás Borge, who went on to become the hard-nosed Interior Minister in the Sandinista government.[17]

Torrijos now had a job for Greene and Chuchu. He proposed that they go, as his emissaries, north to Belize, formerly British Honduras, which had a Caribbean coast and was neighboured by Guatemala and Mexico. Its population was just 140,000. The British had long accepted that it should be fully independent, but Guatemala wanted to seize it and had, on occasion, massed its forces on the frontier, requiring the British to reinforce its garrison. The previous year, the Foreign Office had botched negotiations with Guatemala by indicating an openness to hand over land, a move likely to encourage a comparable claim by Mexico for its own piece of Belize. The Guatemalans were also demanding control of the territory's economy, foreign affairs, and military.

George Price, the premier of Belize and a friend of Torrijos, had conducted a strong international campaign for Belize to be free of Britain and safe from Guatemala, and he especially wanted the British garrison to be switched for a broadly constituted Commonwealth force or one from Latin America. The military regime in Guatemala enjoyed no international support for its claims, and was condemned for its human rights record:[18] political murders, disappearances, and torture were commonplace. Just three months before Greene's visit to the region, Nekchi indigenous people in the Guatemalan town of Panzos had been protesting the loss of their land to oil and nickel interests when soldiers opened fire and killed about 113 men, women, children, and babies.[19] Belize had every reason to be afraid of the regime in Guatemala.

Greene found himself 'charmed' by Belize City, where houses stood on posts seven feet high, and all around was mangrove swamp. The city had been battered by a hurricane in 1961 and was always threatened by the sea: 'Perhaps the charm comes from the temporary, of the precarious, of living on the edge of destruction'. He could understand the interest Torrijos had in this vulnerable place, which belonged, as the General himself did, to 'a world of confrontation with superior powers, of the dangers and uncertainties of what the next day would bring'.[20] This too was Greeneland.

At first, Greene thought George Price all too ingratiating, almost 'servile', but then he realized that here was a truly humble man. Educated by Jesuits, he had tried to become a priest, but then his father died and he had to support his family. He remained celibate and was a daily communicant, and, as Diederich recalled, was so frugal with public funds that he would not take taxis but always went on the bus.[21] He had read Greene's works and once sent him a letter about a short story – Greene could not remember this letter but was glad to learn that he had responded. The two spoke of the theologians Teilhard de Chardin and Hans Küng, and about the works of Thomas Mann.

Price took them in an old black Land Rover to the Mayan ruins of Xunantunich, where the atheist Chuchu hedged his bets and spent some time calling to his ancestors – unsuccessfully, as it turned out. They drove on to the frontier, where Price cheerfully walked into Guatemalan territory and talked to customs officials as old friends. On the way back, he gave lifts to those on foot, and when he waved to people Greene thought he saw in the gesture a priest's blessing.[22]

Of course, not everybody loved George Price. He was a democratic socialist, and his conservative opponents wanted the British simply to stay in Belize. A report appeared in the opposition press about '"the so-called writer called Green" [*sic*] who had been sent by the Communist Torrijos to see his fellow-Communist Price for reasons which were unknown and certainly sinister'.[23] There was not a great deal Greene could do for Price. As discussions dragged on concerning the final status of the colony, in August 1980 he wrote a letter to *The Times* arguing against territorial concessions and defending Price from the accusation that he was a communist.[24] It took another year, but Belize did win its independence, and Price invited Greene in 'gratitude' to attend the national ceremonies on 21 September 1981. Greene was 'touched and honoured' by the invitation, but by then he was so involved in a private war against the mafia in Nice he could not make the journey.[25]

In that summer of August 1978, Greene and Chuchu carried out another important errand for Torrijos, this time in Costa Rica, which, like Panama, had given discreet support to Nicaraguan rebels. Chuchu himself had flown weapons to locations along the border. On this occasion, he was to meet two Sandinista leaders, a man and a woman, at a café in the capital, San José. Greene made small talk with the woman, whom he remembered meeting at the pigeon house the year before. This was the poet Rosario Murillo, who would go on to become vice-president of Nicaragua. At another table, Chuchu did business with 'a tall, dark, serious man' who was not identified to Greene; he later learned that this was Murillo's future husband, Daniel Ortega, who would become the dominant figure in Nicaraguan politics for over forty years.[26] The couple certainly seemed heroic in the 1970s and 80s, leaders in a rebellion that disposed of a dictator who did not hesitate to rain shells and rockets onto villages.

Through the closing months of 1978, Bernard Diederich's life was constantly in danger as he documented atrocities in Nicaragua. At fifty-two, he was now a veteran war reporter, and, as he told Greene, he had seen never seen anything to match the carnage of Nicaragua.[27] He strongly approved of the Sandinista cause. And yet, in 2019, a ninety-three-year-old Diederich, by then in the last months of his life, would remark, 'We are all disappointed, terribly sad'; there was 'no excuse' for the conduct of Ortega and Murillo, who were 'just power hungry'.[28]

Ortega and Murillo were clinging to power much as Anastasio Somoza had once done: by sheer repression. In 1994, Ernesto Cardenal broke with them as dictators; in a Spanish pun on theft, he said they were not running a revolution but a 'robo-lucion'.[29] Things would get much worse. The Inter-American Commission on Human Rights concluded that in suppressing protests beginning on 18 April 2018, the regime had been guilty of 325 deaths, amounting to a 'crime against humanity'.[30] Many of those protesting against Ortega and Murillo had once been their staunch supporters[31] – the couple had abandoned the ideals of the old movement. In Diederich's more pointed phrase, they had 'gone to hell'.[32]

At the time, Greene looked upon the Sandinistas, quite reasonably, as a force for democracy and economic fairness, and he believed that their struggle could loosen America's grip on the region. But he would have had to change his thinking as time passed. He had done so with respect to Cuba once he fully understood how opponents of the regime, religious outsiders, and homosexuals were being abused. Likewise, he would have been distressed by the conduct of former friends in Nicaragua. However, he was intellectually prepared for such things. He had once spoken of his own duty in 'The Virtue of Disloyalty', a lecture given in Hamburg in 1969: '... the writer should always be ready to change sides at the drop of a hat. He stands for the victims, and the victims change.'[33]

71

THE BOMB PARTY

There was something about the Christmas crackers. It was 1978, and Greene was eating Christmas dinner with Caroline and her sons in Jongny, the Swiss village where she now lived. It was then, he said, that the idea for *Doctor Fischer of Geneva or The Bomb Party* came to him.[1] Dr Fischer, an immensely wealthy manufacturer of toothpaste, holds dinners at which he tries to see how much humiliation people not quite as rich as himself will bear to get an expensive present from him; at one dinner he makes his guests choke down cold porridge. At his last, he goes much further and devises a game comparable to Russian roulette involving Christmas crackers: five contain large cheques, one is said to contain a bomb, and they must be drawn out of a bran tub. Will his guests play the game?

Seeing the Christmas crackers on Caroline's table probably reminded Greene of something from childhood reading. William Le Queux's novel *Spies of the Kaiser: Plotting the Downfall of England* became a bestseller in 1909 by claiming that the Germans had planted an army of spies in England, and the book was popular for years afterwards. In its last chapter, German agents attempt to kill two patriotic characters with exploding Christmas crackers.[2] He had certainly read Le Queux as he alludes to him in *The Ministry of Fear*.

Greene's book is not a thriller – it is a fantasy in some ways reminiscent of Henry James's *The Turn of the Screw*. Greene is not writing about ghosts, but he is evoking an atmosphere of evil and the book has supernatural overtones, with Dr Fischer often compared to God or to Satan. He is testing out how much suffering a certain kind of person will bear for a reward, and the exercise has parallels with what the Christian God is thought to do. The narrator is Alfred Jones, a translator for a Swiss chocolate manufacturer. The chocolate causes tooth decay, which Fischer's toothpaste counteracts, an ironic parallel to sin and grace. Jones marries Fischer's estranged daughter and gets drawn into his cruel dinners, which resemble hateful sacraments. The daughter, Anna-Luise, is killed in a skiing accident, and Jones longs for his own death; indeed, he throws off Fischer's last experiment somewhat by seeking the explosive cracker for himself. When Fischer takes his own life, Jones is left to envy his courage, though he allows that Fischer now has no more significance than a dead dog.

If *Doctor Fischer of Geneva* takes up, in a grim allegory, the ideas of *The Honorary Consul*, it focuses only on the darkness of God, what Father Rivas called the 'night-side', and offers little hope of evolution. In this respect, the book is extraordinarily bitter. However, there is another element here. Jones has lost his much-loved wife and has struck up a friendship with a man named Steiner, who once fell in love with her mother, Fischer's wife, now also dead. Steiner hates Fischer for his treatment of himself and of the woman, with whom he only listened to music: 'We were never really lovers, but he made innocence dirty. Now I want to get near enough to him to spit in God Almighty's face.' The book is a study of grief, as Jones puts it: 'I saw the continuous straight falling of the snow as though the world had ceased revolving and lay becalmed at the centre of a blizzard.'[3]

This novel has an inescapable personal context. Greene's relationship with Catherine Walston had made impossible any lasting relationship with another woman in the 1950s, and it was certainly an intolerable complication for Anita Björk. When he took up with Yvonne Cloetta, he made the necessary decision, however slowly, to disengage from Catherine. She remained married to Harry and pursued other relationships, but came to regard Graham's distance, his infrequent, dictated letters, his avoidance of her, as a betrayal.

At the same time, she suffered a great many health problems, and for fifteen years endured chronic pain. In time she developed leukaemia, from which she experienced remissions. It returned, and she deteriorated during 1977–8, with her weight dropping to seven stone.[4]

Graham visited her at Thriplow in November 1977, but it was uncomfortable and she was left thinking him angry about something. In one of her last letters to him, she wrote: 'What a vast amount of pleasure you have given me playing scrabble on the roof at the Rosaio and the 7/30 Bus to Gemma and teaching me [to] swim underwater at Ian Fleming's house, smoking opium and Angkor, ETC . . . There has never been anyone in my life like you . . . '[5] Having feared death, she came to accept it in her last weeks, though it came a little sooner than she expected. She died of a haemorrhage on 2 September 1978.[6] She was just sixty-two.

Graham was returning from Panama when Marie Biche broke the news to him. The funeral took place at St George's Church in Thriplow on 7 September 1978. He did not attend, but Biche sent him a description of it, and a postcard of the church on which she indicated the position of the grave. Graham wrote to Harry expressing sympathy, as well as remorse for suffering he had caused over the years. In his response, Harry wrote that it was difficult to answer the letter, but that while he had indeed caused suffering, remorse was not called for since everyone causes pain: 'But you gave Catherine something (I don't know what) that no one else had given her. It would not be unjust [?] to say it changed her life: but it developed her into a far more deeply feeling human being than before . . . '[7]

Many years earlier, Graham and Catherine had gone through a form of marriage, secretly exchanging vows during a Mass in Tunbridge Wells,[8] and for a time he had put great store by it. It is hard, then, not to think of the death of Anna-Luise in *Doctor Fischer of Geneva* as somehow reflecting Greene's recent experience or the pent-up anger of many years, as if in his relationship with Catherine God had been toying with him. However, the book is not entirely despairing, as at the end Jones takes neither of the options open to him: embrace the corruption of the rich or commit suicide. Instead he returns to an ordinary life, and merely meets a client. A. S. Frere, who admired the novella, discerned its personal dimension and thought it was Greene's most 'self-expressing' work.[9]

Greene left Switzerland, and began writing the novella in Antibes on 30 December 1978. He worked at a tremendous pace and had a version of the story finished by the time he went to London in mid-February. Despite having other projects, including *Monsignor Quixote*, under way, Greene was again, as he had been in the early 1960s, afraid that he was written out. In January he wrote to the American journalist

Gloria Emerson: 'I have just begun re-reading *Moby Dick* in celebration of starting a new book which I thought I would never do.'[10] He chose a sentence from Melville as his epigraph: 'Who has but once dined his friends, has tasted whatever it is to be Caesar.' The speed with which he worked was not just a matter of celebration. He was facing the real possibility of dying very soon, and he wanted to get this book written.

On 20 February 1979 he went into the King Edward VII Hospital in London for the removal of a large portion of his colon; he later described it to Anita as the same operation 'that scoundrel Reagan had' – that is, a colectomy. He told Caroline, at the time, that the procedure would be 'not serious but disagreeable'.[11] In fact, it was very serious, as the surgeon told him his chances were '50–50'.[12] Preparing for the worst, he wrote to Yvonne: 'You have given me so much love & happiness over these 19 years which have been the best of my life.' As it turned out, the malignant polyp was well situated;[13] the operation on the 23rd was a success, and he was spared a colostomy, a possibility that had distressed him. On the 27th he called Elisabeth from hospital and described the experience as 'horrid', and said he did not want visitors as talking gave him hiccups.[14] He spent four days on an intravenous drip and was discharged in about twelve. Left with a fifteen-inch vertical scar on his lower abdomen, he felt altogether 'feeble'.[15] Convalescing in Antibes for two months, he began to feel himself again in mid-April, and was well enough by June to travel to Oxford to receive an honorary doctorate of letters.[16]

During his convalescence, Greene was waiting to learn the fate of two short plays he had written. One, *Yes and No*, is a brief parody of acting and directing styles: a director gives incoherent instructions to a young actor whose only lines are 'Yes' and 'No'. The second, longer one, *For Whom the Bell Chimes*, he described to his dramatic agent Jan Van Loewen as 'a disreputable farce which I don't suppose anyone will want'.[17] He was more or less correct. The story is pure entertainment, with criminals impersonating collectors for a polio charity and a murdered woman's body concealed in a folding bed. Even using the first play as a curtain-raiser for the second, they were too short for a mainstream production in London or New York. In the end, a disappointed Greene had to settle for a production at the Haymarket Studio Theatre in Leicester, which opened on 20 March 1980.[18]

More importantly, he got back to work on *Doctor Fischer of Geneva*.[19] As happened rarely, he liked this book, and thought it auspicious that Josephine Reid, who still took on some jobs for him, wept over the manuscript as she typed.[20] He expanded and revised the story, and had what he thought a 'publishable' version of thirty-four thousand words ready by 15 June. As was his usual method, he read the manuscript into his Dictaphone and sent the belts to Reid for typing.[21] He was able to place the final typescript in Max Reinhardt's hands at the beginning of August.[22]

It reached the bookshops in late March 1980, and even though it was not a major work for Greene it was well received. Margaret Drabble wrote: 'This is a cold and glittering fable, decked with deadly trinkets – crystal glasses, gold watches, dry martinis, Muscat grapes, emeralds. These are the little presents with which Greene serves up the cold porridge of his knowledge. We swallow it, of course.'[23] In the United States, Christopher Lehmann-Haupt thought the theologizing 'glib' but praised it as a 'wickedly inventive piece of black humour'.[24]

72

THREE HOSTAGES

'Graham, I thought you were not there.'

'I was fast asleep, Chuchu. Where are you?'

'In Panama, of course. I have a message for you from the General.'[1]

The telephone had rung in Antibes at 1 a.m. on 30 April 1979. Much as Greene missed his friends in Panama, he had no reason to believe that he would ever go back. Just two months earlier, he had had his colectomy and was still incapable of making the long flight; at the same time, he was beginning to believe that a criminal gang posed a terrible threat to Yvonne's family and that he must remain on post in France.

No matter, Central America was coming to him. The Canal Treaty was settled, and the Sandinistas had driven Somoza out of Nicaragua, but a frightening new civil war was about to break out in El Salvador, the violence of which is now hard to comprehend. The causes of the war can be traced chiefly to land ownership. Almost all the agricultural land was owned by a few families, whose wealth derived from coffee.[2] A brief war with neighbouring Honduras in 1969 caused the border to be closed, ruining the Salvadoran economy and plunging many landless people into destitution. In 1972, José Napoleón Duarte, a Christian Democrat, won election as president but was expelled from the country. The military took over and engaged in repression of the left, both the radical and merely reformist strands, particularly in the countryside, where an outfit named ORDEN (Organización Democrática Nacionalista) held sway through a network of spies and occasional collaborators numbering sixty to one hundred thousand. A persecution set in with union leaders, teachers, and left-leaning church workers being assassinated.[3]

In the mid-1970s the government attempted to quell tensions by embarking on modest land reform, but it was thwarted by the traditional oligarchs and so it seemed that change by political means was an impossibility. By 1977 there was a marked increase in political repression by the military and by paramilitaries. The best known of those killed at this time was Father Rutilio Grande, SJ, a pastor and theologian who supported the formation of *comunidades eclesiales de base* – essentially church-based cooperatives – which made it possible for peasants to press for their rights. He and two other men were ambushed on a country road in March 1977.[4] His friend, the now canonized Archbishop Óscar Romero, was so shocked by the killing that he abandoned his own political conservatism and began to protest economic injustice and the operation of the death squads.

It turned out that the General wanted Greene to help resolve a hostage situation in El Salvador. A messenger from Panama appeared in Antibes and explained that rebels had abducted two bankers. The rebels were willing to drop their original demands for the release of political prisoners and the broadcast of a communiqué, and would settle for a ransom of five million dollars. Greene was to pass this information on to their employer, the little-known Bank of London and Montreal based in Nassau. With the help of Hugh's son, the publisher Graham C. Greene, he made contact with the right official in the firm, who initially treated his approach with scepticism; he may have thought Greene a criminal or fantasist. Greene gave him a number to call in Mexico City and left. The novelist met the General's emissary again shortly after; the man placed a call to Mexico and learned that the bank had already made contact, and soon the men were free. Greene rather resented the bank's lack of gratitude. He thought he had earned at least a case of Scotch, but he supposed that the bank believed he would get a cut of the ransom money. The contact in Mexico City was, in fact, Gabriel García Márquez, who had founded an organization called Habeas, a Central American equivalent of Amnesty International.[5]

Meanwhile the situation in El Salvador was growing dire. As students, workers, peasants, and church leaders were coming together in mass protests and acts of civil disobedience, General Carlos Humberto Romero, the right-winger running the government, initiated a ruthless campaign against anyone assumed to be an opponent of the regime: bodies were frequently found at the sides of roads. In October, the

Carter administration organized a bloodless coup to get rid of this man and install a junta with civilian representation from the centre and left. The junta promised nationalization of foreign trade in coffee and sugar, an investigation of political violence, and land reform. None of it happened, and the civilians withdrew at the end of 1979; a series of juntas would be formed and overthrown in the coming year. A popular front against the government came together in January 1980, and about two hundred thousand people marched through San Salvador in support. Towards the end of 1980, several guerrilla groups would unite as the Farabundo Martí National Liberation Front (FMLN),[6] and Greene would have dealings with them.

Archbishop Óscar Romero happened to be an old friend of Bernard Diederich, and told him on several occasions that he expected to be killed.[7] In the early months of 1980, he spoke against the juntas as a 'cover for repression' and rounded on the United States for providing military aid. On 23 March 1980, Romero spoke of the supposed agrarian reforms as 'bathed in blood', and urged soldiers to disobey their orders. The next morning, as he was saying Mass, a gunman shot him through the heart. At his funeral, a bomb went off outside the cathedral, and the panicking crowd of fifty thousand was machine-gunned, leaving up to forty people dead and another two hundred wounded.[8]

The cruelties were relentless. On 14 May 1980, at least three hundred peasants were killed by the National Guard, ORDEN, and Honduran forces at the Sumpul River in a counter-insurgency sweep. They were shot, bayoneted, or drowned as they fled towards the river, which marked the border with Honduras.[9] In October the army began a campaign in the department of Morazán, killing three thousand people and turning twenty-four thousand into refugees.[10] Church workers were often targets: in December 1980, three American nuns of the Maryknoll Order and a laywoman were raped, machine-gunned, and buried in a shallow grave as supposed communists. Graham Greene later wrote a cover endorsement for Ana Carrigan's *Salvador Witness*, focusing on the life of the murdered laywoman, Jean Donovan.[11]

Socorro Juridico, a group of lawyers sponsored by the archdiocese of San Salvador, documented 8062 political assassinations carried out by the army, national guard, police, and paramilitaries in 1980 alone. This count did not include the disappeared, or those killed in military clashes.[12] With the new Reagan administration seeking to push back what it took to be a communist tide in the region, such numbers would be repeated year after year until a negotiated peace in 1992. In a country of 4.7 million, something like seventy-five thousand people were killed, and eight thousand more disappeared.[13]

At the beginning of 1980, Greene was again asked to help resolve a kidnapping in El Salvador. He received a late-night call from the South African chargé d'affaires in Paris, Jeremy Shearer, who asked for his help in securing the release of Archibald Gardner Dunn, the country's ambassador to El Salvador, who had been abducted on 28 November 1979. The ransom demands were extreme and they did not know who was holding Dunn.

The South Africans would have had to swallow some pride to seek help from the author of *The Human Factor*, but Shearer seems to have liked and admired Greene. The novelist put him in contact with the bank that had been involved in the earlier kidnapping to see if they still had the telephone number in Mexico City.

In the midst of this, Greene got hold of Gabriel García Márquez and explained the details of the case. Gabo foresaw real difficulty. The first task was to determine which of five guerrilla groups were holding the ambassador. More importantly, South Africa had no friends on the left and someone like Dunn would be seen as a fascist, wholly deserving of his fate. Gabo found it hard to involve himself in such a case but did take a hand in it. He advised Greene that it would be far better for the family to make contact than for the South African government to do so.[14] When Greene relayed this information back to Shearer in Paris, he learned that Dunn's wife was suffering from cancer and her children were not up to the job of negotiating. So he suggested a bit of deception: the South African diplomatic service should 'provide a notional brother-in-law'.[15] Nothing worked, and Dunn remained in captivity.

By the summer of 1980, Greene was in much better health, embarking on a longer than usual excursion with Father Durán in July. He also accepted, at short notice, an invitation from the General, who had it in mind to send him back to Nicaragua. He had dinner in Antibes with Jeremy Shearer and asked if there was anything he could do for Ambassador Dunn while he was in the region. The chargé told him that the matter was being handled by the embassy in Washington, and that it would be best not 'to cross lines'.[16] For most of his life, Greene had been crossing lines, and would do so again in trying to help Dunn.

Arriving in Panama on 19 August 1980 for a two-week visit, he spent his first few days with Chuchu and Diederich. He was surprised by changes in Panama City: everywhere were new bank buildings of twenty storeys or higher, a strange sight in a country supposedly dedicated to social democracy.[17] He received word from Gabo that the ambassador's release was now arranged but Salvador Cayetano Carpio, codenamed Comandante Marcial, wanted first to speak with Graham Greene. Marcial was head of the FPN, the largest rebel faction and the group holding the ambassador.

It took a while for Chuchu to track down the General, but on the evening of the 21st they had dinner together at the house of Rory Gonzalez. The leader's young girlfriend was there and he showed off their new baby. He rebuked Greene for addressing him as 'General' rather than by his first name, 'Omar', when other people were present as this placed a distance between them; Greene found this poignant rather than offensive, and wrote of him in his journal as 'A lonely man genuinely affectionate & grasping for friendship.'[18] In what turned into an evening of hard drinking, Torrijos asked that Greene delay his departure for Nicaragua to make sure of meeting Cayetano, as he wanted this negotiation to succeed.

Before meeting the rebel leader, Greene read an interview with Ambassador Dunn in *Granma*, the official newspaper of the Cuban government. He could see that the man was very ill and had been badly treated; the journalist who conducted the interview was also badgering him. Disgusted, Greene threw down the newspaper and swore never to read it again.[19]

Diederich noticed that Greene was still angry when Cayetano appeared at his hotel escorted by a G-2 officer.[20] A small, elderly man in spectacles – this was what a lesser evil looked like. When roused, Greene was formidable, and for this kind of conversation he needed to be, even though Cayetano behaved courteously. The left in El Salvador was very divided: Cayetano, who is often compared to Ho Chi Minh, was the chief advocate for a protracted popular war rather than for socialism achieved through the ballot box; among his followers he encouraged immediate sacrifice for the cause.[21] Once a seminarian, he had been imprisoned and tortured, and grew into a hardline ideologue, essentially indifferent to bloodshed. When Greene came to write about this encounter, he did not wish his words to be construed as endorsing the Salvadoran regime, so offered explanations for how Cayetano had become so harsh. Nonetheless, as Greene told Diederich, he thought the man's eyes hard and would not care to be his prisoner. Writing to his son Francis, he referred to Cayetano as 'creepy'.[22]

It is usually assumed that Greene was swept along by enthusiasm for rebel movements. He wasn't. Certainly, he and Diederich treated Chuchu's passion for the armed struggle in El Salvador with caution, as did the General himself. Greene had good information on what was happening there, and knew that the guerrillas were themselves guilty of atrocities. Of course, no one really knows the full extent of what happened in El Salvador. The UN Truth Commission of 1993 found that of the twenty-two thousand complaints it received of executions, disappearances, and torture over an eleven-year period, representing only 'a significant sample' of all that occurred, 85 per cent were specifically attributed by witnesses to agents of the government and paramilitaries or death squads allied to it. However, the commission also received eight hundred complaints against the rebels, half concerning executions, and the rest disappearances and forced recruitment.[23] Admittedly, this number was a small fraction of the total, but even so it represented a great deal of butchery. Greene had been somewhat critical of the guerrillas in Nicaragua, but judged that they were much better than those in El Salvador.[24]

When the meeting moved to Greene's room, Diederich observed an odd tableau: while discussing the fate of Archibald Dunn, Greene and Cayetano sat separated from each other by the bed, on which Greene had earlier laid the page proofs of Mark Amory's edition of *The Letters of Evelyn Waugh*. It was the sort of thing that happened in Greene's life; he had, after all, been handed a Tintin book in the bell tower at Phat Diem.

Playing his weak hand, Greene appealed for a release purely on humanitarian grounds since Dunn's wife was dying of cancer. There followed a brief silence during which the novelist searched his thoughts for some stronger grounds for appeal, then Cayetano assured him that things were 'all right' apart from a few points such as the ransom.

Greene had the names of people in South Africa and elsewhere who were prepared to pay the money. This pleased Cayetano; he made note of the names, and seemed to warm up.

Cayetano told him that he had some associates downstairs – these were representatives of the other rebel groups – might they come up? Greene knew that they were meeting in Panama to form a united front, so he agreed to meet them – they would need to agree to the release. Diederich was asked to leave the room for what became a two-hour session. One of the rebels could speak English; he acted as interpreter and gave a long propaganda speech. Greene had nothing more to offer them, except that he could write truthfully and dispel 'disinformation'. While all this was going on, Diederich felt the vulnerability of their position: gunmen might burst in at any moment and kill everybody.

At the end, Greene turned the tables and challenged Cayetano about the execution of peasants. The rebels exercised harsh military discipline in areas they controlled and regularly shot 'ears' – those thought to be informers – as well as anyone suspected of belonging to ORDEN.[25] His answer was that the word peasants should be in inverted commas. He would not change his practices simply because a foreign novelist did not like them. When they emerged from the room, Diederich also asked Cayetano about the peasants and was told that those they executed belonged to ORDEN, 'But we have recently changed that policy.' This change of policy occurred between one room and another, but it hardly affected what happened in the field.

Greene was happy: he believed that he had been given an assurance that Archibald Dunn would soon be free. It did not happen. On 8 October 1980, the guerrillas issued a communiqué that Dunn had been executed, so Greene felt he had been deceived by Cayetano. Bernard Diederich's sources[26] then passed on a quite different story that the ambassador, already sick, had died in captivity, rendering the whole business a shambles. In that scenario, the communiqué was an attempt to salvage a little value from the kidnapping; the guerrillas could pretend to have followed through on their threats. Jeremy Shearer inclined to this view, as did Greene.[27]

Strangely enough, the story of the kidnapping of Archibald Dunn raised its head again in 2018, when his grandson launched a lawsuit against the president of El Salvador, Sánchez Cerén, alleging that he was one of Cayetano's senior lieutenants and involved in the abduction, a charge he denies. The suit is merely for habeas corpus and intended to force him to reveal where the body is. The Supreme Court ordered Cerén to testify and his refusal to do so threatened to become a constitutional crisis in El Salvador.[28] Cerén's presidential term ended in June 2019, so presumably the action will proceed. For many years Cerén was protected by an amnesty law, which has since been declared unconstitutional, so prosecutors have opened an investigation into his role in the kidnapping of Dunn, and it seems likely that it will expand to include other kidnappings and deaths.[29]

Having met Cayetano, Greene headed to Managua on 23 August to attend a great demonstration in honour of a highly successful literacy campaign in which five thousand high school students had been sent into the countryside to teach peasants to read. It was an awkward assignment for Greene as the Sandinistas had wanted Torrijos himself to come, but, perhaps insultingly, he sent the Englishman as his representative. The General was uneasy about the new government in Managua: they were doctrinaire and were provoking the United States unnecessarily. They had refused humanitarian aid from the Americans and were bringing in personnel from Cuba and Eastern Europe – the country was beginning to look like a client of the Soviet Union. Torrijos had sent soldiers and arms for the fight against Somoza, but could now see that the Sandinistas were making a trap for themselves and he did not care to join them inside it.[30]

The demonstration was vast, with perhaps hundreds of thousands in attendance, and the speeches went on interminably, especially one by Humberto Ortega, the Defence Minister and brother of Daniel Ortega. Tomás Borge, the Interior Minister, did better, speaking for just five minutes. Although Greene made courtesy visits to Ernesto Cardenal and other ministers, his stay in Managua was mostly focused on Borge, and it did not go especially well. The minister was unhappy when Greene moved out of a remote VIP house in favour of Managua's InterContinental Hotel, where, presumably, surveillance was more difficult. Later, his bodyguards took the cassette out of Diederich's tape recorder, and when he protested to Borge he was told that he should not have been recording. Diederich would later wonder whether Borge thought them Torrijos's spies. Greene was not told that the whole junta had assembled for a dinner with him, so missed one of the most important events planned on his itinerary, doubtless giving offence.[31]

Back in Panama, Greene asked to see Bocas del Toro on the Atlantic coast, the furthest point reached by Christopher Columbus in his voyages; this was the same boyish impulse that had led him on an earlier visit to seek out Francis Drake's grave. Accustomed to the General's recklessness, the pilot flew through a dangerous rainstorm, unnerving the novelist, who would have preferred to go by car. Once the plane had landed, they walked through ankle-deep water and checked in to a hotel room equipped with just two iron bedsteads, a single chair, and a light that did not work. The next morning, the weather had cleared, and 'Bocas was transformed'. In the little houses on stilts with balconies Greene saw something of Freetown, 'a town I had loved'. He also had ideas, mistaken as it turned out, of how he might revive his Panamanian novel, 'On the Way Back'.[32]

Before going home, Greene had to turn down a whimsical request from the General. He wanted to dress the novelist in an officer's uniform and take him for war games with the Americans at Fort Bragg in North Carolina. This amused Greene, but he wondered how convincing he would appear – a Panamanian military officer in his seventies with no Spanish and an English accent.[33] He felt that it was all right to say no; after all, he would be back next year, and he would see the General then.

And so it was that a year later Greene was getting ready for that journey when he heard that Omar Torrijos Herrera was missing, then confirmed as dead. On 31 July 1981, he had flown in a twin-engine de Havilland Otter towards the town of Coclesito in bad weather. Unable to see clearly, his experienced pilot and co-pilot aborted two attempts to land at a dirt airstrip, and as they attempted a third one of the wings hit a tree. The plane crashed into the side of a mountain, and the seven aboard, including Torrijos, were killed. It took a day for the bodies to be recovered.[34]

Greene did not attend the state funeral, but wrote to Chuchu: 'I really loved that man. What an extraordinary thing it was that a tiny country like Panama produced one of the great men of our time … I had already packed my bags to come to you last Wednesday and the shock left me staggered.'[35] For his part, Chuchu believed the worst: he assumed it was a bomb and that Torrijos had been assassinated. He had no proof of this, yet Greene was inclined to believe him. In fact, conspiracy theories abounded. Some people claimed that Manuel Noriega, or another of the General's rivals in the military, had arranged such a bomb. Others claimed that since Torrijos had lately befriended Edén Pastora, the Sandinistas had decided to kill him.

Some believed it was the CIA, even though at the time of the funeral the American ambassador remarked that Torrijos 'talked left, but acted conservatively' and was coming to see the region in terms the United States could accept.[36] As Diederich later noted, people too easily dismissed an expert from the de Havilland firm who put the crash down to the weather.[37] Torrijos had flown into too many rainstorms.

73

J'ACCUSE

'Let me issue a warning to anyone who is tempted to settle for a peaceful life on what is called the Côte d'Azur. Avoid the region of Nice which is the preserve of some of the most criminal organisations in the South of France.'[1] So opened *J'Accuse*, a pamphlet by Graham Greene with text in both English and French published by the Bodley Head on 27 May 1982. He went on to describe how organized crime, referred to in France as the *milieu*, was involved in the drug trade, had fought a war over casinos, was laundering money in the building industry, and was bound up with the Italian mafia. A survey of French newspapers of the time shows all this to have been well documented. Why was Graham Greene taking an interest in it?

In March 1979, immediately after his cancer surgery, Greene learned that one of Yvonne's daughters was getting a divorce from her husband, who ran a property company originally established with Jacques's help.[2] According to Greene's pamphlet, the marriage began with a deception: the man had a long criminal history which he did not disclose. Once married, he began beating his wife, and in February 1979 the abuse reached its limit when, at a country hotel, she feared he would strangle her. Already the mother of one child, she was then four and a half months pregnant with her second. Divorce proceedings began, with the husband aggressively seeking control of the elder child; he purportedly said that he was not interested in the child, but wanted to control his ex-wife. He was able to obtain an extraordinary order from the court, requiring the woman to live within 500 metres of his residence. Moreover, Greene's pamphlet asserted that a witness for the husband perjured himself, owing to threats.

Abusing his visiting rights, the husband again threatened and assaulted his ex-wife. Greene made enquiries and found out about his hidden past. On 15 January 1980, he invited the man to his flat in Antibes, confronted him with the facts of his criminal record, and tried to negotiate a more reasonable set of arrangements for visiting the children. This got nowhere, and the conversation ended with the man raising his fists and declaring, '*Je suis un mur*' – I am a wall. Greene smiled and responded, '*Mais . . . je suis aussi un mur.*'[3] There was no question that Greene was now in danger, and he seems to have obtained a revolver, though he also thought often of Chuchu's maxim, 'A revolver is no defence.'[4]

In early April 1980, according to *J'Accuse*, the man threatened to blow Yvonne's brains out and tried to break into the Cloettas' house. The next day, he attacked Jacques, but was driven off when his ex-wife threw a tear-gas bomb at him. He then absconded with the elder child. Despite all this, a court soon granted him provisional custody of that child. When Greene explained what had been going on to the sympathetic mayor of Antibes, the politician remarked: 'But you are living one of your own books.'[5]

In the months that followed a series of court decisions went mysteriously against the mother. Since the husband had boasted of belonging to the *milieu*, Greene concluded that it had pressured the magistrates and lawyers to favour one of its own. Greene's frustration about what was happening to the Cloettas came out in his last meeting with Omar Torrijos, when he spoke of the situation in France as his reason not to go with him on the jaunt to Fort Bragg. Torrijos proposed first that the young woman and her children take refuge in Panama or that she remain in Europe with a new identity and a Panamanian passport. Greene wrote in his journal, 'We spoke of killing' the husband; Torrijos 'produced the idea of a man whom he has helped with monopolies of fruit machines & wants me to see him through the G2 & discuss the possibilities'.[6] Describing this conversation in *Getting to Know the General*, he adds, 'I pretended that I would think the matter over.'[7]

At the beginning of 1981, things seemed to be getting worse. He learned that the man had assaulted his current mistress and was proposing to sabotage Yvonne's car. He described all this to Francis: 'I thought that at last we had to go to the top. So I sent a letter to the Chancellor of the Legion [of Honour] returning my insignia & saying that I wanted to be free to speak out against the corruption of justice on the Côte. I sent a copy with another letter to Alain Peyrefitte, the Minister of Justice. Immediate action.' The Grand Chancellor returned Greene's insignia, which had been first bestowed in 1967, with the comradely suggestion that it might be useful in the fight. Peyrefitte, himself a well-known author, wrote Greene a letter and then called him: 'he was sending his Inspector General & a colleague down the next day. Two extremely nice men. He had expected to stay 24 hours & stayed four days – he was quite overwhelmed by what he found. Now I think action will not be long delayed. Light at last at the end of the tunnel.'[8]

Not yet. The investigation lost steam when Peyrefitte left office in May with the defeated President Giscard d'Estaing; however, Greene soon found allies within the administration of François Mitterrand. In November 1981, the Inspector General of the Ministry of the Interior assured Greene that a group of corrupt magistrates and policemen in Nice was under surveillance, and that they would one day break through their secrecy.[9]

The newly elected Socialists had every reason to look into corruption there. Nice was controlled by the popular Gaullist mayor Jacques Médecin – he and his father, between them, held that post for a total of sixty-two years. Greene could see that the mayor was a scoundrel. Once the case became public, Médecin repeatedly denounced him for slandering his city. However, Greene, in the last year of his life, had the satisfaction of seeing the mayor flee to Uruguay rather than face prosecution. He was eventually brought home and jailed for malfeasance, embezzlement, and fraud.[10]

For her own safety, Yvonne's daughter moved with the baby to Switzerland and continued to fight for custody of her elder child.[11] By early 1982, Greene decided it was time to throw a petrol bomb. He wrote a short account of the divorce, the domestic violence, and the litigation, asserting that the civic life of Nice was infected by corruption and by the workings of the *milieu*, and he named Jacques Médecin as part of it. He borrowed the title of Emile Zola's *J'Accuse*, written in defence of Alfred Dreyfus, and ended the piece with a crescendo of accusations. He wanted it published as soon as possible, so Reinhardt sent it to his friend and trusted associate the printer Bill Hummerstone at the Stellar Press. Reinhardt's colleague Euan Cameron recalls that no review copies were sent out before publication and that the initial print run went straight to France.[12]

The ability to seize the attention of the world's press was a weapon Graham Greene brought to what he called his war with the *milieu*. He did not much care how he might personally be harmed by publishing the pamphlet, and indeed some of the coverage hinted that he had gone potty. He hadn't. He carried throughout his life a sense of failure in relationships and family, and saw this fight as one he could undertake for people he loved, even if there was a chance that he might take a bullet for his efforts.

What he actually faced was four writs. Relying on France's restrictive libel and privacy laws, the ex-husband quickly sued Graham Greene, the Bodley Head, and the *Sunday Times*, which had run excerpts from the pamphlet. At a hearing of which Greene and the other defendants were not notified, judges in Nice ordered the book destroyed[13] and imposed financial penalties.[14] But it was already too late: according to Euan Cameron, *J'Accuse* sold seventeen thousand copies in France within three weeks.[15] Greene lodged appeals and managed to delay the suppression of the pamphlet for about two years.[16]

The legal battles involving the marriage went on, and no one could feel real confidence about the outcome until July 1983, when Greene told Father Durán that he had 'cause to rejoice' as the Court of Cassation in Paris had overturned the original divorce and cleared the way for a new one.[17] Eventually, the mother won custody of the elder child. However, the litigation hardly stopped in Greene's lifetime. As late as 1990, she had to pursue the ex-husband for unpaid child support of about thirty thousand francs, at a time when he was said to be driving a Maserati.[18]

In the worst times, Greene relied heavily on the advice of a neighbour in Antibes. The Irish honorary consul, Pierre Joannon, was a historian and cultural writer, but also qualified as a lawyer. At certain moments, he reined in Greene's suspicions about the *milieu*; he still believes that Nice has about the same problem of organized crime as any other large city and is not quite the infected place that Greene supposed it. He thought the abusive ex-husband was comparable to a character Greene had created: Pinkie from *Brighton Rock*. He likely did enjoy favours and protection from an old boys' network, but one not nearly so active and sinister as Greene believed.[19]

There is another side to what happened. It was very common at the time, and still is in some jurisdictions, for the police and the courts to treat domestic abuse with indifference. A woman lodging a complaint against her husband might just be ignored. Greene could see that Yvonne's daughter had been subject to outrageous injustice and he put it down to a specific criminal conspiracy. That may have been only part of the truth – the part which his upbringing and experiences equipped him to see most clearly. It is also a sad fact of social welfare that violence in the home sometimes escalates all the way to murder before the victim is taken seriously.[20] Looking at the J'Accuse episode from a distance of forty years, it shows that the civic life of Nice was corrupted not just by the *milieu* but by misogyny.

The battle over the marriage subjected Greene, tough-minded as he was, to unremitting strain for about seven years. It was a daily concern until well after his eightieth birthday in 1984, and it ground him down. Shirley Hazzard, never one to overdo compassion, recalled how court cases interrupted his usual pattern of visits to Capri: 'When we did coincide on the island, he was exceptionally on edge, the need for an adversary not appeased by evils on what he called la Côte d'Ordure.'[21]

Other people could also see the effects. Graham and Yvonne had maintained a pleasant friendship with Mercia Rhynier, Greene's former lover who had trapped wild animals for zoos and later married Rex Harrison (see above, p. 247), but it came to an end when Mercia remarked to Yvonne that Graham looked awful and reproached her for having involved him in her daughter's troubles.[22] This was not entirely fair on Yvonne, as it was always in his personality to take sides, but it does indicate that the business turned Graham Greene, at last, into an old man.

74

I AM THE MESSAGE

C huchu was something of a nag. He had been on the phone urging Greene to come back to Panama, but the novelist did not want to go. Without the General, 'it would be like going to see Hamlet played by an understudy'.[1] Then Chuchu seems to have ratcheted up the pressure by giving Greene's telephone number to Ernesto Cardenal, who invited Greene to Nicaragua on behalf of the junta. This was a more formal request, so Greene politely equivocated.

In August 1982, Greene had 'escaped' from Antibes, where he felt besieged by mafiosi and *avocats*, to England for about ten days and begun a book to be called *Getting to Know the General*, chiefly about Torrijos and Chuchu. He wanted to pay tribute to his dead friend and to write about the troubles of the region. It was also to be an elegy for his failed novel, 'On the Way Back'. By early October, he had about a quarter of it written.[2] Going to Panama again would certainly help with the book.

Finally, Chuchu got him to agree, but since he was still fighting three of the four lawsuits arising from *J'Accuse* he wanted to stay no more than two weeks. He wrote to Vivien that he was undertaking the journey, 'to light a small fire under the fool Reagan'.[3] As the plane entered Panamanian airspace on 3 January 1983, he felt a 'depression, anxiety & sense of frustration' at the thought of being in the country with Torrijos dead.[4] He landed at an airport now named for the General, and was met by Chuchu, who had suggested Greene's visit could be 'of use', though for what was unclear.[5]

When Torrijos's plane went down, so too did his cautious plans for a return to democracy. After a year of upheavals there was still a civilian president, Ricardo de la Espriella, but the real power lay

with three military officers, General Rubén Darío Paredes, Colonel
Manuel Noriega, and Colonel Roberto Díaz Herrera – these were the
understudies to Torrijos. Greene thought none of them comparable to
his old friend, least of all the very crass Paredes who gave him a gold
Rolex watch, of a sort that Greene later saw selling in Paris for sixty-six
thousand francs.[6]

Torrijos had never encouraged him to get to know Noriega, even
though they had met in passing. Greene found him pleasant enough
on this visit, and they discussed whether Greene should accept an
invitation to go to Cuba after his stay in Nicaragua. However, in his
journal, he compared Noriega to Trujillo, the murderous former ruler of
the Dominican Republic – so he evidently had his doubts about him.[7]
He was building a powerbase by consolidating intelligence, the police,
and the National Guard. At the time of Greene's visit, it was believed
that Paredes, a right-winger, would be elected to the largely ceremonial
post of president and that the two colonels would actually be in control,
and so continue the policies of Torrijos. Of the three, Greene found
Díaz, the chief of security and a cousin of Torrijos, the most appealing,
as did Chuchu. By the end of the summer of 1983, Noriega had got rid
of Paredes altogether and was running the country with Díaz as chief
of staff, but Díaz too was eventually sidelined and exiled.[8] Greene later
condemned Noriega but remarked, 'if I have to choose between a drug
dealer and United States imperialism I prefer the drug dealer'.[9]

He went in a helicopter with Chuchu and Omar's daughter to see
the crash site, something Chuchu, for all his certainty about a bomb,
had not done before.[10] The helicopter was bucketing in high winds
and Greene wondered if they might be killed in exactly the spot where
Omar had met his end.[11] Chuchu wanted to fly him around Panama and
Nicaragua in his little Cessna, but Díaz and Paredes put a stop to that.

At a reception on 6 January 1983, President de la Espriella presented
Greene with the Grand Cross of the Order of Vasco Núñez de Balboa.
The novelist felt embarrassed as he got tangled in the ribbon and the
stars: 'I felt like a Christmas tree in process of being hung with presents.' He was glad to be associated with Panama in such a way, but he
was certain that he did not deserve the honour and thought that the
ceremony might be chiefly a signal to the Nicaraguans that he could
be trusted as a messenger.[12]

Greene's visit to Managua seems to have been symbolic: the colonels were sending a famous friend of Torrijos as a sign that they honoured the General's legacy, including his friendly attitude towards the Sandinistas, who were now facing a war with the American-backed Contras, many of whom had once fought for Somoza. More narrowly, Díaz and Noriega wanted to send a message that they would not be pulled to the right, even if Paredes became president. Greene later reflected on whether the Panamanians were using him, and remarked: 'I have never hesitated to be "used" in a cause I believed in, even if my choice might be only for a lesser evil. We can never foresee the future with any accuracy.'[13]

Joined by Diederich in Managua, he met Ernesto Cardenal, Daniel Ortega, Rosario Murillo, Tomás Borge, and Humberto Ortega. From both Humberto Ortega and Borge he heard very sharp criticisms of Noriega, whom they seemed to regard as the rising man in Panama but tainted by association with Paredes. Greene attended a party for the novelist Carlos Fuentes at the Mexican embassy and noted in his journal that the man's last book was 'unreadable'. There was a plan for Fuentes to go that day to the Honduran frontier, where the Contras were making their incursions, 'but he was scared. So am I, but I'll have to go.'[14] He did that on 9 January 1983, and came within 300 metres of the frontier, in an area where indiscriminate mortar fire killed two or three people per day and the actual raids were more deadly still. In this sector, he watched very old and very young people training for the militia, and his escorts were on constant lookout for an ambush. Greene felt that the Land Rover he was in resembled a coffin: if attacked it would be impossible to get out.[15]

Back in Managua, he met Lenin Cerna, the chief of security, who showed him various booby-trapped devices that the Contras were supposedly planting in the countryside. Greene was especially outraged by a child's lunchbox featuring Mickey Mouse but containing an explosive. Diederich noted that not everyone who saw Cerna's displays was certain of their authenticity.[16] Greene had no doubt and often spoke of the Mickey Mouse bombs as a sign of the wickedness of the Contra war.[17]

For all his talk about lesser evils, he did see some things that he regarded as absolutely good. Above all, he was impressed by two Maryknoll nuns from the United States living in poverty in Ciudad

Sandino, a community of sixty thousand on the outskirts of Managua. Their home was a tin-roofed hut with water supplied by a standpipe in the yard. One of them had lived like this for ten years and seen the whole war with Somoza; she had recently observed a great improvement in medical care for the local people. Also, those people now had secure possession of their homes, whereas in the past they could be thrown out at any time by landlords.[18]

He spoke with the nuns about the Miskito indigenous people from the Río Coco area bordering Honduras. Since the Contras were recruiting among this group, the Sandinistas forcibly removed 8500 of them to inland camps; another ten thousand fled to Honduras; and seven thousand were moved to coffee plantations.[19] There were reliable reports of Sandinista soldiers killing or torturing Miskito people to find out about the Contras or to force resettlement.[20] The Reagan administration characterized this as genocide. Greene raised the matter with Borge, who admitted that the soldiers had behaved 'clumsily' and failed to explain to the people that they were being moved from a war zone.

One of the Maryknoll nuns had visited the camps and found the people there had good food and housing, and better medical care than had previously been available to them.[21] What she could not have seen was the manner of their removal from traditional lands, which was certainly repressive. Nonetheless, Greene quoted her, for example in a letter to *The Times* on 15 October 1983, disputing claims made by Reagan's ambassador to the United Nations, Jeane Kirkpatrick, about the 'most brutal maltreatment' of the Miskitos. In 1987, the Sandinista government reversed its policy towards the Miskito people, allowed them to return, and, in a bold move, granted indigenous peoples autonomy in areas amounting to about half the country.[22] Sadly, even this was not enough to repair all the injustices concerning land. Thirty years later, the Miskito people near the Río Coco are still caught in a cycle of violence. Murders are commonplace, as other ethnic groups, notably mestizos, seek to settle near the lush rainforest,[23] and Miskito control of their traditional homeland remains, at best, a theory.

While in Managua, Greene had another meeting with Salvador Cayetano, the rebel leader responsible for the abduction of Ambassador Dunn. This time the novelist was struck by his age rather than by an air of cruelty; he seemed much older than his reported sixty-three years and now wore a wispy 'Ho Chi Minh' beard.[24] He greeted Greene with something like affection, and seemed 'full of optimism' about a quick victory.[25] Unfolding a large map on the floor, he began, like a schoolmaster, to explain the military position in El Salvador. He gave Greene a book he had written under his own name but inscribed it with his codename 'Marcial' – the novelist judged from this that his security arrangements were looser now.[26] That was the last Greene would see of him. About three months later, his second-in-command was killed at a Managua safe house; she was stabbed eighty times and her throat cut. Cayetano was in Libya at the time, but was implicated in her killing. Some days later, he died of a bullet to the heart, said to be self-inflicted.[27] Both deaths remain a mystery.

Greene had no interest in going to Cuba unless he could see Castro again. He certainly did not want to go as the guest of a cultural agency. While in Managua, he received confirmation that the invitation was indeed from Fidel himself, so on 11 January 1983 he made his last visit to Havana aboard a small jet formerly used by Somoza; the pilot was amused to see him choose the very seat that the dictator had always preferred. Greene was lodged in a new hotel in a quarter he was not acquainted with, so could not revisit the places he knew from the past.[28]

The meeting with Fidel was to take place in the evening. Gabriel García Márquez was visiting at the same time, and was glad to see Greene as the two were by now friends. They spoke about Greene's war in Nice, and the Englishman said plainly, 'I'd rather die of a bullet in the head than a cancer of the prostate'.[29] Ever the night owl, Fidel appeared at 1 a.m., and Greene thought that he looked far more relaxed than at their meeting sixteen years earlier.

Fidel was amused by the novelist's greeting: 'I am not a messenger. I am the message.' Of course, Greene was an emissary from the two colonels, and his role was to signal that, regardless of the right-wing General Paredes, Panama would stay the course set by Omar Torrijos. It turned out that Castro was not enthusiastic about the plan for Paredes to run for the presidency, as the conservatives might defeat him and send him back to the army, in which case both the presidency and the army would be under conservative control; this was Greene's view of the matter too. They went on to talk about El Salvador, with Fidel expressing optimism, much as Cayetano had, that the war would be short. In fact, it went on for years, as Colonel Díaz had predicted.

Once the serious talk was over, Gabo thought to spur conversation by asking Greene whether it was true that he had once played Russian roulette. Greene said he had and named the occasions. Fidel was impressed, closed his eyes, did some multiplication of the odds, and told him he ought not to be alive. Indeed, his not being dead took on some interest for him, and he asked what regime of exercise and diet he followed. Greene answered, 'No régime. I eat what I like and drink what I like.'[30] He sensed that his answer rather shocked Fidel, a true believer in health and fitness – that is, apart from the cigars. At some point they discussed books: Fidel had read about a third of *Monsignor Quixote* and wanted to talk about Spanish wine and to hear about Greene's travels in Spain. Their talk went on until the early morning, and it seems that Fidel was thinking through the implications of this odd visit from a pair of novelists. As they said goodbye, he sent a message of support for Díaz, and said, 'Tell them that I have received the message.'[31]

75

BETTER A BAD MAN

'The one good thing about this horrible 80th birthday is the amount of liquor with which my cellars begin to be stacked!'[1] Greene was writing to Pierre Joannon, who had sent a bottle of twelve-year-old Jameson Irish whiskey on 2 October 1984. Joannon had founded the Jameson Irish Club in Juan-les-Pins and whenever Greene was in Antibes he made a point of attending, so Joannon made sure that Greene received a bottle of Jameson every couple of months.[2] Whatever Fidel might think, liquor seemed to contribute to his longevity.

And perhaps he needed a drink, as his birthday saw the release of a book that disappointed him. He had finished *Getting to Know the General* in February, and left the decision as to whether it should be published at all to Chuchu: the Panamanian army paid his way to Antibes so that he could scour the manuscript for errors, but all he found were misspellings of Spanish words. 'He liked the book better than I did and he didn't at all interfere with my picture of himself which is not very complimentary. Or not what the ordinary reader would say was complimentary.'[3] Half the book's Spanish royalties were to go to the FMLN rebels in El Salvador and the other half to the Monastery of Oseira, which Greene visited annually with Father Durán. They hurried to get the book ready for publication before the US election that November, hoping that it might stir up even a few votes against Ronald Reagan; at the time, Greene supported Gary Hart, who eventually lost the Democratic nomination to Walter Mondale, who in turn lost to Reagan.

Greene could see the book 'falling between two stools':[4] it was not exactly a memoir of Torrijos, nor was it an autobiography. The character of Chuchu seemed to take over at times. Of course, the fundamental problem was that he needed to write a novel about Panama and had failed. He was worried again that he did not have another novel in him. When he began *Monsignor Quixote*, he did not really believe that he would ever finish it. For him to complete yet another novel seemed beyond hope.

By the mid-1980s, he was searching his 'rag and bone shop' for the makings of a new novel, and decided, instead, to finish one he had begun and laid aside. Long before, he had written on the short manuscript: 'Picked this up again in Antibes by a curious coincidence on 16 December 1978 when I despaired of ever writing again. I prayed last night without conviction that I could work again. For the first time in months I woke without melancholy. I attributed it to a dream I had of the new Pope and his kindness to me ... In a folder marked Ideas I found a manuscript which I thought I might sell for the *Tablet* fund. However I decided to read it through first and suddenly I saw – anyway part of the road ahead. I sat down and added 400 words – I was working again. Only afterwards I looked at the date and saw that I had begun the book at the same table exactly four years before. Whatever happens now it has given me a happy day ... '[5]

In 1980, he submitted the opening sentences under a pseudonym to a competition in the *Spectator* (12 April 1980), which asked for an extract of up to 150 words from an imaginary Graham Greene novel – it lost. From time to time he wrote more pages, remarking in June 1985, 'The story won't lie down.' One of his main struggles was with the first-person narration: Jim Baxter, perhaps to be understood as 'the enemy', narrates events apart from in the last few pages, which shift to the third person. On 22 November 1987, he completed a first draft.[6]

The story is a very strange one; Father Durán thought it was structured as a dream and that may be so.[7] The events proceed from one another mysteriously. It begins at a school modelled on Berkhamsted; on a number of earlier occasions, Greene had tried to write fictionally about his school years, with scant success. It follows one of his characteristic plotlines, in which the main character betrays a very flawed mentor or dominant friend, and so it resembles *The Man Within*, *The Third Man*, 'The Basement Room', and the unfinished 'Lucius'. The book begins with the boy Jim Baxter being taken away from school by a man referred to as 'the Captain', who has, according to extraordinary opening paragraph, won him from his father in a game of backgammon. The novel proceeds as an exploration of the extreme unreliability of memory, narration, and the language of love.

When Greene began the story, he had not yet visited Panama and had no idea that the novel would end there. Indeed, one of its peculiarities is the tension between the settings of 1950s Britain in the first part and 1970s Panama in the second. The boy is left with a woman the Captain loves, while he disappears in pursuit of fortune; a modern buccaneer, the Captain makes money transporting drugs and at the end is flying arms to Nicaraguan rebels.

Greene made another visit to Central America in December 1985, just as he had reached the stage of a first partial typescript. Full of confidence, he was looking for the right setting for a new conclusion he envisaged. In Panama, he found there was something wrong with Díaz, whom he described then as 'weak'. Also, Greene was settling into a distrust of Noriega;[8] he probably believed that he was working with the CIA to undermine the Sandinistas. He was glad to move on to Managua, where he spent much of his time with Borge, whom he liked more and more.

One of the more spectacular recent events in the region had been the kidnapping of the daughter of José Napoleón Duarte, the ineffectual Christian Democratic president of El Salvador. She and a friend were held for forty-four days, then released in exchange for twenty-two rebel prisoners.[9] Greene reported to Diederich that he had met in Nicaragua with the new head of the FMLN – perhaps he was referring to Salvador Sánchez Cerén, later elected president of El Salvador (see above, pp. 468–9) – who gave him thirteen photographs of Duarte's daughter in captivity, enjoying herself with the rebels. Convinced of their authenticity Greene handed these photographs on to *Le Matin*, which published a selection.[10]

Having finished a full draft of the novel in December 1986, Greene tried immediately go to Central America, but was stymied by flight delays and had to postpone the trip until April, by which time the text of the novel was settled. He was truly disconcerted by what he found then in Panama, where he stopped on the way to and then returning from Nicaragua. After their initial conversation, he felt that Díaz was having psychiatric problems, as he spoke in mystical language about his consultations with a medium. Their second conversation was at least comprehensible; Díaz explained how the 1984 presidential election had been rigged against Arnulfo Arias to preserve the Torrijos reforms.[11]

A few weeks later, Noriega forced Díaz to retire, and the dispute between them became public, with Díaz making the same revelation about the election of 1984 to the press. He added the wilder claim that Noriega had been responsible for a bomb that killed Torrijos; as a relative of Torrijos, Díaz would have been specifically left out of any such conspiracy and he presented no evidence to support his claim. But whatever his mental state, some of what he said was true, particularly that Noriega had arranged the killing of the opposition leader Hugo Spadafora,[12] and that he was trafficking in drugs. The charges had an immediate effect. Riots broke out in Panama, and Noriega came down hard on political dissent.

In early July, the erratic Díaz had Chuchu, his ally, handcuffed and held for a few hours at his house, accusing him of, among other things, having a sexual affair with Graham Greene. Not long afterwards, Greene telephoned Chuchu and offered to fly directly to Panama to create a stir and make sure nothing further happened to him, but Chuchu said it was unnecessary.[13] At the start of a two-day general strike, Noriega sent helicopters and troops to attack Díaz's house and detain him.[14] After a week in custody, Díaz, unsurprisingly, retracted his charges, and[15] a few months later Noriega threw him out of the country.

After the fall of Díaz, Chuchu kept a low profile for a few months and then allied himself with Noriega, whom he now saw as a patriot. Although Noriega signalled that Greene was welcome to return, his visits to Panama were at an end. At one point, he mused to Diederich that either Noriega or the CIA might have him killed there and blame it on the other side.[16] He was emphatic in his distaste for Noriega, but he did admire his recent defiance of the Americans: 'Better a bad man against the USA in Central America than a good man for it.'[17]

Unexpectedly topical, *The Captain and the Enemy* appeared at the beginning of September 1988. Not every reader likes Greene's late fiction: despite a profound admiration for Greene's work, David Cornwell believes, nonetheless, that in his last decade he was written out.[18]

Greene himself did not like the new novel[19] and had no expectation of writing another.

Many critics did like it. Jonathan Coe thought it one of 'his most purely enjoyable' works, 'a small miracle of construction in which traditional narrative is used to allow rather than to compensate for density of ideas'.[20] Brian Moore used similar language, speaking of 'the miraculous shift of gears' into the world of the political thriller in the later pages – he felt that this 'short, skilful book' confirmed V. S. Pritchett's view that Greene was 'one of the two or three living novelists who really count'.[21]

76

TWO FACES

'Please, Graham, don't ask me any questions about the past.'[1] These were Kim Philby's first words to Graham Greene when the novelist entered his flat in Moscow. For years, Greene had hoped for a meeting with Philby on neutral ground, but his efforts had been stymied by the KGB and the Writers' Union, which took a dim view of his appeals on behalf of Daniel, Sinyavsky, Solzhenitsyn, and other dissidents, and of his protests over the invasions of Hungary and Czechoslovakia.

But times were changing. Mikhail Gorbachev had been elected General Secretary of the Communist Party in March 1985 and launched glasnost and perestroika. Even the Writers' Union changed – to a degree. In 1986, it elected the journalist and novelist Genrikh Borovik as its secretary for foreign affairs and he approached various foreign authors, among them Graham Greene. Of course, this man was also an agent of the KGB, specializing in disinformation,[2] so his recollection of what happened is hardly to be taken at face value. He says he contacted Greene and found him anxious to make a journey to the Soviet Union, but, according to Borovik, Greene also made an awkward request: he wanted to see his old friend Philby. This is con-tradicted by Yvonne's recollection that Philby asked for the meeting.[3] Borovik may have been trying to hide the fact that the Soviets were aggressively courting Graham Greene, and using Philby, whose value was otherwise exhausted, as bait. In May 1987, David Cornwell seemed to get the same treatment, when at a Writers' Union cocktail party in Moscow he was approached by Borovik, whom he recalls as 'a big KGB bully boy who made no secret of his profession'; he was invited to meet '"a great admirer of your work, a lover of your country, Kim Philby". . . . I replied rather pompously that since I was about to dine with the

Queen's ambassador, I did not feel I was able to square that with dining with the Queen's traitor. Borovik was angry, and that was that, except that when I departed from Leningrad airport, I was subjected to a full body search.'[4]

It is well known that the KGB never fully trusted Philby and did not give him any meaningful work until the 1970s; before that he lived like a ghost in Moscow and even attempted suicide in 1970.[5] The KGB obviously permitted the late correspondence between Philby and Greene, and perhaps, as Greene thought, took advantage of it to pass notes to MI6. Even so, a personal meeting between Philby and an old colleague from British intelligence was a different matter.

Borovik was able to organize things. In June 1985 he had been granted permission (or perhaps was assigned) to conduct interviews with Philby, and he did so over a period of three years. He was even shown his KGB file in order to write a book about him, and he also produced a television documentary on Graham Greene. Borovik says that he went straight to one of the chief reformers, Alexander Yakovlev, Secretary for Ideology of the Central Committee and soon to be promoted to the Politburo, and explained the problem. 'What idiots,' said Yakovlev. He then picked up a hotline – presumably to Gorbachev – and obtained permission for the meeting between Graham Greene and Kim Philby.[6]

The arrangements were confirmed only at the last minute. Greene arrived in Russia in mid-September 1986 not knowing whether he would meet Philby at all. He and Yvonne landed first in Moscow and were taken to Leningrad and to the Black Sea and Georgia, before returning to Moscow.[7] Along the way, he was delighted to meet a cosmonaut who had stayed a record three months in space; he gave Greene his annotated copy of *Our Man in Havana* that had been his companion in zero gravity.[8]

Kim Philby and his fourth wife, Rufina, lived in a side street near Pushkin Square. As it became clear, everyone involved was nervous about this meeting: there was some doubt whether after all these years the two men could rekindle old conversations especially with watchers and listeners about. For security, Greene's limousine did not stop in front of the building but went around the corner to where Rufina was waiting at an arranged spot. She expected Greene to be as severe as some of his photographs, and was pleasantly surprised when a tall, smiling man popped out of the car. He said, 'I am feeling so shy.' Then he repeated quietly, 'I am so shy.'

They took the lift to the Philbys' flat, a place filled with books. Having not seen Greene in so many years, Kim was himself diffident. He embraced his visitor, and made his point about no questions, but even so, Greene, curious about how English Kim still was, did ask one: had he learned Russian?[9] And, of course, he had, but on this evening he struck Borovik as more English in his manner than ever before.[10] Borovik left them to their conversation, which had to move in very narrow channels since the flat was undoubtedly bugged. As usual, Greene ignored the food that was laid out, and drank up the Stolichnaya, remarking, 'Funny how vodka never makes you drunk.' Philby, who had spent most of the past two decades drunk on vodka, disagreed.[11]

The next night, the four visited Borovik's home, where they were joined by a number of writers, among them one of Russia's leading poets, Andrei Voznesensky, for a cheerful party at which Greene sat beside Philby and the two exchanged reminiscences.[12] For her part, Yvonne found Philby 'seductive'.[13] Once Graham and Yvonne flew back to France, Philby wrote on 24 September 1986: 'Rufa said, without any prompting from me, that the three days we spent on and off together were among the happiest in her life ... I find myself suffering from an acute attack of the esprit d'escalier: so many questions I wanted to ask, but didn't, so many things I wanted to say but didn't. Well, you can't bridge a gap of thirty-five years in a few hours. Zut alors!'[14] Perhaps this was a way of saying, yes, we were listened to.

Greene was no sooner home than he was planning another trip to the Soviet Union. However, there were problems in England. His brother Raymond had battled throat cancer in 1975 and survived, only to die on 6 December 1982 following a heart attack and kidney failure.[15] Graham liked and admired Raymond, and they had often worked together in helping relatives with financial problems, but they were not close. Hugh, however, was his closest male friend, and he was now suffering from lung, bone, and prostate cancer, complicated by severe anaemia.[16] When Graham flew to Moscow in February 1987 to participate in the grand Forum for a Nuclear Free World and the Survival of

Mankind, it was understood that Hugh was likely to recover owing to a new course of treatment.[17]

He was travelling without Yvonne this time, having suggested that the Forum might be tedious for her. Early in the trip, which seems to have lasted just six days, someone put a fur hat on his head and he was pressed to wear it whenever he went into the cold; he remarked later to Gillian Sutro, 'I suppose they did not want me to go back with pneumonia like I did once on one of my visits.'[18] He had not seen a great deal of snow in his life and so forgot to bring boots to Moscow in February. He had to step in Rufa's footprints and hold her hand as he slipped about in the snow – a dangerous matter for an eighty-two-year-old. At the Philbys' flat, he remarked to Kim: 'You and I are suffering from the same incurable disease – old age.' He complained how difficult it was even to have a shower.[19] Though eight years younger than Greene, Philby was facing greater difficulties: he had emphysema and a failing heart. At this point, Greene was merely fragile.

Borovik took Greene and Philby to a dacha owned by Oleg Vukulov, one of Russia's leading artists, and after a while the party moved to the house of Serge Mikoyan, a historian and peace campaigner. There Kim Philby spoke at length about the books that had moved him in his youth, and about *The Quiet American*, particularly praising a description of Pyle: 'He is absolutely convinced of his righteousness and absolutely indifferent.' Greene listened to all this while tossing pine cones onto the fire.[20]

The Forum brought about six hundred foreign and Soviet participants together to promote the cause of arms reduction, but it was also a large-scale PR operation. The Soviets were anxious to assemble foreign intellectuals, including Graham Greene, Norman Mailer, and Fay Weldon, for 'round table' discussions; as it turned out, Greene most admired the contributions of Gore Vidal.[21] However, in the week before the event protests for the release of a detained teacher of Hebrew were brutally put down by the KGB. The British reporter Martin Walker was beaten up and kicked in the kidneys by men who had obviously been trained in hand-to-hand combat. There was speculation that hardliners in the KGB were trying to embarrass Gorbachev and undermine his reforms.[22]

Greene became involved in his own way. He threatened to withdraw from the Forum over the case of a Russian Orthodox prisoner who had been refused a Bible and access to a priest, but Greene was promised on the telephone, presumably by Borovik, that he could have a meeting with the head of the judiciary about the case as soon he reached Moscow. When he got there, he was told that the man had already been released. It was the sort of thing Greene often did when welcomed to a repressive country; for example, he followed up his visit to Cuba in 1983 by sending Fidel a plea for two imprisoned writers whose names were provided by PEN.[23] Of his involvement with the case of the Orthodox prisoner, Greene commented to the Czech novelist Josef Škvorecký: 'Perhaps I did do a tiny bit to help.'[24] Although devoted to Greene as a writer and as a person, Škvorecký did not approve of Greene's late visits to the Soviet Union.[25]

Greene met Gorbachev briefly. Participants at the round tables, which Greene found life-threateningly dull, were taken into a smaller room in the Kremlin before the general meeting. When Greene approached in a group of eight participants, Gorbachev shook his hand and said, rather mysteriously, in English, 'I have known you for some years, Mr Greene.'[26] It is not clear whether Gorbachev was a reader of Graham Greene – there were millions of them in the Soviet Union – or had noticed his name in intelligence reports concerning Latin America. During the Forum, Greene received a good deal of attention from a Siberian he understood to be second to Gorbachev in the Politburo; this was almost certainly his ally and later rival Yegor Ligachyov. He invited Greene to return in the summer and visit Siberia. Gorbachev, Ligachyov, and Yakovlev were the three most powerful men in the Soviet Union – why did they care whether a British novelist came to the country?

Perhaps, the Kremlin hoped – very unrealistically – that this Englishman would defect and become a trophy for the reformed Soviet Union, or at least become a wholehearted advocate for it in the West. It is also conceivable that they hoped he would be useful to them in Latin America. Father Durán tells us that at some point in his Russian travels Greene was offered the Order of Lenin for his literary achievements, but he turned it down because he did not want people to think he was a secret communist.[27]

The Russians, who tended to hold authors in greater esteem than in the West, probably overrated his value. Moreover, they missed a nuance in Greene's thinking. He had written to Bernard Diederich in 1985: 'Russia and the USA seem to be the same face looking at each other in the same glass and there are times when I certainly prefer the Russian face to the American face similar though they both are.'[28] However, Greene fundamentally did not want to align with either side, and would have been content to smash the mirror.

Greene came away from the Forum with a good feeling about Gorbachev, as he put it to Škvorecký: 'Yes, I was very impressed by Gorbachev both in the few moments of meeting him when he struck me as an honest man with a certain inner strength and a sense of humour. I was also very impressed by his speech at the Forum. I see him too as very close to Dubcek, but I think he has a certain political genius which may enable him to survive and to make his changes however gradually. I am an optimist.'[29] It was not often that Greene claimed to be an optimist.

Unexpectedly, Greene was asked to give a short speech before a thousand people in the Kremlin Grand Palace on 16 February 1987. Without notes, he addressed Gorbachev, who listened with a broad smile.[30] He made the case that Catholics and communists were not essentially enemies, and that they were struggling side by side in many just causes: 'We are fighting together against the Death Squads in El Salvador. We are fighting together against the Contras in Nicaragua. We are fighting together against General Pinochet in Chile.' This was greeted with applause. He concluded: 'And I even have a dream, Mr General Secretary, that perhaps one day before I die, I shall know that there is an Ambassador of the Soviet Union giving good advice at the Vatican.'[31] At the time, Greene's suggestion struck many as odd, but he was on to something. Having broken diplomatic ties in 1923, the Vatican and the Soviet Union would exchange ambassadors three years later[32] – and Greene did live to see it.

Then came bad news from England, and he was obliged to cut short his stay in Moscow. Hugh had taken a sudden turn for the worse. He was near the end and had asked to see Graham, who took the first available flight to London. By the time he arrived at the King Edward VII Hospital, Hugh had lost consciousness. Graham stood beside his bed saying repeatedly, 'Poor boy, poor boy.'[33] He later described the experience of listening to Hugh's rattling breath as 'terrible', and his thoughts went to their shared experiences in Malaya and to their childhood, when he had read pirate stories to him – the same sort of tales he was revisiting in The Captain and the Enemy. He suggested to Hugh's wife, Sarah, that they should hasten his death, but she rejected the idea.[34]

Graham was at Bentley's restaurant, near Piccadilly, when he heard from his nephew James that Hugh was gone, and felt relieved that he would no longer be struggling. He later asked James's forgiveness for not attending the funeral: 'I couldn't bear the thought of all the strangers.' Three weeks after the death, he could not get the breathing out of his mind.[35] In the period after Hugh's death, Graham did what he could to help Sarah, who came to regard him as 'a darling man'.[36]

On 25 August 1987, Graham, accompanied by Yvonne, made his return to Russia for a twelve-day visit. Taking up Ligachyov's invitation, they went to Siberia and saw Novosibirsk and Irkutsk, as well as Tomsk, which was ordinarily closed to foreigners because of its nuclear facilities. Yvonne was impressed when a group of five senior KGB officers came to pay their respects.[37] In Moscow, they had a dinner with the Philbys at the well-known Aragvi restaurant, which figured in The Human Factor. Their conversation turned to Peter Wright's then controversial book Spycatcher: The Candid Autobiography of a Senior Intelligence Officer, which claimed that the one-time head of MI5, Sir Roger Hollis, was a mole, and that he was responsible for tipping off Kim Philby prior to his defection. The Thatcher government was trying to ban publication, but in so doing transformed the book into a worldwide bestseller. Once home, Greene asked his American publisher, Michael Korda, to send him some copies, one of which he sent to Philby in Moscow.

Meanwhile, Philby's old friend Nicholas Elliott was distressed about Spycatcher, which reflected badly on him as the British intelligence officer who confronted Philby in Beirut just before his defection. While Graham was in Moscow, Elliott wrote to Elisabeth Dennys dismissing the book as 'balls' and Wright as a 'traitor'. He enclosed a newspaper clipping suggesting that Graham was in Moscow to consult with Philby about a second volume of the defector's memoirs. Such a book would, of course, describe those meetings in Beirut, and Elliott wanted to know what was going on.[38] After Graham returned, Elisabeth, who had been friends with Elliott for many years, wrote back to him that she had spoken to Graham about his recent meeting with Philby, and he said there was no truth to the story about the memoirs. She also said that Graham had read *Spycatcher* and thought it 'not only inaccurate but very boring'.[39] Philby had a good deal of blood on his hands. Given Greene's earlier pattern, it is extremely likely that he consulted with senior officers at MI6 about his meetings in Moscow, but, even so, many of his old colleagues were, like Elliott, baffled by his involvement.

In February 1988, he returned to the Soviet Union for the airing of Borovik's laudatory documentary. This also marked the only occasion that Kim Philby appeared on television during his years in Russia. Sitting in a pinstripe suit beside Rufa, in front of a row of P. D. James novels in his study, he said that Greene 'rather dropped out of my life during my troubles' but made contact again 'when I came over here'.[40] He spoke for ten minutes in praise of Greene and of the 'perfection' of his portrayal of the CIA in *The Quiet American*. He was happy to gloss over any disagreements they had ever had: 'I wouldn't say that our views coincided but he belonged to those few, who at least sympathized with me'.[41]

Greene attended a dinner in honour of Philby at the House of Writers, where he met the poet Andrei Dementyev and Svyatoslav Fyodorov, a pioneering eye surgeon and wealthy entrepreneur. Greene asked Fyodorov pointedly, 'How can you obtain independence from state control when no one else can?' Fyodorov answered smilingly, 'Because I'm pushy. If I can't get in the door, I'll climb through the window.'[42] In 1991, Boris Yeltsin offered him the premiership of Russia, but he refused, and in 1996 was one of many candidates in the presidential election eventually won by Yeltsin.[43]

After this visit, Greene would not see Philby again. Philby's heart was giving out and he was admitted to hospital. In an odd expression of Englishness, he announced one day that he wanted to make tea, so Rufa brought an electric kettle to the intensive care ward, thinking he was on the mend – he wasn't. He died before dawn on 11 May 1988.[44]

The Gorky Institute of World Literature in Moscow wanted to celebrate Greene's eighty-fifth birthday, but since he could not guarantee that he would live that long he returned to the Soviet Union, for the last time, in October 1988, when he was turning eighty-four. Travelling in good weather, he and Yvonne went from Moscow to Kiev and then back again. The University of Moscow gave him an honorary doctorate; also receiving one was the Canadian John Kenneth Galbraith, the only economist whose books Greene found readable.[45] A still-grieving Rufa joined Graham and Yvonne at the birthday reception held by the Writers' Union at the Sovyetskaya Hotel. Greene interrupted a toast to him as guest of honour to propose one of his own: 'I want to drink to the wife of my close friend who died not long ago and to whom I was bound by warm memories.'[46] He then blew out the eighty-four candles on his cake.

77

THE LATE ROUNDS

'I have now received another cutting in which you claim I told you of an aggrieved husband shouting through my window (difficult as I live on the fourth floor.) You are either a liar or you are unbalanced and should see a doctor. I prefer to think that.' It was 13 June 1988, and this was the second time that day that Greene had written to Anthony Burgess. After years of pleasant, though not close, association with Greene, Burgess had spoken scathingly on a French television programme of Greene's age, and in a magazine of his supposedly constant correspondence with Kim Philby. Greene's first letter pointed out he was three years younger than Burgess had claimed and expressed the hope that he too would reach that age. He then confirmed that his contact with Philby was no secret from the intelligence agencies: 'I received ten letters from him in the course of nearly 20 years. You must be very naïf if you believe our letters were clandestine on either side.' He concluded tartly: 'Never mind. I admired your three earliest novels & I remember with pleasure your essay on my work in your collection *Urgent Copy*, your article on me last May in the *Sunday Telegraph* & the novel (not one of your best) which you dedicated to me.'[1] Then he wrote the second letter.

What was this about? One of Burgess's biographers believes that after years of writing adulatory reviews of Greene's work, Burgess noticed that the praise was seldom returned, and grew angry.[2] This is a very plausible explanation. It is also possible that some remark made by Greene had been passed on to Burgess; he wrote, for example, to Bill Igoe in 1984: 'I liked his early books, but I thought *Earthly Powers* was terrible. He writes far too much. Apparently he was wildly indignant that he hadn't got the Nobel Prize instead of [William] Golding and believed himself to be at the top of the list.'[3] A comment like this could have made its way round until someone told Burgess. Pierre Joannon tried to broker a peace, but Greene and Burgess had nothing more to do with each other.[4]

Despite being widely reported, this was at best a tiff between two authors who had never been on intimate terms. There were other conflicts of much greater importance in Greene's last years. Just as he had left Heinemann in the early 1960s in part because of how the publisher had treated A. S. Frere, he now left the Bodley Head because of how Max Reinhardt was treated.[5] Since 1973, the firm had belonged to a consortium with Chatto & Windus and Jonathan Cape, and somewhat later with Virago Press. By 1982, it was clear that the consortium was unwieldy and inefficient. Approaching seventy, Reinhardt wanted a smooth succession so sold many of his shares to two of the other principal figures in the group, Tom Maschler and Graham C. Greene.

Maschler and Graham C. Greene entertained a takeover bid by the American giant Random House, something Reinhardt objected to as he felt it would erase the character of the existing imprints. The disagreements became intense in late 1986 and early 1987, with Graham Greene (the novelist) taking Reinhardt's side entirely. Graham C. Greene unwisely claimed in the press that rumours of changes at the publishing group were 'pure fantasy';[6] the novelist then wrote a letter to the editor suggesting that his nephew was 'living himself in a fantasy world'. That letter reiterated a threat made privately that he would leave the Bodley Head if the appropriate changes in management were not made.[7] Hugh had died a few weeks earlier, so presumably it was easier for one Graham Greene to enter into a dispute with the other.

The Random House deal went through, and Max Reinhardt was sacked within a year.[8] Greene followed through on his threat and gave *The Captain and the Enemy* to Reinhardt Books, an imprint separate from the old consortium, and followed it with four other titles: *Yours Etc: Letters to the Press 1945–89*, edited by Christopher Hawtree; *Reflections*, a collection of prose pieces edited by Judith Adamson; *The Last Word and Other Stories*; and the posthumously published *A World of My Own: A Dream Diary*. Since the relationship with Graham C. Greene was never close, there was, in reality, no bad blood. Graham C. Greene did well by the transaction with Random House, and his uncle went his own way.

This was a dispute about how to make money. One of the peculiarities of the literary world is that merely *giving* money away can lead to rows. The last really public event of Graham Greene's life was to judge a new prize in Irish literature in 1989. The Guinness Peat Aviation (GPA) Prize was set up by Tony Ryan, the co-founder of Ryanair, who had given a good deal of money for the support of the arts in Ireland. This prize was spectacular: IR £50,000 for any Irish book published in the preceding three years. To make a splash for the inaugural award, they wanted the final decision to be made by the outstanding writer in English. An official of the firm, Seán Donlon, met with Greene at a dinner hosted by Pierre Joannon. The novelist agreed to an arrangement whereby he would be given a shortlist of five determined by a committee of eminent critics, and he would choose the winner. It was also agreed, explicitly, that Greene, who would receive IR £25,000 for his efforts, could if he wished ignore the shortlist and simply give the prize to whoever he thought worthy.

Greene told Donlon and Joannon that he wanted to give the prize to the extremely talented Vincent McDonnell for his debut novel, *The Broken Commandment*, published by Reinhardt upon his own recommendation. Greene had already promoted this book, unsuccessfully, for the lucrative *Sunday Express* Book of the Year Award.[9] Donlon had no objection to Greene making that choice. However, when presented with a shortlist that included Roy Foster, Seamus Heaney, and John Banville, Greene saw that he had made a mistake and that the main prize should go to Banville for his novel *The Book of Evidence*. He asked for a separate prize to go to McDonnell, whom he still regarded as outstanding. Donlon quickly came up with a 'first fiction' prize of IR £25,000.

Five years later, when Greene was under ground, a playwright and lecturer named Gerry Dukes called Greene a 'wool merchant' for his dismissal of the shortlist, which Dukes had helped devise, and remarked that 'integrity ... was in short supply in Greene's world'. He even worked the word 'villain' into his account. Dukes had indeed delivered the shortlist to Greene.[10] However, Joannon soon responded that Dukes had nothing to do with the original arrangement or with the creation of the additional prize.[11] Joannon's account was later confirmed by Donlon, who also wrote that Greene had matched the generosity of the GPA by forgoing his own fee, and so effectively paid for the additional prize himself.[12]

Graham and Yvonne went to Ireland, staying first with Tony Ryan at his home in Tipperary. Ryan had them helicoptered to Dublin for the prize-giving on 28 November 1989. Greene's health had been slipping. As late as May 1989, he made a show of hardiness after falling and breaking four ribs: he took some painkillers and went on to a large meeting at the Central Hall in Westminster, where he gave an address introducing Daniel Ortega.[13] However, from about June, he declined rapidly.[14] At the prize-giving, he was in obvious pain and barely got through the ceremony, which was held at the Old Parliament House, now the Bank of Ireland, on College Green. He was troubled by the size of the crowd and needed to be taken outside for a breather before giving a gracious speech in honour of the authors. At the end there was a standing ovation, and he was moved to tears. He remarked later to Joannon, 'It was far better than the Nobel Prize.'[15]

78

A SENSE OF MOVEMENT

In April 1968, Graham Greene had retraced the route of *Stamboul Train* from Paris to Istanbul on the Orient Express. With him was the documentary-maker Christopher Burstall, who filmed the novelist, though not his face, and recorded his conversation (see pp. 369–70). They eventually spoke of what might lie beyond death:

GREENE: I'm a great believer in Purgatory. Purgatory to me makes sense while Hell doesn't.

BURSTALL: You think you have to serve your time in Purgatory, do you?

GREENE: Serve your time, and I think it would be a very interesting experience, and one would have a sense of movement. I can't believe in a Heaven which is just passive bliss. If there's such a thing as a Heaven, it will contain movement and change.

BURSTALL: And do you think it will contain pen and ink?

GREENE: No, I don't believe that. No, I don't follow Kipling there. I think what one might find is that what one is crudely trying with pen and ink, the search one was making for understanding, would be pursued intellectually forever. But in a far more subtle and interesting and painless manner.[1]

Greene was speaking hypothetically. Given that life had often seemed too long, he was not always sure that he wanted more of it, let alone an eternity. And in any event, the proofs of an afterlife were elusive. In the 1980s and 90s there was widespread curiosity about 'near-death experiences'. Even Freddie Ayer, a long-time atheist and an old friend of Graham Greene, seemed to have one. In 1988, he choked on a piece of smoked salmon and was more or less dead. In the four minutes before he was revived, he saw a red light which was responsible for the ordering of the universe, but it was not doing its job well, 'with the result that space, like a badly fitting jigsaw, was slightly out of joint'. Greene read his article, 'What I Saw When I Was Dead',[2] and asked Jocelyn Rickards, who had had affairs with both Greene and Ayer, to pass a question on to Freddie: 'How does he know that the experience he had during those four minutes was not an experience he had immediately his heart began to beat again and before he became fully conscious. I don't see that there is any proof there of the memory existing for a while after death. Do get him to explain that.' Here we have Britain's outstanding Catholic novelist disputing a spiritual experience claimed by its most renowned atheist. Ayer died in a more permanent way in June 1989.[3]

By the slightest of margins, Greene thought an afterlife was more likely than not – this got him into the country of Morin as he could not formulate a solid argument in favour of an afterlife, but his instincts affirmed it. Valentina Ivasheva was a literary scholar in Moscow and a friend of the novelist. In 1980 she wrote him a tragic letter about how her husband had thrown himself from the balcony of their seventh-storey apartment and been killed. Greene offered what consolation he could: 'I don't believe myself that death is the end of everything, or rather my faith tells me that death is not the end of everything and when my belief wavers I tell myself that I am wrong. One can't believe 365 days a year, but my faith tells me that my reasoning is wrong. There is a mystery which we won't be able to solve as long as we are alive. Personally even when I doubt I go on praying at night my own kind of prayers. Why not try at night talking to your husband and telling him all you think. Who knows whether he mightn't be able to hear you and now with a mind unclouded?'[4]

At about the time he wrote this letter, Greene had returned to the sacraments, doubtless owing to the kind-hearted chivvying of Father Durán, and he continued to receive them for the rest of his life.[5] He also placed great store in having people pray for him and Masses said for his intentions. This does not mean that he resolved his doubts. Father

Alberto Huerto, SJ, was an authority on Greene's fiction and a friend. He wrote to him in the summer of 1989 to ask whether there was any truth to the rumour that he had abandoned the church. Greene replied that although he disagreed with much of what Pope John Paul II did, he still went to church fairly frequently: 'I would call myself at the worst a Catholic agnostic.'[6]

The 'agnostic' part of that formulation had to do with the reasoning side of Christianity. In his late years, Greene followed closely the writings of the theologian Father Hans Küng, best known for *Infallible? An Inquiry*, which offered a tough critique of the fundamental claims of the papacy, after which the Vatican withdrew his credentials as a Catholic theologian. Graham Greene was strongly influenced by ideas, and they exchanged letters in 1989, with the novelist expressing gratitude to Küng 'for helping me to keep one foot in the Catholic church'.[7]

Dismissing the papacy, Greene could see that his own beliefs were not that far from the Anglicanism in which he had been raised, and he studied the publications of the Anglican Roman Catholic International Commission, intended to work out common ground between the churches. He could see that if he were a young person again the differences between the beliefs of the two churches would have been insufficient for him to become a Roman Catholic.[8] However, he was still attracted to the 'magical' element in Catholicism, so there was a powerful tug. The Catholic church was where almost a billion of the world's poorest people brought their deepest yearnings, and Graham Greene was unlikely to walk away from that.

In certain respects, Greene's theological views were surprisingly conservative. He did not admire the Dominican theologian Father Edward Schillebeeckx because his account of the Resurrection was overly figurative: he spoke of Easter occurring in the experience of the disciples. For Greene, the Resurrection, if it occurred at all, had to involve an empty tomb, and he pointed to the account in John's Gospel as having the veracity of good journalism, as the sprinting John comes to the tomb first and stops, while Peter rushes in. This was a human touch that fable or myth would be unlikely to generate.[9]

Sadly, Graham Greene was himself sprinting towards the tomb. He came back from Dublin in very poor shape. In late 1989 he visited a doctor in Antibes, who told him that his blood tests were *'déplorable'*;

moreover, his blood pressure was up and his heart weak. This doctor said that it was a 'miracle' that he could even stand up.[10] In this condition, Greene travelled to Switzerland with Yvonne, and on 27 December 1989 fell seriously ill. Gruelling tests at the Hôpital de la Providence in Vevey, involving a needle to the spine and tubes down his nose, confirmed anaemia, with a haemoglobin count about half what was normal. He was given four blood transfusions to relieve the symptoms. After two days, he was released from hospital and then came down with what seemed to be flu. He collapsed in Caroline's bathroom and was returned to hospital on 4 January 1990 for a stay of almost two weeks. He got back to Antibes on the 26th and found a huge pile of letters waiting for reply – uncharacteristically, he tossed most of them into the waste-paper basket.

Further medical tests at the beginning of February showed that his haemoglobin count had plunged again, and confirmed that he was suffering from aplastic anaemia, a condition in which the bone marrow fails to produce enough red blood cells. Transfusions could not get to the root of the problem, and, given his age and frailty, Greene was not a candidate for a bone marrow transplant.[11] He received frequent vitamin B12 injections and was ordered to reduce his drinking, even though the doctor thought a little vodka necessary for 'morale'.[12]

On top of his illness, Greene was outraged by news from Central America. Before dawn on 16 November 1989, thirty uniformed soldiers, carrying arms Washington had paid for, raided a Jesuit residence at the San Salvador campus of the University of Central America, torturing and killing six priests, a cook, and her daughter.[13] On 20 December 1989, the United States launched Operation Just Cause, an invasion of Panama and its largest military venture since Vietnam. There was hard fighting, and Noriega initially avoided capture by taking refuge in the Vatican embassy, which the Americans famously bombarded with rock music and the noise of helicopter blades. He surrendered on 3 January 1989 and was arraigned in Florida the next day on charges of drug trafficking, conspiracy, and racketeering.[14]

At first, there was no word about Chuchu. A rumour reached Greene that he had been shot and killed, but then, unexpectedly, Chuchu called him.[15] He had not been involved in the fighting and was now moving from one refuge to another. He then took to calling Greene late at night; since the novelist could not easily get to the telephone, Yvonne had one installed by his bed.[16] Bernard Diederich recalls that a reporter tracked Chuchu down; he was composing in his head a book for Panamanian children of the future, so that they could understand what terrible things had happened. Although feeling betrayed by Noriega, he had not surrendered to the Americans. He told the reporter, 'We haven't lost very much because we didn't have anything ... Nothing remains of Torrijos. There is nothing to defend. I'm more pessimistic than ever.'[17] A year earlier, Greene might have boarded a plane and headed straight to Panama; now it was a challenge to leave his flat. Even so, he outlived his friend. Chuchu died of a heart attack at his home after a jog on 27 January 1991; he was sixty-one.[18]

Unsurprisingly, Greene abhorred the invasion and maintained that American dominance of the region was worse than Noriega's involvement in the drug trade. Another disappointment was in the works: in an election on 25 February 1990, Daniel Ortega lost the presidency of Nicaragua to a former ally, the publisher Violeta Chamorra, who had broken with him over the Sandinistas' insistence on hard-left orthodoxy.[19]

Greene understood his own situation. He wrote to Francis on 12 February 1990: 'I have just escaped death, but am still not far from it. I shall not write any more books'. His memory was failing, so he turned to his son to handle the transfer of his business to a new agent, Bruce Hunter of David Higham Associates, and to deal with publishers.[20]

His treatments were tedious: blood transfusions every two weeks and vitamin injections every three days.[21] It seems Yvonne and those closest to Graham said little about his condition: they wanted to avoid a press frenzy, and also did not want to worry his sister Elisabeth, who had had a debilitating stroke in 1989, or Rodney, who suffered one at the end of 1990.[22] Elisabeth was much on Graham's mind, and in order to ensure that she was fully provided for he made a gift to her of his archives, which were later sold to Boston College. Yvonne believed that grief over Elisabeth's condition shortened Graham's own life.[23]

In spring 1990, Yvonne convinced Graham that they must move to Switzerland. Antibes was very noisy in summer, and getting away would be a relief. By early May he had sold the much-loved house in

Anacapri; the journey there was now too difficult and he needed to be near a good hospital. They took a two-bedroom flat on Chemin du Châno in Corseaux, which was then part of Vevey.[24] It had a beautiful view of Lake Geneva, and both Graham and Yvonne had daughters and grandchildren living near by. He had arranged for his books from the flat in Paris, now occupied by the ailing Marie Biche, to be brought to Corseaux so he could enjoy having them around him.[25] He made his last visit to Antibes in September.[26]

He did some work in his last months, but it was hard to sustain. He pored over a selection from his dream diaries, a large and enigmatic body of writing which he wisely chose to organize according to theme. Knowing time was short, he entrusted the completion of this work to Yvonne, who collaborated with Louise Dennys on the short volume *A World of My Own*, which appeared in June 1992.

He lost a good deal of weight that summer and by the end of September was less than 140 pounds;[27] in the past he had weighed as much as 180 pounds. He did his best to keep his legs working: even in the days before his death he was still forcing himself to do a hundred paces a day.[28]

A low point came around Christmas 1990, when he was again hospitalized. The first time Yvonne had seen Graham cry had been upon hearing the news of Dorothy Glover's death. On this occasion, he turned his head away and said, 'I love you; you know how much I love you', and wept. For Yvonne, this was the most desolating moment, and she left the hospital near despair. Her spirits were revived, a little, by a long conversation with Caroline and two glasses of whisky.[29]

The exactness of his thinking made him hard to comfort. When Yvonne's daughter reminded him of all the fine books he had written, he answered: 'A few, yes, are good books. Perhaps people will think of me from time to time as they think of Flaubert.'[30] He spoke a good deal about whether there might be an eternal life, coming down, cautiously, in favour of the idea, but he could not accept an eternity without time, change, and movement.

In mid-March he went to the Hôpital de la Providence, where he had been receiving his treatments, and learned that his body was rejecting the transfusions. There was little more that could be done. This news had an odd effect, jolting him out of his depression. According to Caroline, he was very curious about what was now to happen. He said to Yvonne, 'at last I shall know what lies on the other side of the fence'.[31] He was anxious to be on his way.

Clutching a volume of the letters of Ezra Pound, he went into hospital for the last time on 30 March 1991. Among those now in attendance was Elisabeth's daughter Amanda Saunders, who had taken over as his secretary. He had a longstanding arrangement for Father Durán to give him the last rites. When Yvonne asked if they should send for him, he had no strong opinion and allowed her to decide. He received the sacraments on 2 April 1991, and died the next morning, at 11:40 a.m.[32] He had, perhaps, imagined the moment at the end of *The Captain and the Enemy*, when Jim Baxter says: 'I write a line under all this scroll before I throw the whole thing into the same waste-paper basket, where anyone who chooses can find it. The line means Finis. I'm on my own now and I am following my own mules to find my own future.'[33]

NOTES

ABBREVIATIONS

Persons

AB	Anita Björk
BD	Bernard Diederich
CB	Lucy Caroline Bourget (née Greene)
CW	Catherine Walston
ED	Elisabeth Dennys
EL	Etienne Leroux
EW	Evelyn Waugh
FG	Francis Greene
GG	Graham Greene
GS	Gillian Sutro
JR	Josephine Reid
KP	Kim Philby
LD	Father Leopoldo Durán
LP	Laurence Pollinger
MB	Marie Biche
MG	Marion Greene
MK	Michael Korda
ML	Michel Lechat
MR	Max Reinhardt
RD	Rodney Dennys
RG	Richard Greene
VG	Vivien Greene (née Dayrell-Browning)
YC	Yvonne Cloetta

Institutions

Balliol	Balliol College Archives, Oxford
BC	Burns Library, Boston College
BL	British Library
Bod	Bodleian Library
GU	Lauinger Library, Georgetown University
HRC	Harry Ransom Center, University of Texas at Austin
TNA	The National Archives, Kew

Frequently cited works by Graham Greene

(note: the works of Graham Greene are cited in this book in the common Penguin edition, except as otherwise indicated):

Articles	*Articles of Faith: The Collected* Tablet *Journalism of Graham Greene*, ed. Ian Thomson (Oxford: Signal Books, 2006)
BOC	*A Burnt-Out Case*
BR	*Brighton Rock*
CE	*Collected Essays*
CP	*The Collected Plays of Graham Greene*
CS	*Collected Stories*
EA	*The End of the Affair*
GTG	*Getting to Know the General: The Story of an Involvement*
HC	*The Honorary Consul*
HM	*The Heart of the Matter*
JWM	*Journey Without Maps*
Letters	*A Life in Letters*, ed. Richard Greene (London: Little, Brown, 2007)
LR	*The Lawless Roads*
ODNB	*Oxford Dictionary of National Biography*
PG	*The Power and the Glory*
QA	*The Quiet American*
Reflections	*Reflections*, ed. Judith Adamson (1990; rev. edn, London: Vintage, 2014)
SC	*In Search of a Character: Two African Journals*

SOL	A Sort of Life
TC	The Comedians
TCE	The Captain and the Enemy
WOE	Ways of Escape
YE	Yours Etc. Letters to the Press 1945–89, ed. Christopher Hawtree (London: Reinhardt Books, 1989)

Frequently cited works by other authors

Allain	Marie-Françoise Allain, *The Other Man: Conversations with Graham Greene*, trans. Guido Waldman (New York: Simon & Schuster, 1983)
Adamson (1984)	Judith Adamson, *Graham Greene and Cinema* (Norman: Pilgrim Books, 1984)
Adamson (2009)	Judith Adamson, *Max Reinhardt: A Life in Publishing* (London: Palgrave Macmillan, 2009)
Barbara Greene	*Land Benighted* (1938), reprinted as *Too Late to Turn Back* (London: Penguin 1990)
Borovik	Genrikh Borovik, *The Philby Files: The Secret Life of the Master Spy – KGB Archives Revealed*, ed. Phillip Knightley (London: Little, Brown, 1994)
Butcher	Tim Butcher, *Chasing the Devil: On Foot through Africa's Killing Fields* (London: Vintage, 2011)
Cloetta	Yvonne Cloetta with Marie-Françoise Allain, *In Search of a Beginning: My Life with Graham Greene*, trans. Euan Cameron (London: Bloomsbury, 2004)
Diederich and Burt	Bernard Diederich and Al Burt, *Papa Doc and the Tontons Macoutes* (1969; Port-au-Prince: Editions Henri Deschamps, 1986)
Diederich	Bernard Diederich, *Seeds of Fiction: Graham Greene's Adventures in Haiti and Central America 1954–1983* (London and Chicago: Peter Owen, 2012)
Drazin	Charles Drazin, *Korda: Britain's Only Movie Mogul* (London: Sidgwick & Jackson, 2002)
Durán	Father Leopoldo Durán, *Graham Greene: Friend and Brother*, trans. Euan Cameron (London: HarperCollins, 1994)
Edge	*Dangerous Edge: A Life of Graham Greene* (2013), film documentary, produced and written by Thomas P. O'Connor
Falk	Quentin Falk, *Travels in Greeneland: The Cinema of Graham Greene* (1984; 4th edn Dahlonega: University Press of North Georgia, 2014)

Goscha	Christopher E. Goscha, *Historical Dictionary of the Indochina War (1945–1954)* (Honolulu: University of Hawai'i Press, 2012)
Gould	Tony Gould, *Don't Fence Me In: Leprosy in Modern Times* (London: Bloomsbury, 2005)
Hazzard	Shirley Hazzard, *Greene on Capri: A Memoir* (London: Virago, 2000)
Hull	Christopher Hull, *Our Man Down in Havana* (New York: Pegasus, 2019)
Korda	Michael Korda, *Charmed Lives: A Family Romance* (New York: Random House, 1979)
Lechat	Michel Lechat, 'Graham Greene & the Congo 1959: Personal Memories and Background of *A Burnt-Out Case*', *Graham Greene Studies*, 1 (2017), 59–68
Lewis	Jeremy Lewis, *Shades of Greene: One Generation of an English Family* (London: Jonathan Cape, 2010)
Meeuwis	Michael Meeuwis, 'The Furthest Escape of All: Darkness and Refuge in the Belgian Congo', *Graham Greene Studies*, 1 (2017), 69–96
Milne	Tim Milne, *Kim Philby: The Unknown Story of the KGB's Master Spy* (London: Biteback Publishing, 2014)
Mitrokhin	Christopher Andrew and Vasili Mitrokhin, *The Mitrokhin Archive*, vol. 2 (London: Allen Lane, 2005)
Muggeridge (1973)	Malcolm Muggeridge, *The Infernal Grove* (London: William Collins, 1973)
Muggeridge (1981)	Malcolm Muggeridge, Like It Was: The Diaries of Malcolm Muggeridge, ed. John Bright-Holmes (London: Collins, 1981)
Ruane (2012)	'The Hidden History of Graham Greene's Vietnam War: Fact, Fiction and *The Quiet American*', *History*, 97 (July 2012), 431–52
Ruane (2017)	Kevin Ruane, 'Graham Greene in Love and War: French Indochina and the Making of *The Quiet American*', *Graham Greene Studies*, 1 (2017), 112–25
Rufina	Rufina Philby, Mikhail Lyubimov, and Hayden Peake, *The Private Life of Kim Philby: The Moscow Years* (London: St Ermin's Press, 1999)
Shelden	Michael Shelden, *Graham Greene: The Enemy Within* (New York: Random House, 1994)
Sherry	Norman Sherry, *The Life of Graham Greene*, 3 vols (London: Jonathan Cape, 1989–2004)
Walston	Oliver Walston, 'SIMB: A Brief and Unreliable History of the Walston Family', unpublished manuscript

Wapshott	Nicholas Wapshott, *The Man Between: Biography of Carol Reed* (London: Chatto & Windus, 1990)
Waugh (1976)	Evelyn Waugh, *The Diaries of Evelyn Waugh*, ed. Michael Davie (London: Weidenfeld & Nicolson, 1976)
Waugh (1980)	Evelyn Waugh, *The Letters of Evelyn Waugh*, ed. Mark Amory (New Haven and New York: Ticknor & Fields, 1980)
West	Nigel West, *Historical Dictionary of British Intelligence*, 2nd edn (Plymouth: Scarecrow Press, 2014)
West and Tsarev	Nigel West and Oleg Tsarev, *The Crown Jewels: The British Secrets at the Heart of the KGB Archives* (London: HarperCollins, 1998)
Williams	B. H. Garnons Williams, *A History of Berkhamsted School 1541–1972* (privately printed, 1980)
Wise and Hill	Jon Wise and Mike Hill, *The Works of Graham Greene*, 2 vols. Volume 1: *A Reader's Bibliography and Guide* (London: Continuum, 2012). Volume 2: *A Guide to the Graham Greene Archives* (London: Bloomsbury, 2015)

Introduction

1 GG to MG, 28 December 1951, BL.
2 WOE, 140.
3 'Before the Attack', *Reflections*, 202–3.
4 Allain, 172. It may be that he did go to confession later in the 1950s, as suggested in GG to CW, 7 December 1958, GU.
5 'Indo-China: France's Crown of Thorns', trans. Alan Adamson, *Reflections*, 167.
6 I am grateful to Claire Tran, Directrice, Institut de Recherche sur l'Asie du Sud-Est Contemporaine (IRASEC) for information on this priest.
7 GG to CW, 25 December 1952, GU.
8 Journal, 16–18 December 1951, GU.
9 *New York Times* (22 August 2007).
10 *Guardian* (27 February 2019).
11 *Edge*.
12 It is necessary to declare at the outset how indebted this book is to the scholarship on Graham Greene of Judith Adamson, Marie-Françoise Allain, Christopher Hull, Tim Butcher, Quentin Falk, Carlos Villar Flor, Michael Hill, the late Jeremy Lewis, Michael Meeuwis, the late David Pearce, Kevin Ruane, Brigitte Timmerman, and Jonathan Wise. Each of these scholars has assisted me in essential ways, and any errors I make in their special areas of research are mine alone.
13 QA, 172.
14 HM, 26.

1: The Dog in the Pram

1 SOL, 13–14.
2 *Moments of Being: The Random Recollections of Raymond Greene* (London: Heinemann, 1974), ix.
3 SOL, 52–3.
4 SOL, 15.
5 SOL, 28.
6 SOL, 23–4.
7 SOL, 11.
8 Information from Jenny Sherwood of the Berkhamsted Local History and Museum Society.
9 Information from David R. A. Pearce, who served as church warden.

10 SOL, 11.
11 Ashridge Estate: https://www. nationaltrust.org.uk/ashridge-estate (accessed 29 May 2019).
12 Berkhamsted Castle: http://www. english-heritage.org.uk/visit/ places/berkhamsted-castle/history/ (accessed 29 May 2019).
13 SOL, 12.
14 SOL, 21–2; information from Cliff Davies, Keeper of the Archives, Wadham College, Oxford.
15 Williams, 124 and passim.
16 Williams, 157.
17 Lewis, 25.
18 Williams, 230; SOL, 50.; Graham Greene's information came from Kenneth Bell and Father George Trollope.
19 1901 census: familysearch.org.
20 Lewis, 4.
21 David Olusaga, 'Britain's Forgotten Slave Owners', documentary, BBC 2, 13 July 2016. Specific records can be found at 'Legacies of British Slave-ownership' database: https:// www.ucl.ac.uk/lbs/ (accessed 18 June 2019).
22 SOL, 69–71.
23 HG, 'On the Track of Great Uncle Charles', History Today 20:1 (1 January 1970), 61–2.
24 GG to HG, 8 November 1969, BC.
25 American Psychiatric Association, Diagnostic and Statistical Manual of Mental Disorders: Fifth Edition DSM 5 (Washington, DC: APA Publishing, 2013); Neel Burton, 'A Short History of Bipolar Disorder', Psychology Today (21 June 2012): https://www.psychologytoday.com/ us/blog/hide-and-seek/201206/short-history-bipolar-disorder (accessed 17 December 2019); further information from Kay Redfield Jamison.
26 Information from Louise Dennys.
27 SOL, 67.
28 SOL, 67.
29 Information from Louise Dennys, calling on the recollections of Marion's younger sister Nora known as 'Nono'. GG himself did not believe his mother had ever met him.
30 GG to John Gheeraeit, 3 October 1989, BC.
31 GG to Mrs Mirrylees, 16 June 1949, BC; GG to Moray McLaren, 5 July 1949, BC.
32 SOL, 17.
33 Lewis, passim.
34 Lewis, 25. Further information from David R. A. Pearce.
35 Lewis, 25. Further information from David R. A. Pearce.
36 1901 census; SOL, 22.
37 SOL, 14.
38 John, E. Barham, ed., The Mother and the Maiden Aunt: Letters of Eva and Alice Greene 1909–1912 (Kibworth: Matador, 2010), 101.
39 SOL, 19; 'The Lost Childhood', CE, 13.
40 SOL, 52–3.
41 Letters, 326.
42 For a more detailed account of Greene's childhood reading, see SOL, 38–40.
43 'Founder's Day, 1912', The Berkhamstedian (December 1912), 140.
44 School News, The Berkhamstedian (December 1912), 204.
45 SOL, 38.
46 SOL, 44.
47 SOL, 33.
48 See Allain, 33.
49 Letters, 315. GG's correspondence with Saunders is at BC, along with other letters from Old Berkhamstedians responding to SOL.
50 SOL, 35–6.
51 Williams, 216.
52 Peter Quennell, The Marble Foot (London: Collins, 1976), 64.
53 SOL, 46–7.
54 Hilary Rost to RG, 12 March 2006; see Letters, 316.
55 Letters, 123.
56 Editorial, The Berkhamstedian (November 1913), 101–3.
57 'Musketry Competition for the Messum Cup, The Berkhamstedian (June 1912), 75–6.

58 Colonel R. Macgregor, letter, *The Berkhamstedian* (June 1913), 56–7.

59 Editorial, *The Berkhamstedian* (November 1914), 3–4.

60 'Lieutenant Arthur Harding', *The Berkhamstedian* (November 1914), 91.

61 Editorial, *The Berkhamstedian* (March 1915), 1–4.

62 Editorial, *The Berkhamstedian* (June 1915), 42.

63 Supplement, *The Berkhamstedian* (December 1915).

64 *The Berkhamstedian* (December 1916), 80–9.

65 'Founder's Day, 1918', *The Berkhamstedian* (December 1918), 96–7.

66 Memorial plaque, St Peter's Church, Berkhamsted.

2: Flight

1 *LR*, 13.

2 Editorial, *The Berkhamstedian* (April 1917), 2–3.

3 Tracey, 9.

4 *LR*, 14–15.

5 *SOL*, 54–5.

6 *Letters*, 315–17.

7 Information from David R. A. Pearce.

8 Cloetta, 90.

9 American Psychiatric Association, *Diagnostic and Statistical Manual of Mental Disorders: Fifth Edition DSM 5* (Washington, DC: APA Publishing, 2013).

10 Jamison is interviewed in *Edge*. I am grateful to her for further information on this subject.

11 Information from David Pearce.

12 *WOE*, 65.

13 MG to VG, 29 June 1948, McFarlin Library, University of Tulsa.

14 Sherry 1: 85. He bases the suggestion on there only being a record of Mendelssohn being played at a school concert on that day.

15 *LR*, 13–14.

16 Sherry 1: 89.

17 Information from Nicholas Dennys and Louise Dennys.

18 MG to VG, [c. July 1948], McFarlin Library, University of Tulsa.

19 *WOE*, 73–5.

20 GG to MG, 6 October 1921, BL.

21 *WOE*, 75–6.

22 *WOE*, 71; *Letters*, 419.

23 GG to MG, n.d. [c. October 1921], BL.

24 *Letters*, 357–8.

25 Durán, 129–30.

26 *SOL*, 76.

27 *Letters*, 3–4.

28 GG to MG, 29 November 1921, BL.

29 Kenneth Richmond to Charles Greene, 26 November 1921, private collection of FG; George Riddoch to Charles Greene, 26 November 1921, private collection of FG.

30 Claud Cockburn, *I, Claud …* (revised edn; Harmondsworth: Penguin, 1967), 37.

31 Kenneth Bell to C. Bailey, 16 June 1922, Balliol. For information on GG's application to Balliol see the 'Administrative File'.

32 *WOE*, 87–8.

3: Backwards Day

1 GG to MG, 22 October 1922, BL.

2 GG to MG, 17 October 1922, BL.

3 *Letters*, 270.

4 Edith Sitwell to GG, 25 April 1923, GU.

5 GG to MG, 12 June 1923, BL.

6 Sherry 1: 141–2.

7 Edith Sitwell to GG, 15 June 1923, GU.

8 GG to MG, 9 June 1923, BL.

9 GG to MG, 9 June 1923, BL.

10 Pierre Joannon, 'Graham Greene's Other Island', in in A. F. Cassis, ed., *Graham Greene: Man of Paradox* (Chicago: Loyola University Press, 1994), 305.

11 'Impressions of Dublin', *Reflections*, 1–4.

12 'Barrel-organing', *The Times* (27 December 1928); reprinted in *Reflections*, 18–20. See also 'The Mask Remover', *New Statesman* (31 May 1968), 728.

13 *SOL*, 100–1; Knut Hansen, *Albrecht*

Graf von Bernstorff (Frankfurt:
Peter Lang, 1996); Anne Sebba,
Enid Bagnold (London: Weidenfeld
& Nicolson, 1986), 112–16 and
passim.

14 Allain, 40.
15 *SOL*, 104–5.
16 *SOL*, 100–5.
17 GG to MG, *c.* 27 October 1924, BL.
18 *SOL*, 103.

4: The Revolver

1   *SOL*, 86.
2   *SOL*, 87.
3   *SOL*, 90.
4   *SOL*, 89–91.
5   *SOL*, 93.
6   *Letters*, 270.
7   *SOL*, 94.
8   Information from Oliver Greene.
9   Nigel Lewis, 'Graham Greene
    Tapes', BL.
10 'Sensations', *Babbling April* (Oxford:
    Basil Blackwell, 1925), 1.
11 *SOL*, 95–6.
12 J. T.G. *Macleod*, BBC Scotland
    documentary, 1974.
13 GG to VG, 29 August 1925, HRC.
14 *SOL*, 90–1.
15 Harold Acton, review of *Babbling
    April*, *The Cherwell* (9 May 1925).
16 GG, 'The Poets Fight', *The Cherwell*
    (16 May 1925).
17 *Letters*, 177.
18 *WOE*, 12.
199 *Letters*, 16–18.
20 The first chapter of 'The Empty
    Chair' was published in *The Times*
    (13 December 2008); all five
    chapters, with an introduction
    by François Gallix, appeared in
    successive issues of *The Strand*,
    June–September 2009 to October
    2010–January 2011.

5: Casual Corpses

1   GG to MG, 2 August 1925, BL.
2   GG to MG, 8 February 1925, 16
    February 1925, 3 March 1925, 15
    May 1925, 18 May 1925, 22 May
    1925, BL. See also *SOL*, 106–11.

3   'The Average Film', *Oxford Outlook*,
    7:35 (February 1925), 96–7.
4   *Letters*, 10; *SOL*, 118.
5   The dates are given in GG to VG,
    30 July 1925, HRC.
6   She is sometimes said to have
    been a year or two younger. FG
    discovered the correct age from her
    Rhodesian birth certificate.
7   Information from CB.
8   Bevis Hillier, 'A Sort of Wife', *The
    Times Magazine* (20 January 1996).
9   Interview with CB, 20 February
    2014.
10 Hillier, 'A Sort of Wife'.
11 Vivienne Dayrell-Browning, *The
    Little Wings: Poems and Essays*,
    intro. G. K. Chesterton (Oxford: B.
    H. Blackwell, 1921).
12 GG to MG, [*c.* 18 May 1925], BL.
13 GG to VG, 30 May [1925?], HRC.
14 GG, 'The Trial of Pan', *Oxford
    Outlook* (February 1923), 47–50.
15 GG to VG, 22 June 1925, with
    annotation by VG, HRC.
16 GG to VG, 7 August 1925, HRC.
17 Quoted by GG in letter to VG, 23
    August 1925, HRC.
18 GG to VG, 26 September 1925,
    HRC.
19 Typescript draft of *SOL*, HRC.
20 *SOL*, 112–14.
21 GG to MG, 8 September1925, BL.
22 GG to MG, 19 August and 13
    November 1925, BL.
23 GG to VG, 11 November 1925,
    HRC; *SOL*, 111.
24 Carl Cavanagh Hodge,
    *Encyclopedia of the Age of
    Imperialism, 1800–1914* (Westport:
    Greenwood, 2008), 138.
25 GTG, 10–11.
26 *SOL*, 116–24.
27 *Letters*, 23.
28 GG to MG, 4 November 1925.
29 GG to MG, 5 December 1925, BL.
30 See Wise and Hill 1: 89.
31 GG to MG, 17 December 1925, BL.
32 GG to MG, 25 February 1926, BL.
33 The full description of Roberts is
    found in the Bodley Head edition
    of *SOL*, 159–60.
34 Cecil Roberts, 'Graham Greene's

Sort of Life', *Books and Bookmen*
(October 1971), 28–31.
35 *SOL*, 118.
36 GG to VG, 2 November 1925,
HRC.
37 *SOL*, 118.
38 What follows relies heavily on
Margaret Quinn's apparently
unpublished article about Trollope,
of which there is a typescript in the
Graham Greene Collection, BC.
Her research is also described in
'Notebook: Greene Then and Now',
The Tablet (29 September 1984), 9.
39 For GG's account of his dealings
with Trollope, see *SOL*, 118–22.
40 GG to VG, 16 November 1925,
HRC.
41 *SOL*, 119.
42 *Letters*, 25.
43 GG to MG, 16 February 1926 and
19 February 1926, BL.
44 *SOL*, 121; GG to MG, 19 February
1926, BL.
45 GG to VG, 21 January 1926, HRC.
46 GG to VG, 16 and 21 March
1926, HRC; Margaret Quinn,
unpublished article on Trollope,
BC.
47 Baptismal Register 1926, St
Barnabas Cathedral, Nottingham.
48 *SOL*, 121.
49 *SOL*, 122.

6: Marriage

1 *Letters*, 25–7; *SOL*, 125–7.
2 *SOL*, 127.
3 GG to MG, 5 May 1926, 6 May
1926, 8 May 1926, 18 May 1926, BL.
4 *Letters*, 27.
5 *SOL*, 127.
6 Allain, 91.
7 GG to VG, 27 August 1926 and 21
September 1926, HRC.
8 GG to VG, 12 August 1926 and 31
January 1927, HRC.
9 Greene seems to have submitted a
group of poems under pseudonyms,
winning as 'H. Graham'. The
untitled poem appeared in *Saturday
Review* (25 September 1926), 338.
Greene refers to winning the

competition in his letter to MG, 25
September 1926, BL.
10 GG to MG, 4 August 1926, BL.
11 GG to VG, 25 September 1927,
HRC; GG to MG, 21 April 1927,
BL.
12 *Letters*, 127–8.
13 Lord Teignmouth and Charles
G. Harper, *The Smugglers*, 2 vols.
(1923), 1: 42–5. See *Letters*, 63.
14 *WOE*, 11.
15 GG to MG, 18 November 1926, BL;
information about the epilepsy scare
is mainly drawn from *SOL*, 135–8.
16 Greene and Sherry misspell
the name in different ways. He
is correctly identified in E. H.
Reynolds, 'The Impact of Epilepsy
on Graham Greene', *Epilepsia*, 42
(2001), 1091–3.
17 GG to VG, 11 December 1925,
HRC.
18 *SOL*, 137.
19 For further information, see 'Father
James Christie', *Oratory Parish
Magazine* (November 1929), 207–8,
and 'Obituary: The Revd H. J.
Christie, Cong. Orat.', *The Tablet*
(28 September 1929), 26.
20 *SOL*, 137.
21 GG to MG, 13 February 1927, BL.
22 GG, Journal (19 July 1932), HRC.
23 GG to MG, 24 January 1927, BL;
Williams, 250.
24 GG to MG, 29 March 1928, BL.
25 GG to VG, 6 April 1927, HRC.
26 GG to VG, 18? February 1926, 21
March 1926, 22 March 1926, HRC.
27 *Morning Post* (17 October 1927).
28 Sherry 1: 354–5.
29 GG to MG, 31 October 1927, BL.

7: Rats in the Thatch

1 *SOL*, 128.
2 *SOL*, 125.
3 *The Times* (18 May 1951).
4 *SOL*, 129–30; Obituary, *The Times*
(23 November 1979).
5 'A Walk on the Sussex Downs' (9
March 1928) and 'Barrel-organing'
(27 December 1928) are reprinted
in *Reflections*, 18–20 and 21–3.

6   'The Province of the Film: Past Mistakes and Future Hopes', *The Times* (9 April 1928).

7   'A Film Technique: Rhythms of Space and Time', *The Times* (12 June 1928).

8   See Pamela Hutchinson, 'C'mon feel the noise: What happened when the talkies came to Britain?', *Guardian* (21 September 2015).

9   'Film Aesthetic: Its Distinction for Drama – The Province of the Screen', *The Times* (19 March 1929); for Disney, see for example GG to MG, 4 May 1942, BL.

10 *SOL*, 138–40.

11 David Higham, *Literary Gent* (London: Jonathan Cape, 1978), 170.

12 *Letters*, 32.

13 GG to MG, 24 May 1929, BL.

14 *SOL*, 140.

15 *Letters*, 34–5.

16 *SOL*, 133

17 GG to Lints Smith, 7 October 1929, News International Record Office.

18 *WOE*, 14.

19 Journal, 11 June 1932, HRC.

20 GG to MG, 4 April 1929, BL.

21 GG to MG, 24 May 1929, BL.

22 *WOE*, 16.

23 GG to MG, 7 May 1930, 13 May 1930, 15 May 1930, BL.

24 Quoted in GG to MG, 13 May 1930, BL.

25 *SOL*, 140.

26 GG to MG, Tuesday [late July 1930], BL.

27 Review of *The Name of Action*, *The Bookman*, 73 (April 1931), 195.

28 *Letters*, 38–9.

29 *Letters*, 39.

30 Dates and word count are recorded on the manuscript of *Rumour at Nightfall*, HRC.

31 GG to MG, 28 April 1931, BL.

32 *SOL*, 146–7; *WOE*, 15–18; GG to MG, 2 October 1930, BL.

33 *Rumour at Nightfall* (New York: Doubleday Doran, 1932), 240.

34 *Rumour at Nightfall*, 214.

35 *Evening News* (20 November 1931). See *WOE*, 17–18.

36 *WOE*, 17; Wise and Hill 1: 17.

37 GG's letters of instruction, which I have examined, are in the possession of FG.

38 *Letters*, 39.

39 Greene's copy of *Devotional Poets of the XVII Century*, ed. and intro. Sir Henry Newbolt (London & Edinburgh: Thomas Nelson, n.d.) is in the collection at the HRC. In it he marks off his favourite poems from the period. The phrase from Herbert's 'The Church Porch' is singled out on page 62.

40 *Lord Rochester's Monkey* (London: The Bodley Head, 1974), 10. Note that this passage, though consistent with the positions taken in the book, was actually written as part of a preface at the time of publication.

41 *Lord Rochester's Monkey*, 110.

42 GG to Christopher Hill, 15 October 1974, Balliol.

43 The circumstances of the book's rejection are recounted in the preface to *Lord Rochester's Monkey*, 9.

44 *SOL*, 145–6.

45 *Edge*.

46 Journal, 18 July 1932, HRC.

47 *Letters*, 182.

48 GG to MG, 25 May 1931, BL.

49 Information from Caroline Bourget.

50 *SOL*, 147–50.

51 Chipping Campden History Society: https://www.chippingcampdenhistory.org.uk/content/history/religious_life_in_campden_district/father_henry_bilsborrow (accessed 10 September 2019).

52 *SOL*, 148.

53 'Death in the Cotswolds' (24 February 1933), is reprinted in *Reflections*, 24–7. For further information on Seitz, see https://www.chippingcampdenhistory.org.uk/content/history/people-2/campden-characters/charles_francis_seitz_sykes_1858_-_1933 (accessed 10 September 2019).

54 *WOE*, 18–22; Nils Lie, 'The Young

Nordahl Grieg', unpublished translation by Jens Folkman of a speech by Lie at a 1972 commemoration of Grieg, BC.

55 Information from Johanne Elster Hanson.

56 WOE, 22.

8: The Devil Looks After His Own

1 Annotation on MS of *Stamboul Train*, HRC.

2 WOE, 22.

3 See, for example, Stephen Clissold, *A Short History of Yugoslavia From Early Times to 1966* (Cambridge: Cambridge University Press, 1966), 181–4.

4 Anne Applebaum, *Red Famine: Stalin's War on Ukraine* (New York: Doubleday, 2017), xxvi and 280.

5 David R. A. Pearce, '*Stamboul Train*: The Timetable for 1932', 19–37, in *Dangerous Edges of Graham Greene*, eds Dermot Gilvray and Darren J. N. Middleton (New York: Continuum, 2011). I follow Pearce, 30, in placing the events of the story in the politically fraught April 1932.

6 WOE, 23.

7 *Letters*, 398–9.

8 Tracey, 33.

9 Lewis, 139–47.

10 *Letters*, 86.

11 *Letters*, 98.

12 See, for example, Ninian Stewart, *The Royal Navy and the Palestine Patrol* (London: Frank Cass, 2002).

13 PG, 102.

14 Undated entry *c.* March 1941, 'The Defenders' (Blitz journal 1940–41), HRC.

15 MS of *Stamboul Train*, HRC.

16 *Letters*, 46.

17 Journal, 17 July 1932, HRC.

18 SOL, 131.

19 Journal, 23 July 1932, HRC.

20 Journal, 19 and 26 August 1932, HRC.

21 SOL, 153.

22 Journal, 1 September 1932, HRC.

23 Journal, 1 September 1932, HRC.

24 Philip Ziegler, *Rupert Hart-Davis: Man of Letters* (London: Chatto & Windus, 2004), 78–81; Journal, 7 October 1932, HRC.

25 *Letters*, 47; Journal, 20 October 1932, HRC.

26 *Stamboul Train*, 70.

27 Journal, 28 November 1932, HRC.

28 *Letters*, 48. BL has what appears to be a copy of the uncorrected first issue under the call number Cup. 410 f.742.

29 John St John, *William Heinemann: A Century of Publishing 1890–1990* (London: William Heinemann, 1990), 295.

30 GG to MG, [? December 1932], BL.

31 Journal, 28 November 1932 – 4 January 1933, HRC.

32 GG to MG, 3 March 1933, BL. I am grateful to John Baxendale for information about Priestley's reviewing.

33 GG to MG, 3 March 1933, BL.

34 Quoted in GG to MG, 13 April 1933, BL.

35 GG to MG, 21 February and 3 March 1933, BL; Journal, 14 February 1933, HRC.

36 Jeremy Lewis, *Grub Street Irregular* (London: Harper Press, 2008), 18.

37 See Wise and Hill 1: 79–190.

38 GG to MG, 21 February 1933, BL.

39 Bevis Hillier, 'A Sort of Wife', *The Times Magazine* (20 January 1996).

40 Journal, 15 March and 18 April 1933, HRC.

41 GG to MG, 5 May 1933, BL.

42 Journal, 25 April 1933, HRC.

43 Journal, 21–3 May 1933, HRC; *Letters*, 49–50.

44 Wise and Hill 1: 18.

45 Journal, 15 August and 7 October 1932, HRC.

46 See G. D. Turner, 'Aid for Prisoners on Discharge', *Police Journal* (1930), 11–19, and *The Alternatives to Capital Punishment* (London: National Council for the Abolition of the Death Penalty, 1940).

47 Journal, 4 January 1933, HRC.

48 *It's a Battlefield*, 194.

49 The dates of writing are noted on the AMS of 'It's a Battlefield', HRC.
50 Wise and Hill 1: 18.
51 Ford Madox Ford to GG, 4 December 1934, HRC; see Alan Judd, *Ford Madox Ford* (London: Collins 1990), 420.

9: Minty Stepped on Board

1 See George Soloveytchik, *The Financier: The Life of Ivar Kreuger* (London: Peter Davies, 1933), 108–12, 141 and 151.
2 Review of *The Financier: The Life of Ivar Kreugaer* by George Soloveytchik, *The Spectator* (3 March 1993), 308.
3 *WOE*, 30.
4 GG to MG, 3 August 1933, 20 August 1933, 29 August 1933, BL; *Letters*, 51–2; 'Two Capitals', *Reflections*, 31–4.
5 This matter is referred to repeatedly in GG's letters to MG at the BL.
6 *WOE*, 31–2.
7 KP to GG, 23 November 1982, Sutro Collection, Bod; Waugh (1980), 322.
8 L. P. Hartley, 'The Conformer', 85–102, in GG, ed., *The Old School* (London: Jonathan Cape, 1934), 87.
9 *Letters*, 50.
10 Walter Greenwood, 'Langy Road', 73–84, in GG, ed., *The Old School*, 76.
11 GG to MG, 12 November 1933, BL.
12 *Letters*, 52.
13 GG to MG, 12 November 1933, BL.
14 GG to MG, 29 December 1933, BL.
15 Oxford Diary, *Oxford Mail* (20 January 1934). The issue of the 24th makes no reference to the meeting, but does describe a 'black-out' across southern England owing to frost and fog. It is possible the meeting was cancelled.
16 Allain, 55.

17 GG to VG, 14 October 1926, HRC.
18 *The Times* (esp. 12 and 26 January 1934; 8, 12 and 20 February 1934).
19 Desmond Flower, 'Denyse Clarouin', unpublished memoir, GG Collection, BC.
20 'Strike in Paris', *Spectator* (16 February 1934). *Letters*, 56.
21 *Letters*, 58.
22 GG to MG, 9 July 1934, BL.
23 GG to MG, 14 April 1934, BL; *WOE*, 55; *Letters*, 301.
24 *JWM*, 35–6.
25 GG to MG, 14 April 1934, BL.
26 *New York Times* (16 May 1934).
27 *Letters*, 60–2.
28 For a full account of Greene's visit to Tallinn and his friendship with Leslie, see *Articles*, 165–79. See also Greene's letter to Thomson about Tallinn and the abortive film script in *Letters*, 403. I am grateful to Ian Thomson for his generous assistance.
29 *WOE*, 55–6.

10: In Zigi's Town

1 *JWM*, 37.
2 *WOE*, 37.
3 'The International Commission of Enquiry in Liberia' (Geneva: League of Nations Official Publications, 1930), 133–5.
4 'The International Commission of Enquiry in Liberia', 133–5; further information from Tarnue Johnson, *A Critical Examination of Firestone's Operations in Liberia: A Case Study Approach* (Bloomington: AuthorHouse, 2010), esp. 23–8.
5 *The Times* (19 May 1934).
6 My comments here are indebted to an email exchange with Tim Butcher, 13 July 2016. I am grateful to Tim Butcher for his generous assistance.
7 *ODNB*.
8 *Letters*, 67.
9 *WOE*, 39.
10 *ODNB*.
11 Foreign Office memo, 7 December 1934, outline response to Sir John

Harris, TNA, FO 371/ 18044. This archival source was first discovered by Butcher.

12 *Letters*, 65.
13 Barbara Greene, xii; Tracey, 47.
14 *Letters*, 64.
15 Barbara Greene, xii–xiii.
16 Lewis, 99–100, and 161–2.
17 See Butcher, 26.
18 See a series of letters between G. H. Thompson and GG, 13–23 December 1934, TNA, FO 371/ 18044.
19 GG to MG, undated, BL.
20 GG to MG, 14 January 1935, BL.
21 Butcher, 26.
22 Barbara Greene, 6.
23 Barbara Greene, vii.
24 *JWM*, 18.
25 *JWM*, 45–6.
26 *JWM*, 80–1, 122.
27 *JWM*, 41; Butcher, 73.
28 *JWM*, 119.
29 See Chinua Achebe, 'An Image of Africa: Racism in Conrad's *Heart of Darkness*', *Massachusetts Review*, 18. (1977). Reprinted in Joseph Conrad, *Heart of Darkness, An Authoritative Text, Background and Sources Criticism*, ed. Robert Kimbrough (3rd edn; London: W. W Norton and Co., 1988), 251–61.
30 *JWM*, 100–1.
31 Cable to Mr Yapp, 20 December 1934, TNA, FO 371/ 18044.
32 'Journey Without Maps: Notes' (journal), HRC.
33 *JWM*, 106.
34 'Journey Without Maps: Notes' (journal), HRC.
35 *JWM*, 196–207, 231; Butcher, 278, suspects that Greene was somewhat fooled.
36 Report on Greene's remarks to the annual meeting of the Anti-Slavery Society on 18 June 1935: Anon., 'Slavery and the League of Nations: Liberia', *Anti-Slavery Reporter and Aborigine's Friend*, Series V, 25:3 (October 1935), 99–100.
37 Ibid.
38 *JWM*, 174.
39 Barbara Greene, 115.

40 Butcher, 247–54.
41 Barbara Greene, 71.
42 Barbara Greene, 174.
43 'Journey Without Maps: Notes' (journal), HRC.
44 Barbara Greene, 176.
45 *JWM*, 213–14.
46 *JWM*, 214.

11: Raven

1 GG to MG, 1 May 1935, BL.
2 GG to MG, undated, BL.
3 Despite extensive damage in the Blitz, the house survives, now divided into flats; it is grade-II listed and bears an English Heritage blue plaque commemorating Graham Greene's time there: http://www. english-heritage.org.uk/visit/blue-plaques/GrahamGreene. Interview with CB, 20 February 2014.
4 Bevis Hillier, 'A Sort of Wife', *The Times Magazine* (20 December 1996).
5 GG to MG, 29 May 1935, BL.
6 *The Times* (19 June 1935).
7 Wise and Hill 2: 19.
8 GG to MG, undated, BL.
9 Greene's writings on film have been compiled in David Parkinson, ed., *The Graham Greene Film Reader: Mornings in the Dark* (Manchester: Carcanet Press, 1993).
10 WOE, 45.
11 GG to MG, 18 April 1935, BL.
12 GG to MG, undated, BL.
13 R. K. Narayan, *My Days* (1973; London: Picador, 2001), 110–11; Susan Ram and N. Ram, *R. K. Narayan: The Early Years 1906–1945* (New Delhi: Viking, 1996), esp. 143–5; for a learned account of Narayan's life and writing, see Ranga Rao, *R. K. Narayan: The Novelist and his Art* (New Delhi: Oxford University Press, 2017).
14 *Letters*, 68–70.
15 Information from Bruce Hunter.
16 David Higham to GG, 5 January 1953, Pollinger Files, HRC. Higham is quoting a letter he has received from Narayan.

17 GG to MR, 21 September 1964, BL.
18 GG to Marshall Best, 23 March 1974, Viking Press editorial files, New York.
19 Arthur Calder-Marshall, 'The Works of Graham Greene', *Horizon*, 5 (May 1940), 367–75.
20 *JWM*, 19.
21 GG to MG, [?] September 1935, BL.
22 *WOE*, 27–31.
23 GG to MG, 17 January 1936, BL.
24 Allain, 148.
25 Contract between Graham Greene and Paramount Productions, Inc., 12 May 1936, Pollinger Files, HRC.
26 *Letters*, 81.

12: My Worst Film

1 Notebook 1936, HRC.
2 *Letters*, 71.
3 GG to MG, 29 August 1936, BL.
4 Allain, 132–3; for a contrary opinion, see Bergonzi, 28–34, who maintains that the idea of Greene's cinematic method has been exaggerated.
5 Falk, 4–6.
6 *Spectator* (12 January 1940).
7 *Reflections*, 407–10.
8 *Spectator* (4 September 1936). David Parkinson, ed., *The Graham Greene Film Reader: Mornings in the Dark* (Manchester: Carcanet Press, 1993), 135.
9 See Drazin, 212–19 and *passim*.
10 *Letters*, 79.
11 *WOE*, 50.
12 *WOE*, 50.
13 GG to MG, 18 November 1936, BL.
14 Falk, 1.

13: Shirley Temple

1 See Christopher Hawtree, Introduction, Christopher Hawtree, ed., *Night and Day* (London: Chatto & Windus, 1985), viii–xiv.
2 Peter Fleming, 'Minutes of the Week', in Hawtree, ed., *Night and Day*, 20.
3 GG, Preface, in Hawtree, ed., *Night and Day*, vii.
4 *WOE*, 34.
5 'Review of *Wee Willie Winkie* and *The Life of Emile Zola*', in Hawtree, ed., *Night and Day*, 204.
6 I am borrowing and changing slightly a wisecrack by the literary critic Allan Pero.
7 'Is it Criticism?', David Parkinson, ed., *The Graham Greene Film Reader: Mornings in the Dark* (Manchester: Carcanet Press, 1993), 408.
8 Shirley Temple, *Child Star* (New York: McGraw-Hill, 1988), 319–20.
9 *WOE*, 47.
10 *The Times* (23 March 1938).

14: Real Brighton

1 *Nineteen Stories* (New York: Viking, 1949), 210.
2 *WOE*, 57.
3 For example, *WOE*, 58.
4 Review of *After Strange Gods*, *Life and Letters* (April 1934). 112.
5 I am grateful to Edward Short, a biographer of Newman, for his observations on this point.
6 Ian Ker, *The Catholic Revival in English Literature, 1845–1961: Newman, Hopkins, Belloc, Chesterton, Greene, Waugh* (Notre Dame, IN: Notre Dame University Press, 2003), esp. 115–16.
7 Margaret Drabble, *The Dark Flood Rises* (London: Canongate, 2016), 241–2.
8 *WOE*, 61.
9 *The Times* (17 July 1934).
10 *WOE*, 61.
11 *Daily Mail* (31 July, 9 August, 17 August 1928); *The Times* (31 July 1928)
12 'A History of the World in 100 objects: Prince Monolulu's Jackets', BBC Radio 4: http://www.bbc.co.uk/ahistoryoftheworld/objects/mwelEdCnRQ6lPy_v2ZNY9w (accessed 15 January 2020); 'My Brighton and Hove': https://www.mybrightonandhove.org.uk/people/peopchar/colourful-characters-10 (accessed 15 January 2020).

13 Heather Shore, *London's Criminal Underworlds, c. 1720–c. 1930* (Basingstoke: Palgrave Macmillan, 2015), 174.

14 *The Times* (17 June 1936).

15 *The Times* (29 and 30 July 1936).

16 *Racing Post* (29 July 2006): https://www.thefreelibrary.com/ WHEN+GANGS+RULED+ THE+RACECOURSE%3B+As+ Britain+emerged+buoyant+from+ the...-a0147586279 (accessed 22 January 2020); Carl Chinn, *Better Betting with a Decent Fellow: Bookmaking, Betting and the British Working Class, 1750–1990* (London: Harvester Wheatsheaf, 1991), 204–5;

17 *ODNB*; *Letters*, 398.

18 'My Brighton and Hove': https:// www.mybrightonandhove.org.uk/ search?st%5B%5D=pinkie&css_ searchfield%5B%5D=text&fq= (accessed 15 January 2020).

19 Michael Routh to GG, 29 October 1983, BC; GG to Michael Routh, 11 November 1983, BC; *BR*, 5.

20 *BR*, 219–20.

21 *BR*, 52.

22 *BR*, 91.

23 *BR*, 189.

24 *BR*, 246.

25 *Letters*, 88.

26 See Bergonzi, 97.

27 *WOE*, 60.

15: The Lawless Roads

1 NS 1: 613–14.

2 These are commonly accepted figures derived from Antonio Montero Marino, *Historia de la persecución religiosa en España, 1936–1939* (Madrid: Biblioteca de Autores Cristianos, 1961). For comment on them, see Bruce Lincoln, 'Revolutionary Exhumations in Spain, July 1936', *Comparative Studies in Society and History*, 27:2 (April 1985), 241.

3 GG to MG, n.d., BL.

4 *WOE*, 59–60.

5 Francisco Maria Aguilera González,

Cardenal Miguel Darío Miranda: El hombre, el Cristiano, el Obispo (Mexico City: Instituto Mexicano de Doctrina Social Cristiana, 2005), 162–3. I am grateful to Professor Stephen Andes for bringing this source to my attention.

6 *Letters*, 88.

7 See Tom Burns, 'Graham Greene: A Memoir', *Articles*, 146–50.

8 My account here relies heavily on Julia G. Young, *Mexican Exodus: Emigrants, Exiles, and Refugees of the Cristero War* (Oxford and New York: Oxford University Press, 2015), esp. 18–38 and 125–54. I have supplemented her account especially with that of Jean A. Meyer, *The Cristero Rebellion: The Mexican People Between Church and State 1926–1929* (Cambridge: Cambridge University Press, 1976).

9 See Young, *Mexican Exodus*, esp. 22–4.

10 See Young, *Mexican Exodus* 23–4; Meyer, *The Cristero Rebellion*, 13–15.

11 Meyer, 41–3.

12 Young, *Mexican Exodus*, 26–30; Meyer, *The Cristero Rebellion*, 49–56

13 Meyer, *The Cristero Rebellion*, 64.

14 Meyer, *The Cristero Rebellion*, 165.

15 Meyer, *The Cristero Rebellion*, 202.

16 Pope Pius XI, *Acerbo Animi* (1932). See the Vatican website: http:// w2.vatican.va/content/pius-xi/en/ encyclicals/documents/hf_p-xi_ enc_29091932-acerba-animi.html.

17 Young, *Mexican Exodus*, 42.

18 Meyer, *The Cristero Rebellion*, 71–5. The challenge to Meyer's count of priests remaining in the parishes is found in Matthew Butler, 'Keeping the Faith in Revolutionary Mexico: Clerical and Lay Resistance to Religious Persecution, East Michoacan, 1926–1929', *The Americas* 59:1 (July 2002), 9–32.

19 Robert E. Quirk, *The Mexican Revolution and the Catholic Church* (Bloomington: Indiana University

Press, 1973), 212–13; Joseph I. Marmion, SJ, 'Fr. Miguel Pro' in *Jesuits: Biographical Essays*, ed. Robert Nash, SJ, ed. (Westminster, MD: Newman Press, 1956), 139–48.

20 GG to MG, 7 February 1938, BL.

21 Young, *Mexican Exodus*, 58.

22 Mexican Journal, 27 February 1938, Greene-Walston Papers Box 51, Georgetown. For a description of this bishop see Young, *Mexican Exodus*, 135–40. I am grateful to Professor Young for further information conveyed by email.

23 LR, 27.

24 LR, 30.

25 GG to VG, postcard, 27 February 1938, BL.

26 GG, *Getting to Know the General* (London: The Bodley Head, 1984), 23.

27 LR, 67.

28 *The Times* (21 March 1938).

29 LR, 73.

30 LR, 33.

31 GG to Charles Greene, postcard, 7 March 1938, BL.

32 Meyer, *The Cristero Rebellion*, 202–5.

33 LR, 70–5; Journal, 14 March 1938, GU. Professor Stephen Andes has kindly identified Father Tagle for me, citing Pedro Velasquez Hernandez, *El secretariado social mexicano (25 anos de vida)*. (Mexico City: Secretariado Social Mexicano, 1945), 94 and 108.

34 See Pope Pius XI, *Fermissiam Constantiam*: https://w2.vatican. va/content/pius-xi/en/encyclicals/ documents/hf_p-xi_enc_19370328_ firmissimam-constantiam.html.

35 Stephen J. C. Andes, *The Vatican and Catholic Activism in Mexico and Chile: The Politics of Transnational Catholicism, 1920–1940* (Oxford: Oxford University Press, 2014), 170–4. My observations on the attitudes of the bishops, the Vatican, and Catholic Action are drawn more generally from Professor Andes's research. He has also kindly discussed some of these points with me by email and directed me to other sources.

36 Peter Godman, 'Graham Greene's Vatican Dossier', *The Atlantic* (July/August 2001): http://www. theatlantic.com/magazine/ archive/2001/07/graham-greenes-vatican-dossier/302264/ (accessed 11 September 2019).

37 LR, 96.

38 LR, 145.

39 American Psychiatric Association, *Diagnostic and Statistical Manual of Mental Disorders: Fifth Edition DSM 5* (Washington, DC: APA Publishing, 2013).

40 LR, 105.

41 GG to MG, 13 April 1938, BL.

42 Greene uses this phrase as the title for chapter 6 of *LR*.

43 Obituary: 'Don Tomas Garrido Canabal', *Time Magazine* (19 April 1943).

44 LR, 106.

45 *The Times* (2 January 1935).

46 *New York Times* (9 April 1943).

47 LR, 123. Greene is quoting from Rilke's novel, *The Notebooks of Malte Laurids Brigge*.

48 LR, 122 and 141.

49 Massimo De Giuseppe, '"El Indio Gabriel": New Religious Perspectives among the Indigenous in Garrido Canabal's Tabasco (1927–30)', in Matthew Butler trans. and ed., *Faith and Impiety in Revolutionary Mexico* (New York: Palgrave Macmillan, 2007), 225–42.

50 LR, 131.

51 LR, 142–5.

52 JR to Miss Black, 8 November 1965, Fan Mail file, BC. Reid conveys Greene's explanation of the episode to an enquiring reader.

53 Sherry 1: 720.

54 LR, 165.

55 Journal, 11 April 1938, GU.

56 GG to MG, 13 April 1938, BL.

57 Allain, 155.

58 LR, 175.

59 Journal, 14 April 1938, GU.

60 Quoted in 'Translator's Preface' in Léon Bloy, *Letters to his Fiancée*, trans. Barbara Wall (London: Sheed & Ward, 1937), xi.
61 O'Malley, 495–6.

16: Doll

1 *Letters*, 95; *WOE*, 61.
2 Gerald Pollinger to GG, 2 December 1977, HRC.
3 *New York Times* (24 June 1938).
4 *Letters*, 96.
5 *Letters*, 197.
6 *Letters*, 93–4.
7 *CP*, 330.
8 *WOE*, 68–9.
9 *Letters*, 96 and 120.
10 1911 census: www.findmypast. co.uk.
11 J. P. Wearing, *The London Stage 1910–19*, 2 vols. (Metuchen and London: Scarecrow Press, 1982), 1, 641.
12 J. P. Wearing, *The London Stage 1930–1939: A Calendar of Productions, Performers, and Personnel* (Lanham, MD: Rowman and Littlefield, 2014), 129, 130, and 154.
13 Theatricalia database: https:// theatricalia.com/play/33f/the-barretts-of-wimpole-street/ production/759 (accessed 11 September 2019).
14 'Provincial Notes', *The Dancing Times* (October 1938), 91. This reference may be to a different Dorothy Glover.
15 *Letters*, 103.
16 Hill and Wise, 1, 24.
17 Brian Alderson, 'The Four (or Five? ... or Six? ... Seven? ...) Children's Books of Graham Greene', *Children's Literature in Education*, 36 (2005), 325–42.
18 GG to A. S. Frere, Sunday [13 April 1952], Random House Archive, Rushden.
19 GS, transcript of conversation with GG, 21 October 1987, Sutro Collection, Bod.
20 *Letters*, 119.

21 LP to GG, 22 September 1948, HRC.
22 GS, transcript of conversation with YC, 8 June 1995, Sutro Collection, Bod.
23 GG to CW, 1 March 1952, GU.
24 GG to MG, 7 April 1941 and 20 August 1941, BL.
25 *Letters*, 99.
26 *Letters*, 100.
27 Wise and Hill 1: 22.
28 *Confidential Agent*, 62.
29 Wise and Hill 1:22.
30 *Confidential Agent*, 152.
31 Falk, 21–4.
32 *WOE*, 68.
33 *PG*, 40.
34 *PG*, 125.
35 *WOE*, 68.
36 Quoted in 'Translator's Preface' in Léon Bloy, *Letters to his Fiancée*, trans. Barbara Wall (London: Sheed & Ward, 1937), xi.
37 Wise and Hill 1: 22–3.
38 *Saturday Review of Literature* (30 March 1940).
39 *Letters*, 115–16.

17: Bombs and Books

1 *Letters*, 115–16.
2 Muggeridge (1973), 82.
3 *Letters*, 106.
4 Peter Stansky, *The First Day of the Blitz: September 7, 1940* (New Haven: Yale University Press, 2007), 180.
5 *Letters*, 106.
6 Muggeridge (1981), 317.
7 *Letters*, 105.
8 *Letters*, 107; interview with CB, 20 February 2014.
9 Ibid.
10 Muggeridge (1981), 317.
11 *Letters*, 106.
12 *WOE*, 81–94; 'The Defenders' [Journal], GG Collection, HRC. What follows about the raid is drawn mainly from these sources.
13 *The Times* (18 April 1941).
14 *Letters*, 108.
15 *WOE*, 88.
16 *WOE*, 88.

17 See Graham Greene and Hugh Greene, eds, *The Spy's Bedside Book: An Anthology* (London: Rupert Hart-Davis, 1957); John Carter, ed., *Victorian Detective Fiction: A Catalogue of the Collection Made by Dorothy Glover and Graham Greene* (London: The Bodley Head, 1966).

18 Interview with Graham C. Greene, 19 May 2015.

19 GG, Introduction, David Low, *'with all faults'* (Tehran: The Amate Press), xiv.

20 GG, Introduction, Low, *'with all faults'*, xiv.

18: The House in the Swamp

1 Keith Jeffery, *MI6: The History of the Secret Intelligence Service, 1909–1949* (London: Bloomsbury, 2010), 301 and 479–80.

2 GG to MG, 3 October 1941, BL.

3 *Letters*, 110.

4 SC, 85–6.

5 SC, 97.

6 SC, 89.

7 'The Soupsweet Land', CE, 342.

8 GG to MG, 5 February 1942, 6 February 1942, and 14 February 1942, BL.

9 Butcher, 8; *Letters*, 112.

10 *Letters*, 112.

11 'The Soupsweet Land', CE, 341–3; WOE, 77.

12 GG to V. S. Pritchett, 3 March 1978, BC.

13 WOE, 76.

14 JWM, 51; GG to MG, 19 April 1942, BL.

15 *Letters*, 120.

16 *Letters*, 117 and 113.

17 'The Soupsweet Land', CE, 342.

18 WOE, 76.

19 WOE, 75; 'The Soupsweet Land', CE, 341.

20 Jeffery, *MI6*, 355.

21 *Letters*, 420–3.

22 'Denyse Clairouin (1900–45)', Bibliothèque nationale de France: data.bnf.fr; Mauthausen Monument, http://www. monument-mauthausen.org/1431. html?lang=fr (accessed 11 September 2019). Desmond Flower, 'Denyse Clarouin', unpublished memoir, GG Collection, BC.

23 Nicholas Elliott, *Never Judge a Man by his Umbrella* (Wilton: Michael Russell, 1991), 113. I am grateful to David Cornwell (John le Carré) for drawing my attention to this episode.

24 *Letters*, 421.

25 Philby, 81.

26 *Letters*, 123.

27 'Irish Spiritans Remembered', Spiritan Heritage Centre, Dublin: http://kimmagemanor.ie/irish-spiritans.html; I am grateful for information received from Father John Geary, CSSp, Peter O' Mahony, and Margaret Bluett.

28 NS 2: 117 and Sheldon, 294, identify this man cursorily as Captain Brodie. Much further information is available, beginning with, for example, *Who's Who, 1943*. See also, England and Wales Deaths Transcription 1837–2007, TNA: http://search.findmypast. co.uk/record?id=bmd%2fd% 2f1965%2f1%2faz%2f000107% 2f135.

29 1891 and 1901 census.

30 Passenger Lists leaving UK 1890–1960, TNA: http://search. findmypast.co.uk/record?id=tna% 2fbt27%2f0583000080%2f00010.

31 A. E. Capell, *The 2nd Rhodesia Regiment in East Africa* (1923; reprinted Uckfield: Military and Naval Press, 2006), 107; H. Moyse-Bartlett, *The King's African Rifles: A study in the military history of East and Central Africa, 1890–1945* (Aldershot: Gale & Polden, 1956), 394.

32 Gassan Abess, 'Legitimating the Sierra Leone Police: Politics, Corruption, and Public Trust', doctoral dissertation, Department of Criminal Justice and Criminology, Washington State University (2015), 39.

33 *The Times* (1 January 1941).
34 'The Soupsweet Land', CE, 345; SOE, 77–8 and 102.
35 Abess, 'Legitimating the Sierra Leone Police', 39.
36 WOE, 94; see also Shelden, 251.
37 Information from James Greene.
38 Interview with CB, 20 February 2014.
39 *The Times* (7 November 1942); this corrects Sherry 2: 150, and *Letters*, 121.
40 SOL, 20.
41 *Letters*, 122.
42 *Letters*, 119.
43 *Letters*, 121.
44 WOE, 95.

19: The Ministry of Fear

1 WOE, 74.
2 David Gaiman to GG, 4 January 1978, 27 June 1978, and 8 August 1978, BC; ED to David Gaiman, 10 July 1978, BC.
3 WOE, 73–9; GG to MG, 22 July 1942, BL.
4 Wise and Hill 1: 23.
5 WOE, 81.
6 Falk, 15; Film contract: *Ministry of Fear*, 16 February 1943, HRC.
7 'A Graphical History of the Dollar Exchange Rate': http://www. miketodd.net/encyc/dollhist.htm (accessed 19 August 2019).
8 Interview with CB, 20 February 2014.
9 *Letters*, 126–8.
10 *Letters*, 124–5.

20: Canaries and Defectors

1 Milne, 121.
2 Milne, 270; Philby, 42–3 and 47.
3 Philby, 53.
4 Philby, 65.
5 Knightley, 84.
6 Milne, 124.
7 In what follows I am extremely grateful for information from Nigel West.
8 Nigel West to RG, email, 15 May 2015.
9 Milne, 124.
10 Knightley, 105–8.
11 Sherry 2: 177.
12 See 'Selected Historical Papers from the JOSEF Case', TNA, PF 63101/SAV6.
13 Butcher, 228–30.
14 Nigel West to RG, email, 31 May 2017.
15 This paragraph is drawn from Juan Pujol with Nigel West, *Garbo* (London: Weidenfeld & Nicolson, 1985). See also Tomás Harris, *Garbo: The Spy who Saved D-Day*, intro. Mark Seaman (Richmond, Surrey: Public Record Office, 2000) and Jason Webster, *The Spy with 29 Names* (London: Chatto & Windus, 2014).
16 John Cairncross, *The Enigma Spy* (London: Century, 1997), 117–22.
17 West and Tsarev, 219.
18 Peter Wright, *Spycatcher: The Candid Autobiography of a Senior Intelligence Officer* (New York: Penguin, 1987), 222 and *passim*.
19 *The Times* (24 December 1979).
20 *Letters*, 412.
21 Philby, 67–8.
22 GG, 'Kim Philby' in Philby, 7–9.
23 West and Tsarev, 219.
24 Knightley, 119.
25 Philby, 92–8.
26 GG, 'Kim Philby' in Philby, 9.
27 West and Tsarev, 157; Nigel West to RG, email, 15 May 2015.
28 Milne, 138–9.
29 Sherry 2: 183; Shelden, 259.
30 Milne, 138–9.
31 GG to MG, 1 May 1944, BL; Sherry 2: 182.
32 Contract between GG and MGM, 3 February 1944, GG Collection, 92.16, HRC.
33 David Cornwell (John le Carré) interview with RG, 23 August 2013.
34 SOL, 65.

21: Mrs Montgomery

1 Hugh Kingsmill quoted by Muggeridge (1973), 262.
2 ODNB.
3 Muggeridge (1973), 262; for a

detailed and engaging account of Greene's period with the firm, see Lewis, 338–44.

4   GG to MG, 5 July [1944], BL.
5   ODNB; Muggeridge (1973), 262.
6   Douglas Jerrold, 'Graham Greene: Pleasure Hater', Harper's Magazine (August 1952), 50–2.
7   Jerrold, 'Graham Greene: Pleasure Hater'.
8   Letters, 129–30.
9   See G. Peter Winnington, Vast Alchemies: The Life and Work of Mervyn Peake (London: Peter Owen, 2000), 166–9.
10 GG to MG, 2 October 1944, BL. Note: this letter is incorrectly dated 20 October.
11 Letters, 135.
12 Judith Adamson, '"I've always wanted to be in a publisher's office" (Graham Greene, 1933)', lecture, Graham Greene International Festival, Berkhamsted, 24 September 2016.
13 Documents related to this agreement can be found in file 92:16, GG Collection, HRC.
14 Introduction, The Tenth Man (London: The Bodley Head, 1985), 9–11.
15 Mike Hill, 'An Old Man's Memory: The Strange Case of The Tenth Man', A Sort of Newsletter (February 2020), 2–8.
16 GG to LP, 23 March 1967, BC.
17 GG to GP, 10 August 1983, GG Collection, HRC.
18 MR to Jean-Felix Paschoud, 1 May 1987, Max Reinhardt Collection, BL.
19 GG to Maria Aurora Couto, 6 April 1985, BC; Introduction, The Tenth Man, 9–11.
20 GG to LP, 8 March 1951, HRC.

22: Hot Irons

1   VG, notes in a photo album in possession of CB; CB interview with RG, 20 February 2014.
2   CB, interview with RG, 20 February 2014.
3   I. C. B. Dear, gen. ed, The Oxford Companion to World War II (Oxford: Oxford University Press, 1995), 978–9.
4   Letters, 131–2.
5   Letters, 133.
6   GG to MG, Good Friday 1945 [30 March], BL; Peter Ackroyd, London: The Biography (London: Chatto & Windus, 2000), 748–9; London Fire Journal: http://londonfirejournal.blogspot.ca/2005/07/world-war-ii.html.
7   GG to MG [June 1945], BL.
8   GG to 'Liberal Party', 20 August 1962, BC.
9   Sunday Times (1 April 1984).
10 GG to MG, [June 1945] and [October 1945], BL.
11 WOE, 93.
12 GG to Betty Judkins, 8 October 1964, HRC.
13 Letters, 136–7 and 147.
14 WOE, 6; Falk, 25–7.
15 Contract between Graham Greene and Theatrecraft, 7 February 1944, GG Collection (93:14), HRC.
16 See especially Andrew Spicer, Sydney Box (Manchester: Manchester University Press, 2006), 64–8.
17 WOE, 14; Falk, 25–7.
18 Various film contracts are preserved at HRC.

23: Mother of Six

1   Except as otherwise indicated, the main source for the next seven paragraphs is Walston.
2   Passports of Catherine Walston, private papers of Oliver Walston, Thriplow.
3   Information from Dr James Stone of King's College London.
4   John Hayward to CW, 21 July 1949, private papers of Oliver Walston, Thriplow.
5   I am grateful to Karl Orend for information on this point.
6   Letters, 138.
7   Quoted in Walston.
8   GG to CW, 26 December 1946, GU.

9 VG, notes in photograph album in possession of CB.
10 *Letters*, 146.
11 *Letters*, 143.
12 *Letters*, 139.
13 *Letters*, 141.
14 GG to CW, 22 August 1947 and 11 May 1948, GU; *Letters*, 145–6.
15 A series of letters and documents relating to this episode can found in the Graham Greene Papers, Special Collections, University of Tulsa.
16 *Letters*, 159.
17 Bevis Hillier, 'A Sort of Wife', *The Times Magazine* (20 December 1996).
18 GS, transcript of conversation with YC, 17 January 1992, Sutro Collection, Bod.

24: Banned in the Republic of Ireland

1 GG to London Film Productions, 2 October 1947; Contract for film rights between London Film Productions and Graham Greene, 2 October 1947; Contract for services between London Film Productions and Graham Greene, 2 October 1947; all documents in Graham Greene Collection (92:12), HRC. These documents formalized an agreement under which Greene had been working through the late summer.
2 My discussion of *The Fallen Idol* is drawn mainly from Wapshott, 193–206; but see also Falk, 41–7.
3 Wapshott, 197.
4 Adamson (1984), 45–6.
5 GG to MG, 11 June 1947, BL.
6 GG to CW, 8 August 1947, GU.
7 GG to CW, 8 August 1947, GU.
8 Portrait of John Hayward, GG Collection, HRC; see also 'John Hayward, 1904–1965: Some Memories', *Book Collector* (winter 1965).
9 John Hayward to Lord Kinross, 4 November 1941, HRC; quoted in John Smart, *Tarantula's Web: John Hayward, T. S. Eliot and their Circle*

(Norwich: Michael Russell, 2013), 170.
10 John Hayward to CW, 19[?] July 1948 and 20 July 1953, private papers of Oliver Walston, Thriplow.
11 Portrait of John Hayward, GG Collection, HRC; see also 'John Hayward, 1904–1965: Some Memories'.
12 GG to CW, 21 August 1947, GU.
13 GG to A. S. Frere, 1 October 1947, BC.
14 Muggeridge (1981), 170–1.
15 GG to Editor of *Quarto*, 6 August 1981, BC.
16 Wise and Hill 1: 25.
17 *John O'London's Weekly* (28 May 1948).
18 *New Yorker*, 17 July 1948.
19 GG to Sean O' Faolain, 6 July 1948, BC.
20 *The Tablet* (5 June 1948).
21 *The Tablet* (5 June 1948).
22 *Universe* (18 June 1948).
23 *Universe* (3 September 1948).
24 Clifford W. Crouch to Messrs Heinemann, 20 September 1948, BC.

25: Lime

1 *Letters*, 146.
2 *WOE*, 96.
3 Wapshott, 207–8.
4 Drazin, 318.
5 Contract between GG and London Film Productions, 26 August 1948, GG Collection (92:12), HRC.
6 Information from Teresa Hadadi Berezuk.
7 *WOE*, 99.
8 Jeremy Lewis, *David Astor* (London: Jonathan Cape, 2016), 121–2.
9 West, 157–8.
10 Shelden, 266–9.
11 *WOE*, 99–100.
12 GG to CW, 23 February 1948, GU; *WOE*, 101, plays down Greene's desire to see the revolution but it is clearly expressed in the letter.
13 Jean-Luc Fromental and Myles Hyman, *Le Coup de Prague* (ebook, 2017).
14 Egon Hostovský, *Seven Times the*

Leading Man, trans. Fern Long (London: Eyre & Spottiswoode, 1945).

15 *WOE*, 109–12; Lonnie Johnson, *Central Europe: Enemies, Neighbors, Friends* (New York: Oxford University Press, 1996), 88.

16 Korda, 198.

17 Korda, 312.

18 Korda, 313.

19 Korda, 315–16.

20 Korda, 316–17.

21 Mark Holloway, *Norman Douglas: A Biography* (London: Secker & Warburg, 1976), 483.

22 Michelangelo Sabatino, *Pride in Modesty: Modernist Architecture and the Vernacular Tradition in Italy* (Toronto: University of Toronto Press, 2010), 105–6. I am grateful for further information from Professor Sabatino and from Professor Fabio Mangone.

23 *Letters*, 197.

24 See Wyse and Hill 1: 25–6.

25 See 'Norman Douglas', *CE*, 271–4.

26 See Wyse and Hill 2: 97.

27 Holloway, *Norman Douglas*, 483 and 489–91.

28 *WOE*, 96.

29 GG to Mary Pritchett, 7 January 1948, BC.

30 See Adamson (1984), 55.

31 *WOE*, 97.

32 *WOE*, 98.

33 Drazin, 309 and 319–20.

34 GG to CW, 9 August 1948, GU.

35 Wapshott, 216–20.

36 *Letters*, 161; GG to CW, 23 August 1948, GU.

37 Drazin, 318–20; Wapshott, 221–7.

38 *Independent* (7 July 2017).

39 Jimmy Stamp, 'The Past, Present, and Future of the Cuckoo Clock', *Smithsonian Magazine* (17 May 2013): https://www. smithsonianmag.com/arts-culture/ the-past-present-and-future-of-the-cuckoo-clock-65073025/.

40 Wapshott, 232.

26: A Piece of Grit

1   GG to CW, 30 December 1947, GU.

2   Muggeridge (1981), 249 and 298.

3   Hilary Spurling, *Anthony Powell: Dancing to the Music of Time* (London: Hamish Hamilton, 2017), 285 and 305–6; *Letters*, 162.

4   GG to CW, 15 July 1949 and 26 August 1949, GU; Nic Compton, 'A Brief Affair with Graham Greene – A Double-Ender Lists the Author as an Owner', *Yachting World* (19 April 2016): http:// www.yachtingworld.com/features/ brief-affair-graham-greene-lovely-double-ender-lists-author-owner-71110.

5   *Letters*, 163.

6   GS, notes on conversation with GG, 4 October 1989, Sutro Collection, Bod; Muggeridge (1973), 262–3.

7   *Letters*, 164.

8   See 'François Mauriac', *CE*, 91–6.

9   *Letters*, 151

10 'The Virtue of Disloyalty', *Reflections*, 311–16.

27: Points of Departure

1   Waugh (1977), 694.

2   James Salter, 'Like a Retired Confidential Agent, Graham Greene Hides Quietly in Paris', in *Don't Save Anything: The Uncollected Writings of James Salter*, ed. Kay Eldredge (Berkeley: Counterpoint, 2017), 29.

3   Waugh (1980), 322.

4   *WOE*, 200.

5   *Letters*, 175–6; Waugh (1980), 332–3.

6   Waugh (1980), 211

7   Waugh (1980), 353 and 355.

8   Oliver Walston to RG, email, 17 September 2007.

9   Waugh (1980), 283–4; GG to CW, 6 July 1948, GU. Further information from Oliver Walston.

10 Waugh (1977), 702.

11 Waugh (1980), 557.

12 Edith Sitwell to GG, n.d. [1945], Graham Greene Collection, GU.

13 Edith Sitwell to David Horner, 1 June 1948, Osbert Sitwell Collection, HRC.

14 GG to CW, 7 November 1951, GU.

15 VG to LD, 9 August 1994, GU.

16 *Letters*, 165.

17 GG to CW, 9 September 1949, GU.

18 GG to CW, 18 December 1949, GU.

19 *Letters*, 169–72.

20 See Basil Dean, *Mind's Eye: An Autobiography 1927–1972* (London: Hutchinson, 1973), 305–7.

21 GG to CW, 25 February 1950, GU.

22 GG to CW, 28 February 1950, GU.

23 GS, manuscript notes, Sutro Collection, Bod.

24 GG to CW, 24 March 1950, GU.

25 LP to Mary Pritchett, 21 March 1950, BC.

26 Friedhard Knolle, Frank Jacobs and Ewald Schug, '225 Years Uranium and Radioactivity Cross-Links Around the Brocken: Klaproth, Elster and Geitel, Nazi Research, Wismut Prospection, and Recent Anomalies', in Broder J. Merkel and Alireza Arab, eds, *Uranium – Past and Future Challenges* (Switzerland: Springer, 2015), 609–16.

27 GG to LP, 12 January 1950, BC.

28 See Adamson (1984), 73–5.

29 'No Man's Land', HRC; see also GG to LP, 21 April 1950, BC.

30 Sir Alexander Korda to GG, 8 September 1950, BC.

31 GG to CW, 27–28 March 1950, GU.

32 GG to CW, 2 April 1950, GU.

33 *ODNB*.

34 C. C. Martindale, SJ, to GG, 9 October 1950, GU.

35 GG to CW, 12 April 1950, GU.

36 GG to CW, 23 April 1950, GU.

37 Meyer, 124.

38 GG to CW, 21 February 1950, GU.

39 Obituary: E. B. Strauss, *British Medical Journal* (21 January 1961), 214.

40 *The Times* (17 January 1961).

41 *The Times* (20 January 1961).

42 GG to CW, 30 April 1950, GU.

43 GG to CW, 3 May 1950 and 4 May 1950, GU.

44 I am grateful to Kay Redfield Jamison for information on this point.

45 *WOE*, xiii.

46 GG to CW, 4 May 1950, GU.

47 *SOL*, 126; GG to CW, 27 November 1952, GU.

48 GG to CW, 24 June 1950, GU.

49 GG to CW, 29 Feb 1952, GU.

50 See GG to CW, 13 May 1950, 12 July 1950, GU; CW's whereabouts are confirmed by visa stamps in her passport, private papers of Oliver Walston.

51 Michael Korda, *Another Life*, 313–14.

52 GG to CW, 19 May 1948, GU.

53 *WOE*, 113–17; except as indicated my account of the writing of the novel depends on this source.

54 GG to CW, 15 August 1950, GU.

55 See John Locke, *An Essay Concerning Human Understanding*, ed. P. H. Nidditch (Oxford: Oxford University Press, 1975), 345. The origins of the discussion can be traced further back, for example, to Boethius, but that would not be relevant to this biography.

56 'François Mauriac', CE, 91–2.

57 J. W. Lambert, 'Graham Greene: The Next Move', in A. F. Cassis, ed., *Graham Greene: Man of Paradox* (Chicago: Loyola University Press, 1994), 185.

58 *WOE*, 117.

59 *Letters*, 177–8; GG to CW, 19 Oct 50, GU.

60 *Edge*.

28: Malaya

1 *WOE*, 110.

2 Robert Jackson, *The Malayan Emergency* (London: Routledge, 1991), 1–15 and *passim*.

3 See Christopher Hale, *Massacre in Malaya: Exposing Britain's My Lai* (Stroud: The History Press, 2013).

4   *The Times* (15 December 2015).
5   Tracey, 126–37; Lewis, 364–71; Hale, *Massacre in Malaya*, 344–51.
6   Journal, 27 November 1950, GU.
7   GG to CW, 5 December 1950, GU.
8   *New York Times* (6 January 2014).
9   *Letters*, 182–3.
10 Journal, 15 December 1950, GU; GG later said that he felt like shooting himself: Allain, 112.
11 Journal, 15–17 December 1950, GU.
12 *WOE*, 125–7.
13 *WOE*, 81.
14 *Letters*, 183.
15 *SOL*, 82.
16 GG to MG, 19 January 1951, BL.
17 Journal, 19 December 1950, GU.
18 GG to MG, 3 January 1951, BL. GG refers to 'Rong Rong', which I have corrected to Ronggeng on the advice of Professor Andrew Biswell.
19 Journal, 28 December 1950, GU; GG to CW, 31 December 1950, GU.
20 GG to MG, 19 January 1951, BL.

29: Shoulder Flash

1   David G. Marr, *Vietnam: State, War, and Revolution (1945–1946)* (Oakland: University of California Press, 2013), 330.
2   GG to MG, 3 January 1951, BL.
3   Richard J. Aldrich, '"The Value of Residual Empire": Anglo-American Intelligence Co-operation in Asia after 1945', 226–59, in Richard J Aldrich and Michael F Hopkins, eds, *Intelligence, Defence and Diplomacy: British Policy in the Post-war World* (Ilford: Frank Cass, 1994) 239.
4   Information from Sarah Greene.
5   Milne, 102–3.
6   *New York Times* (5 December 1950).
7   *New York Times* (9 January 1951).
8   *New York Times* (23 January 1951).
9   GG to HG, 26 January 1951, GU.
10 Journal, 25 January 1951, GU.
11 GG to MG, Monday [12 February 1951?], BL.
12 My discussion of Greene in Vietnam is very indebted to

Professor Ruane's excellent article on Greene and Wilson (cited here as Ruane, publication information above), which he is developing into a book, and to his lecture 'Our Man in Hanoi: the strange and enduring friendship of Graham Greene and confidential agent Trevor Wilson', Graham Greene International Festival, Berkhamsted, 22 September 2017.
13 *WOE*, 133.
14 GG to MG, [12 February 1951?], BL.
15 *Letters*, 184–6.
16 GG to CW, 18–19 June 1951, GU.

30: The Cards in his Wallet

1   See John Cornford, *Hitler's Pope: The Secret History of Pope Pius XII* (New York: Viking, 1999); Martin Gilbert, *The Righteous: Unsung Heroes of the Holocaust* (New York: Doubleday, 2002). There are other works on this subject, but a listing of them is not relevant to this biography.
2   'The Paradox of a Pope', CE, 291.
3   'The Paradox of a Pope', CE, 297; *Letters*, 413–15.
4   *WOE*, 118.
5   *WOE*, 116.
6   John Cornwell, 'Why I am Still a Catholic: An Interview', in *Articles*, 130–2.

31: 'C'

1   GG to CW, 16 August 1951 and 19 August 1951, GU.
2   Waugh (1980), 352–6; *Letters*, 191–2.
3   GG to CW, 16 September 1951, GU.
4   Quoted in GG to CW, [30 August 1951], GU.
5   GG to FG, 15 October 1951, BC.
6   GG to Margot Fonteyn, 24 March 1952, BC.
7   *WOE*, 116.
8   *Time* (29 October 1951).
9   William Faulkner, *Selected Letters of William Faulkner*, ed. Joseph Blotner

(New York: Random House, 1977), 327–8; GG to CW, 29 February 1952, GU.

32: The Bell Tower

1 Journal, 30 October 1951, GU.
2 Robert Miller and Dennis D. Wainstock, *Indochina and Vietnam: The Thirty-Five Year War, 1940–1975* (New York: Enigma Books, 2013), 90–1.
3 *New York Times* (20 October 1951).
4 This chapter, as does the previous one, is generally indebted to the research of Professor Kevin Ruane on Greene's involvement in Indochina. Specific citations occur as appropriate.
5 Journal, 26 October 1951, GU; Stephen Dorril, *MI6: Inside the Covert World of Her Majesty's Secret Intelligence Service* (New York: Simon & Schuster, 2002), 712.
6 GG to MG, 29 October 1951, BL.
7 Michel Gay, *L'Année de Lattre en Indochine 1951* (Paris: les éditions de l'officine, 2011), 119–20.
8 Charles Keith, *Catholic Vietnam: A Church from Empire to Nation* (Berkeley: University of California Press, 2012), esp. 1, 4, 20, 88, 105, 211–16. I am grateful to Professor Keith for discussing certain points with me by email.
9 Goscha, 326–7.
10 *New York Times* (17 October 1951).
11 Keith, *Catholic Vietnam*, 236; Gay, *L'Année de Lattre en Indochine 1951*, 195; Apostolic Delegation Vietnam: http://www.gcatholic.org/dioceses/nunciature/nunc183.htm.
12 Gay, *L'Année de Lattre en Indochine 1951*, 189–92.
13 *WOE*, 134–6.
14 Journal, 21 January 1952, GU.
15 GG to René de Berval, 4 May 1951, BC.
16 GG to René de Berval, 26 February 1952, BC; Journal, 9 February 1952, GU.
17 GG to CW, 11 Dec 1951, GU.
18 Trevor Wilson to GG, 6 November 1953, BC.
19 GS, transcript of telephone conversation with YC, *c.* 1990, Sutro Collection, Bod.
20 Danielle Floode, *The Unquiet Daughter* (Portsmouth, NH: Piscataqua Press, 2016).
21 I am grateful to the publisher Kent Davis for drawing this book to my attention.
22 *New York Times* (13 May 1975).
23 BD to RG, emails, 4 and 7 January 2018.
24 Diederich, 30.
25 *WOE*, 217.
26 Kevin Ruane, 'Our Man in Hanoi: The Strange and Enduring Friendship of Graham Greene and Confidential Agent Trevor Wilson', lecture, Graham Greene International Festival, Berkhamsted, 22 September 2017.
27 GG to Warren Winkelstein, 29 February 1952, BC.
28 *New York Times* (5 August 2012).
29 'Vertical Raid', *Reflections*, 214.
30 *Letters*, 193.
31 QA, 148.
32 Journal, 18 November 1951, GU.
33 *WOE*, 136–8.
34 *The Times* (12 January 1952).
35 Gay, *L'Année de Lattre en Indochine 1951*, 221.
36 GG to CW, 21 November 1951, GU.
37 GG, introduction, Armand Olichon, *Father Six*, trans. Barbara Hall (London: Burns & Oates, 1954), v–vii.
38 Journal, 13 December 1951, GU.
39 'Catholics at War', *Reflections*, 206. See also Charles-Henri de Pirey, *Vandenberghe: les commandos des tigres noirs* (Paris: Indo éditions, 2003), and Nguyen Cong Luan, *Nationalist in the Vietnam Wars* (Bloomington: Indiana University Press, 2012), 98.
40 Journal, 24 January 1952, GU.
41 Journal, 2 February 1952, GU.
42 Robert Shaplen, *The Lost Revolution* (New York: Harper & Row, 1965), 86–7.

43 *WOE*, 140.
44 Sherry 2: 416–17 disposes of such claims.
45 'Indo-China: France's Crown of Thorns', trans. Alan Adamson, *Reflections*, 156–7.
46 See Tran My-Van, 'Japan and Vietnam's Caodaists: A Wartime Relationship (1939–45)', *Journal of Southeast Asian Studies* 27:1 (March 1996), 179–93.
47 Goscha, 83.
48 Goscha, 468–9.
49 GG to CW, 7 November 1951, GU.
50 Journal fragment in GG Collection, 20:5, HRC.
51 GG to CW, 11 December 1951, GU.
52 Journal, 9 December 1951, GU.

33: Visas

1 *WOE*, 180.
2 *Washington Post* (5 February 1952).
3 GG to CW, 14 February 1952, GU.
4 Contract between Graham Greene Productions Limited and David Lewis, 21 February 1952, HRC.
5 GG to CW, 17 February 1952, GU.
6 *New Statesman* (27 September 1952).
7 See Adamson (2009), 68–76.
8 *New York Times* (20 February 1952).
9 *New York Times* (20 February 1952).
10 Christopher Hitchens, 'I'll Be Damned', review of Sherry 3, *The Atlantic* (March 2005): https://www.theatlantic.com/magazine/archive/2005/03/ill-be-damned/303741/.
11 'Indo-China: France's Crown of Thorns', trans. Alan Adamson, *Reflections*, 149–70.
12 GG to Emmet Hughes, 18 March 1952, 2 May 1952, 9 June 1952, HRC.
13 GG to CW, 5 April 1952, GU.
14 GG to CW, 14 August 1952, GU; Moor, 137–8.
15 Moor, 150–1.

34: The Splinter

1 GG to CW, 10 January 1953, GU.
2 The anthology is preserved in the GG Collection (21:6), HRC.
3 GG to CW, 4 April 1952, GU.
4 GG to CW, 17 April 1952, GU.
5 The typescripts are preserved in the GG Collection (21:9), HRC.
6 *The Times* (3 November 1952).
7 Her role is advertised in the programme for the Swedish production of *The Living Room*, a copy of which is preserved in the Walston Collection, GU; Meyer, 132–4.
8 GG to CW, 7 February 1953, GU.
9 *The Times* (28 December 1953); Donald Albery, Statement of Accounts, BC.
10 *The Times* (18 November 1954).
11 *Letters*, 200–1.
12 See Adamson (1984), 81, and Falk, 70.
13 *WOE*, 188–9; GG to CW, 2 August 1952, 5 August 1952, 6 August 1952, 11 August 1952, GU.
14 GG to CW, 2 September 1952, GU.
15 GG to CW, 7 November 1952, GU. Published in GG, *A Quick Look Behind* (Los Angeles: Sylvester & Orphanos, 1983), 23.
16 GG to CW, 27 November 1952, GU.
17 Durán, 115.
18 GG to George Russo, 27 July 1989, BC.
19 GG to CW, 10 January 1953, GU.
20 Quoted in Waugh (1980), 398.
21 'Albany', in F. H. W. Sheppard, ed., *Survey of London: Volumes 31 and 32, St James Westminster, Part 2* (London: London County Council, 1963), pp. 367–89. Available at British History Online: http://www.british-history.ac.uk/survey-london/vols31-2/pt2/pp367-389 (accessed 17 March 2018).
22 GG, 'Opium in Albany', unpublished ms, GU.
23 *Guardian* (14 July 2005).
24 *Telegraph* (12 July 2005).
25 *Letters*, 384. See also Jocelyn

Rickards, *The Painted Banquet: My Life and Loves* (London: Weidenfeld & Nicolson, 1987), esp. 35–8.

26 Meyer, 124.

27 David Pearce and Mike Hill, 'In the style of Graham Greene', lecture, Graham Greene International Festival, Berkhamsted, 29 September 2007.

28 *New Statesman* (30 April 1949).

29 *New Statesman* (14 May 1949). For an account of this episode and others like it, see YE, 9–13.

30 See Ian Thomson's interview with Soldati, 'Postcard from Turin', *Independent* (12 February 1994).

31 'The Novelist and the Cinema: A Personal Experience', *Reflections*, 240–1.

32 Falk, 79.

33 Falk, 78–9.

35: Mau Mau

1 David Anderson, *Histories of the Hanged: Britain's Dirty War in Kenya and the End of Empire* (London: Weidenfeld & Nicolson, 2005), 1–8. My account in this paragraph follows Professor Anderson's arguments.

2 *Letters*, 213.

3 GG to MG, Friday [28 August 1953?], BL.

4 Anderson, *Histories of the Hanged*, 83, 273–9, 331, and *passim*.

5 Anderson, *Histories of the Hanged*, 126–9.

6 YE, 32.

7 *Sunday Times* (29 November 1953).

8 GG to CW, 2 September 1953, GU.

9 *The Times* (8 March 1954).

10 GG to CW, 2 September 1953, GU.

11 Journal, 6–7 September 1953, GU.

12 David Anderson, email to RG, 17 April 2018.

13 WOE, 162.

14 GG to CW, 2 September 1953, GU.

15 GG to Maria Newall, 28 January 1974, BC.

16 GG to CW, 13 October 1954, GU.

17 David Anderson to RG, email, 12 April 2018; my comments

on Whyatt and Nihill draw on observations made by Professor Anderson.

18 *The Times* (4 December 1953). Reprinted in YE, 32–4.

19 Sir John Barclay Nihill to GG, 11 December 1953, BC. This letter is not included in the finding aid to the Graham Greene collection, but can be found in file 73:36.

20 Durán, 374.

21 *Sunday Times* (27 September 1953 and 4 October 1953).

22 *Guardian* (7 June 2013 and 21 March 2017).

23 The Rt Hon William Hague, 'Statement to Parliament on Settlement of Mau Mau Claims', 6 June 2013: https://www.gov.uk/government/news/statement-to-parliament-on-settlement-of-mau-mau-claims.

36: Dien Bien Phu

1 'Catholics at War', *Reflections*, 209.

2 Journal, 9 January 1954, GU.

3 GG to MG, 28 December 1953, BL.

4 GG to FG, 21 March [1952], BC.

5 Trevor Wilson to GG, 29 September 1953, BC; GG to Trevor Wilson, 8 December 1953, BC.

6 Trevor Wilson to GG, 24 November 1953, BC.

7 Kevin Ruane's research may bring forward further evidence on this point.

8 Goscha, 298.

9 'Return to Indo-China', *Reflections*, 186.

10 'Before the Attack', *Reflections*, 202.

11 Journal, 3–4 January 1954; Ted Morgan, *Valley of Death: The Tragedy at Dien Bien Phu That Led America into the Vietnam War* (New York: Random House, 2010), 169, 185, and 369.

12 GG to Lászlo Róbért, 8 July 1975, BC.

13 Goscha, 141–2.

14 WOE, 141.

15 Journal, 5–7 January 1954, GU.

16 GG, 'Catholics at War', 209–11.

17 http://www.catholic-hierarchy.org/
bishop/blehu.html.
18 'Catholics at War', 207–8.
19 'Catholics at War', 212; Journal, 9
January 1954, GU.
20 Journal, 11 January 1954, GU.
21 Journal, 12–21 January 1954, GU.
22 Journal, 13 January 1954, GU.
23 WOE, 140; Morgan, Valley of Death,
241.
24 Goscha, 146.
25 Morgan, Valley of Death, 634.
26 Journal, 4 January 1954, GU.
27 GG to CW, 27 December 1954,
GU.
28 Peter Ryhiner, as told to Daniel
P. Mannix, The Wildest Game
(London: Cassell, 1959), 10–18, 56,
and 224.
29 Passport of Catherine Walston,
private collection of Oliver
Walston.
30 The chronology is constructed from
a series of letters and telegraphs
from GG to Mercia Ryhiner
Schwob Tinker Harrison at the
Columbia University Library. For
an overview of the relationship,
see especially the letter of 26 April
1954. Greene's relationship with
Ryhiner came to light in Wise and
Hill 2: 194.
31 Nicholas Wapshott, Rex Harrison:
A Biography (London: Chatto &
Windus, 1991), 315.
32 GG to CW, 4 March 1954, GU.
33 Wise and Hill 1: 171.
34 GG to René Cogny, 30 March
1954, BC; René Cogny to GG, 27
May 1956, BC.

37: No One Expects the Inquisition

1 Cardinal Giuseppe Pizzardo
to Cardinal Bernard Griffin,
November 1954, BC. See Stephen
Schloesser, 'Altogether Adverse',
America (11 November 2000),
archived at www.americamagazine.
org. However, my discussion draws
primarily on the more detailed
article published shortly after
Schloesser's: Peter Godman,
'Graham Greene's Vatican Dossier',
The Atlantic Monthly (July–August
2001), 84–9. Drafts of Greene's
correspondence on this issue are
located at BC.
2 Waugh (1980), 422–3.
3 YE, 40–2; Letters, 207–8; Waugh
(1980), 429.
4 See Richard Leon Higdon, 'A
Textual History of Graham Greene's
The Power and the Glory', Studies in
Bibliography, 33 (1980), 234.
5 See Godman, 'Graham Greene's
Vatican Dossier', 86.
6 Letters, 360.
7 See Godman, 'Graham Greene's
Vatican Dossier', 85–6.
8 Stephen J. C. Andes, The Vatican
and Catholic Activism in Mexico and
Chile: The Politics of Transnational
Catholicism, 1920–1940 (Oxford:
Oxford University Press, 2014),
170–4.
9 WOE, 67; Letters, 203–6.
10 Quoted in Godman, 'Graham
Greene's Vatican Dossier', 85–6.
11 Letters, 278.
12 Letters, 349.
13 GG to CW, 12 October 1954, GU.
14 GG to MG, 14 October [1953?], BL.
15 GG to FG, 4 June 1954, BC.
16 WOE, 167–70.
17 Wise and Hill 1: 30–1 and 172.
18 WOE, 167.
19 GG to MG, 10 June [1951], BL.
20 GG to Michael Davie, 18
November 1975, BC.
21 Korda, 350–4.
22 GG to CW, 27 June 1955, GU.
23 Korda, 350–8.
24 WOE, 170; GG to MB, 30 January
1956, Balliol.

38: A Reformed Character

1 GG to Harold Acton, 26 March
1957, BC.
2 GG to CW, 21 June 1954, GU.
3 GG to CW, 30 June 1954, GU.
4 Letters, 209–10.
5 Bernard Diederich, Trujillo:
The Death of the Dictator (1978;

Princeton: Markus Wiener, 2000),
12.

6   BD to RG, email, 8 May 2018.
7   'The Nightmare Republic' (*Sunday Telegraph*, 22 September 1963; *Reflections*, 259) and in *TC*, 179–83.
8   *Letters*, 210–11; *WOE*, 162–7.
9   Diederich, 88.
10 Diederich, 88–90; *Letters*, 210–11; Hull, 5.

39: Accidents Can Always Happen

1   Keith, 7.
2   Seth Jacobs, *America's Miracle Man in Vietnam* (Durham, NC: Duke University Press, 2004), 131.
3   YE, 34–5.
4   Journal, 17 and 18 February 1955, GU. Note: GG incorrectly marked 1956 on the front of this journal.
5   Jacobs, *America's Miracle Man in Vietnam*, 133.
6   Journal, 19 February 1955, GU.
7   Journal, 21 and 23 February 1955, GU.
8   Journal, 20 February 1955, GU.
9   Jacobs, *America's Miracle Man in Vietnam*, 194–5.
10 Goscha, 112.
11 Journal,10 March 1955, GU.
12 *New York Times* (27 December 1966).
13 Jacobs, *America's Miracle Man in Vietnam*, 185–8.
14 Journal, 10 March 1955, GU.
15 Goscha, 462–3.
16 Journal, 21 February 1955, GU.
17 Journal, 4 February, 11 and 8 March 1955, GU; *New York Times* (7 December 1966).
18 Jacobs, *America's Miracle Man in Vietnam*, 206.
19 Journal, 2 March 1955, GU.
20 Wise and Hill 2: 134.
21 Journal, 9 and 21 March 1955, GU.
22 West, 171–2.
23 Ruane (2017).
24 Journal, 4 and 8 March 1955, GU.
25 GG to C. L. Sulzberger, 19 May 1955, BC.
26 Journal, 12 and 13 March 1955, GU.

27 *Sunday Times* (1 May 1955).
28 *New York Times* (19 January 1961).
29 Jacobs, 139–40.
30 Journal, 15–18 March 1955, GU.
31 Journal, 19 March 1955, GU.
32 Journal, 20–24 March 1955, GU.
33 'Last Drama of Indo China', *Sunday Times* (24 April, 1 May and 8 May 1955).

40: Anita

1   GG to CW, 6 and 7 July 1955, GU.
2   FG to GG, 23 March 1955, BC.
3   RG interview with CB, 20 February 2014.
4   GG to MG, 24 August 1955, BL.
5   GG to CW, 27 August 1955, GU.
6   'The Half-Defeated', *Sunday Times* (8 January 1956), and 'Between "Pax" and Patriotism', *Sunday Times* (15 January 1956).
7   GG to CW, 20 November 1955, GU.
8   Wise and Hill 2: 178–9.
9   *New York Times* (2 January 1979).
10 Journal, 22 November 1955, GU.
11 Journal, 25 November 1955, GU.
12 GG to T. S. Eliot, 3 September 1956, BC. T. S. Eliot to Robert Giroux, 20 November 1956, Berg Collection, New York Public Library.
13 Jan T. Gross, *Fear: Anti-Semitism in Poland after Auschwitz* (New York: Random House, 2006), 35 and 148–9.
14 Journal, 11 November 1955, GU.
15 François Truffaut, *Hitchcock* (New York: Simon & Schuster, 1967), 149.
16 *New York Times* (6 June 1952).
17 See http://www.dagerman.us (accessed 17 September 2019). This website is maintained by Lo Dagerman, the daughter of Anita Björk and Stig Dagerman.
18 My account of the beginnings of the relationship between Greene and Björk is drawn chiefly from Meyer, 132–6.
19 Journal, 14 November 1955, GU.
20 GG to AB, 2 October 1989, GU.

41: Our Man on the Potomac

1   *New Yorker* (7 April 1956).
2   *Washington Post* (24 December 1955).
3   See Agreement between Graham Greene and Figaro Incorporated, 4 March 1956, Graham Greene Collection (91.15), HRC. This agreement effectively gave the rights to Lucy Caroline Greene, and they were then sold to Mankiewicz in a separate agreement; GG to CB, [December 1956], private collection of CB.
4   *The Times* (9 January 1957).
5   'The Novelist and the Cinema: A Personal Experience', *Reflections*, 238.
6   Garry O' Connor, *Scofield: The Biography* (London: Sidgwick & Jackson, 2002), 131–5. Olivier's comments, quoted here, appear in Olivier's *Confessions of an Actor* (London: Weidenfeld & Nicolson, 1982), 261–2.

42: The Filthiest Book I Have Ever Read

1   *Sunday Times* (25 December 1955).
2   *Sunday Express* (29 January 1956); YE, 76–88. My discussion of the John Gordon Society is largely based on this source. The papers of the society can be found in the Sutro Collection, Bod.
3   *ODNB*.
4   *Spectator* (30 March 1956).
5   *Spectator* (29 September 1984).
6   'A Thorn on the Yellow Rose', *Daily Telegraph Magazine* (22 November 1974).
7   *The Times* (22 August 1953).
8   Mary Carolyn Hollers George, 'The Anglo-Texan Society 1953–1979: A Cross-Cultural Alliance', *Southwestern Historical Quarterly*, 101:2 (October 1997), 214–38.
9   *Sunday Telegraph* (23 June 1985).
10 Nicholas Shakespeare, *Priscilla: The Hidden Life of an Englishwoman in Wartime France* (London: Harvill Secker, 2013), 46.

11 GS, manuscript notes, Sutro Collection, Bod.
12 *Letters*, 276.
13 Shakespeare, *Priscilla*, 46.
14 GS, manuscript notes, Sutro Collection, Bod.

43: 6½ Raves

1   'Nobody to Blame', *The Tenth Man* (London: The Bodley Head, 1985), 18–30.
2   The details of GG's visit to Haiti are taken from Diederich, 90–5.
3   Diederich, 92.
4   Hull, 109.
5   WOE, 191.
6   *New York Times* (1 December 1956).
7   Antoni Kapcia, *Cuba in Revolution: A History Since the Fifties* (London: Reaktion Books, 2008), 22; information from Christopher Hull and Bernard Diederich.
8   GG to CW, 23 December 1956, GU.
9   *Letters*, 222–3.
10 GG, 'Dear Dr Falkenheim', CSS, 565.
11 GG, 'A Vist to Morin', CSS, 262.
12 GG to Patrick Lawlor, 14 April 1975, BC.
13 See *Letters*, 367 and 409.
14 WOE, 180.
15 Jonathan Croall, *Sybil Thorndike: A Star of Life* (London: Haus Books, 2008), 402–3.
16 GG to MG, Christmas Day [1956], BL.
17 GG to CW, 9 January 1957, GU.
18 GG to CW, 1 February 1957, GU.
19 *New York Times* (6 May 1957).
20 Sheridan Morley, *John G: The Authorised Biography of John Gielgud* (London: Hodder & Stoughton, 2001), 285–6.
21 John Gielgud, *Gielgud's Letters*, ed. Richard Mangan (London: Weidenfeld & Nicolson, 2004), 207.
22 *The Times* (1 April 1958).
23 Gielgud, *Gielgud's Letters*, 207 and 223.
24 WOE, 180–1.
25 *The Potting Shed*, CP, 132.

44: A Mixture of Petrol and Vodka

1 *Letters*, 222.
2 GG to CW, 4 January 1957, GU.
3 GG to GS, 4 December 1957, Bod.
4 GS, transcript of conversation with YC, 3 July 1994, Sutro Collection, Bod.
5 GG to CW, 8 November 1957, GU.
6 The main source for the trip to China is 'A Weed Among the Flowers', *Reflections*, 394–402.
7 *ODNB*.
8 GG to CW, Holy Saturday [20 April 1957], GU. See also, Sherry 3: 74.
9 Alan Bold, *MacDiarmid: A Critical Biography* (London: John Murray, 1988), 411–12.
10 GG to Chen Siming, 27 June 1982, BC.
11 For details about Hu Feng, see, for example, Kirk A. Denton, *The Problematic of Self in Modern Chinese Literature* (Redwood City: Stanford University Press, 1998), 155 and *passim*.
12 See Letters to the Editor, *Daily Telegraph* (4, 10, 20, and 24 June 1957).
13 'A Weed Among the Flowers', 394.

45: Handshakes and Contracts

1 GG to CW, 19 June 1957 and 1 February 1962, GU.
2 Muriel Spark, *Curriculum Vitae* (London: Constable, 1992), 205.
3 Adamson, 32.
4 Adamson (2009), 5–41 and 62–76.
5 GG to MR, 18 June 1957, 6 August 1957, 4 September 1957, 23 September 1957, 18 December 1957, 3 February 1958, Max Reinhardt Collection, BL.
6 MR to Vladimir Nabokov, 19 January 1959, Max Reinhardt Collection, BL; Adamson (2009), 64–7.
7 GG to MR, 21 September 1964, Max Reinhardt Collection, BL.
8 GG to CW, 4 February 1958, GU.

9 GG to Oliver Crosthwaite-Eyre, 6 March 1958, BC.
10 *Letters*, 227.

46: Bombs and Daiquiris

1 GG to CW, 8 November 1957, GU.
2 My discussion of Cuba relies heavily on Christopher Hull, 'Sex, Drugs, and Communism: Graham Greene's Visits to Cuba', lecture, Graham Greene International Festival, Berkhamsted, 29 September 2012.
3 GG to CW, 8 November 1957, GU; Journal, 8 November 1957, GU.
4 Shelden, 303.
5 GG to CW, 19 June 1957, GU.
6 Journal, 8 November 1957, GU; the extent of Fordham's failure is described in Christopher Hull, 'Prophecy and Comedy in Havana: Graham Greene's Spy Fiction and Cold War Reality', in Dermot Gilvary and Darren J. N. Middleton, eds, *Dangerous Edges of Graham Greene: Journeys with Saints and Sinners* (New York: Continuum, 2011), 155–8.
7 Journal, 8 and 12 November 1957, GU.
8 See Thomas D. Schoonover, *Hitler's Man in Havana: Heinz Lüning and Nazi Espionage in Latin America* (Lexington: The University Press of Kentucky, 2008), esp. 141–54.
9 Journal, 10–11 November 1957, GU.
10 Hull, 99.
11 *WOE*, 186.
12 *WOE*, 186.
13 Roberto de Mendoza to GG, 22 October 1957, BC; this chain of connections was explained in Hull, 122–35. See also Mark Gollom, 'I never stayed to see if they were dead: Natalia Bolivar, 82, unsentimental about her role in Cuban Revolution', 4 December 2016, archived at www.cbc.ca; Tom Miller, 'Sex, Spies and Literature', *Washington Post* (14 April 1991); Tom Miller, *Trading with the Enemy:*

A *Yankee Travels Through Castro's
Cuba* (New York: Basic Books,
1992), esp. 186–8.

14   Christopher Hull to RG, email, 25
June 2018.

15   *WOE*, 188.

16   *WOE*, 190–1.

17   My account of the trip to Santiago
draws on *WOE*, 187–91, and an
unpublished account by Bernard
Diederich.

18   Hull, 131.

19   BD to RG, email, 23 June 2018.

20   GG to HG, 24 October 1958, BC.

21   Accounts differ on minor points;
see Hull, 131–3.

22   Hull, 133–5.

23   GG to CW, 8 January 1958, GU.

24   MB to CW, 24 May 1958, GU.

25   GG to Tatiana Lanina, 2 June 1958,
BC.

26   GG to CW, 1 July 1958, GU.

27   GG to CW, 9 July 1958, GU.

47: The Whole Trouble

1   John le Carré, *The Pigeon Tunnel*
(London: Viking, 2016), 17–18.

2   *Letters*, 413.

3   *Sunday Times* (5 October 1958).

4   Servando Valdés Sánchez, 'Anglo-
Cuban Diplomacy: The Economic
and Political Links with Britain
(1945–60)', *International Journal of
Cuban Studies*, 8:1 (spring 2016),
55–73 (esp. 59–63).

5   Hansard (17 March 1958).

6   *WOE*, 190.

7   Hansard (17 March 1958, 19
November 1958, and 15 December
1958).

8   Christopher Hull, 'Prophecy and
Comedy in Havana: Graham
Greene's Spy Fiction and Cold
War Reality', in Dermot Gilvary
and Darren J. N. Middleton, eds,
*Dangerous Edges of Graham Greene:
Journeys with Saints and Sinners*
(New York: Continuum, 2011),
156–8.

9   *WOE*, 191.

10   *Washington Post* (25 May 2001).

11   Various documents relating to this

transaction may be found in the
GG Collection, Box 92, HRC.

12   Robert Emmett Ginna, 'Our Man
in Havana', *Horizon*, 2:2 (November
1959), 31.

13   GG to CW, 21 November 1958 and
7 December 1958, GU.

48: Taxidermy Everywhere

1   *SOL* typescript, GG Collection
(33.1), HRC; Wise and Hill 2: 86–7.

2   *SOL*, 63–4; Williams, 381.

3   GG to CW, 3 January 1959, GU.

4   GG to CW, 17 December 1958,
GU.

5   Journal, 26 July 1963, HRC.

6   Alec Guinness, *Blessings in Disguise*
(London: Hamish Hamilton, 1985),
201–7; GG corrects this account
in GG to Nicholas Wapshott, 3
September 1990, BC.

7   Robert Ostermann, 'Interview
with Graham Greene' (1950), in
A. F. Cassis, ed., *Graham Greene:
Man of Paradox* (Chicago: Loyola
University Press, 1994), 99.

8   GS, manuscript notes, Sutro
Collection, Bod.

9   Roy Perrot, 'A Brief Encounter'
(1969), in Cassis, ed., *Graham
Greene: Man of Paradox*, 198–9.

10   *Letters*, 235.

11   GS, manuscript notes, Sutro
Collection, Bod.

12   John Gielgud, *Gielgud's Letters*,
ed. Richard Mangan (London:
Weidenfeld & Nicolson, 2004), 228.

13   John Miller, *Ralph Richardson: The
Authorized Biography* (London:
Sidgwick & Jackson, 1995), 173–9.

14   *The Times* (4 June 1960).

15   *New York Times* (23 August 1959).

16   *New York Times* (8 June 1960).

17   Irene Mayer Selznick, *A Private
View* (New York: Alfred A. Knopf,
1983), 353–6.

18   Alan Strachan, *Secret Dreams:
The Biography of Michael Redgrave*
(London: Weidenfeld & Nicolson,
2004), 356.

19   *New York Times* (8 January 1962).

49: The Separating Sickness

1 GS, transcript of conversation with GG, 10 May 1985, Sutro Collection, Bod.
2 *HM*, 59 (Vintage edn).
3 GG to CW, 7 July 1955, GU.
4 Gould, 59. This book, recommended to me by Michel Lechat, provides most of the historical and technical information on leprosy referred to in this chapter. It is, in places, supplemented by information from Lechat himself.
5 Gould, 59–102.
6 Gould, 3.
7 Gould, 13.
8 Gould, 15.
9 World Health Organization: http://www.who.int/lep/epidemiology/en/ (accessed 20 July 2018).
10 ML to RG, email, 30 January 2005.
11 ML to RG, email, 30 January 2005.
12 ML to RG, email, 30 January 2005.
13 Michel Lechat, 'Evocation of Graham Greene at Yonda', lecture, Edinburgh, July 1986; the text of this lecture is preserved in the BC collection.
14 Lechat, 60–1.
15 ML to GG, 3 October 1958, BC.
16 *Letters*, 233–4.
17 Ch. Didier Gondola, *The History of Congo* (Westport: Greenwood Press, 2002), 97–114.
18 Gondola, *The History of Congo*, 97–114
19 David Van Reybrouck, *Congo: The Epic History of a People*, trans. Sam Garrett (New York: CCC, 2014), 227–66.
20 Gondola, *The History of Congo*, 115–29.
21 Gondola, *The History of Congo*, 115–29.
22 *Letters*, 238.
23 Lechat, 59.
24 Journal, 31 January 1959, HRC.
25 Lechat, 60–1.
26 Journal, 19 February 1959, HRC.
27 Journal, 10 February 1959, HRC.
28 GG to MB, 26 February 1959, Balliol.
29 Journal, 5 February 1959, HRC. I am extremely grateful to Professor Michael Meeuwis who has provided me with his transcription of this journal. In a lecture given at the Graham Greene International Festival, 'The Five Lives of Graham Greene's Congo Journal', September 2017, Professor Meeuwis traced the history of this journal. I have also relied on his article 'The Furthest Escape of All: Darkness and Refuge in the Belgian Congo', *Graham Greene Studies*, 1 (2017), 69–96. I am also grateful to him for his further assistance on many points related to Greene's sojourn in the Congo. Any mistakes are my own.
30 Lechat, 61.
31 Journal, 27 February 1959, HRC.
32 Lechat, 69; Michael Meeuwis, 'Tiny Bouts of Contentment. Rare Film Footage of Graham Greene in the Belgian Congo, March 1959', *Rozenberg Quarterly* (December 2013): http://rozenbergquarterly.com/tiny-bouts-of-contentment-rare-film-footage-of-graham-greene-in-the-belgian-congo-march-1959/ (accessed 29 August 2018). For other identifications of people Greene encountered, see Gustaaf Hulstaert, 'Graham Greene et les Missionnaires Catholiques au Congo Belges', *Annales Æquatoria*, 15 (1994), 493–503.
33 Meeuwis, 'Tiny Bouts of Contentment'.
34 Lechat, 63.
35 Lechat, 62.
36 R. Van den Brandt to GG, *c.* 3 February 1959, HRC; Journal, 4 February 1959, HRC; Meeuwis (2017), 82.
37 Lechat, 62; Meeuwis (2017), 83.
38 Journal, 11 and 14 February 1959, HRC.
39 *Letters*, 241.
40 Journal, 15 February 1959, HRC.
41 Journal, 12 and 22 February 1959, HRC.
42 Journal, 14 and 24 February 1959, HRC.

43 Journal, 12 February 1959, HRC.
44 GG to Stephen Spender, 24 May 1957, BC.
45 Journal, 15 and 26 February 1959, HRC.
46 Journal, 15–16 February 1959, HRC.
47 Journal, 22–3 February 1959, HRC.
48 Journal, 19–20 February 1959, HRC.
49 GG to Father Andre Blanchet, 14 July 1961, BC.
50 Journal, 21–22 February 1959, HRC.
51 Journal, 26 February 1959, HRC.
52 Journal, 2 March 1959, HRC.
53 Journal, 28 February and 2 March 1959, HRC. See also her obituary in *New York Times* (18 October 2007).

50: Alone in a Lift

1 J. H. Jennings, 'The Eruption of Mount Cameroon, 1959', *Journal of the Geographical Association*, 44:3 (1 July 1959), 207–8.
2 Cloetta, 6; GG to ML, 18 March 1959, BL. Some details of Cloetta's book are distant recollections, so I have corrected minor errors using documents closer to the time.
3 ML to GG, 4 May 1959, BC.
4 GS, transcript of telephone call with YC, November 1981, Sutro Collection, Bod; Hazzard, 83.
5 Cloetta, 11.
6 Cloetta, 8.
7 GG to MB, 29 July 1959, Balliol. Cloetta, 8–10, gives approximate and contradictory dates.
8 GS, notes on conversation with YC, 21 October 1987, Sutro Collection, Bod.
9 Cloetta, 10; GG to MB

51: Changes

1 CB, interview with RG, 22 September 2018. CB is reporting an observation made by VG.
2 I am grateful for observations on this subject by James Greene (son of HG).

3 GG to CW, 11 September 1959 and 22 September 1959 (telegram), GU.
4 *Letters*, 245.
5 *Letters*, 226.
6 *Daily Mail* (17 October 1960).
7 CB, interview with RG, 22 September 2018.
8 *Letters*, 303.
9 Graham C. Greene, interview with RG, 24 September 2015.
10 Information from Sarah Greene.
11 Nicholas Dennys, interview with RG, 1 October 2015.
12 GG to ED, 22 June 1968, BC.
13 Peter Walker, interview with RG, 29 September 2014.
14 Information from Bruce Hunter.
15 GG, interview with Nigel Lewis, 1982, BL.
16 Cloetta, 13–15.
17 GG to MB, 19 May 1960, Balliol.
18 GG to CW, 18 December 1961, GU.
19 Cloetta, 20–23.
20 GG to CW, 31 January 1960, GU.
21 'Bob Kaufman': www.poetryfoundation.org/poets/bob-kaufman (accessed 24 September 2018).
22 *Letters*, 247.
23 CB, interview with RG, 22 September 2018.
24 GG to CW, 5 February 1960, GU.

52: Death and Taxes

1 *The Times* (2 April 1960); West, 312.
2 GG to Tanya Lanina, 13 April 1960, BC; *Letters*, 248.
3 West, 219–20.
4 *Letters*, 248–9, 405–6; Stewart Purvis and Jeff Hulbert, *Guy Burgess: The Spy Who Knew Everybody* (London: Biteback, 2016), 339.
5 Information from Karl Orend.
6 GG to CW, 13 March 1960, GU.
7 GG to CW, 31 March 1960, GU.
8 Pierre Joannon, interview with RG, 12 April 2016.
9 GS, manuscript notes, Sutro Collection, Bod.

10 *Letters*, 256; GG to Jean-Felix Paschoud, 11 March 1966, HRC. For average wages see Gregory Clark, 'What Were the British Earnings and Prices Then? (New Series)', MeasuringWorth, 2018, http://www.measuringworth.com/ukearncpi/ (accessed 1 October 2018).

11 GG to FG, 21 June 1971, BC. Note: there are two letters of the same date on the same subject.

12 George Harrison, 'Taxman' (1966). Lyrics © Sony/ATV Music Publishing LLC.

13 HM Revenue and Customs, Income Tax Today: http://webarchive.nationalarchives.gov.uk/20130127153200/http://www.hmrc.gov.uk/history/taxhis7.htm (accessed 28 September 2018). Harrison is quoted in this article.

14 GG to CW, 31 October 1961, GU.

15 LP to GG, 11 April 1963, C.

16 LP to Jean-Felix Paschoud, 10 May 1968, HRC.

17 Except as otherwise indicated, what follows is drawn from articles on Thomas Roe and Cadco in *The Times* (1 December 1966 and 8–25 February 1967). Also 'Cadco Developments Limited, Royal Victoria Sausages Limited; Victoria Wholesale Meats Limited: Investigation under Section 165 (b) f the Companies Act 1948': https://archive.org/stream/op1268196-1001/op1268196-1001_djvu.txt (accessed 16 June 2020).

18 Hansard (1 December 1964).

19 Murray Pollinger to GG, 29 July 1966, HRC.

20 GG to FG, 21 June 1971, BC. Note: there are two letters of the same date on the same subject.

21 Bruce Hunter to RG, email, 30 September 2018.

53: The End of a Long Rope

1 *Observer* (15 January 1961).

2 BOC, 190–1.

3 BOC, 193.

4 BOC, 50.

5 Waugh (1976), 779.

6 Waugh (1980), 557.

7 *Letters*, 251–2.

8 Waugh (1980), 559–60; see also WOE, 195–8.

9 *Letters*, 253.

10 *Letters*, 255.

11 *Letters*, 408.

12 GG to ML, 10 June 1961, Balliol.

13 For a detailed account, see Adamson (2009), 77–80. For other background, see *Letters*, 261–3.

14 Adamson (2009), 82. Professor Adamson has kindly provided further information.

15 Mike Hill, introduction to film of 'Under the Garden', Graham Greene International Festival, Berkhamsted, 21 September 2018.

16 GG to CW, 26 January 1962, GU.

17 GG to CW, 12 January 1962, GU.

18 The Burns library at BC purchased Greene's library, which includes some volumes, with his marginalia, from the series *The Letters and Diaries of John Henry Newman*, ed. Charles Stephen Dessain (London and New York: Nelson, 1961–); in early 1962, only the volume given number 11 had yet appeared. Publication of this 32-volume edition was eventually taken over by the Oxford University Press. I am grateful to Newman's biographer Edward Short for information on this point.

19 GG to CW, 12 January 1962, GU.

20 GS, transcript of conversation with GG, 27 January 1989, Bod.

54: Plastiques

1 Irwin Wall, *France, the United States, and the Algerian War* (Berkeley: University of California Press, 2001), 1–3.

2 GG to Jean Leroy, 15 March 1957, BC. The same archive holds some cables pertaining to the planned visit and its cancellation.

3 *Letters*, 342.

4 *Evening Standard* (8 January 1978);

see also YE, 98–100. I follow Hawtree in citing this interview.

5 GG to CW, 11 February 1962 [?], GU.

6 GG to CW, 16 March 1962, GU.

55: Masks

1 WOE, 231–7.

2 David Nicolson to GG, 2 May 1989, BC; Amanda Saunders [?] to David Nicolson, 23 May 1989, BC.

3 Letters, 246–7.

4 Letters, 260.

5 University of Cambridge: Speeches of the Orator at the Presentation of the Recipients of Honorary Degrees to the Chancellor (Cambridge University Press: Cambridge, 1962).

6 CB to RG, email, 10 October 2017.

7 GG to CB, 23 June 1962, private collection of CB.

8 RG, interview with CB, 26 September 2015.

9 GG to MB, 20 July 1962, Balliol.

10 GG to Anna T. Zakarija, 4 January 1986, BC. Note: this letter is filed in the BC collection under Georgetown Library correspondence.

11 Knightley, 184–9.

12 Amanda Saunders to RG, email, 1 April 2003.

13 Anthony Cave Brown, Treason in the Blood: H. St John Philby, Kim Philby, and the Spy Case of the Century (London: Robert Hale, 1994), 446.

14 GG to Jill Parwin, 10 August 1975, BC; Andrew Boyle, The Climate of Treason: Five who Spied for Russia (London: Hutchinson, 1979), 422.

15 GG, introduction, Kim Philby, My Silent War: The Autobiography of a Spy (London: MacGibbon & Kee, 1968), 9.

16 Brown, Treason in the Blood, 482.

17 Knightley, 189 and 198.

18 Knightley, 205–6 and passim.

19 Knightley, 212–15.

20 Brown, Treason in the Blood, 506–10.

21 Hansard (1 July 1963).

22 The Times (1 February 1963).

23 The Times (18 April 1963).

24 GG to R. W. Leonhardt, undated, 16 April 1963, 20 April 1963, 10 May 1963, 4 June 1963, BC; R. W. Leonhardt to GG, 2 April 1963, 18 April 1963, BC.

25 'Letter to a West German Friend', Reflections, 244.

26 'Letter to a West German Friend', 249.

27 Sunday Times (14 July 1963).

28 See, for example, GG to GS, 22 January 1968, Sutro Collection, BLO.

56: The Real End of the World

1 GG to MB, 11 August 1963, Balliol.

2 'Return to Cuba', Reflections, 250.

3 Journal, 21 July 1963, HRC.

4 GG to YC, 22 July 1963, GU.

5 Journal, 22 July 1963, HRC.

6 GG to YC, 27 July 1963, GU.

7 GG to YC, 6 August 1963, GU.

8 Journal, 26 July 1963, HRC.

9 YE, 127–8.

10 GG to YC, 27 July 1963, GU.

11 Journal, 31 July 1961, HRC.

12 Sunday Telegraph (22 September 1963).

13 Letters, 265, 379–80.

14 See Bernard Diederich, Bon Papa (Port-au-Prince: Editions Henri Deschamps, 2008), and Bernard Diederich, The Prize: Haiti's National Palace (2nd edn, Port-au-Prince: Editions Henri Deschamps, 2008). My discussion of Haiti is overwhelmingly indebted to the writings and conversation of Bernard Diederich. My errors are my own.

15 Diederich and Burt, 13–20; Diederich, Bon Papa, 359.

16 Diederich and Burt, 126 and 138–9.

17 Bernard Diederich, 1959 (Lincoln, NE: iUniverse, 2007), 71–5.

18 Diederich and Burt, 122.

19 Bernard Diederich, The Fools of April (Port-au-Prince: Editions Henri Deschamps, 2015), 29–30; Diederich and Burt, 109–15, 167.

20 Diederich and Burt, 177–96.
21 Diederich and Burt, 168–70.
22 *New York Times* (18 January 1963).
23 *New York Times* (15 August 1963).
24 Diederich and Burt, 197–8.
25 Diederich and Burt, 199–200.
26 Diederich, 51–5.
27 Diederich, 51–5.
28 *The Times* (1 and 6 May 1963).
29 Diederich and Burt, 240.
30 GG to MB, 11 August 1963, Balliol.
31 GG to YC, 11 August 1963, GU.
32 *WOE*, 205.
33 GG to Roger Coster, 30 September 1963, BC.
34 *WOE*, 205.
35 *Guardian* (18 February 2005).
36 Diederich, 23–4.
37 *Independent* (19 February 2005).
38 Diederich, 24.
39 *WOE*, 205–6.
40 *New York Times* (18 August 1963).
41 GG to MB, 8 May 1963, Balliol.
42 *Sunday Telegraph* (29 September 1963).
43 *WOE*, 206.
44 Diederich, 22–3.

57: Statues and Pigeons

1 *Punch* (23 September 1964).
2 *ODNB*; GG 'Epitaph for a Play', CP, 212.
3 GG to MB, 13 December 1963, Balliol.
4 GG to MB, 12 March 1964, Balliol.
5 *Letters*, 271–2.
6 John Miller, *Ralph Richardson: The Authorized Biography* (London: Sidgwick & Jackson, 1995), 193–7.
7 GG to Irene Selznick, 19 October 1964, BC.
8 Wise and Hill 2: 63.
9 GG to MB, 23 September 1964 and 13 October 1964, Balliol.
10 GG to MB, 1 January 1965, Balliol.
11 The account of Greene's border journey is drawn from Diederich, 21–74, except as otherwise indicated.
12 *Guardian* (15 March 1976).
13 *Letters*, 288–9 and 347. Greg

Chamberlain, email to RG, 26 June 2004.
14 *YE*, 117–8.
15 GG to MB, 5 May 1965, Balliol; GG to MR, 6 Mary 1965, BL.
16 Diederich, 106–8; *WOE*, 203.
17 *New York Times* (2 January 1966).
18 *TC*, 132.
19 *TC*, 57.
20 I am grateful to my student Jane Yearwood for this observation.
21 *TC*, 253.
22 GG to Martin Stannard, 7 November 1989, BC.
23 GG to FG, 24 November 1964, BC; GG to MB, 14 December 1964, Balliol.
24 GG to MR, 6 May 1965, BL.
25 W. H. Auden, 'In Memory of W. B. Yeats', *Selected Poems* (New York: Vintage, 1979).

58: The New Life

1 GG to YC, 6 November 1965, GU.
2 GS, manuscript notes, Sutro Collection, Bod.
3 *New York Times* (26 January 2012).
4 GS, manuscript notes, Sutro Collection, Bod.
5 GG to YC, 20 August 1964, GU.
6 *Letters*, 273–4.
7 GG to YC, 20 May 1965 and 11 July 1965, GU.
8 *WOE*, 219–20.
9 *Letters*, 282.
10 Monica McCall to LP, 21 October 1965, HRC.
11 LP to Sir Carol Reed, 12 October 1965, HRC.
12 LP to GG, 9 December 1965, HRC.
13 GG to YC, 17 December 1965, GU.
14 *The Times* (6 February 1966).
15 MR to GG, 24 March 1966, BL.
16 GG to MB, 4 February 1966, Balliol; see also GG to Peter Glenville, 16 December 1965, BC.
17 Thomas Guinzberg to Monica McCall, 7 February 1966, BC; GG to J.-F. Paschoud, 10 February 1966, BC; GG to Monica McCall, 16 February 1966, BC.
18 GG to MB, 22 April 1966, Balliol.

19 GG to MB, 13 May 1966, Balliol.
20 *The Times* (18 March 1978).
21 RG, interview with Julian Evans, 24 September 2015.
22 Waugh Letters, 635–6.
23 Philip Caraman, SJ, to GG, 8 January 1966, BC.
24 GG to Philip Caraman, SJ, 31 January 1966, BC.
25 *Letters*, 350.
26 *Letters*, 284.

59: Fidel at Night

1 Diederich, 114–37.
2 This quotation from *Le Matin* (6 May 1966) is contained in the letter GG to MR, 2 June 1966, BL.
3 Quoted in Diederich, 137.
4 GG to MB, 4 February 1966, Balliol.
5 Richard Burton to GG, 31 March 1966, BC.
6 GS, manuscript notes, Sutro Collection, Bod.
7 GG to MR, 7 February 1970, BL.
8 The account of the visit to Cuba is drawn from Greene's journal at GU, supplemented slightly by *Letters*, 285–6. As always in matters pertaining to Cuba, I am indebted to the research of Christopher Hull.
9 Journal, 28 August 1966, GU.
10 *Miami Herald* (26 October 2014); *Report on the Situation of Political Prisoners and their Families in Cuba*, Interamerican Commission on Human Rights, OAS, 17 May 1963: http://www.cidh.org/countryrep/Cuba63sp/indice.htm (accessed 28 March 2020).
11 Journal, 17 September 1966, GU.
12 Journal, c. 16 September 1966, GU.
13 Journal, 18 September 1966, GU.
14 R. M. K. Slater to R. H. G. Edmonds, 22 September 1966, TNA FA 371/184888.

60: Papa Doc Honoured Me

1 Journal, 18 September 1966, GU.
2 Falk, 110.
3 *New York Times* (7 May 1967).
4 *New York Times* (7 May 1967).
5 Piers Paul Read, *Alec Guinness: The Authorized Biography* (London: Simon & Schuster, 2003), 473.
6 Bernard Diederich, *Le Prix du sang* Port-au-Prince: Editions Henri Deschamps, 2004), 386 and *passim*; *Letters*, 288–9.
7 *Letters*, 293.
8 *Letters*, 293.
9 Diederich, 122–5 and 132–3. A copy of the book itself may be found in the National Archives (UK): FCO 7/249.
10 Diederich, 125.

61: Morse Code on the Water Pipes

1 V. S. Naipaul, typescript of interview with Graham Greene, BC; a later draft was published in *Daily Telegraph Magazine* (8 March 1968).
2 GG to Roy Arthur, 1 March 1966, BC; GG to KP, 17 May 1968, BC.
3 *Observer* (2 February 1968).
4 GG to Mr Badesi, 17 June 1980, Fan Mail file, BC.
5 RG, interview with David Cornwell, 23 August 2013.
6 Robin Lustig, 'Journalists and Novelists: Facts and Truth', lecture, Graham Greene International Festival, Berkhamsted, 22 September 2018.
7 [JR] to Alewyn Birch, 13 March 1968, BC.
8 E. M. Forster, 'What I Believe', *Nation* (16 July 1938).
9 GG, introduction, Kim Philby, *My Silent War: The Autobiography of a Spy* (London: MacGibbon & Kee, 1968), 7–9.
10 *Letters*, 291.
11 *The Times* (4 September 1967).
12 YE, 135–7.
13 YE, 141–5.
14 GG to Münnich Ferenc, telegram, 26 September 1957, HRC.
15 *Letters*, 234–5.
16 *Listener* (21 September 1972).
17 See Adamson (2009), 110–21.

18 *Letters*, 373.

19 GG to Josef Škvorecký, 28 October 1968, BC.

20 GG to Josef Škvorecký, 5 March 1969, BC; *Letters*, 415–16.

21 Karel Kyncl, 'A Conversation with Graham Greene', in A. F. Cassis, ed., *Graham Greene: Man of Paradox* (Chicago: Loyola University Press, 1994), 368.

22 *The Times* (15 February 1973).

23 Karel Kyncl to GG, 11 February 1980, BC.

24 Vladimir Tosek to GG, 27 February 1980, BC.

25 *Independent* (3 April 1997).

26 GG to Josef Škvorecký, 7 October 1968, BC.

27 Royal Astronomical Society of Canada: https://www.rasc.ca/asteroid/26314 (accessed 20 December 2018). I am grateful to Professor Sam Solecki for drawing this to my attention.

62: Behind the Sand Dune

1 *Letters*, 292.

2 The following account is based on WOE, 211–19.

3 WOE, 217.

4 GG to YC, 28 September 1967, GU.

5 WOE, 218.

6 *The Times* (28 September 1967).

7 GG to YC, 28 Sept 1967, GU.

8 *Letters*, 363–4.

9 *Letters*, 377.

10 Journal, 29 September 1969, GU.

11 GG to Mme Blau, 18 August 1988, BC.

12 GG, telegram to Bruce Kent, 27 September 1988, Reid Collection, Balliol.

13 Amnesty International Press Release (11 May 2016): https://www.amnesty.org.uk/press-releases/israel-should-drop-latest-ludicrous-charges-against-nuclear-whistle-blower-mordecha-o (accessed 12 December 2018).

14 *Telegraph* (23 January 2017).

15 FG, email to RG, 22 December 2018.

16 FG to GG, 20 November 1967, BC.

17 TW to GG, 15 March 1968, BC.

18 FG to GG, 11 December 1967, BC.

19 *Letters*, 294–5.

20 *Telegraph* (8 March 1968).

21 TW to GG, 15 March 1968, BC.

22 FG to GG, 11 March 1964, BC. Further information from FG.

23 *Letters*, 344–5.

24 YE, 149.

63: A House Surrounded by Orange Trees

1 Hazzard, 26.

2 GG to CW, 23 January 1975, BC.

3 GG to MK, 24 June 1974, files of Simon & Schuster.

4 *Letters*, 385.

5 GG to GS, 12 December 1967, Sutro Collection, Bod.

6 *New York Times* (12 September 1971).

7 *Observer Magazine* (19 May 1968).

8 Journal, 23 December 1967, GU.

9 Ian Smillie, Lansana Gberie, and Ralph Hazelton, 'The Heart of the Matter: Sierra Leone, Diamonds & Human Security' (2000): https://web.archive.org/web/20070120121759/http://www.sierra-leone.org/heartmatter.html (accessed 29 December 2018).

10 Butcher, 94.

11 Smillie, Gberie, and Hazelton, 'The Heart of the Matter'.

12 GG to MB, 15 January 1968, Balliol.

13 Barbara Greene, 158–71.

14 GG to GS, 21 February 1968, Sutro Collection, Bod.

15 In the documentary, a line is missing from Greene's recitation.

16 Quotations are taken from Christopher Burstall, 'Graham Greene: The Hunted Man', post-production script. I am grateful to Sue Burstall for allowing me to quote from this and to Professor Andrew Biswell for drawing the interview to my attention.

17 GG to VG, [c. 1930], GG Collection, HRC.

18 Julia J. S. Sarreal, *The Guarani and Their Missions: A Socioeconomic History* (Stanford: Stanford University Press, 2014), 1–2.

19 R. B. Cunninghame Graham, 'A Vanished Arcadia: Being Some Account of the Jesuits in Paraguay, 1607–1767', in Peter Lambert and R. Andrew Nickson, eds, *The Paraguay Reader: History, Culture, Politics* (Durham, NC: Duke University Press, 2013), 41–5.

20 Bridget Chesterton, 'Chaco War', *Oxford Bibliographies*: www.oxfordbibliographies.com (accessed 6 January 2019).

21 *Letters*, 85.

22 'From the Chaco War to the Civil War', in Lambert and Nickson, eds, *The Paraguay Reader*, 193–4.

23 Diederich, 189.

24 Marcial Riquelme, 'Toward a Weberian Characterization of the Stroessner Regime', in Lambert and Nickson, eds, *The Paraguay Reader*, 239–43.

25 J. Patrice McSherry, '"Industrial Repression" and Operation Condor in Latin America', in Marcia Esparza *et al.*, eds., *State Violence and Genocide in Latin America The Cold War Years* (London and New York: Routledge, 2010), 107–23; 'Truth Commission: Paraguay', United States Institute of Peace: https://www.usip.org/publications/2004/06/truth-commission-paraguay (accessed 4 January 2019).

26 BBC News, 10 September 2019.

27 GG to MB, 7 August 1968, Balliol.

28 Javier Sologuren, 'Victoria Ocampo: A Woman in Search of Justice and Spirituality', in Susnigdha Dey, ed., *Victoria Ocampo: An Exercise in Indo-Argentine Relationship* (Delhi: BR Publishing, 1992), 80–8.

29 For biographical information on Ocampo, see especially Doris Meyer, *Victoria Ocampo: Against the Wind and the Tide* (New York: George Braziller, 1979), 3–170.

30 *New York Times* (4 August 1968).

31 See, for example, Jörg Le Blanc, *Political Violence in Latin America: A Cross-Case Comparison of the Urban Insurgency Campaigns of Montoneros, M-19, and FSLN in a Historical Perspective* (Cambridge: Cambridge Scholars Publishing, 2013), esp. 59–66.

32 *Letters*, 311; Journal, undated entry c. 31 July 1968, GU.

33 John Gerassi, ed., *The Complete Writings & Messages of Camilo Torres* (New York: Random House, 1971), xiii and 14–33.

34 *Daily Telegraph Magazine* (3 January 1969).

35 Diederich, 173.

36 *Letters*, 297.

37 Journal, 6 August 1968, GU.

38 *Letters*, 297.

39 Quoted in 'Brazilian Icon of Liberation Theology Moves Closer to Sainthood', *Crux* (7 January 2019): https://cruxnow.com/church-in-the-americas/2019/01/07/brazilian-icon-of-liberation-theology-moves-closer-to-sainthood/ (accessed 7 January 2019).

40 R. Andrew Nickson, 'Tyranny and Longevity: Stroessner's Paraguay', *Third World Quarterly*, 10:1 (January 1988), 237–59.

41 *Daily Telegraph Magazine* (3 January 1969).

64: No One's Poodle

1 Quoted in MK, 'The Third Man', *New Yorker* (25 March 1996), 48.

2 Monica McCall to GG, 25 August 1969, HRC.

3 MK to GG, 25 August 1969, HRC.

4 *Telegraph* (16 November 1969).

5 Cloetta, 27.

6 Contract between Robert Fryer and Verdant, S.A., 5 June 1971, HRC.

7 Falk, 114–16.

8 See Falk, 114–33.

9 Raimo Väyrynen, 'Some Aspects of Theory and Strategy of Kidnapping', *Instant Research on Peace and Violence*, 1:1 (1971), 3–21.

10 GG to BD, 22 November 1969, BC.
11 See Wise and Hill 2: 67–8.
12 Enrique Dussell, *A History of the Church in Latin America* (Grand Rapids: Wm. B. Eerdmans, 1981) 200–1.
13 GG to LP, 20 February 1970, HRC.
14 Journal, 26 March 1970, GU; this visit to Argentina is also described in *WOE*.
15 *Letters*, 307.
16 Journal, 28 March 1970, GU.
17 *El Litoral* (29 March 1970). The translation is preserved at HRC.
18 Journal, 27 March 1970, GU.
19 *WOE*, 206.
20 *New York Times* (12 August 1970).
21 *Norte de Corrientes* (2 November 2016).
22 *The Times* (5 April 1970); *Irish Times* (6 April 1970).
23 GG to MB, 31 July 1971, Balliol; Wise and Hill 2: 67–9.
24 *Guardian* (11 September 1971).
25 GG to CW, 1 September 1947, GU.
26 HC, 228.
27 I am grateful to Professor Gilles Mongeau, SJ, for his observations on this subject.
28 Wise and Hill 2: 5.
29 Ricardo Israel Zipper, *Politics and Ideology in Allende's Chile* (Tempe: Arizona State University, 1989), viii and 167–8.
30 *New York Times* (18 March 1971).
31 GG to Victoria Ocampo, 24 April 1971, BC.
32 *Letters*, 311–12.
33 *Guardian* (23 October 2017).
34 *Guardian* (8 January 2018).
35 Journal, 13 September 1971, HRC.
36 Journal, 14 September 1971, HRC; GG to Janet Adam Smith, 11 February 1974, BC; 'In Memory of Borges, *Reflections*, 385–7.
37 'Chile: The Dangerous Edge', *Reflections*, 323.
38 Journal, 17 September 1971, HRC.
39 Journal, 18 September 1971, HRC.
40 Journal, 21 September 1971, HRC.
41 Journal, 22 September 1971, HRC.
42 Luis Poirot, 'Graham Greene in Chile', unpublished ms (2020).
43 Richard Hall, *My Life with Tiny* (London: Faber & Faber, 1987), 84–5. I am grateful to the late Jeremy Lewis for drawing this source to my attention.

65: Light Bulbs

1 GS, manuscript notes, Sutro Collection, Bod.
2 GG, Dream Diary (vol. 1), 26 December 1964, HRC.
3 Cloetta, 65.
4 GS, transcript of conversation with YC, 8 June 1995, Sutro Collection, Bod. Dorothy Glover's death announcement appeared in *The Times* (30 November 1971).
5 RG interview with Judy Taylor Hough, 12 May 2015; see Wise and Hill 1:30.
6 GG to YC, 27 September 1972, GU.
7 *Letters*, 318–19.
8 Cloetta, 46.
9 RG interview with Julian Evans, 24 September 2015.
10 Judith Adamson to RG, email, 7 December 2014.
11 Cloetta, 90.
12 ED to LD, 3 October 1988, GU.
13 Cloetta, 28
14 *Letters*, 321.
15 Meyer, 219–23.
16 RG interview with CB, 26 September 2015.
17 Journal, 30 January 1977, GU. This journal is otherwise dedicated to his first journey to Panama.
18 *Letters*, 325.
19 RG interview with CB, 25 September 2016.
20 The correspondence between GG and Igoe is preserved at BC. See especially William Igoe to GG, 25 May 1974, BC.
21 GG to FG, 3 June 1977, private collection of FG.
22 NS to GG, 3 July 1975, GG estate files.
23 GG to Anthony Mockler, 12 June 1987, Reinhardt Collection, BL.

66: About My Best

1 GG to GS, 27 July 1967, BC.
2 *New York Times* (7 May 1985).
3 See, for example, Martin Trump, 'Afrikaner Literature and the South African Liberation Struggle', *Journal of Commonwealth Literature*, 25:1 (January 1990), 42–70.
4 *The Times* (26 August and 28 September 1968)
5 *Life* (12 April 1968).
6 EL to GG, undated [c. October 1967], BC.
7 There are several undated letters from Leroux to GG about the itinerary in the collection at BC.
8 See, for example, Ray Swart, *Progressive Odyssey: Towards a Democratic South Africa* (Cape Town: Human & Rousseau, 1991), 140 and *passim*.
9 Journal, 21 July 1973, GU.
10 See Ebbe Dommisse and W. P. Esterhuyse, *Anton Rupert: A Biography* (Cape Town: Tafelberg, 2005).
11 Journal, 30 July 1973, GU.
12 *Letters*, 326.
13 Journal, 13 August 1973, GU; GG to JR, 3 August 1973, Balliol (GG made additions to this letter on several dates including the 13th).
14 GG to YC, 20 August 1973, GU; this letter gives a probable date of arrival.
15 GG to John Anstey, 23 September 1973, BC.
16 *The Times* (13 September 1973).
17 *Daily Mail* (13 September 1973).
18 GG to Bill Igoe, 15 September 1973, BC.

67: Long Spoons

1 GG to GS and JS, 15 December 1973, Sutro Collection, Bod; GG to Mario Soldati, 7 March 1974, BC.
2 GG to Hugh Greene, 12 December 1974, GU.
3 GG to Peter Glenville, 15 October 1974, BC.
4 *The Times* (12 August 1975).

5 GG to YC, 9 June 1975, GU.
6 *The Times* (10 April 1976),
7 GG to Tadeusz Murek, 9 June 1975, BC.
8 *Letters*, 346–7.
9 GG to EL, 17 January 1976, BC.
10 Durán, 233.
11 GG to Monica McCall, 11 May 1977, BC.
12 *Observer* (19 March 1978).
13 MR to GG, 12 June 1978, Reinhardt Collection, BL.
14 See László Róbert, 'The Greene Connection', unpublished memoir. I am also grateful to Dr Tamás Molnár and Dr Ramon Rami Porta for discussing their research on Greene's involvement in Hungary; in this respect, see Tamás Molnár, 'Graham Greene in the Aiming Cross of the Hungarian Secret Service Catch 22 at the Pearl of River Danube', MA thesis, University of Pécs, 2016. For Greene's recollection of these events, see GG to KP, 27 May 1978, BC.
15 KP to Graham C. Greene, 30 October 1977, BC.
16 Maurice Oldfield to RD, 4 January 1978, BC.
17 KP to GG, 25 April 1978, BC.
18 GG to KP, 17 May 1978, BC.
19 KP to GG, 25 April 1978, BC.
20 KP to GG, 2 January 1980, BC.
21 RD to Sir Dick Franks, 22 January 1980, BC.
22 *Letters*, 412.
23 GTG, 157.
24 *New York Times* (11 February 1984).

68: Effervescence and Vibration

1 GG to YC, 23 [?] June 1975, GU.
2 Guya Accornero, *The Revolution Before the Revolution: Late Authoritarianism and Student Protest in Portugal* (New York and Oxford: Berghahn Books, 2016), 1 and 119–24.
3 Ronald H. Chilcote, *The Portuguese Revolution: State and Class in the Transition to Democracy* (Plymouth:

Rowman & Littlefield, 2010), 89–116.

4 GG to YC, 23 [?] June 1975, GU.
5 *El País* (13 December 2013).
6 *New York Times* (25 April 1975).
7 GG to LD, 7 April 1975, BC.
8 Carlos Villar Flor, 'Travels With My Priest: Greene's Spanish Trips 1976–89', lecture, Graham Greene International Festival, Berkhamsted, 27 September 2013; and 'Journey With Maps: The Beginning of Greene's Quixotic Journeys', lecture, Graham Greene International Festival, Berkhamsted, 23 September 2016. This chapter relies on other information from Carlos Villar Flor, who is writing a book on Durán.
9 GG to LD, 18 October 1976, GU.
10 LD to GG, 22 June 1964, BC.
11 LD to GG, 23 September 1968 and 26 January 1972, BC.
12 Durán, 3; JR to LD, 14 August 1975, BC; LD to GG, 6 December 1975, BC.
13 Durán, 94–5.
14 GG to DL, 1 December 1975 and 11 December 1975, BC.
15 GG to DL, 26 May 1976, BC.
16 Durán, 125.
17 Durán, 125.
18 See the monastery's website: http://mosteirodeoseira.org/web/resena-historica-2/ (accessed 11 March 2019).
19 Durán, 128.
20 Durán, 129–30; Charles Wolfe, 'The Burial of Sir John Moore at Corunna': https://rpo.library.utoronto.ca/poems/burial-sir-john-moore-corunna (accessed 11 March 2019).
21 Durán, 129–31.
22 Durán, 134–5.
23 Durán, 324–6.
24 *Letters*, 345–6.
25 Durán, 75.
26 *Letters*, 345–6.
27 *Letters*, 348.
28 *Articles*, 37–76; ED to GP, 8 January 1979, HRC.
29 Wise and Hill 2: 202–3.
30 GG to LD, 11 December 1981, GU.
31 Durán, 203.
32 Durán, 206.
33 *Guardian* (16 September 1982).
34 *Washington Post* (12 September 1978).

69: The Diplomatic Passport

1 Journal, 3 December 1976, GU.
2 John Lindsay-Poland, *Emperors in the Jungle: The Hidden History of the US in Panama* (Durham, NC and London: Duke University Press, 2003), 1–9.
3 Lindsay-Poland, *Emperors in the Jungle*, 17.
4 Carlos Guevara Mann, *Panamanian Militarism: A Historical Interpretation* (Athens, OH: Ohio University Center for International Studies, 1996), 85–91.
5 Diederich, 177.
6 Mann, *Panamanian Militarism*, 95.
7 John Dinges, *Our Man in Panama: The Shrewd Rise and Brutal Fall of Manuel Noriega* (rev. edn; New York: Random House, 1991), 44–8.
8 Sandra W. Meditz and Dennis M. Hanratty, eds, *Panama: A Country Study* (Washington: GPO for the Library of Congress, 1987): http://countrystudies.us/panama/ (accessed 18 April 2019).
9 Dinges, *Our Man in Panama*, 67–9.
10 *Mitrokhin*, 108–14.
11 Robert C. Harding II, *Military Foundations of Panamanian Politics* (New Brunswick and London: Transaction Publishers, 2001), 89.
12 Diederich, 153–4.
13 Journal, 5 December 1976, GU.
14 BD to GG, 19 December 1971, BC.
15 Diederich, 159.
16 *Letters*, 323–4.
17 Diederich, 168.
18 GTG, 23.
19 Journal, 4 December 1976, GU.
20 GTG, 24.
21 BD to GG, 30 January 1977, BC.
22 Journal, 6 December 1976, GU.
23 Diederich, 177.
24 BD to GG, 11 April 1973, BC.

25 *Panama Today* (19 February 2019): https://www.panamatoday.com/panama/countdown-huge-copper-mine-panama-starts-exporting-9296 (accessed 16 April 2019).
26 Diederich, 170.
27 GTG, 26.
28 Journal, 5 December 1976, GU.
29 GTG, 38–9.
30 Department of State: Office of the Historian, 'The Panama Canal and the Torrijos-Carter Treaties': https://history.state.gov/milestones/1977-1980/panama-canal (accessed 17 April 2019).
31 Journal, 7 December 1976, GU.
32 Journal, 17 December 1976, GU.
33 Journal, 21 December 1976, GU.
34 GTG, 34.
35 BD to GG, 11 April 1973, BC.
36 GTG, 57.
37 GTG, 86–7.
38 Journal, 19–20 December 1976, GU.
39 GTG, 50–1.
40 *Letters*, 338.
41 'The Country with Five Frontiers', *Reflections*, 348–63.
42 *Letters*, 342.
43 Interview with Sarah Greene, 21 June 2019.
44 GG to BD, 19 February 1977, BC.
45 GG to BD, 14 June 1977 and 9 July 1977, BC.
46 Meditz and Hanratty, eds., *Panama*.
47 Department of State: Office of the Historian, 'The Panama Canal and the Torrijos-Carter Treaties'.
48 *New York Times* (10 August 1977).
49 Journal, 24 August 1977, GU.
50 'The Great Spectacular', *Reflections*, 370.
51 GTG, 91–2.
52 Journal, 25 August 1977, GU.
53 Bernard Diederich, *Somoza and the Legacy of US Involvement in Central America* (New York: E. P. Dutton, 1981), 106–14.
54 Journal, 29 August 1977, GU.
55 Journal, 5 September 1977, GU.
56 Journal, 4 September 1977, GU.
57 Diederich, 188–9.
58 GTG, 99.
59 *New York Times* (7 September 1977).
60 Journal, 4 September 1977, GU.
61 *The Times* (8 September 1977).
62 Journal, 6 September 1977, GU.
63 'The Great Spectacular', 369–74.

70: Storming the Palace

1 Journal, 22 August 1978, GU. The phrase is Chuchu's.
2 Diederich, 191–2; *Mitrokhin*, 111.
3 Journal, 21 August 1978, GU; GTG, 117.
4 Diederich, 195.
5 Journal, 20 August 1978, GU; GTG, 115.
6 GG to YC, 20 August 1978, GU.
7 Journal, 20 and 21 August 1978, GU; GTG, 118.
8 Diederich, 199.
9 *YE*, 223–5.
10 *America* (18 February 2019).
11 Bernard Diederich, *Somoza and the Legacy of US Involvement in Central America* (New York: E. P. Dutton, 1981), 176.
12 *Telegraph* (24 October 2011).
13 Diederich, 202.
14 *TCE*, 145.
15 Diederich, *Somoza and the Legacy of US Involvement in Central America*, 176–84.
16 *New York Times* (6 November 1978).
17 Journal, 24–5 August 1978, GU; GTG, 119–21.
18 *The Times* (4 July 1978).
19 *Washington Post* (24 June 1978).
20 GTG, 124.
21 BD to RG, email, 5 February 2005.
22 GTG, 123–8.
23 GTG, 127.
24 *The Times* (16 August 1980). YE, 195–6.
25 George Price to GG, 24 August 1981, BC; GG to George Price, telegram, 26 August 1981, BC.
26 GTG, 129.
27 BD to GG, 26 September 1978, BC.
28 BD to RG, email, 29 April 2019, BC.
29 *Washington Post* (30 May 2011).
30 Inter-American Commission on

Human Rights, Press Release: 'CIDH denounces the weakening of the rule of law in the face of serious human rights violations and crimes against humanity in Nicaragua', 10 January 2019: http://www. oas.org/en/iachr/media_center/ PReleases/2019/006.asp (accessed 25 April 2019).

31 *New York Times* (26 April 2018).

32 BD to RG, email, 29 April 2019, BC.

33 'The Virtue of Disloyalty', *Reflections*, 314.

71: The Bomb Party

1 GG, *Doctor Fischer of Geneva or The Bomb Party* (London: The Bodley Head, 1980), 8.

2 See Christopher Andrew, *The Defence of the Realm: The Authorized History of MI5* (London: Penguin, 2009–10), 14.

3 GG, *Doctor Fischer of Geneva or The Bomb Party*, 134 and 106.

4 Betty Boothroyd to JR, 21 September 1978, Balliol.

5 CW to GG, 18 May 1978, BC.

6 *The Times* (5 September 1978).

7 Harry Walston to GG, 18 September 1978, BC.

8 GG to CW, 7 November 1951, GU.

9 Durán, 241.

10 *Letters*, 352.

11 *Letters*, 353.

12 GG to AB, 16 August 1985, GU; *Letters*, 353.

13 GG to YC, 20 February 1979, GU.

14 ED to MB, 27 February 1979, Balliol.

15 GG to BD, 19 March 1979, BC.

16 *The Times* (28 June 1979).

17 GG to Jan Van Loewen, 31 August 1978, BC.

18 See Wise and Hill 2: 156.

19 GG to MB, 16 April 1979, Balliol.

20 GG to Ragnar Svanstrom, 6 April 1979, BC.

21 GG to MR, 15 June 1979, BC.

22 MR to GP, 8 August 1979, BC.

23 *The Listener* (27 March 1980).

24 *New York Times* (19 May 1980).

72: Three Hostages

1 GTG, 133–4.

2 Introduction, Anjali Sundaram and George Gelber, eds, *A Decade of War: El Salvador Confronts the Future* (London: CIIR, 1991), 11.

3 Harald Jung 'Class Struggle and Civil War in El Salvador', in Marvin E. Gettleman et al., eds, *El Salvador: Central America in the New Cold War* (rev. edn; New York: Grove Press, 1986), 64–85. This book also contains a 'Political Chronology', 53–64, which I have relied on extensively in this chapter.

4 'Rutilio Grande SJ', The Archbishop Romero Trust: http://www.romerotrust.org.uk/martyrs/rutilio-grande-sj (accessed 7 May 2019).

5 GTG, 133–6.

6 'Political Chronology', in Gettleman et al., eds, *El Salvador*.

7 BD to GG, 6 June 1980, BC.

8 'Political Chronology', in Gettleman et al., eds, *El Salvador*.

9 UPI, 22 February 1981.

10 'Political Chronology', in Gettleman et al., eds, *El Salvador*.

11 Some letters between GG and Ana Carrigan are preserved at BC.

12 Socorro Juridico, *El Salvador: One Year of Repression* (1981), 11.

13 'El Salvador Government Rejects Court Ruling on Kidnapped Envoy', BBC (12 July 2018): https://www.bbc.com/news/world-latin-america-44794535 (accessed 4 May 2019).

14 GTG, 136–7.

15 GG to Jeremy B. Shearer, 28 January 1980, BC.

16 Jeremy B. Shearer to GG, 26 June 1980 and 4 March 1981, BC; GTG, 136–7.

17 GTG, 138.

18 Journal, 21 August 1980, GU.

19 Diederich, 221.

20 The description of this meeting is drawn from Diederich, 221–4, and GTG, 140–1.

21 'The Salvadoran Rebels: Editors' Introduction', in Gettleman et al., eds, *El Salvador*, 189–91.
22 *Letters*, 368.
23 'Report of the Truth Commission on El Salvador' (1993): http://www.derechos.org/nizkor/salvador/informes/truth.html (accessed 4 May 2019).
24 GG to BD, 28 October 1980, BC.
25 BD to GG, 11 September 1980, BC.
26 BD to GG, Telex, 12 February 1981, BC.
27 *GTG*, 141.
28 *The Times* (13 July 2018). Further information from www.elsalvador.com (accessed 7 April 2019).
29 *La Noticia SV* (3 January 2020): https://lanoticiasv.com/familiares-piden-a-fgr-que-investigue-al-expresidente-sanchez-ceren-y-organizaciones-guerrilleras-po (accessed 8 February 2020).
30 Diederich, 237–8.
31 Diederich, 239–43.
32 *GTG*, 152–7.
33 GG to BD, 28 October 1980, BC.
34 Diederich, 249.
35 *Letters*, 374.
36 *New York Times* (5 August 1981).
37 Diederich, 251–2.

73: J'Accuse

1 GG, *J'Accuse* (London: The Bodley Head, 1982), 7. This chapter relies on the pamphlet for Greene's view of events, unless otherwise indicated. It is meant to indicate only what Greene believed to be true. It is not intended to be an objective report of the facts of the marriage and subsequent litigation.
2 GG to YC, 2 March 1979, GU.
3 GG to LD, 2 February 1980, GU. The ellipses indicate deletion of the man's name.
4 *GTG*, 46.
5 *Letters*, 366.
6 Journal, 31 August 1980, GU.
7 *GTG*, 159.
8 *Letters*, 369–70.
9 GG to LD, 25 November 1981, GU.
10 *New York Times* (19 November 1998).
11 GG to LD, 16 November 1981, GU.
12 Euan Cameron to RG, email, 12 May 2019.
13 *Letters*, 375–6.
14 *Le Monde* (8 August 1982).
15 *Irish Times* (19 June 1982).
16 Euan Cameron to RG, email, 13 May 2019,
17 GG to LD, 21 July 1983, GU.
18 GS, Transcript of conversation with YC, 20 April 1990, Sutro Collection, Bod.
19 Pierre Joannon, Interview with RG, 12 April 2016.
20 I am grateful for advice on this subject from Alanna Greene, MSW.
21 Hazzard, 133.
22 GS, transcript of conversation with YC, 20 April 1990, Sutro Collection, Bod.

74: I Am the Message

1 GG to BD, 30 August 1982, BC.
2 GG to BC, 7 October 1982, BC.
3 *Letters*, 376.
4 Journal, 3 January 1983, GU.
5 *GTG*, 163.
6 GG to BD, 25 April 1983, BC.
7 Journal, 5 January 1983, GU.
8 Diederich, 261.
9 *Letters*, 400.
10 Diederich, 262.
11 *GTG*, 163.
12 *GTG*, 170.
13 *GTG*, 171–2.
14 Journal, 7 January 1983, GU.
15 Diederich, 263.
16 Diederich, 263.
17 See, for example, *GTG*, 177.
18 *GTG*, 174–5.
19 Robert S. Leiken and Barry Rubin, 'The Sandinistas in Power', in Robert S. Leiken and Barry Rubin, eds, *The Central American Crisis Reader* (New York: Summit Books, 1987), 205.
20 Bernard Nietschmann, 'Statement to the OAS', in Leiken and Rubin, eds, *The Central American Crisis Reader*, 271–4.

21 GTG, 175.
22 *New York Times* (16 October 2016).
23 *Guardian* (1 March 2017).
24 Journal, 10 January 1983, GU.
25 GG to BD, 22 May 1983, BC.
26 GTG, 178–81.
27 Diederich, 268–9.
28 GTG, 181–2.
29 *Granma* (14 April 1991); Gabriel García Márquez's recollection of this evening is reprinted in Diederich, 265–7.
30 GTG, 183.
31 Journal, 11 January 1983, GU; GTG, 183.

75: Better a Bad Man

1   GG to Pierre Joannon, 8 October 1984, BC.
2   Pierre Joannon to RG, email, 17 May 2019.
3   GG to William Igoe, 26 March 1984, BC.
4   *Letters*, 383–4.
5   *The Observer* (4 September 1988).
6   See Wise and Hill 2: 207–10, which presents Greene's full 'Apologia' for this novel. I am grateful to Mike Hill for further information about how this novel was written.
7   LD to GG, 15 December 1988, BC.
8   GG to BD, 27 January 1986, BC.
9   *New York Times* (25 October 1985).
10 GG to BD, 28 January 1986, BC.
11 GG to BD, 28 July 1987, BC.
12 BD to RG, email, 21 May 2019.
13 GG to BD, 28 July 1987, BC.
14 *Los Angeles Times* (28 July 1987).
15 *New York Times* (3 August 1987).
16 *Letters*, 400.
17 GG to Joseph Jeffs, 11 March 1988, BC.
18 David Cornwell (John le Carré) interview with RG, 23 August 2013.
19 GS, transcript of telephone conversation with GG, 13 October 1988, Sutro Collection, Bod.
20 *Guardian* (9 September 1988).
21 *New York Times* (23 October 1988).

76: Two Faces

1   Cloetta, 133.
2   Borovik, 370. For Borovik's career, see Mitrokhin, particularly p. 297, and 'Moscow and the Peace Movement: The Soviet Committee for the Defense of Peace', US Department of State Foreign Affairs Note, May 1987.
3   Cloetta, 130–1.
4   David Cornwell to RG, email, 1 August 2019; see Adam Sisman, *John le Carré: The Biography* (Toronto: Knopf Canada, 2015), 453–5.
5   Rufina, 424.
6   Borovik, 370–1; see also Knightley's introduction, vii–xvii.
7   GG to Josef Škvorecký, 15 March 1987, BC.
8   *Letters*, 392.
9   Rufina, 173.
10 Borovik, 371.
11 Rufina, 174.
12 Borovik, 371–2.
13 GS, 'Visit to GG 7 March 1987', Sutro Collection, Bod.
14 KP to GG, 24 September 1986, GU.
15 ED to JR, 12 December 1982, Reid Collection, Balliol.
16 Lewis, 486.
17 Information from Sarah Greene.
18 GS, 'Visit to GG 7 March 1987', Sutro Collection, Bod.
19 Rufina, 177.
20 Borovik, 372
21 GS, 'Visit to GG 7 March 1987', Sutro Collection, Bod.
22 *Guardian* (15 February 1987).
23 *Letters*, 379–80.
24 GG to Josef Škvorecký, 15 March 1987, BC.
25 Information from Professor Sam Solecki.
26 Cloetta, 143.
27 Durán, 24.
288 GG to BD, 27 June 1985, BC.
29 GG to Josef Škvorecký, 15 March 1987, BC.
30 *The Times* (17 February 1987).
31 'The Meeting in the Kremlin', *Reflections*, 405–7.

32 *New York Times* (16 March 1990).
33 Interview with Sarah Greene, 21 June 2019; see Lewis, 486.
34 Interview with Sarah Greene, 21 June 2019.
35 *Letters*, 393–4.
36 Interview with Sarah Greene, 21 June 2019; see Lewis, 486.
37 GS, '21 October 1987 Visit to Antibes', Sutro Collection, Bod.
38 Nicholas Elliott to ED, 1 September 1987, BC.
39 ED to Nicholas Elliott, 21 September 1987, BC.
40 *Daily Telegraph* (19 February 1988).
41 *The Times* (19 February 1988).
42 Rufina, 179.
43 *New York Times* (4 June 2000).
44 Borovik, 374.
45 GS, transcript of telephone conversation with GG, 13 October 1988, Sutro Collection, Bod.
46 Rufina, 179.

77: The Late Rounds

1 *Letters*, 401–2.
2 Information from Andrew Biswell.
3 GG to William Igoe, 26 March 1984, BC.
4 Pierre Joannon, 'Graham Greene and the Honorary Consul', lecture, Graham Greene International Festival, Berkhamsted, 23 September 2017.
5 My account of the mergers is based almost entirely on Adamson (2009), 140–71, and on further information kindly provided by Professor Adamson.
6 *The Times* (24 March 1987).
7 *The Times* (28 March 1987).
8 MR to GG, 11 March 1988, Reinhardt Collection, BL.
9 GS, manuscript notes, 29 January 1990, Sutro Collection, Bod.
10 *London Review of Books* (7 July 1994).
11 *London Review of Books* (22 September 1994).
12 Seán Donlon, 'Graham Greene and the GPA Book Award', in Jane Conroy, ed., *Franco-Irish*

Connections: Essays, Memoirs and Poems in Honour of Pierre Joannon (Dublin: Four Courts Press, 2009), 78–81
13 *Independent* (10 May 1989); GG to Gloria Emerson, 28 July 1989, BC.
14 GS, transcript of telephone conversation with YC, 3 February 1990, Sutro Collection, Bod.
15 *Irish Times* (4 April 1991).

78: A Sense of Movement

1 Christopher Burstall, 'Graham Greene: "The Hunted Man"', post-production script (1968), private collection of Sue Burstall.
2 *National Review* (14 October 1988).
3 *Letters*, 404; I confess to shamelessly recycling a joke here.
4 *Letters*, 367.
5 Durán, 100.
6 *Letters*, 409.
7 *Letters*, 409.
8 *Letters*, 349–50.
9 Mark Abley, interview with GG, *Woman's Journal* (March 1981), 116–18.
10 GS, transcript of telephone conversation with YC, 3 February 1990, Sutro Collection, Bod.
11 I am grateful for information from Dr Ramon Rami Porta. This corrects the assertion in *Letters*, xxxii, that he was suffering from leukaemia.
12 GS, transcript of telephone conversation with YC, 15 February 1990, Sutro Collection, Bod.
13 *New York Times* (18 November 1989).
14 ABC News (4 January 1990).
15 GS, transcript of telephone conversation with YC, 29 January 1990, Sutro Collection, Bod.
16 GS, transcript of telephone conversation with YC, 3 February 1990, Sutro Collection, Bod.
17 *Boston Globe* (14 February 1990); quoted in Diederich, 296.
18 *Washington Post* (30 January 1991). See Diederich, 299.
19 *New York Times* (27 February 1990).

20 GG to FG, 12 February 1990, Reinhardt Collection, BL.
21 GG to LD, 5 August 1990, GU.
22 Durán, 330.
23 Information from Louise Dennys.
24 Pierre Smolik, *Graham Greene: The Swiss Chapter* (Vevey: Call Me Edouard, 2013), 149.
25 GS, transcript of telephone conversation with YC, 14 June 1990, Sutro Collection, Bod.
26 GG to LD, 7 September 1990, BC.
27 GS, transcript of telephone conversation with YC, 27 September 1990, Sutro Collection, Bod.
28 Cloetta, 185.
29 Cloetta, 190–1.
30 Cloetta, 188.
31 Cloetta, 185.
32 Cloetta, 189; Durán, 341–5.
33 TCE, 180.

ACKNOWLEDGEMENTS

My first and greatest obligation is to the children of Graham Greene, Caroline Bourget and Francis Greene, who have treated me with the greatest kindness over many years and steadily encouraged my research, while leaving me at liberty to form my own views of the evidence. I am also indebted to other members of Graham Greene's family: Andrew Bourget, Jonathan Bourget, the late Amanda Dennys, Louise Dennys, Nick Dennys, the late Graham C. Greene, James Greene, Oliver Greene, Sarah Greene, and Peter Walker.

I am very grateful to Graham Greene's literary estate and to Verdant SA for permission to quote from his works and to reproduce images on which they hold the copyright.

I would like to record my debt to friends of Graham Greene, who have helped with my research. Bernard Diederich, who died as this book went to press, was generous to an extraordinary degree, answering a steady stream of enquiries related to Graham Greene's visits to Haiti and Central America – any errors I have made about these matters are entirely my own fault; he also kindly gave permission for his works to be freely quoted and his photographs to illustrate these pages.

Oliver Walston has welcomed me to his home at Thriplow on several occasions, discussed his mother's relationship with Graham Greene, and allowed me, most generously, to quote from his unpublished family memoir.

I am also deeply indebted to friends of Graham Greene, including Judith Adamson, Marie Françoise Allain, David Cornwell, Euan Cameron, Ginette Diederich, Julian Evans, Judy Taylor Hough, the late Alberto Huerta, SJ, Pierre Joannon, Michael Korda, the late Michel Lechat, Luis Poirot, the late Lászlo Róbért, the late Josef Škvorecký, and Ralph Wright, OSB.

It is no longer possible to study Graham Greene without incurring a very great debt to other scholars and writers. I am extremely for the assistance of: David Anderson, Stephen Andes, Andrew Biswell, Margaret

Bluett, Tim Butcher, the late Justin Cartwright, Greg Chamberlain, Kent Davis, Robert Murray Davis, Quentin Falk, Danielle Floode, Carlos Villar Flor, Patrice Fox, the late John Geary, CSSp, Dermot Gilvary, Massimo De Giuseppe, François Gallix, Johanne Elster Hanson, Selena Hastings, Christopher Hawtree, the late Lucy Hill, Michael Hill, Christopher Hull, Kay Redfield Jamison, Charles Keith, the late Jeremy Lewis, J. Patrice McSherry, Fabio Mangone, Carlos Guevara Mann, Michael Meeuwis, Anthony Mockler, Tamas F. Molnar, Gilles Mongeau, SJ, Thomas P. O' Connor, Peter O' Mahony, Karl Orend, the late David Pearce, Ramon Rami Porta, Kevin Ruane, Michelangelo Sabatino, Martyn Sampson, Nicholas Shakespeare, Edward Short, Adam Sisman, Sam Solecki, James Stone, William Sullivan, Nicholas Swarbrick, Margaret Swarbrick, Ian Thomson, Brigitte Timmermann, Claire Tran, Richard Watson, Nigel West, Jon Wise, Alexander Waugh, and Julia G. Young.

I have benefited enormously from the loyalty and shrewd advice of Richard Beswick and Zoe Gullen of Little, Brown UK, and Jill Bialosky of W.W. Norton. My literary agent Andrew Gordon of David Higham Associates has stood behind this book, unfailingly, and encouraged me to write it as I believed the evidence dictated. His retired colleague Bruce Hunter supported my work for over thirty years, and has remained a dear and constant friend.

For permission to quote from the works of Evelyn Waugh, I am grateful to his literary estate and to Alexander Waugh. For permission to quote from the Sutro papers, I am grateful to the President and Fellows of Trinity College, Oxford. For permission to quote from an interview conducted by Christopher Burstall, I am grateful to Sue Burstall. I also thank Giles Clark, Rufina Philby, Helen Womack, Nick Holdsworth and Patrick von Richthofen. For many kinds of assistance, I am grateful to librarians at the Bodleian Library, Oxford, the British Library, the Burns Library, Boston College, the Harry Ransom Humanities Research Center, University of Texas at Austin, the McFarlin Library, University of Tulsa, the Lauinger Library, Georgetown University, The National Archives at Kew, and the Rare Book and Manuscript Library, Columbia University. The research for this book has been handsomely assisted by a research grant from the Social Sciences and Humanities Research Council of Canada.

I am finally most grateful for the love and support of Tanya Berezuk, Samuel Greene, and Sarah Greene, which have lifted my heart in times of difficulty and allowed me to see this work to its end.

INDEX

Abwehr 149, 150, 292

Achebe, Chinua 86

Achill Island (County Mayo) 170–1, 211, 228

Action Française (French royalists) 77

Acton, Harold 24, 33, 34, 252

Adamson, Judith 414, 498

Adzhubei, Alexei 352

'A.E.' (George William Russell) 349

Afghanistan 426, 427

Aguado, Macario Fernández 119–20

Albania 350

Albery, Donald 228, 361

Aldermaston 323

Algeria 341–2

All-African People's Conference (Accra, 1958) 311

Allain, Marie-Françoise 325

Alleg, Henri 341, 342

Allen, Larry 217–18

Allende, Salvador 409, 411–12, 439

Ambler, Eric 339

American Academy of Arts and Letters 393

Amnesty International 363, 391

Anacapri, Villa Rosaio in 197, 227, 230, 252, 263, 289, 330, 369, 371, 394; Korda gives to GG 182–3; productive writing at 183, 231, 407, 422; GG sells (1990) 505–6

Anaconda (American firm) 409

Anderson, George 52, 55

Andropov, Yuri 427

Anglicanism 94, 176, 503

Anglo-Texan Society 273–4

Angola 420, 428

Annakin, Ken 251

Antibes 368–9, 371, 414, 505–6

Anti-Slavery and Aborigines' Protection Society 81–2, 92

Aramburu, Pedro Eugenio 400–1

Ardizzone, Edward 413

Argentina 399, 400–1, 406–7, 410–11, 446, 448

Arias, Arnulfo 437, 441, 444, 450, 486

armadillo, nine-banded 308

Astor, David 180, 412

Asturias, Miguel Angel 410

Attenborough, Richard 165–6

Attlee, Clement 164

Auden, W. H. 75, 316, 329, 367

Auschwitz 264

Ayer, A. J. (Freddie) 210, 232, 273, 502

Baddeley, Hermione 148, 165–6

Bagnold, Enid 27

Bajeux, Jean-Claude 363, 364

Balaguer, Joaquín 365

Ball, Beatrice ('Twinkle') 191, 192

Ballestrino, Esther 401

Baltic States 78–9

Bangkok 247

Bank of London and Montreal 463

Banville, John, Book of Evidence 499

Bao Dai (Annamite emperor) 204, 205, 208, 221, 256–7, 259

Baptiste, Fred 363, 378, 379

Baptiste, Renel 363

Barbot, Clément 354, 355–6, 357, 359

Barclay, Edwin 87

Barrington-Ward, Robert 66
Basque territory 429, 432
Bastos, Augusto Roa 402
Batista, Fulgencio 278–9, 291–2, 293,
    294, 295, 299, 300
Baudouin, King of Belgium 312
Baytelman, David 411
BBC 33, 201, 294–5, 323, 385, 396–8,
    501
Beaton, Cecil 139
Beauclerk, Charles 180
Beaumont, Binkie 362
Begin, Menachem 390
Beirut 346–7, 494
Belfast 138–9
Belgium: missionaries in Vietnam
    xi–xii, 215, 245, 308, 314; and the
    Congo 82, 308–18
Belize 453–5
Bell, Kenneth 4, 22, 60
Bellamy, Ralph 185
Belloc, Hilaire 265
Ben Greet players 42
Ben Tre (Mekong Delta) 207, 221
Benedict XV, Pope 215
Beneš, Edvard 181
Bennett, Arnold 56
Benoit, François 356–7
Benoit, Rigaud 278
Benson, Theodora 75
Bergman, Ingrid 233, 326
Berkhamsted 2–3, 4, 6, 10, 13–17, 50,
    76, 82
Berkhamsted School 3–4, 6, 9–12,
    13–17, 21–2, 50, 202, 301, 349
Berkhamstedian (school magazine)
    23, 24
Berlin 78; Berlin Wall 347–9
Berlin, Isaiah 306
Bernanos, George, The Diary of a
    Country Priest 289–90
Bernstorff, Albrecht Graf von 27, 28,
    78
Berval, René de 217

Betjeman, John 102, 139
Bevan, Nye 298
Biche, Marie (née Schebeko) 188, 220,
    296, 330, 343, 344, 369, 370, 459;
    archive of GG's letters to xiv;
    GG hands Paris flat to 289, 506;
    GG buys a car for 423–4
Bilsborrow, Henry 61
Björk, Anita 229, 266–8, 277, 284–5,
    295–6, 303, 374, 458
Blackwell, Basil 34, 37, 40
Blanco, Luis Carrero 429
Bletchley Park 150, 152
Blixen, Karen, Out of Africa 235
Blond, Anthony 162
Bloy, Léon 122, 130, 198
Blum, Robert 221
Blundell, Michael 236
Blunden, Edmund 66–7
Blunt, Anthony 152
Bodleian Library (Oxford) 276
The Bodley Head 53, 60, 162, 331, 413,
    474–5, 498–9; GG as director
    at 225, 289–90, 338–9; Max
    Reinhardt acquires 289; GG
    moves from Heinemann to 338–9
Bolívar, Natalia 293
Bolivia 399, 411
Book Society 57, 66–7
book trade, second-hand 135–6, 323
Borge, Tomás 453, 469, 479, 485
Borges, Jorge Luis 410–11
Borovik, Genrikh 488–9, 490, 491,
    492, 495
Bosch, Juan 357, 365
Bossom, Sir Alfred 273
Bost, Pierre 270
Boston College 197, 505
Boucarut, Hô, 217, 319, 320, 321
Boucarut, Paul 217, 319–20, 321
Boulting brothers 165–6
Bourget, Caroline (daughter) xiv,
    91, 145, 163, 188, 212; birth of
    (1933) 75–6; on GG 76, 369; as

rancher in western Canada 163, 264, 270, 279–80, 295, 326, 327, 330; marries Jean Bourget 322–3, 344; death of son Richard (1962) 344–5; lives in Switzerland 416, 457, 504, 506

Bourget, Jean 322–3, 344

Bourget, Jonathan 416

Bowen, Elizabeth 102, 139, 180–1, 189

Bowen, Marjorie, *The Viper of Milan* 8–9

Bowlby, Cuthbert 137

Box, Sydney 166

Brain, Russell 195–6

Brandt, R. Van den 315

Brandt, Willy 348

Brazil 77, 399, 411

Brezhnev, Leonid 383, 427

Brighton 106–9, 174, 300

Brighton Rock (1938) xiii, 7, 64, 67, 95, 104, 419, 475–6; Catholic themes in 59, 105, 109–10, 147, 148, 165; and *The Green Cockatoo* 100; gramophone recording in 102, 109; GG on 104–5; mercy of God theme 105, 110; depiction of Brighton in 106, 108–9; plot 107, 108–10; as commercial success 124; GG horrified by stage version 148, 165; collection edition (1970) 339; Yvonne Cloetta on 414

Britain in Pictures series (Collins) 139

British American Tobacco Company 36, 39

British European Airways 328

British Film Institute 97

British Union of Fascists 76, 158

Brodie, Patrick Tait 144

Brompton Oratory 44, 50

Brook, Natasha (née Parry) 252, 253

Brook, Peter 252, 253, 270

Brown, William (Bishop of Southwark) 178

Browne, Sir Thomas, *Religio Medici* 54

Browning, Robert, 'Bishop Blougram's Apology' 397

Brownlow, Earl 2, 9

Bruce, William Speirs 9–10

Brussels 306, 311

Buchan, John 8, 25

Budberg, Moura 78, 79, 329

Bunker, Ellsworth 442

Burgess, Anthony 249, 424, 497–8

Burgess, Guy 152, 153, 328–9, 345, 346, 382

Burns, Tom 112, 434

A Burnt-Out Case (1961) 20, 89, 330, 365, 366, 370; Querry in 281, 313, 314, 315, 317–18, 325, 335–8; Father Damien as influence on 307; GG's research in the Congo 312–18; psychological theme of 313, 317, 318, 335–6; distress of writing of 325, 326, 327, 359; critical reception 335; and Catholicism 336, 337–8

Burstall, Christopher 396–8, 501

Burton, Richard 373–4, 378

Busch, Frederick 435

Bush, George W. xii–xiii

Butcher, Tim 85, 86, 88–9, 151

Buthelezi, Mangosuthu 420

Butler, Christopher 178

Cable Street, Battle of (4 October 1936) 76, 389

Cadco Developments 332–3

Caetano, Marcelo 428

Caine, Michael 405

Cairncross, John 152–3

Calder-Marshall, Arthur 94

Calles, Plutarco Elías 113, 116

Camacho, María de la Luz 123

Câmara, Dom Hélder 402

Cambodia 246

Cameron, A. C. 97

Cameron, Euan 475
Cameroon 319–21
Camp David Accords (1978) 390
Campion, Edmund 114
Camus, Albert 400
Canada 163, 264, 279–80, 295, 322–3, 326, 344–5, 387
Canaris, Wilhelm 150
Candler, James Hardie 237
Cannan, Denis 270
Canning, Victor, *The Limbo Line* 381
Cao Dai (religious sect in Vietnam) 207, 222
Capalbo, Carmen 281–2
capital punishment 71, 238–9
Capote, Truman 252–3, 358, 370
Capri, *see* Anacapri, Villa Rosaio in
Caraman, Philip 196, 230, 231, 371–2
Cardenal, Ernesto 451, 456, 469, 477, 479
Cárdenas, Lázaro 115, 116, 119
Carrigan, Ana, *Salvador Witness* 464
Carter, Jimmy 442, 445, 447–8, 450, 463–4
Carter, Lionel 14, 15, 17–18, 21, 202, 301
Cartmell, Joseph 177
Casson, Hugh 102
Casson, Sir Lewis 281
Castries, Christian de 244
Castro, Fidel 88, 303, 352, 375–7, 409, 411, 439, 448; leads guerrilla war from mountains 279, 293, 294, 295; victory of (1959) 299; political alliance with Moscow, 351, 355; GG's meetings with 376–7, 378, 481–2
Castro, Raúl 375
Catholic Action 117–18, 123, 215, 249
Catholicism: Belgian missionaries in Vietnam xi–xii, 215, 245, 308, 314; GG's confession in Phat Diem xi–xii, 257; doubt as counterpart of belief xiii,

xvi, 19, 43–4, 59–60, 159, 210, 223, 250, 280–1, 431, 502–3; GG's conversion to 4, 41–5, 50; belief-faith distinction 43–4, 59–60, 280–1, 336–7, 430, 433, 502–3; GG makes first confession (28 February 1926) 44–5; and contraception 50, 203; *Humanae Vitae* (encyclical, 1968) 50; marriage doctrine 50, 228; in novels before *Brighton Rock* 58; and deathbed repentance 59; mortal sin 59, 106, 109–10, 176, 203; resistance to the Nazis 64; and Barbara in Liberia 89; and modernity 94; belief in the Devil and Hell 105, 109, 408; Catholic literary revival 105; mercy of God theme 105, 110, 148, 177, 229, 407–8; *Rerum Novarum* (encyclical, 1891) 112; *Acerba Animi* (encyclical, 1932) 113–14; and communism 115, 130, 159, 208, 209, 348–9, 375, 376, 383, 493; theories of the just war 117; black Madonna in Guadalupe 118, 352; 'bootleg' Masses 122; indigenous faiths on the margins of 122, 240, 254; Léon Bloy on sainthood 122, 130; Council of Trent 129; Eucharist/communion 129, 176–7; *ex opere operato* concept 129; conditional absolution during war 135; and Jerrold 158, 159; 'sin of impurity' 176; GG's effect on Catholics 177, 191, 315; Second Vatican Council 178, 372; and Mauriac 189; mystical tradition 194, 196; and Eric Strauss 195, 196; Thomistic teaching 196, 281; dogma of the Assumption 200; GG's private audience with Pius XII 209–10; Pius XII and the Nazis 209; GG

attends Padre Pio's mass 210;
and end of European empires
215–16; in USA 216, 225, 258–9,
349–50, 376; missionaries in
Kenya 237–8; and Dr Tom
Dooley 260; in Poland 265–6;
'anonymous Christian' concept
337; Redemptorists 364; Latin
mass 372; in Cuba 375, 376;
Jesuit *reducciones* in Paraguay
398–9, 402; in Argentina 400,
401; liberation theology 401, 402;
Jesuits in modern Paraguay 402;
Golconda Group in Colombia
405; *Populorum Progressio*
(encyclical, 1967) 407; 'Third
World Movement' of priests
407; in Chile 411–12; Abbey of
St Maurice, Vevey 416; in El
Salvador 463; Maryknoll nuns
464, 479–80; GG returns to the
sacraments 502–3; *see also under*
entries for individual novels,
people, and countries
Caussade, Jean-Pierre de 194
Cavallera, Carlo Maria (Bishop of
Nyeri) 238
Cavendish Association 11
Cedillo, Saturnino 116–17, 119, 125
Céline, Louis-Ferdinand, *Voyage au
bout de la nuit* 101
Cerén, Salvador Sánchez 468–9, 485
Cerio, Edwin 182, 409
Cerio, Laetitia 182
Cerna, Lenin 479
Cervantes, Miguel de, *Don Quixote*
58, 431, 433
Chalmers, René 358–9
Chamberlain, Greg 363
Chamorra, Violeta 505
Chaplin, Charlie 53, 224–5, 290, 330,
333
Chardin, Teilhard de 194, 318, 408,
454

Chatto & Windus 75, 101, 103, 160,
498
Chautemps, Camille 77
Chernenko, Konstantin 427
Chiang Kai-shek 204, 205
Chiapas (Mexico) 120–2, 141
Chiapas, Bishop of 117
Chile 400, 409–10, 411–12, 446, 493
China 36, 39, 62, 205, 285–7
Chipping Campden 60–2, 66, 68–9
Chorley, Robert 285, 286–7
Christie, Cuthbert 80–1, 88
Christie, James 44, 50, 51
Church, Richard 176
Churchill, Randolph 181, 182, 273
Churchill, Winston 6, 20, 99, 164,
233, 236, 324
Cienfuegos, Camilo 279
Clairouin, Denyse 77, 82, 91, 142, 188
Clemons, Walter 395
Cloetta, Jacques 320, 321, 369, 414,
472, 473
Cloetta, Yvonne (née Guével):
memoir published by xv; and
Gillian Sutro 275; background
of 320; children of 320, 369,
415, 416, 472–6, 477; meets GG
320, 321, 322; and GG's mood
disorder 325, 414; personal
qualities of 326, 414–15; and
Catherine Walston 326, 369, 458;
and GG's move to France 368–9;
on Dorothy's death 413; criminal
gang threat to 462, 472–6, 477;
with GG in Soviet Union 488,
489, 490, 494, 495–6; and GG's
final illness 504, 505, 506–7;
moves to Switzerland with GG
(1990) 505–6
Cochrane, Robert 335
Cockburn, Claud 21, 24, 26, 27–8, 29,
52, 111, 288
Coe, Jonathan 487
Coggan, Donald 344

Cogny, General René 243, 244, 247, 260–1

Colette (French author) 248

College of Arms 324

Collins, Joseph Lawton 258

Collins, Michael 25

Colombia 405–6

Columbus, Christopher 470

Colvin, Sidney 5

The Comedians (1966) 253, 254, 334, 354, 357, 359–60, 362–7, 439; the Oloffson as setting for 278, 358, 359, 370, 378; play within a play technique 336, 366; title of 358, 362, 366; as critical and popular success 370, 371; Pap Doc's response to 373, 379–80

communism: British Communist Party 29, 47, 70, 224, 255; and Catholicism 115, 130, 159, 208, 209, 348–9, 375, 376, 383, 493; dialogue with Catholicism in GG's later work 130, 159; coup in Czechoslovakia (1948) 181; MRLA in Malaya 200, 201; in China 205, 285–7; and war in Vietnam 205, 208, 214, 215–16, 222, 226, 244, 393; McCarran Act in USA (1950) 224, 225, 254–5; Tito's Yugoslavia 233, 234; and Castro 299, 375, 409; GG in East Germany (1963) 348–9; and liberation theology 401, 402

Comyns, Barbara 289

Congo 82, 104, 308–18, 419; leproseries in 33, 306, 308, 309–10, 312–15, 316–17, 318, 319; GG's travel in (1959) 311, 312–18

Congreve, William 139

Conrad, Joseph 40, 57, 70, 183, 316, 417; *Heart of Darkness* 86, 104, 307, 309, 316, 443

Conservative Party 164, 165

Contreras, Eduardo 446–7

Contreras, Dr Ramiro 446–7, 451–2

Cooper, Duff 125

Corbett, Harry H. 270

Cordery, Mrs 368

Cornwell, David (John le Carré) xiii, 156–7, 297, 382–3, 486, 488–9

Cornwell, John 209, 210

Costa Rica 119, 455

Cotten, Joseph 185

Coward, Noël 185, 302, 330

Cowgill, Felix 154

Crompton, David and Lillian 167

Crosby, Bing 144

Crosthwaite-Eyre, Oliver 290

Crowborough (East Sussex) 50, 106, 127, 322, 345–6, 413

Cuba: GG's visits to 255, 278–9, 291–5, 298, 300, 302–3, 352–3, 374–7, 481–2; Batista regime 278–9, 291–5, 297–9, 300; Moncada Barracks attack (1953) 279, 295, 374–5; British arms sales to Batista 292, 295, 297–9; victory of Fidel Castro's forces (1959) 299; filming of *Our Man in Havana* 302–3; Cuban Missile Crisis (1962) 347, 351; Bay of Pigs operation (1961) 351; Castro allies with Moscow, 351, 355, 375; human rights abuses under Castro 353, 375, 409, 456; exile raids from Dominican Republic 365; art 376; collectivisation of land in 411; *Granma* (official newspaper of government) 466

Culver, Roland 361

Cunninghame Graham, R. B. 57, 398, 399

Czechoslovakia 124–5, 181, 355, 375, 385–7, 409, 450, 488

Częstochowa, Virgin of 265

Dachau camp 64–5

Dagerman, Stig 229, 266–7, 290, 303

Dahomey 378
Daily Telegraph 64–5, 374, 408–9
Dale, F. 'Dicker' 301
Damien, Father (St Damien of
    Molokai) 307
Dane, Clemence 57
Daniel, Yuliy 383–5, 488
Dansey, Claude ('Z') 98–9
D'Arcy, Martin 169
Darr, Richard 289
Dasnoy, Édith 309, 314
Davis, Elwood 87–8
Dawes Agreement 28
Dawkins, Richard 210
Dawson, Geoffrey 36, 55
Dayan, Moshe 388, 389
Dayan, Yael 388
Dayrell-Browning, Marion 37–8, 47,
    51, 69, 77–8
De Beers 395–6
De Gaulle, Charles 341
De la Espriella, Ricardo 477–8
De la Mare, Walter 18
De Varg, Meredith 343
Dean, Basil 97, 98, 192–3, 229
Déjoie, Louis 353, 360
Delargy, Hugh 298–9, 300
Dementyev, Andrei 495
Dempster, Fergus 260
Denham (village in
    Buckinghamshire) 99
Dennis, Nigel 404
Dennys, Elisabeth (sister) 30, 51,
    227, 239, 323–4, 415, 425,
    494–5; becomes GG's secretary
    (1975) 5, 423; in MI6 G
    Section 5, 137, 205; in Istanbul
    with Rodney 212, 345; GG's
    financial support for children of
    288, 324; lives in Crowborough
    345, 413, 423; GG gifts his
    archives to 505
Dennys, Louise (niece) 324, 387, 409
Dennys, Nick (niece) 324

Dennys, Rodney 323–4, 345, 350, 386,
    413, 425, 426, 505
Déry, Tibor 385
detective fiction 102, 104–5, 110, 136,
    146
Díaz, Porfirio 112
Díaz Herrera Roberto 478, 479, 481,
    482, 485–6
Dickens, Charles, *Great Expectations*
    197
Diederich, Bernard xiv, 218, 254, 294,
    359, 360, 365, 464; as journalist
    in Port-au-Prince 254, 255, 278,
    354, 355, 356, 358; deported to
    Dominican Republic 356; at Port-
    au-Prince memorial service (2013)
    357; visits Dominican Republic
    border with GG (1965) 360, 363–5;
    and Panama 439–43, 445–6, 450–1,
    452, 466, 467, 468, 471, 505; and
    Nicaragua 452–3, 455–6, 469, 479
Disney, Walt 53
Dobraczyński, Jan 265
domestic abuse 472–6
Dominican Republic 356, 357, 360,
    362–5, 478
Donlon, Seán 499–500
Donne, John 59
Donovan, Jean 464
Dooley, John 216
Dooley, Dr Tom 260, 262
Doubleday, Doran (publisher) 54, 55,
    58, 66, 68
Douglas, Norman 183
Doyle, Arthur Conan 422
Drabble, Margaret 106, 461
Drake, Sir Francis 452, 470
Drinan, Adam (Joseph Macleod) 33
Duarte, José Napoleón 462, 485
Dubček, Alexander 385, 493
Duffell, Peter 405
Dukes, Gerry 499–500
Dunn, Archibald Gardner 465,
    467–9, 480–1

Dunne, J. W. *An Experiment with Time* (1927) 19
Durán, Leopoldo xiv, 20, 239, 429–34, 465, 484, 492, 507
Duvalier, François 'Papa Doc' 253, 254, 353–60, 366, 373, 378, 439
Duvalier, Jean-Claude 356

Eden, Anthony 81
Eder, Richard 359
Eisenhower, Dwight D. 226, 246
El Salvador 462–8, 480–1, 483, 485, 493, 504; Castro's view of 481–2
El Taboso (Spain) 433
Elastoplast 178
electro-shock therapy 2, 195, 196, 372
elephantiasis 313
Eliot, T. S. 33, 95, 105, 174, 175, 265
Elliott, Nicholas 142, 155, 346–7, 494–5
Ellison, Ralph, *Invisible Man* 250
The End of the Affair (1951) xiii, 5, 162, 213, 225, 306; and GG's relationship with Catherine xv, 170, 198, 211; and Catholicism 105, 199, 212, 213, 249; first-person narration 197–8
Erskine, George 237
ETA (Basque separatists) 429
Evans, Charles 47–8, 53–4, 55, 56–7, 66, 67, 82
Evans, Julian 371, 414
Eyre & Spottiswoode 155, 158–61, 170, 181, 187, 188, 290

Falk, Quentin 100
Farabundo Martí National Liberation Front (FMLN) 464, 483, 485
fascism 5, 98, 429, 431; Nazis in Germany 63, 64–5, 78, 99, 117, 161, 209; Mosley's Blackshirts 76, 158; in France 77; in Portugal 149, 277, 428–9; in Spain 149, 429, 430, 431

Faulkner, William 199, 213
Fernández, Ernesto 374
Fernández, Pablo Armando 374
Fernando Po (Spanish island) 81
Fignolé, Daniel 353
Fiji 326
film industry: GG's writing about at Oxford 36–7, 53; Cinematograph Films Act (1928) 53; coming of talkies 53; rights for GG novels 67, 68, 95–6, 147, 299–300, 370; GG as film reviewer 68, 92, 97, 98, 102–3; GG on film reviewing 102; GG's contracts with MGM (1944/46) 156, 161–2; awards/prizes for *The Fallen Idol* 174; GG's method of script production 183; blacklists in USA 225; Anita Björk's career 266–7
Finland 78
Firestone (tyre manufacturer) 81, 85, 88
First World War 12, 13, 20–1
Fleming, Ian 231, 297
Fleming, Peter 80, 101
Flemyng, Robert 281
Flood, Danielle 217
Foley, Frank 138
Fonteyn, Margot 212, 344
Footman, David 329
Ford, Ford Madox 71–2, 290
Ford, Gerald 442
Ford, John 130
Ford Motor Company 81
Fordham, Stanley 291–2, 299
Forster, E. M. 198, 383
France: in Vietnam xi–xii, 33, 204–5, 206–7, 214–16, 218–21, 222, 241–6, 247, 257–8; occupation forces in Germany 26–7, 28, 56; GG visits communists in Paris (1925) 29, 70; GG's honeymoon in 51; French resistance 77, 142,

161; Stavisky Affair 77; Colonial Office 82; Vichy forces 142, 143, 204; GG's literary business in 188, 423–4; German occupation 320; Algerian war (1954–62) 341–2; GG becomes resident of (1966) 368–9; organized crime in 455, 472–6, 477; GG returns Legion of Honour insignia 473–4; *see also* Paris

Francis, Pope (Jorge Bergoglio) 401, 451

Franck, Frederick 310

Franco, Francisco 111, 149, 153, 158, 429, 430, 432

Franks, Sir Dick ('C') 426

Franqui, Carlos 375, 376

Fraser, Lionel 338–9

French Guinea 86, 142, 143

Frere, A. S. 54, 199, 273, 339, 415, 424, 459

Friend-Smith, Ernest 107

Frost, Robert 316

Fry, Thomas Charles 3–4, 9, 43

Fryer, Robert 404–5

Fuentes, Carlos 479

Fuller, Father 240

Fulton, James 205

Fyodorov, Svyatoslav 495

Gabon 81

Galbraith, John Kenneth 496

Gambiez, Fernand 246

gang warfare in Britain (1920s and 30s) 107–8

García, Gabriel 120

García, Juan Pujol ('Garbo') 151–2

Garrido y Canabal, Tomás 119, 120, 123

General Strike (May 1926) 46–7, 76

George V's Silver Jubilee (1935) 92

Georges, Jean-Baptiste 379

Germany: occupied Ruhr 26–7, 28; GG visits as journalist (1924) 27–8; GG's support for in 1920s 27–9, 56; research for *Stamboul Train* 63–4; rise of Nazis in 63, 64; Nazi persecution of Jews 64–5; Catholic resistance to Nazis 64; GG visits Berlin (1934) 78; von Stauffenberg's plot (1944) 150; Goslar (Lower Saxony) 193–4; Berlin Wall 347–9

Giap, General Vo Nguyen 243

Gielgud, John 282, 304, 362

Gilbert, Sir Martin 209

Gilby, Thomas 188, 230–1

Gilmour, Ian 272

Gilson,Captain, *The Pirate Aeroplane* 8

Girodias, Maurice 272

Giscard d'Estaing, Valéry 474

Glenalmond House (St Albans) 149, 150, 152, 153

Glenrothes (Fife) 332–3, 366–7

Glenville, Peter 228, 370, 373, 378–80

Glover, Dorothy xv, 126–7, 128, 136, 140–1, 170, 175, 296; children's books by 126–7, 162, 413; GG's financial support for 127, 288, 413; with GG in WW2 London 133, 134, 148, 163–4, 198; designing of book covers 161; affair with GG ends 171; trip to Morocco with GG (1948) 171, 184; death of (1971) 413–14, 506

Gnosticism 408

Goa 361

Golding, William 497–8

Golitsyn, Anatoliy 346

Gollancz, Victor 143

González, Rory 441, 466

Gorbachev, Mikhail 427, 488, 492, 493

Gordon, John 272–3, 290

Gottwald, Klement 181

GPO Film Unit 97

Graham Greene Productions 331

Grand Hotel (Edmund Goulding film, 1932) 63
Grande, Rutilio 463
Graves, Robert 24
Green, Eva (aunt) 6, 20
Green-Armytage, Alfred 51
Green-Armytage, Vivian 69
Greene, Alice (aunt) 7
Greene, Anne (née Cucksey, wife of Francis) 416
Greene, Barbara (cousin) 6, 82–4, 85, 86–7, 88, 89–90, 396
Greene, Benjamin (cousin) 6, 76
Greene, Benjamin (great-grandfather) 4, 81
Greene, Charles (father) 3–4, 16–17, 27, 50, 81, 106, 127; and Berkhamsted School 3–4, 9, 10, 11, 50; death of (1942) 145
Greene, Edward 'Eppy' (uncle) 6, 16, 50, 82–3
Greene, Edward 'Tooter' (cousin) 6, 25, 27–8, 82
Greene, Eva 'Ave' (cousin) 6, 20
Greene, Felix (cousin) 6
Greene, Francis Charles Bartley (son) 96, 163, 170, 188, 212, 263–4, 323, 505; and Russia 323, 350; and *The Quiet American* copyright 331; as war reporter 391–2; married life in Devon 416
Greene, Graham, BIPOLAR ILLNESS: boredom as debilitating feature of xvi, 15, 30, 31, 33, 36, 40, 141; inclination to suicide xvi, 15, 17, 31–3, 49–50, 141, 171, 193, 195, 340, 395; psychoanalytic treatment for 2, 18, 19–20, 31, 49, 171, 195–6, 263; writing as form of therapy 2, 196; mental illness in family 4–5; depression in childhood 13, 15, 16–18; self-harming in childhood 14, 15, 16, 395;

excessive irritability 15, 69–70, 118, 263, 286, 287; crisis at school (summer 1920) 16–17, 157; GG describes to Vivien 171, 195; crises during 1950–62 period 193, 194–5, 201, 325–6, 340; at its worst in the 1950s 193, 195–6, 246–7, 266, 369; suicide attempt 193; improved mood after 1950s 369–70, 414
Greene, Graham, CHARACTER: defence of dissidents/underdogs xvi, 153, 154, 156, 325, 349–50; dislike of children 7, 284; payments to family/friends/ writers 74, 288–9, 322, 323, 331, 423–4; Barbara Greene on 83; fascination with charismatic strongmen 88, 220, 411; quest for absolutes 141; sympathy for the disgraced 152–3, 183, 349–50, 382, 383, 495; Jerrold on 159; practical jokes 159, 180–1, 232–3, 238; appetite for conflict 187, 350; self-loathing 306–7; fear in Haiti 358, 360, 362–3
Greene, Graham, FILMS (GG scripts and/or based on GG's work): *Orient Express* (Paul Martin, 1934) 68, 83; *The Fallen Idol* (Carol Reed, 1948) 92, 162, 173–4; *Twenty-One Days* (Basil Dean, 1940) 97–8, 192; *The Green Cockatoo* (William Cameron Menzies, 1937) 99, 100, 106; *Brighton Rock* (John Boulting, 1948) 127, 165–6; *The Confidential Agent* (Herman Shumlin, 1945) 128–9; *The Fugitive* (John Ford, 1947) 130; *The Third Man* (Carol Reed, 1949) 155, 179–81, 182, 183–4, 185–6; *The Man Within* (Bernard Knowles, 1947) 166; *The Quiet American* (Joseph L.

Mankiewicz, 1958) 166, 270, 300; 'No Man's Land' (abandoned film idea) 193–4; *The End of the Affair* (Edward Dmytryk, 1955) 224; *The Comedians* (Peter Glenville, 1967) 228, 370, 373–4, 378–80; *The Heart of the Matter* (George More O'Ferrall, 1953) 229; *The Stranger's Hand* (Mario Soldati, 1954) 233–4, 415; *Loser Takes All* (Ken Annakin, 1956) 251; *Saint Joan* (Otto Preminger, 1957) 277; *Our Man in Havana* (Carol Reed, 1959) 300, 302–3, 304; *Travels with My Aunt* (1972) 404–5; *England Made Me* (Peter Duffell, 1972) 405; *The Honorary Consul* (*Beyond the Limit*) (John Mackenzie, 1983) 405; *The Human Factor* (Otto Preminger, 1979) 405

Greene, Graham, HEALTH:
adenoids and tonsils removed 2, 7; childhood illnesses 2, 13, 15, 16–18, 21, 49; epilepsy diagnosed 21, 49–50; appendectomy (October 1926) 48, 74; hay fever and asthma 61; serious fever in Liberia 89–90; dysentery in Mexico 122–3; use of amphetamines 125–6, 193, 281–2, 325; haemorrhage in urinary tract (1948) 184–5; use of barbiturates 193; abdominal pains 301–2; cancer as rife in family 302; colectomy (1979) 302, 460; pneumonia (1960) 328–30; Celevac (medication) 420–1; lumbago attack (1973) 420–1; digestive trouble 421; dental problems (1974) 422, 424; decline (from 1989) 500, 503–4, 505–7; *see also* Greene, Graham, BIPOLAR ILLNESS

Greene, Graham, JOURNALISM:
articles on Irish Civil War 25–6; in Germany (1924) 27–8; for *Oxford Outlook* 28, 36–7; on film industry 36–7, 53; at *Nottingham Journal* 40–1; sub-editor on *The Times* 46–7, 52–3; leaves *The Times* (1929) 55; passion play at Oberammergau 56–7; as film reviewer 68, 92, 97, 98, 102–3; reviews fiction for *Spectator* 68, 92, 102; Stavisky Affair in Paris 77; literary editor of *Night and Day* 101–3; literary editor of *Spectator* (1940–1) 134; *Evening Standard* book column 165; for *Life* in Malaya/Vietnam 200, 206, 208, 209, 219, 226–7; article on Pius XII 209–10; public letter to Chaplin 225; 'Indo-China: France's Crown of Thorns' (1952) 226–7; for *Sunday Times* 236, 239–40, 242, 247, 261–2, 264–5, 361; 'A Third Man Entertainment on Security in Room 51' 349–50; for *Sunday Telegraph* 351, 353, 360, 362–3, 388–90, 391; 'Return to Cuba' (article, 1963) 353; 'The Nightmare Republic' (article, 1963) 360, 362–3; for *Daily Telegraph* in Cuba 374–7; 'The Soupsweet Land' (article) 395; on Paraguay 403; 'Chile: The Dangerous Edge' (1971) 412; 'The Country with Five Frontiers' (1977) 444–5, 446; 'The Great Spectacular' 448

Greene, Graham, LITERARY LIFE:
existing biographies of xiv, 416–18; loyalty and betrayal narratives xv–xvi, 49, 58, 148, 155, 173–4, 189, 301, 381, 456, 484; term 'involvement' xv–xvi;

Greene, Graham, LITERARY
LIFE – *continued*

'Catholic novelist' tag xvi,
105–6, 199, 225; faith theme xvi,
105–6, 194–5, 213, 282–3, 284,
336–7, 430; core of nostalgia or
sentimentality 7, 80, 94, 251,
395; fascination with men on
the run 8, 49, 64, 119–20, 128,
129–30; writing in childhood
9; poems 18, 24, 32, 33, 34, 47,
230; attention to dreams 19,
20, 26, 67, 71, 147, 398, 484,
506; first published story 23–4;
early fiction writing 34–5,
47–9, 53–9; five hundred words
per day 41, 197; Nottingham
settings 41; repulsive character
as 'hero' 48–9, 95, 109; traces of
himself in fictional characters
49, 74, 130, 144–5, 175, 336–7;
use of foolscap 49, 291, 407;
Catholicism in before *Brighton
Rock* 58; debt to Heinemann
66, 67; characters taking on
life of their own 74–5, 144–5,
434; female characters 74,
281, 343; arrangement with
Hamish Hamilton 92–3;
discovers/promotes Narayan
93–4; 'Greeneland' 94, 141,
184, 220, 293, 454; 'Novels' and
'Entertainments' distinction
95, 146, 394; pseudonym Hilary
Trench 95; pity and compassion
themes 109, 146, 147, 407–8;
papers sold to US universities
126; comic fiction 146, 251,
361, 394, 402, 404, 430, 435;
works for Eyre & Spottiswoode
155, 158–61, 170, 181, 187, 188;
MGM contracts 156, 161–2; and
first-person narration 197–8;

third-person perspective 197;
writes in longhand 197; and
Nobel Prize 199; numbers as a
leitmotif 212, 251; as director at
the Bodley Head 225, 289–90,
338–9; *Collected Edition* volumes
331, 339, 395, 408–9; play within
a play technique 335–6, 366;
problem of the 'Judas' 349; leaves
Viking for Simon & Schuster
(1970) 370–1, 404; television
interview (April 1968) 396–8,
501; GG on writing a novel 434;
Borovik's documentary on (1988)
489, 495; conflict with Anthony
Burgess 497–8; leaves Bodley
Head 498

Greene, Graham, PERSONAL LIFE:
growth of body of evidence on
xiv–xv; existing biographies of
xiv, 416–18; personal mythology
on trust and betrayal xv–xvi,
13, 14, 231, 270, 300, 349–50,
383, 395; childhood and school
days 1–3, 5–12, 13–17, 18–22,
31, 49–50, 157, 301, 349; phobia
of birds 2, 121, 253; journey on
foot through Liberia 6, 33, 80,
81–4, 86–90, 94, 140, 307–8; at
Balliol 22, 23–5, 27, 29, 30, 31,
32, 33–5; friendship with Waugh
24, 190, 211–12, 248, 336–7, 342,
371; love for Gwen Howell 30–1;
Russian roulette story 31–3,
482; alcohol consumption 31,
184–5, 252, 260, 483, 490; gains
second in History at Oxford 36;
use of prostitutes 39–40, 68–9,
74; as private tutor in Ashover
40; as special constable during
General Strike 46, 76; expresses
gratitude to his parents 50–1;
honeymoon in south of France
51; marries Vivienne (1927) 51;

expects to die young 59; as avid rambler/walker 60–1; lives in Chipping Campden 60–2, 66, 68–9; money problems in early 1930s 65–8, 288; lives in Oxford 69–70; driving 75; at Battle of Cable Street (4 October 1936) 76, 389; as distant father 76, 148, 163, 263–4, 416; flying 77; house at 14 Clapham Common North Side 91, 133–4; at Ministry of Information in WW2, 132–3; book collecting 135–6, 323; WW2 intelligence work 137–45, 146, 149–53, 154–7, 277; gives up smoking during WW2, 140; resigns from MI6 (June 1944) 154–6; flat at 5 St James's Street 187–8, 197, 231; ties to England loosen 188; Dictaphone for personal correspondence 197; closeness to brother Hugh 201, 323, 490–1, 493–4; collects licence-plate numbers 211–12; smoking of opium 223, 231, 246–7, 260, 261, 263; friendship with Chaplin 224–5, 290; refusals to be interviewed 225–6; lives at Albany, Piccadilly 231, 264, 289; affair with Jocelyn Rickards 232, 502; use of heroin 246; liaison with Mercia Ryhiner 247, 266, 476; smoking of marijuana 255; affair with Anita Björk 267–8, 277, 284–5, 295–6, 458; friendship with the Sutros 273–6, 350, 368; flat in Paris's seventeenth arrondissement 289, 330, 342, 506; final break with Anita Björk 296; money worries in early 1960s 330–4; Thomas Roe swindle 330–4, 366–7, 370; as tax exile 330, 331–2, 368; impersonators of

343; honorary doctorate from Cambridge 344; becomes resident of France (1966) 368–9; named Companion of Honour (1966) 368; fortunes restored by *The Comedians* 370, 371; Antibes becomes permanent home 371; meetings with Castro 376–7, 378, 481–2; Jerusalem Prize for the Freedom of the Individual in Society (1981) 391; plays small part in Truffaut's *La Nuit américaine* 415; domestic tasks 416; correspondence with Philby (from 1978) 424–6; wish to meet Philby (1970s/80s) 424–6, 488–9; at Panama treaty signing in Washington (1977) 447–9; war against the mafia in Nice 455, 472–6, 477; and hostages in El Salvador 462, 463, 465–9, 480–1; and FMLN in El Salvador 464, 483, 485; meetings with Philby (Moscow, 1986/87) 488, 489–90, 494–5; death of (3 April 1991) 507

Greene, Graham, VIEWS AND OPINIONS: anti-Americanism xii–xiii, xvi, 115, 349–50, 374, 382, 384, 393, 412, 478, 486; on Cold War xii, xvi, 347, 348–50, 383–4, 493; pro-German in 1920s 27–9, 56; on colour prejudice 28; joins Oxford branch of Communist Party 29, 47, 224, 255; on Joyce's *Ulysses* 29; on General Strike (May 1926) 46–7, 76; on atheism/unbelief 59–60, 210; hatred of income tax 76, 182, 330, 331–2, 368; joins ILP 76; anti-imperialist 85, 86, 236, 238–9; on primitivism 86, 94; on sexualization of children 102–3; on Munich Agreement 125; on

Greene, Graham, VIEWS AND OPINIONS – *continued*

expatriates in Africa 143; on Cambridge spy ring 153, 154, 156, 347, 349–50, 382, 383; interest in the left 158–9; party preference 164–5; on Czechoslovakia 181, 385–7, 488; on the English novel 198–9; on identity in philosophy 198–9; on McCarthyism 224–5; on domino theory 226; on partition in Vietnam 256; on Chinese Communist regime 285–7; on Castro's Cuba 299, 351, 353, 374, 375, 377, 409, 411, 456, 466; on idea of an afterlife 322, 501–2, 506–7; on Algerian war 341–2; response to Philby's defection 347, 349–50, 382, 383; art and political change 367, 378, 379, 393; on Soviet Union 383–5, 488, 492–3; on Israel 390–1; on war reporting 392; on Vietnam War 393; non-Marxist alternatives to capitalism 399; on liberation theology 401, 402; on faith, hope, and charity 416; on KGB 426–7; on mystics 433; preference for social democracy 450; on Sandinistas 456; on rebel movements 467; on Purgatory 501; theological views as conservative 503

Greene, Graham, WORKS: 'Across the Bridge' (short story) 166, 277; 'Anthony Sant' (rejected first novel) 34, 47, 301; 'An Appointment with the General' (short story) 444; *Babbling April* (poems, 1925) 34, 40, 230; 'The Basement Room' (short story) 92, 162, 173–4, 301, 484; *British Dramatists* (non-fiction) 139; *The Captain and the Enemy* 301, 450, 452, 484–5, 486–7, 494, 498, 507; *Carving a Statue* (play, 1964) 304, 352, 361–2; 'Cheap in August' (short story) 325; 'Church Militant' (short story) 238; *The Complaisant Lover* (play, 1959) 270, 301, 303–5, 362; *The Confidential Agent* 125, 128–9, 306; 'Dear Dr Falkenheim' (short story, 1963) 280, 282; *Doctor Fischer of Geneva or The Bomb Party* (novella) 457–8, 459–61; 'The Empty Chair' (unfinished murder mystery, 1926) 35; 'The End of the Party' (short story) 58–9; *England Made Me* 8, 66, 73–5, 92, 104, 152; 'The Episode' (historical novel) 40, 47–8, 49; 'Fanatic Arabia' (unfinished) 104; 'Under the Garden' (short story) 329, 339; *Getting to Know the General* (non-fiction, 1984) 446, 473, 477, 483–4; *The Great Jowett* (radio play, 1939) 125; *A Gun for Sale* 41, 64, 92, 95–6, 104; *The Honorary Consul* (1973) 57, 117–18, 401, 405–8, 409, 421, 458; 'I Do Not Believe' (poem) 230; *It's a Battlefield* (1934) 20, 57, 66, 70–1, 73, 107; *J'Accuse* (pamphlet, 1982) 472–3, 474–5, 476, 477; *Journey Without Maps* 82, 94, 96; 'The Last Decade' (autobiographical memoir, 1964) 395; *The Last Word and Other Stories* 498; *The Lawless Roads* 14, 112, 116, 117, 125; 'The Leader' (plan for novel, 1938) 104; *The Little Fire Engine* (with Glover) 162; *The Little Train* (with Glover) 126–7; *The Living Room* (play) 59, 162, 228–9, 266, 275, 370;

Lord Rochester's Monkey 59–60, 65, 174, 210; *Loser Takes All* (novella, 1955) 250–1, 261, 339; 'Lucius' (unfinished novel) 301, 484; *The Man Within* (1929) 48–9, 52, 53–6, 57, 61–2, 95, 106, 155, 301, 484; 'May We Borrow Your Husband' (short story, 1962) 326, 339–40; 'Men at Work' (short story, 1941) 132; *The Ministry of Fear* (1943) 8, 66, 146–8, 457; *Monsignor Quixote* (1982) xiv, 20, 58, 223, 239, 429–35, 444, 459, 482, 484; 'My Worst Film' (essay, 1987) 98; *The Name of Action* (1930) 57, 58; *Nineteen Stories* (short story collection, 1947) 104, 162, 173; *The Old School* (ed. volume of essays, 1934) 75; 'The Other Side of the Border' (short story) 104; *The Potting Shed* (play) 41, 138–9, 259, 270, 279, 281–3, 284; *Reflections* (prose collection, ed. Judith Adamson) 227, 498; *Refugee Ship* (non-fiction book) 65; *The Return of A. J. Raffles* (play) 422–3, 430; *Rumour at Nightfall* (1931) 57–8, 59, 62, 217; 'Sad Cure' (unpublished poetry collection) 40, 47; *In Search of a Character: Two African Journals* 338; *The Spy's Bedside Book* (anthology, with Hugh Greene) 323; *Stamboul Train* (1932) 63–4, 65, 66–7, 83, 91, 397, 501; 'The Stranger's Hand' (short story) 232–3; *The Tenth Man* (story/film script) 161–2, 165, 183; *The Third Man* (novella) 162, 183, 484; 'Tick Tock' (short story) 23–4; *Travels with My Aunt* (1969) 9, 168, 227, 394–5, 398, 401–3, 404, 407; *Travels with My Aunt* (1972)

419; 'The Virtue of Disloyalty' (lecture in Hamburg, 1969) 189, 456; 'A Visit to Morin' (short story, 1956) 280–1, 336; 'On the Way Back' (unfinished novel) 434, 443–4, 470, 477; *Ways of Escape* (memoir, 1980) 226–7, 282, 298, 408–9; *For Whom the Bell Chimes* (short play) 460; *A World of My Own: A Dream Diary* 20, 498, 506; *Yes and No* (short play) 460; *Yours Etc: Letters to the Press 1945–89* (ed. Christopher Hawtree) 498; *see also* separate entries for: *Brighton Rock* (1938); *A Burnt-Out Case* (1961); *The Comedians* (1966); *The End of the Affair* (1951); *The Heart of the Matter* (1948); *The Human Factor* (1978); *Our Man in Havana* (1958); *The Power and the Glory* (1940); *The Quiet American* (1955); *A Sort of Life* (memoir, 1971)

Greene, Graham C. (nephew) 425, 463, 498–9

Greene, Herbert (brother) 5, 12, 13–14, 20, 74, 104, 111, 322; GG's financial support for 288, 323; death of (1969) 323

Greene, Hugh (brother) 4, 10, 30, 73, 82, 127, 136, 205, 444–5; at BBC 5, 294–5, 323; *Telegraph* correspondent in Berlin 64–5, 78, 99; and psychological warfare in Malaya 200, 201, 203; closeness to GG 201, 323, 490–1, 493–4; ill health 490–1, 493–4; death of (1987) 494

Greene, James (nephew) 494

Greene, Katharine (cousin) 6

Greene, Marion (mother) 4–5, 10, 16, 17, 145, 322; lives in Crowborough 50, 106, 127, 322,

Greene, Marion – *continued*
345, 413; and son Herbert 74,
322; GG's financial support for
288, 322; death of (1959) 322
Greene, Maud (aunt) 5
Greene, Nora 'Nono' (aunt) 5, 322
Greene, Oliver (nephew) 32
Greene, Raymond (brother) 1, 5,
10, 13–14, 20, 46, 51, 195, 322;
and GG's health 18, 48, 50,
301–2; owns revolver 31, 32; sets
standard for daring 80; death of
(1982) 490
Greene, Reverend Carleton 4–5
Greene, Sarah (wife of Hugh) 494
Greene, Sir (William) Graham
(uncle) 5–6, 18, 70, 83
Greene, Vivien (née Dayrell-
Browning, wife): background
of 37–8; Catholicism of 37,
38–9, 41–3, 44, 45, 49–50,
223; character of 37, 127; GG's
courtship of 38–9, 47, 49–50;
marries GG (1927) 51; travel
with GG 55, 56–7, 114–15, 171;
lives in Chipping Campden
60–2, 66, 68–9; money
problems in early 1930s 65–6;
and GG's use of prostitutes
68–9; pregnancy 68–9; lives in
Oxford with GG 69–70; birth
of daughter Lucy Caroline 75–6;
antique furniture collection 91,
133–4; house at 14 Clapham
Common North Side 91, 133–4;
as world's authority on doll's
houses 91, 170, 288; dinner
with T. S. Eliot 95; birth of son
Francis (1936) 96; deterioration
of marriage 126, 127, 133, 148,
163; evacuated to Crowborough
127; in Oxford during WW2,
127, 148, 163; and Catherine
Walston 169, 170–1; break-up

of marriage 171–2, 195, 322;
refuses annulment and divorce
171–2, 191–2; and *The Heart of
the Matter* 175; and GG after
marriage break-up 187, 264, 288,
295, 331, 344; lives at Grove
House at Iffley Turn 187, 288
Greene, William (grandfather) 4
Greenwood, Walter 75
Grieg, Harald 62, 266
Grieg, Nordahl 61–2, 78, 266
Grierson, John 97
Griffin, Bernard (Cardinal
Archbishop of Westminster) 248,
249
Gromyko, Andrei 351
Guaraní people 398–9, 402
Guatemala 118, 120, 405, 453–4
Guest, Eric 21
Guevara, Che 279, 353
Guinea Bissau 428
Guinness, Alec 231, 251, 302, 362,
374, 379
Guinness, Samuel 273
Guinness Peat Aviation (GPA) Prize
499–500
Gurkhas 201–2, 203, 204

Habeas (Márquez's organisation) 463
Hafenrichter, Oswald 186
Haggard, Rider *She* 8, 420
Hague, William 240
Haig, Earl 20
Haiti: GG's visits to 252–5, 278, 357–
60; Duvalier's tyranny/brutality
253, 354–60, 366, 378, 439;
massacre in Dominican Republic
(1937) 253, 364; pre-1950s history
of 253; Oloffson hotel (Port-au-
Prince) 278, 358, 359, 370, 378;
schools of art 278, 360; Duvalier's
takeover of 353–5; Benoit
massacre (1963) 356–7; rebel
bands in Dominican Republic

356, 357–8, 363, 364; Pap Doc's response to *The Comedians* 373, 379–80
Hall, Richard 412
Hamilton, Willie 333
Hamish Hamilton Ltd 92–3
Hanoi 207, 208, 214, 242, 243, 244, 260, 261
Harbottle & Lewis (law firm) 330
Harley, George 88
Harper, Charles 48
Harris, Sir John 81–2, 83, 84
Harris, Tomás 152
Harrison, George 331
Harrison, Rex 247, 476
Harry Ransom Center (Austin, Texas) 39
Harston Hall, Cambridgeshire 5–6, 8, 12
Hart, Armando 295, 297–8, 375
Hart, Gary 483
Hart, Louis Albert 'Boy' 289
Hart-Davis, Rupert 66–7, 71, 75, 91
Hartley, L. P. 24, 75
Hartshorne, Charles 408
Harvey, Ian 298
Hastings, John (16th Earl of Huntingdon) 169, 285
Havana 255, 291–2, 352–3, 481–2
Havel, Václav 181, 386
Hawtree, Christopher 498
Haydon, Benjamin Robert 361
Hayward, John 60, 168, 174–5
Hazzard, Shirley xiii, 394, 476
The Heart of the Matter (1948) xiii, 139, 143, 144, 147, 148, 162; Scobie in xvi, 70, 144–5, 165, 175, 176, 177–8, 288, 306; and Catholicism 105, 176–8, 189, 191, 194, 229, 249; GG's view of 165, 174, 190; as critical and popular success 175–6; theologians' responses to 177–8, 189, 194, 249; failed stage version (1950) 192–3, 229

Heath, Edward 347
Heinemann 5, 41, 65, 92, 112, 130, 173, 199; rejects 'The Episode' 47–8; accepts *The Man Within* 53–4; rejects Rochester biography 60; and GG's debt 66, 67; GG tries to leave (1933) 75; and Hilary Trench pseudonym 95; withdraws *Journey Without Maps* 96; and collected edition of novels 331, 339; GG leaves (1961) 338–9, 498; takeover of (1961) 338–9
Heinl, Robert 354
Heller, Joseph 343
Hemerijckx, Dr Frans 309, 318
Hemingway, Ernest 111, 199, 302–3
Henty, G. A. 8, 20, 57
Herbert, George 59
Herbert, Laura 191
Herr, Michael, *Dispatches* 392
Hervey, Harry *Congai: Mistress of Indochine* (1925) 217
Heyer, Georgette 339
Higham, David 54, 68, 93, 324–5, 423, 505
Hitchcock, Alfred 99, 266–7, 300
Hitchens, Christopher 226
Hitler, Adolf 63, 64, 124, 164, 393, 433
Ho Chi Minh 204–5, 216, 226, 257, 260; GG meets in Hanoi (1955) 261, 262
Hoa Hao (religious sect in Vietnam) 207, 257–8
Hoare, Mike 419, 420
Hobbes, Thomas 60
Hochstetter, Leo 221–2
Hollis, Sir Roger 494
homosexuality 27, 196, 329, 339–40, 374, 375, 456
Honduras 462, 464
Honegger, Arthur, *Pacific 231,* 64
Hong Kong 221, 226, 246–7, 261
Hoover, J. Edgar 346

Hornung, E. W. 422
Horthy, Miklós 98
Hostovský, Egon 181
Howard, Brian 24, 33
Howard, Reginald 'Rex' 137, 138
Howard, Trevor 185, 229, 233–4
Howell, Gwen 30–1
Hoxha, Enver 350
Hu Feng 286–7
Hubbard, L. Ron 146
Huerta, Alberto 172, 502–3
Hügel, Baron von 194
Hughes, Emmet 226
Hugo, Victor 207
Hull, Christopher 299
The Human Factor (1978) 8, 137, 227,
    381, 383, 384, 424, 425, 494;
    treatment of apartheid in 312,
    381, 465; manuscript set-aside
    (1968) 381–2, 394, 421
Hummerstone, Bill 474–5
Hungary 98, 385, 424–5, 488
Hunter, Bruce 334, 505
Hutt, John 91
Huxley, Aldous 57, 185
Hyde, Annie 7
Hyde, Dr Charles McEwen 307

Igoe, Bill 417, 421
Independent Labour Party (ILP) 76
India 257, 343, 361
Inkatha Freedom Party 420
Innes, Michael 146
intelligence services: GG's early
    attempts at espionage 28–9;
    Vansittart's 'private detective
    agency' 98–9; SIS-SOE rivalry
    141–2; MI5, 144, 149, 152, 297,
    345, 346, 494; MI6-MI5 rivalries
    149; Cambridge spy ring 150,
    152–5, 328–9, 345–7, 349–50,
    382; HUMINT 150; signals
    intelligence (SIGINT) 150;
    'Garbo' case 151–2; appeal to

writers 156–7; Smollett
    as Russian spy 180;
    photographing of Yugoslav
    coast 229; GG meets Guy
    Burgess in Moscow (1960)
    328–9; see also MI6 (SIS)
Iran 426
Ireland 170–1, 175, 499–500; Civil
    War (1922–3) 25–6
Isherwood, Christopher 4, 24, 273
Israel 388–91
Italy 209–10, 227, 252
Ivasheva, Valentina 502
Iyonda, leprosy clinic in 309–10,
    312–15, 318, 319

Jacob, Sir Ian 323
Jamaica 278, 326
James, Henry 198, 457
Jameson Irish whiskey 483
Jamison, Dr Kay Redfield 15
Japan 111, 138, 151, 200, 204, 222, 323
Jenkin, Sir William 205
Jenkins, Graham 217
Jerrold, Douglas 158–9, 160, 187
Jesuit order 64, 114, 169, 398–9, 402,
    463, 504
Jews 27, 64–5, 108, 265–6
Joannon, Pierre 475–6, 483, 499–500
Jodl, Field Marshal 152
John Gordon Society 272–3, 290
John Paul II, Pope 114, 248, 265, 451,
    503
John XXIII, Pope 352
Johns Hopkins University 309
Johnson, Lady Bird 448
Johnson, Lyndon B. 259, 365, 437
Jolicoeur, Aubelin 358, 360, 370
Jonathan Cape 47, 75, 498
Jones, David, In Parenthesis 95
Jones, David (theatre director) 422
Jones, James Earl 374, 378–9
Jongh, Andrée de 318
Jowett, Benjamin 125

Joyce, James, *Ulysses* 29
Jumelle, Clément 353–4

Karas, Anton 185
Kasavubu, Joseph 311
Kaufman, Bob 326–7
Keating, Kenneth 351
Keene, Ralph 166
Kempe, Margery 196
Kennedy, John F. 214, 257, 327, 351
Kent, Bruce 391
Kenya 33, 235–40, 312
Kenyatta, Jomo 236, 240
Ker, Ian 105–6
Keyes, Frances Parkinson 160
KGB 346, 425, 426–7, 488–9, 491–2,
    494
Khrushchev, Nikita 350, 351
Kikuyu people 33, 236, 237, 238
King's College London 430
Kinnock, Neil 165
Kipling, Rudyard 501
Kirkpatrick, Jeane 480
Kissinger, Henry 442, 448
Knightley, Philip 346
Knox, Dilly 150
Kollek, Teddy 389
Korda, Alexander 98, 99–100, 128,
    132, 161, 183, 194, 233, 289; and
    intelligence services 98–9; and
    The Fallen Idol 162, 173, 174; and
    The Third Man 179, 180, 182,
    184, 185; the *Elsewhere* (yacht)
    181–2, 197, 212, 229–30, 251;
    gives GG villa on Capri 182–3;
    The Heart of the Matter (film,
    1953) 229; death of (1956) 251
Korda, Michael 181–2, 197, 234, 371,
    404, 494
Korean War 200
Krasker, Robert 185, 186
Kretschmer, Ernst 195
Kreuger, Ivar 73
Küng, Hans 454, 503

Kuznetsov, Anatoly 384–5
KwaZulu territory 420
Kyncl, Karel 386

Labour Party 164
Lagerkvist, Pär 199, 228–9
Lagos 139–40, 142, 144, 145
Lambert, Hansi 306, 308
Lamumba, Patrice 311
Lancaster, Donald 215, 242
Lancaster, Osbert 102
Land Benighted (*Too Late to Turn
    Back*) (Barbara Greene) 83
Lanina, Tanya 328
Lansdale, Edward 222, 257, 269
Lansky, Meyer 279, 353
Lanusse, Alejandro 411
Laos 243, 245–6, 260, 391
Lapautre, Michelle 424
Lattre, Bernard de 215, 220, 221
Lattre de Tassigny, Jean de 207, 208,
    214–15, 216, 219–20, 221, 222
Latvia 78
Lauwerys, Joseph 285, 286
Le Huu Tu (Bishop of Phat Diem)
    207, 216, 245, 257
Le Queux, William, *Spies of the Kaiser*
    457
League of Nations 80–1, 82, 86, 91
Lechat, Michel 308–10, 312–15, 318,
    319, 335, 338, 369
Lehmann-Haupt, Christopher 461
Leigh, Vivien 98, 181, 212
Leo XIII, Pope 112
Leonard, Mary (later Pritchett) 66,
    68, 95–6, 115, 183
Leonhardt, Rudolf Walter 348
leprosy 33, 306, 307–10, 312–15,
    316–17, 319, 335, 338, 443; GG
    encounters in Liberia 89, 307–8;
    psychological effects 313, 317,
    318, 335–6
Leroux, Etienne (Stephanus le Roux)
    414, 419–20, 421

Leroy, Colonel Jean 207, 208, 221,
    257–8, 259, 341
Leslie, Peter 78–9
Letelier, Orlando 448
Lewis, C. S. 169
Lewis, David 224
Lewis, Jeremy 68
Lewis, Peter 421
Lewis, Wilmarth Sheldon 'Lefty' 344
Lhérisson, Camille 365–6
libel law 67, 96, 175, 475, 477; *Wee
    Willie Winkie* review (1937) 102,
    103, 123, 124, 137, 273
Liberal Party 164
liberation theology 401, 402
Liberia 6, 33, 80–90, 94, 137, 140,
    307–8, 312
Lie, Nils 61–2
Liebling, A. J. 269
Life magazine 171, 200, 206, 208, 209,
    219, 226–7
Ligachyov, Yegor 492, 494
Literary Guild 370
lithium 196
Lithuania 78
Llanusa José 376
Lloyd, Selwyn 298
Lloyd George, David 20
Locke, John 198
Lodge, David 417
London: GG at 15 Devonshire
    Terrace 18–21; room at 141
    Albert Palace Mansions 46; flat
    at 8 Heathcroft, Hampstead Way
    51; in *It's a Battlefield* 70–1, 75;
    house at Clapham Common 91,
    133–4; studio in Mecklenburgh
    Square 125, 126, 134, 148; WW2
    in 127–8, 132–6, 148, 149–50,
    163–4; Victoria League building
    destroyed (April 1941) 134–5; flat
    at 18 Gordon Square 148, 164,
    171; V-weapon attacks on 164;
    flat at 5 St James's Street 187–8,

    197, 231; Albany, Piccadilly 231,
        264, 289
London Film Productions 98–9, 173
Longmans, Green & Co 112, 125
Loraine, Denis 332–3
Low, David 135–6
Lu Ling 286
Lublin, University of 265
Luce, Clare Boothe 226
Luce, Henry 226
Luciano, Lucky 279
Lüning, Heinz 292
Lusitania sinking (1915) 167
Lustig, Robin 383
Lyons, Islay de Courcy 183, 394

Macaulay, Rose 91
MacDiarmid, Hugh 285–6
MacDonald, Ramsay 433
MacGregor-Cheers, Joey 202
Mackenzie, Compton 182
Mackey, Michael 143–4, 145
Maclean, Donald 152, 329, 345, 346,
    382
Macleod, Joseph (Adam Drinan) 33
Macmillan, Harold 346
Macowan, Michael 282
Macpherson, Kenneth 183
magic realism 402
Magloire, Paul (President of Haiti)
    253, 353, 365
Mailer, Norman 491
Mais, Priscilla 275
Malaya 33, 200–3, 204, 205, 209
Mallin, Jay 294–5
Malraux, André 341–2
Manichaeism 408
Mankiewicz, Joseph L. 270, 300
Manríquez y Zárate, José de Jesús 115
Mantichorean Society (Oxford) 23
Mao Zedong 285, 286
maps 84–5
Marais, Kowie 420
Marbury, Elisabeth 68

Marcial, Comandante (Salvador
    Cayetano Carpio) 466–9, 480–1,
    482
marijuana 255
Maritain, Jacques 365
Marks, John 101
Marlborough College 13–14
Márquez, Gabriel García ('Gabo') 439,
    447, 463, 465, 466, 481, 482
Martindale, C. C. 178, 194–5, 212
Martínez, Boris 437
Martínez, José de Jesús ('Chuchu')
    434, 440–1, 445, 447, 462, 477,
    483–4; and GG's 1976 trip to
    Panama 440–1, 443–4; 'pigeon
    house' of 441, 446, 455; and
    Nicaraguan rebels 446–7, 450,
    455; and GG's 1978 trip to
    Panama 450–1, 452, 453–4, 466,
    467; and death of Torrijos 470–1,
    478; and Díaz 478, 486; allies
    with Noriega 486, 505; and US
    invasion (1989) 504–5; death of
    (1991) 505
Martinique 285
Marturet Raúl Oscar 407
Masariegos, Don Porfirio 121
Masaryk, Jan 181
Maschler, Tom 498
Mathew, David 212, 249
Mathew, Gervase 135, 212
Mau Mau uprising (1952–60) 33,
    235–40, 312
Maude, A. H. 52
Maugham, Somerset 156
Mauriac, François 188–9, 199
Mauthausen concentration camp 77,
    188
Mayo, Arthur 11
McCall, Monica 299–300, 370, 404
McCarthy, Joseph 225
McDonnell, Vincent, *The Broken
    Commandment* 499
McGill, P. J. 238

Médecin, Jacques 474
Melville, Herman, *Moby Dick* 459–60
Mendoza, Nicolas 293
Menzies, Stewart ('C') 154
Merton, Thomas 194
Mexico xv, 101, 104, 453; Catholicism
    in 14, 44, 112–15, 116–20, 122–3,
    129–30, 249, 352; GG visits
    (1938) 103, 104, 110, 111, 112, 114,
    115–23; oil industry nationalized
    116, 312; black Madonna in
    Guadalupe 118, 352; aboriginal
    communities 119–20, 121–2, 240;
    GG returns to (1963) 351–2
Meyer, Michael 266, 267, 284, 303,
    326, 327, 415
MGM 156, 161–2, 370, 378, 404–5
MI6 (SIS) xiv, 78–9, 297, 346; GG's
    WW2 service in 137–43, 149–53,
    154–7, 277; Section V (counter-
    intelligence) 149–55, 205, 277,
    428; rivalry with MI5, 149;
    counter-intelligence on Soviet
    Union (Section IX) 153–4;
    operations in the Far East 205,
    215, 242, 260, 261; and Rodney
    Dennys 212, 324, 345, 350, 425,
    426; GG in Poland 265; and
    Philby-GG communications 425,
    426, 489, 495, 497
Mikoyan, Serge 491
Milian, Raúl 374, 375
Miller, Henry 272
Miller, Inglis 12
Milne, Tim xiv, 150, 154–5, 205, 346
Miranda, Miguel Darío 112, 117, 123
Miskito people in Nicaragua 480
The Mission (Roland Joffé film, 1986)
    398
Mistinguett (entertainer) 29
Mitterrand, François 474
Mobutu, Joseph Désiré (Mobutu Sese
    Seko) 311
modernist movement 24–5

Monckton, Sir Walter 239
Mondale, Walter 483
Monde, Claudette 169, 170
Monserrat 4, 81
Montagu, Elizabeth 180
Monte Carlo 250, 424
Moor, Elisabeth 227, 263, 288, 301,
     394
Moore, Brian 289, 487
Moore, Peter 233
Moore, Sir John 20, 432
Moret, André 242, 260, 319
Morgan, Charles 55
Morgan, J. P. 73
Morley, Robert 251
Morocco 171, 184
Morrell, Lady Ottoline 57, 70
Morrison, William Shepherd 298–9
Morrow, Jo 302
Moscow 62, 328–9, 346, 347, 426,
     488–90, 494, 495–6
Mosley, Oswald 76
Moss, Geoffrey, *Defeat* 26
Mountbatten, Louis 205
Mozambique 428
Muggeridge, Malcolm 65, 78, 137,
     158, 175, 188, 205; at Ministry of
     Information in WW2, 132; on
     loss of GG's Clapham house 133,
     134; on GG's appetite for conflict
     187; with GG at Aileen Philby's
     house 345–6; and religion 389–90
Muller, Hilgard 420
Munich Agreement (September 1938)
     124–5
Murillo, Rosario 455–6, 479
Murphy, Audie 270
Murphy, John P. 177
Murry, John Middleton 70
Mussolini, Benito 158

Nabokov, Nicolas 306
Nabokov, Vladimir, *Lolita* 272, 273, 290
Naidenoff, Georges 258

Namibia 420
Narayan, R. K. 93–4, 160–1, 290
the *Nausikaa* (double-ended cutter) 188
Navarre, Henri 242, 243
'near-death experiences' 501–2
Neave, Airey, *Little Cyclone* 318
Nekchi people in Guatemala 454
Nelson, Thomas 25
Neruda, Pablo 409–10
Neumann, Therese 193–4
Nevinson, Christopher 18
New Statesman 225, 232–3
New York 171, 184–5, 225–6, 229, 279,
     281–2, 326
New York Review of Books 444–5, 448
New York Times 124, 224, 254, 356
Newall, Maria 239, 429, 433
Newbolt, Sir Henry, *Devotional Poets of
     the XVII Century* 59, 228
Newman, John Henry 105–6, 340
News Chronicle 83, 92
Ngo Dinh Diem 221, 256–7, 258–9,
     260, 261, 270
Ngo Dinh Nhu 257, 258
Nguyen Manh Ha 215–16
Nhu, Madame 258
Nicaragua 446–7, 452–3, 505;
     Sandinistas 451–2, 453, 455–6,
     462, 469–70, 477, 479, 480, 485;
     GG in Managua (1980/3) 469–70,
     478–81; American-backed Contras
     479, 480, 493
Nicoll, Maurice 18
Nicolson, Harold 329
Night and Day (magazine, 1937) 101–3
Nihill, Sir John Barclay 238–9, 240
Nin, Anaïs 272
Niven, David 422
Nixon, Richard 409
Nobel Prize for Literature 199, 228–9,
     266, 284, 410
Noble, Allan 298
Noriega, Manuel 436, 438, 446, 471,
     478, 479, 486; GG distrusts

478, 485, 486; and GG's visit to
Castro (1983) 478, 481–2; and
Chuchu 486, 505; arrested by the
Americans (1989) 504
Northumberland, Duke of 27
Norway 61–2
Nottingham 40–4

Oakley, P. D. 96, 102
Oberammergau, passion play at 56–7
the *Observer* 346, 409, 412
Ocampo, Victoria 400, 401, 406, 409,
410, 444
Odd Man Out (Carol Reed film, 1947)
173
O'Faoláin, Seán 177
O'Grady, Clodagh 30
Ojeda, Fernando 294
Oldfield, Maurice ('C') 205, 260, 425,
428, 429
Olivier, Laurence 98, 212, 271, 342
O'Malley, Ernie 170
On Her Majesty's Secret Service (Peter
R. Hunt, film, 1968) 324
Onganía, Juan Carlos 400
opium 223, 231, 246–7, 260, 261, 263
Opus Dei 430
ORDEN (Organización Democrática
Nacionalista) 462, 464, 468
Ordoñez, German Pomares 451–2
Organisation armée secrète (OAS)
341, 342
Organization of American States 355,
375, 448
Orient Express 63–4, 397–8, 501
Ortega, Daniel 447, 455–6, 479, 500,
505
Ortega, Humberto 469, 479
Orwell, George 132, 139, 161, 176
Osborne, John 232
Oseira, Trappist monastery of 431–2,
433, 434, 483
Österling, Anders 266, 410
Otero, Lisandro 374

Our Man in Havana (1958) 137, 227,
277–9, 288, 291–5, 296, 297,
351, 366, 489; George Herbert
epigraph 59; Lisbon/Tallinn as
possible settings for 78–9, 428;
'Garbo' case as influence on plot
151; numbers as a leitmotif 212,
251; bidding for film rights 299
Oxford 69–70, 163, 187, 288
Oxford University 18, 23–5, 33–5,
127, 163; Wadham College 3,
62; Balliol College 21–2, 23–5,
27, 29, 30, 31, 32, 33–5, 125;
GG's pranks/escapades at 23,
26, 29, 52; *Oxford Outlook*
(undergraduate review) 24, 25,
28, 36–7; GG at 52 Beechcroft
Road 30; Trinity College 127,
163; Oriel College 138; Christ
Church 264, 323

Pachman, Luděk 386
Palestine, British mandate in 65
Panama 434, 436, 438–49, 450–4;
Canal Zone 436–7, 438, 439,
442, 444, 445, 447–9, 462; US
military interventions 436,
504–5; coups of late 1960s
437–8; treaty negotiations
with USA 437, 438, 445–6;
G-2 (intelligence service) 438,
446, 466; GG's trips to 439–44,
445–6, 450–4, 465–9, 470, 477–8,
485–6; search for Drake's body
452, 470; and GG's meeting with
Castro (1983) 481, 482; Noriega
ousts Díaz 486; *see also* Martínez,
José de Jesús ('Chuchu');
Torrijos, Omar
Panama Papers scandal (2016) 438
Paraguay 57, 398–400, 401–3, 406,
410, 417, 420, 448
Paramount 98, 147–8
Paredes, Rubén Darío 478, 479, 481

Paris 188, 192, 195, 208, 212–13, 289, 326; GG visits communists in (1925) 29, 70; flat at 130 Boulevard Malesherbes 289, 330, 342, 506

Parsons, Ian 101, 102

Parsons, Louella 270

Paschoud, Jean-Felix 333

Pasternak, Boris 385

Pastora, Edén 453, 471

Pasture (holding company) 331

the Patriot (right-wing publication) 27

Patrizi, Bernardo 209

Paul VI, Pope (Giovanni Battista Montini) 50, 249–50, 407

Peake, Mervyn 159–60, 252

Peaky Blinders (television show) 108

Pearce, David 6, 16

Péguy, Charles 110, 146, 177

Penang 247

Penguin 331, 332, 333

Peres, Shimon 390

Perón, Juan 400, 410, 444

Pershing, John 20

Peter Jones department store 124

Peters, A. D. 34, 47

Pettiward, Daniel 168

Peyrefitte, Alain 474

Pham Ngoc Chi (Bishop of Bui Chu) 207, 214, 222, 245, 257

Philby, Aileen 345–6

Philby, Eleanor, Kim Philby: The Spy I Loved 382, 425

Philby, Kim xiv, 75, 142–3, 150, 153–5, 156, 275–6, 329; heads MI6 Section IX 154, 155; My Silent War 154, 275–6, 383, 424; exposure of (1963) 345–7, 349–50; as correspondent in Beirut 346; flees to Moscow (1963) 347, 349, 494; Le Carré's Haydon based on 382–3; wish to meet GG (1970s/80s) 424–6, 488–9; correspondence with GG (from 1978) 425–6, 489, 497; meetings

with GG (Moscow, 1986/87) 488, 489–90, 494–5; death of (1988) 495; television appearance in Russia (1988) 495

Philby, Rufina 489–90, 491, 494, 495, 496

Philippe-Auguste (Haitian artist) 360

Phuong (partner of de Berval) 217

Piasecki, Bolesław 265

Pick, Frank 132–3

Pinochet, Augusto 400, 409, 448, 493

Pinto, Vivian de Sola 60

Pio, Padre (Capuchin friar) 210

Pius X, Pope 176

Pius XI, Pope 113–14, 215

Pius XII, Pope 117, 209–10, 216, 249

Pizzardo, Giuseppe 118, 248, 249–50

Playboy magazine 419, 421

poetry 18–19, 24–5, 32, 47, 230, 316; verses on BBC Radio (22 January 1925) 33; poets of the seventeenth century 59–60, 228

Poirot, Luis 411

Poland 264–6

polar exploration 9–10

Pollinger, Laurence 148, 324–5, 332, 370, 423

Portocarrera, René 374

Portugal 142, 149–51, 267, 277, 284, 299, 399, 428; 'Garbo' case in 151, 277; GG travels in with Durán 239, 429–30, 433; 'Carnation Revolution' (1974) 428–9

Il Postino (Michael Radford film, 1994) 409

Potter, Stephen 125

Pound, Ezra, Personae 18–19

Powell, Anthony 175, 187

Powell, Selwyn 97, 101

The Power and the Glory (1940) xiii, 121, 125, 152, 366, 421; whisky priest in 8, 65, 103, 121, 129–30, 306; Catholic themes in 105,

118, 129–30, 147, 248–50,
318; as critical success 130–1;
Hawthornden Prize awarded
for 131; dedication to Gervase
Mathews 135; denounced by the
Inquisition 248–50
The Power and the Glory (play) 270–1
Prague Spring 385, 409
Preminger, Otto 405
Price, George 453–5
Priestley, J. B. 67, 71, 97, 102, 290
Pritchett, Mary (née Leonard) 66, 68,
95–6, 115, 183
Pritchett, V. S. 189, 371, 487
Pro, Miguel 114, 123, 130
process theology 408
Profumo affair 347
psychoanalysis 18, 19–20, 31, 49, 94,
147; and GG's view of Africa
80, 86; GG and Eric Strauss 195,
196, 202, 263; Freudians 196
Purna, Kit 93
Putin, Vladimir 427

Quayle, Anthony 289
Quennell, Peter 10–11, 15, 17, 21
The Quiet American (1955) xv, 58,
216, 219, 222, 242, 250, 336–7,
366; American reaction to
xii–xiii, 269–70; GG has idea
for 208, 221–2; dedication to
René and Phuong 216–17; theme
of American meddling 221–2;
Continental Hotel bombing
(1952) 258; Liebling's review of
269; Russian stage version 328;
copyright given to Francis 331;
Philby on 491, 495
Quinn, Anthony 199

race: black soldiers in occupied Ruhr
28; reference to Jews 64, 108;
inter-racial couples in Vietnam
217; apartheid in South Africa

235, 312, 419, 420, 465; in
colonial Kenya 235; in colonial
Congo 310; skin colour in
Haiti 353, 364, 365–6, 379; and
Panama Canal Zone 436
Radio Free Europe 384
Rahner, Karl 337
Rain Queen in Limpopo Province
420
Random House 498–9
Rank Organisation 173
Ransome, Patrick 101
Ratcliffe, Michael 421
Rattigan, Terence 165
Read, Herbert 94–5, 102, 161
Reagan, Ronald 439, 442, 460, 465,
477, 480, 483
Redgrave, Michael 166, 270, 304–5
Reed, Carol 173–4, 179, 181, 183, 184,
185, 186, 193, 300, 302, 370
Reid, Josephine 325, 368, 423, 461
Reilly, Sir Patrick 328
Reinhardt, Max xiv, 289–90, 321, 331,
338, 368, 385, 461, 474–5, 498–9
Rhodesia 37, 420
Ribbentrop, Joachim von 27
Richardson, Ralph 174, 289, 302, 304,
361, 362
Richmond, Kenneth 18, 19–20, 21, 49
Rickards, Jocelyn 232, 266, 502
Riddoch, George 49, 50
Rilke, Rainer Maria 119
Róbért, László 424–5
Roberts, Cecil 41
Robles, Marco 437
Rochester, Second Earl of 59–60, 174,
210
Rockefeller, Nelson 448
Rodgers and Hammerstein 193
Roe, Thomas 330–4, 366–7, 370
Romero, Carlos Humberto 463–4
Romero, Óscar 463, 464
Roosevelt, Theodore 436
Ross, Noël 201, 203

Rossellini, Roberto 233
Rost, Hilary 11
Rothenstein, Elizabeth 169, 170
Rothenstein, John 168–9
Roturman (Roe's company) 330, 332, 333
Royal Shakespeare Company 422
Royal Victoria Sausage Company 332–3, 366–7
Royde-Smith, Naomi 18, 24
Ruane, Kevin 207–8
Runciman, Steven, The Medieval Manichee 408
Rupert, Anton 420
Russell, Bertrand 199
Ryan, Tony 499, 500
Ryhiner, Mercia 247, 266, 476

Sabini, Charles 'Darby' 108
Sackville-West, Edward 24, 177, 195, 199
Saigon 206–7, 215, 217, 247, 256–60
Saint-Jean-Cap-Ferrat 321
Salamanca 431
Salan, Raoul 219, 220, 341
Salazar, António de Oliveira 149–51, 277, 428
SALT II agreement (1979) 426
Samoa 326
San Antonio (Texas) 115, 129
San Francisco 326–7
San Sebastián 432
Sánchez, Waldemar 406
Sander, Allegra 252, 266
Sanders, George 333
Santamaria, Haydée 295, 374, 375
Santiago (Cuba) 279, 293–5
Santiago de Compostela 432
Sarabia, Nydia 293, 294, 295
Saturday Review of Literature 130–1
Saunders, Amanda (niece) 324, 345, 423, 507
Saunders, W. A. 14
Schack, Baron von 227

Scharansky, Anatoly (Natan) 385
Schillebeeckx, Edward 503
School of the Americas (Panama Canal Zone) 437
Schweitzer, Albert 310
Scofield, Paul 270–1, 304, 362
Scorsese, Martin 185
Scott, Robert 23
Second World War: Macleod as news presenter 33; German occupation of Norway 62; French resistance 77, 142, 161; approach of (1938–9) 124–5; outbreak of (1939) 127–8; GG in London during 128, 132–6, 148, 149–50, 164; GG at Ministry of Information 132–3; Clapham Common house bombed (1940) 133–4; the Blitz in London 133–6; GG as ARP warden 134–6, 164; GG's intelligence work during 137–45, 146, 149–53, 154–7, 277; Portugal during 142, 149–51; Operation Torch (1942) 145; Battle of Kursk (1943) 152; Normandy landings 152; D-Day 154; collaborators 161; Nazi atrocities 161; V-weapons 164; in Indochina 204, 222; and the Congo 310; Comet Line into Spain 318
Seitz, Charles (Charlie Sykes) 61
Selznick, David O. 184, 185, 186, 190, 304
Selznick, Irene Mayer 304, 326
Senate House, University of London 132
Sestigers ('sixtiers') movement of Afrikaans writers 419
Seychelles 419
Shackleton, Sir Ernest 9
Shades of Greene (Thames Television series) 270, 430
Shakespeare, Nicholas, Priscilla 275
Shakespeare, William, Hamlet 336

Shamir, Yitzhak 390

Shaw, Glen Byam 304

Shaw, Run Run (film producer) 201

Shearer, Jeremy 465–6, 468

Sheed, Frank 112, 117

Sheen, Fulton 376

Shelden, Michael xiv

Sheringham (Norfolk) 30–1

Sherry, Norman xiv, 121, 417–18

Siberia 492, 494

Sierra Leone xvi, 137, 139, 175, 395–6;
    GG and Barbara in 84, 85, 86,
    396; Krios or Creoles in 85; GG's
    WW2 service in 140–5, 146

Sight and Sound 102

Simon, Dame Kathleen 82

Simon & Schuster 370–1, 404

Singapore 201, 203, 205, 247

Sinn Féin 25

Sintra (Portugal) 239, 429, 433

Sinyavsky, Andrei 383–5, 488

Sitwell, Edith 24–5, 27, 139, 191, 231

Six Day War (1967) 388–90, 391

Skiathos, island of 212

Skinner, John 343

Škvorecký, Josef 181, 385–6, 387, 492,
    493

slavery: and Greene family history 4,
    81; in Liberia 80–1, 83, 85, 87,
    312

Smollett, Peter 180

Soares, Mário 429

Society for Psychical Research 18

Socorro Juridico 464–5

Soldati, Mario 233, 234, 395

Solomon, Flora 346

Solzhenitsyn, Alexander 385, 488

Somoza, Anastasio 446–7, 452, 453,
    462

the Sorbonne 91, 188, 440

A Sort of Life (memoir, 1971) 39, 41–2,
    43, 47, 50, 395, 408; childhood
    and school days in 1, 2, 11, 14,
    16, 21; and GG's writing for

Strauss 2, 196; as unreliable 14,
    16, 32, 395

South Africa 419–21, 465–6, 467–9;
    apartheid 235, 312, 419, 420, 465

Soviet Union: show trials 62; forced
    collectivization of farms 63;
    human rights abuses 63, 65,
    383–5, 425, 488, 491–2; and
    Baltic States 78; and Cambridge
    spy ring 150, 152–5, 328–9, 382,
    383, 425–6, 489; and Philby 150,
    153–5, 382, 383; Battle of Kursk
    (1943) 152; takeover of Eastern
    Europe 181; support for Viet
    Minh 205; and Poland 264–5; and
    the Congo 311; Francis Greene's
    visits to 323; GG's trips to 328,
    426, 489–93, 494–6; Writers'
    Union 328, 488–9; Golitsyn's
    defection to West 346; Cuban
    alliance with 351, 355, 375;
    invasion of Czechoslovakia (1968)
    375, 385, 488; crushes Hungarian
    revolution (1956) 385, 488;
    Gorbachev in 427, 488, 492, 493;
    Forum for a Nuclear Free World
    (Moscow, 1987) 490–3; courting
    of GG 492–3; celebration of GG's
    eighty-fourth birthday 495–6

Spadafora, Hugo 486

Spain: GG's holiday in (1921) 20, 432;
    Carlist wars in 40, 57–8; Civil
    War (1936–9) 62, 111, 123, 128,
    153, 431; Franco regime 149, 429,
    430, 431; 'Garbo' case in 151, 277;
    GG travels in with Durán 239,
    429–34, 465; Batista flees to 299;
    Valle de los Caídos (Valley of the
    Fallen) 431

Spark, Muriel 288–9

Special Operations Executive (SOE)
    141–2

Spectator 68, 77, 92, 97, 98, 102, 134,
    247, 272, 484

Spellman, Cardinal (of New York) 216, 225, 258–9, 376
Spender, Stephen 306
Spinks, James 108
spiritualism 18, 19, 66
Squire, J. C. 47
St Bartholomew's Hospital, London 195
St Francis Xavier 201
St John of the Cross 433
St John-Stevas, Norman 272
St Kitts (West Indies) 4, 81
St Teresa of Avila 432–3
Stafford, John 233, 251, 277
Stalin, Joseph 62, 433
Stavisky, Alexandre 77
Steinbeck, John, *Travels with Charley* 404
Steiner, Rudolf 38
Stellar Press 474–5
Sterling, John 40
Stern, Karl 279
Stevens, Siaka 396
Stevenson, Robert Louis 5, 8, 307, 410
Stockholm 228–9, 266, 267–8, 284, 295–6; Royal Dramatic Theatre 268, 284–5
Stonor, Jeanne (née Stourton) 302, 352
Stonor, Sherman (6th Baron Camoys) 288, 291, 293, 302
Stopford, Richmond 151
Stoppard, Tom 405
Strachey, Oliver 150
Stratford, Philip 417
Strauss, Eric 15, 195–6, 202, 263, 329
Stroessner, Alfredo 399, 400, 402, 406, 448
Subotica, border crossing at 64
Sun Yat Sen 207
Sunday Express 272, 499
Sunday Telegraph 351, 353, 360, 388
Sunday Times 236, 239–40, 242, 247, 261–2, 264–5, 272, 361, 475

Sutro, Gillian xv, 233, 274–6, 303, 320, 368
Sutro, John 233, 272, 273, 274–5, 303, 330, 350, 368, 372
Suzman, Helen 420
Svanström, Ragnar 266, 267, 284
Sweden 73, 228–9, 266, 267–8, 284–5, 295–6
Swinnerton, Frank 58
Switzerland 416, 457, 474, 504; GG and Yvonne move to (1990) 505–6
Sykes, Christopher 417

Tabasco (Mexico) 33, 117, 118–20, 129–30
The Tablet 247, 434
Tagle, Ernesto Gomez 117, 123
Tagore, Rabindranath 400
Tahiti 326
Tal, General Israel 388–9
Tallinn 78–9, 277, 329
Taylor, Elizabeth 374, 378, 379
Teignmouth, Lord 48
Temple, Shirley 102–3, 123, 124, 137, 273
Teresa, Mother 389
Texas 273–4
Thatcher, Margaret 165
Thé, Trinh Minh 222, 258, 259
The Times 36, 46–7, 52–3, 55, 65, 66, 82, 92, 153
Theatrecraft Limited 166
Thomas Tilling Ltd 338–9
Thompson, Francis, 'The Hound of Heaven' 130
Thompson, G. H. 83
Thorndike, Dame Sybil 281, 282
Thriplow (Cambridgeshire) 191, 230, 458–9
Thurmond, Strom 445
Time magazine 213, 226
Times Literary Supplement 41
Tito, Josip Broz 234

Tomic, Radomiro 411

Tontons Macoutes 253, 354, 356–7, 358, 359, 360, 362–3, 364, 370, 373

Topolski, Feliks 101

Torres, Camilo 401, 405

Torrijos, Omar 437–9, 440–1, 450–1, 467, 469; GG's friendship with 88, 426–7, 442–9, 452, 455, 462, 465, 466, 470–1, 473, 477–8; self-destructive nature of 442–3, 470–1; *Getting to Know the General* 446, 473, 477, 483–4; treaty signing in Washington (1977) 447–9; and Belize 453–4, 455; and hostages in El Salvador 462, 463; death of (1981) 470–1, 477–8, 486

Toussaint L'Ouverture 253

Toynbee, Philip 335

Tran Van Huu 259

Tran Van Soai 257–8

Tran Van Van 259

Trevor, William 435

Trollope, Anthony 116, 120

Trollope, George 4, 42–3, 44, 45

Trotsky, Leon 115

Trudeau, Margaret 376

Trudeau, Pierre Elliott 376

Truffaut, François, *La Nuit américaine* 415

Trujillo, Rafael 356, 364, 478

Trump, Donald xiii

Turner, G. D. 70–1, 127

Turner, Vincent 169, 192

Turnier, Charles 355

Tutin, Dorothy 229

Ukraine, *Holodomor* in 63, 65

Ulmanis, Kārlis 78

Unamuno, Miguel de 431, 433

United African Company 320

United Nations (UN) 420, 467

United States: foreign policy xii–xiii, xvi, 382, 399–400, 409, 411, 436–8, 442, 444–9, 463–4, 465; GG's anti-Americanism xii–xiii, xvi, 115, 349–50, 374, 382, 384, 412, 478, 486; Cold War mentality xii, 205, 222, 226; GG's tangles with immigration authorities 29, 224, 254–5; rubber production in Africa 81, 88; GG in (early 1938) 114–15; *Brighton Rock* as success in 124; *The Power and the Glory* as success in 130–1; GG in California for *The Third Man* 184; and French claim to Vietnam 204, 205, 206, 214, 216, 242; increased involvement in Vietnam 221–2, 242, 258–9; McCarran Act (1950) 224, 225, 254–5; black ops in Indochina 269; and Cuba 294, 298; truck break-down in Utah (1960) 327; and Duvalier's Haiti 354–5, 357, 378, 379; and Dominican Republic coup (1965) 365; and 'Operation Condor' 399–400; backs coup in Chile (1973) 409; and Panama 436–7, 438, 439, 442, 444–6, 447–9, 471, 504–5; and El Salvador 463–4, 465, 504; invasion of Panama (1989) 504–5

Updegraff, Allan 77

Urquhart, F. F. 'Sligger' 22

Vallejo, René 376

Valli, Alida 185, 233–4

Van Molle, Paul 314

Vance, Cyrus 445

Vandenberghe, Roger 221

Vanderslaghmolen, Père Hendrik 314, 315

Vansittart, Sir Robert 98–9

Vanunu, Mordechai 390–1

Velarde, Fabian 440

Venice 233–4

Ventura, Esteban 279, 299

Verdant (holding company) 330, 331, 332, 333

Verschoyle, Derek 68, 134

Vevey (Switzerland) 416, 504, 506

Vicentín, Francisco 407

Vidal, Gore 491

Videla, Jorge Rafael 448

Vienna 179–81, 184

Viet Minh 204–5, 214, 215, 216, 241, 242–6, 256, 260

Vietnam: French colonial forces in xi–xii, 33, 204–5, 206–8, 214–16, 218–21, 222, 241–6, 247, 257–8; GG's trips to xi–xii, 205–8, 213, 214–15, 216–23, 241–7, 257–62; Phat Diem xi–xii, 207–8, 216, 220–1, 226, 244, 245, 257, 389; Catholicism in xi, 207, 208, 214, 215–16, 221–2, 226, 241, 244–5, 256–7, 258–9, 261; 'strategic hamlets' used in 200; Haiphong 204, 206, 218, 223, 260–1; Battle of Route Coloniale 4 (1950) 205; enclave of Bui-Chu 207, 214, 241, 244–5, 257; UMDCs in 207; Sûreté Fédérale in 216, 219, 242; GG dive-bombs in B-26 plane 218–19; American Economic Mission 221–2, 242; GG's brush with land mine 241, 244; Thui-nhai (fortified village) 241, 244–5; Dien Bien Phu 243–4, 246, 247, 256; Geneva Accords (1954) 243, 256, 257; division at the 17th parallel 256; 'Northern Migration' 256, 257; *coup d'état* (1963) 257; Binh Xuyen (criminal gang) 259; Francis Greene reports from (1967–8) 391–2; GG's view on American policy 393; *see also* *The Quiet American* (1955)

Viking 103, 124, 125, 225, 291, 370–1, 404

Virago Press 498

Vitoria (Basque region) 432

Vivian, Valentine 138

Vodou religion 253–4

Voznesensky, Andrei 490

Vukovic, Pedro 411

Vukulov, Oleg 491

Walker, Alice Marion 'Molly' (sister) 5, 7, 16, 24, 324, 352

Walker, John (nephew) 324

Walker, Lionel 24, 324

Walker, Martin 491

Walker, Peter 324

Walpole, Horace 344

Walston, Catherine: Oliver Walston's memoir xiv–xv, 167, 168; and *The End of the Affair* xv, 170, 198, 211; background of 167–8; and Catholicism 168–9, 192, 194, 223, 227; parentage of children of 168; private pilot's licence 168, 170; first meetings with GG (1945/6) 169, 170; affair with GG begins 170–1; John Hayward's love for 174–5; in Capri with GG 183, 197, 227, 231, 252, 369; 5 St James's Street residence 187–8, 231; intensity of GG's love for 191–2, 193, 194, 196, 201, 213, 231; affair with GG as public knowledge 192, 211; refuses to leave children/Harry 192, 195, 212–13; and psychoanalysis 195; in France with GG 197, 208; travel with GG 210, 247, 278–9, 284; reconciliations and break-ups with GG (1950s) 212, 260, 267–8, 284, 295–6; and opium 223; Thomas Gilby's affair with 230–1; GG's slow break with 266, 268, 325–6, 369, 458–9; and GG's relationship with Anita Björk 267–8, 284, 285, 295–6, 458;

Gillian Sutro on 275; ill health in later life 326, 369, 458–9; death of (1978) 459

Walston, David 168

Walston, Harry 167–8, 187–8, 191, 192, 195, 197, 284, 458, 459; and *The End of the Affair* 198, 211

Walston, James 168

Walston, Oliver xiv–xv, 167, 168

Waugh, Auberon 191, 353

Waugh, Evelyn 22, 31, 34, 75, 80, 93, 102, 114, 231; friendship with GG 24, 190, 211–12, 248, 336–7, 342, 371; on *The Heart of the Matter* 177; and Catholicism 190–1, 248, 336–7, 372; *Brideshead Revisited* 190; on *A Burnt-Out Case* 336, 337; and politics 342; declining health and death of (1966) 371–2; Sykes's biography of 417; Amory's edition of the letters of 467

Wayne, John 445

Weaver, John 127, 163

Weaver, Stella 47, 51, 127, 163

Wee Willie Winkie (John Ford film, 1937) 102–3

Weidenfeld & Nicolson 416

Weldon, Fay 491

Welles, Orson 185–6

West, Nigel 151, 154

Westminster Gazette 18, 24, 26, 41, 108

Westminster Hospital 48

Wheeler, Augustus 14–15, 17, 21, 202, 301

White, Antonia 91–2

White, Sir Dick ('C') 297

Whitehead, Alfred 408

Whyatt, John 238

Wijnants, Pierre 314

Wilde, Oscar 3, 422

Wilder, Gene 305

Wilhelm, Prince (of Sweden) 266

Willichs, Father (Belgian priest) xi–xii, 257, 260

Wilson, Colonel 15

Wilson, Margaret 70–1, 127

Wilson, Dr McNair 50

Wilson, Trevor 149, 205–6, 207–8, 214–15, 217, 221, 241–2, 260, 288; GG tainted by association with 216, 219, 220; Laotian posting 391, 392

Winkelstein, Dr Warren 218

Withers, Googie 305

Wolfe, Charles 432

Wolfe, Humbert 47

Wood, Peter 361, 362

Woolf, Virginia 198–9

World Health Organization 308

World Wildlife Fund 420

Wormald, Brian 291

Wormwood Scrubs 71

Wright, Peter, *Spycatcher* 494–5

Wright, Ralph 337–8

Wyszyński, Cardinal Stefan 265–6

Yakovlev, Alexander 489, 492

Yapp, Mr (FO's man in Monrovia) 83, 87

Yeltsin, Boris 495

Yonge, Charlotte M., *The Little Duke* 8

Young, Doris 197, 231, 264

Young, Francis Brett 182

Yugoslavia 63, 229, 233–4

Zaharoff, Sir Basil 64

Zhou Enlai 286

Zola, Emile 474

Zorillo, Américo 411

Zweig, Arnold 348